COLLECTED WORKS OF

James Wilson

JAMES WILSON

COLLECTED WORKS OF

James Wilson

James Wilson

Edited by Kermit L. Hall and Mark David Hall
with an Introduction by Kermit L. Hall
and a Bibliographical Essay by Mark David Hall
Collected by Maynard Garrison

VOLUME I

Liberty Fund

This book is published by Liberty Fund, Inc., a foundation established to encourage study of the ideal of a society of free and responsible individuals.

The cuneiform inscription that serves as our logo and as a design element for Liberty Fund books is the earliest-known written appearance of the word "freedom" (*amagi*), or "liberty." It is taken from a clay document written about 2300 B.C. in the Sumerian city-state of Lagash.

Cover art: James Wilson, etching by Max Rosenthal, 1890.
From Library of Congress, Prints and Photographs Division, James Wilson Biographical File, LC-USZ62-6065.
Frontispiece portrait of James Wilson by James Barton Longacre, after an original by J. P. H. Elouis, c. 1825, by permission of the National Portrait Gallery, Smithsonian Institution.

4th printing (2023),
printed on demand by Lightning Source, Inc.

Library of Congress Cataloging-in-Publication Data
Wilson, James, 1742–1798.
[Works]
Collected works of James Wilson/edited and with an introduction by Kermit L. Hall with a Bibliographical Essay by Mark David Hall; collected by Maynard Garrison.
p. cm.
Includes bibliographical references and index.
ISBN-13: 978-0-86597-682-5 (hardcover—set)
ISBN-13: 978-0-86597-684-9 (hardcover—vol 1)
ISBN-13: 978-0-86597-685-6 (hardcover—vol 2)
ISBN-13: 978-0-86597-683-2 (pbk.—set)
[etc.]
1. Law—United States. I. Hall, Kermit. II. Title.
KF213.W5H35 2007
349.73—dc22 2006102965

Liberty Fund, Inc.
11301 North Meridian Street
Carmel, Indiana 46032
libertyfund.org

CONTENTS

Volume 1

PART I
Political Papers, Speeches, and Judicial Opinions of James Wilson

PART 2
Lectures on Law

Volume 2

COLLECTOR'S ACKNOWLEDGMENTS

The genesis of the *Collected Works of James Wilson* was the chance discovery in 1995 of Andrew Bennett's pamphlet "James Wilson of St. Andrews, an American Statesman" (1928) in a bookstall at the Sunday Antiques Faire at St. Andrews Town Hall. The journey from that initial discovery to this publication was made possible through the help of many scholars, all of whom eagerly shared their knowledge with me. These include: the staff of the University of St. Andrews Library, Jack Rakove (Stanford University), Dennis L. Bark (Hoover Institution), James Billington (Library of Congress), George Carey (Georgetown University), David Kennedy (Earhart Foundation), Hans Eichoz (Liberty Fund), Thomas Vail (Cleveland, *The Plain Dealer*), and Mark David Hall (George Fox University). I am indebted to each of them.

Maynard Garrison
San Francisco, CA

COLLECTOR'S FOREWORD

In 1907 Professor L. H. Alexander of Harvard University observed that "two great figures . . . loom from the Revolutionary era, the one, [James] Wilson's, whose brain conceived and created the nation; the other, [George] Washington's, who wielded the physical forces that made it."[1] Alexander concluded that because of Wilson's intellectual and theoretical contributions to the nation's founding, it was certain that future scholars would shower great attention on him. Compared with others of the founding generation, however, that has not happened. There is not a little irony in this development. For example, in 1997 Lady Margaret Thatcher stated before the annual convention of the American Bar Association that the modern political era began with the signing of the Declaration of Independence and the subsequent adoption of the American Constitution in 1787, both documents Wilson helped to shape and to which he affixed his signature. Government created by consideration and choice, rather than force or accident, had become the universally admired model, Thatcher observed, and Wilson was one of the architects of that model. It was Wilson who wove the intellectual threads of his generation into a theory of popularly based government wedded to the rule of law. In theory and action Wilson, as Alexander argued, created a nation.

The path of Wilson's life, career, and political thought are detailed in Kermit Hall's introduction. As Hall makes clear, Wilson was at the front rank of the founders. He was also in touch with the future. "By adopting this system," Wilson explained in 1787, "we shall probably lay a foundation for erecting temples of liberty, in every part of the earth." He went on to insist that "[t]he advantages resulting from this system will not be confined to the United States; it will draw from Europe many worthy

1. L. H. Alexander, *James Wilson, Nation Builder* (1907), p. 13.

characters, who pant for the enjoyment of freedom."[2] Thus the universal admiration for the American system recognized by Lady Thatcher in 1997 was foretold by James Wilson more than two centuries earlier. It is for this reason that we return with respect to his works.

Maynard Garrison
San Francisco

2. Historical Society of Pennsylvania, *Pennsylvania and the Federal Constitution, 1787–1788* (1888), 2: 488.

INTRODUCTION

The Reputation of James Wilson

James Wilson was a dominant figure in the founding of the American nation, not just in politics and law, but in personal ambition. He had a formidable appetite for fame and wealth matched by a powerful intellect. Wilson was one of only six persons to sign both the Declaration of Independence and the Constitution; only Gouverneur Morris spoke more frequently in the Philadelphia Convention of 1787; and scholars rank Wilson as the second most influential member of that convention, behind only James Madison. Wilson was, in the end, a tragic figure, a founder who understood the future too clearly and pointed to it too directly, both for his own immediate reputation and, as significantly, for his standing among generations to come. These volumes are intended to stimulate new research and analysis of Wilson's contributions in the ongoing effort to determine accurately his rightful place in the founding era.

Wilson's writings have always competed for attention against the better known works of the founding generation, notably *The Federalist Papers* authored by John Jay, James Madison, and Alexander Hamilton.[i] Moreover, scholars have turned repeatedly to the individual writings of Madison, Thomas Jefferson, and John Adams to discern the nature of free institutions. The materials in this volume suggest that Wilson, as the historian Gordon Wood has noted, was one of the most, if not the most, ardent advocates for the people as the sovereign base of the new American constitutional system.[ii]

Wilson deserves attention as well because he sketched a genuinely systematic view of the law. His *Lectures on Law,* while never published in a

i. Alexander Hamilton, James Madison, and John Jay, *The Federalist Papers,* ed. Clinton Rossiter (1961).

ii. Gordon Wood, *The Creation of the American Republic* (1998): 212.

single volume during his life, were nonetheless intended to make him the American equivalent of Sir Edward Blackstone, the great English legal commentator. The *Lectures* reflect Wilson's scholarly approach to matters of public affairs, a quality that set him apart from Thomas Jefferson, Oliver Ellsworth, Edmund Randolph, Tapping Reeve, and George Wythe. Wilson attempted to blend the ideas of liberty and the rule of law with the new idea of popular sovereignty. Moreover, the *Lectures* stand in marked contrast to Wilson's contributions as a justice of the Supreme Court. He crafted few opinions while on the high court; in eight years, Wilson produced about twenty total pages of written opinions, a legacy that reflected neither his talent as a lawyer nor his impact on American law. His most important opinion, in *Chisholm* v. *Georgia* (1793), was quickly overturned by the ratification of the Eleventh Amendment.[iii] In this light his ambitious project to synthesize principles of natural law and popular will in the *Lectures* stands as his most definitive statement about the character of American law.

The *Lectures,* there is no doubt, were a serious contribution to the literature of the law that no student of its early national origins can ignore. Wilson deserves high marks for his efforts to reduce and synthesize American law, a particularly difficult task in light of the jumble of colonial legal practices and the traditions of the English common law. What set him apart from his better-known contemporaries was his gift for addressing the law in broad, often bold strokes that encompassed philosophy, psychology, and political theory.

Despite the obvious importance of his contributions, Wilson continues to struggle for attention in comparison with the other founders at least in part because of his personal life. Wilson's adult life was marked by land-development schemes, a corresponding inability to reconcile his quest for individual wealth with a scrupulous attention to the public interest, and ultimately the distinction of being the only justice of the Supreme Court ever imprisoned for debt. That made Wilson something of a paradox. He was trained in the Scottish Moral Enlightenment tradition of Thomas Reid and Francis Hutcheson, which stressed, among other things, the close relationship among public virtue, moral commitment to the public interest,

iii. 2 U.S. 419 (1793).

and respect for the will of the people based on their intrinsic good. This philosophical perspective, however, collided with Wilson's fabled scramble for wealth, power, and social station. Wilson's articulated philosophy was based on a relatively optimistic view of human nature; his personal conduct betrayed to his critics a more pessimistic assessment. Madison, who was also schooled in the Scottish Moral Enlightenment, diverged from Wilson by rejecting the latter's strongly populist impulses and substituting in their place the belief that if men were angels there would be no need for a constitution in the first place. Wilson has been considered a conservative because of his opposition to the Pennsylvania Constitution of 1776, but at the Constitutional Convention of 1787 he was the only founder to argue for "the direct election of the executive, the direct and proportional election of senators, and the principle of 'one person, one vote.'"[iv]

However, like Chief Justice John Marshall, he also supported the constitutional separation of powers and checks and balances—even suggesting in his *Lectures* that the Supreme Court could strike down an act of Congress if it violated the Constitution or natural law.[v] Although he lost many battles at the Constitutional Convention, America's constitutional system has come to closely resemble that advocated by Wilson. Accordingly, the materials in this volume can help us better understand the political and legal ideas underlying the American experiment in constitutional government.

Beginnings

James Wilson was born in 1742 at Carskerdo, Scotland. His father was a farmer who resided in the vicinity of St. Andrews.[vi] Despite his

iv. Mark David Hall, *The Political and Legal Philosophy of James Wilson, 1742–1798* (1997), 21. For further discussion of Wilson's support of democratic institutions see chapter 4 of this volume.

v. Ibid., chapter 5. Hall argues that a proper understanding of Wilson's political philosophy shows how his acceptance of democratic institutions and countermajoritarian checks may be reconciled (see especially chapters 2, 4, and 5).

vi. The best discussion of Wilson's early life is Charles Page Smith, *James Wilson: Founding Father, 1742–1798* (1956), especially pp. 1–89. More generally see Randolph G. Adams, *Political Ideas of the American Revolution* (1922); Arnaud B. Leavelle, "James Wilson and the Relation of the Scottish Metaphysics to American Political Thought," *Political Science Quarterly* 57 (September 1942): 394–410; George W. Carey, "James Wilson's Political Thought and the Constitutional modest beginnings, Wilson received a splendid classical education at Culpar grammar school, which enabled him to win a scholarship to the University of St. Andrews in 1757. This education served him well throughout his life, training him in scholarly analysis and simultaneously providing a lifelong intellectual compass. The Scottish Moral Enlightenment and the Common Sense school of philosophy associated with it pervaded these institutions and deeply influenced Wilson.

After completing his studies, Wilson moved to America in the midst of the Stamp Act agitations in 1765. Early the next year, he accepted a position as a Latin tutor and then a lecturer in English Literature at the College of Philadelphia (later part of the University of Pennsylvania), only to abandon it to study law under John Dickinson. On borrowed capital, he also began a lifelong passion—speculating in land. The College awarded him an honorary Master of Arts degree in 1766. In 1768, the year after his admission to the Philadelphia bar, Wilson set up practice at Reading, Pennsylvania. Two years later he moved westward to the Scotch-Irish settlement of Carlisle and built up a broad clientele. The following year he married Rachel Bird, the daughter of a wealthy Berks County landowner,

---

Convention," *The Political Science Reviewer* 17 (Fall 1987): 50–107; Morton M. Rosenberg, "James Wilson, Forgotten Founding Father," *International Journal of Social Education* 2 (Spring 1987): 30–43; Arthur E. Wilmarth, Jr., "Elusive Foundation: John Marshall, James Wilson, and the Problem of Reconciling Popular Sovereignty and Natural Law Jurisprudence in the New Republic," *George Washington Law Review* 72 (December 2003): 113–93; Ralph Rossum, "James Wilson and the 'Pyramid of Government': The Federal Republic," *Political Science Reviewer* 6 (Fall 1976): 113–34; Rossum, "James Wilson," in *Encyclopedia of the American Constitution,* 4 vols. (1986), 4: 2068; Stephen A. Conrad, "Metaphor and Imagination in James Wilson's Theory of Federal Union," *Law & Social Inquiry* 13 (1988): 1–70; Conrad, "The Rhetorical Constitution of 'Civil Society' at the Foundation: One Lawyer's Anxious Vision," *Indiana Law Journal* 72 (Spring, 1997): 335–73; Conrad, "Polite Foundation: Citizenship and Common Sense in James Wilson's Republican Theory," *Supreme Court Review* 1984 (1985): 359–86; Conrad, "Undercurrents of Republican Thinking in Modern Constitutional Theory: James Wilson's 'Assimilation of the Common-Law Mind'," *Northwestern University Law Review* 84 (Fall 1989): 186–219; Garry Wills, "James Wilson's New Meaning of Sovereignty," in *Conceptual Change and the Constitution* (1988): 99–106; John V. Jezierski, "Parliament or People: James Wilson and Blackstone on the Nature and Location of Sovereignty," *Journal of the History of Ideas* 32 (January–March 1971): 95–106; Lyle Dennison, "The 'Revolution Principle': Ideology and Constitutionalism in the Thought of James Wilson," *Review of Politics* 39 (1977): 157–91; Daniel Farber, *Lincoln's Constitution* (2003), 47–49, 81–85; Kermit L. Hall, *The Supreme Court and Judicial Review in American History* (1985): 1–10; and Daniel J. McCarthy, "James Wilson and the Creation of the Presidency," *Presidential Studies Quarterly* 17 (Fall 1987): 689–96. In preparing this essay, I have relied heavily on the insights of Conrad, Wilmarth, and McCloskey.

a union that joined her family's considerable wealth with the young lawyer's voracious appetite for speculation in land. The marriage produced six children and lasted until 1786, when Rachel Wilson died. Seven years later Wilson married again, to Hannah Gray, half his age and a resident of Boston, who outlived him.

Of Wilson's children, the best known was his third, Bird, born in 1777. Bird became his father's favorite, and he alone among the children was permitted to enter his study to read while his father worked. Wilson also took the young boy with him as he went about Philadelphia doing business and conferring on matters of politics and law. In 1792 the fifteen-year-old Bird graduated from the University of Pennsylvania and went on to become one of the chief managers of his father's gradually collapsing financial empire. Following the elder Wilson's death, it fell to Bird to arrange for the publication of his father's *Works* in 1804, including the *Lectures on Law.*

While Wilson began his family he also entered the swirl of Revolutionary era politics. In Carlisle in 1774 he assumed the chairmanship of the city's committee of correspondence, attended the first provincial assembly, and completed preparation of *Considerations on the Nature and Extent of the Legislative Authority of the British Parliament.* This tract was an early statement challenging British authority; it was also Wilson's first direct published attack on what became one of his favorite targets, Parliamentary sovereignty. His authorship of the pamphlet established him as a Whig leader, and it is one of the most important documents in this collection.

The next year, voters sent Wilson to the provincial assembly, which in turn sent him to the Continental Congress, where he sat mainly on military and Indian affairs committees. In 1776, bound by the Pennsylvania legislature not to vote for independence, he joined the moderates in Congress, voting for a three-week delay in considering Richard Henry Lee's resolution of June 7 for independence, what ultimately became in the hands of Thomas Jefferson the Declaration of Independence. Wilson, however, after Pennsylvania freed the state delegates to vote their consciences, switched his vote, and on the July 1 and 2 ballots he voted in favor of and ultimately signed the Declaration of Independence.

At the same time, Wilson strenuously opposed the republican Pennsylvania constitution of 1776. That position proved politically costly, and in

1777 he lost his seat in Congress when his aggressive frontier constituents viewed him as out of step with the fast-moving revolution. Wilson relocated to Annapolis during the winter of 1777–78, subsequently taking up residence in Philadelphia, where he resided for the remainder of his life.

Wilson's quest for wealth became increasingly apparent. In Philadelphia he emerged as a spokesperson for and leader of conservative republican groups determined to break with the British without fundamentally losing economic control. Despite the dislocations created by the war, Wilson's economic fortunes blossomed. He became a successful businessman, and the uncertain state created by the conflict served his speculative interest in land well. In June 1779 the French government appointed Wilson its advocate general in the new United States, a post he held until 1781. In this office, Wilson skillfully addressed commercial and maritime matters involving France while defending the Loyalists who opposed the American Revolution. Wilson resigned the post in 1783, however, because the French had failed to honor their agreement to compensate him. Two years later, however, the King of France rewarded him with a lump-sum payment of ten thousand livres.

Wilson's success in the face of the hardship of others made him a target. Motivated by soaring inflation and food shortages brought on by the war, a mob attacked Wilson's home in the fall of 1779. He and thirty-five other prominent businessmen were barricaded inside his home at Third and Walnut Streets, a residence that came to be known as Fort Wilson. The fracas proved a turning point for both Wilson's political fortunes and the conservatives in the city, who gained political traction in the face of casualties. Congress in 1781 selected him to be one of the directors of the Bank of North America, led by Robert Morris. Morris had been not just a client but a fellow investor with Wilson in several speculative land deals. A year later, he was selected to serve again in the Continental Congress, a post that he held until 1787.

The mob violence in Philadelphia also prompted Wilson to adopt an even stronger nationalist position, one that coincided with his self-interest in the success of the Bank of North America. In 1785 the radical elements of the Pennsylvania legislature proposed revoking the bank's charter. In return for a fee of four hundred dollars, Wilson agreed to write a pamphlet in support of the bank. The bank had established a modicum of fiscal stability during the revolutionary crisis, but as significantly, Wilson was indebted to it for more than thirty thousand dollars in loans. His widely circulated pamphlet, *Considerations on the Bank of North America,* offered a vision of the powers of the national government that foreshadowed the new Constitution drafted two years later. Wilson insisted that repeal of the Bank's charter by the Pennsylvania Assembly would be economically foolish.

His position at once aligned him with the conservative elements in Pennsylvania politics and affirmed his strong nationalism. It also was unsuccessful. The Assembly repealed the charter in Pennsylvania; Wilson's opponents painted him as more interested in his own economic advantage than in the well-being of his fellow citizens. Yet even his sharpest critics stood in awe of the erudition of *Considerations* and of Wilson's general intelligence.

The Philadelphia Convention of 1787 and the Ratification of the Constitution

Wilson's greatest moment in public life came in the Philadelphia Convention of 1787.[vii] Wilson was a staunch advocate for separation of powers that included an independent and powerful judiciary, a popularly elected president, and a bicameral legislative branch. He prevailed in his arguments in support of the judiciary, although one of his pet ideas, a Council of Revision, lost not once but three times before the delegates. Wilson's hope of having a popularly elected president with a three-year term also failed, with the delegates instead adopting an electoral college, which Wilson came to support, and a four-year term. Article I did include a bicameral scheme, as Wilson proposed, but with the Senate selected by state legislators rather than the people.

Wilson also advocated for federalism and the related concept of dual sovereignty. Since the people were the foundation of all government, they could construct as many levels of authority as they wished. Thus, the

vii. The best description of Wilson's contributions to the Philadelphia Convention are in Smith, pp. 215–61.

people could not only establish a national government of enumerated powers but simultaneously lend their support to state governments vested with the traditional police powers of health, safety, morals, and welfare. Ironically, both John C. Calhoun and Abraham Lincoln in the years leading up to the Civil War found in Wilson's ideas arguments to support either the limited or the perpetual nature of the Union.

Wilson's colleagues selected him to be one of the six delegates who reported the final document for acceptance, a genuine honor to a person uniformly recognized as one of its chief architects. And Wilson also played a decisive role in the ratification of the Constitution in his important home state. He was the only member of the Pennsylvania state convention of 1787 to ratify the Constitution who had served in the Philadelphia Convention. Following the ratification of the federal constitution in Pennsylvania, Wilson participated in a second state convention to align the state constitution with the new federal document.

The Writings in This Volume: Legal Philosopher and Associate Justice

In 1789 President George Washington appointed Wilson an associate justice of the Supreme Court. At the same time Wilson agreed to give a series of law lectures at the College of Philadelphia. The documents in this collection speak to his role in both.

Wilson used his university position to deliver his *Lectures on Law.* The *Lectures* comprise almost seven hundred pages of text; the first was publicly delivered on December 15, 1790. They were long on theory and short on the kinds of blackletter law issues that might be of practical value to students. The *Lectures* were lectures. They were not finely hewn essays meant to be read rather than spoken.[viii] Only about half of them were delivered over the course of two winter terms at the law school, hardly enough time for Wilson to sketch his ambitious vision of American law. At the same time, Wilson was also busy becoming a justice of the Supreme Court and managing his increasingly chaotic business affairs.

viii. Robert G. McCloskey, ed., *The Works of James Wilson,* 2 vols. (1967), 1: 37–43.

The *Lectures* shed light on Wilson's philosophy of law, on the relationship of politics to law, on the role of God in the development of law, and thus on the landscape of early America in general. The *Lectures* are also one of the most notable examples in American thought of the purported link between popular will and moral sense philosophy. While Wilson owed a great deal to the Scottish Moral Enlightenment, he also infused his lectures with ideas drawn from John Locke, insisting that government depended on a voluntary compact that included the right and duty of every citizen to act in ways that conformed to the laws of God and nature. Wilson also agreed with Locke that the consent of the people was essential to create and maintain the state.

Wilson's *Lectures* underscore that he objected to the Pennsylvania Constitution of 1776 not because it was too democratic but because it granted too much popular authority to the legislative branch at the expense of the two other branches, the executive and the judicial, which he considered to have a popular base as well. Wilson, in other sections of the *Lectures*, objected that an all-powerful, single-house legislature threatened to produce "sudden and violent fits of despotism, injustice, and cruelty."[ix] Wilson wanted the broadest possible popular base for the executive and legislative branches at the same time that he insisted that all three branches, including the appointed judiciary, enjoyed coequal status as agents of the people.

That theoretical proposition collided with practical reality in *Chisholm* v. *Georgia* (1793), the most important Supreme Court case in which he participated.[x] Wilson insisted that the people could at once support both the federal government and each of the separate states. The plaintiff, a citizen of South Carolina and the executor of a merchant in that state, sued the state of Georgia for the value of clothing supplied by the merchant during the Revolutionary War. Georgia ignored a summons to appear in federal court and asserted that it was a sovereign and independent state immune from any federal lawsuit. Article III section 2 of the Constitution extended the federal judicial power to controversies between "a State and Citizens of another State." The Court entered a default judgment against Georgia,

ix. As quoted in Wilmarth, p. 154.
x. 2 U.S. 419.

with four votes cast seriatim by Wilson, John Jay, William Cushing, and John Blair, Jr., and a strong dissent by James Iredell.

Wilson wrote that sovereignty resided in the people of the United States "for the purposes of the Union" and that as to those purposes Georgia was "not a sovereign state."[xi] Georgia stood no higher than any individual; it had to be held to account for the contracts it made, and the place to do so was in the federal courts. The backlash against the decision in general and against the words of Wilson (and Jay) in particular was especially vehement among Anti-Federalists. The result was the speedy ratification in 1795 of the Eleventh Amendment. The new amendment stripped the federal courts of jurisdiction in suits commenced against a state by citizens of another state or another nation. This rebuke of Wilson was particularly poignant since in the constitutional convention he had urged the principle of dual sovereignty. Put to the test on the bench, however, Wilson discovered that his views on the sovereignty of the people had less support than he supposed, at least when that sovereignty trumped state authority.

Wilson's strident nationalism also led him to oppose the addition of the Bill of Rights to the Constitution. Based on his new concept of the perpetually sovereign people, Wilson confidently proclaimed that the proposed Bill of Rights was neither essential nor necessary. Wilson even argued that the addition of a bill of rights would be dangerous because any enumeration of rights would imply that others were not included.

The *Lectures* also remind us that Wilson was something of a legal sociologist. For example, he insisted that the will of the people tended to mirror their needs through the law, and he used the jury system to prove this proposition. The jury, according to Wilson, was the most important embodiment of the will of the people in the legal system and an essential safeguard of liberty. Few early Americans, as the *Lectures* make clear, wrote with greater authority and passion about the jury. Wilson insisted that trial by jury was essential to "just government" and freedom. He, however, was an equally strong critic of jury nullification, the practice by which juries interposed their interpretation of the law in place of that of a judge.

Wilson also covered the subject of equity. He believed that the entire purpose of the legal system was to produce justice; accordingly, the con-

xi. Ibid., 454.

cept of equity was central to the success of the American experiment. Wilson argued that judges should be more than mere voices of precedent; they had also to make certain that what he called "the spirit of the law" was realized.[xii] He also warned that judges should not make law. According to Wilson, a judge should take account of "the immediate sentiments of justice" and should implement "principles and rules of genuine policy and natural justice" for the purpose of promoting a true "science of law."[xiii] He urged common law judges to apply equitable principles in the interest of "continual progression," because "equity may well be deemed the conductor of law towards a state of refinement and perfection."[xiv]

Wilson emerged as a proponent of law as a tool for the commercial growth of the new nation. If the Republic were to prosper, it would do so based on principles of uniformity and predictability. Once again, he drew on his Scottish experience. America's economy, like that of Scotland, would prosper to the extent that it embraced principles of international commercial law or, as it was called then, the law of nations.

The connection that Wilson made among common law, natural law, and the law of nations also informed his thinking about judicial review. For his authority, Wilson drew on Lord Coke's decision in *Dr. Bonham's Case* (1610).[xv] He also took exception to Blackstone's view that judges could not defeat the intention of a legislative body, since in the new American scheme the people rather than Parliament were sovereign. Because judges were also agents of the people, those same judges could strike down an unconstitutional law. The people would expect nothing less of them. His version of judicial review was in part text based. Judges, he believed, were required to take the text of the Constitution and lay it alongside the law that was in question. Judges could not simply do what they felt was best. In the *Lectures*, he went even further. He insisted that any act of a legislature could be subject to the control "arising from natural and revealed law."[xvi]

Wilson argued strongly in the *Lectures* for the importance of federal judicial review. He had insisted in *Hayburn's Case* (1792) that the justices

xii. As quoted in Wilmarth, p. 163.
xiii. As quoted in ibid.
xiv. As quoted in ibid.
xv. 77 English Reports 646, 652 (1610).
xvi. As quoted in Wilmarth, p. 166.

should not hear claims made by Revolutionary War pensioners, even though an act of Congress directed that they do so. He and other members of the Court objected because the law required them to perform nonjudicial duties, thus violating the principle of separation of powers. The decision also prefigured arguments to come that the Court could declare an act of Congress to be unconstitutional, although it did not do so in this particular instance. He expected the people in whom he so trusted to respond with support, but in practice Wilson consistently underestimated how broad the base of opposition was not only to an active federal judiciary but also to the courts' exercise of the equity power.

Wilson's own behavior on and off the bench reminds us of how unworkable his attempt was to establish natural law as a cornerstone of American politics and jurisprudence and to frame a common law of federal crimes. For example, in *Henfield's Case* (1793) he attempted to establish the principle of a common law of federal crimes. The jury hearing the case, however, rejected his direct charge that, even though there was no specific statute that Gideon Henfield had violated, the captain of a privateer had nevertheless acted illegally by bringing a captured British ship to Philadelphia.[xvii]

Disgrace and Death

Wilson's ambition for high station in life collided with his equally strong quest for material gain. Wilson wanted to be Chief Justice, a position that he believed he had earned for his resolute support of the new national government. Wilson was also vain enough to believe that of the members of the Court, he was the one best versed in the law. Such an ambition was entirely in keeping with his goal of becoming the American Blackstone.

When the Supreme Court came into session in February 1796, President George Washington had to replace Chief Justice John Jay. Wilson seemed a likely possibility, but because of his preoccupation with land and

xvii. *Henfield's Case*, 11 F. Cas. 1099 (C.C.D. Pa. 1793) (No. 6360). These developments are more fully discussed in Wilmarth, pp. 167–70, and in Stephen B. Presser and Jamil S. Zainaldin, *Law and Jurisprudence in American History: Cases and Materials*, 5th ed. (2003): 183–93.

business ventures, Washington ultimately turned to Oliver Ellsworth, a Connecticut Federalist, a member of the Philadelphia Convention, and the principal framer of the Judiciary Act of 1789. Wilson was devastated by being passed over, so much so that he wrote privately of his intentions of resigning.

He simply could not afford to do so. His steadily plummeting financial fortunes made his meager Supreme Court salary all the more important, especially since he was borrowing money to cover failed land speculation at rates as high as thirty percent. Wilson confronted financial ruin and, even more tragically for a judge, arrest and imprisonment. After spending a brief period in a New Jersey jail in July 1797, Wilson fled to Edenton, North Carolina. He was unable to return to the February 1798 term of the Court because his creditors would have had him imprisoned. Among the creditors to whom he owed money was Pierce Butler of South Carolina, who, on learning of Wilson's presence across the border, demanded payment of the $197,000 owed him, a huge sum for the time. Wilson could not pay; he was again jailed. Ultimately, Butler agreed to the release of the Supreme Court justice, who took up residence in the Horniblow Tavern. In July he was stricken with malaria; on August 21, 1798, he died, financially ruined.

Legacy

Litigation over Wilson's extensive estate went on for years. Its disposition included hundreds of thousands of dollars in real property in Pennsylvania and the Gibraltar Iron Works in Bucks County. His estate also included an extensive selection of books on farming, a lifelong passion of Wilson and an echo of his childhood in Scotland. Ultimately, his son, Bird, was able to pay the great bulk of his debts in full.

In the end, the real wealth and fame that Wilson sought eluded him. Literally no one had a good word to say about him. "His death," wrote Page Smith, "had been a pathetic one without the nobler dimensions of tragedy."[xviii] Perhaps even more important, Wilson left this life with a

xviii. Smith, p. 390.

string of claims of serious ethical lapses as a legacy. His land-acquisition programs and personal conduct are subjects well worthy of the attention of modern scholars of the Court and the era.

Wilson did leave a legacy in the law and in his contributions to the creation of the American republic. As Arthur Wilmarth reminds us, he was committed to the idea of public virtue, an unwavering belief in the power of popular sovereignty, and an oddly unrealistic view of human nature. What Wilson wanted was, in the end, not within his or even the nation's reach: a more perfect society that not only secured the rights of individuals but actually enlarged them through an appointed federal judiciary. Judges were supposed to be agents of human perfection. In some ways Wilson was the first sociologist of American law; his legacy lingers in his admonition to view law as a system of social adaptation.

The Text

This edition is the most comprehensive collection of materials ever assembled by and about James Wilson. It also has the virtue of gathering all of Wilson's important works in one place.

Although comprehensive, it is not complete. For example, Wilson made a number of charges to grand juries in the course of his circuit court duties while sitting on the Supreme Court between 1789 and 1798, but not all of them were recorded, and of those that were only two merit serious consideration, one from Pennsylvania in 1793 and the other from Virginia in 1797. Scholars uniformly treat these as important contributions by Wilson to the development of American law.[xix] Only two of Wilson's Supreme Court opinions are included, again because of their importance. The first is from the famous case of *Chisholm* (1793); the other, and much briefer, from *Ware* v. *Hylton* (1796).[xx] Wilson possessed one of the finest legal minds of his era, but it seldom found expression in Supreme Court opinions. Wilson was on the Court in only two other significant cases: *Hylton* v.

xix. Maeva Marcus, ed., *The Documentary History of the Supreme Court of the United States, 1789–1800*. Vol. 3 (1990), contains the charges made by Wilson and the other justices to grand juries while on circuit.

xx. 3 U.S. 199 (1796).

United States (1796) and *Calder* v. *Bull* (1798).[xxi] In the case of *Calder*, Wilson did not participate because of his flight from creditors and an illness that ultimately killed him. All commentators agree, however, that *Chisholm* was Wilson's most important Supreme Court opinion and that his opinion in *Ware*, while brief, underscored his basic constitutional values.

In 1967 Robert G. McCloskey produced the last edited volumes of Wilson's works. His two-volume compilation was for the most part a reprint of the 1804 text prepared by Bird Wilson. In 1896 James DeWitt Andrews edited a two-volume collection. Andrews omitted some of the papers that Bird Wilson had included and modestly rearranged some of the materials. Both McCloskey and Andrews followed Bird Wilson's organizational scheme. McCloskey provided an illuminating introduction and supplied footnoted annotations along with the translation of Latin phrases.

Since the publication of McCloskey's two volumes on Wilson, additional materials have come to light. These include Wilson's carefully handwritten notes for the *Lectures on Law*, now in the manuscript collection of the Free Library of Philadelphia. These notes are discussed at the beginning of the section on the *Lectures* in an essay by Wilson scholar Mark David Hall. Hall not only addresses the notes but also offers a substantial commentary on the origins, purposes, and value of the *Lectures*.

In presenting the text, the chief goal has been to make it as authentic as the original 1804 edition of the lectures and to leave the reader to reach his or her own judgments about it. The spelling, capitalization, and punctuation have been left as they were in the 1804 edition. James Wilson's footnotes and those of his son have also been left intact. They are indicated by letters. Footnotes marked by numbers are modern translations of Latin phrases from McCloskey's version of Wilson's works or annotations for individuals who might not be known to even well-educated readers today. Again, the objective has been to intrude as little as possible on the way in which Bird Wilson presented his father's materials. Where "Ed." appears beside a note, it indicates that the annotation was made by Bird Wilson.

This volume is arranged somewhat differently from that of McCloskey, in part to reflect the new material and in part to underscore that the *Lectures* were a self-contained enterprise. Thus, the first materials in the vol-

xxi. 3 U.S. 171 (1796); 3 U.S. 386 (1798).

ume are some of what McCloskey termed "Miscellaneous Papers," which he placed at the end of his volumes. The decision to place these materials first was driven in part by their chronology, since most of them appeared before the *Lectures* were given. In addition to the miscellaneous material included by previous editors, this edition contains Wilson's "An Address to the Inhabitants of the Colonies" (1776), "Remarks of James Wilson in the Federal Convention of 1787," "State House Yard Speech" (1787), and "On the Improvement and Settlement of Lands in the United States (mid-1790s). The materials from the constitutional convention include every instance that Madison recorded Wilson's comments. Although Wilson repeated some of these thoughts in his *Lectures,* the excerpts from the convention shine light on one of his most important contributions to American constitutional history. As well, this edition contains Wilson's remarks at the Pennsylvania ratifying convention and his most important judicial opinions.

Finally, this volume also contains a Bibliographical Glossary, one that McCloskey prepared for his two-volume work. The glossary is helpful because Wilson drew extensively on a rich and varied body of writing, but in indicating the sources to which he turned, he used what McCloskey rightly termed an "often . . . baffling" system of abbreviated citations.[xxii] The glossary will help readers to understand the sources that Wilson relied on and to confirm his ambitions as a serious scholar.

The impetus for this volume originated with Maynard Garrison of San Francisco, a person with a strong interest in Wilson and the Founding Era. Garrison pulled together a collection of materials that makes this volume the most comprehensive assemblage of writings and speeches ever collected by and about Wilson.

In bringing this volume to publication, I have had considerable assistance. I am grateful to James Taylor, Robert Wagner, and Phyllis A. Hall for their assistance with footnote preparation, citation checking, research on the annotations, and proofreading. I also treasure the professional support and patience provided by Laura Goetz of the Liberty Fund press.

Kermit L. Hall
Albany, New York, September 1, 2005

xxii. McCloskey, p. 50.

PART I

Political Papers, Speeches, and Judicial Opinions of James Wilson

"All men are, by nature, equal and free: no one has a right to any authority over another without his consent: all lawful government is founded on the consent of those who are subject to it: such consent was given with a view to ensure and to increase the happiness of the governed, above what they could enjoy in an independent and unconnected state of nature. The consequence is, that the happiness of the society is the *first* law of every government." ("Considerations," August 17, 1774, James Wilson.)

Originally written in 1768, Wilson's pamphlet was one of the first to argue that Parliament had no authority to pass legislation regulating the colonies' internal *or external* affairs.

Considerations on the Nature and Extent of the Legislative Authority of the British Parliament, 1774.

No question can be more important to Great Britain, and to the colonies, than this—does the legislative authority of the British parliament extend over them?

On the resolution of this question, and on the measures which a resolution of it will direct, it will depend, whether the parent country, like a happy mother, shall behold her children flourishing around her, and receive the most grateful returns for her protection and love; or whether, like a step dame, rendered miserable by her own unkind conduct, she shall see their affections alienated, and herself deprived of those advantages which a milder treatment would have ensured to her.

The British nation are generous: they love to enjoy freedom: they love to behold it: slavery is their greatest abhorrence. Is it possible, then, that they would wish themselves the authors of it? No. Oppression is not a plant of the British soil; and the late severe proceedings against the colonies must have arisen from the detestable schemes of interested ministers, who have misinformed and misled the people. A regard for that nation, from whom we have sprung, and from whom we boast to have derived the spirit which prompts us to oppose their unfriendly measures, must lead us to put this construction on what we have lately seen and experienced. When, therefore, they shall know and consider the justice of our claim—that we insist only upon being treated as freemen, and as the descendants of those British ancestors, whose memory we will not dishonour by our degeneracy, it is reasonable to hope, that they will approve of our conduct, and bestow their loudest applauses on our congenial ardour for liberty.

But if these reasonable and joyful hopes should fatally be disappointed, it will afford us at least some satisfaction to know, that the principles on which we have founded our opposition to the late acts of parliament, are the principles of justice and freedom, and of the British constitution. If our righteous struggle shall be attended with misfortunes, we will reflect with exultation on the noble cause of them; and while suffering unmerited distress, think ourselves superiour to the proudest slaves. On the contrary, if we shall be reinstated in the enjoyment of those rights, to which we are entitled by the supreme and uncontrollable laws of nature, and the fundamental principles of the British constitution, we shall reap the glorious fruit of our labours; and we shall, at the same time, give to the world and to posterity an instructive example, that the cause of liberty ought not to be despaired of, and that a generous contention in that cause is not always unattended with success.

The foregoing considerations have induced me to publish a few remarks on the important question, with which I introduced this essay.

Those who allege that the parliament of Great Britain have power to make laws binding the American colonies, reason in the following manner. "That there is and must be in every state a supreme, irresistible, absolute, uncontrolled authority, in which the *jura summi imperii*,[1] or the rights of sovereignty, reside:"[a] "That this supreme power is, by the constitution of Great Britain, vested in the king, lords, and commons:"[b] "That, therefore, the acts of the king, lords, and commons, or, in other words, acts of parliament, have, by the British constitution, a binding force on the American colonies, they composing a part of the British empire."

I admit that the principle, on which this argument is founded, is of great importance: its importance, however, is derived from its tendency to promote the ultimate end of all government. But if the application of it would, in any instance, destroy, instead of promoting, that end, it ought, in that instance, to be rejected: for to admit it, would be to sacrifice the end to the means, which are valuable only so far as they advance it.

All men are, by nature, equal and free: no one has a right to any authority over another without his consent: all lawful government is founded on the consent of those who are subject to it: such consent was given with a view to ensure and to increase the happiness of the governed, above what they could

1. Highest or whole imperious decision.

a. 4. Bl. Com. 48. 49.

b. Id. 50. 51.

enjoy in an independent and unconnected state of nature. The consequence is, that the happiness of the society is the *first* law of every government.[c]

This rule is founded on the law of nature: it must control every political maxim: it must regulate the legislature itself.[d] The people have a right to insist that this rule be observed; and are entitled to demand a moral security that the legislature will observe it. If they have not the first, they are slaves; if they have not the second, they are, every moment, exposed to slavery. For "civil liberty is nothing else but natural liberty, devested of that part which constituted the independence of individuals, by the authority which it confers on sovereigns, attended with a right of insisting upon their making a good use of their authority, and with a moral security that this right will have its effect."[e]

Let me now be permitted to ask—Will it ensure and increase the happiness of the American colonies, that the parliament of Great Britain should possess a supreme, irresistible, uncontrolled authority over them? Is such an authority consistent with their liberty? Have they any security that it will be employed only for their good? Such a security is absolutely necessary. Parliaments are not infallible: they are not always just. The members, of whom they are composed, are human; and, therefore, they may err; they are influenced by interest; and, therefore, they may deviate from their duty. The acts of the body must depend upon the opinions and dispositions of the members: the acts of the body may, then, be the result of errour and of vice. It is no breach of decency to suppose all this: the British constitution supposes it: "it supposes that parliaments may betray their trust, and provides, as far as human wisdom can provide, that they may not be able to do so long, without a sufficient control."[f] Without provisions for this purpose, the temple of British liberty, like a structure of ice, would instantly dissolve before the fire of oppression and despotick sway.

It will be very material to consider the several securities, which the inhabitants of Great Britain have, that their liberty will not be destroyed by the legislature, in whose hands it is intrusted. If it shall appear, that

c. The right of sovereignty is that of commanding finally—but in order to procure real felicity; for if this end is not obtained, sovereignty ceases to be a legitimate authority. 2. Burl. 32, 33.

d. The law of nature is superiour in obligation to any other. 1. Bl. Com. 41.

e. 2. Burl. 19.

f. Bol. Diss, on Part. I. 11. 12. p. 167. 179.

the same securities are not enjoyed by the colonists; the undeniable consequence will be, that the colonists are not under the same obligations to intrust their liberties into the hands of the same legislature: for the colonists are entitled to all[g] the privileges of Britons. We have committed no crimes to forfeit them: we have too much spirit to resign them. We will leave our posterity as free as our ancestors left us.

To give to any thing that passes in parliament the force of a law, the consent of the king, of the lords, and of the commons[h] is absolutely necessary.[i] If, then, the inhabitants of Great Britain possess a sufficient restraint upon any of these branches of the legislature, their liberty is secure, provided they be not wanting to themselves. Let us take a view of the restraints, which they have upon the house of commons.

They elect the members of that house. "Magistrates," says Montesquieu,[j2] "are properly theirs, who have the nomination of them." The members of the house of commons, therefore, elected by the people, are the magistrates of the people; and are bound by the ties of gratitude for the honour and confidence conferred upon them, to consult the interest of their constituents.

The power of elections has ever been regarded as a point of the last consequence to all[k] free governments. The independent exercise of that power is justly deemed the strongest bulwark of the British liberties.[l] As such, it has always been an object of great attention to the legislature; and is expressly stipulated with the prince in the bill of rights. All those are excluded from voting, whose poverty is such, that they cannot live independent, and must therefore be subject to the undue influence of their superiours. Such are

g. As the law is the birthright of every subject, so wheresoever they go, they carry their laws with them. 2. P. Wms. 75.

h. 4. Ins. 25.

i. The commons of England have a great and considerable right in the government; and a share in the legislature without whom no law passes. 2. Ld. Ray. 950.

j. Sp. L. b. 2. c. 2.

2. Charles Louis de Secondat, Baron de La Brède et de Montesquieu (1689–1755) was a French political writer. He inherited from his uncle the office of Président à Mortier in the Parlement of Bordeaux. He is best known for his *The Spirit of the Laws* (1748).

k. The Athenians, justly jealous of this important privilege, punished, with death, every stranger who presumed to interfere in the assemblies of the people.

l. The English freedom will be at an end whenever the court invades the free election of parliament. Rapin.[3]

A right that a man has to give his vote at the election of a person to represent him in parliament, there to concur to the making of laws, which are to bind his liberty and property, is a most transcendant thing and of a high nature. 2. Ld. Ray. 953.

3. Paul de Rapin (1661–1725) was a French historian. He wrote *L'Histoire d'Angleterre.*

supposed to have no will of their own: and it is judged improper that they should vote in the representation of a free state. What can exhibit in a more striking point of view, the peculiar care which has been taken, in order to render the election of members of parliament entirely free? It was deemed an insult upon the independent commons of England, that their uninfluenced suffrages should be adulterated by those who were not at liberty to speak as they thought, though their interests and inclinations were the same. British liberty, it was thought, could not be effectually secured, unless those who made the laws were freely, and without influence, elected by those for whom they were made. Upon this principle is reasonably founded the maxim in law—that every one, who is capable of exercising his will, is party, and presumed to consent, to an act of parliament.

For the same reason that persons, who live dependent upon the will of others, are not admitted to vote in elections, those who are under age, and therefore incapable of judging; those who are convicted of perjury or subornation of perjury, and therefore unworthy of judging; and those who obtain their freeholds by fraudulent conveyances, and would therefore vote to serve infamous purposes, are all likewise excluded from the enjoyment of this great privilege. Corruption at elections is guarded against by the strictest precautions, and most severe penalties. Every elector, before he polls, must, if demanded by a candidate or by two electors, take the oath against bribery, as prescribed by 2. Geo. 2. c. 24. Officers of the excise, of the customs, and of the post offices; officers concerned in the duties upon leather, soap, paper, striped linens imported, hackney coaches, cards and dice, are restrained from interfering in elections, under the penalty of one hundred pounds, and of being incapable of ever exercising any office of trust under the king.

Thus is the freedom of elections secured from the servility, the ignorance, and the corruption of the electors; and from the interposition of officers depending immediately upon the crown. But this is not all. Provisions, equally salutary, have been made concerning the qualifications of those who shall be elected. All imaginable care has been taken, that the commons of Great Britain may be neither awed, nor allured, nor deceived into any nomination inconsistent with their liberties.

It has been adopted as a general maxim, that the crown will take advantage of every opportunity of extending its prerogative, in opposition to the privileges of the people; that it is the interest of those who have pensions or offices at will from the crown, to concur in all its measures; that mankind in general will prefer their private interest to the good of their country; and that, consequently, those who enjoy such pensions or offices are unfit to represent a free nation, and to have the care of their liberties committed to their hands.[m] All such officers or pensioners are declared incapable of being elected members of the house of commons.

But these are not the only checks which the commons of Great Britain have, upon the conduct of those whom they elect to represent them in parliament. The interest of the representatives is the same with that of their constituents. Every measure, that is prejudicial to the nation, must be prejudicial to them and their posterity. They cannot betray their electors, without, at the same time, injuring themselves. They must join in bearing the burthen of every oppressive act; and participate in the happy effects of every wise and good law. Influenced by these considerations, they will seriously and with attention examine every measure proposed to them; they will behold it in every light, and extend their views to its most distant consequences. If, after the most mature deliberation, they find it will be conducive to the welfare of their country, they will support it with ardour: if, on the contrary, it appears to be of a dangerous and destructive nature, they will oppose it with firmness.

Every social and generous affection concurs with their interest, in animating the representatives of the commons of Great Britain to an honest and faithful discharge of their important trust. In each patriotick effort, the heart-felt satisfaction of having acted a worthy part vibrates in delightful unison with the applause of their countrymen, who never fail to express their warmest acknowledgements to the friends and benefactors of their country. How pleasing are those rewards! How much to be preferred to that paltry wealth, which is sometimes procured by meanness and treachery! I say sometimes; for meanness and treachery do not always obtain that pitiful reward. The most useful ministers to the crown, and therefore the most likely to be employed, especially in great emergencies, are those who are best beloved by the people; and those only are beloved by the people, who act steadily and uniformly in support of their liberties. Patriots, therefore, have frequently, and especially upon important occasions, the best chance of being advanced to offices of profit and power. An

m. There are a few exceptions in the case of officers at will.

abject compliance with the will of an imperious prince, and a ready disposition to sacrifice every duty to his pleasure, are sometimes, I confess, the steps, by which only men can expect to rise to wealth and titles. Let us suppose that, in this manner, they are successful in attaining them. Is the despicable prize a sufficient recompense, for submitting to the infamous means by which it was procured, and for the torturing remorse with which the possession of it must be accompanied? Will it compensate for the merited curses of the nation and of posterity?

These must be very strong checks upon the conduct of every man, who is not utterly lost to all sense of praise and blame. Few will expose themselves to the just abhorrence of those among whom they live, and to the excruciating sensations which such abhorrence must produce.

But lest all these motives, powerful as they are, should be insufficient to animate the representatives of the nation to a vigorous and upright discharge of their duty, and to restrain them from yielding to any temptation that would incite them to betray their trust; their constituents have still a farther security for their liberties in the frequent election of parliaments. At the expiration of every parliament, the people can make a distinction between those who have served them well, and those who have neglected or betrayed their interest: they can bestow, unasked, their suffrages upon the former in the new election; and can mark the latter with disgrace, by a mortifying refusal. The constitution is thus frequently renewed, and drawn back, as it were, to its first principles; which is the most effectual method of perpetuating the liberties of a state. The people have numerous opportunities of displaying their just importance, and of exercising, in person, these natural rights. The representatives are reminded whose creatures they are; and to whom they are accountable for the use of that power, which is delegated unto them. The first maxims of jurisprudence are ever kept in view—that all power is derived from the people—that their happiness is the end of government.

Frequent new parliaments are a part of the British constitution: by them only, the king can know the immediate sense of the nation. Every supply, which they grant, is justly to be considered as a testimony of the loyalty and affection, which the nation bear to their sovereign; and by this means, a mutual confidence is created between the king and his subjects. How pleasing must such an intercourse of benefits be! How must a father of his people rejoice in such dutiful returns for his paternal care! With what ardour must his people embrace every opportunity of giving such convincing proofs, that they are not insensible of his wise and indulgent rule!

Long parliaments have always been prejudicial to the prince, who summoned them, or to the people, who elected them. In that called by King Charles I,[4] in the year 1640, the commons proceeded at first, with vigour and a true patriotick spirit, to rescue the kingdom from the oppression under which it then groaned—to retrieve the liberties of the people, and establish them on the surest foundations—and to remove or prevent the pernicious consequences, which had arisen, or which, they dreaded, might arise from the tyrannical exercise of prerogative. They abolished the courts of the star chamber and high commission: they reduced the forests to their ancient bounds: they repealed the oppressive statutes concerning knighthood: they declared the tax of ship money to be illegal: they presented the petition of rights, and obtained a ratification of it from the crown. But when the king unadvisedly passed an act to continue them till such time as they should please to dissolve themselves, how soon—how fatally did their conduct change! In what misery did they involve their country! Those very men, who, while they had only a constitutional power, seemed to have no other aim but to secure and improve the liberty and felicity of their constituents, and to render their sovereign the glorious ruler of a free and happy people—those very men, after they became independent of the king and of their electors, sacrificed both to that inordinate power which had been given them. A regard for the publick was now no longer the spring of their actions: their only view was to aggrandize themselves, and to establish their grandeur on the ruins of their country. Their views unhappily were accomplished. They overturned the constitution from its very foundation; and converted into rods of oppression those instruments of power, which had been put into their hands for the welfare of the state; but which those, who had formerly given them, could not now reassume. What an instructive example is this! How alarming to those, who have no influence over their legislators—who have no security but that the power, which was originally derived from the people, and was delegated for their preservation, may be abused for their destruction! Kings are not the only tyrants: the conduct of the long parliament will justify me in adding, that kings are not the severest tyrants.

4. Charles I (1600–1649) was king of England from 1625 until his execution in 1649.

At the restoration, care was taken to reduce the house of commons to a proper dependence on the king; but immediately after their election, they lost all dependence upon their constituents, because they continued during the pleasure of the crown. The effects soon dreadfully appeared in the long parliament under Charles the second.[5] They seemed disposed ingloriously to surrender those liberties, for which their ancestors had planned, and fought, and bled: and it was owing to the wisdom and integrity of two[n 6] virtuous ministers of the crown, that the commons of England were not reduced to a state of slavery and wretchedness by the treachery of their own representatives, whom they had indeed elected, but whom they could not remove. Secure of their seats, while they gratified the crown, the members bartered the liberties of the nation for places and pensions; and threw into the scale of prerogative all that weight, which they derived from the people in order to counterbalance it.

It was not till some years after the revolution, that the people could rely on the faithfulness of their representatives, or punish their perfidy. By the statute 6. W. & M. c. 2. it was enacted, that parliaments should not continue longer than three years. The insecure situation of the first prince of the Hanoverian line,[7] surrounded with rivals and with enemies, induced the parliament, soon after his accession to the throne, to prolong this term to that of seven years. Attempts have, since that time, been frequently made to reduce the continuance of parliaments to the former term: and such attempts have always been well received by the nation. Undoubtedly they deserve such reception: for long parliaments will naturally forget their dependence on the people: when this dependence is forgotten, they will become corrupt: "Whenever they become corrupt, the constitution of England will lose its liberty—it will perish."[o]

5. Charles II (1630–1685) was king of England from 1660 to 1685.

n. The Earls of Clarendon and Southampton.

6. Edward Hyde, the Earl of Clarendon (1609–1674), was appointed Lord Chancellor during the Restoration. The Earl of Southampton is Thomas Wriothesley (1607–1667). When hostilities broke out between the king and parliament, he originally sided with parliament. He later switched sides, however, and Charles II made him Lord High Treasurer.

7. The Hanoverian line of English kings and queens ruled from 1714 to 1901. The prince in question was George I (1660–1727) who ruled England from 1714–1727.

o. Mont. Sp. L. b. 11. c. 6. If the legislative body were perpetual; or might last for the life of the prince who convened them, as formerly; and were so to be supplied, by occasionally filling the vacancies with new representatives; in these cases, if it were once corrupted, the evil would be past remedy: but when different bodies succeed each other, if the people see cause to disap-

Such is the provision made by the laws of Great Britain, that the commons should be faithfully represented: provision is also made, that faithful representatives should not labour for their constituents in vain. The constitution is formed in such a manner, that the house of commons are able as well as willing to protect and defend the liberties intrusted to their care.

The constitution of Great Britain is that of a limited monarchy; and in all limited monarchies, the power of preserving the limitations must be placed somewhere. During the reigns of the first Norman princes, this power seems to have resided in the clergy and in the barons by turns. But it was lodged very improperly. The clergy, zealous only for the dignity and preeminence of the church, neglected and despised the people, whom, with the soil they tilled, they would willingly have considered as the patrimony of St. Peter. Attached to a foreign jurisdiction, and aspiring at an entire independence of the civil powers, they looked upon the prerogatives of the crown as so many obstacles in the way of their favourite scheme of supreme ecclesiastical dominion; and therefore seized, with eagerness, every occasion of sacrificing the interests of their sovereign to those of the pope. Enemies alike to their king and to their country, their sole and unvaried aim was to reduce both to the most abject state of submission and slavery. The means employed by them to accomplish their pernicious purposes were, sometimes, to work upon the superstition of the people, and direct it against the power of the prince; and, at other times, to work upon the superstition of the prince, and direct it against the liberties of the people.

The power of preserving the limitations of monarchy, for the purposes of liberty, was not more properly placed in the barons. Domineering and turbulent, they oppressed their vassals, and treated them as slaves; they opposed their prince, and were impatient of every legal restraint. Capricious and inconstant, they sometimes abetted the king in his projects of tyranny; and, at other times, excited the people to insurrections and tumults. For these reasons, the constitution was ever fluctuating from one extreme to another; now despotism—now anarchy prevailed.

---

prove of the present, they may rectify its faults in the next. A legislative assembly also, which is sure to be separated again, will think themselves bound, in interest as well as duty, to make only such laws as are good, 1. Bl. Com. 189.

But after the representatives of the commons began to sit in a separate house; to be considered as a distinct branch of the legislature; and, as such, to be invested with separate and independent powers and privileges; then the constitution assumed a very different appearance. Having no interest contrary to that of the people, from among whom they were chosen, and with whom, after the session, they were again to mix, they had no views inconsistent with the liberty of their constituents, and therefore could have no motives to betray it. Sensible that prerogative, or a discretionary power of acting where the laws are silent, is absolutely necessary, and that this prerogative is most properly intrusted to the executor of the laws, they did not oppose the exercise of it, while it was directed towards the accomplishment of its original end: but sensible likewise, that the good of the state was this original end, they resisted, with vigour, every arbitrary measure, repugnant to law, and unsupported by maxims of publick freedom or utility.

The checks, which they possessed over prerogative, were calm and gentle—operating with a secret, but effectual force—unlike the impetuous resistance of factious barons, or the boisterous fulminations of ambitious prelates.

One of the most ancient maxims of the English law is, that no freeman can be taxed at pleasure.[p] But taxes on freemen were absolutely necessary to defray the extraordinary charges of government. The consent of the freemen was, therefore, of necessity to be obtained. Numerous as they were, they could not assemble to give their consent in their proper persons; and for this reason, it was directed by the constitution, that they should give it by their representatives, chosen by and out of themselves. Hence the indisputable and peculiar privilege of the house of commons to grant taxes.[q]

This is the source of that mild but powerful influence, which the commons of Great Britain possess over the crown. In this consists their security, that prerogative, intended for their benefit, will never be exerted for their ruin. By calmly and constitutionally refusing supplies, or by granting them only on certain conditions, they have corrected the extravagancies

p. 1. Bac. 568.

q. Note. It is said in divers records, "per communitatem Angliae nobis concess."[8] Because all grants of subsidies or aids by parliament do begin in the house of commons, and first granted by them: also because in effect the whole profit which the king reapeth, doth come from the commons. 4. Ins. 29.

8. It is conceded that the world belongs to the very common English.

of some princes, and have tempered the headstrong nature of others; they have checked the progress of arbitrary power, and have supported, with honour to themselves, and with advantage to the nation, the character of grand inquisitors of the realm. The proudest ministers of the proudest monarchs have trembled at their censures; and have appeared at the bar of the house, to give an account of their conduct, and ask pardon for their faults. Those princes, who have favoured liberty, and thrown themselves upon the affections of their people, have ever found that liberty which they favoured, and those affections which they cultivated, the firmest foundations of their throne, and the most solid support of their power. The purses of their people have been ever open to supply their exigencies: their swords have been ever ready to vindicate their honour. On the contrary, those princes, who, insensible to the glory and advantage of ruling a free people, have preferred to a willing obedience the abject submission of slaves, have ever experienced, that all endeavours to render themselves absolute were but so many steps to their own downfall.

Such is the admirable temperament of the British constitution! such the glorious fabrick of Britain's liberty—the pride of her citizens—the envy of her neighbours—planned by her legislators—erected by her patriots—maintained entire by numerous generations past! may it be maintained entire by numerous generations to come!

Can the Americans, who are descended from British ancestors, and inherit all their rights, be blamed—can they be blamed *by their brethren in Britain*—for claiming still to enjoy those rights? But can they enjoy them, if they are bound by the acts of a British parliament? Upon what principle does the British parliament found their power? Is it founded on the prerogative of the king? His prerogative does not extend to make laws to bind any of his subjects. Does it reside in the house of lords? The peers are a collective, and not a representative body. If it resides any where, then, it must reside in the house of commons.

Should any one object here, that it does not reside in the house of commons *only,* because that house cannot make laws without the consent of the king and of the lords; the answer is easy. Though the concurrence of all the branches of the legislature is necessary to every law; yet the same laws bind different persons for different reasons, and on different principles. The king is bound, because he assented to them. The lords are bound, because they voted for them. The representatives of the commons, for the same reason, bind themselves, and those whom they represent.

If the Americans are bound neither by the assent of the king, nor by the votes of the lords, to obey acts of the British parliament, the *sole* reason why they are bound is, because the representatives of the commons of Great Britain have given their suffrages in favour of those acts.[r] But are the representatives of the commons of Great Britain the representatives of the Americans? Are they elected by the Americans? Are they such as the Americans, if they had the power of election, would probably elect? Do they know the interest of the Americans? Does their own interest prompt them to pursue the interest of the Americans? If they do not pursue it, have the Americans power to punish them? Can the Americans remove unfaithful members at every new election? Can members, whom the Americans do not elect; with whom the Americans are not connected in interest; whom the Americans cannot remove; over whom the Americans have no influence—can such members be styled, with any propriety, the magistrates of the Americans? Have those, who are bound by the laws of magistrates not their own, any security for the enjoyment of their absolute rights—those rights, "which every man is entitled to enjoy, whether in society or out of it?"[s] Is it probable that those rights will be maintained? Is it "the primary end of government to maintain them?"[t] Shall this primary end be frustrated by a political maxim intended to promote it?

But from what source does this mighty, this uncontrolled authority of the house of commons flow? From the collective body of the commons of Great Britain. This authority must, therefore, originally reside in them: for whatever they convey to their representatives, must ultimately be in themselves.[u] And have those, whom we have hitherto been accustomed to consider as our fellow subjects, an absolute and unlimited power over us? Have they a natural right to make laws, by which we may be deprived of

r. This is allowed even by the advocates for parliamentary power; who account for its extension over the colonies, upon the very absurd principle of their being *virtually* represented in the house of commons.

s. 1. Bl. Com. 123.

t. 1. Bl. Com. 124.

u. It is selfevident that the power, with relation to the part we bear in the legislation, is absolutely, is solely in the electors. We have no legislative authority but what we derive from them. Debates of the Commons, vol. 6. p. 75.

our properties, of our liberties, of our lives? By what title do they claim to be our masters? What act of ours has rendered us subject to those, to whom we were formerly equal? Is British freedom denominated from the *soil,* or from the *people* of Britain? If from the latter, do they lose it by quitting the soil? Do those, who embark, freemen, in Great Britain, disembark, slaves, in America? Are those, who fled from the oppression of regal and ministerial tyranny, now reduced to a state of vassalage to those, who, then, equally felt the same oppression? Whence proceeds this fatal change? Is this the return made us for leaving our friends and our country—for braving the danger of the deep—for planting a wilderness, inhabited only by savage men and savage beasts—for extending the dominions of the British crown—for increasing the trade of the British merchants—for augmenting the rents of the British landlords—for heightening the wages of the British artificers? Britons should blush to make such a claim: Americans would blush to own it.

It is not, however, the ignominy only, but the danger also, with which we are threatened, that affects us. The many and careful provisions which are made by the British constitution, that the electors of members of parliament may be prevented from choosing representatives, who would betray them; and that the representatives may be prevented from betraying their constituents with impunity, sufficiently evince, that such precautions have been deemed absolutely necessary for securing and maintaining the system of British liberty.

How would the commons of Great Britain startle at a proposal, to deprive them of their share in the legislature, by rendering the house of commons independent of them! With what indignation would they hear it! What resentment would they feel and discover against the authors of it! Yet the commons of Great Britain would suffer less inconvenience from the execution of such a proposal, than the Americans will suffer from the extension of the legislative authority of parliament over them.

The members of parliament, their families, their friends, their posterity must be subject, as well as others, to the laws. Their interest, and that of their families, friends, and posterity, cannot be different from the interest of the rest of the nation. A regard to the former will, therefore, direct to such measures as must promote the latter. But is this the case with respect to America? Are the legislators of Great Britain subject to the laws which are made for the colonies? Is their interest the same with that of the colonies? If we consider it in a large and comprehensive view, we shall discern it to be undoubtedly the same; but few will take the trouble to consider it in that view; and of those who do, few will be influenced by the consideration. Mankind are usually more affected with a near though inferiour interest, than with one that is superiour, but placed at a greater distance. As the conduct is regulated by the passions, it is not to be wondered at, if they secure the former, by measures which will forfeit the latter. Nay, the latter will frequently be regarded in the same manner as if it were prejudicial to them. It is with regret that I produce some late regulations of parliament as proofs of what I have advanced. We have experienced what an easy matter it is for a minister, with an ordinary share of art, to persuade the parliament and the people, that taxes laid on the colonies will ease the burthens of the mother country; which, if the matter is considered in a proper light, is, in fact, to persuade them, that the stream of national riches will be increased by closing up the fountain, from which they flow.

As the Americans cannot avail themselves of that check, which interest puts upon the members of parliament, and which would operate in favour of the commons of Great Britain, though they possessed no power over the legislature; so the love of reputation, which is a powerful incitement to the legislators to promote the welfare, and obtain the approbation, of those among whom they live, and whose praises or censures will reach and affect them, may have a contrary operation with regard to the colonies. It may become popular and reputable at home to oppress us. A candidate may recommend himself at his election by recounting the many successful instances, in which he has sacrificed the interests of America to those of Great Britain. A member of the house of commons may plume himself upon his ingenuity in inventing schemes to serve the mother country at the expense of the colonies; and may boast of their impotent resentment against him on that account.

Let us pause here a little.—Does neither the love of gain, the love of praise, nor the love of honour influence the members of the British parliament in favour of the Americans? On what principles, then—on what motives of action, can we depend for the security of our liberties, of our properties, of every thing dear to us in life, of life itself? Shall we depend on their veneration for the dictates of natural justice? A very little share of experience in the world—a very little degree of knowledge in the history of men, will sufficiently convince us, that a regard to justice is by no means the ruling principle in human nature. He would discover himself to be a very sorry statesman, who would erect a system of jurisprudence upon that slender foundation. "He would make," as my Lord Bacon says, "imaginary laws: for imaginary commonwealths; and his discourses, like the stars, would give little light, because they are so high."[v]

But this is not the worst that can justly be said concerning the situation of the colonies, if they are bound by the acts of the British legislature. So far are those powerful springs of action, which we have mentioned, from interesting the members of that legislature in our favour, that, as has been already observed, we have the greatest reason to dread their operation against us. While the happy commons of Great Britain congratulate themselves upon the liberty which they enjoy, and upon the provisions—infallible, as far as they can be rendered so by human wisdom—which are made for perpetuating it to their latest posterity; the unhappy Americans have reason to bewail the dangerous situation to which they are reduced; and to look forward, with dismal apprehension, to those future scenes of woe, which, in all probability, will open upon their descendants.

What has been already advanced will suffice to show, that it is repugnant to the essential maxims of jurisprudence, to the ultimate end of all governments, to the genius of the British constitution, and to the liberty and happiness of the colonies, that they should be bound by the legislative authority of the parliament of Great Britain. Such a doctrine is not less repugnant to the voice of her laws. In order to evince this, I shall appeal to some authorities from the books of the law, which show expressly, or by a necessary implication, that the colonies are not bound by the acts of the British parliament; because they have no share in the British legislature.

The first case I shall mention was adjudged in the second year of Richard the third. It was a solemn determination of all the judges of England, met in the exchequer chamber, to consider whether the people in Ireland were bound by an act of parliament made in England. They resolved, "that they were not, as to such things as were done in Ireland; but that what they did out of Ireland must be conformable to the laws of England, because

v. 2. Ld. Bac. 537.

they were the subjects of England. Ireland," said they, "has a parliament, who make laws; and our statutes do not bind them; *because they do not send knights to parliament:* but their persons are the subjects of the king, in the same manner as the inhabitants of Calais, Gascoigne, and Guienne."[w]

This is the first case which we find in the books upon this subject; and it deserves to be examined with the most minute attention.

1. It appears, that the matter under consideration was deemed, at that time, to be of the greatest importance: for ordinary causes are never adjourned into the exchequer chamber; only such are adjourned there as are of uncommon weight, or of uncommon difficulty. "Into the exchequer chamber," says my Lord Coke,[x] "all cases of difficulty in the king's bench, or common pleas, &c. are, and of ancient time have been, adjourned, and there debated, argued, and resolved, by all the judges of England and barons of the exchequer." This court proceeds with the greatest deliberation, and upon the most mature reflection. The case is first argued on both sides by learned counsel, and then openly on several days, by all the judges. Resolutions made with so much caution, and founded on so much legal knowledge, may be relied on as the surest evidences of what is law.

2. It is to be observed, that the extent of the legislative authority of parliament is the very *point* of the adjudication. The decision was not incidental or indigested: it was not a sudden opinion, unsupported by reason and argument: it was an express and deliberate resolution of that very doubt, which they assembled to resolve.

3. It is very observable, that the reason, which those reverend sages of the law gave, why the people in Ireland were not bound by an act of parliament made in England, was the same with that, on which the Americans have founded their opposition to the late statutes made concerning them. The Irish did not send members to parliament; and, therefore, they were not bound by its acts. From hence it undeniably appears, that parliamentary authority is derived *solely* from representation—that those, who are bound by acts of parliament, are bound for this only reason, because they are represented in it. If it were not the *only* reason, parliamentary authority might subsist independent of it. But as parliamentary authority fails wherever this

w. 4. Mod. 225. 7. Rep. 22. b. Calvin's case.
x. 4. Ins. 110.

reason does not operate, parliamentary authority can be founded on no other principle. The law never ceases, but when the reason of it ceases also.

4. It deserves to be remarked, that no exception is made of any statutes, which bind those who are not represented by the makers of them. The resolution of the judges extends to *every* statute: they say, without limitation—"our statutes do not bind them." And indeed the resolution ought to extend to every statute; because the reason, on which it is founded, extends to every one. If a person is bound only because he is represented, it must certainly follow that wherever he is not represented he is not bound. No sound argument can be offered, why one statute should be obligatory in such circumstances, and not another. If we cannot be deprived of our property by those, whom we do not commission for that purpose; can we, without any such commission, be deprived, by them, of our lives? Have those a right to imprison and gibbet us, who have not a right to tax us?

5. From this authority it follows, that it is by no means a rule, that the authority of parliament extends to all the subjects of the crown. The inhabitants of Ireland were the subjects of the king as of his crown of England; but it is expressly resolved, in the most solemn manner, that the inhabitants of Ireland are not bound by the statutes of England. Allegiance to the king and obedience to the parliament are founded on very different principles. The former is founded on protection: the latter, on representation. An inattention to this difference has produced, I apprehend, much uncertainty and confusion in our ideas concerning the connexion, which ought to subsist between Great Britain and the American colonies.

6. The last observation which I shall make on this case is, that if the inhabitants of Ireland are not bound by acts of parliament made in England, *a fortiori*,[9] the inhabitants of the American colonies are not bound by them. There are marks of the subordination of Ireland to Great Britain, which cannot be traced in the colonies. A writ of errour lies from the king's bench in Ireland,[y] to the king's bench, and consequently to the house of lords, in England; by which means the former kingdom is subject to the control of the courts of justice of the latter kingdom. But a writ of errour does not lie in the king's bench, nor before the house of lords, in

9. From the stronger.
y. 4. Ins. 356.

England, from the colonies of America. The proceedings in their courts of justice can be reviewed and controlled only on an appeal to the king in council.[z]

The foregoing important decision, favourable to the liberty of all the dominions of the British crown that are not represented in the British Parliament, has been corroborated by subsequent adjudications. I shall mention one that was given in the king's bench, in the fifth year of King William and Queen Mary,[10] between Blankard and Galdy.[a][11]

The plaintiff was provost marshal of Jamaica, and by articles, granted a deputation of that office to the defendant, under a yearly rent. The defendant gave his bond for the performance of the agreement; and an action of debt was brought upon that bond. In bar of the action, the defendant pleaded the statute of 5. Ed. 6. made against buying and selling of offices that concern the administration of justice, and averred that this office concerned the administration of justice in Jamaica, and that, by virtue of that statute, both the bond and articles were void. To this plea the plaintiff replied, that Jamaica was an island inhabited formerly by the Spaniards, "that it was conquered by the subjects of the kingdom of England, commissioned by legal and sufficient authority for that purpose; and that since that conquest its inhabitants were regulated and governed by their own proper laws and statutes, and not by acts of parliament or the statutes of the kingdom of England." The defendant, in his rejoinder, admits that, before the conquest of Jamaica by the English, the inhabitants were governed by their own laws, but alleges that "since the conquest it was part of the kingdom of England, and governed by the laws and statutes of the kingdom of England, and not by laws and statutes peculiar to the island." To this rejoinder the plaintiff demurred, and the defendant joined in demurrer.

Here was a cause to be determined judicially upon this single question in law—Were the acts of parliament or statutes of England in force in Jamaica? It was argued on the opposite sides by lawyers of the greatest

z. 1. Bl. Com. 108. 231.

10. William III (1650–1702) and Mary II (1662–1694) were brought to England by Parliament in 1689 after James II fled the country. They reigned jointly until Mary's death in 1694.

a. 4. Mod. 215. Salk. 411.

11. Case decided in 1693 that held that all laws in force in England were in force in a country newly inhabited by English subjects.

eminence, before Lord Chief Justice Holt[12] (a name renowned in the law) and his brethren, the justices of the king's bench. They unanimously gave judgment for the plaintiff; and, by that judgment, expressly determined—That the acts of parliament or statutes of England were not in force in Jamaica. This decision is explicit in favour of America; for whatever was resolved concerning Jamaica is equally applicable to every American colony.

Some years after the adjudication of this case, another was determined in the king's bench, relating to Virginia; in which Lord Chief Justice Holt held, that the laws of England did not extend to Virginia.[b]

I must not be so uncandid as to conceal, that in Calvin's case, where the above mentioned decision of the judges in the exchequer chamber, concerning Ireland, is quoted, it is added, by way of explanation of that authority,—"which is to be understood, unless it (Ireland) be especially named." Nor will I conceal that the same exception[c] is taken notice of, and seems to be allowed, by the judges in the other cases relating to America. To any objection that may, hence, be formed against my doctrine, I answer, in the words of the very accurate Mr. Justice Foster, that "general rules thrown out in argument, and carried farther than the true state of the case then in judgment requireth, have, I confess, no great weight with me."[d]

The question before the judges in the cases I have reasoned from, was not how far the naming of persons in an act of parliament would affect them; though, unless named, they would not be bound by it: the question was, whether the legislative authority of parliament extended over the inhabitants of Ireland or Jamaica or Virginia. To the resolution of the latter question the resolution of the former was by no means necessary, and was, therefore, wholly impertinent to the point of the adjudication.

But farther, the reason assigned for the resolution of the latter question is solid and convincing: the American colonies are not bound by the acts of the British parliament, because they are not represented in it. But what reason can be assigned why they should be bound by those acts, in which they are specially named? Does naming them give those, who do them

12. Lord Chief Justice John Holt (1642–1710) was a jurist known for his impartiality and protection of civil rights.

b. Salk. 666.

c. This exception does not seem to be taken in the case of 2d. Richard III, which was the foundation of all the subsequent cases.

d. Fost. 313.

that honour, a right to rule over them? Is this the source of the supreme, the absolute, the irresistible, the uncontrolled authority of parliament? These positions are too absurd to be alleged; and a thousand judicial determinations in their favour would never induce one man of sense to subscribe his assent to them.[e]

The obligatory force of the British statutes upon the colonies, when named in them, must be accounted for, by the advocates of that power, upon some other principle. In my Lord Coke's[13] Reports, it is said, "that albeit Ireland be a distinct dominion, yet, *the title thereof being by conquest,* the same, by judgment of law, may be, by express words, bound by the parliaments of England." In this instance, the obligatory authority of the parliament is plainly referred to a title by conquest, as its foundation and original. In the instances relating to the colonies, this authority seems to be referred to the same source: for any one, who compares what is said of Ireland, and other conquered countries, in Calvin's case, with what is said of America, in the adjudications concerning it, will find that the judges, in determining the latter, have grounded their opinions on the resolutions given in the former.[f] It is foreign to my purpose to inquire into the reason-

e. Where a decision is manifestly absurd and unjust, such a sentence is not law. 1. Bl. Com. 70.

The legality of the opinion "that the people in Ireland were bound by the statutes of England, when particularly named by them," seems afterwards to have been doubted of by Lord Coke himself, in another place of his works. After having mentioned the resolution in the exchequer chamber in the time of Richard the third, and having taken notice that question is made of it in some of the books, and particularly in Calvin's case, he says, "that the question concerning the binding force of English statutes over Ireland is now by common experience and opinion without any scruple resolved; that the acts of parliament made in England, since the act of the 10th H. 7. (he makes no exceptions) do not bind them in Ireland; but all acts made in England before 10. H. 7. *by the said act made in Ireland An.* 10. H. 7. c. 22, do bind them in Ireland." 12. Rep. 111.

13. Sir Edward Coke (1552–1634) was an English jurist, legal reporter, and author.

f. It is plain that Blackstone understood the opinion of the judges—that the colonies are bound by acts of the British parliament, if named in them—to be founded on the principle of conquest. It will not be improper to insert his commentary upon the resolutions respecting America. "Besides these adjacent islands, (Jersey, &c.) our more distant plantations in America and elsewhere are also, in some respects, subject to the English laws. Plantations, or colonies in distant countries, are either such where the lands are claimed in right of occupancy only, by finding them desart and uncultivated, and peopling them from the mother country; or where, when already cultivated, they have been either gained by conquest, or ceded to us by treaties. Our American plantations are principally of this latter sort; being obtained in the last century, either *by right of conquest,* and driving out the natives (with what natural justice I shall not at present inquire) or by treaties." 1. Bl. Com. 106. 107.

Lord Chief Justice Holt, in a case above cited, calls Virginia a conquered country. Salk. 666.

ableness of founding the authority of the British parliament over Ireland, upon the title of conquest, though I believe it would be somewhat difficult to deduce it satisfactorily in this manner. It will be sufficient for me to show, that it is unreasonable, and injurious to the colonies, to extend that title to them. How came the colonists to be a conquered people? By whom was the conquest over them obtained? By the house of commons? By the constituents of that house? If the idea of conquest must be taken into consideration when we examine into the title by which America is held, that idea, so far as it can operate, will operate in favour of the colonists, and not against them. Permitted and commissioned by the crown, they undertook, at their own expense, expeditions to this distant country, took possession of it, planted it, and cultivated it. Secure under the protection of their king, they grew and multiplied, and diffused British freedom and British spirit, wherever they came. Happy in the enjoyment of liberty, and in reaping the fruits of their toils; but still more happy in the joyful prospect of transmitting their liberty and their fortunes to the latest posterity, they inculcated to their children the warmest sentiments of loyalty to their sovereign, under whose auspices they enjoyed so many blessings, and of affection and esteem for the inhabitants of the mother country, with whom they gloried in being intimately connected. Lessons of loyalty to parliament, indeed, they never gave: they never suspected that such unheard of loyalty would be required. They never suspected that their descendants would be considered and treated as a conquered people; and therefore they never taught them the submission and abject behaviour suited to that character.

I am sufficiently aware of an objection, that will be made to what I have said concerning the legislative authority of the British parliament. It will be alleged, that I throw off all dependence on Great Britain. This objection will be held forth, in its most specious colours, by those, who, from servility of soul, or from mercenary considerations, would meanly bow their necks to every exertion of arbitrary power: it may likewise alarm some, who entertain the most favourable opinion of the connexion between Great Britain and her colonies; but who are not sufficiently acquainted with the nature of that connexion, which is so dear to them. Those of the first class, I hope, are few; I am sure they are contemptible, and deserve to have very little regard paid to them: but for the sake of those of the second class, who may be more numerous, and whose laudable principles atone for their mistakes, I shall take some pains to obviate the objection, and to show that a denial of the legislative authority of the British parliament over America is by no means inconsistent with that connexion, which ought to subsist between the mother country and her colonies, and which, at the first settlement of those colonies, it was intended to maintain between them: but that, on the contrary, that connexion would be entirely destroyed by the extension of the power of parliament over the American plantations.

Let us examine what is meant by a *dependence* on Great Britain: for it is always of importance clearly to define the terms that we use. Blackstone, who, speaking of the colonies, tells us, that "they are no part of the mother country, but distinct (though dependent) dominions,"[g] explains dependence in this manner. "Dependence is very little else, but an obligation to conform to the will or law of that superiour person or state, upon which the inferiour depends. The original and true ground of this superiority, in the case of Ireland, is what we usually call, though somewhat improperly, the right of conquest; a right allowed by the law of nations, if not by that of nature; but which, in reason and civil policy, can mean nothing more, than that, in order to put an end to hostilities, a compact is either expressly or tacitly made between the conqueror and the conquered, that if they will acknowledge the victor for their master, he will treat them for the future as subjects, and not as enemies."[h]

The original and true ground of the superiority of Great Britain over the American colonies is not shown in any book of the law, unless, as I have already observed, it be derived from the right of conquest. But I have proved, and I hope satisfactorily, that this right is altogether inapplicable to the colonists. The original of the superiority of Great Britain over the colonies is, then, unaccounted for; and when we consider the ingenuity and pains which have lately been employed at home on this subject, we may justly conclude, that the only reason why it is not accounted for, is, that it cannot be accounted for. The superiority of Great Britain over the colonies ought, therefore, to be rejected; and the dependence of the colonies upon her, if it is to be construed into "an obligation to conform to the will or law of the superiour state," ought, in *this* sense, to be rejected also.

g. 1. Bl. Com. 107.
h. Id. 103.

My sentiments concerning this matter are not singular. They coincide with the declarations and remonstrances of the colonies against the statutes imposing taxes on them. It was their unanimous opinion, that the parliament have no right to exact obedience to those statutes; and, consequently, that the colonies are under no obligation to obey them. The dependence of the colonies on Great Britain was denied, in those instances; but a denial of it in those instances is, in effect, a denial of it in all other instances. For, if dependence is an obligation to conform to the will or law of the superiour state, any exceptions to that obligation must destroy the dependence. If, therefore, by a dependence of the colonies on Great Britain, it is meant, that they are obliged to obey the laws of Great Britain, reason, as well as the unanimous voice of the Americans, teaches us to disown it. Such a dependence was never thought of by those who left Britain, in order to settle in America; nor by their sovereigns, who gave them commissions for that purpose. Such an obligation has no correspondent right: for the commons of Great Britain have no dominion over their equals and fellow subjects in America: they can confer no right to their delegates to bind those equals and fellow subjects by laws.

There is another, and a much more reasonable meaning, which may be intended by the dependence of the colonies on Great Britain. The phrase may be used to denote the obedience and loyalty, which the colonists owe to the *kings* of Great Britain. If it should be alleged, that this cannot be the meaning of the expression, because it is applied to the kingdom, and not to the king, I give the same answer that my Lord Bacon gave to those who said that allegiance related to the kingdom and not to the king; because in the statutes there are these words—"born within the allegiance of England"—and again—"born without the allegiance of England." "There is no trope of speech more familiar," says he, "than to use the place of addition for the person. So we say commonly, the line of York, or the line of Lancaster, for the lines of the duke of York, or the duke of Lancaster. So we say the possessions of Somerset or Warwick, intending the possessions of the dukes of Somerset, or earls of Warwick. And in the very same manner, the statute speaks, allegiance of England, for allegiance of the king of England."[i]

i. 4. Ld. Bac. 192. 193. Case of the postnati[14] of Scotland.

14. See also *Calvin's Case* (1607–1608). *Calvin's Case* determined that all persons born within territory held by the king of England enjoyed the benefits of English law.

Dependence on the mother country seems to have been understood in this sense, both by the first planters of the colonies, and also by the most eminent lawyers, at that time, in England.

Those who launched into the unknown deep, in quest of new countries and habitations, still considered themselves as subjects of the English monarchs, and behaved suitably to that character; but it no where appears, that they still considered themselves as represented in an English parliament, or that they thought the authority of the English parliament extended over them. They took possession of the country in the *king's* name: they treated, or made war with the Indians by *his* authority: they held the lands under *his* grants, and paid *him* the rents reserved upon them: they established governments under the sanction of *his* prerogative, or by virtue of *his* charters:—no application for those purposes was made to the parliament: no ratification of the charters or letters patent was solicited from that assembly, as is usual in England with regard to grants and franchises of much less importance.

My Lord Bacon's[15] sentiments on this subject ought to have great weight with us. His immense genius, his universal learning, his deep insight into the laws and constitution of England, are well known and much admired. Besides, he lived at that time when settling and improving the American plantations began seriously to be attended to, and successfully to be carried into execution.[j] Plans for the government and regulation of the colonies were then forming: and it is only from the first general idea of these plans, that we can unfold, with precision and accuracy, all the more minute and intricate parts, of which they now consist. "The settlement of colonics," says he, "must proceed from the option of those who will settle them, else it sounds like an exile: they must be raised by the *leave*, and not by the *command* of the *king* At their setting out, they must have their commission, or letters patent, from the *king*, that so they may acknowledge their *dependency upon the crown* of England, and under his protection." In another place he says, "that they still must be subjects of the realm."[k] "In

15. Francis Bacon (1561–1626) was an English scientist, statesman, and legal author.

j. During the reign of Queen Elizabeth, America was chiefly valued on account of its mines. It was not till the reign of James I. that any vigorous attempts were made to clear and improve the soil.

k. The parliament have no subjects. My Lord Bacon gives, in this expression, an instance of the trope of speech before mentioned. He says, the subjects of the *realm*, when he means the subjects of the *king* of the realm.

order to regulate all the inconveniences, which will insensibly grow upon them," he proposes, "that the king should erect a subordinate council in England, whose care and charge shall be, to advise, and put in execution, all things which shall be found fit for the good of those new plantations; who, upon all occasions, shall give an account of their proceedings to the king or the council board, and from *them* receive such directions, as may best agree with the government of that place."[l] It is evident, from these quotations, that my Lord Bacon had no conception that the parliament would or ought to interpose,[m] either in the settlement or the government of the colonies. The only relation, in which he says the colonists must still continue, is that of subjects: the only dependency, which they ought to acknowledge, is a dependency on the crown.

This is a dependence, which they have acknowledged hitherto; which they acknowledge now; and which, if it is reasonable to judge of the future by the past and the present, they will continue to acknowledge hereafter. It is not a dependence, like that contended for on parliament, slavish and unaccountable, or accounted for only by principles that are false and inapplicable: it is a dependence founded upon the principles of reason, of liberty, and of law. Let us investigate its sources.

The colonists ought to be dependent on the king, because they have hitherto enjoyed, and still continue to enjoy, his protection. Allegiance is the faith and obedience, which every subject owes to his prince. This obedience is founded on the protection derived from government: for protection and allegiance are the reciprocal bonds, which connect the prince and his subjects.[n] Every subject, so soon as he is born, is under the royal protection, and is entitled to all the advantages arising from it. He therefore owes obedience to that royal power, from which the protection, which he

l. 1. Ld. Bac. 725, 726.

m. It was chiefly during the confusions of the republick, when the king was in exile, and unable to assert his rights, that the house of commons began to interfere in colony matters.

n. Between the sovereign and subject there is duplex et reciprocum ligamen; quia sicut subditus regi tenetur ad obedientiam; ita ex subdito tenetur ad protectionem: merito igitur ligeantia dicitur a ligando, quia continet in se duplex ligamen[16] 7. Rep. 5a. Calvin's case.

16. Between the sovereign and the subject there is a double and reciprocal bond. Because just as the subject is bound to obey the king, so the king is bound to protect the subject. Rightly, therefore, are kings called "Lieges" from *ligo*, "to bind or tie" because this double tie holds them in it.

enjoys, is derived. But while he continues in infancy and nonage, he cannot perform the duties which his allegiance requires. The performance of them must be respited till he arrive at the years of discretion and maturity. When he arrives at those years, he owes obedience, not only for the protection which he now enjoys, but also for that which, from his birth, he has enjoyed; and to which his tender age has hitherto prevented him from making a suitable return. Allegiance now becomes a duty founded upon principles of gratitude, as well as on principles of interest: it becomes a debt, which nothing but the loyalty of a whole life will discharge.[o] As neither climate, nor soil, nor time entitle a person to the benefits of a subject; so an alteration of climate, of soil, or of time cannot release him from the duties of one. An Englishman, who removes to foreign countries, however distant from England, owes the same allegiance to his king there which he owed him at home; and will owe it twenty years hence as much as he owes it now. Wherever he is, he is still liable to the punishment annexed by law to crimes against his allegiance; and still entitled to the advantages promised by law to the duties of it: it is not cancelled; and it is not forfeited. "Hence all children born in any part of the world, if they be of English parents continuing at that time as liege subjects to the king, and having done no act to forfeit the benefit of their allegiance, are *ipso facto* naturalized: and if they have issue, and their descendants intermarry among themselves, such descendants are naturalized to all generations."[p]

Thus we see, that the subjects of the king, though they reside in foreign countries, still owe the duties of allegiance, and are still entitled to the advantages of it. They transmit to their posterity the privilege of naturalization, and all the other privileges which are the consequences of it.[q]

Now we have explained the dependence of the Americans. They are the subjects of the king of Great Britain. They owe him allegiance. They

o. The king is protector of all his subjects: in virtue of his high trust, he is more particularly to take care of those who are not able to take care of themselves, consequently of infants, who, by reason of their nonage, are under incapacities; from hence natural allegiance arises, as a debt of gratitude, which can never be cancelled, though the subject owing it goes out of the kingdom, or swears allegiance to another prince. 2. P. Wms. 123. 124.

p. 4. Ld. Bac. 192. Case of the postnati of Scotland.

q. Natural born subjects have a great variety of rights, which they acquire by being born in the king's ligeance, and can never forfeit by any distance of place or time, but only by their own misbehaviour; the explanation of which rights is the principal subject of the law. 1. Bl. Com. 371.

have a right to the benefits which arise from preserving that allegiance inviolate. They are liable to the punishments which await those who break it. This is a dependence, which they have always boasted of. The principles of loyalty are deeply rooted in their hearts; and there they will grow and bring forth fruit, while a drop of vital blood remains to nourish them. Their history is not stained with rebellious and treasonable machinations: an inviolable attachment to their sovereign, and the warmest zeal for his glory, shine in every page.

From this dependence, abstracted from every other source, arises a strict connexion between the inhabitants of Great Britain and those of America. They are fellow subjects; they are under allegiance to the same prince; and this union of allegiance naturally produces a union of hearts. It is also productive of a union of measures through the whole British dominions. To the king is intrusted the direction and management of the great machine of government. He therefore is fittest to adjust the different wheels, and to regulate their motions in such a manner as to cooperate in the same general designs. He makes war: he concludes peace: he forms alliances: he regulates domestick trade by his prerogative, and directs foreign commerce by his treaties with those nations, with whom it is carried on. He names the officers of government; so that he can check every jarring movement in the administration. He has a negative on the different legislatures throughout his dominions, so that he can prevent any repugnancy in their different laws.

The connexion and harmony between Great Britain and us, which it is her interest and ours mutually to cultivate, and on which her prosperity, as well as ours, so materially depends, will be better preserved by the operation of the legal prerogatives of the crown, than by the exertion of an unlimited authority by parliament.[r]

r. After considering, with all the attention of which I am capable, the foregoing opinion—that all the different members of the British empire are distinct states, independent of each other, but connected together under the same sovereign in right of the same crown—I discover only one objection that can be offered against it. But this objection will, by many, be deemed a fatal one. "How, it will be urged, can the trade of the British empire be carried on, without some power, extending over the whole, to regulate it? The legislative authority of each part, according to your doctrine, is confined within the local bounds of that part: how, then, can so many interfering interests and claims, as must necessarily meet and contend in the commerce of the whole, be decided and adjusted?"

Permit me to answer these questions by proposing some others in my turn. How has the trade of Europe—how has the trade of the whole globe, been carried on? Have those widely extended plans been formed by one superintending power? Have they been carried into execution by one superintending power? Have they been formed—have they been carried into execution, with less conformity to the rules of justice and equality, than if they had been under the direction of one superintending power?

It has been the opinion of some politicians, of no inferiour note, that all regulations of trade are useless; that the greatest part of them are hurtful; and that the stream of commerce never flows with so much beauty and advantage, as when it is not diverted from its natural channels. Whether this opinion is well founded or not, let others determine. Thus much may certainly be said, that commerce is not so properly the object of laws, as of treaties and compacts. In this manner, it has been always directed among the several nations of Europe.

But if the commerce of the British empire must be regulated by a general superintending power, capable of exerting its influence over every part of it, why may not this power be intrusted to the king, as a part of the royal prerogative? By making treaties, which it is his prerogative to make, he directs the trade of Great Britain with the other states of Europe: and his treaties with those states have, when considered with regard to his subjects, all the binding force of laws upon them. (1. Bl. Com. 252.) Where is the absurdity in supposing him vested with the same right to regulate the commerce of the distinct parts of his dominions with one another, which he has to regulate their commerce with foreign states? If the history of the British constitution, relating to this subject, be carefully traced, I apprehend we shall discover, that a prerogative in the crown, to regulate trade, is perfectly consistent with the principles of law. We find many authorities that the king cannot lay impositions on traffick; and that he cannot restrain it *altogether,* nor confine it to monopolists: but none of the authorities, that I have had an opportunity of consulting, go any farther. Indeed many of them seem to imply a power in the crown to regulate trade, where that power is exerted for the great end of all prerogative—the publick good.

If the power of regulating trade be, as I am apt to believe it to be, vested, by the principles of the constitution, in the crown, this good effect will flow from the doctrine: a perpetual distinction will be kept up between that power, and a power of laying impositions on trade. The prerogative will extend to the former: it can, under no pretence, extend to the latter: as it is given, so it is limited, by the law.

Speech Delivered in the Convention for the Province of Pennsylvania, Held at Philadelphia, in January, 1775.

Whence, Sir, proceeds all the invidious and ill-grounded clamour against the colonists of America? Why are they stigmatized, in Britain, as licentious and ungovernable? Why is their virtuous opposition to the illegal attempts of their governours represented under the falsest colours, and placed in the most ungracious point of view? This opposition, when exhibited in its true light, and when viewed, with unjaundiced eyes, from a proper situation, and at a proper distance, stands confessed the lovely offspring of freedom. It breathes the spirit of its parent. Of this ethereal spirit, the whole conduct, and particularly the late conduct, of the colonists has shown them eminently possessed. It has animated and regulated every part of their proceedings. It has been recognised to be genuine, by all those symptoms and effects, by which it has been distinguished in other ages and other countries. It has been calm and regular: it has not acted without occasion: it has not acted disproportionably to the occasion. As the attempts, open or secret, to undermine or to destroy it, have been repeated or enforced; in a just degree, its vigilance and its vigour have been exerted to defeat or to disappoint them. As its exertions have been sufficient for those purposes hitherto, let us hence draw a joyful prognostick, that they will continue sufficient for those purposes hereafter. It is not yet exhausted; it will still operate irresistibly whenever a necessary occasion shall call forth its strength.

Permit me, sir, by appealing, in a few instances, to the spirit and conduct of the colonists, to evince, that what I have said of them is just. Did they disclose any uneasiness at the proceedings and claims of the British parliament, before those claims and proceedings afforded a reasonable cause for it? Did they even disclose any uneasiness, when a reasonable cause for it was *first* given? Our rights were invaded by their regulations of our internal policy. We submitted to them: we were unwilling to oppose them. The spirit of liberty was slow to act. When those invasions were renewed; when the efficacy and malignancy of them were attempted to be redoubled by the stamp act; when chains were formed for us; and preparations were made for rivetting them on our limbs—what measures did we pursue? The spirit of liberty found it necessary now to act: but she acted with the calmness and decent dignity suited to her character. Were we rash or seditious? Did we discover want of loyalty to our sovereign? Did we betray want of affection to our brethren in Britain? Let our dutiful and reverential petitions to the throne—let our respectful, though firm, remonstrances to the parliament—let our warm and affectionate addresses to our brethren, and (we will still call them) our friends in Great Britain—let all those, transmitted from every part of the continent, testify the truth. By their testimony let our conduct be tried.

As our proceedings during the existence and operation of the stamp act prove fully and incontestably the painful sensations that tortured our breasts from the prospect of disunion with Britain; the peals of joy, which burst forth universally, upon the repeal of that odious statute, loudly proclaim the heartfelt delight produced in us by a reconciliation with her. Unsuspicious, because undesigning, we buried our complaints, and the causes of them, in oblivion, and returned, with eagerness, to our former unreserved confidence. Our connexion with our parent country, and the reciprocal blessings resulting from it to her and to us, were the favourite and pleasing topicks of our publick discourses and our private conversations. Lulled into delightful security, we dreamt of nothing but increasing fondness and friendship, cemented and strengthened by a kind and perpetual communication of good offices. Soon, however, too soon, were we awakened from the soothing dreams! Our enemies renewed their designs against us, not with less malice, but with more art. Under the plausible pretence of regulating our trade, and, at the same time, of making provision for the administration of justice, and the support of government, in some of the colonies, they pursued their scheme of depriving us of our property without our consent. As the attempts to distress us, and to degrade us to a rank inferiour to that of freemen, appeared now to be reduced into a regular system, it became proper, on our part, to form a regular system for counteracting them. We ceased to import goods from Great Britain. Was this measure dictated by selfishness or by licentiousness? Did it not injure ourselves, while it injured the British merchants and manufacturers? Was it inconsistent with the peaceful demeanour of subjects to abstain from making purchases, when our freedom and our safety rendered it necessary for us to abstain from them? A regard for our freedom and our safety was our only motive; for no sooner had the parliament, by repealing part of the revenue laws, inspired us with the flattering hopes that they had departed from their intentions of oppressing and of taxing us, than we forsook our plan for defeating those intentions, and began to import as formerly. Far from being peevish or captious, we took no publick notice even of their declaratory law of dominion over us: our candour led us to consider it as a decent expedient of retreating from the actual exercise of that dominion.

But, alas! the root of bitterness still remained. The duty on tea was reserved to furnish occasion to the ministry for a new effort to enslave and to ruin us; and the East India Company were chosen, and consented, to be the detested instruments of ministerial despotism and cruelty. A cargo of their tea arrived at Boston. By a low artifice of the governour, and by the wicked activity of the tools of government, it was rendered impossible to store it up, or to send it back; as was done at other places. A number of persons unknown destroyed it.

Let us here make a concession to our enemies: let us suppose that the transaction deserves all the dark and hideous colours, in which they have painted it: let us even suppose—for our cause admits of an excess of candour—that all their exaggerated accounts of it were confined strictly to the truth: what will follow? Will it follow, that every British colony in America, or even the colony of Massachussetts Bay, or even the town of Boston in that colony, merits the imputation of being factious and seditious? Let the frequent mobs and riots that have happened in Great Britain upon much more trivial occasions shame our calumniators into silence. Will it follow, because the rules of order and regular government were, in that instance, violated by the offenders, that, for this reason, the principles of the constitution, and the maxims of justice, must be violated by their punishment? Will it follow, because those who were guilty could not be known, that, therefore, those who were known not to be guilty must suffer? Will it follow, that even the guilty should be condemned without being heard?—That they should be condemned upon partial testimony, upon the representations of their avowed and embittered enemies? Why were they not tried in courts of justice known to their constitution, and by juries of their neighbourhood? Their courts and their juries were not, in the case of Captain Preston, transported beyond the bounds of justice by their resentment: why, then, should it be presumed, that, in the case of those offenders, they would be prevented from doing justice by their affection? But the colonists, it seems, must be stript of their judicial, as well as of their legislative powers. They must be bound by a legislature, they must be tried by a jurisdiction, not their own. Their constitutions must be changed: their liberties must be abridged: and those, who shall be most infamously active in changing their constitutions and abridging their liberties, must, by an express provision, be exempted from punishment.

I do not exaggerate the matter, sir, when I extend these observations to all the colonists. The parliament meant to extend the effects of their proceedings to all the colonists. The plan, on which their proceedings are formed, extends to them all. From an incident, of no very uncommon or atrocious nature, which happened in one colony, in one town in that colony, and in which only a few of the inhabitants of that town took a part, an occasion has been taken by those, who probably intended it, and who certainly prepared the way for it, to impose upon that colony, and to lay a foundation and a precedent for imposing upon all the rest, a system of statutes, arbitrary, unconstitutional, oppressive, in every view and in every degree subversive of the rights, and inconsistent with even the name of freemen.

Were the colonists so blind as not to discern the consequences of these measures? Were they so supinely inactive as to take no steps for guarding against them? They were not. They ought not to have been so. We saw a breach made in those barriers, which our ancestors, British and American, with so much care, with so much danger, with so much treasure, and with so much blood, had erected, cemented, and established for the security of their liberties and—with filial piety let us mention it—of ours: we saw the attack actually begun upon one part: ought we to have folded our hands in indolence, to have lulled our eyes in slumbers, till the attack was carried on, so as to become irresistible, in every part? Sir, I presume to think not. We were roused; we were alarmed, as we had reason to be. But still our measures have been such as the spirit of liberty and of loyalty directed; not such as a spirit of sedition or of disaffection would pursue. Our counsels have been conducted without rashness and faction: our resolutions have been taken without phrensy or fury.

That the sentiments of every individual concerning that important object, his liberty, might be known and regarded, meetings have been held, and deliberations carried on in every particular district. That the sentiments of all those individuals might gradually and regularly be collected into a single point, and the conduct of each inspired and directed by the result of the whole united, county committees—provincial conventions—a continental congress have been appointed, have met and resolved. By this means, a chain—more inestimable, and, while the necessity for it continues, we hope, more indissoluble than one of gold—a chain of freedom has been formed, of which every individual in these colonies, who is willing to preserve the greatest of human blessings, his liberty, has the pleasure of beholding himself a link.

Are these measures, sir, the brats of disloyalty, of disaffection? There are miscreants among us—wasps that suck poison from the most salubrious flowers—who tell us they are. They tell us that all those assemblies are unlawful, and unauthorized by our constitutions; and that all their deliberations and resolutions are so many transgressions of the duty of subjects. The utmost malice brooding over the utmost baseness, and nothing but such a hated commixture, must have hatched this calumny. Do not those men know—would they have others not to know—that it was impossible for the inhabitants of the same province, and for the legislatures of the different provinces, to communicate their sentiments to one another in the modes appointed for such purposes, by their different constitutions? Do not they know—would they have others not to know—that all this was rendered impossible by those very persons, who now, or whose minions now, urge this objection against us? Do not they know—would they have others not to know—that the different assemblies, who could be dissolved by the governours, were, in consequence of ministerial mandates, dissolved by them, whenever they attempted to turn their attention to the greatest objects, which, as guardians of the liberty of their constituents, could be presented to their view? The arch enemy of the human race torments them only for those actions, to which he has tempted, but to which he has not necessarily obliged them. Those men refine even upon infernal malice: they accuse, they threaten us (superlative impudence!) for taking those very steps, which we were laid under the disagreeable necessity of taking by themselves, or by those in whose hateful service they are enlisted. But let them know, that our counsels, our deliberations, our resolutions, if not authorized by the forms, because that was rendered impossible by our enemies, are nevertheless authorized by that which weighs much more in the scale of reason—by the spirit of our constitutions. Was the convention of the barons at Running Meade,[1] where the tyranny of John was checked, and magna charta was signed, authorized by the forms of the constitution? Was the convention parliament, that recalled Charles the second, and restored the monarchy, authorized by the forms of the constitution? Was the convention of lords and commons, that placed King William on the throne, and secured the monarchy and liberty likewise, authorized by the forms of the constitution? I cannot conceal my emotions of pleasure, when I observe, that the objections of our adversaries cannot be urged against us, but in common with those venerable assemblies, whose proceedings formed such an accession to British liberty and British renown.

The resolutions entered into, and the recommendations given, by the continental congress, have stamped, in the plainest characters, the genuine and enlightened spirit of liberty upon the conduct observed, and the measures pursued, in consequence of them. As the invasions of our rights have become more and more formidable, our opposition to them has increased in firmness and vigour, in a just, and in no more than a just, proportion. We will not import goods from Great Britain or Ireland: in a little time we will suspend our exportations to them: and, if the same illiberal and destructive system of policy be still carried on against us, in a little time more we will not consume their manufactures. In that colony where the attacks have been most open, immediate, and direct, some farther steps have been taken, and those steps have met with the deserved approbation of the other provinces.

Is this scheme of conduct allied to rebellion? Can any symptoms of

1. Also known as Runnymede, it is a meadow by the River Thames where the Barons and King John met (10 June 1215) to negotiate what eventually became the Magna Carta (15 June 1215).

disloyalty to his majesty, of disinclination to his illustrious family, or of disregard to his authority be traced in it? Those, who would blend, and whose crimes have made it necessary for them to blend, the tyrannick acts of administration with the lawful measures of government, and to veil every flagitious procedure of the ministry under the venerable mantle of majesty, pretend to discover, and employ their emissaries to publish the pretended discovery of such symptoms. We are not, however, to be imposed upon by such shallow artifices. We know, that we have not violated the laws or the constitution; and that, therefore, we are safe as long as the laws retain their force and the constitution its vigour; and that, whatever our demeanour be, we cannot be safe much longer. But another object demands our attention.

We behold—sir, with the deepest anguish we behold—that our opposition has not been as effectual as it has been constitutional. The hearts of our oppressors have not relented: our complaints have not been heard: our grievances have not been redressed: our rights are still invaded: and have we no cause to dread, that the invasions of them will be enforced in a manner, against which all reason and argument, and all opposition of every peaceful kind, will be vain? Our opposition has hitherto increased with our oppression: shall it, in the most desperate of all contingencies, observe the same proportion?

Let us pause, sir, before we give an answer to this question: the fate of us; the fate of millions now alive; the fate of millions yet unborn depends upon the answer. Let it be the result of calmness and of intrepidity: let it be dictated by the principles of loyalty, and the principles of liberty. Let it be such, as never, in the worst events, to give us reason to reproach ourselves, or others reason to reproach us for having done too much or too little.

Perhaps the following resolution may be found not altogether unbefitting our present situation. With the greatest deference I submit it to the mature consideration of this assembly.

"That the act of the British parliament for altering the charter and constitution of the colony of Massachussetts Bay, and those 'for the impartial administration of justice' in that colony, for shutting the port of Boston, and for quartering soldiers on the inhabitants of the colonies, are unconstitutional and void; and can confer no authority upon those who act under colour of them. That the crown cannot, by its prerogative, alter the charter or constitution of that colony: that all attempts to alter the said charter or constitution, unless by the authority of the legislature of that colony, are manifest violations of the rights of that colony, and illegal: that all force employed to carry such unjust and illegal attempts into execution is force without authority: that it is the right of British subjects to resist such force: that this right is founded both upon the letter and the spirit of the British constitution."

To prove, at this time, that those acts are unconstitutional and void is, I apprehend, altogether unnecessary. The doctrine has been proved fully, on other occasions, and has received the concurring assent of British America. It rests upon plain and indubitable truths. We do not send members to the British parliament: we have parliaments (it is immaterial what name they go by) of our own.

That a void act can confer no authority upon those, who proceed under colour of it, is a selfevident proposition.

Before I proceed to the other clauses, I think it useful to recur to some of the fundamental maxims of the British constitution; upon which, as upon a rock, our wise ancestors erected that stable fabrick, against which the gates of hell have not hitherto prevailed. Those maxims I shall apply fairly, and, I flatter myself, satisfactorily to evince every particular contained in the resolution.

The government of Britain, sir, was never an arbitrary government: our ancestors were never inconsiderate enough to trust those rights, which God and nature had given them, unreservedly into the hands of their princes. However difficult it may be, in other states, to prove an original contract subsisting in any other manner, and on any other conditions, than are naturally and necessarily implied in the very idea of the first institution of a state; it is the easiest thing imaginable, since the revolution of 1688, to prove it in our constitution, and to ascertain some of the material articles, of which it consists. It has been often appealed to: it has been often broken, at least on one part: it has been often renewed: it has been often confirmed: it still subsists in its full force: "it binds the king as much as the meanest subject."[a] The measures of his power, and the limits, beyond which he cannot extend it, are circumscribed and regulated by the same authority, and with the same precision, as the measures of the subject's obedience, and the limits, beyond which he is under no obligation

a. Bol. Pat. King. 122.

to practise it, are fixed and ascertained. Liberty is, by the constitution, of equal stability, of equal antiquity, and of equal authority with prerogative. The duties of the king and those of the subject are plainly reciprocal: they can be violated on neither side, unless they be performed on the other.[b] The law is the common standard, by which the excesses of prerogative as well as the excesses of liberty are to be regulated and reformed.

Of this great compact between the king and his people, one essential article to be performed on his part is—that, in those cases where provision is expressly made and limitations set by the laws, his government shall be conducted according to those provisions, and restrained according to those limitations—that, in those cases, which are not expressly provided for by the laws, it shall be conducted by the best rules of discretion, agreeably to the general spirit of the laws, and subserviently to their ultimate end—the interest and happiness of his subjects—that, in no case, it shall be conducted contrary to the express, or to the implied principles of the constitution.

These general maxims, which we may justly consider as fundamentals of our government, will, by a plain and obvious application of them to the parts of the resolution remaining to be proved, demonstrate them to be strictly agreeable to the laws and constitution.

We can be at no loss in resolving, that the king cannot, by his prerogative, alter the charter or constitution of the colony of Massachussetts Bay. Upon what principle could such an exertion of prerogative be justified? On the acts of parliament? They are already proved to be void. On the discretionary power which the king has of acting where the laws are silent? That power must be subservient to the interest and happiness of those, concerning whom it operates. But I go farther. Instead of being supported by law, or the principles of prerogative, such an alteration is totally and absolutely repugnant to both. It is contrary to express law. The charter and constitution we speak of are confirmed by the only legislative power capable of confirming them: and no other power, but that which can ratify, can destroy. If it is contrary to express law, the consequence is necessary, that it is contrary to the principles of prerogative: for prerogative can operate only when the law is silent.

b. Bol. Tracts. 293. The compact between the king and people is mutual, and the parties are mutually bound. 11. Parl. Deb. 455. (Ld. Chesterfield.)

In no view can this alteration be justified, or so much as excused. It cannot be justified or excused by the acts of parliament; because the authority of parliament does not extend to it: it cannot be justified or excused by the operation of prerogative; because this is none of the cases, in which prerogative can operate: it cannot be justified or excused by the legislative authority of the colony; because that authority never has been, and, I presume, never will be given for any such purpose.

If I have proceeded hitherto, as I am persuaded I have, upon safe and sure ground, I can, with great confidence, advance a step farther, and say, that all attempts to alter the charter or constitution of that colony, unless by the authority of its own legislature, are violations of its rights, and illegal.

If those attempts are illegal, must not all force, employed to carry them into execution, be force employed against law, and without authority? The conclusion is unavoidable.

Have not British subjects, then, a right to resist such force—force acting without authority—force employed contrary to law—force employed to destroy the very existence of law and of liberty? They have, sir, and this right is secured to them both by the letter and the spirit of the British constitution, by which the measures and the conditions of their obedience are appointed. The British liberties, sir, and the means and the right of defending them, are not the grants of princes; and of what our princes never granted they surely can never deprive us.

I beg leave, here, to mention and to obviate some plausible but ill founded objections, that have been, and will be, held forth by our adversaries, against the principles of the resolution now before us. It will be observed, that those employed for bringing about the proposed alteration in the charter and constitution of the colony of Massachussetts Bay act by virtue of a commission for that purpose from his majesty: that all resistance of forces commissioned by his majesty, is resistance of his majesty's authority and government, contrary to the duty of allegiance, and treasonable. These objections will be displayed in their most specious colours: every artifice of chicanery and sophistry will be put in practice to establish them: law authorities, perhaps, will be quoted and tortured to prove them. Those principles of our constitution, which were designed to preserve and to secure the liberty of the people, and, for the sake of that, the tranquillity of government, will be perverted on this, as they have been on many other occasions, from their true intention; and will be made use of for the contrary purpose of endangering the latter, and destroying the former. The names of the most exalted virtues, on one hand, and of the most atrocious crimes, on the other, will be employed in direct contradiction to the nature of those virtues, and of those crimes: and, in this manner; those who cannot look beyond names, will be deceived; and those, whose aim it is to deceive by names, will have an opportunity of accomplishing it. But, sir, this disguise will not impose upon us. We will look to things as well as to names: and, by doing so, we shall be fully satisfied, that all those objections rest upon mere verbal sophistry, and have not even the remotest alliance with the principles of reason or of law.

In the first place, then, I say, that the persons who allege, that those, employed to alter the charter and constitution of Massachussetts Bay, act by virtue of a commission from his majesty for that purpose, speak improperly, and contrary to the truth of the case. I say, they act by virtue of no such commission: I say, it is impossible they can act by virtue of such a commission. What is called a commission either contains particular directions for the purpose mentioned; or it contains no such particular directions. In neither case can those, who act for that purpose, act by virtue of a commission. In one case, what is called a commission is void; it has no legal existence; it can communicate no authority. In the other case, it extends not to the purpose mentioned. The latter point is too plain to be insisted on—I prove the former.

"Id rex potest," says the law, "quod de jure potest."[c][2] The king's power is a power according to law. His commands, if the authority of Lord Chief Justice Hale[d][3] may be depended upon, are under the directive power of the law; and consequently invalid, if unlawful. Commissions, says my Lord Coke,[e] are legal; and are like the king's writs; and none are lawful, but such as are allowed by the common law, or warranted by some act of parliament.

c. 9. Rep. 123.

2. The power of the king and who according to right is able.

d. 1. Hale. P.C. 43. 44. Vide on this head. 4. Bac. 149. 9. Parl. Hist. 168, 170, 179, 180. Vent. 63, 169. 3. Ins. 237, 238, 240.

3. Lord Chief Justice Matthew Hale (1609–1676) was an English jurist and author. He is best known for his commitment to neutrality (and lack of partisanship) through the tumultuous years of the English civil war.

e. 3. Ins. 165.

Let us examine any commission expressly directing those to whom it is given, to use military force for carrying into execution the alterations proposed to be made in the charter and constitution of Massachussetts Bay, by the foregoing maxims and authorities; and what we have said concerning it will appear obvious and conclusive. It is not warranted by any act of parliament; because, as has been mentioned on this, and has been proved on other occasions, any such act is void. It is not warranted, and I believe it will not be pretended that it is warranted, by the common law. It is not warranted by the royal prerogative; because, as has already been fully shown, it is diametrically opposite to the principles and the ends of prerogative. Upon what foundation, then, can it lean and be supported? Upon none. Like an enchanted castle, it may terrify those, whose eyes are affected by the magick influence of the sorcerers, despotism and slavery: but so soon as the charm is dissolved, and the genuine rays of liberty and of the constitution dart in upon us, the formidable appearance vanishes, and we discover that it was the baseless fabrick of a vision, that never had any real existence.

I have dwelt the longer upon this part of the objections urged against us by our adversaries; because this part is the foundation of all the others. We have now removed it; and they must fall of course. For if the force, acting for the purposes we have mentioned, does not act, and cannot act, by virtue of any commission from his majesty, the consequence is undeniable, that it acts without his majesty's authority; that the resistance of it is no resistance of his majesty's authority; nor incompatible with the duties of allegiance.

And now, sir, let me appeal to the impartial tribunal of reason and truth—let me appeal to every unprejudiced and judicious observer of the laws of Britain, and of the constitution of the British government—let me appeal, I say, whether the principles on which I argue, or the principles on which alone my arguments can be opposed, are those which ought to be adhered to and acted upon—which of them are most consonant to our laws and liberties—which of them have the strongest, and are likely to have the most effectual, tendency to establish and secure the royal power and dignity.

Are we deficient in loyalty to his majesty? Let our conduct convict, for it will fully convict, the insinuation, that we are, of falsehood. Our loyalty has always appeared in the true form of loyalty—in obeying our sovereign according to law:[f] let those, who would require it in any other form, know, that we call the persons who execute his commands, when contrary to law, disloyal and traitors. Are we enemies to the power of the crown? No, sir: we are its best friends: this friendship prompts us to wish, that the power of the crown may be firmly established on the most solid basis: but we know, that the constitution alone will perpetuate the former, and securely uphold the latter. Are our principles irreverent to majesty? They are quite the reverse: we ascribe to it perfection, almost divine. We say, that the king can do no wrong: we say, that to do wrong is the property, not of power, but of weakness. We feel oppression; and will oppose it; but we know—for our constitution tells us—that oppression can never spring from the throne. We must, therefore, search elsewhere for its source: our infallible guide will direct us to it. Our constitution tells us, that all oppression springs from the ministers of the throne. The attributes of perfection, ascribed to the king, are, neither by the constitution, nor in fact, communicable to his ministers. They may do wrong: they have often done wrong: they have been often punished for doing wrong.

Here we may discern the true cause of all the impudent clamour and unsupported accusations of the ministers and of their minions, that have been raised and made against the conduct of the Americans. Those ministers and minions are sensible, that the opposition is directed, not against his majesty, but against them: because they have abused his majesty's confidence, brought discredit upon his government, and derogated from his justice. They see the publick vengeance collected in dark clouds around them: their consciences tell them, that it should be hurled, like a thunder bolt, at their guilty heads. Appalled with guilt and fear, they skulk behind the throne. Is it disrespectful to drag them into publick view, and make a distinction between them and his majesty, under whose venerable name

f. Rebellion being an opposition, not to persons, but authority, which is founded only in the constitution and laws of the government, those, whoever they be, who by force break through, and by force justify the violation of them, are truly and properly rebels. Puffend.[4] 720. 721. notes.

4. Samuel Baron von Pufendorf was a German jurist and historian. Pufendorf is considered an early international law theorist. Also a natural law theorist, he believed that all individuals had the right to equality and freedom.

they daringly attempt to shelter their crimes? Nothing can more effectually contribute to establish his majesty on the throne, and to secure to him the affections of his people, than this distinction. By it we are taught to consider all the blessings of government as flowing from the throne; and to consider every instance of oppression as proceeding, which in truth is oftenest the case, from the ministers.

If, now, it is true, that all force employed for the purposes so often mentioned, is force unwarranted by any act of parliament; unsupported by any principle of the common law; unauthorized by any commission from the crown—that, instead of being employed for the support of the constitution and his majesty's government, it must be employed for the support of oppression and ministerial tyranny—if all this is true—and I flatter myself it appears to be true—can any one hesitate to say, that to resist such force is lawful: and that both the letter and the spirit of the British constitution justify such resistance?

Resistance, both by the letter and the spirit of the British constitution, may be carried farther, when necessity requires it, than I have carried it. Many examples in the English history might be adduced, and many authorities of the greatest weight might be brought, to show, that when the king, forgetting his character and his dignity, has stepped forth, and openly avowed and taken a part in such iniquitous conduct as has been described; in such cases, indeed, the distinction above mentioned, wisely made by the constitution for the security of the crown, could not be applied; because the crown had unconstitutionally rendered the application of it impossible. What has been the consequence? The distinction between him and his ministers has been lost: but they have not been raised to his situation: he has sunk to theirs.

An Address to the Inhabitants of the Colonies (1776).

AN ADDRESS TO THE INHABITANTS OF THE COLONIES OF NEW HAMPSHIRE, MASSACHUSETTS BAY, RHODE ISLAND AND PROVIDENCE PLANTATIONS, CONNECTICUT, NEW YORK, NEW JERSEY, PENNSYLVANIA, THE COUNTIES OF NEWCASTLE, KENT AND SUSSEX ON DELAWARE, MARYLAND, VIRGINIA, NORTH CAROLINA, SOUTH CAROLINA AND GEORGIA FROM THEIR DELEGATES IN CONGRESS. [13 FEBRUARY, 1776.]

Friends and Countrymen—

History, we believe, cannot furnish an Example of a Trust, higher and more important than that, which we have received from your Hands. It comprehends in it every Thing that can rouse the Attention and interest the Passions of a People, who will not reflect Disgrace upon their Ancestors nor degrade themselves, nor transmit Infamy to their Descendants. It is committed to us at a Time when every Thing dear and valuable to *such* a People is in imminent Danger. This Danger arises from those, whom we have been accustomed to consider as our Friends; who really were so, while they continued friendly to themselves; and who will again be so, when they shall return to a just Sense of their own Interests. The Calamities, which threaten us, would be attended with a total Loss of those Constitutions, formed upon the venerable Model of British Liberty, which have been long our Pride and Felicity. To avert those *Calamities* we are under the disagreeable Necessity of making temporary Deviations from those *Constitutions.*

Such is the Trust reposed in us. Much does it import you and us, that it be executed with Skill and with Fidelity. That we have discharged it with

Reprinted from the Library of Congress edition of the *Journals of the Continental Congress,* IV, 134–46.

Fidelity, we enjoy the Testimony of a good Conscience. How far we have discharged it with Skill must be determined by you, who are our Principals and Judges, to whom we esteem it our Duty to render an Account of our Conduct. To enable you to judge of it, as we would wish you to do, it is necessary that you should be made acquainted with the *Situation,* in which your Affairs have been placed; the *Principles,* on which we have acted; and the *Ends,* which we have kept and still keep in View.

That all Power was originally in the People—that all the Powers of Government are derived from them—that all Power, which they have not disposed of, still continues theirs—are Maxims of the *English* Constitution, which, we presume, will not be disputed. The Share of Power, which the King derives from the People, or, in other Words, the Prerogative of the Crown, is well known and precisely ascertained: It is the same in *Great Britain* and in the Colonies. The Share of Power, which the House of Commons derives from the People, is likewise well known: The Manner in which it is conveyed is by Election. But the House of Commons is not elected by the Colonists; and therefore, from *them* that Body can derive no Authority.

Besides; the Powers, which the House of Commons receives from its Constituents, are entrusted by the Colonies to their Assemblies in the several Provinces. Those Assemblies have Authority to propose and assent to Laws for the Government of their Electors, in the same Manner as the House of Commons has Authority to propose and assent to Laws for the Government of the Inhabitants of *Great Britain.* Now the same collective Body cannot delegate the same Powers to distinct representative Bodies. The undeniable Result is, that the *House of Commons* neither has nor can have any Power deriv'd from the *Inhabitants of these Colonies.*

In the Instance of imposing *Taxes,* this Doctrine is clear and familiar: It is true and just in every *other* Instance. If it would be incongruous and absurd, that the same Property should be liable to be taxed by two Bodies independent of each other; would less Incongruity and Absurdity ensue, if the same Offense were to be subjected to different and perhaps inconsistent Punishments? Suppose the Punishment directed by the Laws of one Body to be Death, and that directed by those of the other Body be Banishment for Life; how could both Punishments be inflicted?

Though the Crown possesses the same Prerogative over the Colonies, which it possesses over the Inhabitants of *Great Britain:* Though the Colonists delegate to their Assemblies the same Powers which our Fellow Subjects in *Britain* delegate to the House of Commons: Yet by some inexplicable Mystery in Politics, which is the Foundation of the odious System that we have so much Reason to deplore, *additional* Powers over you are ascribed to the Crown, as a Branch of the British Legislature: And the House of Commons—*a Body which acts solely by derivative Authority*—is supposed entitled to exert over you an Authority, which *you* cannot *give,* and which *it* cannot *receive.*

The Sentence of universal Slavery gone forth against you is; *that the British Parliament have Power to make Laws,* WITHOUT YOUR CONSENT, *binding you in* ALL *Cases whatever.* Your Fortunes, your Liberties, your Reputations, your Lives, every Thing that can render you and your Posterity happy, all are the Objects of the Laws: All must be enjoyed, impaired or destroyed as the Laws direct. And are you the Wretches, who have Nothing that you *can* or *ought* to call *your own?* Were all the rich Blessings of Nature, all the Bounties of indulgent Providence poured upon you, not for your own Use; but for the Use of those, upon whom neither Nature nor Providence hath bestowed Qualities or Advantages superior to yours?

From this Root of Bitterness numerous are the Branches of Oppression that have sprung. Your most undoubted and highest-priz'd Rights have been invaded: Heavy and unnecessary Burthens have been imposed on you: Your Interests have been neglected, and sometimes wantonly sacrificed to the Interests, and even to the Caprice of others. When you felt, for your Enemies have not yet made any Laws to divest you of feeling, Uneasiness under your Grievances, and expressed it in the natural Tone of Complaint; your Murmurs were considered and treated as the Language of Faction; and your Uneasiness was ascribed to a restive Disposition, impatient of Controul.

In proportion, however, as your Oppressions were multiplied and increased, your Opposition to them became firm and vigourous. Remonstrances succeeded Petitions: A Resolution carried into Effect, not to import Goods from *Great Britain* succeeded both. The Acts of Parliament then complained of were in Part, repealed. Your Good-Humour and unsuspicious Fondness returned. Short—alas! *too* short—was the Season allowed for indulging them. The former System of Rigour was renewed.

The Colonies, wearied with presenting fruitless Supplications and Petitions *separately;* or prevented, by arbitrary and abrupt Dissolutions of their Assemblies, from using even those fruitless Expedients for Redress, determined to *join* their Counsels and their Efforts. Many of the Injuries flowing from the unconstitutional and ill-advised Acts of the British Legislature, affected all the Provinces equally; and even in those Cases, in which the Injuries were confined, by the Acts, to one or to a few, the *Principles,* on which they were made, extended to all. If common Rights, common Interests, common Dangers and common Sufferings are Principles of Union, what could be more natural than the Union of the Colonies?

Delegates authorised by the several Provinces from Nova Scotia to Georgia to represent them and act in their Behalf, met in GENERAL CONGRESS.

It has been objected, that this Measure was unknown to the Constitution; that the Congress was, of Consequence, an illegal Body; and that its Proceedings could not, in any Manner, be recognised by the Government of Britain. To those, who offer this Objection, and have attempted to vindicate, by its supposed Validity, the Neglect and Contempt, with which the Petition of that Congress to his Majesty was treated by the Ministry, we beg Leave, in our Turn, to propose, that they would explain the Principles of the Constitution, which warranted the *Assembly of the Barons at* RUNNINGMEDE, when MAGNA CHARTA was signed, the *Convention-Parliament* that recalled Charles 2d, and the *Convention of Lords and Commons* that placed King William on the Throne. When they shall have done this, we shall perhaps, be able to apply their Principles to prove the Necessity and Propriety of a Congress.

But the Objections of those, who have done so much and aimed so much against the Liberties of America, are not confined to the *Meeting* and the *Authority* of the Congress: They are urged with equal Warmth against the *Views* and *Inclinations* of those who composed it. We are told, in the Name of Majesty itself, "that the Authors and Promoters of this *desperate Conspiracy,*" as those who have framed his Majesty's Speech are pleased to term our *laudable Resistance;* "have, in the Conduct of it, derived great Advantage from the Difference of his Majesty's Intentions and theirs. That they meant only to amuse by vague Expressions of Attachment to the Parent State, and the strongest Protestations of Loyalty to the King, whilst they were preparing for a general Revolt. That on the Part of his Majesty and the Parliament, the Wish was rather to reclaim than to subdue." It affords us some Pleasure to find that the Protestations of Loyalty to his Majesty, which have been made, are allowed to be strong; and that Attachment to the Parent State is owned to be expressed. Those Protestations of Loyalty and Expressions of Attachment ought, by every Rule of Candour, to be presumed to be sincere, unless Proofs evincing their Insincerity can be drawn from the Conduct of those who used them.

In examining the Conduct of those who directed the Affairs of the Colonies at the Time when, it is said, they were preparing for a general Revolt, we find it an easy Undertaking to shew, that they merited no Reproach from the British Ministry by making any Preparations *for that Purpose.* We wish it were as easy to shew, that they merited no Reproach from their Constituents, by neglecting the necessary Provisions *for their Security.* Has a single Preparation been made, which has not been found requisite for our Defense? Have we not been attacked in Places where fatal Experience taught us, we were not sufficiently prepared for a successful Opposition? On which Side of this unnatural Controversy was the *ominous Intimation* first given, that it must be decided by Force? Were Arms and Ammunition imported into *America,* before the Importation of them was prohibited? What Reason can be assigned for this Prohibition, unless it be this, that those who made it had determined upon such a System of Oppression, as they knew, would *force* the Colonies into Resistance? And yet, they "wished only to reclaim!"

The Sentiments of the Colonies, expressed in the Proceedings of their Delegates assembled in 1774 were far from being disloyal or disrespectful. Was it disloyal to offer a Petition to your Sovereign? Did your still anxious Impatience for [an] answer, which your *Hopes,* founded only on your *Wishes,* as you too soon experienced, flattered you would be a gracious one—did this Impatience indicate a Disposition only to amuse? Did the keen Anguish, with which the Fate of the Petition filled your Breasts, betray an Inclination to avail yourselves of the Indignity with which you were treated, for forwarding favourite Designs of Revolt?

Was the Agreement not to import Merchandise from *Great Britain* or *Ireland;* nor after the tenth Day of September last, to export our Produce to those Kingdoms and the *West Indies*—was this a disrespectful or an hostile Measure? Surely we have a Right to withdraw or to continue our own Commerce. Though the British Parliament have exercised a Power of *directing* and *restraining* our Trade; yet, among all their extraordinary Pretensions, we recollect no Instance of their attempting to *force* it contrary to our Inclinations. It was well known, before this Measure was adopted, that it would be detrimental to our own Interest, as well as to that of our fellow-Subjects. We deplored it on both Accounts. We deplored the Necessity that produced it. But we were willing to sacrifice our Interest to any probable Method of regaining the Enjoyment of those Rights, which, by Violence and Injustice, had been infringed.

Yet even this peaceful Expedient, which Faction surely never suggested, has been represented, and by high Authority too, as a seditious and unwarrantable Combination. We are, we presume, the first Rebels and Conspirators, who commenced their Conspiracy and Rebellion with a System of Conduct, immediately and directly frustrating every Aim, which Ambition or Rapaciousness could propose: Those, whose Fortunes are desperate, may upon slight Evidence be charged with desperate Designs: But how improbable is it, that the Colonists, who have been happy, and have known their Happiness in the quiet Possession of their Liberties; who see no Situation more to be desired than that, in which, till lately, they have been placed; and whose warmest Wish is to be re-instaled in the Enjoyment of that Freedom, which they claim and are entitled to as Men and as British Subjects—how improbable it is that *such* would, without any Motives that could tempt even the most *profligate* Minds to Crimes, plunge themselves headlong into all the Guilt and Danger and Distress with which those that endeavour to overturn the Constitution of their Country are always surrounded and frequently overwhelmed?

The humble unaspiring Colonists asked only for "Peace, Liberty and Safety." This, we think, was a reasonable Request: Reasonable as it was, it has been refused. Our ministerial Foes, dreading the Effects, which our commercial Opposition might have upon their favourite Plan of reducing the Colonies to Slavery, were determined not to hazard it upon that Issue. They employed military Force to carry it into Execution. Opposition of Force by Force, or unlimited Subjection was now our only Alternative. Which of them did it become Freemen determined never to surrender that Character, to chuse? The Choice was worthily made. We wish for Peace—we wish for Safety: But we will not, to obtain either or both of them, part with our Liberty. The sacred Gift descended to us from our Ancestors: We cannot dispose of it: We are bound by the strongest Ties to transmit it, as we have received it, pure and inviolate to our Posterity.

We have taken up Arms in the best of Causes. We have adhered to the virtuous Principles of our Ancestors, who expressly stipulated, in their Favour, *and in ours,* a Right to resist every Attempt upon their Liberties. We have complied with our Engagements to our Sovereign. He should be the *Ruler* of a *free* People: We will not, as far as his Character depends upon us, permit him to be degraded into a *Tyrant* over *Slaves.*

Our Troops are animated with the Love of Freedom. They have fought and bled and conquered in the Discharge of their Duty as good Citizens as well as brave Soldiers. Regardless of the Inclemency of the Seasons, and of the Length and Fatigue of the March, they go, with Chearfulness, wherever the Cause of Liberty and their Country requires their Service. We confess that they have not the Advantages arising from Experience and Discipline: But Facts have shewn, that native Courage warmed with Patriotism, is sufficient to counterbalance these Advantages. The Experience and Discipline of our Troops will daily increase: Their Patriotism will receive no Diminution: The longer those, who have forced us into this War, oblige us to continue it, the more formidable we shall become.

The Strength and Resources of *America* are not confined to Operations *by Land.* She can exert herself likewise *by Sea.* Her Sailors are hardy and brave: She has all the Materials for Shipbuilding: Her Artificers can Work them into Form. We pretend not to vie with the Royal Navy of England though that Navy had *its Beginnings:* But still we may be able in a great Measure to defend our own Coasts, and may intercept, as we have been hitherto successful in doing, Transports and Vessels laden with Stores and Provisions.

Possessed of so many Advantages; favoured with the Prospect of so many more; Threatened with the Destruction of our constitutional Rights; cruelly and illiberally attacked, because we will not subscribe to our own Slavery; ought we to be animated with Vigour, or to sink into Despondency? When the Forms of our Governments are, by those entrusted with the Direction of them, perverted from their original Design; ought we to submit to this Perversion? Ought we to sacrifice the *Forms,* when the Sacrifice becomes necessary for preserving the *Spirit* of our Constitution? Or ought we to neglect and neglecting, to lose the Spirit by a superstitious Veneration for the Forms? We regard those Forms, and wish to preserve them as long as we can consistently with higher Objects: But much more do we regard essential Liberty, which, at all Events, we are determined not to lose, but with our Lives. In contending for this Liberty, we are willing to go through good Report, and through evil Report.

In our present Situation, in which we are called to oppose an Attack upon your Liberties, made under bold Pretentions of Authority from that Power, to which the executive Part of Government is, in the ordinary Course of affairs, committed—in the Situation, every Mode of Resistance, though directed by Necessity and by Prudence, and authorised by the Spirit of the Constitution, will be exposed to plausible Objections drawn from its Forms. Concerning such Objections, and the Weight that may be allowed to them, we are little solicitous. It will not discourage us to find ourselves represented as "labouring to enflame the Minds of the People of America, and openly avowing Revolt, Hostility and Rebellion." We deem it an Honour to "have raised Troops, and collected a naval Force"; and, *cloathed with the sacred Authority of the People, from* WHOM *all* LEGITIMATE AUTHORITY *proceeds* "to have exercised legislative, executive and judicial Powers." For what Purposes were those Powers instituted? For your Safety and Happiness. You and the World will judge whether those Purposes have been best promoted by us; or by those who claim the Powers, which they charge us with assuming.

But while we feel no Mortification at being misrepresented with Regard to the *Measures* employed by us for accomplishing the great Ends, which you have appointed us to pursue; we cannot sit easy under an Accusation, which charges us with laying aside those *Ends,* and endeavouring to accomplish *such as are very different.* We are accused of carrying on the War "for the Purpose of establishing an independent Empire."

We disavow the Intention. We declare, that what we aim at, and what we are entrusted by you to pursue, *is the Defence and the Re-establishment of the constitutional Rights of the Colonies.* Whoever gives impartial Attention to the Facts, we have already stated, and to the Observations we have already made, must be fully convinced that all the Steps, which have been taken by us in this unfortunate Struggle, can be accounted for as rationally and as satisfactorily by supposing that the Defence and Re-establishment of their Rights were the Objects which the Colonists and their Representatives had in View; as by supposing that an independent Empire was their Aim. Nay, we may safely go farther and affirm, without the most distant Apprehension of being refuted, that many of those steps can be accounted for rationally and satisfactorily only upon the former Supposition, and cannot be accounted for, in that Manner, upon the latter. The numerous Expedients that were tried, though fruitlessly, for avoiding Hostilities: The visible and unfeigned Reluctance and Horrour, with which we entered into them: The Caution and Reserve, with which we have carried them on: The Attempts we have made by petitioning the Throne and by every other Method, which might probably, or could possibly be of any Avail for procuring an accommodation—These are not surely the usual Characteristics of Ambition.

In what Instance have we been the Aggressors? Did our Troops take the Field before the ministerial Forces began their hostile March to *Lexington* and Concord? Did we take Possession, or did we form any Plan for taking Possession of *Canada,* before we knew that it was a Part of the ministerial System to pour the *Canadians* upon our Frontiers? Did we approach the *Canadians,* or have we treated them as Enemies? Did we take the Management of the *Indian* Tribes into our Hands, before we were well assured that the Emissaries of Administration were busy in persuading them to strike us? When we treated with them, did we imitate the barbarous Example? Were not our Views and Persuasions confined to keeping them in a State of Neutrality? Did we seise any Vessel of our Enemies, before our Enemies had seised some of ours? Had we yet seised any, except such as were employed in the Service of Administration, and in supplying those that were in actual Hostilities against us? Cannot our whole Conduct be reconciled to *Principles and Views of Self-Defence?* Whence then the uncandid Imputation of *aiming at an independent Empire?*

Is no regard to be had to the Professions and Protestations made by us, on so many different Occasions, of Attachment to Great Britain, of Allegiance to his Majesty; and of Submission to his Government upon the Terms, on which the Constitution points it out as a Duty, and on which alone a *British Sovereign* has the Right to demand it?

When the Hostilities commenced by the ministerial Forces in Massachusetts Bay, and the imminent Dangers threatening the other Colonies rendered it absolutely necessary that they should be put into a State of Defence—even on that Occasion, we did not forget our Duty to his Majesty, and our Regard for our fellow Subjects in Britain. Our words are these: "But as we most ardently wish for a Restoration of the Harmony formerly subsisting between our Mother-Country and these Colonies, the Interruption of which must at all Events, be exceedingly injurious to both Countries: Resolved, that with a sincere Design of contributing, by all Means in our Power, not incompatible with a just Regard for the undoubted Rights and true Interests of these Colonies, to the Promotion of this most desirable Reconciliation, an humble and dutiful Address be presented to his Majesty."

If the Purposes of establishing an independent Empire had lurked in our Breasts, no fitter Occasion could have been found for giving Intimations of them, than in our Declaration setting forth the Causes and Necessity of our taking up Arms. Yet even there no Pretence can be found for fixing such an Imputation on us. "Lest this Declaration should disquiet the Minds of our Friends and fellow Subjects in any Part of the Empire, we assure them that we mean not to dissolve that Union, which has so long and so happily subsisted between us, and which we sincerely wish to see restored. Necessity has not yet driven us into that desperate Measure, or induced us to excite any other Nation to war against them. We have not raised Armies with the ambitious Designs of separating from Great Britain, and establishing independent States." Our Petition to the King has the following Asseveration: "By such Arrangements as your Majesty's Wisdom can form for collecting the united Sense of your American People, we are convinced your Majesty would receive such satisfactory Proofs of the Disposition of the Colonists towards their Sovereign and the Parent State, that the wished for Opportunity would be soon restored to them, of evincing the Sincerity of their Professions by every Testimony of Devotion becoming the most dutiful Subjects and the most affectionate Colonists." In our Address to the Inhabitants of Great Britain, we say. "We are accused of aiming at Independence: But how is this Accusation supported? By the Allegations of your Ministers, not by our Actions. Give us leave, most solemnly to assure you, that we have not yet lost Sight of the Object we have ever had in View, a Reconciliation with you on constitutional Principles, and a Restoration of that friendly Intercourse, which to the Advantage of both we till lately maintained."

If we wished to detach you from your Allegiance to his Majesty, and to wean your Affections from a Connexion with your fellow-Subjects in

Great Britain, is it likely that we would have taken so much Pains, upon every proper Occasion, to place those Objects before you in the most agreeable Points of View?

If any equitable Terms of Accommodation had been offered us, and we had rejected them, there would have been some Foundation for the Charge that we endeavoured to establish an independent Empire. But no Means have been used either by Parliament or by Administration for the Purpose of bringing this Contest to a Conclusion besides Penalties directed by Statutes, or Devastations occasioned by War. Alas! how long will Britons forget that Kindred-Blood flows in your Veins? How long will they strive, with hostile Fury to sluice it out from Bosoms that have already bled in their Cause; and, in their Cause, would still be willing to pour out what remains, to the last precious Drop?

We are far from being insensible of the Advantages, which have resulted to the Colonies as well as to Britain from the Connexion which has hitherto subsisted between them: We are far from denying them, or wishing to lessen the Ideas of their Importance. But the Nature of this Connexion, and the Principles, on which it was originally formed and on which alone it can be maintained, seem unhappily to have been misunderstood or disregarded by those, who laid or conducted the late destructive Plan of Colony-Administration. It is a Connexion founded upon mutual Benefits; upon Religion, Laws, Manners, Customs and Habits common to both Countries. Arbitrary Exertions of Power on the Part of Britain, and servile Submission on the [part of the] Colonies, if the Colonies should ever become degenerate enough to [accept] it, would immediately rend every generous Bond asunder. An intimate Connexion between Freemen and Slaves cannot be continued without Danger and, at last, Destruction to the former. Should your Enemies be able to reduce you to Slavery, the baneful Contagion would spread over the whole Empire. We verily believe that the Freedom, Happiness, and Glory of Great Britain, and the Prosperity of his Majesty and his Family depend upon the Success of your Resistance. You are now expending your Blood, and your Treasure in promoting the Welfare and the true Interests of your Sovereign and your fellow-Subjects in Britain, in Opposition to the most dangerous Attacks that have been ever made against them.

The Ideas of deriving Emolument to the Mother Country by taxing you, and depriving you of your Constitutions and Liberties were not introduced till lately. The Experiments, to which those Ideas have given Birth, have proved disastrous: The Voice of Wisdom calls loudly that they should be laid aside. Let them not, however, be removed from View. They may serve as Beacons to prevent future Shipwrecks.

Britain and these Colonies have been Blessings to each other. Sure we are, that they might continue to be so. Some salutary System might certainly be devised, which would remove from both Sides, Jealousies that are ill-founded, and Causes of Jealousies that are well-founded; which would restore to both Countries those important Benefits that Nature seems to have intended them reciprocally to confer and to receive; and which would secure the Continuance and the Encrease of those Benefits to numerous succeeding Generations. That such a System may be formed is our ardent Wish.

But as such a System must affect the Interest of the Colonies as much as that of the Mother-Country, why should the Colonies be excluded from a Voice in it? Should not, to say the least upon this Subject, their Consent be asked and obtained as to the *general Ends,* which it ought to be calculated to answer? Why should not its Validity depend upon us as well as upon the Inhabitants of Great Britain? No Disadvantage will result to them: An important Advantage will result to [us]. We shall be affected by no Laws, the Authority of which, as far as they regard us, is not *founded on our own Consent.* This Consent may be expressed as well by a solemn Compact, as if the Colonists, by their Representatives, had an immediate Voice in passing the Laws. In a Compact we would *concede* liberally to Parliament: For the *Bounds* of our Concessions would be known.

We are too much attached to the English Laws and Constitution, and know too well their happy Tendency to diffuse Freedom, Prosperity and Peace wherever they prevail, to desire an independent Empire. If one Part of the Constitution be pulled down, it is impossible to foretell whether the other Parts of it may not be shaken, and, perhaps, overthrown. It is a Part of our Constitution to be under Allegiance to the Crown, Limited and ascertained as the Prerogative is, the Position—*that a King can do no wrong*—may be founded in *Fact* as well as in *Law,* if you are not wanting to yourselves.

We trace your Calamities to the House of Commons. *They* have undertaken to *give* and *grant* your Money. From a supposed virtual Representation in *their* House it is argued, that *you* ought to be bound by the Acts of the British Parliament in all Cases whatever. This is no Part of the Constitution. This is the Doctrine, to which we will never subscribe our Assent: This is the Claim, to which we adjure you, as you tender your own Freedom and Happiness, and the Freedom and Happiness of your Posterity, never to submit. The same Principles, which directed *your Ancestors* to oppose the exorbitant and dangerous Pretensions of the Crown, should direct *you* to oppose the no less exorbitant and dangerous Claims of the House of Commons. Let all Communication of despotic Power through that Channel be cut off, and your Liberties will be safe.

Let neither our Enemies nor our Friends make improper Inferences from the Solicitude, which we have discovered to remove the Imputation of aiming to establish an independent Empire. Though an independent Empire is not our *Wish;* it may—let your Oppressors attend—it may be the Fate of our Countrymen and ourselves. It is in the Power of your Enemies to render Independency or Slavery your and our Alternative. Should we—will you, in such an Event, hesitate a Moment about the Choice? Let those, who drive us to it, answer to their King and to their Country for the Consequences. We are *desirous* to continue Subjects: But we are *determined* to continue Freemen. We shall deem ourselves bound to renounce; and, we hope, you will follow our Example in renouncing the *former* Character whenever it shall become incompatible with the *latter.*

While we shall be continued by you in the very important Trust, which you have committed to us, we shall keep our Eyes constantly and steadily fixed upon the Grand Object of the Union of the Colonies—the RE-ESTABLISHMENT AND SECURITY OF THEIR CONSTITUTIONAL RIGHTS. Every measure that we employ shall be directed to the Attainment of this great End: No Measure, necessary, in our Opinion, for attaining it, shall be declined. If any such Measure should, against our principal Intention, draw the Colonies into Engagements that may suspend or dissolve their Union with their fellow-Subjects in Great Britain, we shall lament the Effect; but shall hold ourselves justified in adopting the Measure. That the Colonies may continue connected, as they have been, with Britain, is our second Wish: Our first is—THAT AMERICA MAY BE FREE.

An Address to the Inhabitants of the Colonies Submitted to the Continental Congress.

The manuscript of this, in Wilson's handwriting, is in the Papers of the Continental Congress, Library of Congress, No. 24, ff. 217–232. It is reprinted in the Library of Congress edition of the *Journals of the Continental Congress,* IV, 134–46. The Committee of which this was the report, was appointed by a resolution of January 24th, 1776, and consisted of John Dickinson, James Wilson, William Hooper, James Duane and Robert Alexander. A note by James Madison to a copy of this paper reads, "This address was drawn by Mr. Wilson, who informed the transcriber that it was meant to lead the public mind into the idea of Independence, of which the necessity was plainly foreseen by Congress: but that before it could be carried through Congress, the language became evidently short of the subsisting maturity for that measure, and the Address was in consequence dropped" Worthington C. Ford, ed. *Journals of the Continental Congress,* IV, 146.

Considerations on the Bank of North America 1785.[a]

An attack is made on the credit and institution of the Bank of North America. Whether this attack is justified by the principles of law and sound policy, is a natural subject of inquiry. The inquiry is as necessary and interesting, as it is natural: for, though some people represent the bank as injurious and dangerous, while others consider it as salutary and beneficial to the community, all view it as an object of high importance; deserving and demanding the publick attention.

In the investigation of this subject, it will be requisite to discuss some great and leading questions concerning the constitution of the United States, and the relation which subsists between them and each particular state in the Union. Perhaps it is to be wished that this discussion had not been rendered necessary; and that those questions had rested some time longer among the *arcana imperii:*[1] but they are now presented to the publick; and the publick should view them with firmness, with impartiality, and with all the solicitude befitting such a momentous occasion.

A gentleman,[b] who had the best opportunities of observing, and who possesses the best talents for judging on the subject, informs his fellow citizens officially, that "it may be not only asserted, but demonstrated, that, without the establishment of the national bank, the business of the department of finance could not have been performed" in the late war.

The millennium is not yet come. War, with all the horrours and miseries

a. The publication of these considerations was occasioned by a bill, introduced into the legislature of Pennsylvania, to repeal an act of assembly passed in the year 1782, by which a charter of incorporation had been granted to the Bank of North America. The bill was passed into a law, in September 1785. *Ed.*

1. State secrets.

b. Vide[2] preface to the statement of the accounts of the United States.

2. Direct attention to something.

in his train, may revisit us. The finances may again be deranged: "publick credit may, again, be at an end: no means may be afforded adequate to the publick expenses." Is it wise or politick to deprive our country, in such a situation, of a resource, which happy experience has shown to be of such essential importance? Will the citizens of the United States be encouraged to embark their fortunes on a similar bottom in a future war, by seeing the vessel, which carried us so successfully through the last, thrown aside, like a useless hulk, upon the return of peace?

It will not be improper to recal to our remembrance the origin, the establishment, and the proceedings of the Bank of North America.

In May, 1781, the superintendant of finance laid before congress a plan of a bank. On the 26th of that month, congress passed the following resolution concerning it.

> Resolved, That congress do approve of the plan for establishing a national bank in these United States, submitted to their consideration by Mr. Robert Morris,[3] the 17th May, 1781, and that they will promote and support the same by such ways and means, from time to time, as may appear necessary for the institution, and consistent with the publick good.
>
> That the subscribers to the said bank shall be incorporated, agreeably to the principles and terms of the plan, under the name of "The President, Directors, and Company of the Bank of North America," so soon as the subscription shall be filled, the directors and president chosen, and application made to congress for that purpose, by the president and directors elected.
>
> Resolved, That it be recommended to the several States, by proper laws for that purpose, to provide that no other bank or bankers shall be established or permitted within the said states respectively during the war.
>
> Resolved, That the notes hereafter to be issued by the said bank, payable on demand, shall be receivable in payment of all taxes, duties, and debts, due or that may become due or payable to the United States.
>
> Resolved, that congress will recommend to the several legislatures to pass laws, making it felony without benefit of clergy, for any person to counterfeit bank notes, or to pass such notes, knowing them to be counterfeit; also making it felony without benefit of clergy, for any president, inspector, director, officer, or servant of the bank, to convert any of the property, money, or credit

3. Robert Morris (1734–1806) was a highly successful merchant and financier of the American Revolution. He was a member of the Continental Congress (1775–1778), a signer of the Declaration of Independence, the Articles of Confederation, and the Constitution.

of the said bank to his own use, or in any other way to be guilty of fraud or embezzlement, as officers or servants of the bank.

Under these resolutions a subscription was opened for the national bank: this subscription was not confined to Pennyslvania: the citizens of other States trusted their property to the publick faith; and before the end of December, 1781, the subscription was filled, "from an expectation of a charter of incorporation from congress." Application was made to congress by the president and directors, then chosen, for an act of incorporation. "The exigencies of the United States rendered it indispensably necessary that such an act should be immediately passed." Congress, at the same time that they passed the act of incorporation, recommended to the legislature of each state, to pass such laws as they might judge necessary for giving its ordinance its full operation, agreeably to the true intent and meaning thereof, and according to the recommendations contained in the resolution of the 26th day of May preceding.

The bank immediately commenced its operations. Its seeds were small, but they were vigorous. The sums paid in by individuals upon their subscriptions did not amount in the whole, to seventy thousand dollars. The sum invested by the United States, in bank stock, amounted to something more than two hundred and fifty thousand dollars: but this sum may be said to have been paid in with one hand and borrowed with the other; and before the end of the first three months, farther sums were advanced to the United States, and an advance was made to this state. Besides, numerous accommodations were afforded to individuals. Little was it then imagined that the bank would ever be represented as unfriendly to circulation. It was viewed as the source and as the support of credit, both private and publick: as such, it was hated and dreaded by the enemies of the United States: as such, it was loved and fostered by their friends.

Pennsylvania, distinguished on numerous occasions by her faithful and affectionate attachment to federal principles, embraced, in the first session of her legislature after the establishment of the bank, the opportunity of testifying her approbation of an act, which had been found to be indispensably necessary. Harmonizing with the sentiments and recommendations of the United States, the assembly passed an act,[c] "for preventing

c. 18th of March, 1782.

and punishing the counterfeiting of the common seal, bank bills, and bank notes, of the president, directors, and company of the Bank of North America." In the preamble to this act, which, according to the constitution of this state, expresses the reasons and motives for passing it, the "necessity" of taking "effectual measures for preventing and punishing frauds and cheats which may be put upon the president, directors, and company of the Bank of North America," is explicitly declared by the legislature.

The sentiments and conduct of other states, respecting the establishment of the national bank by congress, were similar to those of Pennsylvania. The general assembly of Rhode Island and Providence Plantations[d] made it felony, without benefit of clergy, "to counterfeit any note or notes issued, or to be issued, from the Bank of North America, as approved and *established* by the United States in Congress assembled." The state of Connecticut enacted,[e] that a tax should be laid, payable in money, or "notes issued by the directors of the national bank, *established* by an ordinance of the United States in congress assembled." By a law of Massachussetts, the subscribers to the national bank, approved of by the United States, were "incorporated, on the behalf of that commonwealth, by the name of the president, directors and company of the Bank of North America, according to the terms of the ordinance to incorporate the said subscribers, passed by the United States in congress assembled on the thirty first day of December, 1781." The same law further enacts, "that all notes or bills, which have been or shall be issued by, for, or in the name of the said president, directors, and company, and payable on demand, shall be receivable in the payment of all taxes, debts and duties, due or that may become due, or payable to, or for account of, the said United States." In the preamble of this law, the legislature declares that "a national bank is of great service, as well to the publick as to individuals."

The president and directors of the bank had a delicate and a difficult part to act. On one hand, they were obliged to guard against the malice and exertions of their enemies: on the other, it was incumbent on them to sooth the timidity of some of their friends. The credit of a bank, as well as all other credit, depends on opinion. Opinion, whether well or ill founded, produces, in each case, the same effects upon conduct. Some thought that

d. January Sessions, 1782.
e. 10th January, 1782.

an act of incorporation from the legislature of this state would be beneficial; none apprehended that it could ever be hurtful to the national bank. Prudence, therefore, and a disposition, very natural in that season of doubt and diffidence, to gratify the sentiments, and even the prejudices, of such as might become subscribers or customers to the bank, directed an application to the assembly for "a charter, similar to that granted by the United States in congress assembled." But though the directors were willing to avail themselves of encouragement from every quarter, they meant not to relinquish any of their rights, or to change the foundation on which they rested. They made their application in their *corporate* character. They expressly mentioned to the assembly, that the United States in congress assembled had granted to the bank a charter of incorporation, and that the institution was to be carried on under their immediate auspices. The legislature thought that it was proper and reasonable to grant[f] the request of the *president and directors of the Bank of North America;* and assigned, as a reason for the act, "that the United States in congress assembled, from a conviction of the support which the finances of the United States would receive from the establishment of a *national bank,* passed an ordinance to incorporate the subscribers for this purpose, by the name and style of the president, directors, and company of the Bank of North America."

The first clause of the law enacts, that "those who are, and those who shall become subscribers to the said bank, be, and forever hereafter shall be, a corporation and body politick, to all intents and purposes."

It is further enacted, that "the said corporation be, and shall be forever hereafter, able and capable in law to do and execute all and singular matters and things, that to them shall or may appertain to do."

To show, in the most striking light, the kind sentiments of the legislature towards the institution, it is further enacted, that "this act shall be construed and taken most favourably and beneficially for the said corporation."

On these facts and proceedings, two questions of much national importance present themselves to our view and examination.

I. Is the Bank of North America legally and constitutionally instituted and organized, by the charter of incorporation granted by the United States in congress assembled?

f. 1st. of April, 1782.

II. Would it be wise or politick in the legislature of Pennsylvania, to revoke the charter which it has granted to the institution?

The discussion of these two questions will naturally lead us to the proper conclusions concerning the validity and the utility of the bank.

I. Had the United States in congress assembled a legal and constitutional power to institute and organize the Bank of North America, by a charter of incorporation?

The objection, under this head, will be—that the articles of confederation express all the powers of congress, that in those articles no power is delegated to that body to grant charters of incorporation, and that, therefore, congress possess no such power.

It is true, that, by the second article of the confederation, "each state retains its sovereignty, freedom and independence, and every power, jurisdiction, and right, which is not, by the confederation, *expressly* delegated to the United States in congress assembled."

If, then, any or each of the states possessed, previous to the confederation, a power, jurisdiction, or right, to institute and organize, by a charter of incorporation, a bank for North America; in other words—commensurate to the United States; such power, jurisdiction, and right, unless expressly delegated to congress, cannot be legally or constitutionally exercised by that body.

But, we presume, it will not be contended, that any or each of the states could exercise any power or act of sovereignty extending over all the other states, or any of them; or, in other words, incorporate a bank, commensurate to the United States.

The consequence is, that this is not an act of sovereignty, or a power, jurisdiction, or right, which, by the second article of the confederation, must be expressly delegated to congress, in order to be possessed by that body.

If, however, any person shall contend that any or each of the states can exercise such an extensive power or act of sovereignty as that above mentioned; to such person we give this answer—The state of Massachussetts has exercised such power and act: it has incorporated the Bank of North America. But to pursue my argument.

Though the United States in congress assembled derive *from the particular states* no power, jurisdiction, or right, which is not expressly delegated by the confederation, it does not thence follow, that the United States in congress have *no other* powers, jurisdiction, or rights, than those delegated by the particular states.

The United States have general rights, general powers, and general obligations, not derived from any particular states, nor from all the particular states, taken separately; but resulting from the union of the whole: and, therefore, it is provided, in the fifth article of the confederation, "that for the more convenient management of the *general interests* of the United States, delegates shall be annually appointed to meet in congress."

To many purposes, the United States are to be considered as one undivided, independent nation; and as possessed of all the rights, and powers, and properties, by the law of nations incident to such.

Whenever an object occurs, to the direction of which no particular state is competent, the management of it must, of necessity, belong to the United States in congress assembled. There are many objects of this extended nature. The purchase, the sale, the defence, and the government of lands and countries, not within any state, are all included under this description. An institution for circulating paper, and establishing its credit over the whole United States, is naturally ranged in the same class.

The act of independence was made before the articles of confederation. This act declares, that "*these United Colonies,*" (not enumerating them separately) "are free and independent states; and that, as free and independent states, *they* have full power to do *all* acts and things which independent states may, of right, do."

The confederation was not intended to weaken or abridge the powers and rights, to which the United States were previously entitled. It was not intended to transfer any of those powers or rights to the particular states, or any of them. If, therefore, the power now in question was vested in the United States before the confederation; it continues vested in them still. The confederation clothed the United States with many, though, perhaps, not with sufficient powers: but of none did it disrobe them.

It is no new position, that rights may be vested in a political body, which did not previously reside in any or in all the members of that body. They may be derived solely from the union of those members.[g] "The case,"

g. 2. Burl. 42.

says the celebrated Burlamaqui,[4] "is here very near the same as in that of several voices collected together, which, by their union, produce a harmony, that was not to be found separately in each."

A number of unconnected inhabitants are settled on each side of a navigable river; it belongs to none of them; it belongs not to them all, for they have nothing in common: let them unite; the river is the property of the united body.

The arguments drawn from the political associations of individuals into a state will apply, with equal force and propriety, to a number of states united by a confederacy.

New states must be formed and established: their extent and boundaries must be regulated and ascertained. How can this be done, unless by the United States in congress assembled?

States are corporations or bodies politick of the most important and dignified kind.

Let us now concentre the foregoing observations, and apply them to the incorporation of the Bank of North America by congress.

By the civil law, corporations seem to have been created by the mere and voluntary association of their members, provided such convention was not contrary to law.[h]

By the common law, something more is necessary—All the methods whereby corporations exist are, for the most part, reducible to that of the king's letters patent, or charter of incorporation.[i]

From this it will appear that the creation of a corporation is, by the common law, considered as the act of the executive rather than of the legislative powers of government.

Before the revolution, charters of incorporation were granted by the proprietaries of Pennsylvania, under a derivative authority from the crown, and those charters have been recognised by the constitution and laws of the commonwealth since the revolution.

4. Jean Jacques Burlamaqui (1694–1748) was a Swiss publicist and jurist who was a professor of ethics and the law of nature at the University of Geneva. He espoused a philosophy that most closely resembles rational utilitarianism. His major works are *Principles of Natural Law* (1747) and *Principles of Political Law* (1751).

h. 1. Bl. Com. 472.

i. 1. Bl. Com. 472. 473.

From analogy, therefore, we may justly infer, that the United States in congress assembled, possessing the executive powers of the union, may, in virtue of such powers, grant charters of incorporation for accomplishing objects that comprehend the general interests of the United States.

But the United States in congress assembled possess, in many instances, and to many purposes, the legislative as well as the executive powers of the union; and therefore, whether we consider the incorporation of the bank as a law, or as a charter, it will be equally within the powers of congress: for the object of this institution could not be reached without the exertion of the combined sovereignty of the union.

I have asked—how can new states, which are bodies politick, be formed, unless by the United States in congress assembled? Fact, as well as argument, justifies my sentiments on this subject. The conduct of congress has been similar on similar occasions. The same principles have directed the exercise of the same powers.

In the month of April, 1784, congress resolved, that part of the western territory "should be divided into distinct states."

They further resolved, that the settlers should, "either on their own petition, or on the order of congress, receive authority from *them* to meet together, for the purpose of establishing a temporary government, to adopt the constitution and laws of any one of the original states."

"When any such state shall have acquired twenty thousand free inhabitants, on giving due proof thereof to congress, they shall receive from *them* authority to call a convention of representatives, to establish a permanent constitution and government for themselves."

"The preceding articles," among others, "shall be formed into a charter of compact; shall be duly executed by the president of the United States in congress assembled, under his hand and the seal of the United States; shall be promulgated; and shall stand as fundamental constitutions between the thirteen original states, and each of the several states now newly described, unalterable from and after the sale of any part of the territory of such state, but by the joint consent of the United States in congress assembled, and of the particular state within which such alteration is proposed to be made."

It will be difficult, I believe, to urge against the power of congress to grant a charter to the Bank of North America, any argument, which may not, with equal strength and fitness, be urged against the power of that body to form, execute, and promulgate a charter of compact for the new states.

The sentiments of the representatives of the United States, as to their power of incorporating the bank, ought to have much weight with us. Their sentiments are strongly marked by their conduct, in their first resolutions respecting the bank. These resolutions are made at the same time, and on the same subject: but there is a striking difference in their manner. It was thought proper "that no other bank should be permitted within any of the states, during the war." Congress "*recommended* to the several states to make provision, for that purpose, by proper laws." It was thought prudent that the bank should be protected, by penal laws, from fraud, embezzlement, and forgery. Congress *recommended* it to the several legislatures to pass such laws. It was deemed expedient that bank notes should be received in payment of sums payable to the United States: congress *resolve,* that the notes "shall be receivable" in such payments. It was judged necessary that the bank should have a charter of incorporation: congress *resolve,* that the bank "shall be incorporated," on application made "*to congress*" for that purpose. The line of distinction between those things in which congress could only recommend, and those in which they could act, is drawn in the clearest manner. The incorporation of the national bank is ranked among those things, in which they could act.

This act of congress has, either expressly, or by implication, received the approbation of every state in the union. It was officially announced to every state by the superintendant of finance. Had any one state considered it as an exercise of usurped power, would not that state have remonstrated against it? But there is no such remonstrance.

This act of congress has been most explicitly recognised by the legislature of Pennsylvania. The law for preventing and punishing frauds and cheats upon the bank was passed on the 18th of March, 1782, and before the bank had obtained a charter from this state. By that law it is made felony without benefit of clergy, to forge the common seal of the president, directors, and company of the Bank of North America. Who were the president, directors, and company of the Bank of North America? Those whom congress had made "a corporation and body politick, to all intents and purposes, by that name and style." How came that body by a "common seal?" The act of congress ordained that that body "should have full power and authority to make, have and use a common seal." In the act to incorporate the subscribers to the Bank of North America, the legislature, after reciting that the United States in congress assembled had "passed an ordinance to incorporate them," say, "the president and directors of the said bank have applied to this house for a similar act of incorporation, which request it is proper and reasonable to grant."

When the foregoing facts and arguments are considered, compared, and weighed, they will, it is hoped, evince and establish, *satisfactorily* to all, and *conclusively* on the legislature of Pennsylvania, the truth of this position—That the Bank of North America was legally and constitutionally instituted and organized, by the charter of incorporation granted by the United States in congress assembled.

II. Would it, then, be wise or politick in the legislature of Pennsylvania, to revoke the charter which it has granted to this institution? It would not be wise or politick—

1st. Because the proceeding would be nugatory. The recal of the charter of Pennsylvania would not repeal that of the United States, by which we have proved the bank to be legally and constitutionally instituted and organized.

2d. Because, though the legislature may destroy the legislative *operation*, yet it cannot undo the legislative *acknowledgment* of its own act. Though a statute be repealed, yet it shows the sense and opinion of the legislature concerning the subject of it, in the same manner as if it continued in force.[j] The legislature declared, in the law, that it was proper and reasonable to grant the request of the president and directors of the bank, for an act of incorporation similar to the ordinance of congress: no repeal of the law can weaken the force of that declaration.

3d. Because such a proceeding would wound that confidence in the engagements of government, which it is so much the interest and duty of every state to encourage and reward. The act in question formed a charter of compact between the legislature of this state, and the president, directors, and company of the Bank of North America. The latter asked for nothing but what was proper and reasonable: the former granted nothing but what was proper and reasonable: the terms of the compact were, therefore,

j. Foster, 394.

fair and honest: while these terms are observed on one side, the compact cannot, consistently with the rules of good faith, be departed from on the other.

It may be asked—Has not the state power over her own laws?—May she not alter, amend, extend, restrain, and repeal them at her pleasure?

I am far from opposing the legislative authority of the state: but it must be observed, that, according to the practice of the legislature, publick acts of very different kinds are drawn and promulgated under the same form. A law to vest or confirm an estate in an individual—a law to incorporate a congregation or other society—a law respecting the rights and properties of all the citizens of the state—are all passed in the same manner; are all clothed in the same dress of legislative formality; and are all equally acts of the representatives of the freemen of the commonwealth. But surely it will not be pretended, that, after laws of those different kinds are passed, the legislature possesses over each the same discretionary power of repeal. In a law respecting the rights and properties of all the citizens of the state, this power may be safely exercised by the legislature. Why? Because, in this case, the interest of those who make the law (the members of assembly and their constituents) and the interest of those who are to be affected by the law (the members of assembly and their constituents) is the same. It is a common cause, and may, therefore, be safely trusted to the representatives of the community. None can hurt another, without, at the same time, hurting himself. Very different is the case with regard to a law, by which the state grants privileges to a congregation or other society. Here two parties are instituted, and two distinct interests subsist. Rules of justice, of faith, and of honour must, therefore, be established between them: for, if interest alone is to be viewed, the congregation or society must always lie at the mercy of the community. Still more different is the case with regard to a law, by which an estate is vested or confirmed in an individual: if, in this case, the legislature may, at discretion, and without any reason assigned devest or destroy his estate, then a person seized of an estate in fee simple, under legislative sanction, is, in truth, nothing more than a solemn tenant at will.

For these reasons, whenever the objects and makers of an instrument, passed under the form of a law, are not the same, it is to be considered as a compact, and to be interpreted according to the rules and maxims, by which compacts are governed. A foreigner is naturalized by law: is he a citizen only during pleasure? He is no more, if, without any cause of forfeiture assigned and established, the law, by which he is naturalized, may at pleasure be repealed. To receive the legislative stamp of stability and permanency, acts of incorporation are applied for from the legislature. If these acts may be repealed without notice, without accusation, without hearing, without proof, without forfeiture; where is the stamp of their stability? Their motto should be, "Levity." If the act for incorporating the subscribers to the Bank of North America shall be repealed in this manner, a precedent will be established for repealing, in the same manner, every other legislative charter in Pennsylvania. A pretence, as specious as any that can be alleged on this occasion, will never be wanting on any future occasion. Those acts of the state, which have hitherto been considered as the sure anchors of privilege and of property, will become the sport of every varying gust of politicks, and will float wildly backwards and forwards on the irregular and impetuous tides of party and faction.

4th. It would not be wise or politick to repeal the charter granted by this state to the Bank of North America, because such a measure would operate, as far as it would have any operation, against the credit of the United States, on which the interest of this commonwealth and her citizens so essentially depends. This institution originated under the auspices of the United States: the subscription to the national bank was opened under the recommendations and the engagements of congress: citizens of this state, and of the other states, and foreigners have become stockholders, on the publick faith: the United States have pledged themselves "to promote and support the institution by such ways and means, from time to time, as may appear necessary for it, and consistent with the publick good."[k] They have recommended to the legislature of each state, "to pass such laws as they might judge necessary for giving the ordinance incorporating the bank its full operation." Pennsylvania has entered fully into the views, the recommendations, and the measures of congress respecting the bank. She has declared in the strongest manner her sense of their propriety, their reasonableness, and their necessity: she has passed laws for giving them their full operation. Will it redound to the credit of the United States to adopt and pursue a contrary system of conduct? The acts

k. 26th May, 1781.

and recommendations of congress subsist still in all their original force. Will it not have a tendency to shake all confidence in the councils and proceedings of the United States, if those acts and recommendations are now disregarded, without any reason shown for disregarding them? What influence will such a proceeding have upon the opinions and sentiments of the citizens of the United States and of foreigners? In one year they see measures respecting an object of confessed publick importance adopted and recommended with ardour by congress; and the views and wishes of that body zealously pursued by Pennsylvania: in another year they see those very measures, without any apparent reason for the change, warmly reprobated by that state: they must conclude one of two things:—that congress adopted and recommended those measures hastily and without consideration; or that Pennsylvania has reprobated them undutifully and disrespectfully. The former conclusion will give rise to very unfavourable reflections concerning the discernment both of the state and of the United States: the latter will suggest very inauspicious sentiments concerning the federal disposition and character of this commonwealth. The result of the conclusion will be—that the United States do not deserve, or that they will not receive, support in their system of finance.—These deductions and inferences will have particular weight, as they will be grounded on the conduct of Pennsylvania, hitherto one of the most federal, active, and affectionate states in the Union.

5th. It would not be wise or politick in the legislature to repeal their charter to the bank; because the tendency of such a step would be to deprive this state and the United States of all the advantages, publick and private, which would flow from the institution, in times of war, and in times of peace.

Let us turn our attention to some of the most material advantages resulting from a bank.

1st. It increases circulation, and invigorates industry. "It is not," says Dr. Smith,[5] in his Treatise on the Wealth of Nations,[1]

> by augmenting the capital of the country, but by rendering a greater part of that capital active and productive than would otherwise be so, that

5. Adam Smith (1723–1790) was a Scottish political economist and moral philosopher. His *Inquiry into the Nature and Causes of the Wealth of Nations* was published in 1776.

1. Vol. 1. p. 483, 484.

> the most judicious operations of banking can increase the industry of the country. The part of his capital which a dealer is obliged to keep by him unemployed, and in ready money, for answering occasional demands, is so much dead stock, which, so long as it remains in this situation, produces nothing either to him or to his country. The judicious operations of banking enable him to convert this dead stock into active and productive stock: into materials to work upon, into tools to work with, and into provisions and subsistence to work for; into stock which produces something both to himself and to his country. The gold and silver money which circulates in any country, and by means of which the produce of its land and labour is annually circulated and distributed to the proper consumers, is, in the same manner as the ready money of the dealer, all dead stock. It is a very valuable part of the capital of the country, which produces nothing to the country. The judicious operations of banking, by substituting paper in the room of a great part of this gold and silver, enables the country to convert a great part of this dead stock into active and productive stock; into stock which produces something to the country. The gold and silver money which circulates in any country may very properly be compared to a highway, which, while it circulates and carries to market all the grass and corn of the country, produces, itself, not a single pile of either. The judicious operations of banking, by providing, if I may be allowed so violent a metaphor, a sort of wagon-way through the air, enable the country to convert, as it were, a great part of its highways into good pasture and corn fields, and thereby to increase very considerably the annual produce of its land and labour.

The same sensible writer informs us, in another place, that "the[m] substitution of paper in the room of gold and silver money, replaces a very expensive instrument of commerce with one much less costly, and sometimes equally convenient. Circulation comes to be carried on by a new wheel, which it costs less both to erect and to maintain than the old one.—There are several sorts of paper money; but the circulating notes of banks and bankers is the species which is best known, and which seems best adapted for this purpose."—"These notes come to have the same currency as gold and silver money, from the confidence that such money can at any time be had for them."

m. Vol. 1. p. 434, 435.

Sir James Stewart[6] calls banking "the great engine,[n] by which domestick circulation is carried on."

To have a free, easy, and equable instrument of circulation is of much importance in all countries: it is of peculiar importance in young and flourishing countries, in which the demands for credit, and the rewards of industry, are greater than in any other. When we view the extent and situation of the United States, we shall be satisfied that their inhabitants may, for a long time to come, employ profitably, in the improvement of their lands, a greater stock than they will be able easily to procure. In such a situation, it will always be of great service to them to save as much as possible the expense of so costly an instrument of commerce as gold and silver, to substitute in its place one cheaper, and, for many purposes, not less convenient; and to convert the value of the gold and silver into the labour and the materials necessary for improving and extending their settlements and plantations.

"To the banks of Scotland," says Sir James Stewart,[o] "the improvement of that country is entirely owing; and until they are generally established in other countries of Europe, where trade and industry are little known, it will be very difficult to set those great engines to work."

2d. The influence of a bank on credit is no less salutary than its influence on circulation. This position is, indeed, little more than a corollary from the former. Credit is confidence; and, before we can place confidence in a payment, we must be convinced that he who is to make it will be both able and willing to do so at the time stipulated. However unexceptionable his character and fortune may be, this conviction can never take place, unless in a country where solid property can be, at any time, turned into a circulating medium.

3d. Trade, as well as circulation and credit, derives great support and assistance from a bank. Credit and circulation produce punctuality; and punctuality is the soul of commerce. Let us appeal to experience as well as reason.

6. Sir James Stewart (1713–1780), of Coltness, Baronet, was the father of political economy in Britain.

n. 2. Pol. Ec. 350.

o. 2. Pol. Ec. 356.

Dr. Smith says,[p] he has heard it asserted, that the trade of the city of Glasgow doubled in about fifteen years after the first erection of the banks there; and that the trade of Scotland has more than quadrupled since the first erection of the two publick banks at Edinburgh, of which one was established in 1695, and the other in 1727. Whether the increase has been in so great a proportion, the author pretends not to know. But that the trade of Scotland has increased very considerably during this period, and that the banks have contributed a good deal to this increase, cannot, he says, be doubted.

These observations, and observations similar to these, have induced Sir James Stewart to conclude,—that

> Banking,[q] in the age we live, is that branch of credit which best deserves the attention of a statesman. Upon the right establishment of banks depends the prosperity of trade, and the equable course of circulation. By them solid property may be melted down. By the means of banks, money may be constantly kept at a due proportion to alienation. If alienation increases, more property may be melted down. If it diminishes, the quantity of money stagnating will be absorbed by the bank, and part of the property formerly melted down in the securities granted to them will be, as it were, consolidated anew. These must pay, for the country, the balance of their trade with foreign nations: these keep the mints at work: and it is by these means, principally, that private, mercantile, and publick credit is supported.

I make no apology for the number and length of the quotations here used. They are from writers of great information, profound judgment, and unquestioned candour. They appear strictly and strongly applicable to my subject: and being so, should carry with them the greatest weight and influence; for the sentiments, which they contain and inculcate, must be considered as resulting from general principles and facts, and not as calculated for any partial purpose in this commonwealth.

But, here, it will probably be asked—Has your reasoning been verified by experience in this country? What advantages have resulted from the bank to commerce, circulation, and credit? Was our trade ever on such an

p. Vol. 1. p. 442.
q. 2. Pol. Ec. 358.

undesirable footing? Is not the country distressed by the want of a circulating medium? Is not credit almost totally destroyed?

I answer—There is, unfortunately, too much truth in the representation: but if events are properly distinguished, and traced to their causes, it will be found—that none of the inconveniences abovementioned have arisen from the bank—that some of them have proceeded, at least in part, from the opposition which has been given to it—and that, as to others, its energy has not been sufficient to counteract or control them.

The disagreeable state of our commerce has been the effect of extravagant and injudicious importation. During the war, our ports were in a great measure blocked up. Imported articles were scarce and dear; and we felt the disadvantages of a stagnation in business. Extremes frequently introduce one another. When hostilities ceased, the floodgates of commerce were opened; and an inundation of foreign manufactures overflowed the United States: we seemed to have forgot, that to pay was as necessary in trade as to purchase; and we observed no proportion between our imports, and our produce and other natural means of remittance. What was the consequence? Those who made any payments made them chiefly in specie; and in that way diminished our circulation. Others made no remittances at all, and thereby injured our credit. This account of what happened between the European merchants and our importers, corresponds exactly with what happened between our importers and the retailers spread over the different parts of the United States. The retailers, if they paid at all, paid in specie: and thus every operation, foreign and domestick, had an injurious effect on our credit, our circulation, and our commerce. But are any of these disadvantages to be ascribed to the bank? No. Is it to be accounted a fault or defect in the bank, that it did not prevent or remedy those disadvantages? By no means. Because one is not able to stem a torrent, is he therefore to be charged with augmenting its strength? The bank has had many difficulties to encounter. The experiment was a new one in this country: it was therefore necessary that it should be conducted with caution. While the war continued, the demands of the publick were great, and the stock of the bank was but inconsiderable; it had its active enemies, and its timid friends. Soon after the peace was concluded, its operations were restrained and embarrassed by an attempt to establish a new bank. A year had not elapsed after this, when the measure, which has occasioned these considerations, was introduced into the legislature, and caused, for some time, a total stagnation in the business of the institution. When all these circumstances are recollected and attended to, it will be matter of surprise that the bank has done so much, and not that it has done no more. Let it be deemed, as it ought to be, the object of publick confidence, and not of publick jealousy: let it be encouraged, instead of being opposed, by the counsels and proceedings of the state: then will the genuine effects of the institution appear; then will they spread their auspicious influence over agriculture, manufactures, and commerce.

4th. Another advantage to be expected from the Bank of North America is, the establishment of an undepreciating paper currency through the United States. This is an object of great consequence, whether it be considered in a political, or in a commercial view. It will be found to have a happy effect on the collection, the distribution, and the management of the publick revenue: it will remove the inconveniences and fluctuation attending exchange and remittances between the different states. "It is the interest of every trading state to have a sufficient quantity of paper, well secured, to circulate through it, so as to facilitate payments every where, and to cut off inland exchanges, which are a great clog upon trade, and are attended with the risk of receiving the paper of people, whose credit is but doubtful."[r]

Such are the advantages which may be expected to flow from a national bank, in times of peace. In times of war, the institution may be considered as essential. We have seen that, without it, the business of the department of finance could not have been carried on in the late war. It will be of use to recollect the situation of the United States with regard to this subject. The two or three first years of the war were sufficient to convince the British government, and the British armies, that they could not subdue the United States by military force. Their hopes of success rested on the failure of our finances. This was the source of our fears, as well as of the hopes of our enemies. By this thread our fate was suspended. We watched it with anxiety: we saw it stretched and weakened every hour: the deathful instrument was ready to fall upon our heads: on our heads it must have fallen, had not publick credit, in the moment when it was about to break asunder, been entwined and supported by the credit of the bank. Congress, to speak without metaphors, had not money or credit to hire an express, or purchase a cord of wood. General Washington, on one occasion,

r. 2. Pol. Ec. 415.

and probably more than one, saw his army literally unable to march. Our distress was such, that it would have been destruction to have divulged it: but it ought to be known now; and when known, ought to have its proper influence on the publick mind and the publick conduct.

The expenses of a war must be defrayed, either—1st, by treasures previously accumulated—or 2dly, by supplies levied and collected within the year, as they are called for—or 3dly, by the anticipation of the publick revenues. No one will venture to refer us to the first mode. To the second the United States, as well as every state in Europe, are rendered incompetent by the modern system of war, which, in the military operations of one year, concentres the revenue of many. While our enemies adhere to this system, we must adopt it. The anticipation of revenue, then, is the only mode, by which the expenses of a future war can be defrayed. How the revenues of the United States can be anticipated without the operations of a national bank, I leave to those who attack the Bank of North America to show. They ought to be well prepared to show it; for they must know, that to be incapable of supporting a war is but a single step from being involved in one.

The result of the whole, under this head, is,—that in times of peace, the national bank will be highly advantageous; that in times of war, it will be essentially necessary, to the United States.

I flatter myself, that I have evinced the validity and the utility of the institution.

It has been surmised, that the design of the legislature is not to destroy, but to modify, the charter of the bank; and that if the directors would assent to reasonable amendments, the charter, modified, might continue in force. If this is the case, surely to repeal the law incorporating the bank is not the proper mode of doing the business. The bank was established and organized under the authority and auspices of congress. The directors have a trust and duty to discharge to the United States, and to all the particular states, each of which has an equal interest in the bank. They could not have received, from this state, a charter, unless it had been *similar* to that granted by congress. Without the approbation of congress, where all the states are represented, the directors would not be justified in agreeing to any alteration of the institution. If alterations are necessary; they should be made through the channel of the United States in congress assembled.

Wilson is widely regarded by scholars as being second only to James Madison, and perhaps on a par with him, in terms of his influence at the constitutional convention. The following excerpts include every instance that James Madison recorded him speaking in the convention. For the most complete record of the convention's proceedings, see Max Farrand, ed. *The Records of the Federal Convention of 1787*, 3 vols.

Remarks of James Wilson in the Federal Convention, 1787.

Friday 25 of May, when the following members appeared to wit: see Note A.

viz, From *Massachusetts* Rufus King. *N. York* Robert Yates, Alex[r] Hamilton. *N. Jersey,* David Brearly, William Churchill Houston, William Patterson. *Pennsylvania,* Robert Morris, Thomas Fitzsimmons, James Wilson, Govurneur Morris. *Delaware,* George Read, Richard Basset, Jacob Broome. *Virginia,* George Washington, Edmund Randolph, John Blair, James Madison, George Mason, George Wythe, James M[c]Clurg. *N. Carolina,* Alexander Martin, William Richardson Davie, Richard Dobbs Spaight, Hugh Williamson. *S. Carolina,* John Rutlidge, Charles Cotesworth Pinckney, Charles Pinckney, Pierce Butler. *Georgia,* William Few.[1]

1. Rufus King (1755–1827) was recognized as a statesman (both state and federal) and orator of the highest caliber. He supported the Constitution of 1787. Robert Yates (1738–1801) was a justice of the supreme court of New York. He was a leader of the Antifederalists who opposed the Constitution and subsequently left the convention early on July 5, 1787. He later published letters in opposition to the Constitution under the names Brutus and Sydney. David Brearly (1745–1790) fervently backed the Revolution and participated in the New Jersey militia. He later served as the chief justice of the New Jersey supreme court and was appointed by Washington as a federal district court judge. William Churchill Houston (1740–1788) was a professor of mathematics and natural philosophy at Princeton. He fought in the Revolutionary War and was later admitted to the New Jersey bar. Houston was very ill during the convention and did not sign the final document. William Paterson (1745–1806) was a very capable statesman, serving as attorney general of New Jersey, U.S. senator, governor, and associate justice of the Supreme Court. He was at the constitutional convention only until late July (he returned to sign) but figured prominently in it because of his advocacy of the New Jersey, or Paterson, plan. Thomas Fitzsimmons (1741–1811) was a prominent businessman who supported the Revolution. A Federalist, he was active in state politics and later served in the U.S. House of Representatives. Gouverneur Morris (1752–1816) was a statesman and jurist. He was an ardent Federalist who spoke frequently in the constitutional convention. George Read (1734–1798) was an able jurist and statesman who served in the state politics of Delaware, a U.S. senator, and later chief

Mr Robert Morris informed the members assembled that by the instruction & in behalf, of the deputation of Pena he proposed George Washington Esqr late Commander in chief for president of the Convention. Mr Jno Rutlidge seconded the motion; expressing his confidence that the choice would be unanimous, and observing that the presence of Genl Washington forbade any observations on the occasion which might otherwise be proper.

---

justice of the supreme court of Delaware. Richard Basset (1745–1815) was a wealthy jurist and planter who was a U.S. senator from Delaware and later as governor. He supported the Federalist cause but did little in the constitutional convention. Jacob Broom (1752–1810) was active in state and local politics in Delaware. He never missed a session of the convention but did not play a major role. Edmund Randolph (1753–1813) aided George Washington during the Revolutionary War and was highly involved in the local and state politics of Virginia. He presented the Virginia plan at the constitutional convention, and though he declined to sign the final document, he supported it when it came time for ratification. John Blair (1732–1800) held legislative and judicial offices in Virginia. He supported the Constitution, though he played a minor role in the convention. Later he served as an associate justice of the Supreme Court. George Wythe (1726–1806) was active in the politics of Virginia, but his main contribution came from his role in the judicial and academic life of that state. He could count Thomas Jefferson, John Marshall, James Monroe, and Henry Clay as his pupils. He supported the Constitution, but he left the convention early and did not sign. James McClurg (1746–1823) was an eminent physician in Virginia who served as a surgeon during the Revolutionary War. During the convention, he advocated greater power for the executive. He left the convention in early August and did not sign the Constitution. Alexander Martin (1740–1807) served in the North Carolina Senate, as governor, and as a U.S. senator. He left the convention in late August and did not sign the Constitution. William Richardson Davie (1756–1820) was an extremely capable soldier, jurist, and educator. He supported a strong federal government and was a strong supporter of the Constitution, though he left the convention early in mid-August. Richard Dobbs Spaight, Sr. (1758–1802), was a state representative, governor, and member of the U.S. House of Representatives. He attended every session of the convention and strongly supported the Constitution. Hugh Williamson (1735–1819) pursued the Presbyterian ministry, philosophy, medicine, and science in general. He fought in the Revolutionary War and played a significant role during the convention. John Rutledge (1739–1800) was the governor of South Carolina during the Revolutionary War. He participated in all three branches of state government and served as an associate justice of the Supreme Court for a short time. He took a moderately nationalist stance at the convention. Charles Cotesworth Pinckney (1746–1825) was educated as a jurist but was mainly a soldier. He served through many battles of the Revolutionary War. He advocated a strong national government during the convention and defended the Constitution upon returning to South Carolina. Charles Pinckney (1757–1824) was a state legislator and governor, as well as a member of the U.S. House of Representatives. He was one of the more influential members at the convention. Pierce Butler (1744–1822) was a planter and soldier who later served as a U.S. senator. Nominally a Federalist, he supported the Constitution but often crossed party lines. William Few (1748–1828) served in the U.S. Congress as both a representative and senator. Few missed many summer sessions of the convention but was supportive of the Constitution.

General Washington was accordingly unanimously elected by ballot, and conducted to the Chair by Mr R. Morris and Mr Rutlidge; from which in a very emphatic manner he thanked the Convention for the honor they had conferred on him, reminded them of the novelty of the scene of business in which he was to act, lamented his want of better qualifications, and claimed the indulgence of the House towards the involuntary errors which his inexperience might occasion.

[The nomination came with particular grace from Penna. as Doc^r Franklin alone could have been thought of as a competitor. The Doc^r was himself to have made the nomination of General Washington, but the state of the weather and of his health confined him to his house.]

Mr Wilson moved that a Secretary be appointed, and nominated Mr Temple Franklin.[2]

. . .

Thursday May 31

William Pierce[3] from Georgia took his seat.

In Committee of the whole on Mr Randolph's propositions.

The 3^d Resolution "that the national Legislature ought to consist of two branches" was agreed to without debate or dissent, except that of Pennsylvania, given probably from complaisance to Doc^r Franklin who was understood to be partial to a single House of Legislation.

Resol: 4. first clause "that the members of the first branch of the National Legislature ought to be elected by the people of the several States" being taken up,

. . .

Mr Wilson contended strenuously for drawing the most numerous branch of the Legislature immediately from the people. He was for raising the federal pyramid to a considerable altitude, and for that reason wished

2. William Temple Franklin (1760–1823) was the son of William Franklin, Royal Governor of New Jersey, and the grandson of Benjamin Franklin.

3. William Leigh Pierce (1740–1789) was a merchant who served in the U.S. House of Representatives. He left the convention early, playing only a minor role. The notes he took of the proceedings have proved valuable, as they provide character sketches of the lesser known members of the convention.

to give it as broad a basis as possible. No government could long subsist without the confidence of the people. In a republican Government this confidence was peculiarly essential. He also thought it wrong to increase the weight of the State Legislatures by making them the electors of the national Legislature. All interference between the general and local Governm[ts] should be obviated as much as possible. On examination it would be found that the opposition of States to federal measures had proceeded much more from the officers of the States, than from the people at large.

. . .

The Committee proceeded to Resolution 5. "that the second, [or senatorial] branch of the National Legislature ought to be chosen by the first branch out of persons nominated by the State Legislatures."

. . .

M[r] Wilson opposed both a nomination by the State Legislatures and an election by the first branch of the national Legislature, because the second branch of the latter, ought to be independent of both. He thought both branches of the National Legislature ought to be chosen by the people, but was not prepared with a specific proposition. He suggested the mode of chusing the Senate of N. York to wit of uniting several election districts, for one branch, in chusing members for the other branch, as a good model.

. . .

Friday June 1st 1787

William Houston from Georgia took his seat.

The Committee of the whole proceeded to Resolution 7. "that a national Executive be instituted, to be chosen by the national Legislature—for the term of   years &c to be ineligible thereafter, to possess the executive powers of Congress &c."

. . .

M[r] Wilson moved that the Executive consist of a single person.

. . .

M[r] Wilson preferred a single magistrate, as giving most energy, dispatch and responsibility to the office. He did not consider the Prerogatives of the British Monarch as a proper guide in defining the Executive powers. Some of these prerogatives were of Legislative nature. Among others that of war & peace &c. The only powers he conceived strictly Executive were those of executing the laws, and appointing officers, not appertaining to and appointed by the Legislature.

. . .

Mr Wilson said that unity in the Executive instead of being the fetus of monarchy would be the best safeguard against tyranny. He repeated that he was not governed by the British Model which was inapplicable to the situation of this Country; the extent of which was so great, and the manners so republican, that nothing but a great confederated Republic would do for it.

Mr Wilson's motion for a single magistrate was postponed by common consent, the Committee seeming unprepared for any decision on it; and the first part of the clause agreed to, viz—"that a National Executive be instituted."

Mr Madison thought it would be proper, before a choice sh^d be made between a unity and a plurality in the Executive, to fix the extent of the Executive authority; that as certain powers were in their nature Executive, and must be given to that departm^t whether administered by one or more persons, a definition of their extent would assist the judgment in determining how far they might be safely entrusted to a single officer. He accordingly moved that so much of the clause before the Committee as related to the powers of the Executive sh^d be struck out & that after the words "that a national Executive ought to be instituted" there be inserted the words following viz. "with power to carry into effect the national laws, to appoint to offices in cases not otherwise provided for, and to execute such other powers 'not Legislative nor Judiciary in their nature,' as may from time to time be delegated by the national Legislature." The words "not legislative nor judiciary in their nature" were added to the proposed amendment in consequence of a suggestion by Genl Pinkney that improper powers might otherwise be delegated.

Mr Wilson seconded this motion—

. . .

The next clause in Resolution 7, relating to the mode of appointing, & the duration of, the Executive being under consideration.

Mr Wilson said he was almost unwilling to declare the mode which he wished to take place, being apprehensive that it might appear chimerical.

He would say however at least that in theory he was for an election by the people. Experience, particularly in N. York & Mass[ts], shewed that an election of the first magistrate by the people at large, was both a convenient & successful mode. The objects of choice in such cases must be persons whose merits have general notoriety.

. . .

The *mode of appointing* the Executive was the next question.

M[r] Wilson renewed his declarations in favor of an appointment by the people. He wished to derive not only both branches of the Legislature from the people, without the intervention of the State Legislatures but the Executive also; in order to make them as independent as possible of each other, as well as of the States;

Col. Mason favors the idea, but thinks it impracticable. He wishes however that M[r] Wilson might have time to digest it into his own form.—the clause "to be chosen by the National Legislature"—was accordingly postponed.—

. . .

Saturday June 2[d]. In Committee of whole

. . .

M[r] Wilson made the following motion, to be substituted for the mode proposed by M[r] Randolph's resolution, "that the Executive Magistracy shall be elected in the following manner: That the States be divided into   districts: & that the persons qualified to vote in each district for members of the first branch of the national Legislature elect   members for their respective districts to be electors of the Executive magistracy, that the said Electors of the Executive magistracy meet at   and they or any   of them so met shall proceed to elect by ballot, but not out of their own body   person in whom the Executive authority of the national Government shall be vested."

M[r] Wilson repeated his arguments in favor of an election without the intervention of the States. He supposed too that this mode would produce more confidence among the people in the first magistrate, than an election by the national Legislature.

. . .

Mr Dickenson[4] moved "that the Executive be made removeable by the National Legislature on the request of a majority of the Legislatures of individual States." It was necessary he said to place the power of removing somewhere. He did not like the plan of impeaching the Great officers of State. He did not know how provision could be made for removal of them in a better mode than that which he had proposed. He had no idea of abolishing the State Governments as some gentlemen seemed inclined to do. The happiness of this Country in his opinion required considerable powers to be left in the hands of the States.

. . .

Mr Madison & Mr Wilson observed that it would leave an equality of agency in the small with the great States; that it would enable a minority of the people to prevent ye removal of an officer who had rendered himself justly criminal in the eyes of a majority; that it would open a door for intrigues agst him in States where his administration tho' just might be unpopular, and might tempt him to pay court to particular States whose leading partizans he might fear, or wish to engage as his partizans. They both thought it bad policy to introduce such a mixture of the State authorities, where their agency could be otherwise supplied.

. . .

Monday June 4. In Committee of the whole

The Question was resumed on motion of Mr Pinkney 2^{ded} by Wilson, "shall the blank for the number of the Executive be filled with a single person?"

Mr Wilson was in favor of the motion. It had been opposed by the gentleman from Virg^{a} [Mr Randolph] but the arguments used had not convinced him. He observed that the objections of Mr R. were levelled not so much agst the measure itself, as agst its unpopularity. If he could suppose that it would occasion a rejection of the plan of which it should form a part,

4. John Dickenson (1732–1808) represented Delaware at the convention. He was an orator and author of the highest caliber who served in various political capacities. He is best known for his *Letters from a Farmer in Pennsylvania.*

though the part was an important one, yet he would give it up rather than lose the whole. On examination he could see no evidence of the alledged antipathy of the people. On the contrary he was persuaded that it does not exist. All know that a single magistrate is not a King. One fact has great weight with him. All the 13 States tho agreeing in scarce any other instance, agree in placing a single magistrate at the head of the Govern^{t}. The idea of three heads has taken place in none. The degree of power is indeed different; but there are no co-ordinate heads. In addition to his former reasons for preferring a unity, he would mention another. The *tranquility* not less than the vigor of the Gov^{t} he thought would be favored by it. Among three equal members, he foresaw nothing but uncontrouled, continued, & violent animosities; which would not only interrupt the public administration; but diffuse their poison thro' the other branches of Gov^{t}, thro' the States, and at length thro' the people at large. If the members were to be unequal in power the principle of the opposition to the unity was given up. If equal, the making them an odd number would not be a remedy. In Courts of Justice there are two sides only to a question. In the Legislative & Executive departm^{ts} questions have commonly many sides. Each member therefore might espouse a separate one & no two agree.

. . .

Mr Williamson asks Mr Wilson whether he means to annex a Council.

Mr Wilson means to have no Council, which oftener serves to cover, than prevent malpractices.

. . .

First Clause of Proposition 8th relating *to a Council of Revision* taken into consideration.

Mr Gerry[5] doubts whether the Judiciary ought to form a part of it, as they will have a sufficient check agst encroachments on their own department by their exposition of the laws, which involved a power of deciding on their Constitutionality. In some States the Judges had actually set aside laws as being agst the Constitution. This was done too with general approbation. It was quite foreign from the nature of ye office to make

5. Elbridge Gerry (1744–1814), a merchant who represented Massachusetts at the convention. He vacillated greatly in his political stances and was initially opposed to the Constitution. He later came to support it and served as governor of Massachusetts and as vice president under James Madison. The term "gerrymander" is named after him.

them judges of the policy of public measures. He moves to postpone the clause in order to propose "that the National Executive shall have a right to negative any Legislative act which shall not be afterwards passed by parts of each branch of the national Legislature."

. . .

Mr Wilson thinks neither the original proposition nor the amendment go far enough. If the Legislative Exetv & Judiciary ought to be distinct & independent. The Executive ought to have an absolute negative. Without such a self-defense the Legislature can at any moment sink it into non-existence. He was for varying the proposition in such a manner as to give the Executive & Judiciary jointly an absolute negative.

On the question to postpone in order to take Mr Gerry's proposition into consideration it was agreed to, Mass^{a} ay. Con^{t} no. N. Y. ay. P^{a} ay. Del. no. Mary^{d} no. Virg^{a} no. N. C. ay. S. C. ay. G^{a} ay.

Mr Gerry's proposition being now before Committee, Mr Wilson & Mr Hamilton move that the last part of it [viz. "wch s^{l} not be afterw^{ds} passed unless by parts of each branch of the National legislature"] be struck out, so as to give the Executive an absolute negative on the laws. There was no danger they thought of such a power being too much exercised. It was mentioned by Col: Hamilton that the King of G. B. had not exerted his negative since the Revolution.

. . .

Mr Wilson believed as others did that this power would seldom be used. The Legislature would know that such a power existed, and would refrain from such laws, as it would be sure to defeat. Its silent operation would therefore preserve harmony and prevent mischief. The case of Pen^{a} formerly was very different from its present case. The Executive was not then as now to be appointed by the people. It will not in this case as in the one cited be supported by the head of a Great Empire, actuated by a different & sometimes opposite interest. The salary too is now proposed to be fixed by the Constitution, or if D^{r}. F.'s idea should be adopted all salary whatever interdicted. The requiring a large proportion of each House to overrule the Executive check might do in peaceable times; but there might be tempestuous moments in which animosities may run high between the Executive and Legislative branches, and in which the former ought to be able to defend itself.

. . .

Tuesday June 5. In Committee of the whole

Governor Livingston[6] from New Jersey, took his seat.

The words, "one or more" were struck out before "inferior tribunals" as an amendment to the last clause of Resol^{n} 9th. The Clause—"that the National Judiciary be chosen by the National Legislature," being under consideration.

Mr Wilson opposed the appointm^{t} of Judges by the National Legisl: Experience shewed the impropriety of such appointm^{ts} by numerous bodies. Intrigue, partiality, and concealment were the necessary consequences. A principal reason for unity in the Executive was that officers might be appointed by a single, responsible person.

. . .

Mr Wilson gave notice that he should at a future day move for a reconsideration of that clause which respects "inferior tribunals."

. . .

Propos. 15 for "*recommending Conventions under appointment of the people to ratify the new Constitution*" &c. being taken up.

. . .

Mr Wilson took this occasion to lead the Committee by a train of observations to the idea of not suffering a disposition in the plurality of States to confederate anew on better principles, to be defeated by the inconsiderate or selfish opposition of a few States. He hoped the provision for ratifying would be put on such a footing as to admit of such a partial union, with a door open for the acession of the rest.

. . .

Mr Rutlidge hav^{g} obtained a rule for reconsideration of the clause for establishing *inferior* tribunals under the national authority, now moved that that part of the clause in propos. 9. should be expunged: arguing that the State Tribunals might and ought to be left in all cases to decide in the first instance the right of appeal to the supreme national tribunal being sufficient to secure the national rights & uniformity of Judgm^{ts}: that it was making an unnecessary encroachment on the jurisdiction of the

6. William Livingston (1723–1790) served as the governor of New Jersey from 1776 until his death.

States and creating unnecessary obstacles to their adoption of the new system.—Mr Sherman[7] 2^{ded} the motion.

. . .

Mr Wilson opposed the motion on like grounds, he said the admiralty jurisdiction ought to be given wholly to the national Government, as it related to cases not within the jurisdiction of particular states, & to a scene in which controversies with foreigners would be most likely to happen.

. . .

Mr Wilson & Mr Madison then moved, in pursuance of the idea expressed above by Mr Dickinson, to add to Resol: 9. the words following "that the National Legislature be empowered to institute inferior tribunals." They observed that there was a distinction between establishing such tribunals absolutely, and giving a discretion to the Legislature to establish or not establish them. They repeated the necessity of some such provision.

. . .

Wednesday June 6th. In Committee of the whole

Mr Pinkney according to previous notice & rule obtained, moved "that the first branch of the national Legislature be elected by the State Legislatures, and not by the people." contending that the people were less fit Judges in such a case, and that the Legislatures would be less likely to promote the adoption of the new Government, if they were to be excluded from all share in it.

Mr Rutlidge 2^{ded} the motion.

. . .

Mr Wilson. He wished for vigor in the Gov^{t}, but he wished that vigorous authority to flow immediately from the legitimate source of all authority. The Gov^{t} ought to possess not only 1st the *force*, but 2dly the *mind or sense* of the people at large. The Legislature ought to be the most exact transcript of the whole Society. Representation is made necessary only be-

7. Roger Sherman (1721–1793) was a delegate from Connecticut. In his home state he served simultaneously as a member of the upper house in the general assembly and as a superior court judge. He later served in the U.S. House and the U.S. Senate.

cause it is impossible for the people to act collectively. The opposition was to be expected he said from the *Governments,* not from the Citizens of the States. The latter had parted as was observed [by Mr King] with all the necessary powers; and it was immaterial to them, by whom they were exercised, if well exercised. The State officers were to be the losers of power. The people he supposed would be rather more attached to the national Gov^{t} than to the State Gov^{ts} as being more important in itself, and more flattering to their pride. There is no danger of improper elections if made by *large* districts. Bad elections proceed from the smallness of the districts which give an opportunity to bad men to intrigue themselves into office.

. . .

Mr Wilson, would not have spoken again, but for what had fallen from Mr Read; namely, that the idea of preserving the State Gov^{ts} ought to be abandoned. He saw no incompatibility between the National & State Gov^{ts} provided the latter were restrained to certain local purposes; nor any probability of their being devoured by the former. In all confederated Systems antient & modern the reverse had happened; the Generality being destroyed gradually by the usurpations of the parts composing it.

. . .

Mr Wilson moved to reconsider the vote excluding the Judiciary from a share in the revision of the laws, and to add after "National Executive" the words "with a convenient number of the national Judiciary"; remarking the expediency of reinforcing the Executive with the influence of that Department.

. . .

Mr Wilson remarked, that the responsibility required belonged to his Executive duties. The revisionary duty was an extraneous one, calculated for collateral purposes.

. . .

Thursday June 7th 1787—In Committee of the whole

. . .

The Clause providing for ye appointment of the 2^{d} branch of the national Legislature, having lain blank since the last vote on the mode of electing it, to wit, by the 1st branch, Mr Dickenson now moved "that the members of the 2d branch ought to be chosen by the individual Legislatures."

. . .

Mr Wilson. If we are to establish a national Government, that Government ought to flow from the people at large. If one branch of it should be chosen by the Legislatures, and the other by the people, the two branches will rest on different foundations, and dissensions will naturally arise between them. He wished the Senate to be elected by the people as well as the other branch, and the people might be divided into proper districts for the purpose & moved to postpone the motion of Mr Dickenson, in order to take up one of that import.

Mr Morris 2ded him.

. . .

Friday June 8th. In Committee of the whole

On a reconsideration of the clause giving the Natl Legislature a negative on such laws of the States as might be contrary to the articles of Union, or Treaties with foreign nations.

. . .

Mr Wilson would not say what modifications of the proposed power might be practicable or expedient. But however novel it might appear the principle of it when viewed with a close & steady eye, is right. There is no instance in which the laws say that the individual shd be bound in one case, & at liberty to judge whether he will obey or disobey in another. The cases are parallel. Abuses of the power over the individual person may happen as well as over the individual States. Federal liberty is to States, what civil liberty, is to private individuals. And States are not more unwilling to purchase it, by the necessary concession of their political sovereignty, than the savage is to purchase civil liberty by the surrender of his personal sovereignty, which he enjoys in a State of nature. A definition of the cases in which the Negative should be exercised, is impracticable. A discretion must be left on one side or the other? will it not be most safely lodged on the side of the Natl Govt? Among the first sentiments expressed in the first Congs one was that Virga is no more, that Masts is no that Pa is no more &c. We are now one nation of brethren. We must bury all local interests & distinctions. This language continued for some time. The tables at length began to turn. No sooner were the State Gov^{ts} formed than their jealousy & ambition began to display themselves. Each endeavoured to cut a slice from the common loaf, to add to its own morsel, till at length the confederation became frittered down to the impotent condition in which it now stands. Review the progress of the articles of Confederation thro' Congress & compare the first & last draught of it. To correct its vices is the business of this convention. One of its vices is the want of an effectual controul in the whole over its parts. What danger is there that the whole will unnecessarily sacrifice a part? But reverse the case, and leave the whole at the mercy of each part, and will not the general interest be continually sacrificed to local interests?

. . .

Saturday June 9th. Mr Luther Martin[8] from Maryland took his seat. In Committee of the whole

Mr Gerry, according to previous notice given by him, moved that the National Executive should be elected by the Executives of the States whose proportion of votes should be the same with that allowed to the States in the election of the Senate."

. . .

Mr Wilson hoped if the Confederacy should be dissolved, that a *majority*, that a *minority* of the States would unite for their safety. He entered elaborately into the defence of a proportional representation, stating for his first position that as all authority was derived from the people, equal numbers of people ought to have an equal n° of representatives, and different numbers of people different numbers of representatives. This principle had been improperly violated in the Confederation, owing to the urgent circumstances of the time. As to the case of A. & B, stated by Mr Patterson,[9] he

8. Luther Martin (1748–1826) was the attorney general in Maryland for 28 consecutive years. He was strongly opposed to the Constitution and left the convention early.

9. William Paterson (1745–1806) of New Jersey was a member of the constitutional convention. Wilson's reference to Paterson's "A & B" refers to Paterson's explanation of state representation, as recorded by James Madison, on June 9.

observed that in districts as large as the States, the number of people was the best measure of their comparative wealth. Whether therefore wealth or numbers were to form the ratio it would be the same. Mr P. admitted persons, not property to be the measure of suffrage. Are not the Citizens of Pena equal to those of N. Jersey? does it require 150 of the former to balance 50 of the latter? Representatives of different districts ought clearly to hold the same proportion to each other, as their respective Constituents hold to each other. If the small States will not confederate on this plan, Pena & he presumed some other States, would not confederate on any other. We have been told that each State being sovereign, all are equal. So each man is naturally a sovereign over himself, and all men are therefore naturally equal. Can he retain this equality when he becomes a member of Civil Government? He can not. As little can a Sovereign State, when it becomes a member of a federal Governt If N. J. will not part with her Sovereignty it is in vain to talk of Govt A new partition of the States is desireable, but evidently & totally impracticable.

. . .

Monday June 11th. Mr Abraham Baldwin[10] from Georgia took his seat. In Committee of the whole

The clause concerning the rule of suffrage in the natl Legislature postponed on Saturday was resumed.

. . .

Mr King & Mr Wilson, in order to bring the question to a point moved "that the right of suffrage in the first branch of the national Legislature ought not to be according the rule established in the articles of Confederation, but according to some equitable ratio of representation." The clause so far as it related to suffrage in the first branch was postponed in order to consider this motion.

. . .

Mr Wilson & Mr Hamilton moved that the right of suffrage in the 2d branch ought to be according to the same rule as in the 1st branch. On this

10. Abraham Baldwin (1754–1807) served for a total of eighteen years in the U.S. Congress as a member of both the House and the Senate. He was largely inconspicuous at the convention.

question for making the ratio of representation the same in the 2[d] as in the 1st branch it passed in the affirmative:

. . .

Saturday June 16. In Committee of the whole on Resolutions propos[d] by M[r] P. & M[r] R

M[r] Lansing[11] called for the reading of the 1st resolution of each plan, which he considered as involving principles directly in contrast; that of M[r] Patterson says he sustains the sovereignty of the respective States, that of M[r] Randolph distroys it: the latter requires a negative on all the laws of the particular States; the former, only certain general powers for the general good. The plan of M[r] R. in short absorbs all power except what may be exercised in the little local matters of the States which are not objects worthy of the supreme cognizance.

. . .

M[r] Wilson entered into a contrast of the principal points of the two plans so far he said as there had been time to examine the one last proposed. These points were 1. in the Virg[a] plan there are 2 & in some degree 3 branches in the Legislature: in the plan from N.J. there is to be a *single* legislature only—2. Representation of the people at large is the basis of the one:—the State Legislatures, the pillars of the other—3. proportional representation prevails in one:—equality of suffrage in the other—4. A single Executive Magistrate is at the head of the one:—a plurality is held out in the other.—5. in the one the majority of the people of the U. S. must prevail:—in the other a minority may prevail. 6. the Nat[l] Legislature is to make laws in all cases to which the separate States are incompetent &–:—in place of this Cong[s] are to have additional power in a few cases only—7. A negative on the laws of the States:—in place of this coertion to be substituted—8. The Executive to be removeable on impeachment & conviction;—in one plan: in the other to be removeable at the instance of majority of the Executives

11. Refers to John Lansing Jr. (1754–1829), a member of the convention from New York, who was vehemently against the Constitution and convention and left early. He later served as an associate justice and chief justice of the New York Supreme Court and as chancellor of that state.

of the States—9. Revision of the laws provided for in one:—no such check in the other—10. inferior national tribunals in one:—none such in the other. 11. In ye one jurisdiction of Nat^{l} tribunals to extend &c—; an appellate jurisdiction only allowed in the other. 12. Here the jurisdiction is to extend to all cases affecting the Nation^{l} peace & harmony: there, a few cases only are marked out. 13. finally ye ratification is in this to be by the people themselves:—in that by the legislative authorities according to the 13 art: of Confederation.

With regard to the *power of the Convention,* he conceived himself authorized to *conclude nothing,* but to be at liberty to *propose any thing.* In this particular he felt himself perfectly indifferent to the two plans.

With *regard to the sentiments of the people,* he conceived it difficult to know precisely what they are. Those of the particular circle in which one moved, were commonly mistaken for the general voice. He could not persuade himself that the State Govt^{ts} & Sovereignties were so much the idols of the people, nor a Nat^{l} Gov^{t} so obnoxious to them, as some supposed. Why s^{d} a Nat^{l} Gov^{t} be unpopular? Has it less dignity? will each Citizen enjoy under it less liberty or protection? Will a Citizen of *Delaware* be degraded by becoming a Citizen of the *United States*? Where do the people look at present for relief from the evils of which they complain? Is it from an internal reform of their Gov^{ts}? no, Sir. It is from the Nat^{l} Councils that relief is expected. For these reasons he did not fear, that the people would not follow us into a national Gov^{t} and it will be a further recommendation of Mr R.'s plan that it is to be submitted to *them,* and not to the *Legislatures,* for ratification.

Proceeding now to the 1st point on which he had contrasted the two plans, he observed that anxious as he was for some augmentation of the federal powers, it would be with extreme reluctance indeed that he could ever consent to give powers to Cong^{s} he had two reasons either of wch was sufficient. 1. Cong^{s} as a Legislative body does not stand on the people. 2. it is a *single* body. 1. He would not repeat the remarks he had formerly made on the principles of Representation. He would only say that an inequality in it, has ever been a poison contaminating every branch of Gov^{t} In G. Britain where this poison has had a full operation, the security of private rights is owing entirely to the purity of Her tribunals of Justice, the Judges of which are neither appointed nor paid, by a venal Parliament.

The political liberty of that Nation, owing to the inequality of representation is at the mercy of its rulers. He means not to insinuate that there is any parallel between the situation of that Country & ours at present. But it is a lesson we ought not to disregard, that the smallest bodies in G. B. are notoriously the most corrupt. Every other source of influence must also be stronger in small than large bodies of men. When Lord Chesterfield[12] had told us that one of the Dutch provinces had been seduced into the views of France, he need not have added, that it was not Holland, but one of the *smallest* of them. There are facts among ourselves which are known to all. Passing over others, he will only remark that the *Impost,* so anxiously wished for by the public was defeated not by any of the *larger* States in the Union. 2. *Congress is a single Legislature.* Despotism comes on Mankind in different Shapes, sometimes in an Executive, sometimes in a Military, one. Is there no danger of a Legislative despotism? Theory & practice both proclaim it. If the Legislative authority be not restrained, there can be neither liberty nor stability; and it can only be restrained by dividing it within itself, into distinct and independent branches. In a single House there is no check, but the inadequate one, of the virtue & good sense of those who compose it.

On another great point, the contrast was equally favorable to the plan reported by the Committee of the whole. It vested the Executive powers in a single Magistrate. The plan of N. Jersey, vested them in a plurality. In order to controul the Legislative authority, you must divide it. In order to controul the Executive you must unite it. One man will be more responsible than three. Three will contend among themselves till one becomes the master of his colleagues. In the triumvirates of Rome first Caesar, then Augustus, are witnesses of this truth. The Kings of Sparta, & the Consuls of Rome prove also the factious consequences of dividing the Executive Magistracy. Having already taken up so much time he w^{d} not he s^{d} proceed to any of the other points. Those on which he had dwelt, are sufficient of themselves: and on a decision of them, the fate of the others will depend.

. . .

12. Philip Dormer Stanhope, the fourth Earl of Chesterfield (1694–1773), was an able orator, statesman, and politician who is mostly known for his administration of Ireland.

Tuesday June 19th. In Committee of whole on the Propositions of Mr Patterson

. . .

(Of Mr Randolph's plan as reported from the Committee). the 1. propos: "that a Nat^{l} Gov^{t} ought to be established consisting &c." being taken up in the House.

Mr Wilson observed that by a Nat^{l} Gov^{t} he did not mean one that would swallow up the State Gov^{ts} as seemed to be wished by some gentlemen. He was tenacious of the idea of preserving the latter. He thought, contrary to the opinion of [Col. Hamilton] that they might not only subsist but subsist on friendly terms with the former. They were absolutely necessary for certain purposes which the former could not reach. All large Governments must be subdivided into lesser jurisdictions. As Examples he mentioned Persia, Rome, and particularly the divisions & subdivisions of England by Alfred.[13]

. . .

Mr Wilson, could not admit the doctrine that when the Colonies became independent of G. Britain, they became independent also of each other. He read the declaration of Independence, observing thereon that the *United Colonies* were declared to be free & independent States; and inferring that they were independent, not *individually* but *Unitedly* and that they were confederated as they were independent, States.

. . .

Wednesday June 20. 1787. In Convention

Mr William Blount[14] from N. Carolina took his seat.

1st propos: of the Report of Com^{e} of the whole before the House.

. . .

13. Probably refers to Alfred the Great (849–899), who was famous for his defense of England against the Danes (or Vikings) and his reorganization of English society.

14. William Blount (1749–1800) was a member of both the lower and upper houses of the North Carolina legislature. He did not attend the convention and signed the Constitution reluctantly. He was later active in state and national politics in Tennessee.

Mr Wilson, urged the necessity of two branches; observed that if a proper model were not to be found in other Confederacies it was not to be wondered at. The number of them was small & the duration of some at least short. The Amphyctionic & Achaean were formed in the infancy of political Science; and appear by their History & fate, to have contained radical defects. The Swiss & Belgic Confederacies were held together not by any vital principle of energy but by the incumbent pressure of formidable neighbouring nations: The German owed its continuance to the influence of the H. of Austria.[15] He appealed to our own experience for the defects of our Confederacy. He had been 6 years in the 12 since the commencement of the Revolution, a member of Congress, and had felt all its weaknesses. He appealed to the recollection of others whether on many important occasions, the public interest had not been obstructed by the small members of the Union. The success of the Revolution was owing to other causes, than the Constitution of Congress. In many instances it went on even ag^st the difficulties arising from Cong^s themselves. He admitted that the large States did accede as had been stated, to the Confederation in its present form. But it was the effect of necessity not of choice. There are other instances of their yielding from the same motive to the unreasonable measures of the small States. The situation of things is now a little altered. He insisted that a jealousy would exist between the State Legislatures & the General Legislature: observing that the members of the former would have views & feelings very distinct in this respect from their constituents. A private Citizen of a State is indifferent whether power be exercised by the Genl or State Legislatures, provided it be exercised most for his happiness. His representative has an interest in its being exercised by the body to which he belongs. He will therefore view the National Legisl: with the eye of a jealous rival. He observed that the addresses of Cong^s to the people at large, had always been better received & produced greater effect than those made to the Legislatures.

. . .

15. House of Austria.

Thursday June 21. In Convention

Mr Jonathan Dayton[16] from N. Jersey took his seat.

Doc^{r} Johnson.[17]

. . .

Mr Wilson's respect for Doc^{r} Johnson, added to the importance of the subject led him to attempt, unprepared as he was, to solve the difficulty which had been started. It was asked how the Genl Gov^{t} and individuality of the particular States could be reconciled to each other; and how the latter could be secured agst the former? Might it not, on the other side be asked how the former was to be secured agst the latter? It was generally admitted that a jealousy & rivalship would be felt between the Genl & particular Gov^{ts}. As the plan now stood, tho' indeed contrary to his opinion, one branch of the Genl (the Senate or second branch) was to be appointed by the State Legislatures. The State Legislatures, therefore, by this participation in the Genl Gov^{t} would have an opportunity of defending their rights. Ought not a reciprocal opportunity to be given to the Genl Gov^{t} of defending itself by having an appointment of some one constituent branch of the State Gov^{ts}. If a security be necessary on one side, it w^{d} seem reasonable to demand it on the other. But taking the matter in a more general view, he saw no danger to the States from the Genl Gov^{t}. In case a combination should be made by the large ones it w^{d} produce a general alarm among the rest; and the project w^{d} be frustrated. But there was no temptation to such a project. The States having in general a similar interest, in case of any proposition in the National Legislature to encroach on the State Legislatures, he conceived a general alarm w^{d} take place in the National Legislature itself, that it would communicate itself to the State Legislatures, and w^{d} finally spread among the people at large. The Genl Gov^{t} will be as ready to preserve the rights of the States as the latter

16. Jonathan Dayton (1760–1824) was a Federalist who, although objecting to some provisions of the Constitution, signed it. He was later the speaker of the U.S. House of Representatives in the fourth and fifth Congresses and a U.S. senator. Dayton, Ohio, was named after him.

17. William Samuel Johnson (1727–1819) was a wealthy merchant and jurist from Connecticut. He served in various capacities in the state judiciary, in the legislature, and in the U.S. Senate. He did not arrive at the convention until June 2, but he supported the Constitution and worked towards its ratification

are to preserve the rights of individuals; all the members of the former, having a common interest, as representatives of all the people of the latter, to leave the State Gov[ts] in possession of what the people wish them to retain. He could not discover, therefore any danger whatever on the side from which it had been apprehended. On the contrary, he conceived that in spite of every precaution the general Gov[t] would be in perpetual danger of encroachments from the State Gov[ts].

. . .

The *third* resolution of the Report taken into consideration.

Gen[l] Pinkney moved "that the 1st branch, instead of being elected by the people, sh[d] be elected in such manner as the Legislature of each State should direct." He urged 1. that this liberty would give more satisfaction, as the Legislatures could then accomodate the mode to the conveniency & opinions of the people 2. that it would avoid the undue influence of large Counties which would prevail if the elections were to be made in districts as must be the mode intended by the Report of the Committee. 3. that otherwise disputed elections must be referred to the General Legislature which would be attended with intolerable expence and trouble to the distant parts of the republic.

M[r] L. Martin seconded the Motion.

. . .

M[r] Wilson considered the election of the 1st branch by the people not only as the corner Stone, but as the foundation of the fabric: and that the difference between a mediate & immediate election was immense. The difference was particularly worthy of notice in this respect: that the Legislatures are actuated not merely by the sentiment of the people; but have an official sentiment opposed to that of the Gen[l] Gov[t] and perhaps to that of the people themselves.

. . .

Election of the 1st branch "for the term of three years," considered

M[r] Randolph moved to strike out, "three years" and insert "two years"— he was sensible that annual elections were a source of great mischiefs in the States, yet it was the want of such checks ag[st] the popular intemperence as were now proposed, that rendered them so mischievous.

. . .

Mr Wilson being for making the 1st branch an effectual representation of the people at large, preferred an annual election of it. This frequency was most familiar & pleasing to the people. It would be not more inconvenient to them, than triennial elections, as the people in all the States have annual meetings with which the election of the National representatives might be made to co-incide. He did not conceive that it would be necessary for the Nat^{l} Legisl: to sit constantly; perhaps not half—perhaps not one fourth of the year.

. . .

Friday June 22. In Convention

The clause in Resol. 3. "to receive fixed stipends to be paid out of the Nation^{l} Treasury" considered.

. . .

Mr Wilson was agst *fixing* the compensation as circumstances would change and call for a change of the amount. He thought it of great moment that the members of the Nat^{l} Gov^{t} should be left as independent as possible of the State Gov^{ts} in all respects.

. . .

Mr Wilson moved that the Salaries of the 1st branch "*be ascertained by the National Legislature,*" and be paid out of the Nat^{l} Treasury.

. . .

The present Mr Pitt[18] and Lord Bolingbroke[19] were striking instances.

Mr Ghorum[20] moved to strike out the last member of 3 Resol: concerning ineligibility of members of the 1st branch to offices during the term of their membership & for one year after. He considered it as unnecessary & injurious. It was true abuses had been displayed in G. B. but no one c^{d} say how

18. William Pitt the Younger (1759–1806) became a member of the House of Commons in 1781 and the Prime Minister in 1783.

19. Henry St. John, the first Viscount Bolingbroke (1678–1751), an English statesman, orator, and writer, who first took a seat in parliament in 1701.

20. Nathaniel Gorham (1738–1796) was a merchant who served in various political offices in Massachusetts. He was a moderate nationalist who attended all sessions of the convention and later pushed for ratification in his home state.

far they might have contributed to preserve the due influence of the Govt nor what might have ensued in case the contrary theory had been tried.

. . .

Mr Wilson was agst fettering elections, and discouraging merit. He suggested also the fatal consequence in time of war, of rendering perhaps the best Commanders ineligible: appealing to our situation during the late war, and indirectly leading to a recollection of the appointment of the Commander in Chief out of Congress.

. . .

Saturday June 23. In Convention

. . .

Mr Madison renewed his motion yesterday made & waved to render the members of the 1st branch "ineligible during their term of service, & for one year after—to such offices only as should be established, or the emoluments thereof, augmented by the Legislature of the U. States during the time of their being members." He supposed that the unnecessary creation of offices, and increase of salaries, were the evils most experienced, & that if the door was shut agst them: it might properly be left open for the appointt of members to other offices as an encouragemt to the Legislative service.

. . .

Mr Wilson supported the motion. The proper cure he said for corruption in the Legislature was to take from it the power of appointing to offices. One branch of corruption would indeed remain, that of creating unnecessary offices, or granting unnecessary salaries, and for that the amendment would be a proper remedy. He animadverted on the impropriety of stigmatizing with the name of venality the laudable ambition of rising into the honorable offices of the Government; an ambition most likely to be felt in the early & most incorrupt period of life, & which all wise & free Govts had deemed it sound policy, to cherish, not to check. The members of the Legislature have perhaps the hardest & least profitable task of any who engage in the service of the state. Ought this merit to be made a disqualification?

. . .

Monday June 25. In Convention

The mode of constituting the 2^{d} branch being under consideration.

The word "national" was struck out and "United States" inserted.

. . .

Mr Wilson. the question is shall the members of the 2^{d} branch be chosen by the Legislatures of the States? When he considered the amazing extent of Country—the immense population which is to fill it, the influence which the Gov^{t} we are to form will have, not only on the present generation of our people & their multiplied posterity, but on the whole Globe, he was lost in the magnitude of the object. The project of Henry the 4th & his Statesmen was but the picture in miniature of the great portrait to be exhibited. He was opposed to an election by the State Legislatures. In explaining his reasons it was necessary to observe the twofold relation in which the people would stand. 1. as Citizens of the Genl Gov^{t} 2. as Citizens of their particular State. The Genl Gov^{t} was meant for them in the first capacity: the State Gov^{ts} in the second. Both Gov^{ts} were derived from the people—both meant for the people—both therefore ought to be regulated on the same principles. The same train of ideas which belonged to the relation of the Citizens to their State Gov^{ts} were applicable to their relation to the Genl Gov^{t} and in forming the latter, we ought to proceed, by abstracting as much as possible from the idea of State Gov^{ts}. With respect to the province & objects of the Genl Gov^{t} they should be considered as having no existence. The election of the 2^{d} branch by the Legislatures, will introduce & cherish local interests & local prejudices. The Genl Gov^{t} is not an assemblage of States, but of individuals for certain political purposes—it is not meant for the States, but for the individuals composing them; the *individuals* therefore not the *States,* ought to be represented in it: A proportion in this representation can be preserved in the 2^{d} as well as in the 1st branch; and the election can be made by electors chosen by the people for that purpose. He moved an amendment to that effect which was not seconded.

. . .

Tuesday June 26. In Convention

The duration of the 2d branch under consideration.

Mr Ghorum moved to fill the blank with "six years," one third of the members to go out every second year.

Mr Wilson 2ded the motion.

. . .

Mr Wilson did not mean to repeat what had fallen from others, but wd add an observation or two which he believed had not yet been suggested. Every nation may be regarded in two relations 1. to its own citizens. 2 to foreign nations. It is therefore not only liable to anarchy & tyranny within, but has wars to avoid & treaties to obtain from abroad. The Senate will probably be the depositary of the powers concerning the latter objects. It ought therefore to be made respectable in the eyes of foreign Nations. The true reason why G. Britain has not yet listened to a commercial treaty with us has been, because she had no confidence in the stability or efficacy of our Government. 9 years with a rotation, will provide these desirable qualities; and give our Govt an advantage in this respect over Monarchy itself. In a monarchy much must always depend on the temper of the man. In such a body, the personal character will be lost in the political. He wd add another observation. The popular objection agst appointing any public body for a long term was that it might by gradual encroachments prolong itself first into a body for life, and finally become a hereditary one. It would be a satisfactory answer to this objection that as ⅓ would go out triennially, there would be always three divisions holding their places for unequal terms, and consequently acting under the influence of different views, and different impulses—On the question for 9 years, ⅓ to go out triennially.

. . .

Mr Butler moved to strike out the ineligibility of Senators to *State offices.*

Mr Williamson seconded the motion.

Mr Wilson remarked the additional dependence this wd create in the Senators on the States. The longer the time he observed allotted to the officer, the more compleat will be the dependance, if it exists at all.

. . .

Thursday June 28th. In Convention

. . .

Mr Wilson. The leading argument of those who contend for equality of votes among the States is that the States as such being equal, and being represented not as districts of individuals, but in their political & corporate capacities, are entitled to an equality of suffrage. According to this mode of reasoning the representation of the boroughs in Eng^{ld} which has been allowed on all hands to be the rotten part of the Constitution, is perfectly right & proper. They are like the States represented in their corporate capacity; like the States therefore they are entitled to equal voices, old Sarum[21] to as many as London. And instead of the injury supposed hitherto to be done to London, the true ground of complaint lies with old Sarum: for London instead of two which is her proper share, sends four representatives to Parliament.

. . .

Saturday June 30. 1787. In Convention

Mr Brearly moved that the Presid^{t} write to the Executive of N. Hamshire, informing it that the business depending before the Convention was of such a nature as to require the immediate attendance of the deputies of that State.

. . .

Mr Wilson wished to know whether it would be consistent with the rule or reason of secresy, to communicate to N. Hamshire that the business was of such a nature as the motion described. It w^{d} spread a great alarm. Besides he doubted the propriety of soliciting any State on the subject; the meeting being merely voluntary—on the motion of Mr Brearly Mas^{ts} no. Con^{t} no. N. Y. ay. N. J. ay P^{a} not on ye floor. Del. not on floor. M^{d} div^{d} V^{a} no. N. C. no. S. C. no. Geo. not on floor.

21. An ancient hilltop used since the Iron Age and the site of what once was the city of Wiltshire.

The motion of Mr Elseworth[22] resumed for allowing each State an equal vote in y[e] 2[d] branch.

M[r] Wilson did not expect such a motion after the establishment of y[e] contrary principle in the 1st branch; and considering the reasons which would oppose it, even if an equal vote had been allowed in the 1st branch. The Gentleman from Connecticut [M[r] Elseworth] had pronounced that if the motion should not be acceded to, of all the States North of Pen[a] one only would agree to any Gen[l] Government. He entertained more favorable hopes of Conn[t] and of the other Northern States. He hoped the alarms exceeded their cause, and that they would not abandon a Country to which they were bound by so many strong and endearing ties. But should the deplored event happen, it would neither stagger his sentiments nor his duty. If the minority of the people of America refuse to coalesce with the majority on just and proper principles, if a separation must take place, it could never happen on better grounds. The votes of yesterday ag[st] the just principle of representation, were as 22 to 90 of the people of America. Taking the opinions to be the same on this point, and he was sure if there was any room for change, it could not be on the side of the majority, the question will be shall less than ¼ of the U. States withdraw themselves from the Union; or shall more than ¾ renounce the inherent, indisputable, and unalienable rights of men, in favor of the artificial systems of States. If issue must be joined, it was on this point he would chuse to join it. The gentlemen from Connecticut in supposing that the prepondenancy secured to the majority in the 1st branch had removed the objections to an equality of votes in the 2[d] branch for the security of the minority, narrowed the case extremely. Such an equality will enable the minority to controul in all cases whatsoever, the sentiments and interests of the majority. Seven States will controul six: Seven States, according to the estimates that had been used, composed 24/90 of the whole people. It would be in the power then of less than ⅓ to overrule ⅔ whenever a question should happen to divide the States in that manner. Can we forget for whom we are forming a Government? Is it for *men*, or for the imaginary beings called *States*? Will

22. Oliver Ellsworth (1745–1807) was a representative from Connecticut who later was a U.S. senator and chief justice of the Supreme Court. He left the convention in early August but supported ratification.

our honest Constituents be satisfied with metaphysical distinctions? Will they, ought they to be satisfied with being told that the one third compose the greater number of States? The rule of suffrage ought on every principle to be the same in the 2^{d} as in the 1st branch. If the Government be not laid on this foundation, it can be neither solid nor lasting. Any other principle will be local, confined & temporary. This will expand with the expansion, and grow with the growth of the U. States.—Much has been said of an imaginary combination of three States. Sometimes a danger of monarchy, sometimes of aristocracy, has been charged on it. No explanation however of the danger has been vouchsafed. It would be easy to prove both from reason & history that rivalships would be more probable than coalitions; and that there are no coinciding interests that could produce the latter. No answer has yet been given to the observations of [Mr Madison] on this subject. Should the Executive Magistrate be taken from one of the large States would not the other two be thereby thrown into the scale with the other States? Whence then the danger of monarchy? Are the people of the three large States more aristocratic than those of the small ones? Whence then the danger of aristocracy from their influence? It is all a mere illusion of names. We talk of States, till we forget what they are composed of. Is a real & fair majority, the natural hot-bed of aristocracy? It is a part of the definition of this species of Gov^{t} or rather of tyranny, that the smaller number governs the greater. It is true that a majority of States in the 2^{d} branch can not carry a law agst a majority of the people in the 1st. But this removes half only of the objection. Bad Govern^{ts} are of two sorts. 1. that which does too little. 2. that which does too much: that which fails thro' weakness; and that which destroys thro' oppression. Under which of these evils do the U. States at present groan? under the weakness and inefficiency of its Govern^{t}. To remedy this weakness we have been sent to this Convention. If the motion should be agreed to, we shall leave the U. S. fettered precisely as heretofore; with the additional mortification of seeing the good purposes of ye fair represention of the people in the 1st branch, defeated in 2^{d}. Twenty four will still controul sixty six. He lamented that such a disagreement should prevail on the point of representation, as he did not forsee that it would happen on the other point most contested, the boundary between the Genl & the local authorities. He thought the States necessary & valuable parts of a good system.

. . .

Mr Wilson admitted the question concerning the number of Senators, to be embarrassing. If the smallest States be allowed one, and the others in proportion, the Senate will certainly be too numerous. He looked forward to the time when the smallest States will contain 100,000 souls at least. Let there be then one Senator in each for every 100,000 souls and let the States not having that n° of inhabitants be allowed one. He was willing himself to submit to this temporary concession to the small States; and threw out the idea as a ground of compromise.

. . .

Monday July 2^d. In Convention

On the question for allowing each State one vote in the second branch as moved by Mr Elseworth,

. . .

General Pinkney. was willing the motion might be considered. He did not entirely approve it. He liked better the motion of Doc^r Franklin. Some compromise seemed to be necessary: the States being exactly divided on the question for an equality of votes in the 2^d branch. He proposed that a Committee consisting of a member from each State should be appointed to devise & report some compromise.

. . .

Mr Wilson objected to the Committee, because it would decide according to that very rule of voting which was opposed on one side. Experience in Cong^s had also proved the inutility of Committees consisting of members from each State.

. . .

Thursday July 5th. In Convention

Mr Gerry delivered in from the Committee appointed on Monday last the following Report.

"The Committee to whom was referred the 8th Resol. of the Report from the Committee of the whole House, and so much of the 7th as has not been decided on, submit the following Report: That the subsequent propositions be recommended to the Convention on condition that both shall be generally adopted. I. that in the I[st] branch of the Legislature each of the States now in the Union shall be allowed 1 member for every 40,000 inhabitants of the description reported in the 7th Resolution of the Com[e] of the whole House: that each State not containing that number shall be allowed 1 member: that all bills for raising or appropriating money, and for fixing the Salaries of the officers of the Govern[t] of the U. States shall originate in the 1st branch of the Legislature, and shall not be altered or amended by the 2[d] branch: and that no money shall be drawn from the public Treasury. But in pursuance of appropriations to be originated in the 1st branch" II. That in the 2[d] branch each State shall have an equal vote."

. . .

M[r] Wilson thought the Committee had exceeded their powers.

. . .

M[r] Wilson was for a division of the question: otherwise it w[d] be a leap in the dark.

. . .

Friday July 6th. In Convention

M[r] Gov[r] Morris moved to commit so much of the Report as relates to "1 member for every 40,000 inhabitants"

. . .

M[r] Wilson 2[ded] the motion; but with a view of leaving the Committee under no implied shackles.

. . .

M[r] Wilson signified that his view in agreeing to the commitm[t] was that the Com[e] might consider the propriety of adopting a scale similar to that established by the Constitution of Mast[s] which w[d] give an advantage to y[e] small States without substantially departing from a rule of proportion.

M[r] Wilson & M[r] Mason moved to postpone the clause relating to money bills in order to take up the clause relating to an equality of votes in the second branch.

. . .

The 1st clause relating to the originating of money bills was then resumed.

. . .

Mr Wilson could see nothing like a concession here on the part of the smaller States. If both branches were to say yes or no, it was of little consequence which should say yes or no first, which last. If either was indiscriminately to have the right of originating, the reverse of the Report, would he thought be most proper; since it was a maxim that the least numerous body was the fittest for deliberation; the most numerous for decision. He observed that this discrimination had been transcribed from the British into several American constitutions. But he was persuaded that on examination of the American experiments it would be found to be a trifle light as air. Nor could he ever discover the advantage of it in the Parliamentary history of G. Britain. He hoped if there was any advantage in the privilege, that it would be pointed out.

. . .

Mr Wilson. If he had proposed that the 2d branch should have an independent disposal of public money, the observations of [Col Mason] would have been a satisfactory answer. But nothing could be farther from what he had said. His question was how is the power of the 1st branch increased or that of the 2d diminished by giving the proposed privilege to the former? Where is the difference, in which branch it begins if both must concur, in the end?

. . .

Mr Martin said that it was understood in the Committee that the difficulties and disputes which had been apprehended, should be guarded agst in the detailing of the plan.

Mr Wilson. The difficulties & disputes will increase with the attempts to define & obviate them. Queen Anne was obliged to dissolve her Parliamt in order to terminate one of these obstinate disputes between the two Houses. Had it not been for the mediation of the Crown, no one can say what the result would have been. The point is still *sub judice*[23] in England. He approved of the principles laid down by the Hon'ble President [Doctr Franklin] his Colleague, as to the expediency of keeping the

23. Before the court for its consideration and determination.

people informed of their money affairs. But thought they would know as much, and be as well satisfied, in one way as in the other.

. . .

Saturday July 7. In Convention

"Shall the clause allowing each State one vote in the 2^{d} branch, stand as part of the Report"? being taken up—

. . .

Mr Wilson was not deficient in a conciliating temper, but firmness was sometimes a duty of higher obligation. Conciliation was also misapplied in this instance. It was pursued here rather among the Representatives, than among the Constituents; and it w^{d} be of little consequence, if not established among the latter; and there could be little hope of its being established among them if the foundation should not be laid in justice and right.

. . .

Wednesday July 11. In Convention

Mr Randolph's motion requiring the Legisl^{re} to take a periodical census for the purpose of redressing inequalities in the Representation, was resumed.

. . .

Mr Williamson was for making it the duty of the Legislature to do what was right & not leaving it at liberty to do or not do it. He moved that Mr Randolph's proposition be postpon^{d} in order to consider the following "that in order to ascertain the alterations that may happen in the population & wealth of the several States, a census shall be taken of the free white inhabitants and 3/5^{ths} of those of other descriptions on the 1st year after this Government shall have been adopted and every   year thereafter; and that the Representation be regulated accordingly."

. . .

M[r] Wilson had himself no objection to leaving the Legislature entirely at liberty. But considered wealth as an impracticable rule.

. . .

the next clause as to 3/5 of the negroes considered.

. . .

M[r] Wilson did not well see on what principle the admission of blacks in the proportion of three fifths could be explained. Are they admitted as Citizens? then why are they not admitted on an equality with White Citizens? are they admitted as property? then why is not other property admitted into the computation? These were difficulties however which he thought must be overruled by the necessity of compromise. He had some apprehensions also from the tendency of the blending of the blacks with the whites, to give disgust to the people of Pen[a] as had been intimated by his Colleague [M[r] Gov[r] Morris]. But he differed from him in thinking numbers of inhab[ts] so incorrect a measure of wealth. He had seen the Western settlem[ts] of P[a] and on a comparison of them with the City of Philad[a] could discover little other difference, than that property was more unequally divided among individuals here than there. Taking the same number in the aggregate in the two situations he believed there would be little difference in their wealth and ability to contribute to the public wants.

. . .

Thursday July 12. In Convention

M[r] Gov[r] Morris moved to add to the clause empowering the Legislature to vary the Representation according to the principles of wealth & number of inhab[ts] a "proviso that taxation shall be in proportion to Representation."

. . .

M[r] Wilson approved the principle, but could not see how it could be carried into execution; unless restrained to direct taxation.

. . .

M[r] Wilson observed that less umbrage would perhaps be taken ag[st] an admission of the slaves into the Rule of representation, if it should be so expressed as to make them indirectly only an ingredient in the rule, by saying that they should enter into the rule of taxation: and as representation was to be according to taxation the end would be equally attained. He accordingly moved & as 2^{ded} so to alter the last clause adopted by the House, that together with the amendment proposed the whole should read as follows "provided always that the representation ought to be proportioned according to direct taxation, and in order to ascertain the alterations in the direct taxation which may be required from time to time by the changes in the relative circumstances of the States. Resolved that a census be taken within two years from the first meeting of the Legislature of the U. States, and once within the term of every   years afterwards of all the inhabitants of the U. S. in the manner and according to the ratio recommended by Congress in their Resolution of April 18. 1783; and that the Legislature of the U. S. shall proportion the direct taxation accordingly."

. . .

Friday July 13. In Convention

It being moved to postpone the clause in the Report of the Committee of Eleven as to the originating of money bills in the *first* branch, in order to take up the following—"that in the 2^{d} branch each State shall have an equal voice."

. . .

Mr Wilson hoped the motion would not be withdrawn. If it sh^{d} it will be made from another quarter. The rule will be as reasonable & just before, as after a Census. As to fractional numbers, the Census will not distroy, but ascertain them. And they will have the same effect after as before the Census: for as he understands the rule, it is to be adjusted not to the number of *inhabitants*, but of *Representatives*.

. . .

On the motion of Mr Randolph, the vote of saturday last authorising the Legisl^{re} to adjust from time to time, the representation upon the principles of *wealth* & numbers of inhabitants was reconsidered by common consent in order to strike out "Wealth" and adjust the resolution to that requiring periodical revisions according to the number of whites & three fifths of the blacks: the motion was in the words following—"But as the present situation of the States may probably alter in the number of their inhabitants, that the Legislature of the U. S. be authorized from time to time to apportion the number of representatives: and in case any of the States shall hereafter be divided or any two or more States united or new States created within the limits of the U. S. the Legislature of U. S. shall possess authority to regulate the number of Representatives in any of the foregoing cases, upon the principle of their number of inhabitants; according to the provisions hereafter mentioned."

. . .

Mr Wilson. If a general declaration would satisfy any gentleman he had no indisposition to declare his sentiments. Conceiving that all men wherever placed have equal rights and are equally entitled to confidence, he viewed without apprehension the period when a few States should contain the superior number of people. The majority of people wherever found ought in all questions to govern the minority. If the interior Country should acquire this majority, it will not only have the right, but will avail themselves of it whether we will or no. This jealousy misled the policy of G. Britain with regard to America. The fatal maxims espoused by her were that the Colonies were growing too fast, and that their growth must be stinted in time. What were the consequences? first. enmity on our part, then actual separation. Like consequences will result on the part of the interior settlements, if like jealousy & policy be pursued on ours. Further, if numbers be not a proper rule, why is not some better rule pointed out. No one has yet ventured to attempt it. Cong^s^ have never been able to discover a better. No State as far as he had heard, has suggested any other. In 1783, after elaborate discussion of a measure of wealth all were satisfied then as they are now that the rule of numbers, does not differ much from the combined rule of numbers & wealth. Again he could not agree that property was the sole or the primary object of Govern^t^ & society. The cultivation & improvement of the human mind was the most noble object. With respect to this object, as well as to other *personal* rights, numbers were surely the natural & precise measure of Representation. And with respect to property, they could not vary much from the precise measure. In no point of view however could the establishm^t^ of numbers as the rule of representation in the 1st branch vary his opinion as to the impropriety of letting a vicious principle into the 2^d^ branch.—On the Question to strike out *wealth* & to make the change as moved by Mr Randolph, it passed in the affirmative—

. . .

Saturday July 14. In Convention

Mr L. Martin called for the question on the whole report including the parts relating to the origination of money bills, and the equality of votes in the 2^d^ branch.

. . .

Mr Wilson traced the progress of the report through its several stages, remarking y^t^ when on the question concerning an equality of votes, the House was divided, our Constituents had they voted as their representatives did, would have stood as ⅔ ag^st^ the equality, and ⅓ only in favor of it. This fact would ere long be known and it will appear that this fundamental point has been carried by ⅓ ag^st^ ⅔. What hopes will our Constituents entertain when they find that the essential principles of justice have been violated in the outset of the Governm^t^ As to the privilege of originating money bills, it was not considered by any as of much moment, and by many as improper in itself. He hoped both clauses w^d^ be reconsidered. The equality of votes was a point of such critical importance, that every opportunity ought to be allowed, for discussing and collecting the mind of the Convention on it.

. . .

Mr Wilson was not surprised that those who say that a minority is more than the majority should say that the minority is stronger than the majority. He supposed the next assertion will be that they are richer also; though he hardly expected it would be persisted in when the States shall be called on for taxes & troops—

. . .

Mr Pinkney moved that instead of an equality of votes the States should be represented in the 2^d^ branch as follows: N. H. by 2. members. Mas. 4. R. I. 1. Con^t^ 3. N. Y. 3. N. J. 2. P^a^ 4. Del 1. M^d^ 3. Virg^a^ 5. N. C. 3. S. C. 3. Geo. 2. making in the whole 36.

Mr Wilson seconds the motion.

. . .

Mr Wilson would add a few words only. If equality in the 2d branch was an error that time would correct, he should be less anxious to exclude it being sensible that perfection was unattainable in any plan; but being a fundamental and a perpetual error, it ought by all means to be avoided. A vice in the Representation, like an error in the first concoction, must be followed by disease, convulsions, and finally death itself. The justice of the general principle of proportional representation has not in argument at least been yet contradicted. But it is said that a departure from it so far as to give the States an equal vote in one branch of the Legislature is essential to their preservation. He had considered this positon maturely, but could not see its application. That the States ought to be preserved he admitted. But does it follow that an equality of votes is necessary for the purpose? Is there any reason to suppose that if their preservation should depend more on the large than on the small States the security of the States agst the Genl Government would be diminished? Are the large States less attached to their existence, more likely to commit suicide, than the small? An equal vote then is not necessary as far as he can conceive: and is liable among other objections to this insuperable one: The great fault of the existing confederacy is its inactivity. It has never been a complaint agst Congs that they governed overmuch. The complaint has been that they have governed too little. To remedy this defect we were sent here. Shall we effect the cure by establishing an equality of votes as is proposed? no: this very equality carries us directly to Congress: to the system which it is our duty to rectify. The small States cannot indeed act, by virtue of this equality, but they may controul the Govt as they have done in Congs This very measure is here prosecuted by a minority of the people of America. Is then the object of the Convention likely to be accomplished in this way? Will not our Constituents say, we sent you to form an efficient Govt and you have given us one more complex indeed, but having all the weakness of the former Governt. He was anxious for uniting all the States under one Governt. He knew there were some respectable men who preferred three confederacies, united by offensive & defensive alliances. Many things may be plausibly said, some things may be justly said, in favor of such a project. He could not however concur in it himself; but he thought nothing so pernicious as bad first principles.

. . .

Tuesday July 17. In Convention

The 6th Resol^{n} in the Report of the Com^{e} of the Whole relating to the powers, which had been postponed in order to consider the 7 & 8th relating to the constitution of the Nat^{l} Legislature, was now resumed.

Mr Sherman observed that it would be difficult to draw the line between the powers of the Genl Legislatures, and those to be left with the States; that he did not like the definition contained in the Resolution, and proposed in place of the words "of individual Legislation" line 4. inclusive, to insert "to make laws binding on the people of the United States in all cases which may concern the common interests of the Union; but not to interfere with the Government of the individual States in any matters of internal police which respect the Gov^{t} of such States only, and wherein the general welfare of the U. States is not concerned."

Mr Wilson 2^{ded} the amendment as better expressing the general principle.

. . .

9th Resol: "that Nat^{l} Executive consist of a single person." Ag^{d} to nem. con.

"To be chosen by the National Legisl:"

. . .

Mr Wilson. two arguments have been urged agst an election of the Executive Magistrate by the people. 1 the example of Poland where an Election of the supreme Magistrate is attended with the most dangerous commotions. The cases he observed were totally dissimilar. The Polish nobles have resources & dependents which enable them to appear in force, and to threaten the Republic as well as each other. In the next place the electors all assemble in one place: which would not be the case with us. The 2^{d} arg^{t} is that a *majority* of the people would never concur. It might be answered that the concurrence of a majority of people is not a necessary principle of election, nor required as such in any of the States. But allowing the objection all its force, it may be obviated by the expedient used in Mas^{ts} where the Legislature by majority of voices, decide in case a majority of people do not concur in favor of one of the candidates. This would restrain the choice to a good nomination at least, and prevent in a great degree intrigue & cabal. A particular objection with him agst an absolute election by the Legisl^{re} was that the Exec: in that case would be too dependent to stand the mediator between the intrigues & sinister views of the Representatives and the general liberties & interests of the people.

. . .

Mr Wilson. could not see the contrariety stated [by Col. Mason] The Legisl^{re} might deserve confidence in some respects, and distrust in others. In acts which were to affect them & y^{r} Constituents precisely alike confidence was due. In others jealousy was warranted. The appointment to great offices, where the Legisl^{re} might feel many motives, not common to the public confidence was surely misplaced. This branch of business it was notorious was most corruptly managed of any that had been committed to legislative bodies.

. . .

Wednesday July 18. In Convention

. . .

Resol. 11 "that a Nat^{l} Judiciary be estab^{d} to consist of one supreme tribunal." ag^{d} to nem. con.

"The Judges of which to be appoint^{d} by the 2^{d} branch of the Nat^{l} Legislature."

. . .

Mr Wilson, still w^{d} prefer an appointm^{t} by the Executive; but if that could not be attained, w^{d} prefer in the next place, the mode suggested by Mr Ghorum. He thought it his duty however to move in the first instance "that the Judges be appointed by the Executive." Mr Govr Morris 2^{ded} the motion.

. . .

Resol. 15. that provision ought to be made for the continuance of Cong^{s} &c. & for the completion of their engagements.

. . .

Mr Wilson did not entirely approve of the manner in which the clause relating to the engagements of Cong^{s} was expressed, but he thought some provision on the subject would be proper in order to prevent any suspicion that the obligations of the Confederacy might be dissolved along with the Govern^{t} under which they were contracted.

. . .

Resol. 16. "That a Republican Constitution & its. existing laws ought to be guarantied to each State by the U. States."

. . .

Mr Wilson. The object is merely to secure the States agst dangerous commotions, insurrections and rebellions.

. . .

Mr Wilson moved as a better expression of the idea, "that a Republican form of Governmt shall be guarantied to each State & that each State shall be protected agst foreign & domestic violence.

This seeming to be well received, Mr Madison & Mr Randolph withdrew their propositions & on the Question for agreeing to Wilson's motion, it passed nem. con.

. . .

Thursday July 19. In Convention

On reconsideration of the vote rendering the Executive re-eligible a 2d time, Mr Martin moved to reinstate the words "to be ineligible a 2d time."

. . .

Mr Wilson. It seems to be the unanimous sense that the Executive should not be appointed by the Legislature, unless he be rendered ineligible a 2d time: he perceived with pleasure that the idea was gaining ground, of an election mediately or immediately by the people.

. . .

Friday July 20. In Convention

. . .

"to be removable on impeachment and conviction for mal practice or neglect of duty." see Resol: 9.

. . .

Mr Wilson concurred in the necessity of making the Executive impeachable whilst in office.

. . .

Mr Wilson observed that if the idea were to be pursued, the Senators who are to hold their places during the same term with the Executive, ought to be subject to impeachment & removal.

. . .

Doc^{r} McClurg asked whether it would not be necessary, before a Committee for detailing the Constitution should be appointed, to determine on the means by which the Executive is to carry the laws into effect, and to resist combinations agst them. Is he to have a military force for the purpose, or to have the command of the Militia, the only existing force that can be applied to that use? As the Resolutions now stand the Committee will have no determinate directions on this great point.

Mr Wilson thought that some additional directions to the Committee w^{d} be necessary.

. . .

Saturday July 21. In Convention

. . .

Mr Wilson moved as an amendment to Resol^{n} 10. that the supreme Nat^{l} Judiciary should be associated with the Executive in the Revisionary power. This proposition had been before made and failed: but he was so confirmed by reflection in the opinion of its utility, that he thought it incumbent on him to make another effort: The Judiciary ought to have an opportunity of remonstrating agst projected encroachments on the people as well as on themselves. It had been said that the Judges, as expositors of the Laws would have an opportunity of defending their constitutional rights. There was weight in this observation; but this power of the Judges did not go far enough. Laws may be unjust, may be unwise, may be dangerous, may be destructive; and yet may not be so unconstitutional as to justify the Judges in refusing to give them effect. Let them have a share in the Revisionary power, and they will have an opportunity of taking notice of these characters of a law, and of counteracting, by the weight of their opinions the improper views of the Legislature.—

. . .

Mr Wilson. The separation of the departments does not require that they should have separate objects but that they should act separately tho' on the same objects. It is necessary that the two branches of the Legislature should be separate and distinct, yet they are both to act precisely on the same object.

. . .

Mr Wilson. The proposition is certainly not liable to all the objections which have been urged agst it. According [to Mr Gerry] it will unite the Executive & Judiciary in an offensive & defensive alliance agst the Legislature. According to Mr Ghorum it will lead to a subversion of the Executive by the Judiciary influence. To the first gentleman the answer was obvious; that the joint weight of the two departments was necessary to balance the single weight of the Legislature. To the 1st objection stated by the other Gentleman it might be answered that supposing the prepossion to mix itself with the exposition, the evil would be overbalanced by the advantages promised by the expedient. To the 2^{d} objection, that such a rule of voting might be provided in the detail as would guard agst it.

. . .

Monday July 23. In Convention

Mr John Langdon & Mr Nicholas Gilman[24] from N. Hampshire, took their seats.

Resol^{n}: 17. that provision ought to be made for future amendments of the articles of Union, agreed to, nem. con.

Resol^{n} 18. "requiring the Legis: Execut: & Jud^{y} of the States to be bound by oath to support the articles of Union," taken into consideration.

. . .

Mr Wilson said he was never fond of oaths, considering them as a left handed security only. A good Gov^{t} did not need them, and a bad one could not or ought not to be supported. He was afraid they might too

24. John Langdon (1741–1819) was an active soldier and politician during the Revolutionary War. He served as the speaker of the house in the assembly of New Hampshire as well as the state's chief executive on more than one occasion. He was a Federalist during the convention and for the first half of his senatorial career, but later aligned himself with the Democratic-Republicans. Nicholas Gilman (1755–1814) served in the New Hampshire legislature, and the U.S. House of Representatives and Senate. He began his career as a Federalist but later aligned himself with the Democratic-Republicans.

much trammel the members of the Existing Govt–in case future alterations should be necessary; and prove an obstacle to Resol: 17. just agd to.

. . .

Tuesday July 24. In Convention

. . .

Mr L. Martin & Mr Gerry moved to re-instate the ineligibility of the Executive a 2d time.

. . .

Mr Wilson. The difficulties & perplexities into which the House is thrown proceed from the election by the Legislature which he was sorry had been reinstated. The inconveniency of this mode was such that he would agree to almost any length of time in order to get rid of the dependence which must result from it. He was persuaded that the longest term would not be equivalent to a proper mode of election; unless indeed it should be during good behaviour. It seemed to be supposed that at a certain advance in life, a continuance in office would cease to be agreeable to the officer, as well as desirable to the public. Experience had shewn in a variety of instances that both a capacity & inclination for public service existed—in very advanced stages. He mentioned the instance of a Doge of Venice[25] who was elected after he was 80 years of age. The popes have generally been elected at very advanced periods, and yet in no case had a more steady or a better concerted policy been pursued than in the Court of Rome. If the Executive should come into office at 35. years of age, which he presumes may happen & his continuance should be fixt at 15 years. at the age of 50. in the very prime of life, and with all the aid of experience, he must be cast aside like a useless hulk. What an irreparable loss would the British Jurisprudence have sustained, had the age of 50. been fixt there as the ultimate limit of capacity or readiness to serve the public. The great luminary [Ld Mansfield] held his seat for thirty years after his arrival at that age. Notwithstanding what had been done he could not but hope that a better mode of election would yet be adopted; and one that would be more agreeable to

25. The title of the chief magistrate of Venice when it was a Republic.

the general sense of the House. That time might be given for further deliberation he w^{d} move that the present question be postponed till tomorrow.

. . .

Mr Wilson. As the great difficulty seems to spring from the mode of election, he w^{d} suggest a mode which had not been mentioned. It was that the Executive be elected for 6 years by a small number, not more than 15 of the Nat^{l} Legislature, to be drawn from it, not by ballot, but by lot and who should retire immediately and make the election without separating. By this mode intrigue would be avoided in the first instance, and the dependence would be diminished. This was not he said a digested idea and might be liable to strong objections.

. . .

Mr Wilson did not move this as the best mode. His opinions remained unshaken that we ought to resort to the people for the election. He seconded the postponement.

. . .

Wednesday July 25. In Convention

Clause relating to the Executive again under consideration.

. . .

Mr Gerry & Mr Butler moved to refer the resolution relating to the Executive (except the clause making it consist of a single person) to the Committee of detail.

. . .

Mr Wilson hoped that so important a branch of the system w^{d} not be committed until a general principle sh^{d} be fixed by a vote of the House.

. . .

Thursday July 26. In Convention

. . .

"The 2^{d} part, for disqualifying debtors, and persons having unsettled accounts," being under consideration.

. . .

Mr Wilson was for striking them out. They put too much power in the hands of the Auditors, who might combine with rivals in delaying settlements in order to prolong the disqualifications of particular men. We should consider that we are providing a Constitution for future generations, and not merely for the peculiar circumstances of the moment. The time has been, and will again be, when the public safety may depend on the voluntary aids of individuals which will necessarily open acc^{ts} with the public, and when such acc^{ts} will be a characteristic of patriotism. Besides a partial enumeration of cases will disable the Legislature from disqualifying odious & dangerous characters.

. . .

On July 23 the convention's delegates created the Committee of Detail to "prepare and report a Constitution" "conformable" to previously passed resolutions. James Wilson, John Rutledge, Edmund Randolph, and Oliver Ellsworth were appointed to the committee. According to Clinton Rossiter, Wilson "took upon himself the major responsibility for putting the resolutions of the Convention and the thoughts of his colleagues into the language of fundamental law" (*1787: The Grand Convention,* 202). Among the notable additions of this first draft of the Constitution was the list of enumerated powers which eventually became Article I, section 8 of the U.S. Constitution.

The Constitution as Reported by the Committee of Detail, August 6, 1787.

Monday August 6th In Convention

Mr John Francis Mercer from Maryland took his seat.

Mr Rutlidge delivered in the Report of the Committee of detail as follows: a printed copy being at the same time furnished to each member:

We the people of the States of New Hampshire, Massachussetts, Rhode-Island and Providence Plantations, Connecticut, New-York, New-Jersey, Pennsylvania, Delaware, Maryland, Virginia, North-Carolina, South-Carolina, and Georgia, do ordain, declare, and establish the following Constitution for the Government of Ourselves and our Posterity.

Article I

The stile of the Government shall be, "The United States of America."

II

The Government shall consist of supreme legislative, executive; and judicial powers.

III

The legislative power shall be vested in a Congress, to consist of two separate and distinct bodies of men, a House of Representatives and a Senate;

each of which shall in all cases have a negative on the other. The Legislature shall meet on the first Monday in December every year.

IV

Sect. 1. The members of the House of Representatives shall be chosen every second year, by the people of the several States comprehended within this Union. The qualifications of the electors shall be the same, from time to time, as those of the electors in the several States, of the most numerous branch of their own legislatures.

Sect. 2. Every member of the House of Representatives shall be of the age of twenty five years at least; shall have been a citizen in the United States for at least three years before his election; and shall be, at the time of his election, a resident of the State in which he shall be chosen.

Sect. 3. The House of Representatives shall, at its first formation, and until the number of citizens and inhabitants shall be taken in the manner herein after described, consist of sixty five Members, of whom three shall be chosen in New-Hampshire, eight in Massachusetts, one in Rhode-Island and Providence Plantations, five in Connecticut, six in New-York, four in New-Jersey, eight in Pennsylvania, one in Delaware, six in Maryland, ten in Virginia, five in North-Carolina, five in South-Carolina, and three in Georgia.

Sect. 4. As the proportions of numbers in different States will alter from time to time; as some of the States may hereafter be divided; as others may be enlarged by addition of territory; as two or more States may be united; as new States will be erected within the limits of the United States, the Legislature shall, in each of these cases, regulate the number of representatives by the number of inhabitants, according to the provisions herein after made, at the rate of one for every forty thousand.

Sect. 5. All bills for raising or appropriating money, and for fixing the salaries of the officers of Government, shall originate in the House of Representatives, and shall not be altered or amended by the Senate. No money shall be drawn from the Public. Treasury, but in pursuance of appropriations that shall originate in the House of Representatives.

Sect. 6. The House of Representatives shall have the sole power of impeachment. It shall choose its Speaker and other officers.

Sect. 7. Vacancies in the House of Representatives shall be supplied by writs of election from the executive authority of the State, in the representation from which it shall happen.

V

Sect. 1. The Senate of the United States shall be chosen by the Legislatures of the several States. Each Legislature shall chuse two members. Vacancies may be supplied by the Executive until the next meeting of the Legislature. Each member shall have one vote.

Sect. 2. The Senators shall be chosen for six years; but immediately after the first election they shall be divided, by lot, into three classes, as nearly as may be, numbered one, two and three. The seats of the members of the first class shall be vacated at the expiration of the second year, of the second class at the expiration of the fourth year, of the third class at the expiration of the sixth year, so that a third part of the members may be chosen every second year.

Sect. 3. Every member of the Senate shall be of the age of thirty years at least; shall have been a citizen in the United States for at least four years before his election; and shall be, at the time of his election, a resident of the State for which he shall be chosen.

Sect. 4. The Senate shall chuse its own President and other officers.

VI

Sect. 1. The times and places and manner of holding the elections of the members of each House shall be prescribed by the Legislature of each State; but their provisions concerning them may at any time be altered by the Legislature of the United States.

Sect. 2. The Legislature of the United States shall have authority to establish such uniform qualifications of the members of each House, with regard to property, as to the said Legislature shall seem expedient.

Sect. 3. In each House a majority of the members shall constitute a quorum to do business; but a smaller number may adjourn from day to day.

Sect. 4. Each House shall be the judge of the elections, returns and qualifications of its own members.

Sect. 5. Freedom of speech and debate in the Legislature shall not be impeached or questioned in any Court or place out of the Legislature; and the members of each House shall, in all cases, except treason felony and breach of the peace, be privileged from arrest during their attendance at Congress, and in going to and returning from it.

Sect. 6. Each House may determine the rules of its proceedings; may punish its members for disorderly behaviour; and may expel a member.

Sect. 7. The House of Representatives, and the Senate, when it shall be acting in a legislative capacity, shall keep a journal of their proceedings, and shall, from time to time, publish them: and the yeas and nays of the members of each House, on any question, shall at the desire of one-fifth part of the members present, be entered on the journal.

Sect. 8. Neither House, without the consent of the other, shall adjourn for more than three days, nor to any other place than that at which the two Houses are sitting. But this regulation shall not extend to the Senate, when it shall exercise the powers mentioned in the   article.

Sect. 9. The members of each House shall be ineligible to, and incapable of holding any office under the authority of the United States, during the time for which they shall respectively be elected: and the members of the Senate shall be ineligible to, and incapable of holding any such office for one year afterwards.

Sect. 10. The members of each House shall receive a compensation for their services, to be ascertained and paid by the State, in which they shall be chosen.

Sect. 11. The enacting stile of the laws of the United States shall be. "Be it enacted by the Senate and Representatives in Congress assembled."

Sect. 12. Each House shall possess the right of originating bills, except in the cases beforementioned.

Sect. 13. Every bill, which shall have passed the House of Representatives and the Senate, shall, before it become a law, be presented to the President of the United States for his revision: if, upon such revision, he approve of it, he shall signify his approbation by signing it: But if, upon such revision, it shall appear to him improper for being passed into a law, he shall return it, together with his objections against it, to that House in which it shall have originated, who shall enter the objections at large on their journal and proceed to reconsider the bill. But if after such reconsideration, two thirds of that House shall, notwithstanding the objections of the President, agree to pass it, it shall together with his objections, be sent to the other House, by which it shall likewise be reconsidered, and if approved by two thirds of the other House also, it shall become a law. But in all such cases, the votes of both Houses shall be determined by yeas and nays; and the names of the persons voting for or against the bill shall be entered on the journal of each House respectively. If any bill shall not be returned by the President within seven days after it shall have been presented to him, it shall be a law, unless the legislature, by their adjournment, prevent its return; in which case it shall not be a law.

VII

Sect. 1. The Legislature of the United States shall have the power to lay and collect taxes, duties, imposts and excises;

To regulate commerce with foreign nations, and among the several States;

To establish an uniform rule of naturalization throughout the United States;

To coin money;

To regulate the value of foreign coin;

To fix the standard of weights and measures;

To establish Post-offices;

To borrow money, and emit bills on the credit of the United States;

To appoint a Treasurer by ballot;

To constitute tribunals inferior to the Supreme Court;

To make rules concerning captures on land and water;

To declare the law and punishment of piracies and felonies committed on the high seas, and the punishment of counterfeiting the coin of the United States, and of offenses against the law of nations;

To subdue a rebellion in any State, on the application of its legislature;

To make war;

To raise armies;

To build and equip fleets;

To call forth the aid of the militia, in order to execute the laws of the Union, enforce treaties, suppress insurrections, and repel invasions;

And to make all laws that shall be necessary and proper for carrying into execution the foregoing powers, and all other powers vested, by this constitution, in the government of the United States, or in any department or officer thereof.

Sect. 2. Treason against the United States shall consist only in levying war against the United States, or any of them; and in adhering to the enemies of the United States, or any of them. The Legislature of the United States shall have power to declare the punishment of treason. No person shall be convicted of treason, unless on the testimony of two witnesses. No attainder of treason shall work corruption of blood, nor forfeiture, except during the life of the person attainted.

Sect. 3. The proportions of direct taxation shall be regulated by the whole number of white and other free citizens and inhabitants of every age, sex, and condition, including those bound to servitude for a term of years, and three fifths of all other persons not comprehended in the foregoing description, (except Indians not paying taxes); which number shall, within six years after the first meeting of the Legislature, and within the term of every ten years afterwards, be taken in such manner as the said Legislature shall direct.

Sect. 4. No tax or duty shall be laid by the Legislature on articles exported from any State; nor on the migration or importation of such persons as the several States shall think proper to admit; nor shall such migration or importation be prohibited.

Sect. 5. No capitation tax shall be laid, unless in proportion to the census hereinbefore directed to be taken.

Sect. 6. No navigation act shall be passed without the assent of two thirds of the members present in each House.

Sect. 7. The United States shall not grant any title of nobility.

VIII

The acts of the Legislature of the United States made in pursuance of this Constitution, and all treaties made under the authority of the United

States shall be the supreme law of the several States, and of their citizens and inhabitants; and the judges in the several States shall be bound thereby in their decisions; any thing in the Constitution or laws of the several States to the contrary notwithstanding.

IX

Sect. 1. The Senate of the United States shall have power to make treaties, and to appoint Ambassadors, and Judges of the Supreme Court.

Sect. 2. In all disputes and controversies now subsisting, or that may hereafter subsist between two or more States, respecting jurisdiction or territory, the Senate shall possess the following powers. Whenever the Legislature, or the Executive authority, or lawful agent of any State, in controversy with another, shall by memorial to the Senate, state the matter in question, and apply for a hearing; notice of such memorial and application shall be given by order of the Senate, to the Legislature or the Executive authority of the other State in Controversy. The Senate shall also assign a day for the appearance of the parties, by their agents, before the House. The Agents shall be directed to appoint, by joint consent, commissioners or judges to constitute a Court for hearing and determining the matter in question. But if the Agents cannot agree, the Senate shall name three persons out of each of the several States; and from the list of such persons each party shall alternately strike out one, until the number shall be reduced to thirteen; and from that number not less than seven nor more than nine names, as the Senate shall direct, shall in their presence, be drawn out by lot; and the persons whose names shall be so drawn, or any five of them shall be commissioners or Judges to hear and finally determine the controversy; provided a majority of the Judges, who shall hear the cause, agree in the determination. If either party shall neglect to attend at the day assigned, without shewing sufficient reasons for not attending, or being present shall refuse to strike, the Senate shall proceed to nominate three persons out of each State, and the Clerk of the Senate shall strike in behalf of the party absent or refusing. If any of the parties shall refuse to submit to the authority of such Court; or shall not appear to prosecute or defend their claim or cause, the Court shall nevertheless proceed to pronounce judgment. The judgment shall be final and conclusive. The proceedings shall be transmitted to the President of the Senate, and shall be lodged among the public records, for the security of the parties concerned. Every Commissioner shall, before he sit in judgment, take an oath, to be administred by one of the Judges of the Supreme or Superior Court of the State where the cause shall be tried, "well and truly to hear and determine the matter in question according to the best of his judgment, without favor, affection, or hope of reward."

Sect. 3. All controversies concerning lands claimed under different grants of two or more States, whose jurisdictions, as they respect such lands shall have been decided or adjusted subsequent to such grants, or any of them, shall, on application to the Senate, be finally determined, as near as may be, in the same manner as is before prescribed for deciding controversies between different States.

X

Sect. 1. The Executive Power of the United States shall be vested in a single person. His stile shall be, "The President of the United States of America;" and his title shall be, "His Excellency." He shall be elected by ballot by the Legislature. He shall hold his office during the term of seven years; but shall not be elected a second time.

Sect. 2. He shall, from time to time, give information to the Legislature, of the state of the Union: he may recommend to their consideration such measures as he shall judge necessary, and expedient: he may convene them on extraordinary occasions. In case of disagreement between the two Houses, with regard to the time of adjournment, he may adjourn them to such time as he thinks proper: he shall take care that the laws of the United States be duly and faithfully executed: he shall commission all the officers of the United States; and shall appoint officers in all cases not otherwise provided for by this Constitution. He shall receive Ambassadors, and may correspond with the supreme Executives of the several States. He shall have power to grant reprieves and pardons; but his pardon shall not be pleadable in bar of an impeachment. He shall be commander in chief of the Army and Navy of the United States, and of the Militia of the several States. He shall, at stated times, receive for his services, a compensation, which shall neither be increased nor diminished during his continuance in office. Before he shall enter on the duties of his department, he shall take the following oath or affirmation; "I ——— solemnly swear, (or affirm) that that I will faithfully execute the office of President of the United States of America." He shall be removed from his office on impeachment by the House of Representatives, and conviction in the supreme Court, of treason, bribery or corruption. In case of his removal as aforesaid, death, resignation, or disability to discharge the powers and duties of his office, the President of the Senate shall exercise those powers and duties, until another President of the United States be chosen, or until the disability of the President be removed.

XI

Sect. 1. The Judicial Power of the United States shall be vested in one Supreme Court, and in such inferior Courts as shall, when necessary, from time to time, be constituted by the Legislature of the United States.

Sect. 2. The Judges of the Supreme Court, and of the Inferior Courts, shall hold their offices during good behaviour. They shall, at stated times, receive for their services, a compensation, which shall not be diminished during their continuance in office.

Sect. 3. The Jurisdiction of the Supreme Court shall extend to all cases arising under laws passed by the Legislature of the United States; to all cases affecting Ambassadors, other Public Ministers and Consuls; to the trial of impeachments of officers of the United States; to all cases of Admiralty and maritime jurisdiction; to controversies between two or more States, (except such as shall regard Territory or Jurisdiction) between a State and Citizens of another State, between Citizens of different States, and between a State or the Citizens thereof and foreign States, citizens or subjects. In cases of impeachment, cases affecting Ambassadors, other Public Ministers and Consuls, and those in which a State shall be party, this jurisdiction shall be original. In all the other cases beforementioned, it shall be appellate, with such exceptions and under such regulations as the Legislature shall make. The Legislature may assign any part of the jurisdiction abovementioned (except the trial of the President of the United States) in the manner, and under the limitations which it shall think proper, to such Inferior Courts, as it shall constitute from time to time.

Sect. 4. The trial of all criminal offences (except in cases of impeachments) shall be in the State where they shall be committed; and shall be by Jury.

Sect. 5. Judgment, in cases of Impeachment, shall not extend further than to removal from office, and disqualification to hold and enjoy any office of honour, trust or profit, under the United States. But the party convicted shall, nevertheless be liable and subject to indictment, trial, judgment and punishment according to law.

XII

No State shall coin money; nor grant letters of marque and reprisal; nor enter into any Treaty, alliance, or confederation; nor grant any title of Nobility.

XIII

No State, without the consent of the Legislature of the United States, shall emit bills of credit, or make any thing but specie a tender in payment of debts; nor lay imposts or duties on imports; nor keep troops or ships of war in time of peace; nor enter into any agreement or compact with another State, or with any foreign power; nor engage in any war, unless it shall be actually invaded by enemies, or the danger of invasion be so imminent, as not to admit of delay, until the Legislature of the United States can be consulted.

XIV

The Citizens of each State shall be entitled to all privileges and immunities of citizens in the several States.

XV

Any person charged with treason, felony or high misdemeanor in any State, who shall flee from justice, and shall be found in any other State, shall, on demand of the Executive power of the State from which he fled, be delivered up and removed to the State having jurisdiction of the offence.

XVI

Full faith shall be given in each State to the acts of the Legislatures, and to the records and judicial proceedings of the Courts and magistrates of every other State.

XVII

New States lawfully constituted or established within the limits of the United States may be admitted, by the Legislature, into this Government; but to such admission the consent of two thirds of the members present in each House shall be necessary. If a new State shall arise within the limits of any of the present States, the consent of the Legislatures of such States shall be also necessary to its admission. If the admission be consented to, the new States shall be admitted on the same terms with the original States. But the Legislature may make conditions with the new States, concerning the public debt which shall be then subsisting.

XVIII

The United States shall guaranty to each State a Republican form of Government; and shall protect each State against foreign invasions, and, on the application of its Legislature, against domestic violence.

XIX

On the application of the Legislatures of two thirds of the States in the Union, for an amendment of this Constitution, the Legislature of the United States shall call a Convention for that purpose.

XX

The members of the Legislatures, and the Executive and Judicial officers of the United States, and of the several States, shall be bound by oath to support this Constitution.

XXI

The ratifications of the Conventions of   States shall be sufficient for organizing this Constitution.

XXII

This Constitution shall be laid before the United States in Congress assembled, for their approbation; and it is the opinion of this Convention, that it should be afterwards submitted to a Convention chosen, under the recommendation of its legislature, in order to receive the ratification of such Convention.

XXIII

To introduce this government, it is the opinion of this Convention, that each assenting Convention should notify its assent and ratification to the United States in Congress assembled; that Congress, after receiving the assent and ratification of the Conventions of   States, should appoint and publish a day, as early as may be, and appoint a place for commencing proceedings under this Constitution; that after such publication, the Legislatures of the several States should elect members of the Senate, and direct the election of members of the House of Representatives; and that the members of the Legislature should meet at the time and place assigned by Congress, and should, as soon as may be, after their meeting, choose the President of the United States, and proceed to execute this Constitution.

Tuesday August 7th. In Convention

The Report of the Committee of detail being taken up,

Mr Pinkney moved that it be referred to a Committee of the whole. This was strongly opposed by Mr Ghorum & several others, as likely to produce unnecessary delay; and was negatived, Delaware Maryd & Virga only being in the affirmative.

The preamble of the Report was agreed to nem. con. So were Art: I & II.

Art: III. considered. Col. Mason doubted the propriety of giving each branch a' negative on the other "in all cases." There were some cases in which it was he supposed not intended to be given as in the case of balloting for appointments.

Mr Govr Morris moved to insert "legislative acts" instead of "all cases"

Mr Williamson 2ds him.

Mr Sherman. This will restrain the operation of the clause too much. It will particularly exclude a mutual negative in the case of ballots, which he hoped would take place.

Mr Ghorum contended that elections ought to be made by *joint ballot.* If separate ballots should be made for the President, and the two branches should be each attached to a favorite, great delay contention & confusion may ensue. These inconveniences have been felt in Masts in the election of officers of little importance compared with the Executive of the U. States. The only objection agst a joint ballot is that it may deprive the Senate of their due weight; but this ought not to prevail over the respect due to the public tranquility & welfare.

M[r] Wilson was for a joint ballot in several cases at least; particularly in the choice of the President, and was therefore for the amendment. Disputes between the two Houses during & concern[g] the vacancy of the Executive might have dangerous consequences.

. . .

M[r] Madison wished to know the reasons of the Com[e] for fixing by y[e] Constitution the time of Meeting for the Legislature; and suggested, that it be required only that one meeting at least should be held every year leaving the time to be fixed or varied by law.

. . .

M[r] Wilson thought on the whole it would be best to fix the day.

. . .

M[r] Gov[r] Morris moved to strike out Dec[r] & insert May. It might frequently happen that our measures ought to be influenced by those in Europe, which were generally planned during the Winter and of which intelligence would arrive in the Spring.

M[r] Madison 2[ded] the motion, he preferred May to Dec[r] because the latter would require the travelling to & from the seat of Gov[t] in the most inconvenient seasons of the year.

M[r] Wilson. The Winter is the most convenient season for business.

"Art IV. Sect. 1. taken up."

M[r] Gov[r] Morris moved to strike out the last member of the section beginning with the words "qualifications of Electors," in order that some other provision might be substituted which w[d] restrain the right of suffrage to freeholders.

M[r] Fitzimmons 2[ded] the motion.

. . .

M[r] Wilson. This part of the Report was well considered by the Committee, and he did not think it could be changed for the better. It was difficult to form any uniform rule of qualifications for all the States. Unnecessary innovations he thought too should be avoided. It would be very hard & disagreeable for the same persons at the same time, to vote for representatives in the State Legislature and to be excluded from a vote for those in the Nat[l] Legislature.

. . .

Wednesday Augst 8. In convention

. . .

Art IV. Sect. 2 taken up.

Col. Mason was for opening a wide door for emigrants; but did not chuse to let foreigners and adventurers make laws for us & govern us. Citizenship for three years was not enough for ensuring that local knowledge which ought to be possessed by the Representative. This was the principal ground of his objection to so short a term. It might also happen that a rich foreign Nation, for example Great Britain, might send over her tools who might bribe their way into the Legislature for insidious purposes. He moved that "seven" years instead of "three," be inserted.

Mr Govr Morris 2^{ded} the Motion, & on the question, all the States agreed to it except Connecticut.

Mr Sherman moved to strike out the word "resident" and insert "inhabitant," as less liable to miscontruction.

. . .

Mr Wilson preferred "inhabitant."

. . .

Mr Rutlidge urged & moved that a residence of 7 years sh^{d} be required in the State Wherein the Member sh^{d} be elected. An emigrant from N. England to S. C. or Georgia would know little of its affairs and could not be supposed to acquire a thorough knowledge in less time.

Mr Read reminded him that we were now forming a *Nati^{l}* Gov^{t} and such a regulation would correspond little with the idea that we were one people.

Mr Wilson enforced the same consideration.

. . .

Mr Dickenson proposed that it should read "inhabitant actually resident for   year." This would render the meaning less indeterminate.

Mr Wilson. If a short term should be inserted in the blank, so strict an expression might be construed to exclude the members of the Legislature, who could not be said to be actual residents in their States whilst at the Seat of the Genl Government.

. . .

Mr Pinkney, considered the fisheries & the Western frontier as more burdensome to the U. S. than the slaves. He thought this could be demonstrated if the occasion were a proper one.

Mr Wilson. thought the motion premature. An agreement to the clause would be no bar to the object of it.

. . .

Mr Mercer[1] considered the exclusive power of originating Money bills as so great an advantage, that it rendered the equality of votes in the Senate ideal & of no consequence.

Mr Butler was for adhering to the principle which had been settled.

Mr Wilson was opposed to it on its merits without regard to the compromise

. . .

Thursday Aug^st^ 9. In Convention

Art: IV. Sect. 6. Mr Randolph expressed his dissatisfaction at the disagreement yesterday to Sect. 5. concerning money bills, as endangering the success of the plan, and extremely objectionable in itself; and gave notice that he should move for a reconsideration of the vote.

. . .

Mr Wilson, gave notice that he sh^d^ move to reconsider the vote, requiring seven instead of three years of Citizenship as a qualification of candidates for the House of Representatives.

Art. IV. Sect. 6 & 7. Agreed to nem. con.

Art. V. Sect 1. taken up.

Mr Wilson objected to vacancies in the Senate being supplied by the Executives of the States. It was unnecessary as the Legislatures will meet so frequently. It removes the appointment too far from the people; the Executives in most of the States being elected by the Legislatures. As he

1. John Francis Mercer (1759–1821) was strongly opposed to centralization and the Constitution as a whole. He served as a member of the state house in Maryland, U.S. representative, and later as governor.

had always thought the appointment of the Executives by the Legislative department wrong: so it was still more so that the Executive should elect into the Legislative department.

. . .

Mr Read did not consider the section as to money bills of any advantage to the larger States and had voted for striking it out as being viewed in the same light by the larger States. If it was considered by them as of any value, and as a condition of the equality of votes in the Senate, he had no objection to its being re-instated.

Mr Wilson—Mr Elseworth & Mr Madison urged that it was of no advantage to the larger States, and that it might be a dangerous source of contention between the two Houses. All the principal powers of the Natl Legislature had some relation to money.

. . .

Mr Wilson. It seems to have been supposed by some that the section concerning money bills is desirable to the large States. The fact was that two of those States [Pa & Va] had uniformly voted agst it without reference to any other part of the system.

. . .

Art: V. Sect. 3. taken up.

Mr Govr Morris moved to insert 14 instead of 4 years citizenship as a qualification for Senators: urging the danger of admitting strangers into our public Councils. Mr Pinkney 2ds him.

. . .

Mr Wilson said he rose with feelings which were perhaps peculiar; mentioning the circumstance of his not being a native, and the possibility, if the ideas of some gentlemen should be pursued, of his being incapacitated from holding a place under the very Constitution, which he had shared in the trust of making. He remarked the illiberal complexion which the motion would give to the System, & the effect which a good system would have in inviting meritorious foreigners among us, and the discouragement & mortification they must feel from the degrading discrimination, now proposed. He had himself experienced this mortification. On his removal into Maryland, he found himself from defect of residence, under certain legal incapacities which never ceased to produce chagrin, though he assuredly did not desire & would not have accepted the offices to which they related. To be appointed to a place may be matter of indifference. To be incapable of being appointed, is a circumstance grating and mortifying.

. . .

Friday Augst 10. In Convention

Art VI. Sect. 2. taken up.

. . .

Mr Wilson thought it would be best on the whole to let the Section go out. A uniform rule would probably be never fixed by the Legislature, and this particular power would constructively exclude every other power of regulating qualifications.

. . .

Art: VI. Sect. 3. taken up.

. . .

Mr Elseworth was opposed to it. It would be a pleasing ground of confidence to the people that no law or burden could be imposed on them, by a few men. He reminded the movers that the Constitution proposed to give such a discretion with regard to the number of Representatives that a very incovenient number was not to be apprehended. The inconveniency of secessions may be guarded agst by giving to each House an authority to require the attendance of absent members.

. . .

Art: VI. Sect. 7 taken up.

. . .

Mr Govr Morris & Mr Wilson observed that if the minority were to have a right to enter their votes & reasons, the other side would have a right to complain, if it were not extended to them & to allow it to both, would fill the Journals, like the records of a Court, with replications, rejoinders &c.

. . .

Saturday Augst 11. In Convention

Mr Madison & Mr Rutlidge moved "that each House shall keep a journal of its proceeding, & shall publish the same from time to time except such part of the proceedings of the Senate, when acting not in its Legislative capacity as may be judged by that House to require secrecy."

. . .

Mr Wilson thought the expunging of the clause would be very improper. The people have a right to know what their Agents are doing or have done, and it should not be in the option of the Legislature to conceal their proceedings. Besides as this is a clause in the existing confederation, the not retaining it would furnish the adversaries of the reform with a pretext by which week & suspicious minds may be easily misled.

. . .

Monday Augst 13. In Convention

Art IV. Sect. 2. reconsidered—

Mr Wilson & Mr Randolph moved to strike out "7 years" and insert "4 years," as the requisite term of Citizenship to qualify for the House of Reps. Mr Wilson said it was very proper the electors should govern themselves by this consideration; but unnecessary & improper that the Constitution should chain them down to it.

. . .

Mr Wilson, cited Pennsylva as a proof of the advantage of encouraging emigrations. It was perhaps the youngest [except Georgia] settlemt on the Atlantic; yet it was at least among the foremost in population & prosperity. He remarked that almost all the Genl officers of the Pena line of the late army were foreigners. And no complaint had ever been made against their fidelity or merit. Three of her deputies to the Convention [Mr R. Morris; Mr Fitzimmons & himself] were also not natives. He had no objection to Col. Hamiltons motion & would withdraw the one made by himself.

. . .

M[r] Wilson's renewed the motion for 4 years instead of 7. & on question.

. . .

M[r] Gov[r] Morris moved to add to the end of the section [art IV. S. 2] a proviso that the limitation of seven years should not affect the rights of any person now a Citizen.

M[r] Mercer 2[ded] the motion. It was necessary he said to prevent a disfranchisement of persons who had become Citizens under and on the faith & according to the laws & Constitution from being on a level in all respects with natives.

. . .

M[r] Wilson read the clause in the Constitution of Pen[a] giving to foreigners after two years residence all the rights whatsoever of citizens, combined it with the article of Confederation making the Citizens of one State Citizens of all, inferred the obligation Pen[a] was under to maintain the faith thus pledged to her citizens of foreign birth, and the just complaints which her failure would authorize: He observed likewise that the Princes & States of Europe would avail themselves of such breach of faith to deter their subjects from emigrating to the U. S.

. . .

M[r] Wilson moved that [in Art: V. Sect. 3.] 9 years be reduced to seven, which was disag[d] to and the 3[d] section [Art. V.] confirmed by the following vote.

N. H. ay. Mas. ay. C[t] no. N. J. ay. P[a] no. Del. ay. M[d] no. V[a] ay. N. C. ay. S. C. ay. Geo. ay.

Art. IV. Sec 5. being reconsidered.

M[r] Randolph moved that the clause be altered so as to read—"Bills for raising money for the *purpose of revenue* or for appropriating the same shall originate in the House of Representatives and shall not be so amended or altered by the Senate as to increase or diminish the sum to be raised, or change the mode of levying it, or the objects of its appropriation."—He would not repeat his reasons, but barely remind the members from the smaller States of the compromise by which the larger States were entitled to this privilege.

. . .

Mr Wilson was himself directly opposed to the equality of votes granted to the Senate by its present Constitution. At the same time he wished not to multiply the vices of the system. He did not mean to enlarge on a subject which had been so much canvassed, but would remark as an insuperable objection agst the proposed restriction of money bills to the H. of Reps that it would be a source of perpetual contentions where there was no mediator to decide them. The Presidt here could not like the Executive Magistrate in England interpose by a prorogation, or dissolution. This restriction had been found pregnant with altercation in every State where the Constitution had established it. The House of Reps will insert other things in money bills, and by making them conditions of each other, destroy the deliberative liberty of the Senate. He stated the case of a Preamble to a money bill sent up by the House of Commons in the reign of Queen Anne,[2] to the H. of Lords, in which the conduct of the displaced Ministry, who were to be impeached before the Lords, was condemned; the Commons thus extorting a premature judgmt without any hearing of the Parties to be tried, and the H. of Lords being thus reduced to the poor & disgraceful expedient of opposing to the authority of a law, a protest on their Journals agst its being drawn into precedent. If there was any thing like Poynings law[3] in the present case, it was in the attempt to vest the exclusive right of originating in the H. of Reps and so far he was agst it. He should be equally so if the right were to be exclusively vested in the Senate. With regard to the purse strings, it was to be observed that the purse was to have two strings, one of which was in the hands of the H. of Reps the other in those of the Senate. Both houses must concur in untying, and of what importance could it be which untied first, which last. He could not conceive it to be any objection to the Senate's preparing the bills, that they would have leisure for that purpose and would be in the habits of business. War, Commerce, & Revenue were the great objects of the Genl Government. All of them are connected with money. The restriction in favor of the H. of Represts would exclude the Senate from originating any important bills whatever—

. . .

2. Anne (1665–1714) was queen of England from 1702 to 1714.

3. Poynings's law refers to the Statutes of Drogheda (created by the parliament of Drogheda, and summoned by Sir Edward Poynings), which made the Irish legislature entirely subordinate to the English parliament from 1494 to 1782.

Tuesday Aug. 14. In Convention

Article VI. Sect. 9. taken up.

M[r] Pinkney argued that the making the members ineligible to offices was *degrading* to them, and the more improper as their election into the Legislature implied that they had the confidence of the people; that it was *inconvenient*, because the Senate might be supposed to contain the fittest men. He hoped to see that body become a School of public Ministers, a nursery of Statesmen: that it was *impolitic*, because the Legislature would cease to be a magnet to the first talents and abilities. He moved to postpone the section in order to take up the following proposition viz—"the members of each House shall be incapable of holding any office under the U. S. for which they or any of others for their benefit receive any salary, fees, or emoluments of any kind—and the acceptance of such office shall vacate their seats respectively."

Gen[l] Mifflin[4] 2[ded] the motion.

. . .

M[r] Wilson could not approve of the Section as it stood, and could not give up his judgment to any supposed objections that might arise among the people. He considered himself as acting & responsible for the welfare of millions not immediately represented in this House. He had also asked himself the serious question what he should say to his constituents in case they should call upon him to tell them why he sacrified his own Judgment in a case where they authorised him to exercise it? Were he to own to them that he sacrificed it in order to flatter their prejudices, he should dread the retort: did you suppose the people of Penn[a] had not good sense enough to receive a good Government? Under this impression he should certainly follow his own Judgment which disapproved of the section. He would remark in addition to the objections urged ag[st] it, that as one branch of the Legislature was to be appointed by the Legislatures of the States, the other by the people of the States, as both are to be paid by the States, and to be appointable to State offices, nothing seemed to be wanting to prostrate the Nat[l] Legislature, but to render its members ineligible to Nat[l] offices, & by that means take away its power of attracting those talents

4. Thomas Mifflin (1744–1800) was a general in the Continental Army and a political leader in Pennsylvania. He attended the convention regularly but did not make a significant impact.

which were necessary to give weight to the Govern[t] and to render it useful to the people. He was far from thinking the ambition which aspired to Offices of dignity and trust, an ignoble or culpable one. He was sure it was not politic to regard it in that light, or to withold from it the prospect of those rewards, which might engage it in the career of public service. He observed that the State of Penn[a] which had gone as far as any State into the policy of fettering power, had not rendered the members of the Legislature ineligible to offices of Gov[t].

. . .

M[r] Wilson was by no means satisfied with the answer given by M[r] Elseworth to the argument as to the discouragement of merit. The members must either go a second time into the Legislature, and disqualify themselves—or say to their Constituents, we served you before only from the mercenary view of qualifying ourselves for offices, and have[g] answered this purpose we do not chuse to be again elected.

. . .

Wednesday August 15. In Convention

. . .

M[r] Madison moved that all acts before they become laws should be submitted both to the Executive and Supreme Judiciary Departments, that if either of these should object ⅔ of each House, if both should object, ¾ of each House, should be necessary to overrule the objections and give to the acts the force of law—

See the motion at large in the Journal of this date, page 253, & insert it here.

["Every bill which shall have passed the two houses, shall, before it become a law, be severally presented to the President of the United States, and to the judges of the supreme court for the revision of each. If, upon such revision, they shall approve of it, they shall respectively signify their approbation by signing it, but if, upon such revision, it shall appear improper to either, or both, to be passed into a law, it shall be returned, with the objections against it, to that house, in which it shall have originated, who shall enter the objections at large on their journal, and proceed to reconsider the bill: but if, after such reconsideration, two thirds of that house, when either the President, or a majority of the judges shall object, or three fourths, where both shall object, shall agree to pass it, it shall, together with the objections, be sent to the other house, by which it shall likewise be reconsidered; and, if approved by two thirds, or three fourths of the other house, as the case may be, it shall become a law."]

Mr Wilson seconds the motion.

. . .

Mr Carrol[5] when the negative to be overruled by ⅔ only was agreed to, the *quorum* was not fixed. He remarked that as a majority was now to be the quorum, 17. in the larger, and 8 in the smaller house might carry points. The advantage that might be taken of this seemed to call for greater impediments to improper laws. He thought the controuling power however of the Executive could not be well decided, till it was seen how the formation of that department would be finally regulated. He wished the consideration of the matter to be postponed.

. . .

Mr Wilson; after viewing the subject with all the coolness and attention possible was most apprehensive of a dissolution of the Gov^t^ from the legislature swallowing up all the other powers. He remarked that the prejudices ag^st^ the Executive resulted from a misapplication of the adage that the parliament was the palladium of liberty. Where the Executive was really formidable, *King* and *Tyrant,* were naturally associated in the minds of people; not *legislature* and *tyranny.* But where the Executive was not formidable, the two last were most properly associated. After the destruction of the King in Great Britain, a more pure and unmixed tryanny sprang up in the parliament than had been exercised by the monarch. He insisted that we had not guarded ag^st^ the danger on this side by a sufficient self-defensive power either to the Executive or Judiciary department.

. . .

Mr Williamson moved to change "⅔ of each House" into "¾" as requisite to overrule the dissent of the President. He saw no danger in this, and preferred giving the power to the Presid^t^ alone, to admitting the Judges into the business of legislation.

5. Daniel Carroll (1730–1796) was a prominent planter from Maryland. He arrived late to the convention but supported the Constitution and later served in the U.S. House of Representatives.

Mr Wilson 2ds the motion; referring to and repeating the ideas of Mr Carroll.

On this motion for ¾. instead of two thirds; it passed in the affirmative.

. . .

Thursday August 16. In Convention

. . .

Art: VII. Sect. I. taken up.

Mr L. Martin asked what was meant by the Committee of detail in the expression "*duties*" and "*imposts*." If the meaning were the same, the former was unnecessary; if different, the matter ought to be made clear.

Mr Wilson, *duties* are applicable to many objects to which the word *imposts* does not relate. The latter are appropriated to commerce; the former extend to a variety of objects as stamp duties &c.

. . .

Mr Wilson was decidedly agst prohibiting general taxes on exports. He dwelt on the injustice and impolicy of leaving N. Jersey Connecticut &c any longer subject to the exactions of their commercial neighbours.

. . .

Mr Elseworth thought this a favorable moment to shut and bar the door against paper money. The mischiefs of the various experiments which had been made, were now fresh in the public mind and had excited the disgust of all the respectable part of America. By witholding the power from the new Governt more friends of influence would be gained to it than by almost any thing else. Paper money can in no case be necessary. Give the Government credit, and other resources will offer. The power may do harm never good.

Mr Randolph, notwithstanding his antipathy to paper money, could not agree to strike out the words, as he could not foresee all the occasions which might arise.

Mr Wilson. It will have a most salutary influence on the credit of the U. States to remove the possibility of paper money. This expedient can never succeed whilst its mischiefs are remembered, and as long as it can be resorted to, it will be a bar to other resources.

. . .

Friday August 17th. In Convention

Art VII. Sect. 1. resumed on the clause "to appoint Treasurer by ballot."

. . .

Mr Madison moved to strike out "and punishment" &c.

. . .

Mr Wilson was in favor of the motion. Strictness was not necessary in giving authority to enact penal laws; though necessary in enacting & expounding them.

. . .

Mr Wilson, thought "felonies" sufficiently defined by common law.

. . .

Art VII. Sect. 2. concerning Treason which see.

. . .

Mr Randolph thought the clause defective in adopting the words "in adhering" only. The British Stat: adds, "giving them aid and comfort" which had a more extensive meaning.

Mr Elseworth considered the definition as the same in fact with that of the Statute.

Mr Govr Morris "adhering" does not go so far as "giving aid and Comfort" or the latter words may be restrictive of adhering," in either case the Statute is not pursued.

Mr Wilson held "giving aid and comfort" to be explanatory, not operative words; and that it was better to omit them.

. . .

Mr Wilson & Doc^{r} Johnson moved, that "or any of them" after "United States" be struck out in order to remove the embarrassment: which was agreed to nem. con.

. . .

It was then moved to insert after "two witnesses" the words "to the same overt act."

Doc^{r} Franklin wished this amendment to take place—prosecutions for treason were generally virulent; and perjury too easily made use of against innocence.

Mr Wilson. much may be said on both sides. Treason may sometimes be practised in such a manner, as to render proof extremely difficult—as in a traitorous correspondence with an Enemy.

. . .

Mr Wilson in cases of a general nature, treason can only be agst the U— States. and in such they sh^{d} have the sole right to declare the punishment—yet in many cases it may be otherwise. The subject was however intricate and he distrusted his present judgment on it.

. . .

N. H. ay. Mas. ay. C^{t} no. N. J. no. P^{a} ay. Del. ay. M^{d} no. V^{a} no. N. C. no. S. C. ay. Geo. no.—

Mr Wilson. the clause is ambiguous now. "Sole" ought either to have been inserted—or "against the U. S." to be re-instated.

. . .

Tuesday August 21. In Convention

. . .

Art. VII. Sect. 4.—Mr Langdon. by this section the States are left at liberty to tax exports. N. H. therefore with other non-exporting States, will be subject to be taxed by the States exporting its produce. This could not be admitted. It seems to be feared that the Northern States will oppress the trade of the South^{n}. This may be guarded agst by requiring the concurrence of ⅔ or ¾ of the legislature in such cases.

. . .

Mr Wilson. Pennsylvania exports the produce of Mary^{d}, N. Jersey, Delaware & will by & by when the River Delaware is opened, export for N- York. In favoring the general power over exports therefore, he opposed the particular interest of his State. He remarked that the power had been attacked by reasoning which could only have held good in case the Genl Gov^{t} had been *compelled,* instead of *authorized,* to lay duties on exports. To deny this power is to take from the Common Gov^{t} half the regulation of trade. It was his opinion that a power over exports might be more effectual than that over imports in obtaining beneficial treaties of commerce.

. . .

Mr Madison. In order to require ⅔ of each House to tax exports—as a lesser evil than a total prohibition moved to insert the words "unless by consent of two thirds of the Legislature."

Mr Wilson 2^{ds} and on this question, it passed in the Negative.

. . .

Wednesday August 22. In Convention

Art VII sect 4. resumed. M[r] Sherman was for leaving the clause as it stands. He disapproved of the slave trade; yet as the States were now possessed of the right to import slaves, as the public good did not require it to be taken from them, & as it was expedient to have as few objections as possible to the proposed scheme of Government, he thought it best to leave the matter as we find it. He observed that the abolition of Slavery seemed to be going on in the U. S. & that the good sense of the several States would probably by degrees compleat it. He urged on the Convention the necessity of despatching its business.

. . .

M[r] Wilson observed that if S. C. & Georgia were themselves disposed to get rid of the importation of slaves in a short time as had been suggested, they would never refuse to Unite because the importation might be prohibited. As the Section now stands all articles imported are to be taxed. Slaves alone are exempt. This is in fact a bounty on that article.

. . .

M[r] Pinkney & M[r] Langdon moved to commit Sect. 6. as to navigation act by two thirds of each House.

. . .

M[r] Wilson wished for a commitment in order to reduce the proportion of votes required.

. . .

M[r] Gerry & M[r] M[c]Henry[6] moved to insert after the 2[d] sect.

Art: 7, the Clause following, to wit, "The Legislature shall pass no bill of attainder nor any ex post facto law."

. . .

M[r] Wilson was against inserting any thing in the Constitution as to ex post facto laws. It will bring reflexions on the Constitution and proclaim that we are ignorant of the first principles of legislation, or are constituting a Government which will be so. The question being divided,

6. James McHenry (1753–1816) began his career in medicine but later entered the fields of politics and administration, serving in various legislative offices in Maryland and as the secretary of war under Washington and Adams. He missed significant portions of the convention because of the illness of his brother, but strenuously supported the Constitution.

The first part of the motion relating to bills of attainder was agreed to nem. contradicente.

. . .

Mr Wilson. If these prohibitions in the State Constitutions have no effect it will be useless to insert them in this Constitution. Besides both sides will agree to the principle, & will differ as to its application.

. . .

Art. IX being next for consideration,

Mr Govr Morris argued agst the appointment of officers by the Senate. He considered the body as too numerous for the purpose; as subject to cabal; and as devoid of responsibility. If Judges were to be tried by the Senate according to a late report of a Committee it was particularly wrong to let the Senate have the filling of vacancies which its own decrees were to create.

Mr Wilson was of the same opinion & for like reasons.

. . .

M^{r} C- Pinkney moved to add as an additional power to be vested in the Legislature of the U. S. "To negative all laws passed by the several States interfering in the opinion of the Legislature with the general interests and harmony of the Union; provided that two thirds of the members of each House assent to the same."

This principle he observed had formerly been agreed to. He considered the precaution as essentially necessary: The objection drawn from the predominance of the large States had been removed by the equality established in the Senate. Mr Broome 2^{ded} the proposition.

. . .

Mr Wilson considered this as the key-stone wanted to compleat the wide arch of Government, we are raising. The power of self-defence had been urged as necessary for the State Governments. It was equally necessary for the General Government. The firmness of Judges is not of itself sufficient. Something further is requisite. It will be better to prevent the passage of an improper law, than to declare it void when passed.

. . .

Art IX. Sect. 1. being resumed, to wit "The Senate of the U. S. shall have power to make treaties, and to appoint Ambassadors and Judges of the Supreme Court."

. . .

Mr Wilson. In the most important Treaties, the King of G. Britain being obliged to resort to Parliament for the execution of them, is under the same fetters as the amendment of Mr Morris will impose on the Senate. It was refused yesterday to permit even the Legislature to lay duties on exports. Under the clause, without the amendment, the Senate alone can make a Treaty, requiring all the Rice of S. Carolina to be sent to some one particular port.

. . .

Friday August 24. 1787. In Convention

. . .

Sect: 2 & 3 of art: IX being taken up,

Mr Rutlidge said this provision for deciding controversies between the States was necessary under the Confederation, but will be rendered unnecessary by the National Judiciary now to be established, and moved to strike it out.

Doc^{r} Johnson 2^{ded} the Motion.

. . .

Mr Wilson urged the striking out, the Judiciary being a better provision.

. . .

Mr Carrol moved to strike out "by the Legislature" and insert "by the people." Mr Wilson 2^{ded} him & on the question.

. . .

Mr Wilson urged the reasonableness of giving the larger States a larger share of the appointment, and the danger of delay from a disagreement of the two Houses. He remarked also that the Senate had peculiar powers balancing the advantage given by a joint balot in this case to the other branch of the Legislature.

. . .

Mr Wilson remarked that as the President of the Senate was to be President of the U. S. that Body in cases of vacancy might have an interest in throwing dilatory obstacles in the way, if its separate concurrence should be required.

. . .

Mr Dickinson moved to strike out the words "and shall appoint to offices in all cases not otherwise provided for by this Constitution" and insert—"and shall appoint to all offices established by this Constitution, except in cases herein otherwise provided for, and to all offices which may hereafter be created by law."

. . .

Mr Dickinson then moved to annex to his last amendment "except where by law the appointment shall be vested in the Legislatures or Executives of the several States." Mr Randolph 2ded the motion.

Mr Wilson—If this be agreed to it will soon be a standing instruction from the State Legislatures to pass no law creating offices, unless the appts be referred to them.

. . .

Monday Augst 27th 1787. In Convention

Art X. Sect. 2. being resumed.

Mr L. Martin moved to insert the words "after conviction" after the words "reprieves and pardons"

Mr Wilson objected that pardon before conviction might be necessary in order to obtain the testimony of accomplices. He stated the case of forgeries in which this might particularly happen.—Mr L. Martin withdrew his motion.

. . .

Col: Mason & Mr Madison, moved to add to the oath to be taken by the supreme Executive "and will to the best of my judgment and power preserve protect and defend the Constitution of the U. S."

Mr Wilson thought the general provision for oaths of office, in a subsequent place, rendered the amendment unnecessary—

. . .

Mr Dickinson moved as an amendment to sect. 2. art XI after the words "good behavior" the words "provided that they may be removed by the Executive on the application by the Senate and House of Representatives."

Mr Gerry 2ded the motion.

. . .

Mr Wilson considered such a provision in the British Government as less dangerous than here, the House of Lords & House of Commons being less likely to concur on the same occasions. Chief Justice Holt, he remarked, had *successively* offended by his independent conduct, both houses of Parliament. Had this happened at the same time, he would have been ousted. The judges would be in a bad situation if made to depend on every gust of faction which might prevail in the two branches of our Gov[t].

. . .

M[r] Gov[r] Morris wished to know what was meant by the words "In all the cases before mentioned it [jurisdiction] shall be appellate with such exceptions &c," whether it extended to matters of fact as well as law—and to cases of Common law as well as Civil law.

M[r] Wilson. The Committee he believed meant facts as well as law & Common as well as Civil law. The jurisdiction of the federal Court of Appeals had he said been so construed.

. . .

Tuesday August 28. 1787. In Convention

M[r] Gov[r] Morris moved that "The privilege of the writ of Habeas Corpus shall not be suspended; unless where in cases of Rebellion or invasion the public safety may require it."

M[r] Wilson doubted whether in any case a suspension could be necessary, as the discretion now exists with Judges, in most important cases to keep in Gaol or admit to Bail.

. . .

Art. XII. being taken up.

M[r] Wilson & M[r] Sherman moved to insert after the words "coin money" the words "nor emit bills of credit, nor make anything but gold & silver coin a tender in payment of debts" making these prohibitions absolute, instead of making the measures allowable (as in the XIII art:) *with the consent of the Legislature of the U. S.*

. . .

M[r] King moved to add, in the words used in the Ordinance of Cong[s] establishing new States, a prohibition on the States to interfere in private contracts.

. . .

Mr Wilson was in favor of Mr King's motion.

. . .

Col: Mason. This is carrying the restraint too far. Cases will happen that can not be foreseen, where some kind of interference will be proper & essential. He mentioned the case of limiting the period for bringing actions on open account—that of bonds after a certain lapse of time—asking whether it was proper to tie the hands of the States from making provision in such cases?

Mr Wilson. The answer to these objections is that *retrospective* interferences only are to be prohibited.

. . .

Art: XV being taken up, the words "high misdemesnor," were struck out, and "other crime" inserted, in order to comprehend all proper cases: it being doubtful whether "high misdemeanor" had not a technical meaning too limited.

Mr Butler and Mr Pinkney moved "to require fugitive slaves and servants to be delivered up like criminals."

Mr Wilson. This would oblige the Executive of the State to do it at the public expence.

. . .

Wednesday August 29th 1787. In Convention

Art: XVI. taken up.

Mr Williamson moved to substitute in place of it, the words of the Articles of Confederation on the same subject. He did not understand precisely the meaning of the article.

Mr Wilson & Docr Johnson supposed the meaning to be that Judgments in one State should be the ground of actions in other States, & that acts of the Legislatures should be included, for the sake of Acts of insolvency &c.

. . .

Art VII Sect. 6 by ye Committee of eleven reported to be struck out (see the 24 instant) being now taken up.

. . .

Mr Wilson took notice of the several objections and remarked that if every peculiar interest was to be secured, *unanimity* ought to be required. The majority he said would be no more governed by interest than the minority. It was surely better to let the latter be bound hand and foot than the former. Great inconveniences had, he contended, been experienced in Congress from the article of confederation requiring nine votes in certain cases.

. . .

Art. XVII—before the House, as amended.

. . .

Mr Wilson. When the *majority* of a State wish to divide they can do so. The aim of those in opposition to the article, he perceived, was that the Genl Government should abet the *minority,* & by that means divide a State against its own consent.

. . .

Thursday August 30th 1787. In Convention

Art XVII resumed for a question on it as amended by Mr Govr Morris's substitutes.

Mr Carrol moved to strike out so much of the article as requires the consent of the State to its being divided.

. . .

Mr Wilson was against the committment. Unanimity was of great importance, but not to be purchased by the majority's yielding to the minority. He should have no objection to leaving the case of new States as heretofore. He knew of nothing that would give greater or juster alarm than the doctrine, that a political society is to be torne asunder without its own consent.

. . .

Mr Dickinson moved to add the following clause to the last—

"Nor shall any State be formed by the junction of two or more States or parts thereof, without the consent of the Legislature of such States, as well as of the Legislature of the U. States," which was agreed to without a count of the votes.

. . .

Mr Wilson was agst the motion. There was nothing in the Constitution affecting one way or the other the claims of the U. S. & it was best to insert nothing leaving every thing on that litigated subject in statu quo.

. . .

Art: XXI. taken up. viz: The ratifications of the Conventions of   States shall be sufficient for organizing this Constitution."

Mr Wilson proposed to fill the blank with "seven" that being a majority of the whole number & sufficient for the commencement of the plan.

. . .

Mr Wilson mentioned "eight" as preferable.

. . .

Mr Madison, remarked that if the blank should be filled with "seven" eight, or "nine"—the Constitution as it stands might be put in force over the whole body of the people, tho' less than a majority of them should ratify it.

Mr Wilson. As the Constitution stands, the States only which ratify can be bound. We must he said in this case go to the original powers of Society. The House on fire must be extinguished, without a scrupulous regard to ordinary rights.

. . .

Friday August 31st 1787. In Convention

. . .

Mr Madison proposed to fill the blank in the article with "any seven or more States entitled to thirty three members at least in the House of Representatives according to the allotment made in the 3 Sect: of art: 4." This he said would require the concurrence of a majority both of the States and people.

. . .

Mr Wilson supported the motion of Mr Madison, requiring a majority both of the people and of States.

. . .

Monday Sep[r] 3. 1787. In Convention

M[r] Gov[r] Morris moved to amend the Report concerning the respect to be paid to Acts Records &c of one State, in other States (see Sep[r] 1.) by striking out "judgments obtained in one State shall have in another" and to insert the word "thereof" after the word "effect"

Col: Mason favored the motion, particularly if the "effect" was to be restrained to judgments & Judicial proceedings.

M[r] Wilson remarked, that if the Legislature were not allowed to *declare the effect* the provision would amount to nothing more than what now takes place among all Independent Nations.

. . .

M[r] Pinkney moved to postpone the Report of the Committee of Eleven (see Sep[r] 1) in order to take up the following,

"The members of each House shall be incapable of holding any office under the U. S. for which they or any other for their benefit, receive any salary, fees or emoluments of any kind, and the acceptance of such office shall vacate their seats respectively."

. . .

M[r] Wilson considered the exclusion of members of the Legislature, as increasing the influence of the Executive as observed by Mr Gov[r] Morris at the same time that it would diminish, the general energy of the Government. He said that the legal disqualification for office would be odious to those who did not wish for office, but did not wish either to be marked by so degrading a distinction.

. . .

Tuesday Sep[r] 4. 1787. In Convention

M[r] Brearly from the Committee of eleven made a further partial Report as follows

"The Committee of Eleven to whom sundry resolutions &c were referred on the 31st of August, report that in their opinion the following additions and alterations should be made to the Report before the Convention, viz

. . .

Mr Wilson. This subject [election of the president] has greatly divided the House, and will also divide people out of doors. It is in truth the most difficult of all on which we have had to decide. He had never made up an opinion on it entirely to his own satisfaction. He thought the plan on the whole a valuable improvement on the former. It gets rid of one great evil, that of cabal & corrup-tion; & Continental Characters will multiply as we more & more coalesce, so as to enable the electors in every part of the Union to know & judge of them. It clears the way also for a discussion of the question of re-eligibility on its own merits, which the former mode of election seems to forbid. He thought it might be better however to refer the eventual appointment to the Legislature than to the Senate, and to confine it to a smaller number than five of the Candidates. The eventual election by the Legislature w^d^ not open cabal anew, as it would be restrained to certain designated objects of choice, and as these must have had the previous sanction of a number of the States: and if the election be made as it ought as soon as the votes of the electors are opened & it is known that no one has a majority of the whole, there can be little danger of corruption. Another reason for preferring the Legislature to the Senate in this business, was that the House of Rep^s^ will be so often changed as to be free from the influence & faction to which the permanence of the Senate may subject that branch.

. . .

Mr Pinkney moved a clause declaring "that each House should be judge of the privilege of its own members." Mr Govr Morris 2^ded^ the motion.

. . .

Mr Wilson thought the power involved, and the express insertion of it needless. It might beget doubts as to the power of other public bodies, as Courts &c. Every Court is the judge of its own privileges.

. . .

Wednesday Sepr 5. 1787. In Convention

. . .

Col. Mason admitted that there were objections to an appointment by the Legislature as originally planned. He had not yet made up his mind, but would state his objections to the mode proposed by the Committee. 1. It puts the appointment in fact into the hands of the Senate, as it will rarely happen that a majority of the whole votes will fall on any one candidate: and as the Existing President will always be one of the 5 highest, his reappointment will of course depend on the Senate. 2. Considering the powers of the President & those of the Senate, if a coalition should be established between these two branches, they will be able to subvert the Constitution—The great objection with him would be removed by depriving the Senate of the eventual selection. He accordingly moved to strike out the words "if such number be a majority of that of the electors."

. . .

M[r] Wilson moved to strike out "Senate" and insert the word "Legislature"

. . .

Thursday Sep[r] 6. 1787. In Convention

. . .

M[r] Gerry proposed, as the President was to be elected by the Senate out of the five highest candidates, that if he should not at the end of his term be re-elected by a majority of the Electors, and no other candidate should have a majority, the eventual election should be made by the Legislature. This he said would relieve the president from his particular dependence on the Senate for his continuance in office.

. . .

M[r] Wilson said that he had weighed carefully the report of the Committee for remodelling the constitution of the Executive; and on combining it with other parts of the plan, he was obliged to consider the whole as having a dangerous tendency to aristocracy; as throwing a dangerous power into the hands of the Senate. They will have in fact, the appointment of the President, and through his dependence on them, the virtual appointment to offices; among others the offices of the Judiciary Department. They are to make Treaties; and they are to try all impeachments. In allowing them thus to make the Executive & Judiciary appointments, to be the Court of impeachments, and to make Treaties which are to be laws of the land, the Legislative, Executive & Judiciary powers are all blended in one branch of the Government. The power of making Treaties involves the case of subsidies, and here as an additional evil, foreign influence is to be dreaded. According to the plan as it now stands, the President will not be the man of the people as he ought to be, but the Minion of the Senate. He cannot even appoint a tide-waiter without the Senate. He had always thought the Senate too numerous a body for making appointments to office. The Senate, will moreover in all probability be in constant Session. They will have high salaries. And with all those powers, and the President in their interest, they will depress the other branch of the Legislature, and aggrandize themselves in proportion. Add to all this, that the Senate sitting in conclave, can by holding up to their respective States various and improbable candidates, contrive so to scatter their votes, as to bring the appointment of the President ultimately before themselves. Upon the whole, he thought the new mode of appointing the President, with some amendments, a valuable improvement; but he could never agree to purchase it at the price of the ensuing parts of the Report, nor befriend a system of which they make a part.

. . .

The Section 4.—to wit, "The President by & with the advice and consent of the Senate shall have power to make Treaties &c."

M[r] Wilson moved to add, after the word "Senate" the words, "and House of Representatives." As treaties he said are to have the operation of laws, they ought to have the sanction of laws also. The circumstance of secrecy in the business of treaties formed the only objection; but this he thought, so far as it was inconsistent with obtaining the Legislative sanction, was outweighed by the necessity of the latter.

. . .

"He shall nominate &c Appoint Ambassadors &c."

M[r] Wilson objected to the mode of appointing, as blending a branch of the Legislature with the Executive. Good laws are of no effect without a good Executive; and there can be no good Executive without a responsible appointment of officers to execute. Responsibility is in a manner destroyed by such an agency of the Senate. He would prefer the council proposed by Col. Mason, provided its advice should not be made obligatory on the President.

. . .

On motion of M[r] Spaight—"that the President shall have power to fill up all vacancies that may happen during the recess of the Senate by granting Commissions which shall expire at the end of the next Session of the Senate" It was agreed to nem: con:

Section 4. "The President by and with the advice and consent of the Senate shall have power to make Treaties"—"*But no treaty shall be made without the consent of two thirds of the members present*"—this last being before the House.

Mr Wilson thought it objectionable to require the concurrence of ⅔ which puts it in the power of a minority to controul the will of a majority.

. . .

Col: Mason said that in rejecting a Council to the President we were about to try an experiment on which the most despotic Governments had never ventured. The Grand Signor himself had his Divan. He moved to postpone the consideration of the clause in order to take up the following

"That it be an instruction to the Committee of the States to prepare a clause or clauses for establishing an Executive Council, as a Council of State, for the President of the U. States, to consist of six members, two of which from the Eastern, two from the middle, and two from the Southern States, with a Rotation and duration of office similar to those of the Senate; such Council to be appointed by the Legislature or by the Senate."

. . .

Mr Wilson approved of a Council in preference to making the Senate a party to appointm^{ts}.

. . .

Saturday September 8th. In Convention

The last Report of Committee of Eleven (see Sepr 4) was resumed.

Mr King moved to strike out the "exception of Treaties of peace" from the general clause requiring two thirds of the Senate for making Treaties.

Mr Wilson wished the requisition of two thirds to be struck out altogether. If the majority cannot be trusted, it was a proof, as observed by Mr Ghorum, that we were not fit for one Society.

A reconsideration of the whole clause was agreed to.

. . .

Mr Wilson If two thirds are necessary to make peace, the minority may perpetuate war, against the sense of the majority.

. . .

Mr Wilson & Mr Dayton move to strike out the clause requiring two thirds of the Senate for making Treaties—on which,

. . .

Mr McHenry observed that the President had not yet been any where authorised to convene the Senate, and moved to amend Art. X. sect. 2. by striking out the words "he may convene them [the Legislature] on extraordinary occasions" & insert "He may convene both or either of the Houses on extraordinary occasions." This he added would also provide for the case of the Senate being in Session at the time of convening the Legislature.

Mr Wilson said he should vote agst the motion, because it implied that the senate might be in Session, when the Legislature was not, which he thought improper.

. . .

Monday Sepr 10. 1787. In Convention

Mr Sherman moved to add to the article "or the Legislature may propose amendments to the several States for their approbation, but no amendments shall be binding until consented to by the several States."

Mr Gerry 2ded the motion.

Mr Wilson moved to insert "two thirds of" before the words "several States"—on which amendment to the motion of Mr Sherman.

. . .

Mr Wilson then moved to insert "three fourths of" before "the several Sts" which was agreed to nem: con:

. . .

Mr Gerry moved to reconsider art: XXI and XXII. from the latter of which "for the approbation of Congs" had been struck out. He objected to proceeding to change the Government without the approbation of Congress, as being improper and giving just umbrage to that body. He repeated his objections also to an annulment of the confederation with so little scruple or formality.

. . .

M[r] Wilson was against a reconsideration for any of the purposes which had been mentioned.

. . .

M[r] Hamilton then moved to postpone art XXI in order to take up the following, containing the ideas he had above expressed, viz

Resolved that the foregoing plan of a Constitution be transmitted to the U. S. in Congress assembled, in order that if the same shall be agreed to by them, it may be communicated to the Legislatures of the several States, to the end that they may provide for its final ratification by referring the same to the Consideration of a Convention of Deputies in each State to be chosen by the people thereof, and that it be recommended to the said Legislatures in their respective acts for organizing such convention to declare, that if the said Convention shall approve of the said Constitution, such approbation shall be binding and conclusive upon the State, and further that if the said Convention should be of opinion that the same upon the assent of any nine States thereto, ought to take effect between the States so assenting, such opinion shall thereupon be also binding upon such State, and the said Constitution shall take effect between the States assenting thereto"

. . .

M[r] Wilson. This motion being seconded, it is necessary now to speak freely. He expressed in strong terms his disapprobation of the expedient proposed, particularly the suspending the plan of the Convention on the approbation of Congress. He declared it to be worse than folly to rely on the concurrence of the Rhode Island members of Cong[s] in the plan. Maryland has voted on this floor, for requiring the unanimous assent of the 13 States to the proposed change in the federal System. N. York has not been represented for a long time past in the Convention. Many individual deputies from other States have spoken much against the plan. Under these circumstances can it be safe to make the assent of Congress necessary. After spending four or five months in the laborious & arduous task of forming a Government for our Country, we are ourselves at the close throwing insuperable obstacles in the way of its success.

. . .

Friday Sepr 14th 1787. In Convention

The Report of the Committee of Stile & arrangement being resumed.

. . .

To define & punish piracies and felonies on the high seas, and "punish" offences against the law of nations.

Mr Govr Morris moved to strike out "punish" before the words "offences agst the law of nations," so as to let these be *definable* as well as punishable, by virtue of the preceding member of the sentence.

Mr Wilson hoped the alteration would by no means be made. To pretend to *define* the law of nations which depended on the authority of all the civilized nations of the world, would have a look of arrogance, that would make us ridiculous.

. . .

Doc^{r} Franklin moved to add after the words "post roads" Art I. Sect. 8. "a power to provide for cutting canals where deemed necessary"

Mr Wilson 2^{ded} the motion.

Mr Sherman objected. The expence in such cases will fall on the U. States, and the benefit accrue to the places where the canals may be cut.

Mr Wilson. Instead of being an expence to the U. S. they may be made a source of revenue.

Mr Madison suggested an enlargement of the motion into a power "to grant charters of incorporation where the interest of the U. S. might require & the legislative provisions of individual States may be incompetent." His primary object was however to secure an easy communication between the States which the free intercourse now to be opened, seemed to call for. The political obstacles being removed, a removal of the natural ones as far as possible ought to follow. Mr Randolph 2^{ded} the proposition.

Mr King thought the power unnecessary.

Mr Wilson. It is necessary to prevent a *State* from obstructing the *general* welfare.

Mr King. The States will be prejudiced and divided into parties by it. In Philad^{a} & New York, it will be referred to the establishment of a Bank, which has been a subject of contention in those Cities. In other places it will be referred to mercantile monopolies.

Mr Wilson mentioned the importance of facilitating by canals, the communication with the Western Settlements. As to Banks he did not think with Mr King that the power in that point of view would excite the prejudices & parties apprehended. As to mercantile monopolies they are already included in the power to regulate trade.

Col: Mason was for limiting the power to the single case of Canals. He was afraid of monopolies of every sort, which he did not think were by any means already implied by the Constitution as supposed by Mr Wilson.

. . .

Mr Wilson supported the motion.

. . .

Mr Wilson 2^ded^ & supported the motion. Many operations of finance can not be properly published at certain times.

. . .

Saturday Sepr 15th 1787. In Convention

. . .

Art: II. Sect. 2. "he shall have power to grant reprieves and pardons for offences against the U. S. &c"

. . .

Mr Wilson. Pardon is necessary for cases of treason, and is best placed in the hands of the Executive. If he be himself a party to the guilt he can be impeached and prosecuted.

. . .

Monday Sepr 17. 1787. In Convention

The engrossed Constitution being read,

Doc^r^ Franklin rose with a speech in his hand, which he had reduced to writing for his own conveniency, and which Mr Wilson read in the words following.

. . .

Mr King suggested that the Journals of the Convention should be either destroyed, or deposited in the custody of the President. He thought if suffered to be made public, a bad use would be made of them by those who would wish to prevent the adoption of the Constitution.

Mr Wilson prefered the second expedient, he had at one time liked the first best; but as false suggestions may be propagated it should not be made impossible to contradict them.

A question was then put on depositing the Journals and other papers of the Convention in the hands of the President, on which, N. H. ay. M^{tts} ay. C^{t} ay. N. J. ay. Pen^{a} ay. Del. ay. M^{d} no. V^{a} ay. N. C. ay. S. C. ay. Geo. ay.

The President having asked what the Convention meant should be done with the Journals &c, whether copies were to be allowed to the members if applied for. It was Resolved nem: con "that he retain the Journal and other papers, subject to the order of the Congress, if ever formed under the Constitution."

The members then proceeded to sign the instrument.

Whilst the last members were signing it Doct^{r} Franklin looking towards the Presidents Chair, at the back of which a rising sun happened to be painted, observed to a few members near him, that Painters had found it difficult to distinguish in their art a rising from a setting sun. I have said he, often and often in the course of the Session, and the vicisitudes of my hopes and fears as to its issue, looked at that behind the President without being able to tell whether it was rising or setting: But now at length I have the happiness to know that it is a rising and not a setting Sun.

The Constitution being signed by all the members except Mr Randolph, Mr Mason, and Mr Gerry who declined giving it the sanction of their names, the Convention dissolved itself by an Adjournment sine die—[7]

7. Adjournment without a subsequent day being set to meet again.

Wilson's "State House Yard Speech" was one of the first major public defenses of the proposed constitution. By the end of 1787 it had been reprinted in thirty-four newspapers in twelve states and circulated throughout the colonies as a pamphlet. Bernard Bailyn notes that "in the 'transient circumstances' of the time it was not so much the *Federalist* papers that captured most people's imaginations as James Wilson's speech of October 6, 1787, the most famous, to some the most notorious, federalist statement of the time" (*Ideological Origins*, 328).

James Wilson's State House Yard Speech
October 6, 1787.

> Mr. Wilson then rose, and delivered a long and eloquent speech upon the principles of the Foederal Constitution proposed by the late convention. The outlines of this speech we shall endeavour to lay before the public, as tending to reflect great light upon the interesting subject now in general discussion.

Mr. Chairman and Fellow Citizens, Having received the honor of an appointment to represent you in the late convention, it is perhaps, my duty to comply with the request of many gentlemen whose characters and judgments I sincerely respect, and who have urged, that this would be a proper occasion to lay before you any information which will serve to explain and elucidate the principles and arrangements of the constitution, that has been submitted to the consideration of the United States. I confess that I am unprepared for so extensive and so important a disquisition; but the insidious attempts which are clandestinely and industriously made to pervert and destroy the new plan, induce me the more readily to engage in its defence; and the impressions of four months constant attention to the subject, have not been so easily effaced as to leave me without an answer to the objections which have been raised.

It will be proper however, before I enter into the refutation of the charges that are alledged, to mark the leading descrimination between the state constitutions, and the constitution of the United States. When the people established the powers of legislation under their separate governments, they invested their representatives with every right and authority which they did not in explicit terms reserve; and therefore upon every question, respecting the jurisdiction of the house of assembly, if the frame of government is silent, the jurisdiction is efficient and complete. But in delegating foederal powers, another criterion was necessarily introduced, and the congressional authority is to be collected, not from tacit implication, but from the positive grant expressed in the instrument of union. Hence it is evident, that in the former case every thing which is not reserved is given, but in the latter the reverse of the proposition prevails, and every thing which is not given, is reserved. This distinction being recognized, will furnish an answer to those who think the omission of a bill of rights, a defect in the proposed constitution: for it would have been superfluous and absurd to have stipulated with a foederal body of our own creation, that we should enjoy those privileges, of which we are not divested either by the intention or the act, that has brought that body into existence. For instance, the liberty of the press, which has been a copious source of declamation and opposition, what controul can proceed from the foederal government to shackle or destroy that sacred palladium of national freedom? If indeed, a power similar to that which has been granted for the regulation of commerce, had been granted to regulate literary publications, it would have been as necessary to stipulate that the liberty of the press should be preserved inviolate, as that the impost should be general in its operation. With respect likewise to the particular district of ten miles, which is to be made the seat of foederal government, it will undoubtedly be proper to observe this salutary precaution, as there the legislative power will be exclusively lodged in the president, senate, and house of representatives of the United States. But this could not be an object with the convention, for it must naturally depend upon a future compact, to which the citizens immediately interested will, and ought to be parties; and there is no reason to suspect that so popular a privilege will in that case be neglected. In truth then, the proposed system possesses no influence whatever upon the press, and it would have been merely nugatory to have introduced a formal declaration upon the subject—nay, that very declaration might have been construed to imply that some degree of power was given, since we undertook to define its extent.

Another objection that has been fabricated against the new constitution, is expressed in this disingenuous form—"the trial by jury is abolished in civil cases." I must be excused, my fellow citizens, if upon this point, I take advantage of my professional experience to detect the futility of the assertion. Let it be remembered then, that the business of the Foederal Convention was not local, but general; not limited to the views and establishments of a single state, but co-extensive with the continent, and comprehending the views and establishments of thirteen independent sovereignties. When therefore, this subject was in discussion, we were involved in difficulties which pressed on all sides, and no precedent could be discovered to direct our course. The cases open to a trial by jury differed in the different states, it was therefore impracticable on that ground to have made a general rule. The want of uniformity would have rendered any reference to the practice of the states idle and useless; and it could not, with any propriety, be said that "the trial by jury shall be as heretofore," since there has never existed any foederal system of jurisprudence to which the declaration could relate. Besides, it is not in all cases that the trial by jury is adopted in civil questions, for causes depending in courts of admiralty, such as relate to maritime captures, and such as are agitated in courts of equity, do not require the intervention of that tribunal. How then, was the line of discrimination to be drawn? The convention found the task too difficult for them, and they left the business as it stands, in the fullest confidence that no danger could possibly ensue, since the proceedings of the supreme court, are to be regulated by the congress, which is a faithful representation of the people; and the oppression of government is effectually barred, by declaring that in all criminal cases the trial by jury shall be preserved.

This constitution, it has been further urged, is of a pernicious tendency, because it tolerates a standing army in the time of peace.—This has always been a topic of popular declamation; and yet, I do not know a nation in the world, which has not found it necessary and useful to maintain the appearance of strength in a season of the most profound tranquility. Nor is it a novelty with us; for under the present articles of confederation, congress certainly possesses this reprobated power, and the exercise of that power is proved at this moment by her cantonments along the banks of the Ohio. But what would be our national situation were it otherwise? Every principle of policy must be subverted, and the government must declare war, before they are prepared to carry it on. Whatever may be the provocation, however important the object in view, and however necessary dispatch and secrecy may be, still the declaration must precede the preparation, and the enemy will be informed of your intention, not only before you are equipped for an attack, but even before you are fortified for a defence. The consequence is too obvious to require any further delineation, and no man, who regards the dignity and safety of his country, can deny the necessity of a military force, under the controul and with the restrictions which the new constitution provides.

Perhaps there never was a charge made with less reasons than that which predicts the institution of a baneful aristocracy in the foederal senate. This body branches into two characters, the one legislative, and the other executive. In its legislative character it can effect no purpose, without the cooperation of the house of representatives, and in its executive character, it can accomplish no object, without the concurrence of the president. Thus fettered, I do not know any act which the senate can of itself perform, and such dependance necessarily precludes every idea of influence and superiority. But I will confess that in the organization of this body, a compromise between contending interests is descernible; and when we reflect how various are the laws, commerce, habits, population, and extent of the confederated states, this evidence of mutual concession and accommodation ought rather to command a generous applause, than to excite jealousy and reproach. For my part, my admiration can only be equalled by my astonishment, in beholding so perfect a system, formed from such heterogeneous materials.

The next accusation I shall consider, is that which represents the foederal constitution as not only calculated, but designedly framed, to reduce the state governments to mere corporations, and eventually to annihilate them. Those who have employed the term corporation upon this occasion, are not perhaps aware of its extent. In common parlance, indeed, it is generally applied to petty associations for the ease and conveniency of a few individuals; but in its enlarged sense, it will comprehend the government of Pennsylvania, the existing union of the states, and even this projected system is nothing more than a formal act of incorporation. But upon what pretence can it be alledged that it was designed to annihilate the state governments? For, I will undertake to prove that upon their existence, depends the existence of the foederal plan. For this purpose, permit me to call your attention to the manner in which the president, senate, and house of representatives, are proposed to be appointed. The president is to be chosen by electors, nominated in such manner as the legislature of each state may direct; so that if there is no legislature, there can be no electors, and consequently the office of president cannot be supplied. The senate is to be composed of two senators from each state, chosen by the legislature; and therefore if there is no legislature, there can be no senate. The house of representatives, is to be composed of members chosen every second year by the people of the several states, and the electors in each state shall have the qualifications requisite for electors of the most numerous branch of the state legislature,—unless therefore, there is a state legislature, that qualification cannot be ascertained, and the popular branch of the foederal constitution must likewise be extinct. From this view, then it is evidently absurd to suppose, that the annihilation of the separate governments will result from their union; or, that having that intention, the authors of the new system would have bound their connection with such indissoluble ties. Let me here advert to an arrangement highly advantageous, for you will perceive, without prejudice to the powers of the legislature in the election of senators, the people at large will acquire an additional privilege in returning members to the house of representatives—whereas, by the present confederation, it is the legislature alone that appoints the delegates to Congress.

The power of direct taxation has likewise been treated as an improper delegation to the foederal government; but when we consider it as the duty of that body to provide for the national safety, to support the dignity of the union, and to discharge the debts contracted upon the collective faith of the states for their common benefit, it must be acknowledged, that those upon whom such important obligations are imposed, ought in justice and in policy to possess every means requisite for a faithful performance of their trust. But why should we be alarmed with visionary evils? I will venture to predict, that the great revenue of the United States must, and always will be raised by impost, for, being at once less obnoxious, and more productive, the interest of the government will be best promoted by the accommodation of the people. Still however, the objects of direct taxation should be within reach in all cases of emergency; and there is no more reason to apprehend oppression in the mode of collecting a revenue from this resource, than in the form of an impost, which, by universal assent, is left to the authority of the foederal government. In either case, the force of civil institutions will be adequate to the purpose; and the dread of military violence, which has been assiduously disseminated, must eventually prove the mere effusion of a wild imagination, or a factious spirit. But the salutary consequences that must flow from thus enabling the government to receive and support the credit of the union, will afford another answer to the objections upon this ground. The State of Pennsylvania particularly, which has encumbered itself with the assumption of a great proportion of the public debt, will derive considerable relief and advantage; for, as it was the imbecility of the present confederation, which gave rise to the funding law, that law must naturally expire, when a competent and energetic foederal system shall be substituted—the state will then be discharged from an extraordinary burthen, and the national creditor will find it to be his interest to return to his original security.

After all, my fellow citizens, it is neither extraordinary or unexpected, that the constitution offered to your consideration, should meet with opposition. It is the nature of man to pursue his own interest, in preference to the public good; and I do not mean to make any personal reflection, when I add, that it is the interest of a very numerous, powerful, and respectable body to counteract and destroy the excellent work produced by the late convention. All the offices of government, and all the appointments for the administration of justice and the collection of the public revenue, which are transferred from the individual to the aggregate sovereignty of the states, will necessarily turn the stream of influence and emolument into a new channel. Every person therefore, who either enjoys, or expects to enjoy, a place of profit under the present establishment, will object to the proposed innovation; not, in truth, because it is injurious to the liberties of his country, but because it affects his schemes of wealth and consequence. I will confess indeed, that I am not a blind admirer of this plan of government, and that there are some parts of it, which if my wish had prevailed, would certainly have been altered. But, when I reflect how widely men differ in their opinions, and that every man (and the observation applies likewise to every state) has an equal pretension to assert his own, I am satisfied that any thing nearer to perfection could not have been accomplished. If there are errors, it should be remembered, that the seeds of reformation are sown in the work itself, and the concurrence of two thirds of the congress may at any time introduce alterations and amendments. Regarding it then, in every point of view, with a candid and disinterested mind, I am bold to assert, that it is the best form of government which has ever been offered to the world.

Mr. Wilson's speech was frequently interrupted with loud and unanimous testimonies of approbation, and the applause which was reiterated at the conclusion, evinced the general sense of its excellence, and the conviction which it had impressed upon every mind.

Wilson's remarks at the Pennsylvania Ratifying Convention are taken from volume 2 of Jonathan Elliot's *The Debates in the Several State Conventions on the Adoption of the Federal Constitution,* 1836. For the most complete account of the Pennsylvania Ratifying Convention see *The Documentary History of the Ratification of the Constitution, Vol. 2, Ratification by the States: Pennsylvania,* ed. Merrill Jensen, John P. Kaminski, Gasparc J. Saladino, 1976.

Remarks of James Wilson in the Pennsylvania Convention to Ratify the Constitution of the United States, 1787.

Monday, *November* 26, P.M.—Mr. WILSON. The system proposed, by the late convention, for the government of the United States, is now before you. Of that convention I had the honour to be a member. As I am the only member of that body who have the honour to be also a member of this, it may be expected that I should prepare the way for the deliberations of this assembly, by unfolding the difficulties which the late convention were obliged to encounter; by pointing out the end which they proposed to accomplish; and by tracing the general principles which they have adopted for the accomplishment of that end.

To form a good system of government for a single city or state, however limited as to territory, or inconsiderable as to numbers, has been thought to require the strongest efforts of human genius. With what conscious diffidence, then, must the members of the convention have revolved in their minds the immense undertaking which was before them. Their views could not be confined to a small or a single community, but were expanded to a great number of states; several of which contain an extent of territory, and resources of population, equal to those of some of the most respectable kingdoms on the other side of the Atlantick. Nor were even these the only objects to be comprehended within their deliberations. Numerous states yet unformed, myriads of the human race, who will inhabit regions hitherto uncultivated, were to be affected by the result of their proceedings. It was necessary, therefore, to form their calculations on a scale commensurate to a large portion of the globe.

For my own part, I have been often lost in astonishment at the vastness of the prospect before us. To open the navigation of a single river was lately thought, in Europe, an enterprise adequate to imperial glory. But could the commercial scenes of the Scheldt be compared with those that, under a good government, will be exhibited on the Hudson, the Delaware, the Potowmack, and the numerous other rivers, that water and are intended to enrich the dominions of the United States?

The difficulty of the business was equal to its magnitude. No small share of wisdom and address is requisite to combine and reconcile the jarring interests, that prevail, or seem to prevail, in a single community. The United States contain already thirteen governments mutually independent. Those governments present to the Atlantick a front of fifteen hundred miles in extent. Their soil, their climates, their productions, their dimensions, their numbers are different. In many instances a difference and even an opposition subsists among their interests; and a difference and even an opposition is imagined to subsist in many more. An apparent interest produces the same attachment as a real one; and is often pursued with no less perseverance and vigour. When all these circumstances are seen and attentively considered, will any member of this honourable body be surprised, that such a diversity of things produced a proportioned diversity of sentiment? will he be surprised that such a diversity of sentiment rendered a spirit of mutual forbearance and conciliation indispensably necessary to the success of the great work? and will he be surprised that mutual concessions and sacrifices were the consequences of mutual forbearance and conciliation? When the springs of opposition were so numerous and strong, and poured forth their waters in courses so varying, need we be surprised that the stream formed by their conjunction was impelled in a direction somewhat different from that, which each of them would have taken separately?

I have reason to think that a difficulty arose in the minds of some members of the convention from another consideration—their ideas of the temper and disposition of the people, for whom the constitution is proposed. The citizens of the United States, however different in some other respects, are well known to agree in one strongly marked feature of their character—a warm and keen sense of freedom and independence. This sense has been heightened by the glorious result of their late struggle against all the efforts of one of the most powerful nations of Europe. It was apprehended, I believe, by some, that a people so high spirited would ill brook the restraints of an efficient government. I confess that this consideration did not influence my conduct. I knew my constituents to be high spirited; but I knew them also to possess sound sense. I knew that, in the event, they would be best pleased with that system of government, which would best promote their freedom and happiness. I have often revolved this subject in my mind. I have supposed one of my constituents to ask me, why I gave such a vote on a particular question? I have always thought it would be a satisfactory answer to say—because I judged, upon the best consideration I could give, that such a vote was right. I have thought that it would be but a very poor compliment to my constituents to say, that, in my opinion, such a vote would have been proper, but that I supposed a contrary one would be more agreeable to those who sent me to the convention. I could not, even in idea, expose myself to such a retort as, upon the last answer, might have been justly made to me. Pray, sir, what reasons have you for supposing that a right vote would displease your constituents? Is this the proper return for the high confidence they have placed in you? If they have given cause for such a surmise, it was by choosing a representative, who could entertain such an opinion of them. I was under no apprehension, that the good people of this state would behold with displeasure the brightness of the rays of delegated power, when it only proved the superiour splendour of the luminary, of which those rays were only the reflection.

A very important difficulty arose from comparing the extent of the country to be governed, with the kind of government which it would be proper to establish in it. It has been an opinion, countenanced by high authority, "that the natural property of small states is, to be governed as a republick; of middling ones, to be subject to a monarch; and of large empires, to be swayed by a despotick prince; and that the consequence is, that, in order to preserve the principles of the established government, the state must be supported in the extent it has acquired; and that the spirit of the state will alter in proportion as it extends or contracts its limits." This opinion seems to be supported, rather than contradicted, by the history of the governments in the old world. Here then the difficulty appeared in full view. On one hand, the United States contain an immense extent of territory, and, according to the foregoing opinion, a despotick government is best adapted to that extent. On the other hand, it was well known, that, however the citizens of the United States might, with pleasure, submit to the legitimate restraints of a republican constitution, they would reject, with indignation, the fetters of despotism. What then was to be done? The idea of a confederate republick presented itself. This kind of constitution has been thought to have "all the internal advantages of a republican, together with the external force of a monarchical government." Its description is, "a convention, by which several states agree to become members of a larger one, which they intend to establish. It is a kind of assemblage of societies, that constitute a new one, capable of increasing by means of farther association." The expanding quality of such a government is peculiarly fitted for the United States, the greatest part of whose territory is yet uncultivated.

But while this form of government enabled us to surmount the difficulty last mentioned, it conducted us to another, of which I am now to take notice. It left us almost without precedent or guide; and consequently, without the benefit of that instruction, which, in many cases, may be derived from the constitution, and history, and experience of other nations. Several associations have frequently been called by the name of confederate states, which have not, in propriety of language, deserved it. The Swiss cantons are connected only by alliances. The United Netherlands are indeed an assemblage of societies; but this assemblage constitutes no *new one;* and, therefore, it does not correspond with the full definition of a confederate republick. The Germanick body is composed of such disproportioned and discordant materials, and its structure is so intricate and complex, that little useful knowledge can be drawn from it. Ancient history discloses, and barely discloses to our view, some confederate republicks—the Achaean league, the Lycian confederacy, and the Amphyctionick council.[1] But the facts recorded concerning their constitutions are so few and general, and their histories are so unmarked and defective, that no satisfactory information can be collected from them concerning many particular circumstances, from an accurate discernment and comparison of which alone, legitimate and practical inferences can be made from one constitution to another. Besides, the situation and dimensions of those confederacies, and the state

1. The Achaean league refers to a group of twelve ancient Greek city-states in the Peloponnesus. The Lycian confederacy was a group of twenty-three ancient Greek city-states. The Amphyctionick council was a council of twelve Greek nations that met twice a year.

of society, manners, and habits in them, were so different from those of the United States, that the most correct descriptions could have supplied but a very small fund of applicable remark. Thus, in forming this system, we were deprived of many advantages, which the history and experience of other ages and other countries would, in other cases, have afforded us.

Permit me to add, in this place, that the science even of government itself seems yet to be almost in its state of infancy. Governments, in general, have been the result of force, of fraud, and of accident. After a period of six thousand years has elapsed since the creation, the United States exhibit to the world the first instance, as far as we can learn, of a nation, unattacked by external force, unconvulsed by domestick insurrections, assembling voluntarily, deliberating fully, and deciding calmly, concerning that system of government, under which they would wish that they and their posterity should live. The ancients, so enlightened on other subjects, were very uninformed with regard to this. They seem scarcely to have had any idea of any other kinds of governments, than the three simple forms designated by the epithets, monarchical, aristocratical, and democratical. I know that much and pleasing ingenuity has been exerted, in modern times, in drawing entertaining parallels between some of the ancient constitutions and some of the mixed governments that have since existed in Europe. But I much suspect that, on strict examination, the instances of resemblance will be found to be few and weak; to be suggested by the improvements, which, in subsequent ages, have been made in government, and not to be drawn immediately from the ancient constitutions themselves, as they were intended and understood by those who framed them. To illustrate this, a similar observation may be made on another subject. Admiring criticks have fancied, that they have discovered in their favourite Homer the seeds of all the improvements in philosophy, and in the sciences, made since his time. What induces me to be of this opinion is, that Tacitus,[2] the profound politician Tacitus, who lived towards the latter end of those ages which are now denominated ancient, who undoubtedly had studied the constitutions of all the states and kingdoms known before and in his time, and who certainly was qualified, in an un-

2. Gaius Cornelius Tacitus, or Publius, (55–117) was a Roman lawyer, orator, historian, and senator. His works include at least 16 books on Roman history including *The Annals*, *The Histories*, *Germania*, *Agricola*, and *Dialogus*.

common degree, for understanding the full force and operation of each of them, considers, after all he had known and read, a mixed government, composed of the three simple forms, as a thing rather to be wished than expected: and he thinks, that if such a government could even be instituted, its duration could not be long. One thing is very certain, that the doctrine of representation in government was altogether unknown to the ancients. Now the knowledge and practice of this doctrine is, in my opinion, essential to every system, that can possess the qualities of freedom, wisdom, and energy.

It is worthy of remark, and the remark may, perhaps, excite some surprise, that representation of the people is not, even at this day, the sole principle of any government in Europe. Great Britain boasts, and she may well boast, of the improvement she has made in politicks, by the admission of representation: for the improvement is important as far as it goes; but it by no means goes far enough. Is the executive power of Great Britain founded on representation? This is not pretended. Before the revolution, many of the kings claimed to reign by divine right, and others by hereditary right; and even at the revolution, nothing farther was effected or attempted, than the recognition of certain parts of an original contract, supposed at some remote period to have been made between the king and the people. A contract seems to exclude, rather than to imply, delegated power. The judges of Great Britain are appointed by the crown. The judicial authority, therefore, does not depend upon representation, even in its most remote degree. Does representation prevail in the legislative department of the British government? Even here it does not predominate; though it may serve as a check. The legislature consists of three branches, the king, the lords, and the commons. Of these, only the latter are supposed by the constitution to represent the authority of the people. This short analysis clearly shows, to what a narrow corner of the British constitution the principle of representation is confined. I believe it does not extend farther, if so far, in any other government in Europe. For the American States were reserved the glory and the happiness of diffusing this vital principle through all the constituent parts of government. Representation is the chain of communication between the people, and those to whom they have committed the exercise of the powers of government. This chain may consist of one or more links; but in all cases it should be sufficiently strong and discernible.

To be left without guide or precedent was not the only difficulty, in which the convention were involved, by proposing to their constituents a plan of a confederate republick. They found themselves embarrassed with another of peculiar delicacy and importance; I mean that of drawing a proper line between the national government and the governments of the several states. It was easy to discover a proper and satisfactory principle on the subject. Whatever object of government is confined in its operation and effects within the bounds of a particular state, should be considered as belonging to the government of that state; whatever object of government extends in its operation or effects beyond the bounds of a particular state, should be considered as belonging to the government of the United States. But though this principle be sound and satisfactory, its application to particular cases would be accompanied with much difficulty; because, in its application, room must be allowed for great discretionary latitude of construction of the principle. In order to lessen or remove the difficulty arising from discretionary construction on this subject, an enumeration of particular instances, in which the application of the principle ought to take place, has been attempted with much industry and care. It is only in mathematical science, that a line can be described with mathematical precision. But I flatter myself that, upon the strictest investigation, the enumeration will be found to be safe and unexceptionable; and accurate too, in as great a degree as accuracy can be expected in a subject of this nature. Particulars under this head will be more properly explained, when we descend to the minute view of the enumeration which is made in the proposed constitution.

After all, it will be necessary, that, on a subject so peculiarly delicate as this, much prudence, much candour, much moderation, and much liberality should be exercised and displayed, both by the federal government and by the governments of the several states. It is to be hoped, that those virtues in government will be exercised and displayed, when we consider, that the powers of the federal government and those of the state governments are drawn from sources equally pure. If a difference can be discovered between them, it is in favour of the federal government; because that government is founded on a representation of the whole union; whereas the government of any particular state is founded only on the representation of a part, inconsiderable when compared with the whole. Is it not more reasonable to suppose, that the counsels of the whole will embrace the interest of every part, than that the counsels of any part will embrace the interests of the whole.

I intend not, sir, by this description of the difficulties with which the convention were surrounded, to magnify their skill or their merit in surmounting them, or to insinuate that any predicament, in which the convention stood, should prevent the closest and most cautious scrutiny into the performance, which they have exhibited to their constituents and to the world. My intention is of far other and higher aim—to evince by the conflicts and difficulties which must arise from the many and powerful causes which I have enumerated, that it is hopeless and impracticable to form a constitution, which will, in every part, be acceptable to every citizen, or even to every government in the United States; and that all which can be expected is, to form such a constitution as, upon the whole, is the best that can possibly be obtained. Man and perfection!—a state and perfection!—an assemblage of states and perfection! Can we reasonably expect, however ardently we may wish, to behold the glorious union?

I can well recollect, though I believe I cannot convey to others, the impression, which, on many occasions, was made by the difficulties which surrounded and pressed the convention. The great undertaking, at some times, seemed to be at a stand; at other times, its motions seemed to be retrograde. At the conclusion, however, of our work, many of the members expressed their astonishment at the success with which it terminated.

Having enumerated some of the difficulties which the convention were obliged to encounter in the course of their proceedings, I shall next point out the end which they proposed to accomplish. Our wants, our talents, our affections, our passions, all tell us that we were made for a state of society. But a state of society could not be supported long or happily without some civil restraint. It is true that, in a state of nature, any one individual may act uncontrolled by others; but it is equally true, that, in such a state, every other individual may act uncontrolled by him. Amidst this universal independence, the dissensions and animosities between interfering members of the society would be numerous and ungovernable. The consequence would be, that each member, in such a natural state, would enjoy less liberty, and suffer more interruption, than he would in a regulated society. Hence the universal introduction of governments of some kind or other into the social state. The liberty of every member is increased by this introduction; for each gains more by the limitation of the freedom of every other member, than he loses by the limitation of his own. The result is, that civil government is necessary to the perfection and happiness of man. In forming this government, and carrying it into execution, it is essential that the interest and authority of the whole community should be binding on every part of it.

The foregoing principles and conclusions are generally admitted to be just and sound with regard to the nature and formation of single governments, and the duty of submission to them. In some cases they will apply, with much propriety and force, to states already formed. The advantages and necessity of civil government among individuals in society are not greater or stronger than, in some situations and circumstances, are the advantages and necessity of a federal government among states. A natural and a very important question now presents itself. Is such the situation—are such the circumstances of the United States? A proper answer to this question will unfold some very interesting truths.

The United States may adopt any one of four different systems. They may become consolidated into one government, in which the separate existence of the states shall be entirely absorbed. They may reject any plan of union or association, and act as separate and unconnected states. They may form two or more confederacies. They may unite in one federal republick. Which of these systems ought to have been proposed by the convention?—To support with vigour, a single government over the whole extent of the United States, would demand a system of the most unqualified and the most unremitted despotism. Such a number of separate states, contiguous in situation, unconnected and disunited in government, would be, at one time, the prey of foreign force, foreign influence, and foreign intrigue; at another, the victim of mutual rage, rancour, and revenge. Neither of these systems found advocates in the late convention: I presume they will not find advocates in this. Would it be proper to divide the United States into two or more confederacies? It will not be unadvisable to take a more minute survey of this subject. Some aspects, under which it may be viewed, are far from being, at first sight, uninviting. Two or more confederacies would be each more compact and more manageable, than a single one extending over the same territory. By dividing the United States into two or more confederacies, the great collision of interests, apparently or really different and contrary, in the whole extent of their dominion, would be broken, and in a great measure disappear in the several parts. But these advantages, which are discovered from certain points of view, are greatly overbalanced by inconveniences that will appear on a more accurate examination. Animosities, and perhaps wars, would arise from assigning the extent, the limits, and the rights of the different confederacies. The expenses of governing would be multiplied by the number of federal governments. The danger resulting from foreign influence and mutual dissensions would not, perhaps, be less great and alarming in the instance of different confederacies, than in the instance of different though more numerous unassociated states. These observations, and many others that might be made on the subject, will be sufficient to evince, that a division of the United States into a number of separate confederacies would probably be an unsatisfactory and an unsuccessful experiment. The remaining system which the American States may adopt is, a union of them under one confederate republick. It will not be necessary to employ much time or many arguments to show, that this is the most eligible system that can be proposed. By adopting this system, the vigour and decision of a wide spreading monarchy may be joined to the freedom and beneficence of a contracted republick. The extent of territory, the diversity of climate and soil, the number, and greatness, and connexion of lakes and rivers, with which the United States are intersected and almost surrounded, all indicate an enlarged government to be fit and advantageous for them. The principles and dispositions of their citizens indicate, that in this government liberty shall reign triumphant. Such indeed have been the general opinions and wishes entertained since the era of our independence. If those opinions and wishes are as well founded as they have been general, the late convention were justified in proposing to their constituents one confederate republick, as the best system of a national government for the United States.

In forming this system, it was proper to give minute attention to the interest of all the parts; but there was a duty of still higher import—to feel and to show a predominating regard to the superiour interests of the whole. If this great principle had not prevailed, the plan before us would never have made its appearance. The same principle that was so necessary in forming it, is equally necessary in our deliberations, whether we should reject or ratify it.

I make these observations with a design to prove and illustrate this great and important truth—that in our decisions on the work of the late convention, we should not limit our views and regards to the state of

Pennsylvania. The aim of the convention was, to form a system of good and efficient government on the more extensive scale of the United States. In this, as in every other instance, the work should be judged with the same spirit with which it was performed. A principle of duty as well as of candour demands this.

We have remarked, that civil government is necessary to the perfection of society: we now remark, that civil liberty is necessary to the perfection of civil government. Civil liberty is natural liberty itself, devested only of that part, which, placed in the government, produces more good and happiness to the community, than if it had remained in the individual. Hence it follows, that civil liberty, while it resigns a part of natural liberty, retains the free and generous exercise of all the human faculties, so far as it is compatible with the publick welfare.

In considering and developing the nature and end of the system before us, it is necessary to mention another kind of liberty, which has not yet, as far as I know, received a name. I shall distinguish it by the appellation of *federal liberty.* When a single government is instituted, the individuals of which it is composed surrender to it a part of their natural independence, which they before enjoyed as men. When a confederate republick is instituted, the communities of which it is composed surrender to it a part of their political independence, which they before enjoyed as states. The principles which directed, in the former case, what part of the natural liberty of the man ought to be given up, and what part ought to be retained, will give similar directions in the latter case. The states should resign to the national government that part, and that part only, of their political liberty, which, placed in that government, will produce more good to the whole, than if it had remained in the several states. While they resign this part of their political liberty, they retain the free and generous exercise of all their other faculties as states, so far as it is compatible with the welfare of the general and superintending confederacy.

Since states as well as citizens are represented in the constitution before us, and form the objects on which that constitution is proposed to operate, it was necessary to notice and define federal as well as civil liberty.

These general reflections have been made in order to introduce, with more propriety and advantage, a practical illustration of the end proposed to be accomplished by the late convention.

It has been too well known—it has been too severely felt—that the present confederation is inadequate to the government and to the exigencies of the United States. The great struggle for liberty in this country, should it be unsuccessful, will probably be the last one which she will have for her existence and prosperity, in any part of the globe. And it must be confessed, that this struggle has, in some of the stages of its progress, been attended with symptoms that foreboded no fortunate issue. To the iron hand of tyranny, which was lifted up against her, she manifested, indeed, an intrepid superiority. She broke in pieces the fetters which were forged for her, and showed that she was unassailable by force. But she was environed by dangers of another kind, and springing from a very different source. While she kept her eye steadily fixed on the efforts of oppression, licentiousness was secretly undermining the rock on which she stood.

Need I call to your remembrance the contrasted scenes, of which we have been witnesses? On the glorious conclusion of our conflict with Britain, what high expectations were formed concerning us by others! What high expectations did we form concerning ourselves! Have those expectations been realized? No. What has been the cause? Did our citizens lose their perseverance and magnanimity? No. Did they become insensible of resentment and indignation at any high handed attempt, that might have been made to injure or enslave them? No. What then has been the cause? The truth is, we dreaded danger only on one side: this we manfully repelled. But on another side, danger, not less formidable, but more insidious, stole in upon us; and our unsuspicious tempers were not sufficiently attentive, either to its approach or to its operations. Those, whom foreign strength could not overpower, have well nigh become the victims of internal anarchy.

If we become a little more particular, we shall find that the foregoing representation is by no means exaggerated. When we had baffled all the menaces of foreign power, we neglected to establish among ourselves a government, that would ensure domestick vigour and stability. What was the consequence? The commencement of peace was the commencement of every disgrace and distress, that could befal a people in a peaceful state. Devoid of national power, we could not prohibit the extravagance of our importations, nor could we derive a revenue from their excess. Devoid of national importance, we could not procure for our exports a tolerable sale at foreign markets. Devoid of national credit, we saw our publick securities melt in the hands of the holders, like snow before the sun. Devoid of national dignity, we could not, in some instances, perform our treaties on our parts; and, in other instances, we could neither obtain nor compel the performance of them on the part of others. Devoid of national energy, we could not carry into execution our own resolutions, decisions, or laws.

Shall I become more particular still? The tedious detail would disgust me: nor is it now necessary. The years of languor are past. We have felt the dishonour, with which we have been covered: we have seen the destruction with which we have been threatened. We have penetrated to the causes of both, and when we have once discovered them, we have begun to search for the means of removing them. For the confirmation of these remarks, I need not appeal to an enumeration of facts. The proceedings of congress, and of the several states, are replete with them. They all point out the weakness and insufficiency of the present confederation as the cause, and an efficient general government as the only cure of our political distempers.

Under these impressions, and with these views, was the late convention appointed; and under these impressions, and with these views, the late convention met.

We now see the great end which they proposed to accomplish. It was to frame, for the consideration of their constituents, one federal, and national constitution—a constitution that would produce the advantages of good, and prevent the inconveniences of bad government—a constitution, whose beneficence and energy would pervade the whole union, and bind and embrace the interests of every part—a constitution that would ensure peace, freedom, and happiness, to the states and people of America.

We are now naturally led to examine the means, by which they proposed to accomplish this end. This opens more particularly to our view the important discussion before us. But previously to our entering upon it, it will not be improper to state some general and leading principles of government, which will receive particular applications in the course of our investigations.

There necessarily exists in every government a power, from which there is no appeal; and which, for that reason, may be termed supreme, absolute, and uncontrollable. Where does this power reside? To this question, writers on different governments will give different answers. Sir William Blackstone will tell you, that in Britain, the power is lodged in the British parliament; that the parliament may alter the form of the government; and that its power is absolute and without control. The idea of a constitution, limiting and superintending the operations of legislative authority, seems not to have been accurately understood in Britain. There are, at least, no traces of practice, conformable to such a principle. The British constitution is just what the British parliament pleases. When the parliament transferred legislative authority to Henry the eighth, the act transferring it could not, in the strict acceptation of the term, be called unconstitutional.

To control the power and conduct of the legislature by an overruling constitution, was an improvement in the science and practice of government reserved to the American States.

Perhaps some politician, who has not considered, with sufficient accuracy, our political systems, would answer, that, in our governments, the supreme power was vested in the constitutions. This opinion approaches a step nearer to the truth, but does not reach it. The truth is, that, in our governments, the supreme, absolute, and uncontrollable power remains in the people. As our constitutions are superiour to our legislatures; so the people are superiour to our constitutions. Indeed the superiority, in this last instance, is much greater; for the people possess, over our constitutions, control in act, as well as in right.

The consequence is, that the people may change the constitutions, whenever and however they please. This is a right, of which no positive institution can ever deprive them.

These important truths, sir, are far from being merely speculative: we, at this moment, speak and deliberate under their immediate and benign influence. To the operation of these truths, we are to ascribe the scene, hitherto unparallelled, which America now exhibits to the world—a gentle, a peaceful, a voluntary, and a deliberate transition from one constitution of government to another. In other parts of the world, the idea of revolutions in government is, by a mournful and indissoluble association, connected with the idea of wars, and all the calamities attendant on wars. But happy experience teaches us to view such revolutions in a very different light—to consider them only as progressive steps in improving the knowledge of government, and increasing the happiness of society and mankind.

Oft have I viewed with silent pleasure and admiration the force and prevalence, through the United States, of this principle—that the supreme power resides in the people; and that they never part with it. It may be called the *panacea* in politicks. There can be no disorder in the community but may here receive a radical cure. If the errour be in the legislature, it may be corrected by the constitution; if in the constitution, it may be corrected by the people. There is a remedy, therefore, for every distemper in government, if the people are not wanting to themselves. For a people wanting to themselves, there is no remedy: from their power, as we have seen, there is no appeal: to their errour, there is no superiour principle of correction.

There are three simple species of government—monarchy, where the supreme power is in a single person—aristocracy, where the supreme power is in a select assembly, the members of which either fill up, by election, the vacancies in their own body, or succeed to their places in it by inheritance, property, or in respect of some personal right or qualification—a republick or democracy, where the people at large retain the supreme power, and act either collectively or by representation.

Each of these species of government has its advantages and disadvantages.

The advantages of a monarchy are, strength, despatch, secrecy, unity of counsel. Its disadvantages are, tyranny, expense, ignorance of the situation and wants of the people, insecurity, unnecessary wars, evils attending elections or successions.

The advantages of aristocracy are, wisdom, arising from experience and education. Its disadvantages are, dissensions among themselves, oppression to the lower orders.

The advantages of democracy are, liberty, equal, cautious, and salutary laws, publick spirit, frugality, peace, opportunities of exciting and producing abilities of the best citizens. Its disadvantages are, dissensions, the delay and disclosure of publick counsels, the imbecility of publick measures retarded by the necessity of a numerous consent.

A government may be composed of two or more of the simple forms abovementioned. Such is the British government. It would be an improper government for the United States; because it is inadequate to such an extent of territory; and because it is suited to an establishment of different orders of men. A more minute comparison between some parts of the British constitution, and some parts of the plan before us, may, perhaps, find a proper place in a subsequent period of our business.

What is the nature and kind of that government, which has been proposed for the United States, by the late convention? In its principle, it is purely democratical: but that principle is applied in different forms, in order to obtain the advantages, and exclude the inconveniences of the simple modes of government.

If we take an extended and accurate view of it, we shall find the streams of power running in different directions, in different dimensions, and at different heights, watering, adorning, and fertilizing the fields and meadows, through which their courses are led; but if we trace them, we shall discover, that they all originally flow from one abundant fountain. In this constitution, all authority is derived from the people.

Fit occasions will hereafter offer for particular remarks on the different parts of the plan. I have now to ask pardon of the house for detaining them so long.

Wednesday, *October*[3] 28, 1787, A.M.—Mr. WILSON. This will be a proper time for making an observation or two on what may be called the preamble to this Constitution. I had occasion, on a former day, to mention that the leading principle in the politics, and that which pervades the American constitutions, is, that the supreme power resides in the people. This Constitution, Mr. President, opens with a solemn and practical recognition of that principle:—"We, the *people of the United States,* in order to form a more perfect union, establish justice, &c., *do* ordain and establish this Constitution for the United States of America." It is announced in *their* name—it receives its political existence from *their* authority: they ordain and establish. What is the necessary consequence? Those who ordain and establish have the power, if they think proper, to repeal and annul. A proper attention to this principle may, perhaps, give ease to the minds of some who have heard much concerning the necessity of a bill of rights.

Its establishment, I apprehend, has more force than a volume written on the subject. It renders this truth evident—that the people have a right to do what they please with regard to the government. I confess I feel a kind of pride in considering the striking difference between the foundation on which the liberties of this country are declared to stand in this Constitution, and the footing on which the liberties of England are said to be

3. This is a misprint in Elliot's *Debates.* The date should read November 28.

placed. The Magna Charta of England is an instrument of high value to the people of that country. But, Mr. President, from what source does that instrument derive the liberties of the inhabitants of that kingdom? Let it speak for itself. The king says, "*We* have *given* and *granted* to all archbishops, bishops, abbots, priors, earls, barons, and to all the freemen of this our realm, these liberties following, to be kept in our kingdom of England forever." When this was assumed as the leading principle of that government, it was no wonder that the people were anxious to obtain bills of rights, and to take every opportunity of enlarging and securing their liberties. But here, sir, the fee-simple remains in the people at large, and by this Constitution they do not part with it.

I am called upon to give a reason why the Convention omitted to add a bill of rights to the work before you. I confess, sir, I did think that, in point of propriety, the honorable gentleman ought first to have furnished some reasons to show such an addition to be necessary; it is natural to prove the affirmative of a proposition; and, if he had established the propriety of this addition, he might then have asked why it was not made.

I cannot say, Mr. President, what were the reasons of every member of that Convention for not adding a bill of rights. I believe the truth is, that such an idea never entered the mind of many of them. I do not recollect to have heard the subject mentioned till within about three days of the time of our rising; and even then, there was no direct motion offered for any thing of the kind. I may be mistaken in this; but as far as my memory serves me, I believe it was the case. A proposition to adopt a measure that would have supposed that we were throwing into the general government every power not expressly reserved by the people, would have been spurned at, in that house, with the greatest indignation. Even in a single government, if the powers of the people rest on the same establishment as is expressed in this Constitution, a bill of rights is by no means a necessary measure. In a government possessed of enumerated powers, such a measure would be not only unnecessary, but preposterous and dangerous. Whence comes this notion, that in the United States there is no security without a bill of rights? Have the citizens of South Carolina no security for their liberties? They have no bill of rights. Are the citizens on the eastern side of the Delaware less free, or less secured in their liberties, than those on the western side? The state of New Jersey has no bill of rights. The state of New York has no bill of rights. The states of Connecticut and Rhode Island have no bill of rights. I know not whether I have exactly enumerated the states who have not thought it necessary to add *a bill of rights* to their constitutions; but this enumeration, sir, will serve to show by experience, as well as principle, that, even in single governments, a bill of rights is not an essential or necessary measure. But in a government consisting of enumerated powers, such as is proposed for the United States, a bill of rights would not only be unnecessary, but, in my humble judgment, highly imprudent. In all societies, there are many powers and rights which cannot be particularly enumerated. A bill of rights annexed to a constitution is *an enumeration of the powers* reserved. If we attempt an enumeration, every thing that is not enumerated is presumed to be given. The consequence is, that an imperfect enumeration would throw all implied power into the scale of the government, and the rights of the people would be rendered incomplete. On the other hand, an imperfect enumeration of the powers of government reserves all implied power to the people; and by that means the constitution becomes incomplete. But of the two, it is much safer to run the risk on the side of the constitution; for an omission in the enumeration of the powers of government is neither so dangerous nor important as an omission in the enumeration of the rights of the people.

Mr. President, as we are drawn into this subject, I beg leave to pursue its history a little farther. The doctrine and practice of declarations of rights have been borrowed from the conduct of the people of England on some remarkable occasions; but the principles and maxims, on which their government is constituted, are widely different from those of ours. I have already stated the language of Magna Charta. After repeated confirmations of that instrument, and after violations of it repeated equally often, the next step taken in this business was, when the petition of rights was presented to Charles I.

It concludes in this manner: "All of which they most humbly *pray* to be allowed, as their rights and liberties, according to the laws and statutes of this realm." (8*th Par. Hist.* 150.) One of the most material statutes of the realm was Magna Charta; so that we find they continue upon the old ground, as to the foundation on which they rest their liberties. It was not till the era of the revolution that the two houses assume a higher tone, and "*demand* and insist upon all the premises as their undoubted rights and liberties." (*Par. Deb.* 261.) But when the whole transaction is considered, we shall find that those rights and liberties are claimed only on the foundation of an original contract, supposed to have been made, at some former period, between the king and the people. (1 *Blackstone,* 233.)

But, in this Constitution, the citizens of the United States appear dispensing a part of their original power in what manner and what proportion they think fit. They never part with the whole; and they retain the right of recalling what they part with. When, therefore, they possess, as I have already mentioned, the fee-simple of authority, why should they have recourse to the minute and subordinate remedies, which can be necessary only to those who pass the fee, and reserve only a rent-charge?

To every suggestion concerning a bill of rights, the citizens of the United States may always say, WE reserve the right to do what we please.

I concur most sincerely with the honorable gentleman who was last up in one sentiment—that if our liberties will be insecure under this system of government, it will become our duty not to adopt, but to reject it. On the contrary, if it will secure the liberties of the citizens of America,—if it will not only secure their liberties, but procure them happiness,—it becomes our duty, on the other hand, to assent to and ratify it. With a view to conduct us safely and gradually to the determination of that important question, I shall beg leave to notice some of the objections that have fallen from the honorable gentleman from Cumberland, (Whitehill).[4] But, before I proceed, permit me to make one general remark. Liberty has a formidable enemy on each hand; on one there is tyranny, on the other licentiousness. In order to guard against the latter, proper powers ought to be given to government: in order to guard against the former, those powers ought to be properly distributed. It has been mentioned, and attempts have been made to establish the position, that the adoption of this Constitution will necessarily be followed by the annihilation of all the state governments. If this was a necessary consequence, the objection would operate in my mind with exceeding great force. But, sir, I think the inference is rather unnatural, that a government will produce the annihilation of others, upon the very existence of which its own existence depends.

4. Robert Whitehill (1738–1813) was a member of the House of Representatives and state senate of Pennsylvania, and Republican congressman from 1805 to 1813.

Let us, sir, examine this Constitution, and mark its proportions and arrangements. It is composed of three great constituent parts—the legislative department, the executive department, and the judicial department. The legislative department is subdivided into two branches—the House of Representatives and the Senate. Can there be a House of Representatives in the general government, after the state governments are annihilated? Care is taken to express the character of the electors in such a manner, that even the popular branch of the general government cannot exist unless the governments of the states continue in existence.

How do I prove this? By the regulation that is made concerning the important subject of giving suffrage. Article 1, section 2: "And the electors in each state shall have the qualifications for electors of the most numerous branch of the state legislature." Now, sir, in order to know who are qualified to be electors of the House of Representatives, we are to inquire who are qualified to be electors of the legislature of each state. If there be no legislature in the states, there can be no electors of them: if there be no such electors, there is no criterion to know who are qualified to elect members of the House of Representatives. By this short, plain deduction, the existence of state legislatures is proved to be essential to the existence of the general government.

Let us proceed now to the second branch of the legislative department. In the system before you, the senators, sir,—those tyrants that are to devour the legislatures of the states,—are to be chosen by the state legislatures themselves. Need any thing more be said on this subject? So far is the principle of each state's retaining the power of self-preservation from being weakened or endangered by the general government, that the Convention went further, perhaps, than was strictly proper, in order to secure it; for, in this second branch of the legislature, each state, without regard to its importance, is entitled to an equal vote. And in the articles respecting amendments of this Constitution, it is provided "That no state, without its consent, shall be deprived of its equal suffrage in the Senate."

Does it appear, then, that provision for the continuance of the state governments was neglected, in framing this Constitution? On the contrary, it was a favorite object in the Convention to secure them.

The President of the United States is to be chosen by electors appointed in the different states, in such manner as the legislature shall direct. Unless there be legislatures to appoint electors, the President cannot be chosen: the idea, therefore, of the existing government of the states, is presupposed in the very mode of constituting the legislative and the executive departments of the general government. The same principle will apply to the judicial department. The judges are to be nominated by the President, and appointed by him, with the advice and consent of the Senate. This shows that the judges cannot exist without the President and Senate. I have already shown that the President and Senate cannot exist without the existence of the state legislatures. Have I misstated any thing? Is not the evidence indisputable, that the state governments will be preserved, or that the general government must tumble amidst their ruins? It is true, indeed, sir, although it presupposes the existence of state governments, yet this Constitution does not suppose them to be the sole power to be respected.

In the Articles of Confederation, the people are unknown, but in this plan they are represented; and in one of the branches of the legislature, they are represented immediately by persons of their own choice.

I hope these observations on the nature and formation of this system are seen in their full force; many of them were so seen by some gentlemen of the late Convention. After all this, could it have been expected that assertions such as have been hazarded on this floor would have been made—"that it was the business of their deliberations to destroy the state governments; that they employed four months to accomplish this object; and that such was their intentions"? That honorable gentleman may be better qualified to judge of their intentions than themselves. I know my own; and as to those of the other members, I believe that they have been very improperly and unwarrantably represented. Intended to destroy! Where did *he* obtain his information? Let the tree be judged of by its fruit.

Mr. President, the only proof that is attempted to be drawn from the work itself, is that which has been urged from the fourth section of the first article. I will read it: "The times, places, and manner, of holding elections for senators and representatives, shall be prescribed in each state by the legislature thereof; but the Congress may at any time, by law, make or alter such regulations, except as to the places of choosing senators."

And is this a proof that it was intended to carry on this government after the state governments should be dissolved and abrogated? This clause is not only a proper, but necessary one. I have already shown what pains have been taken in the Convention to secure the preservation of the state governments. I hope, sir, that it was no crime to sow the seed of self-preservation in the federal government; without this clause, it would not possess self-preserving power. By this clause, the times, places, and manner of holding elections, shall be prescribed in each state, by the legislature thereof. I think it highly proper that the federal government should throw the exercise of this power into the hands of the state legislatures; but not that it should be placed there entirely without control.

If the Congress had it not in their power to make regulations, what might be the consequences? Some states might make no regulations at all on the subject. And shall the existence of the House of Representatives, the immediate representation of the people in Congress, depend upon the will and pleasure of the state governments? Another thing may possibly happen; I don't say it will; but we were obliged to guard even against possibilities, as well as probabilities. A legislature may be willing to make the necessary regulations; yet the minority of that legislature may, by absenting themselves, break up the house, and prevent the execution of the intention of the majority. I have supposed the case, that some state governments may make no regulations at all; it is possible, also, that they may make improper regulations. I have heard it surmised by the opponents of this Constitution, that the Congress may order the election for Pennsylvania to be held at Pittsburg, and thence conclude that it would be improper for them to have the exercise of the power. But suppose, on the other hand, that the assembly should order an election to be held at Pittsburg; ought not the general government to have the power to alter such improper election of one of its own constituent parts? But there is an additional reason still that shows the necessity of this provisionary clause. The members of the Senate are elected by the state legislatures. If those legislatures possessed, uncontrolled, the power of prescribing the times, places, and manner, of electing members of the House of Representatives, the members of one branch of the general legislature would be the tenants at will of the electors of the other branch; and the general government would lie prostrate at the mercy of the legislatures of the several states.

I will ask, now, Is the inference fairly drawn, that the general government was intended to swallow up the state governments? Or was it calculated to answer such end? Or do its framers deserve such censure from honorable gentlemen? We find, on examining this paragraph, that it contains nothing more than the maxims of self-preservation, so abundantly secured by this Constitution to the individual states. Several other objections have been mentioned. I will not, at this time, enter into a discussion of them, though I may hereafter take notice of such as have any show of weight; but I thought it necessary to offer, at this time, the observations I have made, because I consider this as an important subject, and think the objection would be a strong one, if it was well founded.

Friday, *November* 30, 1787, A.M.—Mr. WILSON. It is objected that the number of members in the House of Representatives is too small. This is a subject somewhat embarrassing, and the Convention who framed the article felt the embarrassment. Take either side of the question, and you are necessarily led into difficulties. A large representation, sir, draws along with it a great expense. We all know that expense is offered as an objection to this system of government; and certainly, had the representation been greater, the clamor would have been on that side, and perhaps with some degree of justice. But the expense is not the sole objection; it is the opinion of some writers, that a deliberative body ought not to consist of more than one hundred members. I think, however, that there might be safety and propriety in going beyond that number; but certainly there is some number so large that it would be improper to increase them beyond it. The British House of Commons consists of upwards of five hundred. The senate of Rome consisted, it is said, at some times, of one thousand members. This last number is certainly too great.

The Convention endeavored to steer a middle course; and, when we consider the scale on which they formed their calculation, there are strong reason why the representation should not have been larger. On the ratio that they have fixed, of one for every thirty thousand, and according to the generally received opinion of the increase of population throughout the United States, the present number of their inhabitants will be doubled in twenty-five years, and according to that progressive proportion, and the ratio of one member for thirty thousand inhabitants, the House of Representatives will, within a single century, consist of more than six hundred members. Permit me to add a further observation on the numbers—that a large number is not so necessary in this case as in the cases of state legislatures. In them there ought to be a representation sufficient to declare the situation of every county, town, and district; and if of every individual, so much the better, because their legislative powers extend to the particular interest and convenience of each. But in the general government, its objects are enumerated, and are not confined, in their causes or operations, to a county, or even to a single state. No one power is of such a nature as to require the minute knowledge of situations and circumstances necessary in state governments possessed of general legislative authority. These were the reasons, sir, that, I believe, had influence on the Convention, to agree to the number of thirty thousand; and when the inconveniences and conveniences, on both sides, are compared, it would be difficult to say what would be a number more unexceptionable.

Saturday, *December* 1, 1787, A.M.—Mr. WILSON. The secret is now disclosed, and it is discovered to be a dread, that the boasted *state sovereignties* will, under this system, be disrobed of part of their power. Before I go into the examination of this point, let me ask one important question. Upon what principle is it contended that the sovereign power resides in the state governments? The honorable gentleman has said truly, that there can be no subordinate sovereignty. Now, if there cannot, my position is, that the sovereignty resides in the people; they have not parted with it; they have only dispensed such portions of power as were conceived necessary for the public welfare. This Constitution stands upon this broad principle. I know very well, sir, that the people have hitherto been shut out of the federal government; but it is not meant that they should any longer be dispossessed of their rights. In order to recognize this leading principle, the proposed system sets out with a declaration that its existence depends upon the supreme authority of the people alone. We have heard much about a consolidated government. I wish the honorable gentleman would condescend to give us a definition of what he meant by it. I think this the more necessary, because I apprehend that the term, in the numerous times it has been used, has not always been used in the same sense. It may be said, and I believe it has been said, that a consolidated government is such as will absorb and destroy the governments of the several states. If it is taken in this view, the plan before us is not a consolidated government, as I showed on a former day, and may, if necessary, show further on some future occasion. On the other hand, if it is meant that the general government will take from the state governments their power in some particulars, it is confessed, and evident, that this will be its operation and effect.

When the principle is once settled that *the people* are the source of authority, the consequence is, that they may take from the subordinate governments powers with which they have hitherto trusted them, and place those powers in the general government, if it is thought that there they will be productive of more good. They can distribute one portion of power to the more contracted circle, called *state governments;* they can also furnish another proportion to the government of the United States. Who will undertake to say, as a state officer, that the people may not give to the general government what powers, and for what purposes, they please? How comes it, sir, that these state governments dictate to their superiors—to the majesty of the people? When I say the *majesty of the people,* I mean the thing, and not a mere compliment to them. The honorable gentleman went further, and said that the state governments were kept out of this government altogether. The truth is,—and it is a leading principle in this system,—that not the states only, but the people also, shall be here represented. And if this is a crime, I confess the general government is chargeable with it; but I have no idea that a safe system of power in the government, sufficient to manage the general interest of the United States, could be drawn from any other source, or vested in any other authority, than that of the people at large; and I consider this authority as the rock on which this structure will stand. If this principle is unfounded, the system must fall. If the honorable gentlemen, before they undertake to oppose this principle, will show that the people have parted with their power to the state governments, then I confess I cannot support this Constitution. It is asked, Can there be *two taxing powers?* Will the people submit to two taxing powers? I think they will, when the taxes are required for the public welfare, by persons appointed immediately by their fellow-citizens.

But I believe this doctrine is a very disagreeable one to some of the state governments. All the objects that will furnish an increase of revenue are eagerly seized by them. Perhaps this will lead to the reason why a state government, when she was obliged to pay only about an eighth part of the loan-office certificates, should voluntarily undertake the payment of about one third part of them. This power of taxation will be regulated in the general government upon equitable principles. No state can have more than her just proportion to discharge; no longer will government be obliged to assign her funds for the payment of debts she does not owe. Another objection has been taken, that the judicial powers are coextensive with the objects of the national government. As far as I can understand the idea of magistracy in every government, this seems to be a proper arrangement; the judicial department is considered as a part of the executive authority of government. Now, I have no idea that the authority should be restricted so as not to be able to perform its functions with full effect. I would not have the legislature sit to make laws which cannot be executed. It is not meant here that the laws shall be a dead letter: it is meant that they shall be carefully and duly considered before they are enacted, and that then they shall be honestly and faithfully executed. This observation naturally leads to a more particular consideration of the government before us. In order, sir, to give permanency, stability, and security to any government, I conceive it of essential importance, that its legislature should be restrained; that there should not only be what we call a *passive,* but an *active* power over it; for, of all kinds of despotism, this is the most dreadful, and the most difficult to be corrected. With how much contempt have we seen the authority of the people treated by the legislature of this state! and how often have we seen it making laws in one session, that have been repealed the next, either on account of the fluctuation of party, or their own impropriety.

This could not have been the case in a compound legislature; it is therefore proper to have efficient restraints upon the legislative body. These restraints arise from different sources. I will mention some of them. In this Constitution, they will be produced, in a very considerable degree, by a *division of the power* in the legislative body itself. Under this system, they may arise likewise from the interference of those officers who will be introduced into the executive and judicial departments. They may spring also from another source—the election by the people; and finally, under this Constitution, they may proceed from the great and last resort—from the *people* themselves. I say, under this Constitution, the legislature may be restrained, and kept within its prescribed bounds, by the interposition of the judicial department. This I hope, sir, to explain clearly and satisfactorily. I had occasion, on a former day, to state that the power of the Constitution was paramount to the power of the legislature acting under that Constitution; for it is possible that the legislature, when acting in that capacity, may transgress the bounds assigned to it, and an act may pass, in the usual *mode*, notwithstanding that transgression; but when it comes to be discussed before *the judges*,—when they consider its principles, and find it to be incompatible with the superior power of the Constitution,—it is their duty to pronounce it *void;* and judges independent, and not obliged to look to every session for a continuance of their salaries, will behave with intrepidity, and refuse to the act the sanction of judicial authority. In the same manner, the President of the United States could shield himself, and refuse to carry into effect an act that *violates* the Constitution.

In order to secure the President from any dependence upon the legislature as to his salary, it is provided that he shall, at stated times, receive for his services a compensation that shall neither be increased nor diminished during the period for which he shall have been elected, and that he shall not receive, within that period, any other emolument from the United States, or any of them.

To secure to the judges this independence, it is ordered that they shall receive for their services a compensation which shall not be diminished during their continuance in office. The Congress may be restrained by the election of its constituent parts. If a legislature shall make a law contrary to the Constitution, or oppressive to the people, they have it in their power, every second year, in one branch, and every sixth year, in the other, to displace the men who act thus inconsistently with their duty; and if this is not sufficient, they have still a further power; they may assume into their own hands the alteration of the Constitution itself; they may revoke the lease when the conditions are broken by the tenant. But the most useful restraint upon the legislature, because it operates constantly, arises from the division of its power among two branches, and from the qualified negative of the President upon both. As this government is formed, there are two sources from which the representation is drawn, though they both ultimately flow from the people. *States* now exist, and others will come into existence; it was thought proper that they should be represented in the general government. But gentlemen will please to remember this Constitution was not framed merely for the states; it was framed for the *people* also; and the popular branch of the Congress will be the objects of their immediate choice.

The two branches will serve as checks upon each other; they have the same legislative authorities, except in one instance. Money bills must originate in the House of Representatives. The Senate can pass no law without the concurrence of the House of Representatives; nor can the House of Representatives without the concurrence of the Senate. I believe, sir, that the observation which I am now going to make will apply to mankind in every situation: they will act with more caution, and perhaps more integrity, if their proceedings are to be under the inspection and control of another, than when they are not. From this principle, the proceedings of Congress will be conducted with a degree of circumspection not common in single bodies, where nothing more is necessary to be done than to carry the business through amongst themselves, whether it be right or wrong. In compound legislatures, every object must be submitted to a distinct body, not influenced by the arguments, or warped by the prejudices, of the other; and I believe that the persons who will form the Congress will be cautious in running the risk, *with a bare majority,* of having the negative of the President put on their proceedings. As there will be more circumspection in forming the laws, so there will be more stability in the laws when made. Indeed, one is the consequence of the other; for what has been well considered, and founded in good sense, will in practice be useful and salutary, and, of consequence, will not be liable to be soon repealed. Though two bodies may not possess more wisdom or patriotism than what may be found in a single body, yet they will necessarily introduce a greater degree of precision. An indigested and inaccurate code of laws is one of the most dangerous things that can be introduced into any government. The force of this observation is well known by every gentleman who has attended to the laws of this state. This, sir, is a very important advantage, that will arise from this division of the legislative authority.

I will proceed now to take some notice of a still further restraint upon the legislature—I mean the qualified *negative* of the President. I think this will be attended with very important advantages for the security and happiness of the people of the United States. The President, sir, will not be a stranger to our country, to our laws, or to our wishes. He will, under this Constitution, be placed in office as the President of the whole Union, and will be chosen in such a manner that he may be justly styled *the man of the people.* Being elected by the different parts of the United States, he will consider himself as not particularly interested for any one of them, but will watch over the whole with paternal care and affection. This will be the natural conduct to recommend himself to those who placed him in that high chair, and I consider it as a very important advantage, that such a man must have every law presented to him, before it can become binding on the United States. He will have before him the fullest information of our situation; he will avail himself not only of records and official communications, foreign and domestic, but he will have also the advice of the executive officers in the different departments of the general government.

If, in consequence of this information and advice, he exercise the authority given to him, the effect will not be lost. He returns his *objections,* together with the bill; and, unless *two thirds* of both branches of the legislature are now found to approve it, it does not become a law. But, even if his objections do not prevent its passing into a law, they will not be useless; they will be kept, together with the law, and, in the archives of Congress, will be valuable and practical materials, to form the minds of posterity for legislation. If it is found that the law operates inconveniently, or oppressively, the people may discover in the President's objections the source of that inconvenience or oppression. Further, sir, when objections shall have been made, it is provided, in order to secure the greatest degree of caution and responsibility, that the *votes* of both houses shall be determined by *yeas* and *nays,* and the names of the persons voting for and against the bill shall be entered in the journal of each house respectively. This much I have thought proper to say, with regard to the distribution of the legislative authority, and the restraints under which it will be exercised.

The gentleman in opposition strongly insists that the general clause at the end of the eighth section gives to Congress a power of legislating generally; but I cannot conceive by what means he will render the words susceptible of that expansion. Can the words, "The Congress shall have power to make all laws which shall be necessary and proper to carry into execution the foregoing powers," be capable of giving them general legislative power? I hope that it is not meant to give to Congress merely an illusive show of authority, to deceive themselves or constituents any longer. On the contrary, I trust it is meant that they shall have the power of carrying into effect the laws which they shall make under the powers vested in them by this Constitution. In answer to the gentleman from Fayette, (Mr. Smilie,)[5] on the subject of the press, I beg leave to make an observation. It is very

5. John Smilie (1741–1812) was a Republican member of the Pennsylvania state legislature and U.S. Representative (1793–1795 and 1799–1812).

true, sir, that this Constitution says nothing with regard to that subject, nor was it necessary; because it will be found that there is given to the general government no power whatsoever concerning it; and no law, in pursuance of the Constitution, can possibly be enacted to destroy that liberty.

I heard the honorable gentleman make this general assertion, that the Congress was certainly vested with power to make such a law; but I would be glad to know by what part of this Constitution such a power is given? Until that is done, I shall not enter into a minute investigation of the matter, but shall at present satisfy myself with giving an answer to a question that has been put. It has been asked, If a law should be made to punish libels, and the judges should proceed under that law, what chance would the printer have of an acquittal? And it has been said he would drop into a den of devouring monsters!

I presume it was not in the view of the honorable gentleman to say there is no such thing as a libel, or that the writers of such ought not to be punished. The idea of the liberty of the press is not carried so far as this in any country. What is meant by the liberty of the press is, that there should be no antecedent restraint upon it; but that every author is responsible when he attacks the security or welfare of the government, or the safety, character, and property of the individual.

With regard to attacks upon the public, the mode of proceeding is by a prosecution. Now, if a libel is written, it must be within some one of the United States, or the district of Congress. With regard to that district, I hope it will take care to preserve this as well as the other rights of freemen; for, whatever district Congress may choose, the cession of it cannot be completed without the consent of its inhabitants. Now, sir, if this *libel* is to be tried, it must be tried where the offence was committed; for, under this Constitution, as declared in the 2d section of the 3d article, the trial must be held in the state; therefore, on this occasion, it must be tried where it was published, if the indictment is for publishing; and it must be tried likewise by a jury of that state. Now, I would ask, is the person prosecuted in a worse situation under the general government, even if it had the power to make laws on this subject, than he is at present under the state government? It is true, there is no particular regulation made, to have the jury come from the body of the county in which the offence was committed; but there are some states in which this mode of collecting juries is contrary to their established custom, and gentlemen ought to consider that this Constitution was not meant merely for Pennsylvania. In some states, the juries are not taken from a single country. In Virginia, the sheriff, I believe, is not confined even to the inhabitants of the state, but is at liberty to take any man he pleases, and put him on the jury. In Maryland, I think, a set of jurors serve for the whole western shore, and another for the eastern shore.

I beg to make one remark on what one gentleman has said, with respect to amendments being proposed to this Constitution. To whom are the Convention to make report of such amendments? He tells you, to the present Congress. I do not wish to report to that body, the representatives only of the state governments; they may not be disposed to admit the people into a participation of their power. It has also been supposed that a wonderful unanimity subsists among those who are enemies to the proposed system. On this point I also differ from the gentleman who made the observation. I have taken every pains in my power, and read every publication I could meet with, in order to gain information; and, as far as I have been able to judge, the opposition is inconsiderable and inconsistent. Instead of agreeing in their objections, those who make them bring forward such as are diametrically opposite. On one hand, it is said that the representation in Congress is too small; on the other, it is said to be too numerous. Some think the authority of the Senate too great; some, that of the House of Representatives; and some, that of both. Others draw their fears from the powers of the President; and, like the iron race of *Cadmus*,[6] these opponents rise only to destroy each other.

Monday, *December* 3, 1787, A.M.—Mr. WILSON. Take detached parts of any system whatsoever, in the manner these gentlemen have hitherto taken this Constitution, and you will make it absurd and inconsistent with itself. I do not confine this observation to human performances alone; it will apply to divine writings. An anecdote, which I have heard, exemplifies this observation. When Sternhold and Hopkins's[7] version of the Psalms was usually sung in the churches, a line was first read by the clerk,

6. Cadmus, ruler of Thebes, slew a dragon. The dragon's teeth, when planted in the ground, produced a horde of armed "earthborn" men, who were tricked into destroying each other.

7. Thomas Sternhold and John Hopkins were the first to publish an English metrical psalter (with a first edition appearing in 1548, and all 150 psalms appearing in 1562). Their versions were popular for the next 150 years despite translation flaws.

and then sung by the congregation. A sailor had stepped in, and heard the clerk read this line—

"The Lord will come, and he will not—"

the sailor stared, and when the clerk read the next line—

"Keep silence, but speak out—"

the sailor left the church, thinking the people were not in their senses.

This story may convey an idea of the treatment of the plan before you; for, although it contains sound sense when connected, yet, by the detached manner of considering it, it appears highly absurd.

Much fault has been found with the mode of expression used in the 1st clause of the 9th section of the 1st article. I believe I can assign a reason why that mode of expression was used, and why the term *slave* was *not* admitted in this *Constitution;* and as to the manner of laying taxes, this is not the first time that the subject has come into the view of the United States, and of the legislatures of the several states. The gentleman, (Mr. Findley)[8] will recollect that, in the present Congress, the quota of the federal debt, and general expenses, was to be in proportion to the value of land, and other enumerated property, within states. After trying this for a number of years, it was found, on all hands, to be a mode that could not be carried into execution. Congress were satisfied of this; and, in the year 1783, recommended, in conformity with the powers they possessed under the Articles of Confederation, that the quota should be according to the number of free people, including those bound to servitude, and excluding Indians not taxed. These were the expressions used in 1783; and the fate of this recommendation was similar to all their other resolutions. It was not carried into effect, but it was adopted by no fewer than eleven out of thirteen states; and it cannot but be matter of surprise to hear gentlemen, who agreed to this very mode of expression at that time, come forward and state it as an objection on the present occasion. It was natural, sir, for the late Convention to adopt the mode after it had been agreed to by eleven states, and to use the expression which they found had been received as unexceptionable before.

8. William Findley (1741/42–1821) was a Revolutionary War soldier, state politician, and U.S. representative (1791–1799 and 1803–1817).

With respect to the clause restricting Congress from prohibiting the *migration or importation of such persons* as any of the states now existing shall think proper to admit, prior to the year 1808, the honorable gentleman says that this clause is not only dark, but intended to grant to Congress, for that time, the power to admit the importation of *slaves.* No such thing was intended. But I will tell you what was done, and it gives me high pleasure that so much was done. Under the present Confederation, the states may admit the importation of slaves as long as they please; but by this article, after the year 1808, the Congress will have power to prohibit such importation, notwithstanding the disposition of any state to the contrary. I consider this as laying the foundation for banishing slavery out of this country; and though the period is more distant than I could wish, yet it will produce the same kind, gradual change, which was pursued in Pennsylvania. It is with much satisfaction I view this power in the general government, whereby they may lay an interdiction on this reproachful trade: but an immediate advantage is also obtained; for a tax or duty may be imposed on such importation, not exceeding ten dollars for each person; and this, sir, operates as a partial prohibition; it was all that could be obtained. I am sorry it was no more; but from this I think there is reason to hope, that yet a few years, and it will be prohibited altogether; and in the mean time, the *new* states which are to be formed will be under *the control* of Congress in this particular, and slaves will never be introduced amongst them. The gentleman says that it is unfortunate in another point of view: it means to prohibit the introduction of white people from Europe, as this tax may deter them from coming amongst us. A little impartiality and attention will discover the care that the Convention took in selecting their language. The words are, "the migration or importation of such persons, &c., shall not be prohibited by Congress prior to the year 1808, but a tax or duty may be imposed on such importation." It is observable here that the term *migration* is dropped, when a tax or duty is mentioned, so that Congress have power to impose the tax only on those imported.

Tuesday, *December* 4, 1787, A.M.—Mr. WILSON. I shall take this opportunity of giving an answer to the objections already urged against the Constitution; I shall then point out some of those qualities that entitle it to the attention and approbation of this Convention; and, after having done this, I shall take a fit opportunity of stating the consequences which, I apprehend, will result from rejecting it, and those which will probably result from its adoption. I have given the utmost attention to the debates, and the objections that, from time to time, have been made by the three gentlemen who speak in opposition. I have reduced them to some order, perhaps not better than that in which they were introduced. I will state them; they will be in the recollection of the house, and I will endeavor to give an answer to them: in that answer, I will interweave some remarks, that may tend to elucidate the subject.

A good deal has already been said concerning *a bill of rights.* I have stated, according to the best of my recollection, all that passed in Convention relating to that business. Since that time, I have spoken with a gentleman, who has not only his memory, but full notes that he had taken in that body, and he assures me that, upon this subject, no direct motion was ever made at all; and certainly, before we heard this so violently supported out of doors, some pains ought to have been taken to have tried its fate within; but the truth is, a bill of rights would, as I have mentioned already, have been not only unnecessary, but improper. In some governments, it may come within the gentleman's idea, when he says it can do no harm; but even in these governments, you find bills of rights do not uniformly obtain; and do those states complain who have them not? Is it a maxim in forming governments, that not only all the powers which are given, but also that all those which are reserved, should be enumerated? I apprehend that the powers given and reserved form the whole rights of the people, as men and as citizens. I consider, that there are very few, who understand the whole of these rights. All the political writers, from *Grotius*[9] and *Puffendorf,* down to *Vattel,*[10] have treated on this subject, but in no one of those books, nor in the aggregate of them all, can you find a complete enumeration of rights, appertaining to the people as men and as citizens.

There are two kinds of government; that where general power is intended to be given to the legislature, and that where the powers are par-

9. Hugo Grotius (1583–1645) was a Dutch philosopher, jurist, and legal theorist. He wrote extensively in the areas of international law and theology.

10. Emmerich de Vattel (1714–1767) was a Swiss philosopher, diplomat, and legal theorist. His most significant work was in the area of international law.

ticularly enumerated. In the last case, the implied result is, that nothing more is intended to be given, than what is so enumerated, unless it results from the nature of the government itself. On the other hand, when general legislative powers are given, then the people part with their authority, and on the gentleman's principle of government, retain nothing. But in a government like the proposed one, there can be no necessity for a bill of rights. For, on my principle, the people never part with their power. Enumerate all the rights of men! I am sure, sir that no gentleman in the late convention would have attempted such a thing. I believe the honorable speakers in opposition on this floor were members of the assembly which appointed delegates to that convention; if it had been thought proper to have sent them into that body, how luminous would the dark conclave have been! So the gentleman has been pleased to denominate that body. Aristocrats as they were, they pretended not to define the rights of those who sent them there. We ask repeatedly, what harm could the addition of a bill of rights do? If it can do no good, I think that a sufficient reason to refuse having any thing to do with it. But to whom are we to report this bill of rights, if we should adopt it? Have we authority from those who sent us here to make one?

It is true, we may propose as well as any other private persons: but how shall we know the sentiments of the citizens of this state and of the other states? Are we certain that any one of them will agree with our definitions and enumerations?

In the second place, we are told, that there is no check upon the government but the people: it is unfortunate, sir, if their superintending authority is allowed as a check; but I apprehend that in the very construction of this government, there are numerous checks. Besides those expressly enumerated, the two branches of the legislature are mutual checks upon each other. But this subject will be more properly discussed when we come to consider the form of the government itself; and then I mean to show the reason why the right of habeas corpus was secured by a particular declaration in its favor.

In the third place we are told, that there is no security for the rights of conscience. I ask the honorable gentleman, what part of this system puts it in the power of congress to attack those rights? When there is no power to attack, it is idle to prepare the means of defence.

After having mentioned, in a cursory manner, the foregoing objections, we now arrive at the leading ones against the proposed system:

The very manner of introducing this constitution, by the recognition of the authority of the people, is said to change the principle of the present confederation, and to introduce a *consolidating* and absorbing government.

In this confederated republic, the sovereignty of the states, it is said, is not preserved. We are told, that there cannot be two sovereign powers, and that a subordinate sovereignty is no sovereignty.

It will be worth while, Mr President, to consider this objection at large. When I had the honor of speaking formerly on this subject, I stated, in as concise a manner as possible, the leading ideas that occurred to me, to ascertain where the supreme and sovereign power resides. It has not been, nor I presume, will be denied, that somewhere there is, and of necessity must be, a supreme, absolute and uncontrollable authority. This, I believe, may justly be termed the sovereign power; for from that gentleman's [Mr Findley] account of the matter, it cannot be sovereign unless, it is supreme; for says he, a subordinate soverergnty is no sovereignty at all. I had the honor of observing, that if the question was asked, where the supreme power resided, different answers would be given by different writers. I mentioned, that *Blackstone* will tell you, that in Britain, it is lodged in the British Parliament; and I believe there is no writer on this subject on the other side of the Atlantic, but supposed it to be vested in that body. I stated further, that if the question was asked, some politicians who had not considered the subject with sufficient accuracy, where the supreme power resided in our governments, he would answer, that it was vested in the state constitutions. This opinion approaches near the truth, but does not reach it; for the truth is, that the supreme, absolute, and uncontrollable authority *remains* with the people. I mentioned, also, that the practical recognition of this truth was reserved for the honor of this country. I recollect no constitution founded on this principle; but we have witnessed the improvement, and enjoy the happiness of seeing it carried into practice. The great and penetrating mind of *Locke* seems to be the only one that pointed towards even the theory of this great truth.

When I made the observation that some politicians would say the supreme power was lodged in our state constitutions, I did not suspect that the honorable gentleman from Westmoreland (Mr. Findley) was included in that description; but I find myself disappointed; for I imagined his opposition would arise from another consideration. His position is, that the supreme power resides in the states, as governments; and mine is, that it *resides* in the people, as the fountain of government; that the people have not—that the people meant not—and that the people ought not—to part with it to any government whatsoever. In their hands it remains secure. They can delegate it in such proportions, to such bodies, on such terms, and under such limitations, as they think proper. I agree with the members in opposition, that there cannot be two sovereign powers on the same subject.

I consider the people of the United States as forming one great community; and I consider the people of the different states as forming communities, again, on a lesser scale. From this great division of the people into distinct communities, it will be found necessary that different proportions of legislative powers should be given to the governments, according to the nature, number, and magnitude of their objects.

Unless the people are considered in these two views, we shall never be able to understand the principle on which this system was constructed. I view the states as made *for* the people, as well as by them, and not the people as made for the states; the people, therefore, have a right, whilst enjoying the undeniable powers of society, to form either a general government, or state governments, in what manner they please, or to accommodate them to one another, and by this means preserve them all. This, I say, is the inherent and unalienable right of the people; and as an illustration of it, I beg to read a few words from the Declaration of Independence, made by the representatives of the United States, and recognized by the whole Union.

> We hold these truths to be self-evident, that all men are created equal; that they are endowed by their Creator with certain unalienable rights; that among these are life, liberty, and the pursuit of happiness; that, to secure these rights, *governments* are instituted among men, *deriving their just powers from the consent of the governed;* that, whenever any form of government becomes destructive of these ends, it is the right of the people to alter or abolish it, and institute new government, laying its foundation on such principles, and organizing its powers in such forms, as to them shall seem most likely to effect their safety and happiness.

This is the broad basis on which our independence was placed: on the same certain and solid foundation this system is erected.

State sovereignty, as it is called, is far from being able to support its weight. Nothing less than the authority of the people could either support it or give it efficacy. I cannot pass over this subject without noticing the different conduct pursued by the late federal Convention, and that observed by the Convention which framed the Constitution of Pennsylvania. On that occasion you find an attempt made to deprive the people of this right, so lately and so expressly asserted in the Declaration of Independence. We are told, in the preamble to the declaration of rights, and frame of government, that *we* "do, by virtue of the authority vested in *us,* ordain, declare, and establish, the following declaration of rights and frame of government, to be the Constitution of this commonwealth, and to remain in force therein unaltered, except in such articles as shall hereafter, on experience, be found to require improvement, and which shall, by the same authority of the people, fairly delegated *as this frame of government directs.*"—An honorable gentleman (Mr. Chambers)[11] was well warranted in saying that all that could be done was done, to cut off the people from the right of amending; for it cannot be amended by any other mode than that which it directs; then, any number more than one third may control any number less than two thirds.

But I return to my general reasoning. My position is, sir, that, in this country, the supreme, absolute, and uncontrollable power resides in the people at large; that they have vested certain proportions of this power in the state governments; but that the fee-simple continues, resides, and remains, with the body of the people. Under the practical influence of this great truth, we are now sitting and deliberating, and under its operation, we can sit as calmly and deliberate as coolly, in order to change a constitution, as a legislature can sit and deliberate under the power of a constitution, in order to alter or amend a law. It is true, the exercise of this power will not probably be so frequent, nor resorted to on so many occasions, in one case as in the other; but the recognition of the principle cannot fail to establish it more firmly. But, because this recognition is made in the proposed Constitution, an exception is taken to the whole of it; for we are

11. Stephen Chambers (1750–1789) was a Revolutionary War soldier and lawyer.

told it is a violation of the present Confederation—*a Confederation of sovereign states.* I shall not enter into an investigation of the present Confederation, but shall just remark that its principle is not the principle of free governments. The people of the United States are not, as such, represented in the present Congress; and, considered even as the component parts of the several states, they are not represented in proportion to their numbers and importance.

In this place I cannot help remarking on the general inconsistency which appears between one part of the gentleman's objections and another. Upon the principle we have now mentioned, the honorable gentleman contended that the powers ought to flow from the states; and that all the late Convention had to do, was to give additional powers to Congress. What is the present form of Congress? A single body, with some legislative, but little executive, and no effective judicial power. What are these additional powers that are to be given? In some cases, legislative are wanting; in others, judicial; and in others, executive. These, it is said, ought to be allotted to the general government. But the impropriety of delegating such extensive trust to one body of men is evident; yet in the same day, and perhaps in the same hour, we are told by honorable gentlemen that those three branches of government are not kept sufficiently distinct in this Constitution; we are told, also, that the Senate, possessing some executive power, as well as legislative, is such a monster, that it will swallow up and absorb every other body in the general government, after having destroyed those of the particular states.

Is this reasoning with consistency? Is the Senate, under the proposed Constitution, so tremendous a body, when checked in their legislative capacity by the House of Representatives, and in their executive authority by the President of the United States? Can this body be so tremendous as the present Congress, a single body of men, possessed of legislative, executive, and judicial powers? To what purpose was Montesquieu read to show that this was a complete tyranny? The application would have been more properly made, by the advocates of the proposed Constitution, against the patrons of the present Confederation.

It is mentioned that this federal government will annihilate and absorb all the state governments. I wish to save, as much as possible, the time of the house: I shall not, therefore, recapitulate what I had the honor of saying last week on this subject. I hope it was then shown that, instead of being abolished, (as insinuated,) from the very nature of things, and from the organization of the system itself, the state governments must exist, or the general governments must fall amidst their ruins. Indeed, so far as to the forms, it is admitted they may remain; but the gentlemen seem to think their power will be gone.

I shall have occasion to take notice of this power hereafter; and, I believe, if it was necessary, it could be shown that the state governments, as states, will enjoy as much power, and more dignity, happiness, and security, than they have hitherto done. I admit, sir, that some of the powers will be taken from them by the system before you; but it is, I believe, allowed on all hands—at least it is not among us a disputed point—that the late Convention was appointed with a particular view to give more power to the government of the Union. It is also acknowledged that the intention was to obtain the advantage of an efficient government over the United States. Now, if power is to be given by that government, I apprehend it must be taken from some place. If the state governments are to retain all the powers they held before, then, of consequence, every new power that is given to Congress must be taken from the people at large. Is this the gentleman's intention? I believe a strict examination of this subject will justify me in asserting that the states, as governments, have assumed too much power to themselves, while they left little to the people. Let not this be called cajoling the people—the elegant expression used by the honorable gentleman from Westmoreland, (Mr. Findley.) It is hard to avoid censure on one side or the other. At some time, it has been said that I have not been at the pains to conceal my contempt of the people; but when it suits a purpose better, it is asserted that I cajole them. I do neither one nor the other. The voice of approbation, sir, when I think that approbation well earned, I confess, is grateful to my ears; but I would disdain it, if it is to be purchased by a sacrifice of my duty or the dictates of my conscience. No, sir; I go practically into this system; I have gone into it practically when the doors were shut, when it could not be alleged that I cajoled the people; and I now endeavor to show that the true and only safe principle for a free people, is a practical recognition of their original and supreme authority.

I say, sir, that it was the design of this system to take some power from the state governments, and to place it in the general government. It was also the design that the people should be admitted to the exercise of some powers which they did not exercise under the present federation. It was thought proper that the citizens, as well as the states, should be represented. How far the representation in the Senate is a representation of states, we shall see by and by, when we come to consider that branch of the federal government.

This system, it is said, "unhinges and eradicates the state governments, and was systematically intended so to do." To establish the intention, an argument is drawn from art. 1st, sect. 4th, on the subject of elections. I have already had occasion to remark upon this, and shall therefore pass on to the next objection—

That the last clause of the 8th section of the 1st article, gives the power of self-preservation to the general government, independent of the states; for, in case of their abolition, it will be alleged, in behalf of the general government, that self-preservation is the first law, and necessary to the exercise of all other powers.

Now, let us see what this objection amounts to. Who are to have this self-preserving power? The Congress. Who are Congress? It is a body that will consist of a Senate and a House of Representatives. Who compose this Senate? Those who are elected by the *legislature* of the different states? Who are the electors of the House of Representatives? Those who are qualified to vote for the most numerous branch of the *legislature* in the separate states. Suppose the state legislatures annihilated; where is the criterion to ascertain the qualification of electors? and unless this be ascertained, they cannot be admitted to vote; if a state legislature is not elected, there can be no Senate, because the senators are to be chosen by the *legislatures only.*

This is a plain and simple deduction from the Constitution; and yet the objection is stated as conclusive upon an argument expressly drawn from the last clause of this section.

It is repeated with confidence, "that this is not a *federal government,* but a complete one, with legislative, executive, and judicial powers: it is a consolidating government." I have already mentioned the misuse of the term; I wish the gentleman would indulge us with his definition of the word. If, when he says it is a consolidation, he means so far as relates to the general objects of the Union,—so far it was intended to be a consolidation, and on such a consolidation, perhaps, our very existence, as a nation, depends. If, on the other hand, (as something which has been said seems to indicate,) he (Mr. Findley) means that it will absorb the governments of the individual states,—so far is this position from being admitted, that it is unanswerably controverted.

The existence of the state governments is one of the most prominent features of this system. With regard to those purposes which are allowed to be for the general welfare of the Union, I think it no objection to this plan, that we are told it is a complete government. I think it no objection, that it is alleged the government will possess legislative, executive, and judicial powers. Should it have only legislative authority, we have had examples enough of such a government to deter us from continuing it. Shall Congress any longer continue to make requisitions from the several states, to be treated sometimes with silent and sometimes with declared contempt? For what purpose give the power to make laws, unless they are to be executed? and if they are to be executed, the executive and judicial powers will necessarily be engaged in the business.

Do we wish a return of those insurrections and tumults to which a sister state was lately exposed? or a government of such insufficiency as the present is found to be? Let me, sir, mention one circumstance in the recollection of every honorable gentleman who hears me. To the determination of Congress are submitted all disputes between states concerning boundary, jurisdiction, or right of soil. In consequence of this power, after much altercation, expense of time, and considerable expense of money, this state was successful enough to obtain a decree in her favor, in a difference then subsisting between her and Connecticut; but what was the consequence? The Congress had no power to carry the decree into execution. Hence the distraction and animosity, which have ever since prevailed, and still continue in that part of the country. Ought the government, then, to remain any longer incomplete? I hope not. No person can be so insensible to the lessons of experience as to desire it.

It is brought as an objection "that there will be a rivalship between the state governments and the general government; on each side endeavors will be made to increase power."

Let us examine a little into this subject. The gentlemen tell you, sir, that they expect the states will not possess any power. But I think there is reason to draw a different conclusion. Under this system, their respectability and power will increase with that of the general government. I believe their happiness and security will increase in a still greater proportion. Let us attend a moment to the situation of this country. It is a maxim of every government, and it ought to be a maxim with us, that the increase of numbers increases the dignity and security, and the respectability, of all governments. It is the first command given by the Deity to man, Increase and multiply. This applies with peculiar force to this country, the smaller part of whose territory is yet inhabited. We are representatives, sir, not merely of the present age, but of future times; not merely of the territory along the sea-coast, but of regions immensely extended westward. We should fill, as fast as possible, this extensive country, with men who shall live happy, free, and secure. To accomplish this great end ought to be the leading view of all our patriots and statesmen. But how is it to be accomplished, but by establishing peace and harmony among ourselves, and dignity and respectability among foreign nations? By these means, we may draw members from the other side of the Atlantic, in addition to the natural sources of population. Can either of these objects be attained without a protecting head? When we examine history, we shall find an important fact, and almost the only fact which will apply to all confederacies:—

They have all fallen to pieces, and have not absorbed the government.

In order to keep republics together, they must have a strong binding force, which must be either external or internal. The situation of this country shows that no foreign force can press us together; the bonds of our union ought therefore to be indissolubly strong.

The *powers of the states,* I apprehend, will increase with the population and the happiness of their inhabitants. Unless we can establish a character abroad, we shall be unhappy from foreign restraints or internal violence. These reasons, I think, prove sufficiently the necessity of having a federal head. Under it, the advantages enjoyed by the whole Union would be participated by every state. I wish honorable gentlemen would think not only of themselves, not only of the present age, but of others, and of future times.

It has been said "that the *state governments* will not be able to make head against the *general government;*" but it might be said, with more propriety, that the general government will not be able to maintain the powers given it against the encroachments and combined attacks of the state governments. They possess some particular advantages from which the general government is restrained. By this system there is a provision made in the Constitution, that no senator or representative shall be appointed to any civil office under the authority of the United States, which shall have been created, or the emoluments whereof shall have been increased, during the time for which he was elected; and no person holding any office under the United States can be a member of either house. But there is no similar security against state influence, as a representative may enjoy places, and even sinecures, under the state governments. On which side is the door most open to *corruption*? If a person in the legislature is to be influenced by an office, the general government can give him none unless he vacate his seat. When the influence of office comes from the state government, he can retain his seat and salary too. But it is added, under this head, "that state governments will lose the attachment of the people, by losing the power of conferring advantages, and that the people will not be at the expense of keeping them up." Perhaps the state governments have already become so expensive as to alarm the gentlemen on that head. I am told that the civil list of this state amounted to £40,000 in one year. Under the proposed government, I think it would be possible to obtain, in Pennsylvania, every advantage we now possess, with a civil list that shall not exceed one third of that sum.

How differently the same thing is talked of, if it be a favorite or otherwise! When advantages to an officer are to be derived from the general government, we hear them mentioned by the name of *bribery;* but when we are told of the state governments' losing the power of conferring advantages, by the disposal of offices, it is said they will lose the attachment of the people. What is in one instance corruption and bribery, is in another the power of conferring advantages.

We are informed "that the state elections will be ill attended, and that the state governments will become mere boards of electors." Those who have a due regard for their country will discharge their duty and attend; but those who are brought only from interest or persuasion had better stay away; the public will not suffer any disadvantage from their absence. But the honest citizen, who knows the value of the privilege, will undoubtedly attend, to secure the man of his choice. The power and business of the state legislatures relate to the great objects of life, liberty and property; the same are also objects of the general government.

Certainly, the citizens of America will be as tenacious in the one instance as in the other. They will be interested, and I hope will exert themselves, to secure their rights not only from being injured by the state governments, but also from being injured by the general government.

"The power over elections, and of judging of elections, gives absolute sovereignty." This power is given to every state legislature; yet I see no necessity that the power of absolute sovereignty should accompany it. My general position is, that the absolute sovereignty never goes from the people.

We are told "that it will be in the power of the Senate to prevent any addition of representatives to the lower house."

I believe their power will be pretty well balanced; and though the Senate should have a desire to do this, yet the attempt will answer no purpose, for the House of Representatives will not let them have a farthing of public money till they agree to it; and the latter influence will be as strong as the other.

"Annual assemblies are necessary," it is said; and I answer, in many instances they are very proper. In Rhode Island and Connecticut, they are elected for six months. In larger states, that period would be found very inconvenient; but, in a government as large as that of the United States, I presume that annual *elections* would be more disproportionate than elections for six months would be in some of our largest states.

"The British Parliament took to themselves the prolongation of their sitting to seven years. But, even in the British Parliament, the appropriations are annual."

But, sir, how is the argument to apply here? How are the Congress to assume such a power? They cannot assume it under the Constitution, for that expressly provides, "The members of the House of Representatives shall be chosen, every two years, by the people of the several states, and the senators for six years." So, if they take it at all, they must take it by usurpation and force.

Appropriations may be made for two years, though in the British Parliament they are made but for one. For some purposes, such appropriations may be made annually; but for every purpose, they are not: even for a standing army, they may be made for seven, ten, or fourteen years: the civil list is established during the life of a prince. Another objection is, "that the members of the Senate may enrich themselves; they may hold their office as long as they live, and there is no power to prevent them; the Senate will swallow up every thing." I am not a blind admirer of this system. Some of the powers of the senators are not, with me, the favorite parts of it; but as they stand connected with other parts, there is still security against the efforts of that body. It was with great difficulty that security was obtained, and I may risk the conjecture that, if it is not now accepted, it never will be obtained again from the same states. Though the *Senate* was not a favorite of mine, as to some of its powers, yet it was a favorite with a majority in the Union; and we must submit to that majority, or we must break up the Union. It is but fair to repeat those reasons that weighed with the Convention: perhaps I shall not be able to do them justice; but yet I will attempt to show why additional powers were given to the Senate rather than to the House of Representatives. These additional powers, I believe, are, that of trying impeachments, that of concurring with the President in making *treaties*, and that of concurring in the appointment of officers. These are the powers that are stated as improper. It is fortunate, that, in the extent of every one of them, the Senate stands controlled. If it is that monster which it is said to be, it can only show its teeth; it is unable to bite or devour. With regard to *impeachments*, the Senate can try none but such as will be brought before them by the House of Representatives.

The Senate can make no treaties: they can approve of none, unless the President of the United States lays it before them. With regard to the appointment of officers, the President must nominate before they can vote; so that, if the powers of either branch are perverted, it must be with the approbation of some one of the other branches of government. Thus checked on each side, they can do no one act of themselves.

"The powers of Congress extend to taxation—to direct taxation—to internal taxation—to poll taxes—to excises—to other state and internal purposes." Those who possess the power to tax, possess all other sovereign power. That their powers are thus extensive is admitted; and would any thing short of this have been sufficient? Is it the wish of these gentlemen—if it is, let us hear their sentiments—that the general government should subsist on the bounty of the states? Shall it have the power to contract, and no power to fulfil the contract? Shall it have the power to borrow money, and no power to pay the principal or interest? Must we go on in the track that we have hitherto pursued? And must we again compel those in Europe, who lent us money in our distress, to advance the money to pay themselves interest on the certificates of the debts due to them?

This was actually the case in Holland the last year. Like those who have shot one arrow, and cannot regain it, they have been obliged to shoot another in the same direction, in order to recover the first. It was absolutely necessary, sir, that this government should possess these rights; and why should it not, as well as the state governments? Will this government be fonder of the exercise of this authority than those of the states are? Will the states, who are equally represented in one branch of the legislature, be more opposed to the payment of what shall be required by the future, than what has been required by the present Congress? Will the people, who must indisputably pay the whole, have more objections to the payment of this tax, because it is laid by persons of their own immediate appointment, even if those taxes were to continue as oppressive as they now are? But, under the general power of this system, that cannot be the case in Pennsylvania. Throughout the Union, direct taxation will be lessened, at least in proportion to the increase of the other objects of revenue. In this Constitution, a power is given to Congress to collect imposts, which is not given by the present Articles of the Confederation. A very considerable part of the revenue of the United States will arise from that source; it is the easiest, most just, and most productive mode of raising revenue; and it is a safe one, because it is voluntary. No man is obliged to consume more than he pleases, and each buys in proportion only to his consumption. The price of the commodity is blended with the tax, and the person is often not sensible of the payment. But would it have been proper to rest the matter there? Suppose this fund should not prove sufficient; ought the public debts to remain unpaid, or the exigencies of government be left unprovided for? should our tranquillity be exposed to the assaults of foreign enemies, or violence among ourselves, because the objects of commerce may not furnish a sufficient revenue to secure them all? Certainly, Congress should possess the power of raising revenue from their constituents, for the purpose mentioned in the 8th section of the 1st article; that is, "to pay the debts and provide for the common defence and general welfare of the United States." It has been common with the gentlemen, on this subject, to present us with frightful pictures. We are told of the hosts of tax-gatherers that will swarm through the land; and whenever taxes are mentioned, military force seems to be an attending idea. I think I may venture to predict, that the taxes of the general government, if any shall be laid, will be more equitable, and much less expensive than those imposed by state governments.

I shall not go into an investigation of this subject, but it must be confessed, that scarcely any mode of laying and collecting taxes can be more burdensome than the present.

Another objection is, "that Congress may borrow money, keep up standing armies, and command the militia." The present Congress possesses the power of borrowing money and of keeping up standing armies. Whether it will be proper at all times to keep up a body of troops, will be a question to be determined by Congress; but I hope the necessity will not subsist at all times. But if it should subsist, where is the gentleman that will say that they ought not to possess the necessary power of keeping them up?

It is urged, as a general objection to this system, that "the powers of Congress are unlimitted and undefined, and that they will be the judges in all cases, of what is necessary and proper for them to do." To bring this subject to your view, I need do no more than to point to the words in the constitution, beginning at the 8th sect. art. 1st. "The Congress (it says) shall have power, &c." I need not read over the words, but I leave it to every gentleman to say whether the powers are not as accurately and minutely defined, as can be well done on the same subject, in the same language. The old constitution is as strongly marked on this subject, and even the concluding clause, with which so much fault has been found, gives no more, or other powers; nor does it in any degree go beyond the particular enumeration; for when it is said, that Congress shall have power to make all laws which shall be necessary and proper, those words are limited, and defined by the following, "for carrying into execution the foregoing powers." It is saying no more than that the powers we have already particularly given, shall be effectually carried into execution.

I shall not detain the house at this time, with any further observations on the liberty of the press, until it is shown that Congress have any power whatsoever to interfere with it, by licensing it to declaring what shall be a libel.

I proceed to another objection, which was not so fully stated as I believe it will be hereafter; I mean the objection against the *judicial department.* The gentleman from Westmoreland only mentioned it to illustrate his objection to the legislative department.

He said "that the judicial powers were co-extensive with the legislative powers, and extend even to capital cases." I believe they ought to be co-extensive, otherwise laws would be framed that could not be executed. Certainly, therefore, the executive and judicial departments ought to have power commensurate to the extent of the laws; for, as I have already asked, are we to give power to make laws, and no power to carry them into effect?

I am happy to mention the punishment annexed to one crime. You will find the current running strong in favor of humanity. For this is the first instance, in which it has not been left to the legislature to extend the crime and punishment of treason so far as they thought proper. This punishment, and the description of this crime, are the great sources of danger and persecution, on the part of government against the citizen. Crimes against the state! and against the officers of the state! History informs us that more wrong may be done on this subject than on any other whatsoever. But under this constitution there can be no treason against the United States, except such as is defined in this constitution. The manner of trial is clearly pointed out; the positive testimony of two witnesses to the same overt act, or a confession in open court, is required to convict any person of treason. And, after all, the consequences of the crime shall extend no further than the life of the criminal; for no attainder of treason shall work corruption of blood or forfeiture, except during the life of the person attainted.

I come now to consider the last set of objections that are offered gainst this constitution. It is urged, that this is not such a system as was within the powers of the convention; they assumed the *power of proposing.* I believe they might have made proposals without going beyond their powers. I never heard before, that to make a proposal was an exercise of power. But if it is an exercise of power, they certainly did assume it; yet they did not act as that body who framed the present constitution of Pennsylvania acted; they did not by an ordinance attempt to rivet the constitution on the people, before they could vote for members of Assembly under it. Yet such was the effect of the ordinance that attended the Constitution of this commonwealth.

I think the late Convention has done nothing beyond their powers. The fact is, they have exercised no power at all; and, in point of validity, this Constitution, proposed by them for the government of the United States, claims no more than a production of the same nature would claim, flowing from a private pen. It is laid before the citizens of the United States, unfettered by restraint; it is laid before them to be judged by the natural, civil, and political rights of men. By their *fiat*, it will become of value and authority; without it, it will never receive the character of authenticity and power. The business, we are told, which was intrusted to the late Convention, was merely to amend the present Articles of Confederation. This observation has been frequently made, and has often brought to my mind a story that is related of Mr. Pope,[12] who, it is well known, was not a little deformed. It was customary with him to use this phrase, "God mend me!" when any little accident happened. One evening, a link-boy was lighting him along, and, coming to a gutter, the boy jumped nimbly over it. Mr. Pope called to him to turn, adding, "God mend me!" The arch rogue, turning to light him, looked at him, and repeated, "God mend you! He would sooner make half-a-dozen new ones." This would apply to the present Confederation; for it would be easier to make another than to amend this. The gentlemen urge that this is such a government as was not expected by the people, the legislatures, nor by the honorable gentlemen who mentioned it. Perhaps it was not such as was expected, but it may be better; and is that a reason why it should not be adopted? It is not worse, I trust, than the former. So that the argument of its being a system not expected, is an argument more strong in its favor than against it.

The letter which accompanies this Constitution must strike every person with the utmost force.

> The friends of our country have long seen and desired that the power of war, peace, and treaties, that of levying money and regulating commerce, and the corresponding executive and judicial authorities, should be fully

12. Alexander Pope (1688–1744) was an English poet.

and effectually vested in the general government of the Union; but the impropriety of delegating such extensive trust to one body of men, is evident. *Hence results the necessity of a different organization.*

I therefore do not think that it can be urged, as an objection against this system, that it was not expected by the people. We are told, to add greater force to these objections, that they are not on local but on general principles, and that they are uniform throughout the United States. I confess I am not altogether of that opinion; I think some of the objections are inconsistent with others, arising from a different quarter, and I think some are inconsistent even with those derived from the same source. But, on this occasion, let us take the fact for granted, that they are all on general principles, and uniform throughout the United States. Then we can judge of their full amount; and what are they, but trifles light as air? We see the whole force of them; for, according to the sentiments of opposition, they can nowhere be stronger, or more fully stated, than here. The conclusion, from all these objections, is reduced to a point, and the plan is declared to be inimical to our liberties. I have said nothing, and mean to say nothing, concerning the dispositions or characters of those that framed the work now before you. I agree that it ought to be judged by its own intrinsic qualities. If it has not merit, weight of character ought not to carry it into effect. On the other hand, if it has merit, and is calculated to secure the blessings of liberty, and to promote the general welfare, then such objections as have hitherto been made ought not to influence us to reject it.

I am now led to consider those qualities that this system of government possesses, which will entitle it to the attention of the United States. But as I have somewhat fatigued myself, as well as the patience of the honorable members of this house, I shall defer what I have to add on this subject until the afternoon.

Eodem Die,[13] P.M.—Mr. WILSON. Before I proceed to consider those qualities in the Constitution before us, which I think will insure it our approbation, permit me to make some remarks—and they shall be very concise—upon the objections that were offered this forenoon, by the member from Fayette, (Mr. Smilie.) I do it at this time, because I think it will be better to give a satisfactory answer to the whole of the objections, before I

13. On the same day.

proceed to the other part of my subject. I find that the doctrine of a single legislature is not to be contended for in this Constitution. I shall therefore say nothing on that point. I shall consider that part of the system, when we come to view its excellences. Neither shall I take particular notice of his observation on the *qualified negative* of the President; for he finds no fault with it: he mentions, however, that he thinks it a vain and useless power, because it can never be executed. The reason he assigns for this is, that the king of Great Britain, who has an absolute negative over the laws proposed by Parliament, has never exercised it, at least for many years. It is true, and the reason why he did not exercise it was that, during all that time, the king possessed a negative before the bill had passed through the two houses—a much stronger power than a negative after debate. I believe, since the revolution, at the time of William III., it was never known that a bill disagreeable to the crown passed both houses. At one time, in the reign of Queen Anne, when there appeared some danger of this being effected, it is well known that she created twelve peers, and by that means effectually defeated it. Again: there was some risk, of late years, in the present reign, with regard to Mr. Fox's East India Bill, as it is usually called, that passed through the House of Commons; but the king had interest enough in the House of Peers to have it thrown out; thus it never came up for the royal assent. But that is no reason why this negative should not be exercised here, and exercised with great advantage. Similar powers are known in more than one of the states. The governors of Massachusetts and New York have a power similar to this, and it has been exercised frequently to good effect.

I believe the governor of New York, under this power, has been known to send back five or six bills in a week; and I well recollect that, at the time the funding system was adopted by our legislature, the people in that state considered the negative of the governor as a great security that their legislature would not be able to encumber them by a similar measure. Since that time, an alteration has been supposed in the governor's conduct, but there has been no alteration in his power.

The honorable gentleman from Westmoreland, (Mr. Findley,) by his highly-refined critical abilities, discovers an inconsistency in this part of the Constitution, and that which declares, in section 1, "All legislative powers, herein granted, shall be vested in a Congress of the United States, which shall consist of a Senate and a House of Representatives;" and yet here, says he, is a power of legislation given to the President of the United States, because every bill, before it becomes a law, shall be presented to him. Thus he is said to possess legislative powers. Sir, the Convention observed, on this occasion, strict propriety of language: "If he approve the bill, when it is sent, he shall sign it, but if not, he shall return it;" but no bill passes in consequence of having his assent: therefore, he possesses no legislative authority.

The *effect* of this power, upon this subject, is merely this: if he disapproves a bill, two thirds of the legislature become necessary to pass it into a law, instead of a bare majority. And when two thirds are in favor of the bill, it becomes a law, not by his, but by authority of the two houses of the legislature. We are told, in the next place, by the honorable gentleman from Fayette, (Mr. Smilie,) that, in the different orders of mankind, there is that of a natural aristocracy. On some occasions there is a kind of magical expression, used to conjure up ideas that may create uneasiness and apprehension. I hope the meaning of the words is understood by the gentleman who used them. I have asked repeatedly of gentlemen to explain, but have not been able to obtain the explanations of what they meant by a consolidated government. They keep round and round about the thing, but never define. I ask now what is meant by a natural aristocracy. I am not at a loss for the etymological definition of the term; for, when we trace it to the language from which it is derived, an aristocracy means nothing more or less than a government of the best men in the community, or those who are recommended by the words of the Constitution of Pennsylvania, where it is directed that the representatives should consist of those most noted for wisdom and virtue. Is there any danger in such representation? I shall never find fault that such characters can be obtained! If this is meant by a natural aristocracy,—and I know no other,—can it be objectionable that men should be employed that are most noted for their virtue and talents? And are attempts made to mark out these as the most improper persons for the public confidence?

I had the honor of giving a definition—and I believe it was a just one—of what is called an *aristocratic government.* It is a government where the supreme power is not retained by the people, but resides in a select body of men, who either fill up the vacancies that happen, by their own choice and election, or succeed on the principle of descent, or by virtue of territorial possessions, or some other qualifications that are not the result of personal properties. When I speak of personal properties, I mean the qualities of the head and the disposition of the heart.

We are told that the representatives will not be known to the people, nor the people to the representatives, because they will be taken from large districts, where they cannot be particularly acquainted. There has been some experience, in several of the states, upon this subject; and I believe the experience of all who had experience, demonstrates that the larger the district of election, the better the representation. It is only in remote corners of a government that little demagogues arise. Nothing but real weight of character can give a man real influence over a large district. This is remarkably shown in the commonwealth of Massachusetts. The members of the House of Representatives are chosen in very small districts; and such has been the influence of party cabal, and little intrigue in them, that a great majority seem inclined to show very little disapprobation of the conduct of the insurgents in that state.

The governor is chosen by the people at large, and that state is much larger than any district need be under the proposed Constitution. In their choice of their governor, they have had warm disputes; but, however warm the disputes, their choice only vibrated between the most eminent characters. Four of their candidates are well known—Mr. Hancock, Mr. Bowdoin, General Lincoln, and Mr. Goreham, the late president of Congress.

I apprehend it is of more consequence to be able to know the true interest of the people than their faces, and of more consequence still to have virtue enough to pursue the means of carrying that knowledge usefully into effect. And surely, when it has been thought, hitherto, that a representation, in Congress, of from five to two members, was sufficient to represent the interest of this state, is it not more than sufficient to have ten members in that body—and those in a greater comparative proportion than heretofore? The citizens of Pennsylvania will be represented by eight, and the state by two. This, certainly, though not gaining enough, is gaining a good deal; the members will be more distributed through the state, being the immediate choice of the people, who hitherto have not been represented in that body. It is said, that the House of Representatives will be subject to corruption, and the *Senate* possess the means of corrupting, by the share they have in the appointment to office. This was not spoken in the soft language of attachment to government. It is, perhaps, impossible, with all the caution of legislators and statesmen, to exclude corruption and undue influence entirely from government. All that can be done, upon this subject, is done in the Constitution before you. Yet it behoves us to call out, and add every guard and preventive in our power. I think, sir, something very important, on this subject, is done in the present system; for it has been provided, effectually, that the man that has been bribed by an office shall have it no longer in his power to earn his wages. The moment he is engaged to serve the Senate, in consequence of their gift, he no longer has it in his power to sit in the House of Representatives; for "No representative shall, during the term for which he was elected, be appointed to any civil office, under the authority of the United States, which shall have been created, or the emoluments whereof shall have been increased, during such time." And the following annihilates corruption of that kind: "And no person holding any office under the United States shall be a member of either house during his continuance in office." So the mere acceptance of an office, as a bribe, effectually destroys the end for which it was offered. Was this attended to when it was mentioned that the members of the one house could be bribed by the other? "But the members of the Senate may enrich themselves," was an observation made as an objection to this system.

As the mode of doing this has not been pointed out, I apprehend the objection is not much relied upon. The Senate are incapable of receiving any money, except what is paid them out of the public treasury. They cannot vote to themselves a single penny, unless the proposition originates from the other house. This objection, therefore, is visionary, like the following one—"that pictured group, that numerous host, and prodigious swarm of officers, which are to be appointed under the general government." The gentlemen tell you that there must be judges of the supreme, and judges of the inferior courts, with all their appendages: there will be tax-gatherers swarming throughout the land. "O!" say they, "if we could enumerate the offices, and the numerous officers that must be employed every day in collecting, receiving, and comptrolling, the moneys of the United States, the number would be almost beyond imagination."

I have been told, but I do not vouch for the fact, that there are, in one shape or another, more than a thousand persons, in this very state, who get their living by assessing and collecting our revenues from the other citizens. Sir, when this business of revenue is conducted on a general plan, we may be able to do the business of the thirteen states with an equal, nay, with a less number: instead of thirteen comptroller-generals, one comptroller will be sufficient. I apprehend that the number of officers, under this system, will be greatly reduced from the number now employed; for, as Congress can now do nothing effectually, the states are obliged to do every thing; and in this very point I apprehend that we shall be great gainers.

Sir, I confess I wish the *powers of the Senate* were not as they are. I think it would have been better if those powers had been distributed in other parts of the system. I mentioned some circumstances, in the forenoon, that I had observed on this subject. I may mention now, we may think ourselves very well off, sir, that things are as well as they are, and that that body is even so much restricted. But surely objections of this kind come with a bad grace from the advocates, or those who prefer the present Confederation, and who wish only to increase the powers of the present Congress. A single body, not constituted with checks, like the proposed one, who possess not only the power of making treaties, but executive powers, would be a perfect despotism; but further, these powers are, in the present Confederation, possessed without control.

As I mentioned before, so I will beg leave to repeat, that this Senate can do nothing without the concurrence of some other branch of the government. With regard to their concern in the appointment to offices, the President must nominate before they can be chosen; the President must acquiesce in that appointment. With regard to their power in forming treaties, they can make none; they are only auxiliaries to the President. They must try all impeachments; but they have no power to try any until presented by the House of Representatives; and when I consider this subject, though I wish the regulation better, I think no danger to the liberties of this country can arise even from that part of the system. But these objections, I say, come with a bad grace from those who prefer the present Confederation, who think it only necessary to add more powers to a body organized in that form. I confess, likewise, that by combining those powers of trying impeachments, and making treaties, in the same body, it will not be so easy, as I think it ought to be, to call the senators to an account for any improper conduct in that business.

Those who proposed this system were not inattentive to do all they could. I admit the force of the observation made by the gentleman from Fayette, (Mr. Smilie,) that, when two thirds of the Senate concur in forming a bad treaty, it will be hard to procure a vote of two thirds against them, if they should be impeached. I think such a thing is not to be expected; and so far they are without that *immediate* degree of responsibility which I think requisite to make this part of the work perfect. But this will not be always the case. When a member of the Senate shall behave criminally, the criminality will not expire with his office. The senators may be called to account after they shall have been changed, and the body to which they belonged shall have been altered. There is a rotation; and every second year one third of the whole number go out. Every fourth year two thirds of them are changed. In six years the whole body is supplied by a new one. Considering it in this view, responsibility is not entirely lost. There is another view in which it ought to be considered, which will show that we have a greater degree of security. Though they may not be convicted on impeachment before the Senate, they may be tried by their country; and if their criminality is established, the law will punish. A grand jury may present, a petty jury may convict, and the judges will pronounce the punishment. This is all that can be done under the present Confederation, for under it there is no power of impeachment; even here, then, we gain something. Those parts that are exceptionable, in this Constitution, are improvements on that concerning which so much pains are taken, to persuade us that it is preferable to the other.

The last observation respects the judges. It is said that, if they are to decide against the law, one house will impeach them, and the other will convict them. I hope gentlemen will show how this can happen; for bare supposition ought not to be admitted as proof. The judges are to be impeached, because they decide an act null and void, that was made in defiance of the Constitution! What House of Representatives would dare to impeach, or Senate to commit, judges for the performance of their duty? These observations are of a similar kind to those with regard to the liberty of the press.

I will proceed to take some notice of those qualities in this Constitution that I think entitle it to our respect and favor. I have not yet done, sir, with the great principle on which it stands; I mean the practical recognition of this doctrine—that, in the United States, the people retain the supreme power.

In giving a definition of the simple kinds of government known throughout the world, I had occasion to describe what I meant by a democracy; and I think I termed it, that government in which the people retain the supreme power, and exercise it either collectively or by representation. This Constitution declares this principle, in its terms and in its consequences, which is evident from the manner in which it is announced. "We, the People of the United States." After all the examination which I am able to give the subject, I view this as the only sufficient and most honorable basis, both for the people and government, on which our Constitution can possibly rest. What are all the contrivances of states, of kingdoms, and empires? What are they all intended for? They are all intended for man; and our natural character and natural rights are certainly to take place, in preference to all artificial refinements that human wisdom can devise.

I am astonished to hear the ill-founded doctrine, that the states alone ought to be represented in the federal government; these must possess sovereign authority, forsooth, and the people be forgot. No. Let us *re-ascend* to first principles. That expression is not strong enough to do my ideas justice.

Let us *retain* first principles. The people of the United States are now in the possession and exercise of their original rights; and while this doctrine is known, and operates, we shall have a cure for every disease.

I shall mention another good quality belonging to this system. In it the legislative, executive, and judicial powers are kept nearly independent and distinct. I express myself in this guarded manner, because I am aware of some powers that are blended in the Senate. They are but few; and they are not dangerous. It is an exception; yet that exception consists of but few instances, and none of them dangerous. I believe in no constitution for any country on earth is this great principle so strictly adhered to, or marked with so much precision and accuracy, as this. It is much more accurate than that which the honorable gentleman so highly extols: I mean, the constitution of England. There, sir, one branch of the legislature can appoint members of another. The king has the power of introducing members into the House of Lords. I have already mentioned that, in order to obtain a vote, twelve peers were poured into that house at one time. The operation is the same as might be under this Constitution, if the President had a right to appoint the members of the Senate. This power of the king extends into the other branch, where, though he cannot immediately introduce a member, yet he can do it remotely, by virtue of his prerogative, as he may create boroughs with power to send members to the House of Commons. The House of Lords form a much stronger exception to this principle than the Senate in this system; for the House of Lords possess judicial powers—not only that of trying impeachments, but that of trying their own members, and civil causes, when brought before them from the courts of chancery and the other courts in England.

If we therefore consider this Constitution with regard to this special object, though it is not so perfect as I could wish, yet it is more perfect than any government that I know.

I proceed to another property, which I think will recommend it to those who consider the effects of beneficence and wisdom; I mean the *division of this legislative authority* into two branches. I had an opportunity of dilating somewhat on this subject before; and as it is not likely to afford a subject of debate, I shall take no further notice of it than barely to mention it. The next good quality that I remark is, that the *executive authority is one.* By this means we obtain very important advantages. We may discover from history, from reason, and from experience, the security which this furnishes. The executive power is better to be trusted when it has no screen. Sir, we have a responsibility in the person of our President; he cannot act improperly, and hide either his negligence or inattention; he cannot roll upon any other person the weight of his criminality; no appointment can take place without his nomination; and he is responsible for every nomination he makes. We secure *vigor.* We well know what numerous executives are. We know there is neither vigor, decision, nor responsibility, in them. Add to all this, that officer is placed high, and is possessed of power far from being contemptible; yet not a *single privilege* is annexed to his character; far from being above the laws, he is amenable to them in his private character as a citizen, and in his public character by *impeachment.*

Sir, it has often been a matter of surprise, and frequently complained of even in Pennsylvania, that the *independence of the judges* is not properly secured. The servile dependence of the judges, in some of the states that have neglected to make proper provision on this subject, endangers the liberty and property of the citizen; and I apprehend that, whenever it has happened that the appointment has been for a less period than during good behavior, this object has not been sufficiently secured; for if, every five or seven years, the judges are obliged to make court for their appointment to office, they cannot be styled independent. This is not the case with regard to those appointed under the general government; for the judges here shall hold their offices during good behavior. I hope no further objections will be taken against this part of the Constitution, the consequence of which will be, that private property, so far as it comes before their courts, and personal liberty, so far as it is not forfeited by crimes, will be guarded with firmness and watchfulness.

It may appear too professional to descend into observations of this kind; but I believe that public happiness, personal liberty, and private property, depend essentially upon the able and upright determinations of independent judges.

Permit me to make one more remark on the subject of the judicial department. Its objects are extended *beyond* the bounds or power of every particular state, and therefore must be proper objects of the general government. I do not recollect any instance where a case can come before the judiciary of the United States, that could possibly be determined by a particular state, except one—which is, where citizens of the same state claim lands under the grant of different states; and in that instance, the power of the two states necessarily comes in competition; wherefore there would be great impropriety in having it determined by either.

Sir, I think there is another subject with regard to which this Constitution deserves approbation. I mean the accuracy with which the *line is drawn* between the powers of the *general government* and those of the *particular state governments.* We have heard some general observations, on this subject, from the gentlemen who conduct the opposition. They have asserted that these powers are unlimited and undefined. These words are as easily pronounced as *limited* and *defined.* They have already been answered by my honorable colleague, (Mr. M'Kean)[14] therefore I shall not

14. Thomas McKean (1734–1817) was an able statesman. He served in a variety of legislative and judicial offices in Delaware and Pennsylvania, including governor and chief justice of the latter.

enter into an explanation. But it is not pretended that the line is drawn with mathematical precision; the inaccuracy of language must, to a certain degree, prevent the accomplishment of such a desire. Whoever views the matter in a true light, will see that the powers are as minutely enumerated and defined as was possible, and will also discover that the general clause, against which so much exception is taken, is nothing more than what was necessary to render effectual the particular powers that are granted.

But let us suppose—and the supposition is very easy in the minds of the gentlemen on the other side—that there is some difficulty in ascertaining where the true line lies. Are we therefore thrown into despair? Are *disputes* between the *general* government and the *state* governments to be necessarily the consequence of inaccuracy? I hope, sir, they will not be the enemies of each other, or resemble comets in conflicting orbits, mutually operating destruction; but that their motion will be better represented by that of the planetary system, where each part moves harmoniously within its proper sphere, and no injury arises by interference or opposition. Every part, I trust, will be considered as a part of the United States. Can any cause of distrust arise here? Is there any increase of risk? Or, rather, are not the enumerated powers as well defined here, as in the present Articles of Confederation?

Permit me to proceed to what I deem another excellency of this system: all authority, of every kind, *is derived by* REPRESENTATION *from the* PEOPLE, *and the* DEMOCRATIC *principle is carried into every part of the government.* I had an opportunity, when I spoke first, of going fully into an elucidation of this subject. I mean not now to repeat what I then said.

I proceed to another quality, that I think estimable in this system: *it secures, in the strongest manner, the right of suffrage. Montesquieu,* book 2d, chap. 2d, speaking of laws relative to democracy, says,—

> When the body of the people is possessed of the supreme power, this is called a *democracy.* When the supreme power is lodged in the hands of a part of the people, it is then an *aristocracy.*
>
> In a democracy the people are in some respects the sovereign, and in others the subject.
>
> There can be no exercise of sovereignty but by their suffrages, which are their own will. Now, the sovereign's will is the sovereign himself. The laws, therefore, which establish the right of suffrage, are fundamental to this government. And, indeed, it is as important to regulate, in a republic, in

what manner, by whom, to whom, and concerning what, suffrages are to be given, as it is, in a monarchy, to know who is the prince, and after what manner he ought to govern.

In this system, it is declared that the electors in each state shall have the qualifications requisite for electors of the most numerous branch of the state legislature. This being made the criterion of the right of suffrage, it is consequently secured, because the same Constitution guaranties to every state in the Union a republican form of government. The right of suffrage is fundamental to republics.

Sir, there is another principle that I beg leave to mention. *Representation and direct taxation,* under this Constitution, are to be according to numbers. As this is a subject which I believe has not been gone into in this house, it will be worth while to show the sentiments of some respectable writers thereon. *Montesquieu,* in considering the requisites in a confederate republic, book 9th, chap. 3d, speaking of Holland, observes,

> It is difficult for the united states to be all of equal power and extent. The Lycian (*Strabo,* lib. 14) republic was an association of twenty-three towns; the large ones had three votes in the common council, the middling ones two, and the small towns one. The Dutch republic consists of seven provinces, of different extent of territory, which have each one voice.
>
> The cities of Lycia (*Strabo,* lib. 14) contributed to the expenses of the state, according to the proportion of suffrages. The provinces of the United Netherlands cannot follow this proportion; they must be directed by that of their power.
>
> In *Lycia,* (*Strabo,* lib. 14,) the judges and town magistrates were elected by the common council, and according to the proportion already mentioned. In the republic of Holland, they are not chosen by the common council, but each town names its magistrates. Were I to give a model of an excellent confederate republic, I should pitch upon that of *Lycia.*

I have endeavored, in all the books that I have access to, to acquire some information relative to the *Lycian republic;* but its history is not to be found; the few facts that relate to it are mentioned only by Strabo;[15] and however excellent the model it might present, we were reduced to the

15. Strabo (64/63 B.C.–c. 24 A.D.) was a Greek philosopher, historian, and geographer. He is perhaps most famous for his *Geographia.*

necessity of working without it. Give me leave to quote the sentiments of another author, whose peculiar situation and extensive worth throw a lustre on all he says. I mean Mr. *Necker*,[16] whose ideas are very exalted, both in theory and practical knowledge, on this subject. He approaches the nearest to the truth in his calculations from experience, and it is very remarkable that he makes use of that expression. His words are, (*Necker on Finance*, vol. i. p. 308,) —

> Population can therefore be only looked on as an exact measure of comparison when the provinces have resources nearly equal; but even this imperfect rule of proportion ought not to be neglected; and of all the objects which may be subjected to a determined and positive calculation, that of the taxes, to the population, approaches nearest to the truth.

Another good quality in this Constitution is, that the members of the Legislature cannot hold offices under the authority of this government. The operation of this I apprehend would be found to be very extensive, and very salutary in this country, to prevent those intrigues, those factions, that corruption, that would otherwise rise here, and have risen so plentiful in every other country. The reason why it is necessary in England to continue such influence, is that the crown, in order to secure its own influence against two other branches of the legislature, must continue to bestow places, but those *places produce the opposition* which frequently runs so strong in the British parliament.

Members who do not enjoy offices, combine against those who do enjoy them. It is not from principle that they thwart the ministry in all its operations. No; their language is, let us turn them out and succeed to their places. The great source of corruption, in that country, is, that persons may hold offices under the crown, and seats in the legislature at the same time.

I shall conclude at present; and I have endeavored to be as concise as possible, with mentioning, that in my humble opinion, the powers of the general government are necessary, and well defined—that the restraints imposed on it, and those imposed on the state governments, are rational and salutary, and that it is entitled to the approbation of those for whom it was intended.

16. Jacques Necker (1723–1804) was an important French statesman. He was finance minister for Louis XVI.

I recollect on a former day, the honorable gentleman from Westmoreland, (Mr. Findley,) and the honorable gentleman from Cumberland, (Mr. Whitehill,) took exceptions against the first clause of the 9th section, art. 1, arguing very unfairly, that because congress might impose a tax or duty of ten dollars on the importation of slaves, within any of the United States, congress might therefore permit slaves to be imported within this state, contrary to its laws. I confess I little thought that this part of the system would be excepted to.

I am sorry that it could be extended no further; but so far as it operates, it presents us with the pleasing prospect, that the rights of mankind will be acknowledged and established throughout the union.

If there was no other lovely feature in the constitution but this one, it would diffuse a beauty over its whole countenance. Yet the lapse of a few years, and congress will have power to exterminate slavery from within our borders.

How would such a delightful prospect expand the breast of a benevolent and philanthrophic European! Would he cavil at an expression? catch at a phrase? Now, sir, that is only reserved for the gentleman on the other side of your chair to do. What would be the exultation of that great man, whose name I have just now mentioned, we may learn from the following sentiments on this subject; they cannot be expressed so well as in his own words (vol. 1, page 329).

> The colonies of France contain, as we have seen, near five hundred thousand slaves, and it is from the number of these wretches, the inhabitants set a value on their plantations. What a fatal prospect, and how profound a subject for reflection! Alas! how inconsequent we are, both in our morality, and our principles. We preach up humanity, and yet go every year to bind in chains twenty thousand natives of Africa! We call the Moors barbarians and ruffians, because they attack the liberty of Europeans, at the risk of their own; yet these Europeans go, without danger, and as mere speculators, to purchase slaves, by gratifying the cupidity of their masters; and excite all those bloody scenes which are the usual preliminaries of this traffic! In short, we pride ourselves on the superiority of man, and it is with reason that we discover this superiority, in the wonderful and mysterious unfolding of the intellectual faculties; and yet the trifling difference in the hair of the head, or in the color of the epidermis, is sufficient to change our respect into contempt, and to engage us to place beings like ourselves, in the rank

of those animals devoid of reason, whom we subject to the yoke; that we may make use of their strength, and of their instinct at command.

I am sensible, and I grieve at it, that these reflections, which others have made much better than me, are unfortunately of very little use! The necessity of supporting sovereign power has its peculiar laws, and the wealth of nations is one of the foundations of this power: thus the sovereign who should be the most thoroughly convinced of what is due to humanity, would not singly renounce the service of slaves in his colonies: time alone could furnish a population of free people to replace them, and the great difference that would exist in the price of labor would give so great an advantage to the nation that should adhere to the old custom, that the others would soon be discouraged in wishing to be more virtuous. And yet, would it be a chimercial project to propose a general compact, by which all the European nations should unanimously agree to abandon the traffic of African slaves! they would in that case, find themselves exactly in the same proportion relative to each other as at present; for it is only on comparative riches that the calculations of power are founded.

We cannot as yet indulge such hopes; statesmen in general, think that every common idea must be a low one; and since the morals of private people, stand in need of being curbed, and maintained by the laws, we ought not to wonder, if those of sovereigns conform to their independence.

The time may nevertheless arrive, when, fatigued of that ambition which agitates them, and of the continual rotation of the same anxieties, and the same plans, they may turn their views to the great principles of humanity; and if the present generation is to be witness of this happy revolution, they may at least be allowed to be unanimous in offering up their vows for the perfection of the social virtues, and for the progress of public beneficial institutions.

These are the enlarged sentiments of that great man.

Permit me to make a single observation, in this place, on the restraints placed on the state governments. If only the following lines were inserted in this Constitution, I think it would be worth our adoption: "No state shall hereafter *emit bills of credit;* make any thing but gold and silver coin a *tender* in payment of debts; pass any bills of attainder, ex post facto law, *or law impairing the obligation of contracts.*" Fatal experience has taught us, dearly taught us, the value of these restraints. What is the consequence even at this moment? It is true, we have no tender law in Pennsylvania; but the moment you are conveyed across the Delaware, you find it haunt your journey, and follow close upon your heels. The paper passes commonly at twenty-five or thirty per cent, discount. How insecure is property!

These are a few of those properties in this system, that, I think, recommend it to our serious attention, and will entitle it to receive the adoption of the United States. Others might be enumerated, and others still will probably be disclosed by experience.

Friday, *December* 7, 1787, A.M.—Mr. WILSON. This is the first time that the article respecting the *judicial department* has come directly before us. I shall therefore take the liberty of making such observations as will enable honorable gentlemen to see the extent of the views of the Convention in forming this article, and the extent of its probable operation.

This will enable gentlemen to bring before this house their objections more pointedly than, without any explanation, could be done. Upon a distinct examination of the different powers, I presume it will be found that not one of them is unnecessary. I will go farther—there is not one of them but will be discovered to be of such a nature as to be attended with very important advantages. I shall beg leave to premise one remark—that the Convention, when they formed this system, did not expect they were to deliver themselves; their relations, and their posterity, into the hands of such men as are described by the honorable gentlemen in opposition. They did not suppose that the legislature, under this Constitution, would be an *association of demons*. They thought that a proper attention would be given, by the citizens of the United States, at the general election for members to the House of Representatives; they also believed that the particular states would nominate as good men as they have heretofore done, to represent them in the Senate. If they should now do otherwise, the fault will not be in Congress, but in the people or states themselves. I have mentioned, oftener than once, that for a people wanting to themselves there is no remedy.

The Convention thought further, (for on this very subject there will appear caution, instead of imprudence, in their transactions;) they considered, that, if suspicions are to be entertained, they are to be entertained with regard to the objects in which government have separate interests and separate views from the interest and views of the people. To say that officers of government will oppress, when nothing can be got by oppression, is making an inference, bad as human nature is, that cannot be allowed. When persons can derive no advantage from it, it can never be expected they will sacrifice either their duty or their popularity.

Whenever the general government can be a party against a citizen, the trial is guarded and secured in the Constitution itself, and therefore it is not in its power to oppress the citizen. In the case of treason, for example, though the prosecution is on the part of the United States, yet the Congress can neither define nor try the crime. If we have recourse to the history of the different governments that have hitherto subsisted, we shall find that a very great part of their tyranny over the people has arisen from the extension of the definition of treason. Some very remarkable instances have occurred, even in so free a country as England. If I recollect right, there is one instance that puts this matter in a very strong point of view. A person possessed a favorite buck, and, on finding it killed, wished the horns in the belly of the person who killed it. This happened to be the king: the injured complainant was tried, and convicted of treason for wishing the king's death.

I speak only of free governments; for, in despotic ones, treason depends entirely upon the will of the prince. Let this subject be attended to, and it will be discovered where the dangerous power of the government operates on the oppression of the people. Sensible of this, the Convention has guarded the people against it, by a particular and accurate definition of treason.

It is very true that trial by jury is not mentioned in civil cases; but I take it that it is very improper to infer from hence that it was not meant to exist under this government. Where the people are represented, where the interest of government cannot be separate from that of the people, (and this is the case in trial between citizen and citizen,) the power of making regulations with respect to the mode of trial may certainly be placed in the legislature; for I apprehend that the legislature will not do wrong in an instance from which they can derive no advantage. These were not all the reasons that influenced the Convention to leave it to the future Congress to make regulations on this head.

By the Constitution of the different states, it will be found that no particular mode of trial by jury could be discovered that would suit them all. The manner of summoning jurors, their qualifications, of whom they should consist, and the course of their proceedings, are all different in the different states; and I presume it will be allowed a good general principle, that, in carrying into effect the laws of the general government by the judicial department, it will be proper to make the regulations as agreeable to the habits and wishes of the particular states as possible; and it is easily discovered that it would have been impracticable, by any general regulation, to give satisfaction to all. We must have thwarted the custom of eleven or twelve to have accommodated any one. Why do this when there was no danger to be apprehended from the omission? We could not go into a particular detail of the manner that would have suited each state.

Time, reflection, and experience, will be necessary to suggest and mature the proper regulations on this subject; time and experience were not possessed by the Convention; they left it therefore to be particularly organized by the legislature—the representatives of the United States—from time to time, as should be most eligible and proper. Could they have done better?

I know, in every part where opposition has arisen, what a handle has been made to this objection; but I trust, upon examination, it will be seen that more could not have been done with propriety. Gentlemen talk of bills of rights. What is the meaning of this continual clamor, after what has been urged? Though it may be proper, in a single state, whose legislature calls itself the sovereign and supreme power, yet it would be absurd in the body of the people, when they are delegating from among themselves persons to transact certain business, to add an enumeration of those things which they are not to do. "But trial by jury is secured in the bill of rights of Pennsylvania; the parties have a right to trials by jury, which *ought* to be held sacred." And what is the consequence? There have been more violations of this right in Pennsylvania, since the revolution, than are to be found in England in the course of a century.

I hear no objection made to the tenure by which the judges hold their offices; it is declared that the judges shall hold them during good behavior;—nor to the security which they will have for their salaries; they shall, at stated times, receive for their services a compensation which shall not be diminished during their continuance in office.

The article respecting the judicial department is objected to as going too far, and is supposed to carry a very indefinite meaning. Let us examine this: "The judicial power shall extend to all cases, in law and equity, *arising under this Constitution and the laws of the United States.*" Controversies may certainly arise under this Constitution and the laws of the United States, and is it not proper that there should be judges to decide them? The honorable gentleman from Cumberland (Mr. Whitehill) says that laws may be made inconsistent with the Constitution; and that therefore the powers given to the judges are dangerous. For my part, Mr. President, I think the contrary inference true. If a law should be made inconsistent with those powers vested by this instrument in Congress, the judges, as a consequence of their independence, and the particular powers of government being defined, will declare such law to be null and void; for the power of the Constitution predominates. Any thing, therefore, that shall be enacted by Congress contrary thereto, will not have the force of law.

The judicial power extends to all cases arising under treaties made, or which shall be made, by the United States. I shall not repeat, at this time, what has been said with regard to the power of the states to make treaties; it cannot be controverted, that, when made, they ought to be observed. But it is highly proper that this regulation should be made; for the truth is,—and I am sorry to say it,—that, in order to prevent the payment of British debts, and from other causes, our treaties have been violated, and violated, too, by the express laws of several states in the Union. Pennsylvania—to her honor be it spoken—has hitherto done no act of this kind; but it is acknowledged on all sides, that many states in the Union have infringed the treaty; and it is well known that, when the minister of the United States made a demand of Lord Carmarthen[17] of a surrender of the western posts, he told the minister, with truth and justice, "The treaty under which you claim those possessions has not been performed on your part; until that is done, those possessions will not be delivered up." This clause, sir, will show the world that we make the faith of treaties a constitutional part of the character of the United States; that we secure its performance no longer nominally, for the judges of the United States will be enabled to carry it into effect, let the legislatures of the different states do what they may.

The power of judges extends to all cases affecting ambassadors, other

17. Lord Carmarthen was Francis Godolphin Osborne, the fifth Duke of Leeds (1751–1799).

public ministers, and consuls. I presume very little objection will be offered to this clause; on the contrary, it will be allowed proper and unexceptionable.

This will also be allowed with regard to the following clause: "*all cases of admiralty and maritime jurisdiction.*"

The next is, "*to controversies to which the United States shall be a party.*" Now, I apprehend it is something very incongruous, that, because the United States are a party, it should be urged, as an objection, that their judges ought not to decide, when the universal practice of all nations has, and unavoidably must have, admitted of this power. But, say the gentlemen, the sovereignty of the states is destroyed, if they should be engaged in a controversy with the United States, because a suiter in a court must acknowledge the jurisdiction of that court, and it is not the custom of sovereigns to suffer their names to be made use of in this manner. The answer is plain and easy: the government of each state ought to be subordinate to the government of the United States.

"*To controversies between two or more states.*" This power is vested in the present Congress; but they are unable, as I have already shown, to enforce their decisions. The additional power of carrying their decree into execution, we find, is therefore necessary, and I presume no exception will be taken to it.

"*Between a state and citizens of another state.*" When this power is attended to, it will be found to be a necessary one. Impartiality is the leading feature in this Constitution; it pervades the whole. When a citizen has a controversy with another state, there ought to be a tribunal where both parties may stand on a just and equal footing.

"*Between citizens of different states, and between a state, or the citizens thereof, and foreign states, citizens, or subjects.*" This part of the jurisdiction, I presume, will occasion more doubt than any other part; and, at first view, it may seem exposed to objections well founded and of great weight; but I apprehend this can be the case only at first view. Permit me to observe here, with regard to this power, or any other of the foregoing powers given to the federal court, that they are not exclusively given. In all instances, the parties may commence suits in the courts of the several states. Even the United States may submit to such decision if they think proper. Though the citizens of a state, and the citizens or subjects of foreign states, may sue in the federal court, it does not follow that they must sue. These are the instances in which the jurisdiction of the United States may be exercised; and we have all the reason in the world to believe that it will be exercised impartially; for it would be improper to infer that the judges would abandon their duty, the rather for being independent. Such a sentiment is contrary to experience, and ought not to be hazarded. If the people of the United States are fairly represented, and the President and Senate are wise enough to choose men of abilities and integrity for judges, there can be no apprehension, because, as I mentioned before, the government can have no interest in injuring the citizens.

But when we consider the matter a little further, is it not necessary, if we mean to restore either public or private credit, that foreigners, as well as ourselves, have a just and impartial tribunal to which they may resort? I would ask how a merchant must feel to have his property lie at the mercy of the laws of Rhode Island. I ask, further, How will a creditor feel who has his debts at the mercy of tender laws in other states? It is true that, under this Constitution, these particular iniquities may be restrained in future; but, sir, there are other ways of avoiding payment of debts. There have been instalment acts, and other acts of a similar effect. Such things, sir, destroy the very sources of credit.

Is it not an important object to extend our manufactures and our commerce? This cannot be done, unless a proper security is provided for the regular discharge of contracts. This security cannot be obtained, unless we give the power of deciding upon those contracts to the general government.

I will mention, further, an object that I take to be of particular magnitude, and I conceive these regulations will produce its accomplishment. The object, Mr. President, that I allude to, is *the improvement of our domestic navigation,* the instrument of trade between the several states. Private credit, which fell to decay from the destruction of public credit, by a too inefficient general government, will be restored; and this valuable intercourse among ourselves must give an increase to those useful improvements that will astonish the world. At present, how are we circumstanced! Merchants of eminence will tell you that they cannot trust their property to the laws of the state in which their correspondents live. Their friend may die, and may be succeeded by a representative of a very different character. If there is any particular objection that did not occur to me on this part of the Constitution, gentlemen will mention it; and I hope, when this article is examined, it will be found to contain nothing but what is proper to be annexed to the general government. The next clause, so far as it gives original jurisdiction in cases affecting ambassadors, I apprehend, is perfectly unexceptionable.

It was thought proper to give the citizens of foreign states full opportunity of obtaining justice in the general courts, and this they have by its appellate jurisdiction; therefore, in order to restore credit with those foreign states, that part of the article is necessary. I believe the alteration that will take place in their minds when they learn the operation of this clause, will be a great and important advantage to our country; nor is it any thing but justice: they ought to have the same security against the state laws that may be made, that the citizens have; because regulations ought to be equally just in the one case as in the other. Further, it is necessary in order to preserve peace with foreign nations. Let us suppose the case, that a wicked law is made in some one of the states, enabling a debtor to pay his creditor with the fourth, fifth, or sixth part of the real value of the debt, and this creditor, a foreigner, complains to his prince or sovereign, of the injustice that has been done him. What can that prince or sovereign do? Bound by inclination, as well as duty, to redress the wrong his subject sustains from the hand of perfidy, he cannot apply to the particular guilty state, because he knows that, by the Articles of Confederation, it is declared that no state shall enter into treaties. He must therefore apply to the United States; the United States must be accountable. "My subject has received a flagrant injury: do me justice, or I will do myself justice." If the United States are answerable for the injury, ought they not to possess the means of compelling the faulty state to repair it? They ought; and this is what is done here. For now, if complaint is made in consequence of such injustice, Congress can answer, "Why did not your subject apply to the General Court, where the unequal and partial laws of a particular state would have had no force?"

In two cases the Supreme Court has original jurisdiction—that affecting ambassadors, and when a state shall be a party. It is true it has appellate jurisdiction in more, but it will have it under such restrictions as the Congress shall ordain. I believe that any gentleman, possessed of experience or knowledge on this subject, will agree that it was impossible to go further with any safety or propriety, and that it was best left in the manner in which it now stands.

"*In all the other cases before mentioned, the Supreme Court shall have appellate jurisdiction, both as to law and fact.*" The jurisdiction as to fact may be thought improper; but those possessed of information on this head see that it is necessary. We find it essentially necessary from the ample experience we have had in the courts of admiralty with regard to captures. Those gentlemen who, during the late war, had their vessels retaken, know well what a poor chance they would have had when those vessels were taken in their states and tried by juries, and in what a situation they would have been if the Court of Appeals had not been possessed of authority to reconsider and set aside the verdicts of those juries. Attempts were made by some of the states to destroy this power; but it has been confirmed in every instance.

There are other cases in which it will be necessary; and will not Congress better regulate them, as they rise from time to time, than could have been done by the Convention? Besides, if the regulations shall be attended with inconvenience, the Congress can alter them as soon as discovered. But any thing done in Convention must remain unalterable but by the power of the citizens of the United States at large.

I think these reasons will show that the powers given to the Supreme Court are not only safe, but constitute a wise and valuable part of the system.

Tuesday, *December* 11, 1787, A.M.—Mr. Wilson. Three weeks have now elapsed since this Convention met. Some of the delegates attended on Tuesday, the 20th November; a great majority within a day or two afterwards; and all but one on the 4th day. We have been since employed in discussing the business for which we are sent here. I think it will now become evident to every person who takes a candid view of our discussions, that it is high time our proceedings should draw towards a *conclusion*.

Perhaps our debates have already continued as long, nay, longer than is sufficient for every good purpose. The business which we were intended to perform is necessarily reduced to a very narrow compass. The single question to be determined is, Shall we assent to and ratify the Constitution proposed?

As *this* is the *first* state whose Convention has met on the subject, and as the subject itself is of very great importance, not only to Pennsylvania, but to the United States, it was thought proper fairly, openly, and candidly to canvass it. This has been done. You have heard, Mr. President, from day to day, and from week to week, the objections that could be offered from any quarter. We have heard these objections once: we have heard a great number of them repeated much oftener than once. Will it answer any valuable end, sir, to protract these debates longer? I suppose it will not. I apprehend it may serve to promote very pernicious and destructive purposes. It may, perhaps, be insinuated to other states, and even to distant parts of this state, by people in opposition to this system, that the expediency of adopting is at most very doubtful, and that the business lingers among the members of the Convention.

This would not be a true representation of the fact; for there is the greatest reason to believe that there is a very considerable majority who do not hesitate to ratify the Constitution. We were sent here to express the voice of our constituents on the subject, and I believe that many of them expected to hear the echo of that voice before this time.

When I consider the attempts that have been made on this floor, and the many misrepresentations of what has been said among us that have appeared in the public papers, printed in this city, I confess that I am induced to suspect that opportunity may be taken to pervert and abuse the principles on which the friends of this Constitution act. If attempts are made here, will they not be repeated when the distance is greater, and the means of information fewer? Will they not at length produce an uneasiness, for which there is, in fact, no cause? Ought we not to prohibit any such uses being made of the continuance of our deliberations? We do not wish to preclude debate: of this our conduct has furnished the most ample testimony. The members in opposition have not been prevented a repetition of all their objections that they could urge against this plan.

The honorable gentleman from Fayette, (Mr. Smilie,) the other evening, claimed for the minority the merit of contending for the rights of mankind; and he told us that it has been the practice of all ages to treat such minorities with contempt; he further took the liberty of observing, that, if the majority had the power, they do not want the inclination, to consign the minority to punishment. I know that claims, self-made, form no small part of the merit to which we have heard undisguised pretences; but it is one thing to claim, and it is another thing, very different indeed, to support that claim. The minority, sir, are contending for the rights of mankind; what, then, are the majority contending for? If the minority are contending for the rights of mankind, the majority must be contending for the doctrines of tyranny and slavery. Is it probable that that is the case? Who are the majority in this assembly?—Are they not the people? are they not the representatives of the people, as well as the minority? Were they not elected by the people, as well as the minority? Were they not elected by the greater part of the people? Have we a single right separate from the rights of the people? Can we forge fetters for others that will not be clasped round our own limbs? Can we make heavy chains that shall not cramp the growth of our own posterity? On what fancied distinction shall the minority assume to themselves the merit of contending for the rights of mankind?

Sir, if the system proposed by the late Convention, and the conduct of its advocates who have appeared in this house, deserve the declarations and insinuations that have been made concerning them, well may we exclaim, "Ill-fated America! thy crisis was approaching! perhaps it was come! Thy various interests were neglected—thy most sacred rights were insecure. Without a government, without energy, without confidence internally, without respect externally, the advantages of society were lost to thee! In such a situation, distressed, but not despairing, thou desiredst to reassume thy native vigor, and to lay the foundation of future empire. Thou selectedst a number of thy sons, to meet together for the purpose. The selected and honored characters met; but, horrid to tell, they not only consented, but they combined in an aristocratic system, calculated and intended to enslave their country! Unhappy Pennsylvania! thou, as a part of the Union, must share in its unfortunate fate; for when this system, after being laid before thy citizens, comes before the delegates selected by them for its consideration, there are found but *three* of the numerous members that have virtue enough to raise their voices in support of the rights of mankind!" America, particularly Pennsylvania, must be ill-starred, indeed, if this is a true state of the case. I trust we may address our country in far other language.

> Happy America! thy crisis was indeed alarming, but thy situation was not desperate. We had confidence in our country; though, on whichever side we turned, we were presented with scenes of distress. Though the jarring interests of the various states, and the different habits and inclinations of their inhabitants, all lay in the way, and rendered our prospect gloomy and discouraging indeed, yet such were the generous and mutual sacrifices offered up, that, amidst *forty-two* members, who represented twelve of the United States, there were only *three* who did not attest the instrument, as a confirmation of its goodness. Happy Pennsylvania! this plan has been laid before thy citizens for consideration; they have sent delegates to express their voice; and listen—with rapture listen!—from only *three* opposition has been heard against it.

The singular unanimity that has attended the whole progress of their business, will, in the minds of those considerate men who have not had opportunity to examine the general and particular interest of their country, prove, to their satisfaction, that it is an excellent Constitution, and worthy to be adopted, ordained, and established, by the people of the United States.

After having viewed the arguments drawn from probability, whether this is a good or a bad system, whether those who contend for it, or those who contend against it, contend for the rights of mankind, let us step forward and examine the fact.

We were told, some days ago, by the honorable gentleman from Westmoreland, (Mr. Findley,) when speaking of this system and its objects, that the Convention, no doubt, thought they were forming a compact, or contract, of the greatest importance. Sir, I confess I was much surprised; at so late a stage of the debate, to hear such principles maintained. It was a matter of surprise to see the great leading principle of this system still so very much misunderstood. "The Convention, no doubt, thought they were forming a *contract!*" I cannot answer for what every member thought; but I believe it cannot be said that they thought they were making a contract, because I cannot discover the least trace of a compact in that system. There can be no compact unless there are more parties than one. It is a new doctrine that one can make a compact with himself. "The Convention were forming compacts!" With whom? I know no bargains that were made there. I am unable to conceive who the parties could be. The state governments make a bargain with one another; that is the doctrine that is endeavored to be established by gentlemen in opposition,—that state sovereignties wish to be represented! But far other were the ideas of the Convention, and far other are those conveyed in the system itself.

As this subject has been often mentioned, and as often misunderstood, it may not be improper to take some further notice of it. This, Mr. President, is not a government founded upon compact; it is founded upon the power of the people. They express in their name and their authority—"*We, the people, do ordain and establish,*" &c.; from their ratification alone it is to take its constitutional authenticity; without that, it is no more than *tabula rasa*.

I know very well all the common-place rant of state sovereignties, and that government is founded in original compact. If that position was examined, it will be found not to accede very well with the true principle of free government. It does not suit the language or genius of the system before us. I think it does not accord with experience, so far as I have been able to obtain information from history.

The greatest part of governments have been founded on conquest: perhaps a few early ones may have had their origin in paternal authority. Sometimes a family united, and that family afterwards extended itself into a community. But the greatest governments which have appeared on the face of the globe have been founded in conquest. The great empires of Assyria, Persia, Macedonia, and Rome, were all of this kind. I know well that in Great Britain, since the revolution, it has become a principle that the constitution is founded in contract; but the form and time of that contract, no writer has yet attempted to discover. It was, however, recognized at the time of the revolution, therefore is politically true. But we should act very imprudently to consider our liberties as placed on such foundation.

If we go a little further on this subject, I think we shall see that the doctrine of original compact cannot be supported consistently with the best principles of government. If we admit it, we exclude the idea of amendment; because a contract once entered into between the governor and governed becomes obligatory, and cannot be altered but by the mutual consent of both parties. The citizens of united America, I presume, do not wish to stand on that footing with those to whom, from convenience, they please to delegate the exercise of the general powers necessary for sustaining and preserving the Union. They wish a principle established, by the operation of which the legislatures may feel the direct authority of the people. The people, possessing that authority, will continue to exercise it by amending and improving their own work. This Constitution may be found to have defects in it; hence amendments may become necessary; but the idea of a government founded on contract destroys the means of improvement. We hear it every time the gentlemen are up, "Shall we violate the Confederation, which directs every alteration that is thought necessary to be established by the state legislatures only!" Sir, those gentlemen must ascend to a higher source: the people fetter themselves by no contract. If your state legislatures have cramped themselves by compact, it was done without the authority of the people, who alone possess the supreme power.

I have already shown that this system is not a compact, or contract; the system itself tells you what it is; it is an ordinance and establishment of the people. I think that the force of the introduction to the work must by this time have been felt. It is not an unmeaning flourish. The expressions declare, in a practical manner, the principle of this Constitution. It is ordained and established by the people themselves; and we, who give our votes for it, are merely the proxies of our constituents. We sign it as their attorneys, and, as to ourselves, we agree to it as individuals.

We are told, by honorable gentlemen in opposition, "that the present Confederation should have been continued, but that additional powers should have been given to it; that such was the business of the late Convention, and that they had assumed to themselves the power of proposing another in its stead; and that which is proposed is such a one as was not expected by the legislature nor by the people." I apprehend this would have been a very insecure, very inadequate, and a very pernicious mode of proceeding. Under the present Confederation, Congress certainly do not possess sufficient power; but one body of men we know they are; and were they invested with additional powers, they must become dangerous. Did not the honorable gentleman himself tell us that the powers of government, vested either in one man or one body of men, formed the very description of tyranny? To have placed in the present the legislative, the executive, and judicial authority, all of which are essential to the general government, would indubitably have produced the severest despotism.

From this short deduction, one of these two things must have appeared to the Convention, and must appear to every man who is at the pains of thinking on the subject. It was indispensably necessary either to make a new distribution of the powers of government, or to give such powers to one body of men as would constitute a tyranny. If it is proper to avoid tyranny, it becomes requisite to avoid placing additional powers in the hands of a Congress constituted like the present; hence the conclusion is warranted, that a different organization ought to take place.

Our next inquiry ought to be, whether this is the most proper disposition and organization of the necessary powers. But before I consider this subject, I think it proper to notice one sentiment, expressed by an honorable gentleman from the county of Cumberland, (Mr. Whitehill.) He asserts that the extent of the government is too great, and this system cannot be executed. What is the consequence, if this assertion is true? It strikes directly at the root of the Union.

I admit, Mr. President, there are great difficulties in adapting a system of good and free government to the extent of our country. But I am sure that our interests, as citizens, as states, and as a nation, depend essentially upon a union. This Constitution is proposed to accomplish that great and desirable end. Let the experiment be made; let the system be fairly and candidly tried, before it is determined that it cannot be executed.

I proceed to another objection; for I mean to answer those that have been suggested since I had the honor of addressing you last week. It has been alleged, by honorable gentlemen, that this general government possesses powers for internal purposes, and that the general government cannot exercise internal powers. The honorable member from Westmoreland (Mr. Findley) dilates on this subject, and instances the opposition that was made by the colonies against Great Britain, to prevent her imposing internal taxes or excises. And before the federal government will be able to impose the one, or obtain the other, he considers it necessary that it should possess power for every internal purpose.

Let us examine these objections: If this government does not possess internal as well as external power, and that power for internal as well as external purposes, I apprehend that all that has hitherto been done must go for nothing. I apprehend a government that cannot answer the purposes for which it was intended is not a government for this country. I know that Congress, under the present Articles of Confederation, possess no internal power, and we see the consequences: they can recommend—they can go further, they can make requisitions; but there they must stop; for, as far as I recollect, after making a law, they cannot take a single step towards carrying it into execution. I believe it will be found, in experience, that, with regard to the exercise of internal powers, the general government will not be unnecessarily rigorous. The future collection of the duties and imposts will, in the opinion of some, supersede the necessity of having recourse to internal taxation. The United States will not, perhaps, be often under the necessity of using this power at all; but if they should, it will be exercised only in a moderate degree. The good sense of the citizens of the United States is not to be alarmed by the picture of taxes collected at the point of the bayonet. There is no more reason to suppose that the delegates and representatives in Congress, any more than the legislature of Pennsylvania, or any other state, will act in this manner. Insinuations of this kind, made against one body of men, and not against another, though both the representatives of the people, are not made with propriety; nor will they have the weight of argument. I apprehend the greatest part of the revenue will arise from external taxation. But certainly it would have been very unwise in the late Convention to have omitted the addition of the other powers; and I think it would be very unwise in this Convention to refuse to adopt this Constitution, because it grants Congress power to lay and collect taxes, for the purpose of providing for the common defence and general welfare of the United States.

What is to be done to effect these great purposes, if an impost should be found insufficient? Suppose a war was suddenly declared against us by a foreign power, possessed of a formidable navy; our navigation would be laid prostrate, our imposts must cease; and shall our existence as a nation depend upon the peaceful navigation of our seas? A strong exertion of maritime power, on the part of an enemy, might deprive us of these sources of revenue in a few months. It may suit honorable gentlemen, who live at the western extremity of this state, that they should contribute nothing, by internal taxes, to the support of the general government. They care not what restraints are laid upon our commerce; for what is the commerce of Philadelphia to the inhabitants on the other side of the Alleghany Mountains? But though it may suit them, it does not suit those in the lower part of the state, who are by far the most numerous. Nor can we agree that our safety should depend altogether upon a revenue arising from commerce.

Excise may be a necessary mode of taxation; it takes place in most states already.

The capitation tax is mentioned as one of those that are exceptionable. In some states, that mode of taxation is used; but I believe, in many, it would be received with great reluctance; there are one or two states where it is constantly in use, and without any difficulties and inconveniences arising from it. An excise, in its very principles, is an improper tax, if it could be avoided; but yet it has been a source of revenue in Pennsylvania, both before the revolution and since; during all which time we have enjoyed the benefit of free government.

I presume, sir, that the executive powers of government ought to be commensurate with the government itself, and that a government which cannot act in every part is, so far, defective. Consequently, it is necessary that Congress possess powers to tax internally, as well as externally.

It is objected to this system, that under it there is no sovereignty left in the state governments. I have had occasion to reply to this already; but I should be very glad to know at what period the state governments became possessed of the supreme power. On the principle on which I found my arguments,—and that is, the principle of this Constitution,—the supreme power resides in the people. If they choose to indulge a part of their sovereign power to be exercised by the state governments, they may. If they have done it, the states were right in exercising it; but if they think it no longer safe or convenient, they will resume it, or make a new distribution, more likely to be productive of that good which ought to be our constant aim.

The powers both of the general government and the state governments, under this system, are acknowledged to be so many emanations of power from the people. The great object now to be attended to, instead of disagreeing about who shall possess the supreme power, is, to consider whether the present arrangement is well calculated to promote and secure the tranquillity and happiness of our common country. These are the dictates of sound and unsophisticated sense, and what ought to employ the attention and judgment of this honorable body.

We are next told by the honorable gentleman in opposition, (as indeed we have been, from the beginning of the debates in this Convention, to the conclusion of their speeches yesterday,) that this is a consolidated government, and will abolish the state governments.

Definitions of a consolidated government have been called for; the gentlemen gave us what they termed definition, but it does not seem to me, at least, that they have as yet expressed clear ideas upon that subject. I will endeavor to state their different ideas upon this point. The gentleman from Westmoreland, (Mr. Findley,) when speaking on this subject, says that he means, by a consolidation, that government which puts the thirteen states into one.

The honorable gentleman from Fayette (Mr. Smilie) gives you this definition: "What I mean by a consolidated government, is one that will transfer the sovereignty from the state governments to the general government."

The honorable member from Cumberland, (Mr. Whitehill,) instead of giving you a definition, sir, tells you again, that "it is a consolidated government, and we have proved it so."

These, I think, sir, are the different descriptions given to us of a consolidated government. As to the first, that it is a consolidated government, that puts the thirteen United States into one,—if it is meant that the general government will destroy the governments of the states, I will admit that such a government would not suit the people of America. It would be improper for this country, because it could not be proportioned to its extent, on the principles of freedom. But that description does not apply to the system before you. This, instead of placing the state governments in jeopardy, is founded on their existence. On this principle its organization depends; it must stand or fall, as the state governments are secured or ruined. Therefore, though this may be a very proper description of a consolidated government, yet it must be disregarded, as inapplicable to the proposed Constitution. It is not treated with decency when such insinuations are offered against it.

The honorable gentleman (Mr. Smilie) tells you that a consolidated government "is one that will transfer the sovereignty from the state governments to the general government." Under this system, the sovereignty is not in the possession of the governments, therefore it cannot be transferred from them to the general government; so that in no point of view of this definition can we discover that it applies to the present system.

In the exercise of its powers will be insured the exercise of their powers to the state governments; it will insure peace and stability to them; their strength will increase with its strength; their growth will extend with its growth.

Indeed, narrow minds—and some such there are in every government—narrow minds and intriguing spirits will be active in sowing dissensions and promoting discord between them. But those whose understandings and whose hearts are good enough to pursue the general welfare, will find that what is the interest of the whole, must, on the great scale, be the interest of every part. It will be the duty of a state, as of an individual, to sacrifice her own convenience to the general good of the Union.

The next objection that I mean to take notice of is, that the powers of the several parts of this government are not kept as distinct and independent as they ought to be. I admit the truth of this general sentiment. I do not think that, in the powers of the Senate, the distinction is marked with so much accuracy as I wished, and still wish; but yet I am of opinion that real and effectual security is obtained, which is saying a great deal. I do not consider this part as wholly unexceptionable; but even where there are defects in this system, they are improvements upon the old. I will go a little further; though, in this system, the distinction and independence of power is not adhered to with entire theoretical precision, yet it is more strictly adhered to than in any other system of government in the world. In the Constitution of Pennsylvania, the executive department exercises judicial powers in the trial of public officers; yet a similar power, in this system, is complained of; at the same time, the Constitution of Pennsylvania is referred to as an example for the late Convention to have taken a lesson by.

In New Jersey, in Georgia, in South Carolina, and North Carolina, the executive power is blended with the legislative. Turn to their constitutions, and see in how many instances.

In North Carolina, the Senate and House of Commons elect the governor himself: they likewise elect seven persons to be a council of state, to advise the governor in the execution of his office. Here we find the whole executive department under the nomination of the legislature, at least the most important part of it.

In South Carolina, the legislature appoints the governor and commander-in-chief, lieutenant-governor and privy council. "Justices of the peace shall be nominated by the legislature, and commissioned by the governor;" and what is more, they are appointed during pleasure. All other judicial officers are to be appointed by the Senate and House of Representatives. I might go further, and detail a great multitude of instances, in which the legislative, executive, and judicial powers are blended; but it is unnecessary; I only mention these to show, that, though this Constitution does not arrive at what is called perfection, yet it contains great improvements, and its powers are distributed with a degree of accuracy superior to what is termed accuracy in particular states.

There are four instances in which improper powers are said to be blended in the Senate. We are told that this government is imperfect, because the Senate possess the power of trying impeachments; but here, sir, the Senate are under a check, as no impeachment can be tried until it is made; and the House of Representatives possess the sole power of making impeachments. We are told that the share which the Senate have in making treaties is exceptionable; but here they are also under a check, by a constituent part of the government, and nearly the immediate representative of the people—I mean the President of the United States. They can make no treaty without his concurrence. The same observation applies in the appointment of officers. Every officer must be nominated solely and exclusively by the President.

Much has been said on the subject of treaties; and this power is denominated a blending of the legislative and executive powers in the Senate. It is but justice to represent the favorable, as well as unfavorable, side of a question, and from thence determine whether the objectionable parts are of a sufficient weight to induce a rejection of this Constitution.

There is no doubt, sir, but, under this Constitution, treaties will become the supreme law of the land; nor is there any doubt but the Senate and President possess the power of making them. But though the treaties are to have the force of laws, they are in some important respects very different from other acts of legislation. In making laws, our own consent alone is necessary. In forming treaties, the concurrence of another power becomes necessary. Treaties, sir, are truly contracts, or compacts, between the different states, nations, or princes, who find it convenient or necessary to enter into them. Some gentlemen are of opinion that the power of making treaties should have been placed in the legislature at large; there are, however, reasons that operate with great force on the other side. Treaties are frequently (especially in time of war) of such a nature, that it would be extremely improper to publish them, or even commit the secret of their negotiation to any great number of persons. For my part, I am not an advocate for secrecy in transactions relating to the public; not generally even in forming treaties, because I think that the history of the diplomatic corps will evince, even in that great department of politics, the truth of an old adage, that "honesty is the best policy," and this is the conduct of the most able negotiators; yet sometimes secrecy may be necessary, and therefore it becomes an argument against committing the knowledge of these transactions to too many persons. But in their nature treaties originate differently from laws. They are made by equal parties, and each side has half of the bargain to make; they will be made between us and powers at the distance of three thousand miles. A long series of negotiation will frequently precede them; and can it be the opinion of these gentlemen that the legislature should be in session during this whole time? It well deserves to be remarked, that, though the House of Representatives possess no active part in making treaties, yet their legislative authority will be found to have strong restraining influences upon both President and Senate. In England, if the king and his ministers find themselves, during their negotiation, to be embarrassed because an existing law is not repealed, or a new law is not enacted, they give notice to the legislature of their situation, and inform them that it will be necessary, before the treaty can operate, that some law be repealed, or some be made. And will not the same thing take place here? Shall less prudence, less caution, less moderation, take place among those who negotiate treaties for the United States, than among those who negotiate them for the other nations of the earth? And let it be attended to, that, even in the making of treaties, the states are immediately represented, and the people mediately represented; two of the constituent parts of government must concur in making them. Neither the President nor the Senate, solely, can complete a treaty; they are checks upon each other, and are so balanced as to produce security to the people.

I might suggest other reasons, to add weight to what has already been offered; but I believe it is not necessary; yet let me, however, add one thing—the Senate is a favorite with many of the states, and it was with difficulty that these checks could be procured; it was one of the last exertions of conciliation, in the late Convention, that obtained them.

It has been alleged, as a consequence of the small number of representatives, that they will not know, as intimately as they ought, the interests, inclinations, or habits, of their constituents.

We find, on an examination of all its parts, that the objects of this government are such as extend beyond the bounds of the particular states. This is the line of distinction between this government and the particular state governments.

This principle I had an opportunity of illustrating on a former occasion. Now, when we come to consider the objects of this government, we shall find that, in making our choice of a proper character to be a member of the House of Representatives, we ought to fix on one whose mind and heart are enlarged; who possesses a general knowledge of the interests of America, and a disposition to make use of that knowledge for the advantage and welfare of his country. It belongs not to this government to make an act for a particular township, country, or state.

A defect in *minute* information has not certainly been an objection in the management of the business of the United States; but the want of enlarged ideas has hitherto been chargeable on our councils; yet, even with regard to minute knowledge, I do not conceive it impossible to find eight characters that may be very well informed as to the situation, interests, and views, of every part of this state, and who may have a concomitant interest with their fellow-citizens; they could not materially injure others without affecting their own fortunes.

I did say that, in order to obtain that enlarged information in our representatives, a large district for election would be more proper than a small one. When I speak of large districts, it is not agreeably to the idea entertained by the honorable member from Fayette, (Mr. Smilie,) who tells you that elections for large districts must be ill attended, because the people will not choose to go very far on this business. It is not meant, sir, by me, that the votes should be taken at one place; no, sir; the elections may be held through this state in the same manner as elections for members of the General Assembly; and this may be done, too, without any additional inconvenience or expense.

If it could be effected, all the people of the same society ought to meet in one place, and communicate freely with each other on the great business of representation. Though this cannot be done in fact, yet we find that it is the most favorite and constitutional idea. It is supported by this principle too, that every member is the representative of the whole community, and not of a particular part. The larger, therefore, the district is, the greater is the probability of selecting wise and virtuous characters, and the more agreeable it is to the constitutional principle of representation.

As to the objection that the House of Representatives may be bribed by the Senate, I confess I do not see that bribery is an objection against *this system;* it is rather an objection against human nature. I am afraid that bribes in every government may be offered and received; but let me ask of the gentlemen who urge this objection to point out where any power is given to *bribe under this Constitution.* Every species of influence is guarded against as much as possible. Can the Senate procure money to effect such design? All public moneys must be disposed of by law, and it is necessary that the House of Representatives originate such law. Before the money can be got out of the treasury, it must be appropriated by law. If the legislature had the effrontery to set aside three or four hundred thousand pounds for this purpose, and the people would tamely suffer it, I grant it might be done; and in Pennsylvania the legislature might do the same; for, by a law, and that conformably to the Constitution, they might divide among themselves what portion of the public money they pleased. I shall just remark, sir, that the objections which have repeatedly been made with regard to "the number of representatives being too small, and that they may possibly be made smaller; that the districts are too large, and not within the reach of the people; and that the House of Representatives may be bribed by the Senate," come with an uncommon degree of impropriety from those who would refer us back to the Articles of Confederation; for, under these, the representation of this state cannot exceed seven members, and may consist of only two; and these are wholly without the reach or control of the people. Is there not also greater danger that the majority of such a body might be more easily bribed than the majority of one not only more numerous, but checked by a division of two or three distinct and independent parts? The danger is certainly better guarded against in the proposed system than in any other yet devised.

The next objections, which I shall notice, are, "that the powers of the Senate are too great; that the representation therein is unequal; and that the Senate, from the smallness of its number, may be bribed." Is there any propriety in referring us to the Confederation on this subject? Because, in one or two instances, the Senate possess more power than the House of Representatives, are these gentlemen supported in their remarks, when they tell you they wished and expected more powers to be given to the present Congress—a body certainly much more exceptionable than any instituted under this system?

That "the representation in the Senate is unequal," I regret, because I am of opinion that the states ought to be represented according to their importance; but in this system there is a considerable improvement; for the true principle of representation is carried into the House of Representatives, and into the choice of the President; and without the assistance of one or the other of these, the Senate is inactive, and can do neither good nor evil.

It is repeated, again and again, by the honorable gentleman, that "the power over elections, which is given to the general government in this system, is a dangerous power." I must own I feel, myself, surprised that an objection of this kind should be persisted in, after what has been said by the honorable colleague in reply. I think it has appeared, by a minute investigation of the subject, that it would have been not only unwise, but highly improper, in the late Convention, to have omitted this clause, or given less power than it does over elections. Such powers, sir, are enjoyed by every state government in the United States. In some they are of a much greater magnitude; and why should this be the only one deprived of them? Ought not these, as well as every other legislative body, to have the power of judging of the qualifications of its own members? "The times, places, and manner of holding elections for representatives, may be altered by Congress." This power, sir, has been shown to be necessary, not only on some particular occasions, but even to the very existence of the federal government. I have heard some very improbable suspicions indeed suggested with regard to the manner in which it will be exercised. Let us suppose it may be improperly exercised; is it not more likely so to be by the particular states than by the government of the United States?—because the general government will be more studious of the good of the whole than a particular state will be; and therefore, when the power of regulating the time, place, or manner of holding elections, is exercised by the Congress, it will be to correct the improper regulations of a particular state.

I now proceed to the second article of this Constitution, which relates to the executive department.

I find, sir, from an attention to the arguments used by the gentlemen on the other side of the house, that there are but few exceptions taken to this part of the system. I shall take notice of them, and afterwards point out some valuable qualifications, which I think this part possesses in an eminent degree.

The objection against the powers of the President is not that they are too many or too great; but, to state it in the gentlemen's own language, they are so trifling, that the President is no more than the *tool* of the Senate.

Now, sir, I do not apprehend this to be the case, because I see that he may do a great many things independently of the Senate; and, with respect to the executive powers of government in which the Senate participate, they can do nothing without him. Now, I would ask, which is most likely to be the tool of the other? Clearly, sir, he holds the helm, and the vessel can proceed neither in one direction nor another, without his concurrence. It was expected by many, that the cry would have been against the powers of the President as a monarchical power; indeed, the echo of such sound was heard some time before the rise of the late Convention. There were men, at that time, determined to make an attack upon whatever system should be proposed; but they mistook the point of direction. Had the President possessed those powers, which the opposition on this floor are willing to consign him, of making treaties and appointing officers, with the advice of a council of state, the clamor would have been, that the House of Representatives and the Senate were the *tools* of the monarch. This, sir, is but conjecture; but I leave it to those who are acquainted with the current of the politics pursued by the enemies of this system, to determine whether it is a reasonable conjecture or not.

The manner of appointing the President of the United States, I find, is not objected to; therefore I shall say little on that point. But I think it well worth while to state to this house how little the difficulties, even in the most difficult part of this system, appear to have been noticed by the honorable gentlemen in opposition. The Convention, sir, were perplexed with no part of this plan so much as with the mode of choosing the President of the United States. For my own part, I think the most unexceptionable mode, next after the one prescribed in this Constitution, would be that practised by the Eastern States and the state of New York; yet, if gentlemen object that an eighth part of our country forms a district too large for election, how much more would they object, if it was extended to the whole Union! On this subject, it was the opinion of a great majority in Convention, that the thing was impracticable; other embarrassments presented themselves.

Was the President to be appointed by the legislature? Was he to continue a certain time in office, and afterwards was he to become ineligible?

To have the executive officers dependent upon the legislative, would certainly be a violation of that principle, so necessary to preserve the freedom of republics, that the legislative and executive powers should be separate and independent. Would it have been proper that he should be appointed by the Senate? I apprehend that still stronger objections could be urged against that: cabal—intrigue—corruption—every thing bad, would have been the necessary concomitant of every election.

To avoid the inconveniences already enumerated, and many others that might be suggested, the mode before us was adopted. By it we avoid corruption; and we are little exposed to the lesser evils of party intrigue; and when the government shall be organized, proper care will undoubtedly be taken to counteract influence even of that nature. The Constitution, with the same view, has directed, that the day on which the electors shall give their votes shall be the same throughout the United States. I flatter myself the experiment will be a happy one for our country.

The choice of this officer is brought as nearly home to the people as is practicable. With the approbation of the state legislatures, the people may elect with only one remove; for "each state shall appoint, in such manner as the legislature thereof may direct, a number of electors equal to the whole number of senators and representatives to which the state may be entitled in Congress." Under this regulation, it will not be easy to corrupt the electors, and there will be little time or opportunity for tumult or intrigue. This, sir, will not be like the elections of a Polish diet, begun in noise and ending in bloodshed.

If gentlemen will look into this article, and read for themselves, they will find that there is no well-grounded reason to suspect the President will be the *tool* of the Senate. "The President shall be commander-in-chief of the army and navy of the United States, and of the militia of the several states, when called into the actual service of the United States. He may require the opinion, in writing, of the principal officers in each of the executive departments, upon any subject relative to the duties of their respective offices; and he shall have power to grant reprieves and pardons for offences against the United States." Must the President, after all, be called the *tool* of the Senate? I do not mean to insinuate that he has more powers than he ought to have, but merely to declare that they are of such a nature as to place him above expression of contempt.

There is another power of no small magnitude intrusted to this officer. "He shall take care that the laws be faithfully executed."

I apprehend that, in the administration of this government, it will not be found necessary for the Senate always to sit. I know some gentlemen have insinuated and conjectured that this will be the case; but I am inclined to a contrary opinion. If they had employment every day, no doubt but it might be the wish of the Senate to continue their session; but, from the nature of their business, I do not think it will be necessary for them to attend longer than the House of Representatives. Besides their legislative powers, they possess three others, viz., trying impeachments, concurring in making treaties, and in appointing officers. With regard to their power in making treaties, it is of importance that it should be very seldom exercised. We are happily removed from the vortex of European politics, and the fewer and the more simple our negotiations with European powers, the better they will be. If such be the case, it will be but once in a number of years that a single treaty will come before the Senate. I think, therefore, that on this account it will be unnecessary to sit constantly. With regard to the trial of impeachments, I hope it is what will seldom happen. In this observation, the experience of the ten last years supports me. Now, there is only left the power of concurring in the appointment of officers; but care is taken, in this Constitution, that this branch of business may be done without their presence. The president is authorized to fill up all vacancies that may happen, during the recess of the Senate, by granting commissions, which shall expire at the end of their next session; so that, on the whole, the Senate need not sit longer than the House of Representatives, at the public expense; and no doubt, if apprehensions are entertained of the Senate, the House of Representatives will not provide pay for them one day longer than is necessary. But what (it will be asked) is this great power of the President? He can fill the offices only by temporary appointments. True; but every person knows the advantage of being once introduced into an office; it is often of more importance than the highest recommendation.

Having now done with the legislative and executive branches of this government, I shall just remark, that, upon the whole question of the executive, it appears that the gentlemen in opposition state nothing as exceptionable but the deficiency of powers in the President; but rather seem to allow some degree of political merit in this department of government.

I now proceed to the judicial department; and here, Mr. President, I meet an objection, I confess, I had not expected; and it seems it did not occur to the honorable gentleman (Mr. Findley) who made it until a few days ago.

He alleges that the judges, under this Constitution, are not rendered sufficiently independent, because they may hold other offices; and though they may be independent as judges, yet their other office may depend upon the legislature. I confess, sir, this objection appears to me to be a little wire-drawn. In the first place, the legislature can appoint to no office; therefore, the dependence could not be on them for the office, but rather on the President and Senate; but then these cannot add the salary, because no money can be appropriated but in consequence of a law of the United States. No sinecure can be bestowed on any judge but by the concurrence of the whole legislature and the President; and I do not think this an event that will probably happen.

It is true that there is a provision made in the Constitution of Pennsylvania, that the judges shall not be allowed to hold any other office whatsoever; and I believe they are expressly forbidden to sit in Congress; but this, sir, is not introduced as a principle into this Constitution. There are many states in the Union, whose constitutions do not limit the usefulness of their best men, or exclude them from rendering those services to their country for which they are found eminently qualified. New York, far from restricting their chancellor, or judges of the Supreme Court, from a seat in

Congress, expressly provide for sending them there on extraordinary occasions. In Connecticut, the judges are not precluded from enjoying other offices. Judges from many states have sat in Congress. Now, it is not to be expected that eleven or twelve states are to change their sentiments and practice, on this subject, to accommodate themselves to Pennsylvania.

It is again alleged, against this system, that the powers of the judges are too extensive; but I will not trouble you, sir, with a repetition of what I had the honor of delivering the other day. I hope the result of those arguments gave satisfaction, and proved that the judicial were commensurate with the legislative powers; that they went no farther, and that they ought to go so far.

The laws of Congress being made for the Union, no particular state can be alone affected; and as they are to provide for the general purposes of the Union, so ought they to have the means of making the provisions effectual over all that country included within the Union.

Eodem die, 1787, P.M.—Mr. WILSON. I shall now proceed, Mr. President, to notice the remainder of the objections that have been suggested by the honorable gentlemen who oppose the system now before you.

We have been told, sir, by the honorable member from Fayette, (Mr. Smilie,) "that the trial by jury was intended to be given up, and the civil law was intended to be introduced into its place, in civil cases."

Before a sentiment of this kind was hazarded, I think, sir, the gentleman ought to be prepared with better proof in its support than any he has yet attempted to produce. It is a charge, sir, not only unwarrantable, but cruel: the idea of such a thing, I believe, never entered into the mind of a single member of that Convention; and I believe further, that they never suspected there would be found, within the United States, a single person that was capable of making such a charge. If it should be well founded, sir, they must abide by the consequences; but if (as I trust it will fully appear) it is ill founded, then he or they who make it ought to abide by the consequences.

Trial by jury forms a large field for investigation, and numerous volumes are written on the subject; those who are well acquainted with it may employ much time in its discussion; but in a country where its excellences are so well understood, it may not be necessary to be very prolix in pointing them out. For my part, I shall confine myself to a few observations in reply to the objections that have been suggested.

The member from Fayette (Mr. Smilie) has labored to infer that, under the Articles of Confederation, the Congress possessed no appellate jurisdiction; but this being decided against him by the words of that instrument, by which is granted to Congress the power of "establishing courts for receiving, and determining finally, appeals in all cases of capture," he next attempts a distinction, and allows the power of appealing from the decisions of the judges, but not from the verdict of a jury; but this is determined against him also by the practice of the states; for, in every instance which has occurred, this power has been claimed by Congress, and exercised by the Courts of Appeals. But what would be the consequence of allowing the doctrine for which he contends? Would it not be in the power of a jury, by their verdict, to involve the whole Union in a war? They may condemn the property of a neutral, or otherwise infringe the law of nations; in this case, ought their verdict to be without revisal? Nothing can be inferred from this to prove that trials by jury were intended to be given up. In Massachusetts, and all the Eastern States, their causes are tried by juries, though they acknowledge the appellate jurisdiction of Congress.

I think I am not now to learn the advantages of a trial by jury. It has excellences that entitle it to a superiority over any other mode, in cases to which it is applicable.

Where jurors can be acquainted with the characters of the parties and the witnesses,—where the whole cause can be brought within their knowledge and their view,—I know no mode of investigation equal to that by a jury: they hear every thing that is alleged; they not only hear the words, but they see and mark the features of the countenance; they can judge of weight due to such testimony; and moreover, it is a cheap and expeditious manner of distributing justice. There is another advantage annexed to the trial by jury; the jurors may indeed return a mistaken or ill-founded verdict, but their errors cannot be systematical.

Let us apply these observations to the objects of the judicial department, under this Constitution. I think it has been shown, already, that they all extend beyond the bounds of any particular state; but further, a great number of the civil causes there enumerated depend either upon the law of nations, or the marine law, that is, the general law of mercantile countries. Now, sir, in such cases, I presume it will not be pretended that this mode of decision ought to be adopted; for the law with regard to them is the same here as in every other country, and ought to be administered in the same manner. There are instances in which I think it highly probable that the trial by jury will be found proper; and if it is highly probable that it will be found proper, is it not equally probable that it will be adopted? There may be causes depending between citizens of different states; and as trial by jury is known and regarded in all the states, they will certainly prefer that mode of trial before any other. The Congress will have the power of making proper regulations on this subject, but it was impossible for the Convention to have gone minutely into it; but if they could, it must have been very improper, because alterations, as I observed before, might have been necessary; and whatever the Convention might have done would have continued unaltered, unless by an alteration of the Constitution. Besides, there was another difficulty with regard to this subject. In some of the states they have courts of chancery, and other appellate jurisdictions, and those states are as attached to that mode of distributing justice as those that have none are to theirs.

I have desired, repeatedly, that honorable gentlemen, who find fault, would be good enough to point out what they deem to be an improvement. The member from Westmoreland (Mr. Findley) tells us that the trial between citizens of different states ought to be by a jury of that state in which the cause of action rose. Now, it is easy to see that, in many instances, this would be very improper and very partial; for, besides the different manner of collecting and forming juries in the several states, the plaintiff comes from another state; he comes a stranger, unknown as to his character or mode of life, while the other party is in the midst of his friends, or perhaps his dependants. Would a trial by jury, in such a case, insure justice to the stranger? But again: I would ask that gentleman whether, if a great part of his fortune was in the hands of some person in Rhode Island, he would wish that his action to recover it should be determined by a jury of that country, under its present circumstances.

The gentleman from Fayette (Mr. Smilie) says that, if the Convention found themselves embarrassed, at least they might have done thus much—

they should have declared that the substance should be secured by Congress. This would be saying nothing unless the cases were particularized.

Mr. Smilie. I said the Convention ought to have declared that the legislature should establish the trial by jury by proper regulations.

Mr. Wilson. The legislature shall establish it by proper regulations! So, after all, the gentleman has landed us at the very point from which we set out. He wishes them to do the very thing they have done—to leave it to the discretion of Congress. The fact, sir, is, nothing more could be done.

It is well known that there are some cases that should not come before juries; there are others, that, in some of the states, never come before juries, and in those states where they do come before them, appeals are found necessary, the facts reëxamined, and the verdict of the jury sometimes is set aside; but I think, in all cases where the cause has come originally before a jury, that the last examination ought to be before a jury likewise.

The power of having appellate jurisdiction, as to facts, has been insisted upon as a proof, "that the Convention *intended* to give up the trial by jury in civil cases, and to introduce the civil law." I have already declared my own opinion on this point, and have shown not merely that it is founded on reason and authority;—the express declaration of Congress (*Journals of Congress,* March 6, 1779) is to the same purpose. They insist upon this power, as requisite to preserve the peace of the Union; certainly, therefore, it ought always to be possessed by the head of the confederacy. We are told, as an additional proof, that the trial by jury was intended to be given up; "that appeals are unknown to the common law; that the term is a civil-law term, and with it the civil law is intended to be introduced." I confess I was a good deal surprised at this observation being made; for Blackstone, in the very volume which the honorable member (Mr. Smilie) had in his hand, and read us several extracts from, has a chapter entitled "Of Proceeding in the Nature of Appeals,"—and in that chapter says, that the principal method of redress for erroneous judgments, in the king's courts of record, is by writ of error to some superior "*court of appeal.*" (3 *Blackstone,* 406.) Now, it is well known that his book is a commentary upon the common law. Here, then, is a strong refutation of the assertion, "that appeals are unknown to the common law."

I think these were all the circumstances adduced to show the truth of the assertion, that, in this Constitution, the trial by jury was *intended* to be given up by the late Convention in framing it. Has the assertion been proved? I say not; and the allegations offered, if they apply at all, apply in a contrary direction. I am glad that this objection has been stated, because it is a subject upon which the enemies of this Constitution have much insisted. We have now had an opportunity of investigating it fully; and the result is, that there is no foundation for the charge, but it must proceed from ignorance, or something worse.

I go on to another objection which has been taken to this system: "that the expense of the general government and of the state governments will be too great, and that the citizens will not be able to support them." If the state governments are to continue as cumbersome and expensive as they have hitherto been, I confess it would be distressing to add to their expenses, and yet it might be necessary; but I think I can draw a different conclusion on this subject, from more conjectures than one. The additional revenue to be raised by a general government will be more than sufficient for additional expense; and a great part of that revenue may be so contrived as not to be taken from the citizens of this country; for I am not of opinion that the consumer always pays the impost that is laid on imported articles; it is paid sometimes by the importer, and sometimes by the foreign merchant who sends them to us. Had a duty of this nature been laid at the time of the peace, the greatest part of it would have been the contribution of foreigners. Besides, whatever is paid by the citizens is a *voluntary* payment.

I think, sir, it would be very easy and laudable to lessen the expenses of the state governments. I have been told (and perhaps it is not very far from the truth) that there are *two thousand* members of assembly in the several states. The business of revenue is done in consequence of requisitions from Congress; and whether it is furnished or not, it commonly becomes a subject of discussion. Now, when this business is executed by the legislature of the United States, I leave it to those who are acquainted with the expense of long and frequent sessions of Assembly, to determine the great saving that will take place. Let me appeal to the citizens of Pennsylvania, how much time is taken up in this state every year, if not every session, in providing for the payment of an amazing interest due on her funded debt. There will be many sources of revenue, and many opportunities for economy, when the business of finance shall be administered under one government: the funds will be more productive, and the taxes, in all probability, less burdensome, than they are now.

I proceed to another objection that is taken against the power, given to Congress, of raising and keeping up standing armies. I confess I have been surprised that this objection was ever made; but I am more so that it is still repeated and insisted upon. I have taken some pains to inform myself how the other governments of the world stand with regard to this power, and the result of my inquiry is, that there is not one which has not the power of raising and keeping up standing armies. A government without the power of defence! it is a solecism.

I well recollect the principle insisted upon by the patriotic body in Great Britain; it is, that, in time of peace, a standing army ought not to be kept up without the consent of Parliament. Their only apprehension appears to be, that it might be dangerous, were the army kept up without the concurrence of the representatives of the people. Sir, we are not in the millennium. Wars may happen; and when they do happen, who is to have the power of collecting and appointing the force, then become immediately and indispensably necessary?

It is not declared, in this Constitution, that the Congress shall raise and support armies. No, sir: if they are not driven to it by necessity, why should we suppose they would do it by choice, any more than the representatives of the same citizens in the state legislatures? For we must not lose sight of the great principle upon which this work is founded. The authority here given to the general government flows from the same source as that placed in the legislatures of the several states.

It may be frequently necessary to keep up standing armies in time of peace. The present Congress have experienced the necessity, and seven hundred troops are just as much a standing army as seventy thousand. The principle which sustains them is precisely the same. They may go further, and raise an army, without communicating to the public the purpose for which it is raised. On a particular occasion they did this. When the commotions existed in Massachusetts, they gave orders for enlisting an additional body of two thousand men. I believe it is not generally known on what a perilous tenure we held our freedom and independence at that period. The flames of internal insurrection were ready to burst out in every quarter; they were formed by the correspondents of state officers, (to whom an allusion was made on a former day,) and from one end to the other of the continent, we walked on ashes, concealing fire beneath our feet; and ought Congress to be deprived of power to prepare for the defence and safety of our country? Ought they to be restricted from arming, until they divulge the motive which induced them to arm? I believe the *power* of raising and keeping up an army, in time of peace, is essential to every government. No government can secure its citizens against dangers, internal and external, without possessing it, and sometimes carrying it into execution. I confess it is a power in the exercise of which all wise and moderate governments will be as prudent and forbearing as possible. When we consider the situation of the United States, we must be satisfied that it will be necessary to keep up some troops for the protection of the western frontiers, and to secure our interest in the internal navigation of that country. It will be not only necessary, but it will be economical on the great scale. Our enemies, finding us invulnerable, will not attack us; and we shall thus prevent the occasion for larger standing armies. I am now led to consider another charge that is brought against this system.

It is said that Congress should not possess the power of calling out the militia, to execute the laws of the Union, suppress insurrections, and repel invasions; nor the President have the command of them when called out for such purposes.

I believe any gentleman, who possesses military experience, will inform you that men without a uniformity of arms, accoutrements, and discipline, are no more than a mob in a camp; that, in the field, instead of assisting, they interfere with one another. If a soldier drops his musket, and his companion, unfurnished with one, takes it up, it is of no service, because his cartridges do not fit it. By means of this system, a uniformity of arms and discipline will prevail throughout the United States.

I really expected that, for this part of the system at least, the framers of it would have received plaudits instead of censures, as they here discover a strong anxiety to have this body put upon an effective footing, and thereby, in a great measure, to supersede the necessity of raising or keeping up standing armies.

The militia formed under this system, and trained by the several states, will be such a bulwark of internal strength, as to prevent the attacks of foreign enemies. I have been told that, about the year 1744, an attack was intended by France upon Massachusetts Bay, but was given up on reading the militia law of the province.

If a single state could deter an enemy from such attempts, what influence will the proposed arrangement have upon the different powers of Europe?

In every point of view, this regulation is calculated to produce good effects. How powerful and respectable must the body of militia appear under general and uniform regulations! How disjointed, weak, and inefficient are they at present! I appeal to military experience for the truth of my observations.

The next objection, sir, is a serious one indeed; it was made by the honorable gentleman from Fayette, (Mr. Smilie.) "The Convention knew this was not a free government; otherwise, they would not have asked the powers of the purse and sword." I would beg to ask the gentleman what free government he knows that has not the powers of both? There was, indeed, a government under which we unfortunately were for a few years past, that had them not; but it does not now exist. A government without these powers is one of the improvements with which opposition wish to astonish mankind.

Have not the freest governments those powers? And are they not in the fullest exercise of them? This is a thing so clear, that really it is impossible to find facts or reasons more clear, in order to illustrate it. Can we create a government without the power to act? How can it act without the assistance of men? And how are men to be procured without being paid for their services? Is not the one power the consequence of the other?

We are told,—and it is the last and heaviest charge,—"that this government is an aristocracy, and was *intended* so to be by the late Convention;" and we are told (the truth of which is not disputed) that an aristocratical government is incompatible with freedom. I hope, before this charge is believed, some stronger reasons will be given in support of it than any that have yet been produced.

The late Convention were assembled to devise some plan for the security, safety, and happiness of the people of the United States. If they have devised a plan that robs them of their power, and constitutes an aristocracy, they are the parricides of their country, and ought to be punished as such. What part of this system is it that warrants the charge?

What is an aristocratic government? I had the honor of giving a definition of it at the beginning of our debates. It is, sir, the government of a few over the many—elected by themselves, or possessing a share in the government by inheritance, or in consequence of territorial rights, or some quality independent of the choice of the people. This is an aristocracy, and this Constitution is said to be an aristocratical form of government; and it is also said that it was intended so to be by the members of the late Convention who framed it. What peculiar rights have been reserved to any class of men, on any occasion? Does even the first magistrate of the United States draw to himself a single privilege or security that does not extend to every person throughout the United States? Is there a single distinction attached to him, in this system, more than there is to the lowest officer in the republic? Is there an office from which any one set of men whatsoever are excluded? Is there one of any kind in this system but is as open to the poor as to the rich? to the inhabitant of the country, as well as to the inhabitant of the city? And are the places of honor and emoluments confined to a few? And are these few the members of the late Convention? Have they made any particular provisions in favor of themselves, their relations, or their posterity? If they have committed their country to the demon of aristocracy, have they not committed themselves also, with every thing they held near and dear to them?

Far, far other is the genius of this system. I have had already the honor of mentioning its general nature; but I will repeat it, sir. In its principle it is purely democratical; but its parts are calculated in such manner as to obtain those advantages, also, which are peculiar to the other forms of government in other countries. By appointing a single magistrate, we secure strength, vigor, energy, and responsibility in the executive department. By appointing a Senate, the members of which are elected for six years, yet, by a rotation already taken notice of, changing every second year, we secure the benefit of experience, while, on the other hand, we avoid the inconveniences that arise from a long and detached establishment. This body is periodically renovated from the people, like a tree, which, at the proper season, receives its nourishment from its parent earth.

In the other branch of the legislature, the House of Representatives, shall we not have the advantages of benevolence and attachment to the people, whose immediate representatives they are?

A free government has often been compared to a pyramid. This allusion is made with peculiar propriety in the system before you; it is laid on the broad basis of the people; its powers gradually rise, while they are confined, in proportion as they ascend, until they end in that most permanent of all forms. When you examine all its parts, they will invariably be found to preserve that essential mark of free governments—a chain of connection with the people.

Such, sir, is the nature of this system of government; and the important question at length presents itself to our view—Shall it be ratified, or shall it be rejected, by this Convention? In order to enable us still further to form a judgment on this truly momentous and interesting point, on which all we have, or can have, dear to us on earth is materially depending, let us for a moment consider the consequences that will result from one or the other measure. Suppose we reject this system of government; what will be the consequence? Let the farmer say, he whose produce remains unasked for; nor can he find a single market for its consumption, though his fields are blessed with luxuriant abundance. Let the manufacturer, and let the mechanic, say; they can feel, and tell their feelings. Go along the wharves of Philadelphia, and observe the melancholy silence that reigns. I appeal not to those who enjoy places and abundance under the present government; they may well dilate upon the easy and happy situation of our country. Let the merchants tell you what is our commerce; let them say what has been their situation since the return of peace—an era which they might have expected would furnish additional sources to our trade, and a continuance, and even an increase, to their fortunes. Have these ideas been realized? or do they not lose some of their capital in every adventure, and continue the unprofitable trade from year to year, subsisting under the hopes of happier times under an efficient general government? The ungainful trade carried on by our merchants has a baneful influence on the interests of the manufacturer, the mechanic, and the farmer; and these, I believe, are the chief interests of the people of the United States.

I will go further. Is there now a government among us that can do a single act that a national government ought to do? Is there any power of the United States that can *command* a single shilling? This is a plain and a home question.

Congress may recommend; they can do no more: they may require; but they must not proceed one step further. If things are bad now,—and that they are not worse is only owing to hopes of improvement or change in the system,—will they become better when those hopes are disappointed? We have been told, by honorable gentlemen on this floor, (Mr. Smilie, Mr. Findley, and Mr. Whitehill,) that it is improper to urge this kind of argument in favor of a new system of government, or against the old one: unfortunately, sir, these things are too severely felt to be omitted; the people feel them; they pervade all classes of citizens, and every situation from New Hampshire to Georgia: the argument of necessity is the patriot's defence, as well as the tyrant's plea.

Is it likely, sir, that, if this system of government is rejected, a better will be framed and adopted? I will not expatiate on this subject; but I believe many reasons will suggest themselves to prove that such expectation would be illusory. If a better could be obtained at a future time, is there any thing essentially wrong in this? I go further. Is there any thing wrong that cannot be amended more easily by the mode pointed out in the system itself, than could be done by calling convention after convention, before the organization of the government? Let us now turn to the consequences that will result if we assent to and ratify the instrument before you. I shall trace them as concisely as I can, because I have trespassed already too long on the patience and indulgence of the house.

I stated, on a former occasion, one important advantage; by adopting this system, we become a *nation;* at present, we are not one. Can we perform a single national act? Can we do any thing to procure us dignity, or to preserve peace and tranquillity? Can we relieve the distress of our citizens? Can we provide for their welfare or happiness? The powers of our government are mere sound. If we offer to treat with a nation, we receive this humiliating answer: "You cannot, in propriety of language, make a treaty, because you have no power to execute it." Can we borrow money? There are too many examples of unfortunate creditors existing, both on this and the other side of the Atlantic, to expect success from this expedient. But could we borrow money, we cannot command a fund, to enable us to pay either the principal or interest; for, in instances where our friends have advanced the principal, they have been obliged to advance the interest also, in order to prevent the principal from being annihilated in their hands by depreciation. Can we raise an army? The prospect of a war is highly probable. The accounts we receive, by every vessel from Europe, mention that the highest exertions are making in the ports and arsenals of the greatest maritime powers. But whatever the consequence may be, are we to lie supine? We know we are unable, under the Articles of Confederation, to exert ourselves; and shall we continue so, until a stroke be made on our commerce, or we see the debarkation of a hostile army on our unprotected shores? Who will guaranty that our property will not be laid waste, that our towns will not be put under contribution, by a small naval force, and subjected to all the horror and devastation of war? May not this be done without opposition, at least effectual opposition, in the present situation of our country? There may be safety over the Appalachian Mountains, but there can be none on our sea-coast. With what propriety can we hope our flag will be respected, while we have not a single gun to fire in its defence?

Can we expect to make internal improvement, or accomplish any of those great national objects which I formerly alluded to, when we cannot find money to remove a single rock out of a river?

This system, sir, will at least make us a nation, and put it in the power of the Union to act as such. We shall be considered as such by every nation in the world. We shall regain the confidence of our citizens, and command the respect of others.

As we shall become a nation, I trust that we shall also form a national character, and that this character will be adapted to the principles and genius of our system of government: as yet we possess none; our language, manners, customs, habits, and dress, depend too much upon those of other countries. Every nation, in these respects, should possess originality; there are not, on any part of the globe, finer qualities for forming a national character, than those possessed by the children of America. Activity, perseverance, industry, laudable emulation, docility in acquiring information, firmness in adversity, and patience and magnanimity under the greatest hardships;—from these materials, what a respectable national character may be raised! In addition to this character I think there is strong reason to believe that America may take the lead in literary improvements and national importance. This is a subject which, I confess, I have spent much pleasing time in considering. That language, sir, which shall become most generally known in the civilized world, will impart great importance over the nation that shall use it. The language of the United States will, in future times, be diffused over a greater extent of country than any other that we know. The French, indeed, have made laudable attempts toward establishing a universal language; but, beyond the boundaries of France, even the French language is not spoken by one in a thousand. Besides the freedom of our country, the great improvements she has made, and will make, in the science of government, will induce the patriots and *literati* of every nation to read and understand our writings on that subject; and hence it is not improbable that she will take the lead in political knowledge.

If we adopt this system of government, I think we may promise security, stability, and tranquillity, to the governments of the different states. They would not be exposed to the danger of competition on questions of territory, or any other that have heretofore disturbed them. A tribunal is here found to decide, justly and quietly, any intefering claim; and now is accomplished what the great mind of Henry IV.[18] of France had in contemplation—a system of government for large and respectable dominions, united and bound together, in peace, under a superintending head, by which all their differences may be accommodated, without the destruction of the human race. We are told by Sully[19] that this was the favorite pursuit of that good king during the last years of his life; and he would probably have carried it into execution, had not the dagger of an assassin deprived the world of his valuable life. I have, with pleasing emotion, seen the wisdom and beneficence of a less efficient power under the Articles of Confederation, in the determination of the controversy between the states of Pennsylvania and Connecticut; but I have lamented that the authority of Congress did not extend to extinguish, entirely, the spark which has kindled a dangerous flame in the district of Wyoming.

Let gentlemen turn their attention to the amazing consequences which

18. Henry IV (1553–1610) ruled France from 1589 to 1610. In 1598 he enacted the Edict of Nantes, which guaranteed religious toleration for Protestants. He is often referred to as Henry the Great.

19. Maximilien de Bethune, Duke of Sully (1560–1641), was the unwavering right-hand man of Henry IV of France.

this principle will have in this extended country. The several states cannot war with each other; the general government is the great arbiter in contentions between them; the whole force of the Union can be called forth to reduce an aggressor to reason. What a happy exchange for the disjointed, contentious state sovereignties!

The adoption of this system will also secure us from danger, and procure us advantages from foreign nations. This, in our situation, is of great consequence. We are still an inviting object to one European power at least; and, if we cannot defend ourselves, the temptation may become too alluring to be resisted. I do not mean that, with an efficient government, we should mix with the commotions of Europe. No, sir, we are happily removed from them, and are not obliged to throw ourselves into the scale with any. This system will not hurry us into war; it is calculated to guard against it. It will not be in the power of a single man, or a single body of men, to involve us in such distress; for the important power of declaring war is vested in the legislature at large: this declaration must be made with the concurrence of the House of Representatives: from this circumstance we may draw a certain conclusion that nothing but our national interest can draw us into a war. I cannot forbear, on this occasion, the pleasure of mentioning to you the sentiments of the great and benevolent man, whose works I have already quoted on another subject. Mr. Necker has addressed this country in language important and applicable in the strictest degree to its situation and to the present subject. Speaking of war, and the greatest caution that all nations ought to use in order to avoid its calamities,—"And you, rising nation," says he, "whom generous efforts have freed from the yoke of Europe! let the universe be struck with still greater reverence at the sight of the privileges you have acquired, by seeing you continually employed for the public felicity: do not offer it as a sacrifice at the unsettled shrine of political ideas, and of the deceitful combinations of warlike ambition; avoid, or, at least, delay, participating in the passions of our hemisphere; make your own advantage of the knowledge which experience alone has given to our old age, and preserve, for a long time, the simplicity of childhood; in short, honor human nature, by showing that, when left to its own feelings, it is still capable of those virtues that maintain public order, and of that prudence which insures public tranquillity."

Permit me to offer one consideration more, that ought to induce our acceptance of this system. I feel myself lost in the contemplation of its magnitude. By adopting this system, we shall probably lay a foundation for erecting temples of liberty in every part of the earth. It has been thought by many, that on the success of the struggle America has made for freedom will depend the exertions of the brave and enlightened of other nations. The advantages resulting from this system will not be confined to the United States, but will draw from Europe many worthy characters, who pant for the enjoyment of freedom. It will induce princes, in order to preserve their subjects, to restore to them a portion of that liberty of which they have for many ages been deprived. It will be subservient to the great designs of Providence with regard to this globe—the multiplication of mankind, their improvement in knowledge, and their advancement in happiness.

Oration Delivered on the Fourth of July 1788, at the Procession Formed at Philadelphia to Celebrate the Adoption of the Constitution of the United States.

My friends and fellow citizens,

Your candid and generous indulgence I may well bespeak, for many reasons. I shall mention but one. While I express it, I feel it in all its force. My abilities are unequal—abilities far superiour to mine would be unequal—to the occasion on which I have the honour of being called to address you.

A people free and enlightened, establishing and ratifying a system of government, which they have previously considered, examined, and approved! This is the spectacle, which we are assembled to celebrate; and it is the most dignified one that has yet appeared on our globe. Numerous and splendid have been the triumphs of conquerors. But from what causes have they originated?—Of what consequences have they been productive? They have generally begun in ambition: they have generally ended in tyranny. But nothing tyrannical can participate of dignity: and to freedom's eye, Sesostris[1] himself appears contemptible, even when he treads on the necks of kings.

The senators of Rome, seated on their curule chairs, and surrounded with all their official lustre, were an object much more respectable: and we view, without displeasure, the admiration of those untutored savages, who considered them as so many gods upon earth. But who were those senators? They were only a part of a society: they were vested only with inferiour powers.

1. Likely refers to Sesostris I, pharaoh of Egypt from 1971 to 1926 B.C.

What is the object exhibited to our contemplation? A whole people exercising its first and greatest power—performing an act of sovereignty, original and unlimited!

The scene before us is unexampled as well as magnificent. The greatest part of governments have been the deformed offspring of force and fear. With these we deign not comparison. But there have been others which have formed bold pretensions to higher regard. You have heard of Sparta, of Athens, and of Rome; you have heard of their admired constitutions, and of their high-prized freedom. In fancied right of these, they conceived themselves to be elevated above the rest of the human race, whom they marked with the degrading title of barbarians. But did they, in all their pomp and pride of liberty, ever furnish, to the astonished world, an exhibition similar to that which we now contemplate? Were their constitutions framed by those, who were appointed for that purpose, by the people? After they were framed, were they submitted to the consideration of the people? Had the people an opportunity of expressing their sentiments concerning them? Were they to stand or fall by the people's approving or rejecting vote? To all these questions, attentive and impartial history obliges us to answer in the negative. The people were either unfit to be trusted, or their lawgivers were too ambitious to trust them.

The far-famed establishment of Lycurgus[2] was introduced by deception and fraud. Under the specious pretence of consulting the oracle concerning his laws, he prevailed on the Spartans to make a temporary experiment of them during his absence, and to swear that they would suffer no alteration of them till his return. Taking a disingenuous advantage of their scrupulous regard for their oaths, he prevented his return by a voluntary death, and, in this manner, endeavoured to secure a proud immortality to his system.

Even Solon[3]—the mild and moderating Solon—far from considering himself as employed only to *propose* such regulations as he should think

2. Said to have lived around 800 B.C., Lycurgus was the ancient lawgiver of Sparta. He instituted the reforms that would become the trademarks of Sparta, including the creation of a senate, the separation of the military from the common man, and the strict regimentation of youth.

3. Solon (c. 638–558 B.C.) was one of the seven wise men of ancient Greece. He instituted laws and political institutions that led Athens to great prosperity.

best calculated for promoting the happiness of the commonwealth, made and promulgated his laws with all the haughty airs of absolute power. On more occasions than one, we find him boasting, with much selfcomplacency, of his extreme forbearance and condescension, because he did not establish a despotism in his own favour, and because he did not reduce his equals to the humiliating condition of his slaves.

Did Numa[4] submit his institutions to the good sense and free investigation of Rome? They were received in precious communications from the goddess Egeria,[5] with whose presence and regard he was supremely favoured; and they were imposed on the easy faith of the citizens, as the dictates of an inspiration that was divine.

Such, my fellow citizens, was the origin of the most splendid establishments that have been hitherto known; and such were the arts, to which they owed their introduction and success.

What a flattering contrast arises from a retrospect of the scenes which we now commemorate! Delegates were appointed to deliberate and propose. They met and performed their delegated trust. The result of their deliberations was laid before the people. It was discussed and scrutinized in the fullest, freest, and severest manner—by speaking, by writing, and by printing—by individuals and by publick bodies—by its friends and by its enemies. What was the issue? Most favourable and most glorious to the system. In state after state, at time after time, it was ratified—in some states unanimously—on the whole, by a large and very respectable majority.

It would be improper now to examine its qualities. A decent respect for those who have accepted it, will lead us to presume that it is worthy of their acceptance. The deliberate ratifications, which have taken place, at once recommend the system, and the people by whom it has been ratified.

But why, methinks I hear some one say—why is so much exultation displayed in celebrating this event? We are prepared to give the reasons of our joy. We rejoice, because, under this constitution, we hope to see just government, and to enjoy the blessings that walk in its train.

4. Numa Pompilius was a legendary king of Rome and successor of Romulus. Roman ceremonial law and religious rites are ascribed to him. He died in 673 B.C.

5. Egeria was Numa Pompilius's wife, a goddess of childbirth, wisdom, and prophecy. She taught Numa Pompilius how to be a wise and just king.

Let us begin with Peace—the mild and modest harbinger of felicity! How seldom does the amiable wanderer choose, for her permanent residence, the habitations of men! In their systems, she sees too many arrangements, civil and ecclesiastical, inconsistent with the calmness and benignity of her temper. In the old world, how many millions of men do we behold, unprofitable to society, burthensome to industry, the props of establishments that deserve not to be supported, the causes of distrust in the times of peace, and the instruments of destruction in the times of war? Why are they not employed in cultivating useful arts, and in forwarding publick improvements? Let us indulge the pleasing expectation, that such will be the operation of government in the United States. Why may we not hope, that, disentangled from the intrigues and jealousies of European politicks, and unmolested with the alarm and solicitude to which these intrigues and jealousies give birth, our counsels will be directed to the encouragement, and our strength will be exerted in the cultivation, of all the arts of peace?

Of these, the first is agriculture. This is true in all countries: in the United States, its truth is of peculiar importance. The subsistence of man, the materials of manufactures, the articles of commerce—all spring originally from the soil. On agriculture, therefore, the wealth of nations is founded. Whether we consult the observations that reason will suggest, or attend to the information that history will give, we shall, in each case, be satisfied of the influence of government, good or bad, upon the state of agriculture. In a government, whose maxims are those of oppression, property is insecure. It is given, it is taken away, by caprice. Where there is no security for property, there is no encouragement for industry. Without industry, the richer the soil, the more it abounds with weeds. The evidence of history warrants the truth of these general remarks. Attend to Greece; and compare her agriculture in ancient and in modern times. Then, smiling harvests bore testimony to the bountiful boons of liberty. Now, the very earth languishes under oppression. View the Campania of Rome. How melancholy the prospect! Whichever way you turn your afflicted eyes, scenes of desolation crowd before them. Waste and barrenness appear around you in all their hideous forms. What is the reason? With double tyranny the land is cursed. Open the classick page: you trace, in chaste description, the beautiful reverse of every thing you have seen. Whence proceeds the difference? When that description was made, the force of liberty pervaded the soil.

But is agriculture the only art, which feels the influence of government? Over manufactures and commerce its power is equally prevalent. There the same causes operate—and there they produce the same effects. The industrious village, the busy city, the crowded port—all these are the gifts of liberty; and without a good government, liberty cannot exist.

These are advantages, but these are not all the advantages, that result from a system of good government.—Agriculture, manufactures, and commerce will ensure to us plenty, convenience, and elegance. But is there not something still wanting to finish the man? Are internal virtues and accomplishments less estimable, or less attracting than external arts and ornaments? Is the operation of government less powerful upon the former than upon the latter? By no means. Upon this as upon a preceding topick, reason and history will concur in their information and advice. In a serene mind, the sciences and the virtues love to dwell. But can the mind of a man be serene, when the property, liberty, subsistence of himself, and of those for whom he feels more than he feels for himself, depend on a tyrant's nod. If the dispirited subject of oppression can, with difficulty, exert his enfeebled faculties, so far as to provide, on the incessant demands of nature, food just enough to lengthen out his wretched existence, can it be expected that, in such a state, he will experience those fine and vigorous movements of the soul, without the full and free exercise of which, science and virtue will never flourish? Look around you to the nations that now exist. View, in historick retrospect, the nations that have heretofore existed. The collected result will be, an entire conviction of these all-interesting truths—where tyranny reigns, there is the country of ignorance and vice—where good government prevails, there is the country of science and virtue. Under a good government, therefore, we must look for the accomplished man.

But shall we confine our views even here? While we wish to be accomplished men and citizens, shall we wish to be nothing more? While we perform our duty, and promote our happiness in this world, shall we bestow no regards upon the next? Does no connexion subsist between the two? From this connexion flows the most important of all the blessings of good government. But here let us pause—unassisted reason can guide us no farther—she directs us to that heaven-descended science, by which life and immortality have been brought to light.

May we not now say, that we have reason for our joy? But while we cherish the delightful emotion, let us remember those things, which are requisite to give it permanence and stability. Shall we lie supine, and look in listless langour, for those blessings and enjoyments, to which exertion is inseparably attached? If we would be happy, we must be active. The constitution and our manners must mutually support and be supported. Even on this festivity, it will not be disagreeable or incongruous to review the virtues and manners that both justify and adorn it.

Frugality and temperance first attract our attention. These simple but powerful virtues are the sole foundation, on which a good government can rest with security. They were the virtues, which nursed and educated infant Rome, and prepared her for all her greatness. But in the giddy hour of her prosperity, she spurned from her the obscure instruments, by which it was procured; and, in their place, substituted luxury and dissipation. The consequence was such as might have been expected. She preserved, for some time, a gay and flourishing appearance; but the internal health and soundness of her constitution were gone. At last, she fell a victim to the poisonous draughts, which were administered by her perfidious favourites. The fate of Rome, both in her rising and in her falling state, will be the fate of every other nation that shall follow both parts of her example.

Industry appears next among the virtues of a good citizen. Idleness is the nurse of villains. The industrious alone constitute a nation's strength. I will not expatiate on this fruitful subject. Let one animating reflection suffice. In a well constituted commonwealth, the industry of every citizen extends beyond himself. A common interest pervades the society. Each gains from all, and all gain from each. It has often been observed, that the sciences flourish all together: the remark applies equally to the arts.

Your patriotick feelings attest the truth of what I say, when, among the virtues necessary to merit and preserve the advantages of a good government, I number a warm and uniform attachment to liberty, and to the constitution. The enemies of liberty are artful and insidious. A counterfeit steals her dress, imitates her manner, forges her signature, assumes her name. But the real name of the deceiver is licentiousness. Such is her effrontery, that she will charge liberty to her face with imposture: and she will, with shameless front, insist that herself alone is the genuine character, and that herself alone is entitled to the respect, which the genuine character deserves. With the giddy and undiscerning, on whom a deeper impression is made by dauntless impudence than by modest merit, her pretensions are often successful. She receives the honours of liberty, and liberty herself is treated as a traitor and a usurper. Generally, however, this bold impostor acts only a secondary part. Though she alone appear upon the stage, her motions are regulated by dark ambition, who sits concealed behind the curtain, and who knows that despotism, his other favourite, can always follow the success of licentiousness. Against these enemies of liberty, who act in concert, though they appear on opposite sides, the patriot citizen will keep a watchful guard.

A good constitution is the greatest blessing, which a society can enjoy. Need I infer, that it is the duty of every citizen to use his best and most unremitting endeavours for preserving it pure, healthful, and vigorous? For the accomplishment of this great purpose, the exertions of no one citizen are unimportant. Let no one, therefore, harbour, for a moment, the mean idea, that he is and can be of no value to his country: let the contrary manly impression animate his soul. Every one can, at *many* times, perform, to the state, *useful* services; and he, who steadily pursues the road of patriotism, has the most inviting prospect of being able, at *some* times, to perform *eminent* ones. Allow me to direct your attention, in a very particular manner, to a momentous part, which, by this constitution, every citizen will frequently be called to act. All those in places of power and trust will be elected either immediately by the people, or in such a manner that their appointment will depend ultimately on such immediate election. All the derivative movements of government must spring from the original movement of the people at large. If to this they give a sufficient force and a just direction, all the others will be governed by its controlling power. To speak without a metaphor, if the people, at their elections, take care to choose none but representatives that are wise and good, their representatives will take care, in their turn, to choose or appoint none but such as are wise and good also. The remark applies to every succeeding election and appointment. Thus the characters proper for publick officers will be diffused from the immediate elections of the people over the remotest parts of administration. Of what immense consequence is it, then, that this primary duty should be faithfully and skilfully discharged! On the faithful and skilful discharge of it, the publick happiness or infelicity, under this and every other constitution, must, in a very great measure, depend. For, believe me, no government, even the best, can be happily administered by ignorant or vicious men. You will forgive me, I am sure, for endeavouring to impress upon your minds, in the strongest manner, the importance of this great duty. It is the first concoction in politicks; and if an errour is committed here, it can never be corrected in any subsequent process: the certain consequence must be disease. Let no one say, that he is but a single citizen; and that his ticket will be but one in the box. That one ticket may turn the election. In battle, every soldier should consider the publick safety as depending on his single arm: at an election, every citizen should consider the publick happiness as depending on his single vote.

A progressive state is necessary to the happiness and perfection of man. Whatever attainments are already reached, attainments still higher should be pursued. Let us, therefore, strive with noble emulation. Let us suppose we have done nothing, while any thing yet remains to be done. Let us, with fervent zeal, press forward, and make unceasing advances in every thing that can support, improve, refine, or embellish society. To enter into particulars under each of these heads, and to dilate them according to their importance, would be improper at this time. A few remarks on the last of them will be congenial with the entertainments of this auspicious day.

If we give the slightest attention to nature, we shall discover, that with utility, she is curious to blend ornament. Can we imitate a better pattern? Publick exhibitions have been the favourite amusements of some of the wisest and most accomplished nations. Greece, in her most shining era, considered her games as far from being the least respectable among her publick establishments. The shows of the circus evince that, on this subject, the sentiments of Greece were fortified by those of Rome.

Publick processions may be so planned and executed as to join both the properties of nature's rule. They may instruct and improve, while they entertain and please. They may point out the elegance or usefulness of the sciences and the arts. They may preserve the memory, and engrave the importance of great political events. They may represent, with peculiar felicity and force, the operation and effects of great political truths. The picturesque and splendid decorations around me furnish the most beautiful and most brilliant proofs, that these remarks are far from being imaginary.

The commencement of our government has been eminently glorious: let our progress in every excellence be proportionably great. It will—it must be so. What an enrapturing prospect opens on the United States! Placid husbandry walks in front, attended by the venerable plough. Lowing herds adorn our vallies: bleating flocks spread over our hills: verdant meadows, enamelled pastures, yellow harvests, bending orchards, rise in rapid succession from east to west. Plenty, with her copious horn, sits easy smiling, and, in conscious complacency, enjoys and presides over the scenes. Commerce next advances in all her splendid and embellished forms. The rivers, and lakes, and seas, are crowded with ships. Their shores are covered with cities. The cities are filled with inhabitants. The arts, decked with elegance, yet with simplicity, appear in beautiful variety, and well adjusted arrangement. Around them are diffused, in rich abundance, the necessaries, the decencies, and the ornaments of life. With heartfelt contentment, industry beholds his honest labours flourishing and secure. Peace walks serene and unalarmed over all the unmolested regions—while liberty, virtue, and religion go hand in hand, harmoniously, protecting, enlivening, and exalting all! Happy country! May thy happiness be perpetual!

Speech on Choosing the Members of the Senate by Electors; Delivered, on the 31st December, 1789, in the Convention of Pennsylvania, Assembled for the Purpose of Reviewing, Altering, and Amending the Constitution of the State.[a]

Well assured I am, that the subject now before the convention must appear to honourable members, for whom I have much regard, under an aspect very different from that, in which it makes its approaches to me. Indeed it has not always appeared to myself in precisely the same light, in which I now view it. One reason may be, that I have not formerly been accustomed to contemplate it from the point of sight, at which I now stand, and from which it is my duty, enjoined by the strongest ties, to make the most attentive and accurate observations. I have considered it as a subject of speculative discussion. I have taken of it such a slight and general survey, as one person would take of the estate of another, without any expectation that it, or one similar to it, would ever become his own. On such a vague and superficial examination, I have not studied or investigated its inconveniences or defects.

a. The debate, in the course of which this speech was delivered, related to the following provisions in the draft of a constitution reported to the convention by a committee appointed for the purpose.

The citizens of the city of Philadelphia and of the several counties in this state, qualified to elect representatives, when assembled for that purpose, shall, if occasion require, at the same time, at the same places, and in the same manner, for every representative, elect two persons resident within their city or county respectively, as electors of the senator or senators of their district.

The very respectable senate of Maryland, chosen by electors, furnishes with letters of recommendation every institution, to which it bears even a distant resemblance. The moderation, the firmness, the wisdom, and the consistency, which have characterized the proceedings of that body, have been of signal benefit to the state, of whose government it forms a part; and have been the theme of just applause in her sister states. It is by no means surprising, that a favourable opinion has been entertained concerning the principles and manner of its constitution.

But now that the question relative to those points comes before us, in the discharge of our high trust, we must devest ourselves of every prepossession, which we may have hitherto indulged; and must scrutinize the subject closely, strictly, deeply, and minutely. It is incumbent upon us to weigh well, 1. Whether the qualities, that so deservedly appreciate the senate of Maryland, may not be secured to a senate, formed and organized upon very different and more eligible principles. 2. Whether the principles, upon which that senate has been formed and organized, are applicable to the plan laid before the convention.

It is admitted, on one side, that the electors should be chosen by the same persons, by whom it is contended, on the other side, that the senators should be chosen. The only question, then, is, whether an intermediate grade of persons, called electors, should be introduced between the senators and the people.

I beg leave to state to the house the light, in which this subject has appeared to me, on an examination which I may venture to style attentive; and to make some remarks, naturally resulting, in my opinion, from the views I have taken of it on different sides.

When I am called upon to appoint other persons to make laws for me, I do it because such an appointment is of absolute necessity; for the citizens

---

Within days after their election, the electors of each district shall meet together at some convenient place within the district, and elect the senator or senators for their district.

No elector shall be chosen a senator.

No person shall be chosen an elector, who shall not have resided in the district three years next before his election. And no person shall be chosen an elector, who is a member of the legislature, or who holds any office in the appointment of the executive department. *Ed.*

of Pennsylvania can neither assemble nor deliberate together in one place. When I reflect, that the laws which are to be made may affect my own life, my own liberty, my own property, and the lives, liberties, properties, and prospects of others likewise, who are dearest to me, I consider the trust, which I place in those for whom I vote to be legislators, as the greatest that one man can, in the course of the business of life, repose in another. I know none, indeed, that can be greater, except that, with which the members of this convention are now honoured; and which happens not but once, and often not once, in the successive revolutions of numerous centuries. But I console myself, that the same trust, which is committed by me, is also committed by others, who are as deeply interested in its exercise as I am. I console myself further, that those, to whom this trust is committed, are the *immediate* choice of myself, and of those others equally interested with myself.

But, by the plan before you, I am now called upon to delegate this trust in a manner, and to transfer it to a distance, which I have never experienced before—I am called upon, not to appoint legislators of my own choice, but to impower others to appoint whomsoever they shall think proper, to be legislators over me, and over those nearest to me in the different relations of life—I am called upon to do this, not only for myself, but for thousands of my constituents, who have confided to me their interests and rights in this convention.—I am called upon to do this for my constituents, and for myself, for the avowed purpose of introducing a choice, different from that which they or I would make. I say *different;* because, if the people and the electors would choose the same senators, there cannot be even a shadow of pretence for acting by the nugatory intervention of electors. I am called upon to do this, not only for the purpose of introducing a choice of senators different from that which the people would make; but for the additional purpose of introducing a new state of things and relations hitherto unknown between the people and their legislators. On the principles of representation, as hitherto understood and practised, there was a trust, and one of the most intimate and important kind, between the people and their representatives, and a responsibility of the latter to the former. On the plan reported, that trust and that responsibility will certainly be weakened: it is doubtful whether they will not be wholly destroyed. Can a trust subsist without some mutual agreement or consent? Can responsibility, resulting from an election, operate in behalf of those who do not choose? Suppose one of the citizens, who chose an elector, who chose a senator, to expostulate with that senator concerning some part of his senatorial conduct; might not the senator retort upon him—Sir, I know not you in this business: I was not chosen a senator by you: I was chosen by——. To them I am ready to account for what I have done. You chose them my electors: if any thing is amiss, you will please to look to them for satisfaction. For, give me leave to tell you, that I know not you nor the other people of your district in my conduct as a senator: neither you nor they chose me. The constitution, sir, supposes that neither they nor you would have chosen me, if you had been indulged with a choice; for the constitution supposes an election made by electors to be very different indeed from that which would be made by the people.—What answer could be made to this?

But if this must be styled a trust, it is certainly one of a new and of a very extraordinary nature. It may subsist not only without the will or knowledge of those from whom it originates; but, on the principles of this plan, it may subsist against their will declared in the most publick and explicit manner. Suppose a senator to behave altogether to the dissatisfaction of a district, for which he is appointed: suppose the people unanimously inclined to remove him at the next election. Can they do it? No. Suppose them to give the most unequivocal instructions to the electors for this purpose: the electors may choose him, the instructions notwithstanding: and the senator may brave them and tell them that he will legislate for them, and make them feel all the effects of his legislative power, in spite of their unavailing efforts to the contrary.

Sir, I will consider well—I will ponder long—before I consent that legislators be introduced in a shape so very questionable. I am placed in a new situation. Permit me to view it again. I am called upon to transfer a right—the right of *immediate* representation in the legislature—a right which I have hitherto retained unalienated—a right which has never, heretofore, been transferred by the citizens of Pennsylvania. Certainly, sir, this new situation requires that I should make a solemn pause—look around me, and reflect what my constituents and I have been, and what we are likely to be.

Many honourable members of this convention are, I presume, in the same predicament with myself; both as it respects their constituents, and as it respects themselves. On every account, it is proper to weigh this subject well.

Those who advocate the plan of electors must do so, either to avoid inconveniences which cannot be avoided, or to obtain advantages which cannot be obtained, in an election by the people themselves. We are, therefore, naturally led to institute a comparison between the two modes of election; and to estimate and balance the qualities and consequences of each.

The subject is of high and extensive importance in the theory and practice of government; and well deserves a full, a patient, and a candid investigation.

The works of human invention are progressive; and frequently are not completed, till after a slow and lengthened series of gradual improvements, remotely distant from one another both in place and in time. To the theory and practice of government this observation is applicable with peculiar justness and peculiar force. In this science, few opportunities have been given to the human mind of indulging itself in easy and unrestrained investigation: still fewer opportunities have offered of verifying and correcting investigation by experiment. An age—a succession of ages elapses, before a system of jurisprudence rises from its first rude beginnings. When we have made a little progress, and look forward, a few eminences in prospect are fondly supposed the greatest elevation we shall be obliged to ascend. But these, once gained, disclose, behind them, new and superiour degrees of excellence yet unattained. In beginning and continuing the pursuit of those arduous paths, through which this science leads us, the tracts, which we explore, point to others, which yet remain to be explored.

If the *discoveries* in government are difficult and slow; how much more arduous must it be to attain, in practice, the advantage of those discoveries, after they have been made! Of some governments, the foundation has been laid in necessity; of others, in fraud; of others, in force; of how few, in deliberate and discerning choice! If, in their commencement, they have been so unpropitious to the principles of freedom, and to the means of happiness; shall we wonder that, in their progress, they have been equally unfavourable to advances in virtue and excellence?

Let us ransack the records of history: in all our researches, how few fair instances shall we be able to find, in which a government has been formed, whose end has been the happiness of those for whom it was designed? how few fair instances shall we be able to find, in which such a government has been administered with a steady direction towards that end?

To these considerations, we must add others, which show still further the numerous and strong obstacles, that lie in the way of improvement in jurisprudence. Government founded on improper principles, and directed to improper objects, has a powerful and pernicious bias both upon those who rule, and those who are ruled. Its bias upon the first will occasion no surprise: its bias upon the second, however surprising, is not, perhaps, less efficacious, whether we consider their sentiments or their conduct. Thus the principles of despotism become the principles of a whole nation, blinded and degraded by its destructive influence. Power, splendour, influence, prejudice, fashion, habit, pride, and meanness, are all arranged to countenance and support those principles.

When we revolve, when we compare, when we combine the remarks we have been now making; when we take a slight glance of others that might be offered; we shall be at no loss to account for the slow and small progress, that, after a long lapse of ages, has been made in the science and practice of government.

This progress has been peculiarly slow and small in the discovery and improvement of the interesting doctrines and rules of election and representation. If government, with regard to other subjects, may be said, as with propriety it has been said, to be still in its infancy; we may well consider it, with regard to this subject, as only in its childhood. And yet this is the subject, which must form the basis of every government, that is, at once, efficient, respectable, and free. The pyramid of government—and a republican government may well receive that beautiful and solid form—should be raised to a dignified altitude: but its foundations must, of consequence, be broad, and strong, and deep. The authority, the interests, and the affections of the people at large are the only basis, on which a superstructure, proposed to be at once durable and magnificent, can be rationally erected.

Representation is the chain of communication between the people, and those to whom they have committed the exercise of the powers of government. If the materials, which form this chain, are sound and strong; I shall not be very anxious about the degree to which they are polished.

But, in order to impart the true republican lustre to freemen, I know no means more efficacious, than to invite and admit them to the rights of suffrage, and to enhance, as much as possible, the value of that right.

I well know how shamefully this right, all-important as it is, has been neglected—I well know how often we have seen the election ground, thinly frequented, or almost deserted, bear mournful testimony to the indolence or to the indifference of the electors. I well know by what frivolous causes they have sometimes been induced to forego the enjoyment of the noblest right of men. But we will indulge the fond conjecture, that this supineness has been owing neither to defect nor degeneracy in the minds and principles of our citizens, nor to ignorance or disregard of the exalted rank, to which, as citizens of a free commonwealth, they are entitled. It has been occasioned, we flatter ourselves, by the narrow point of view, in which the right of election, before the revolution, was considered; and by the few objects, to which the exercise of it was directed. Before that event, the doctrine and the exercise of authority by representation was confined in Pennsylvania, as in England, to one branch of one of the great powers, into which we have seen government divided: and over even that branch a double negative was held suspended by two powers, neither of them professing to derive their authority from the people. Our surprise will be diminished, and our reprehension will be softened, by reflecting, that, in this dependent situation, the ardour of citizenship was probably *damped* as well as confined. Habits, once formed and become familiar, are not soon or easily laid aside. Our customs do not always or immediately vary in proportion to the variation of their causes. Indifference to elections, once less important, has continued, though their importance has been amazingly increased. But this, we hope, will not be the case long. The magnitude of the right will, we trust, secure, in future, the merited attention to the exercise of it.

What is the right of suffrage, which we now display, to be viewed, admired, and enjoyed by our constituents? Is it to go to an obscure tavern in an obscure corner of an obscure district, and to vote, amidst the fumes of spiritous liquors, for a justice of the peace? There, indeed, no lesson would probably be learned, but that of low vice; no example would probably be shown, but that of illiberal cunning. Is it even to choose the members of one part of a legislature, the patriotick counsels and efforts of which part are liable, at every moment, to be controlled and frustrated by the negatives of other powers, independent of the authority, and indifferent, perhaps unfriendly, to the interests of the people? Here, indeed, there might be room for lessons of frigid caution, and timid prudence. It might not be thought advisable to elect a representative of bold, undissembled, and inflexible virtue: he might be obnoxious to his superiours in the other line; and, instead of averting, might provoke the exercise of their overruling power.

Of much higher import—of much more improving efficacy, is that right, which is now the object of our contemplation. It is a right to choose, in large and respectable assemblies, all the legislative, and many of the executive officers of the government; it is a right to choose those, who shall be invested with the authority and with the confidence of the people, and who may employ that authority and that confidence for the noblest interests of the commonwealth, without the apprehension of disappointment or control.

This, surely, must have a powerful tendency to open, to enlighten, to enlarge, and to exalt the mind. I cannot sufficiently express my own ideas of the dignity and value of this right. In real majesty, an independent and unbiassed elector stands superiour to princes, addressed by the proudest titles, attended by the most magnificent retinues, and decorated with the most splendid regalia. His sovereignty is original: theirs is only derivative.

The benign influence flowing from the possession and exercise of this right deserves to be fully and clearly pointed out. The man who enjoys the right of suffrage on the extensive scale which we have marked, will naturally turn his attention to the contemplation of publick men and publick measures. The inquiries he will make, the information he will receive, and his own reflections on both will afford a beneficial and amusing employment to his mind. I am far from insinuating that every citizen should be an enthusiast in politicks, or that the interests of himself, his family, and those who depend on him for their comfortable situation in life, should be absorbed in Quixote speculations about the management or the reformation of the state. But there is surely a golden mean in things; and there can be no real incompatibility between the discharge of one's publick and that of his private duty. Let private industry receive the warmest encouragement; for it is the basis of publick happiness. But must the bow of honest industry be always bent? At no moment shall a little relaxation be allowed?

That relaxation, if properly directed, may prove to be instructive as well as agreeable. It may consist in reading a newspaper, or in conversing with a fellow citizen. May not the newspaper convey some interesting intelligence, or contain some useful essay? For all newspapers are not dedicated to the demon of slander. May not the conversation take a pleasing and an improving turn? Many hours, I believe, are every where spent in talking about the unimportant occurrences of the day or in the neighbourhood; and, perhaps, the frailties or the involuntary imperfections of a neighbour form too often one of the sweet but poisonous ingredients of the discourse. Would it be any great detriment to society or to individuals, if other characters, and with different views, were brought upon the carpet?

At every election, a number of important appointments must be made. To do this, is, indeed, the business of a day. But it ought to be the business of much more than a day to be prepared for doing it well. When a citizen elects to office—give me leave to repeat it—he performs an act of the first political consequence. He should be employed, on every convenient occasion, in making researches after proper persons for filling the different departments of power; in discussing, with his neighbours and fellow citizens, the qualities that should be possessed by those who fill the several offices; and in acquiring information, with the spirit of manly candour, concerning the manners, and history, and characters of those, who are likely to be candidates for the publick choice. A habit of conversing and reflecting on these subjects, and of governing his actions by the result of his deliberations, will form, in the mind of the citizen, a uniform, a strong, and a lively sensibility to the interests of his country. The same causes will produce a warm and an enlightened attachment to those, who are best fitted and best disposed to support and advance those interests.

By these means, and in this manner, pure and genuine patriotism—that kind, which consists in liberal investigation and disinterested conduct—is produced, cherished, and strengthened in the mind: by these means, and in this manner, the warm and generous emotion glows and is reflected from breast to breast.

Investigations of this nature would be useful and improving not to their authors only: they would be so to their objects likewise. The love of honest and well-earned fame is deeply rooted in honest and susceptible minds. Can there be a stronger incentive to the energy of this passion, than the hope of becoming the object of wellfounded and distinguishing applause? Can there be a more complete gratification of this passion, than the satisfaction of knowing that this applause is given—that it is given upon the most honourable principles, and acquired by the most honourable pursuits? To souls truly ingenuous, indiscriminate praise, misplaced praise, flattering praise, interested praise have no bewitching charms. But when publick approbation is the result of publick discernment, it must be highly pleasing to those who give, and to those who receive it.

Let us now review a little the steps we have trod: let us reconsider the ground we have passed over, and the observations we have made. Have I painted the rights of election in colours too flattering?—Have I placed their importance in a light too strong?—Have I described their influence in language, or in sentiments, that have been exaggerated? I presume that I have not.

If, then, the remarks which I have made, and the deductions which I have drawn, will bear—and I trust they will bear—the test of strict and sober scrutiny; what is the result necessarily flowing from the whole? It is undeniably this—that the rights of suffrage, properly understood, properly valued, properly cultivated, and properly exercised, is a rich mine of intelligence and patriotism—that it is an abundant source of the most rational, the most improving, and the most endearing connexion among the citizens—and that it is a most powerful, and, at the same time, a most pleasing bond of union between the citizens, and those whom they select for the different offices and departments of government.

If these things are so; why should this right, so valuable and important, the cause of so many blessings, moral, intellectual, and political, be weakened—why should it be interrupted by the interjection of electors? Reasons irresistibly cogent will certainly be urged and supported, before such a measure will be adopted by the members of this convention.

It has been already mentioned, that those who advocate the plan of electors must do so, either to avoid inconveniences which cannot be avoided, or to obtain advantages which cannot be obtained, in an election by the people. What inconveniences will be avoided?

Will the meetings of the people be less frequent, less troublesome, or less expensive in choosing electors than in choosing senators? In respect both of frequency and of trouble they will be precisely the same. In respect of expense, the inconvenience will be increased by choosing electors; for it will be but reasonable that an allowance be made to them for their time, their trouble, and their services. In these respects, therefore, no inconvenience will be avoided, but an inconvenience will be incurred, by choosing electors.

Will inconveniences respecting the objects of choice attend elections by the people, and be avoided in elections by electors? What are those inconveniences?

Will the choice of the people be less valid than the choice of electors? That will not be pretended, since the electors themselves will derive *all* their authority from the people.

Will the choice of the people be less honourable than the choice of electors? In republican governments, the people are the fountain of honour as well as of power.

Will the choice of the people be less disinterested than the choice of electors? Interest will probably be consulted in both choices: but, in the first, the interests of the individuals, added together, will form precisely the aggregate interest of the whole; whereas, in the last, the interests of the electors, added together, will form but a small part of the interests of the whole; and that small part may be altogether unattached, nay, it may be altogether repugnant, to the remainder.

Will the choice of the people be less impartial than the choice of electors? The answer to this question is determined by the answer to the last. An impartial choice, in the case before us, is a choice that embraces the interests of the whole; a partial choice is that which embraces the interests only of a part. A choice by the people is most likely to suit the first description: a choice by electors is most likely to suit the last.

Will the choice of the people be made with less solicitude and fewer precautions for their common advantage than the choice of electors? If every individual among the people attends to his own advantage; the common advantage, which is the joint result of the whole, will be provided for. But every elector may be very attentive to his own advantage; and yet the common advantage may be left wholly unprovided for.

Will the choice of the people be less wise than the choice of electors? We have already seen that it will not be less valid, nor less honourable, nor less disinterested, nor less impartial, nor less for the common advantage: having seen all this, we may pronounce the presumption to be violent, that it will not be less wise. Upon this presumption we shall leave the matter for the present.

Permit me to observe, in the mean time, that inconveniences unavoidable in elections by the people, but altogether foreign from elections by electors, ought to be shown clearly and undeniably on the other side.

The next inquiry is—what advantages can be obtained in elections by electors, that are unattainable in elections by the people.

This side of the inquiry is, in my view, very much anticipated by the discussion of the other side: indeed it appears to me wholly unproductive. To those who think and speak in favour of electors, it may disclose sources of abundant fertility: to their investigations and discoveries I cheerfully leave it; observing, under this head, that the advantages to be gained, as well as the inconveniences to be avoided, ought to be shown clearly and undeniably on the other side. For if, upon the whole, the balance shall hang in equilibrio; the predilection, for the strong reason already mentioned, will certainly be in favour of a choice by the people themselves, and not by electors.

This predilection ought to operate for another reason, which has not yet been mentioned. It will be cheerfully admitted, that all power is originally in the people: the consequence, unavoidable, is, that power ought to be exercised personally by the people, when this can be done without inconvenience and without disadvantage. In some of the small republicks of Greece, and in the first ages of the commonwealth of Rome, the people voted, even on the passing of laws, in their aggregate capacity. Among the ancient Germans this was also done upon great occasions. "De minoribus consultant principes," says Tacitus, in his masterly account of Germany, "de majoribus omnes."[1] And from the practices of the ancient Germans, some of the finest maxims of modern government are drawn. If, therefore, no inconvenience will be avoided, and no advantage will be obtained by

1. Wilson paraphrased Tacitus's claim "de minoribus consultant principes, de majoribus omnes" (*Germani* 11.1), which means "while the leading men alone deliberate concerning minor issues, all the people together deliberate about major ones."

the plan of electors—and this is the case, so far as we have yet seen—that plan should not be substituted in the place of a choice of senators by the people themselves.

Were we to satisfy ourselves with this partial and incomplete consideration of the subject; I apprehend we should be extremely unwilling to transfer the choice of senators from the people to electors. But if we pursue the examination a little further, we shall find still stronger reasons for this reluctance: for we shall find, I believe, that, by such a transfer, instead of avoiding inconveniences and obtaining advantages, we shall sacrifice advantages for the acquisition of inconveniences.

The political connexion between the people and those whom they distinguish by elective offices, and the reciprocal sensations and engagements resulting from that connexion, I consider as most interesting in their nature, and most momentous in their consequences. This connexion should be as intimate as possible: if possible, it should be indissoluble. Confidence—mutual and endearing confidence—between those who impart power and those to whom power is imparted, is the brightest gem in the diadem of a republick. Let us sedulously avoid every danger of its being broken or lost.

Will there be the same generous emotions of confidence in the body of citizens towards the senators?—Will there be the same warm effusions of gratitude in the senators towards the body of the citizens, if the cold breath of electors is suffered to blow between them? Can the senator say to the people—you are my constituents; for you chose me? Can the people say to the senator—you are our trustee, for you are the object of our choice? Will not these relations, equally delightful and attractive on both sides, be greatly weakened—will not their influence be greatly diminished, by the interposition of electors?

But let us contemplate this subject in a still more serious and important point of view. The great desideratum in politicks is, to form a government, that will, at the same time, deserve the seemingly opposite epithets—efficient and free. I am sanguine enough to think that this can be done. But, I think, it can be done only by forming a popular government. To render government efficient, powers must be given liberally: to render it free as well as efficient, those powers must be drawn from the people, as directly and as immediately as possible. Every degree of removal is attended with a corresponding degree of danger. I know that removals, or at least one removal, is, in many instances, necessary in the executive and judicial departments. But is this a reason for multiplying or lengthening them without necessity? Is it a reason for introducing them into the legislative department, the most powerful, and, if ill constituted, the most dangerous, of all? No. But it is a strong reason for excluding them wherever they can be excluded; and for shortening them as much as possible wherever they necessarily take place. Corruption and putridity are more to be dreaded from the length, than from the strength, of the streams of authority.

On this great subject, I offer my sentiments, as it is my duty to do, without reserve. I think—that all the officers in the legislative department should be the immediate choice of the people—that only one removal should take place in the officers of the executive and judicial departments—and that, in this last department, a very important share of the business should be transacted by the people themselves.

These are, in a few words, the great outlines of the government, which I would choose. I fondly flatter myself that all the parts of it might be safely, compactly, and firmly knit together; and that the qualities of goodness, wisdom, and energy might animate, sustain, and pervade the whole.

And for what should we sacrifice all the valuable connexions, principles, and advantages, which have been mentioned? For electors?—Who are those electors to be? Logicians sometimes describe the subjects of their profound lucubrations negatively as well as positively. Let us borrow a hint from them, on this occasion. Who are those electors *not* to be? 1. They will be such as the people will think not the fittest to represent them in the most numerous branch of the legislature; for no representatives can be electors. 2. They will be such as the people will think not the fittest to be senators; for no elector can be a senator; and therefore the people will not choose those to be electors, whom they would wish to see in the senate. 3. They will be such as the governour *has* thought not the fittest for any office in the executive or judicial departments; for persons holding appointments in any of those departments cannot be electors. I was going to say, in the fourth place, that they will be such as will be thought not the fittest for any office under the executive department in future. But here, I find, I am mistaken. For they may hold offices the moment after their election of senators; and I will not assert it to be impossible, that they will acquire their qualifications for those offices by their conduct in that election.

Thus far we have pursued their negative descriptions. The task of expatiating on their positive qualities, I beg leave, for the present, to assign to those who must be supposed to understand them much better. For they must certainly know well the purifying virtues of those political alembicks, through which they wish to see our senators sublimated and refined.

Among the numerous good qualities of the electors, we hope, one will be—that they will be unsusceptible of intrigue or cabal among themselves. A second, we hope, will be—that they will be inaccessible to the impressions of intrigue and cabal from others. A third, we hope, will be—that as the people, by choosing them electors, have intimated decently that they think *them* not the fittest persons to be senators, *they* will cultivate the same decent reserve with regard to their brothers, their cousins, their other relations, their friends, their dependents, and their patrons.

Speech Delivered, on 19th January, 1790, in the Convention of Pennsylvania, Assembled for the Purpose of Reviewing, Altering, and Amending the Constitution of the State.

ON A MOTION THAT

"No member of congress from this state, nor any person holding or exercising any office of trust or profit under the United States, shall, at the same time, hold and exercise any office whatever in this state."

It has frequently been my lot to plead the cause of others; sometimes of individuals, sometimes of publick bodies, oftener than once of the commonwealth of Pennsylvania. It is now my lot to be under the hard necessity of pleading my own. That commonwealth, whose cause I have pleaded—and pleaded successfully—that commonwealth, in whose service I have laboured faithfully—I defy even my enemies to refute the assertion—though, to myself, very unprofitably—that commonwealth, which I have served in times of safety and in times of danger, through good report, and through bad report—that commonwealth, sir, if the present motion shall be adopted, is about to strip me of the most valuable rights of citizenship. And this is to be done without any offence or cause of forfeiture on my part; unless to have been highly honoured by the president and senate of the United States is, in her consideration, now become a crime, and to have accepted of the high honour is, in her eye, become a cause of forfeiture.

Well, then, may I say, that I am now to plead my own cause. All the citizen is roused within me; and I dissemble neither my feelings nor my interest: for both my interest and my feelings as a citizen of Pennsylvania assure me, in a manner which I cannot mistake, but which, at the same time, I cannot express, that this cause is personally my own. As such, therefore, I shall openly and directly consider and plead it. I am afraid, however, that I shall acquit myself but awkwardly: the task is new and unfamiliar: the path before me I have not hitherto trod. But a ray of consolation darts upon me. Though the cause is personally, it is not exclusively my own. I plead the cause likewise of some of the most distinguished citizens of Pennsylvania: I plead what will soon be the cause of others of her citizens equally distinguished: I plead what will continue, in future ages, to be the cause of her best, and those who ought to be her most favoured sons: I plead, sir, the cause of Pennsylvania herself: for Pennsylvania herself will certainly suffer, if she shall be deprived of the services of such of her citizens, as shall be best qualified for serving her. To deprive her of the services of such citizens is the evident tendency, the evident object, and the evident principle of the present motion: for such will be the citizens selected for the offices of the United States.

But here, sir, I must beg not to be misunderstood. When I speak of the principle and object and tendency of the motion, I mean not to apply those expressions to the principles, the views, or the wishes of its honourable mover. Between the first and the last there may be, and, I think, there probably is, a very considerable difference. In suggesting this, I pay not, to his principles, a compliment at the expense of his understanding; for to the most enlightened mind it is no disparagement to suppose, that, at first sight, it does not perceive all the distant bearings and relations and dependencies, which a motion, especially one so extensive as this, may, on investigation, be found to have.

The motion is in these words: "No member of congress from this state, nor any person holding or exercising any office of trust or profit under the United States, shall, at the same time, hold and exercise any office whatever in this state." It embraces all this broad and comprehensive position—every person, who is employed or trusted by the United States, ought, for that reason, to be incapacitated from being employed or trusted by the commonwealth of Pennsylvania, one of those states who compose the union. This position, your adoption of the motion will establish in its fullest force and extent. It will become a part, not merely of the law, but of the constitution of the land; and will be a binding and perpetual rule for the future conduct of this commonwealth. This, sir, and nothing short of this, is the true and necessary import of the question before you.

It is not, that some offices under the United States may, in point of propriety, or in point of policy, in the nature of their exercise, or in the place where they are exercised, be inconsistent with some offices under Pennsylvania. This, I will readily admit, may be the case under those different governments. It has been admitted to be the case in an instance already agreed to without opposition—I mean that of the governour. This may often be the case with regard to different offices even under the same government. Of this there are many examples in the system before you. They have encountered no disapprobation from me or any other member.

Again: the position, in the motion before you, is not, that it would be inconsistent or improper for the same person to hold, in any case, more offices than one. No, sir: this motion may be adopted, and yet one person may have twenty different offices accumulated upon him under this very constitution. For the position is not, "that no person, holding any one office, shall, at the same time, hold any other office, under this state:" but the position is, "that every person, holding an office under the United States, should be excluded from every office whatsoever in this state." For this reason, sir, all the numerous observations, which we heard on Saturday, from the honourable mover, concerning the profuse and improvident donations of offices, which the people, in a fit of fondness, might heap on the head of a popular favourite, however they might suit other purposes, were evidently beside the purpose of the motion. The motion, though adopted, will not prevent, nor is it calculated to prevent, such thoughtless and injudicious accumulations.

I have always flattered myself, that the constitution of the United States would be a bond of union, and not a principle of inveterate alienage, far less of hostility, between the several states; certainly and more particularly, between each of them and the United States. "A more perfect union" is declared to be one end of that constitution. That constitution, I believe, was intended to be the centre of attraction for that "more perfect union." Shall we convert that constitution, as far as it can depend on Pennsylvania—fortunately for the union, we can convert it no farther—into a principle of repulsion? If that is the design of this committee; if that is an object, for the accomplishment of which our constituents sent us here; the motion before you is well fitted for fulfilling that design; it is well fitted for accomplishing that object. Under the operation of this motion, if the government of the United States shall hereafter distinguish a citizen of Pennsylvania with an "office of profit or trust;" that government must become, however reluctantly, the repulsive agent in destroying the better half of his right of citizenship; and, consequently, of diminishing, by the better half, his political connexion with this commonwealth.

This, sir, is no inflated or exaggerated representation of the matter: the account is strictly and severely true. The right of citizenship consists in these two things: 1. A right to elect. 2. A right to be elected into office. Of the two, the last is certainly not the least valuable or important. Of the last I shall be deprived by your adoption of the motion before you. I call for the principles and reasons of deprivation. I demand, sir—for I have a right to demand—from the justice of this committee, that those principles and reasons be clearly shown and incontestably proved, before the sentence of deprivation be passed against me. I think I heard, on Saturday, an opinion mentioned as being decidedly formed. I trust that the expression was used inadvertently: I trust that the honourable members of this committee will hear, and weigh, and consider, before they decide.

Believe me, sir, the principle, more than any foreseen consequence, of disfranchisement wounds and alarms me. We are told in history, that a person, whose inclination had never led him beyond the gates of Rome, sickened and died, when Augustus, in a wanton trick of his absolute power, confined him within those very limits, beyond which he had never previously wished to go. 'Tis one thing, sir, to be without an office: 'tis a very different thing to be disqualified from holding an office, and to wander about like a person attainted and cut off from the community. The first is often the effect of choice; the last never is; it is the result of dire necessity. The idea of disqualification is a most mortifying idea, when applied by one to himself: it is a most insulting idea, when applied to him by others. And can you think, sir, that I would wish to become or continue the constant mark of mortification or insult? No, sir; I can, at least, comfort myself, that I will not be reduced to this situation. The motion of the honourable gentleman is not armed—fortunately it cannot be armed—with the sting of the edict of Augustus: it may prompt me to go; but it cannot compel me to stay. I can cross the Delaware. In New Jersey, I shall be received as a citizen—a full citizen—of the state; and, at the same time, may hold a dignified and important office under the United States. What I say concerning New Jersey, I may say concerning New Hampshire, Massachusetts, Connecticut, New York, Delaware, Maryland, North Carolina, South Carolina, and Georgia. For none of those states, so far as I know or have been informed, view honourable employments under the national government through the inverted speculum of the motion, which presents them as causes of disqualification and disfranchisement. Nay, sir, I believe I can go to Rhode Island, and be received there as more than a half citizen, if I choose it; for I have not heard, that that state, antifederal as it is, has passed an act of incapacity against the officers of the United States.

But we are told, that the commonwealth of Virginia has observed a different conduct; and has exhibited an example, which we are now solicited to imitate. I wish, sir, to know if this favourite example forms a part of the constitution of Virginia. If it does not—and I presume it does not—I wish to see the law that has produced it: I wish to examine that law: I wish to know the reason of that law: I wish to know the time when, and the occasion on which, that law was made: I wish to know the temper and the *national* principles of the legislature, which made that law. I have been informed, how correctly I will not undertake to vouch, that an antifederal leader in Virginia, foiled by the convention of that commonwealth in his opposition to the national government, introduced into the legislature, and succeeded in fixing some stigma, as far as that legislature could fix a stigma, upon the federal characters of that state. Perhaps, sir, my information is correct; and this law may be the very thing. Perhaps, sir, it may have been the production of the convulsive throes of an antifederal fit. If so—and I think the conjecture a probable one—so soon as the fit shall be over—and, I hope, it will be over soon, if it is not over already—Virginia will remove its effects by considerately repealing the law, which it had precipitately occasioned.

But shall we, sir, suffer ourselves to become infected with the transient, though violent disorder of a neighbouring state? Shall we do more, sir?—shall we inoculate this disorder to become a perpetual and incurable poison in the very vitals of our constitution? I confess I did not expect to see the symptoms of this distemper reappear so soon in Pennsylvania, after all the successful efforts that have been made to expel them from her borders.

It seems that I ought to be incapacitated from enjoying the confidence of this state, while I hold an office under the United States. And yet I may hold *one* office in this state, and not be incapacitated from holding twenty or thirty more. And yet I may hold an office under New Jersey, and not be incapacitated. I may hold an office under *any* other, and even under *every* other state in the Union, and not be incapacitated. I may hold an office under France, under any other state in Europe, under any other state in the world, and not be incapacitated. I may have held an office under Great Britain, and, under that office, may have acted against the United States and against this state, during all the late war; I may still hold that very office, and not be incapacitated. But—the position occurs again—if I hold an office under the United States, I must be incapacitated from any trust under Pennsylvania.

Whence, sir?—in the name of wonder—whence this principle of hostility—this principle of hostility, operating solely and peculiarly—between this commonwealth and the United States? Let it be explained: let us know its origin: let us know its nature: let us know its extent: let us know its effects.

If this principle exists, and ought to be provided against; it is surprising that no such provision was made or recommended against it, by the general convention, formed of members from all the states in the Union—a convention, which, I believe, understood the interests of the Union and of all its parts. If it ought to be a part of our constitution that "no person, holding any office under the United States, shall, at the same time, hold any office in this state;" it ought to have been a part of the constitution of the United States, that "no person holding any office under Pennsylvania, or any other state in the Union, shall, at the same time, hold any office in the national government." But no such part is to be found in that constitution. We may presume—I suggest it with deference—we may presume, that the whole knew the proper connexion between itself and its parts; and provided for the preservation, the strength, and the limits of that connexion, as well as *one* of the parts can know and provide for the preservation, the strength, and the limits of its connexion with the whole. But no such provision as this is made by those, who had the whole state of the Union before them: the inference is fair, that this provision is dictated, not by a general and comprehensive, but by a partial and contracted view of the subject.

Will the principle of this motion contribute to preserve or to strengthen the political connexion between the United States and the commonwealth of Pennsylvania? Will it not, on the other hand, contribute to weaken, to interrupt, or to dissolve it? The principle of this motion, sir, is a principle of political alienage: I go farther—it contains a declaration of political hostility by this commonwealth against the United States. It declares that this commonwealth ought not to trust or employ any person, whom the United States have thought worthy of trust or employment. On what foundation can such a declaration rest? It can have no reasonable foundation, unless the interests and views of the United States are, in their nature and tendency, hostile to the interests and views of this commonwealth. Let it be shown wherein this hostility of views and interests consists.

I have already admitted, that there are many instances, in which offices under different governments are incompatible in point of propriety, or in point of policy, in the nature of their exercise, or in the place where they are exercised. I have admitted also, that an accumulation of offices may be very improper under the same government. But it has appeared, that the principle, the tendency, and the object of this motion are not to prevent any incompatibilities or improprieties of these kinds.

On the other hand, there are many instances, in which different offices, not only under the same government, but even under different governments, may be held, not only with great propriety, but even with great advantage to the publick, by the same persons. Against the enjoyment of this publick advantage, the motion before you is levelled and directed.

And yet, sir, our own experience has attested its happy effects. During the late war, we reaped solid benefits from the exertions and talents of officers—in one instance, of a very distinguished officer—in the service of France. Would we have reaped those benefits, had France adopted, against the United States, the unfriendly principle, which is now recommended to a state, hitherto one of the most federal and one of the most affectionate in the Union? Suppose the sovereign of those officers to have declared to them in the spirit of this motion—"the moment you accept any office under the United States, you shall be disqualified, by that acceptance, from holding any office in my service,"—what would have been the consequence? The United States would have been deprived of their military skill and assistance. But, happily for us, the king of France was not actuated by the spirit of this motion: shall I risk the expression, that he was more federal?

On how many sudden and unforeseen emergencies may the services of a stated officer of the United States be useful, perhaps, in the opinion of the publick, necessary for this commonwealth! On how many sudden and unforeseen emergencies may the services of a stated officer of this commonwealth be useful, perhaps, in the opinion of the publick, necessary for the United States? Why, in both cases, should the door of mutual, useful, necessary, and patriotick exertion be constitutionally shut? For this motion will operate both ways. If the officers of the United States are to be considered as aliens with regard to their capacity of holding offices under this commonwealth: the officers of this commonwealth must be considered as aliens with regard to their capacity of holding offices under the United States.

When I say, sir, that, in both instances, they must be considered as aliens; I use an expression much too soft: for under both constitutions—that of the United States and that which we propose—aliens may be employed in many offices. This motion, if adopted, will, therefore, introduce, between the United States, and this state, as to offices, more than a state of alienage. I was justified in saying, that this motion contained a principle and declaration of political hostility, as to offices, between this commonwealth and the United States. Before the sentence of disfranchisement from office in Pennsylvania be passed, by the adoption of this motion, against the officers of the United States; I again demand that it be clearly shown wherein the principle of political hostility between the two governments consists.

I think it has been suggested, that unless the principle of this motion be introduced into the constitution, the government of the United States may acquire, in Pennsylvania, an influence dangerous to her counsels, dangerous to her interests, and dangerous even to her existence. That government, it was supposed, might, by appointing to its offices the officers of this state, attach them to the measures, the interests, and the counsels of the United States, in opposition to the measures, the interests, and the counsels of Pennsylvania. Like the motion, this reasoning in support of it is founded on an implied principle of hostility between the two governments. Before the committee subscribe to the reasoning, they will require that the principle of hostility be shown.

But let us, for a moment, suppose it to exist: let us suppose that the measures, and interests, and counsels of the United States are in diametrical and inveterate opposition to those of Pennsylvania: let us suppose, that, in order to promote those adverse interests, to establish those adverse counsels, and to carry into effect those adverse measures, the president and senate of the United States should call to their aid, and associate in their designs, the officers of Pennsylvania; would it be politick or wise in Pennsylvania to cooperate, in the most effectual manner, with the president and senate for the accomplishment of their plans? Could she do this more effectually by any means, than by detaching from her all the officers of the state, whom the president and senate would wish to attach to them? Could she detach them from her more effectually by any means, than by disfranchising them from their offices, and by treating them as aliens, nay, worse than aliens? Could she do this more effectually by any means, than by cutting asunder the strongest ties of political connexion and political affection between her and them?

I believe, sir, you may hear, from some states, a series of reasoning, very opposite to that before mentioned: you may hear a train of reflection to the following purpose: What! shall we part with the interests, with the affections, and with the services of our citizens, because they are called into the service of the United States? No. Let us retain their interests; for their interests will be ours: let us retain their affections; for these, at least, may remain with us: let us retain their services, as far as they shall be compatible—and, in many instances, they will be compatible—with their superiour duty to the United States.

Whether this train of reflection and reasoning be just and strong, I shall not pretend to determine. I shall only observe, that, as far as I know, the conduct of every state in the union has been consonant to it, excepting only that of the commonwealth of Virginia—and shall I, after some time, be obliged to make the cruel addition—and excepting likewise that of the commonwealth of Pennsylvania?

'Tis possible, sir, though I will not allow it to be probable, that this cruel addition must be made. 'Tis possible, though, again, I will not allow it to be probable, that Pennsylvania may become as infamous for her antifederal, as she has hitherto been renowned for her federal principles. 'Tis possible, though, still, I will not allow it to be probable, that she may hereafter be as much dishonoured by the littleness, as she has heretofore been admired for the liberality, of her politicks. Her counsels may take an inverted and diminishing turn. Those, sir, who cannot shine in a spacious sphere, will wish to draw some notice in a contracted one. Those, who cannot be distinguished by acting a part in an enlarged system, will endeavour to distinguish themselves by acting as the little but principal puppets in a narrow and separated scene. Into such hands, sir, it is possible—though I once more enter my protest against the probability of the event,—that Pennsylvania, for her sins, may fall.

If this very improbable, but very possible event should take place; then, indeed, the cruel addition, which I have already mentioned, must be made. Yet even then, this cruel circumstance would carry with it, in some degree, its own alleviation. In such a circumstance, the pangs of separation from Pennsylvania would become less severe. Even in such a circumstance, I hope one consolation might be constitutionally allowed me. On my way to the government of the United States, I might turn and look back from the opposite shore of the Delaware; and though Pennsylvania should reject my faithful services, she might permit me, with a fluttering heart and faultering tongue, to wish her well.

But, sir, I will not pursue the consideration of an event so irreconcilable with the present genius and principles of Pennsylvania. Is *she* jealous, because her sons are received into the arms of the United States? No, sir. Was she to open her lips upon this occasion, we should hear the following, or some such as the following, accents: "Though I cheerfully resign you to the service of the Union, in which my own service is, to many important purposes, included; yet I renounce not your affections; nor do I abdicate my well founded claim to your duty. You may still be of use to me; and I retain my right to the exertions of your usefulness, whenever I shall call upon you on a proper occasion. In the mean time, employ your utmost efforts for the interest of the United States: by doing this, you will essentially promote mine; and you will be likewise better prepared, and better disposed for serving me, whenever I shall particularly require your service." Such would be the language, such would be the sentiments, of our venerable political parent. Such, sir, without personification, and without an allegory, I believe to be literally and strictly the language and sentiments of a great majority of the people of this commonwealth. This language and these sentiments are in direct contradiction to the language and principles of the motion before you. To which will this committee pay the greatest regard?

A Charge Delivered to the Grand Jury in the Circuit Court of the United States, for the District of Virginia, in May, 1791.

Gentlemen of the Grand Jury,

To prevent crimes is the noblest end and aim of criminal jurisprudence. To punish them is one of the means necessary for the accomplishment of this noble end and aim. The impunity of an offender encourages him to repeat his offences. The witnesses of his impunity are tempted to become his disciples in his guilt. These considerations form the strongest—some view them as the sole argument for the infliction of punishments by human laws.

There are, in punishments, three qualities, which render them the fit preventives of crimes. The first is their moderation. The second is their speediness. The third is their certainty.

We are told by some writers, that the number of crimes is unquestionably diminished by the severity of punishments. If we inspect the greatest part of the criminal codes; their unwieldy bulk and their ensanguined hue will force us to acknowledge, that this opinion may plead, in its favour, a very high antiquity, and a very extensive reception. On accurate and unbiassed examination, however, it will appear to be an opinion unfounded and pernicious, inconsistent with the principles of our nature, and, by a necessary consequence, with those of wise and good government.

So far as any sentiment of generous sympathy is suffered, by a merciless code, to remain among the citizens, their abhorrence of crimes is, by the barbarous exhibitions of human agony, sunk in their commiseration of criminals. These barbarous exhibitions are productive of another bad effect—a latent and gradual, but a powerful, because a natural, aversion to the laws. Can laws, which are a natural and a just object of aversion, receive a cheerful obedience, or secure a regular and uniform execution?

The expectation is forbidden by some of the strongest principles in the human frame. Such laws, while they excite the compassion of society for those who suffer, rouse its indignation against those who are active in the steps preparatory to their sufferings.

We may easily conjecture the result of those combined emotions, operating vigorously in concert. The criminal will, probably, be dismissed without prosecution by those whom he has injured. If prosecuted and tried, the jury will probably find, or think they find, some decent ground, on which they may be justified, or at least excused, in giving a verdict of acquittal. If convicted, the judges will, with avidity, receive and support every, the nicest exception to the proceedings against him; and, if all other things should fail, will have recourse to the last expedient within their reach for exempting him from rigorous punishment—that of recommending him to the mercy of the pardoning power. In this manner, the acerbity of punishment deadens the execution of the law.

The criminal, pardoned, repeats the crime, under the expectation that the impunity also will be repeated. The habits of vice and depravity are gradually formed within him. Those habits acquire, by exercise, continued accessions of strength and inveteracy. In the progress of his career, he is led to engage in some desperate attempt. From one desperate attempt he boldly proceeds to another, till, at last, he necessarily becomes the victim of that preposterous rigour, which repeated impunity had taught him to despise, because it had persuaded him that he might always escape.

When, on the other hand, punishments are moderate and mild, every one will, from a sense of interest and of duty, take his proper part in detecting, in exposing, in trying, and in passing sentence on crimes. The consequence will be, that criminals will seldom elude the vigilance, or baffle the energy, of publick justice.

True it is, that, on some emergencies, excesses of a temporary nature may receive a sudden check from rigorous penalties: but their continuance and their frequency introduce and diffuse a hardened insensibility among the citizens; and this insensibility, in its turn, gives occasion or pretence to the farther extension and multiplication of those penalties. Thus one degree of severity opens and smooths the way for another, till, at length, under the specious appearance of necessary justice, a system of cruelty is established by law.

Such a system is calculated to eradicate all the manly sentiments of the soul, and to substitute, in their place, dispositions of the most depraved and degrading kind. It is the parent of *pusillanimity.* A nation broke to cruel punishments becomes dastardly and contemptible. For, in nations, as well as individuals, cruelty is always attended by cowardice. It is the parent of *slavery.* In every government, we find the genius of freedom depressed in proportion to the sanguinary spirit of the laws. It is hostile to the prosperity of nations, as well as to the dignity and virtue of men. The laws, which Draco[1] framed for Athens, are said emphatically to have been written in blood. What did they produce? An aggravation of those very calamities, which they were intended to remove. A scene of the greatest and most complicated distress was accordingly exhibited by the miserable Athenians, till they found relief in the wisdom and moderation of Solon. It is a standing observation in China—and China has enjoyed a very long experience—that in proportion as the punishments of criminals are increased, the empire approaches to a new revolution. The Porcian law provided, that no citizen of Rome should be exposed to a sentence of death. Under the Porcian law, the commonwealth grew and flourished. Severe punishments were established by the emperours. Under the emperours, Rome declined and fell.

The principles both of utility and of justice require, that the commission of a crime should be followed by a speedy infliction of its punishment.

The association of ideas has vast power over the sentiments, the passions, and the conduct of men. When a penalty marches close in the rear of the offence, against which it is denounced; an association, strong and striking, is produced between them: and they are viewed in the inseparable relation of cause and effect. When, on the contrary, the punishment is procrastinated to a remote period; this connexion is considered as weak and precarious; and the execution of the law is beheld and suffered as a detached instance of severity, warranted by no cogent reason, and springing from no laudable motive.

It is just, as well as useful, that the punishment should be inflicted soon after the commission of the crime. It should never be forgotten, that imprisonment, though often necessary for the safe custody of the person

1. Draco provided Athens with its first written laws in c. 621 B.C. Under his code, many crimes were punished by death.

accused, is, nevertheless, in itself, a punishment—a punishment galling to some of the finest feelings of the heart—a punishment too, which, since it precedes conviction, may be as undeserved as it is distressing. But imprisonment is not the only penalty, which an accused person undergoes before his trial. He undergoes also the corroding torment of suspense—the keenest agony, perhaps, which falls to the lot of suffering humanity. This agony is by no means to be estimated by the real probability or danger of conviction: it bears a compound proportion to the delicacy of sentiment and the strength of imagination possessed by him, who is doomed to become its prey.

These observations show, that those accused of crimes should be speedily tried, and that those convicted of them should be speedily punished. But with regard to this, as with regard to almost every other subject, there is an extreme on one hand as well as on the other; and the extremes on each hand should be avoided with equal care. In some cases, at some times, and under some circumstances, a delay of the trial and of the punishment, instead of being hurtful or pernicious, may, in the highest degree, be salutary and beneficial, both to the publick, and to him who is accused or convicted.

Prejudices may naturally arise, or may be artfully fomented, against the crime, or against the man who is charged with having committed it. A delay should be allowed, that those prejudices may subside, and that neither jurors nor judges may, at the trial, act under the fascinating impression of sentiments conceived before the evidence is heard, instead of the calm influence of those which should be only its impartial and deliberate result. A sufficient time should be given to prepare the prosecution on the part of the state, and the defence of it on the part of the prisoner. This time must vary according to different persons, different crimes, and different situations.

After conviction, the punishment assigned to an inferiour offence should be inflicted with much expedition. This will strengthen the useful association between them; one appearing as the immediate and unavoidable consequence of the other. When a sentence of death is pronounced, such an interval should be permitted to elapse before its execution as will render the language of political expediency consonant to the language of religion.

Under these qualifications, the speedy punishment of crimes should form a part in every system of criminal jurisprudence.

But the certainty of punishments is that quality, which is of the greatest importance in order to constitute them fit preventives of crimes. This quality is, in its operation, most merciful as well as most powerful. When a criminal determines on the commission of a crime, he is not so much influenced by the lenity of the punishment, as by the expectation that, in some way or other, he may be fortunate enough to avoid it. This is particularly the case with him, when this expectation is cherished by examples or by experience of impunity. It was the saying of Solon, that he had completed his system of laws by the combined energy of justice and strength. By this expression he meant to denote, that laws, of themselves, would be of very little service, unless they were enforced by a faithful and an effectual execution of them. The strict execution of every *criminal* law is the dictate of humanity as well as of wisdom.

This strict execution is greatly promoted by accuracy in the publick police, by vigilance and activity in the ministerial officers of justice, by a prompt and regular communication of intelligence, and by a proper distribution of rewards for the discovery and apprehension of criminals.

Among all the plans and establishments, however, which have been devised for securing the wise and uniform execution of the criminal laws, the institution of grand juries holds the most distinguished place. This institution is, at least in the present times, the peculiar boast of the common law. The era of its commencement, and the particulars attending its gradual progress and improvement, are concealed behind the thick veil of a very remote antiquity. But one thing concerning it is certain. In the annals of the world, there is not found another institution so well adapted for avoiding all the inconveniences and abuses, which would otherwise arise from malice, from rigour, from negligence, or from partiality in the prosecution of crimes.

Among the Romans, any one of the citizens, as well as the person more immediately injured, might prosecute a publick offence. This practice produced mischiefs very great, and of very opposite kinds. Prosecutions were conducted, on some occasions, from motives of rancour and revenge. On other occasions, they were undertaken by a friend, perhaps a confederate of the criminal, with a view to ensure his impunity.

In several of the *feudal* nations, the judge himself was originally the prosecutor. The gross impropriety of such a regulation appears at the first view. The prosecutor is a party: can the same person be both a party and a judge? To remove the grievances, to which this regulation gave birth, a publick prosecutor was appointed to manage the judicial business of the crown, or of the community, before the proper tribunals.

But that crimes may be prosecuted duly and regularly, it is necessary that impartial and authentick information of their existence should be obtained. To furnish such information is the great object of the institution of grand juries.

Sometimes the grand jury bring forward accusations of their own proper motion: sometimes they proceed upon particular charges formally laid before them by the publick prosecutor. These two modes are distinguished by the well known appellations of *presentment* and *indictment.* In both, it is the right, and it is the duty of a grand jury, to inquire diligently, and to present truly.

It is your immediate business, gentlemen, to make inquiries and give official information concerning such crimes and offences as may have been committed against the constitution and laws of the United States, and are cognizable by this circuit court held for the district of Virginia in the middle circuit. To assist you in those inquiries, I shall describe to you the jurisdiction, which, in criminal matters, is vested in the circuit courts; and I shall give you a very plain and concise account of the crimes and offences known to the constitution and laws of the United States, and of the punishments denounced against those crimes and offences.

The circuit courts have *exclusive* jurisdiction of all crimes and offences, which are cognizable under the authority of the United States, except where it is or shall be provided otherwise by law. They have also *concurrent* jurisdiction with the district courts, of the crimes and offences, which are cognizable in those courts[a] The crimes and offences, of which the district courts have jurisdiction, and of which, consequently, the circuit courts have *concurrent* jurisdiction, are all such as are cognizable under the authority of the United States, provided they be committed within the respective districts, or on the high seas; and provided they be those on

a. Laws U. S. Cong. 1. sess. 1. c. 20. s. 11.

which no other punishment than a fine not exceeding one hundred dollars, imprisonment not exceeding six months, or whipping not exceeding thirty stripes is to be inflicted.[b]

Treason generally occupies the first place in the long catalogue of crimes. On this subject, so interesting to the publick and to the citizens, a very important improvement has been ingrafted by the constitution of the United States.

If the description of treason be vague and indeterminate under any government; this alone will be a sufficient cause why that government should degenerate into tyranny. If the denomination and the penalties of treason be communicated to offences of a different and inferiour kind; the horrour, which would otherwise attend this complicated crime, is weakened by the association with things, to which, in truth, it has neither relation nor resemblance.

In the reign of Henry the eighth,[2] a law was made in England by which any one, who predicted the death of the king, was declared guilty of treason. Arbitrary power, on some occasions, recoils upon those who exert it. When this capricious and tyrannical prince lay on his death bed, his physicians would not inform him of his danger, because they would not incur the penalties of his law. We are told by the English parliament itself, that, at another period, so many "pains of treason were ordained by statute; that no man knew how to behave himself, to do, speak, or say, for doubt of such pains."

Under our national government, we have not only a legal, but a constitutional security against arbitrary and constructive treasons.

1. Under that government, treason against the United States can be committed *only* by levying war against them, or by adhering to their enemies, giving them aid and comfort.[c]

2. Misprision of treason consists in knowing the commission of treason, and not disclosing it, as soon as may be, to the president or some one of the judges of the United States, or to the first executive magistrate or some one of the judges or justices of a particular state.[d]

b. Laws U. S. Con. 1. sess. 1. c. 20. s. 9.

2. Henry VIII (1491–1547) was King of England from 1509 to 1547.

c. Con. U. S. art. 3. s. 3.

d. Laws U. S. Con. 1. sess. 2. c. 9. s. 2.

Other crimes and offences against the United States may be comprised under the following enumeration.—3. Wilful murder, committed in any place under the exclusive jurisdiction of the United States,[e] or upon the high seas, or in any river, haven, basin or bay not within the jurisdiction of any particular state.[f] 4. Manslaughter committed in any place under the exclusive jurisdiction of the United States,[g] or upon the high seas.[h] 5. Robbery committed upon the high seas, or in any river, haven or bay not within the jurisdiction of any particular state.[i] 6. The piratical and felonious running away with any vessel, or with any goods to the value of fifty dollars, or yielding up such vessel voluntarily to any pirate, by any captain or mariner of such vessel.[j] 7. The laying of violent hands, by a seaman, upon his commander, in order to hinder his fighting in defence of his ship or goods committed to his trust.[k] 8. The making of a revolt in a ship by any seaman.[l] 9. Piracy or robbery (as specified in the law) or any act of hostility against the United States or a citizen thereof, committed by any citizen upon the high seas, on pretence of authority from any person, or under colour of a commission from a foreign prince or state.[m] 10. Confederacy with pirates.[n] 11. The false making, altering, forging, or counterfeiting of any certificate, indent, or other publick security of the United States.[o] 12. The causing or procuring of any certificate, indent, or other publick security of the United States to be falsely made, altered, forged, or counterfeited.[p] 13. Acting or assisting willingly in the false making, altering, forging, or counterfeiting of any such certificate, indent, or other publick security.[q] 14. The uttering, putting off, or offering, in payment or for sale, of any such false, forged, altered, or counterfeited certificate, indent, or other

e. Laws U. S. con. 1. sess. 2. c. 9. s. 3.
f. Id. s. 8.
g. Id. s. 7.
h. Id. s. 12.
i. Id. s. 8.
j. Id. ibid.
k. Laws U. S. con. 1. sess. 2. c. 9. s. 8.
l. Id. ibid.
m. Id. s. 9.
n. Id. s. 12.
o. Id. s. 14.
p. Id. ibid.
q. Id. ibid.

publick security, with intention to defraud any person, and with knowledge that the same is false, altered, forged, or counterfeited.[r] 15. The causing of any such false, forged, altered, or counterfeited certificate, indent, or other publick security to be uttered, put off, or offered, in payment or for sale, with the knowledge and intention already mentioned.[s] 16. The setting at liberty by force, and the rescuing of any person, convicted of a capital crime, or, before conviction, committed for a capital crime, or committed for or convicted of any other offence.[t] 17. Misprision of felony, which consists in knowing the commission of wilful murder or other felony upon the high seas, or within any fort, arsenal, dock yard, magazine, or other place or district of country under the sole and exclusive jurisdiction of the United States, and not disclosing it as soon as may be to some one of the judges or other person in civil or military authority under the United States.[u] 18. The cutting off of the ear, the cutting out or disabling of the tongue, the putting out of an eye, the slitting of the nose, the cutting off of the nose or a lip, the cutting off or disabling of any limb or member of any person, unlawfully, on purpose and of malice aforethought, and with intention, in so doing, to maim or disfigure such person: provided these crimes be committed in any place under the exclusive jurisdiction of the United States, or upon the high seas, in any vessel belonging to the United States or to any citizen of the United States.[v] 19. Perjury committed wilfully and corruptly on oath or affirmation in any suit or matter before any court, or in any deposition taken pursuant to a law, of the United States.[w] 20. The procuring of any person to commit corrupt and wilful perjury in any of the cases just mentioned.[x] 21. The giving, directly or indirectly, of any sum of money, or any other bribe, present, or reward, or any promise, contract, obligation, or security for the payment or delivery of any money, present, or reward, or any other thing, to procure the opinion, judgment, or decree of any judge of the United States in any suit or matter depending before him.[y] 22. The

r. Id. ibid.
s. Id. ibid.
t. Id. s. 23.
u. Laws U. S. con. 1. sess. 2. c. 9. s. 6.
v. Id. s. 13.
w. Id. s. 18.
x. Id. ib.
y. Id. s. 21.

accepting by any judge of any such sum of money, bribe, present, reward, promise, contract, obligation, or security.[z] 23. Oppression or extortion by any supervisor or officer of inspection, in the execution of his office.[a] 24. The landing, in any place within the limits of the United States, of goods entered for exportation, with a view to draw back the duties.[b] 25. The resisting or impeding of any officer of the customs, or any person assisting him, in the execution of his duty.[c] 26. The resisting or opposing, knowingly and wilfully, of any officer of the United States in serving or attempting to serve process of any court of the United States: and the assaulting, beating, or wounding of any officer, or other person duly authorized, in serving or attempting to serve such process.[d] 27. The felonious stealing, taking away, altering, falsifying, or otherwise avoiding of any record, writ, process, or other proceeding in any court of the United States, by means whereof any judgment shall not take effect, or shall be reversed or made void.[e] 28. The acknowledging or procuring to be acknowledged, in any court of the United States, of any recognizance, bail, or judgment, in the name of any person not privy or consenting to it. There is an exception with regard to attornies duly admitted.[f] 29. Taking and carrying away, with an intent to steal or purloin the personal goods of another, upon the high seas, or in any place within the exclusive jurisdiction of the United States.[g] 30. The embezzling, purloining, or conveying away of any victuals provided for any soldiers, gunners, marines, or pioneers, or of any arms, ordnance, munition, shot, powder, or habiliments of war, belonging to the United States, by any person having the charge or custody thereof; provided such embezzling, purloining, or carrying away be for lucre, or willingly, advisedly and of purpose to impede the service of the United States.[h] 31. The suing forth, or prosecuting, or executing of any writ or process, by which the person of any publick foreign minister, received as such by the president of

z. Laws U. S. con. 1. sess. 2. c. 9. s. 21.
a. Id. sess. 3. c. 15. s. 39.
b. Id. sess. 2. c. 35. s. 59.
c. Id. sess. 2. c. 35. s. 50.
d. Id. sess. 2. c. 9. s. 22.
e. Id. sess. 2. c. 9. s. 15.
f. Id. ibid.
g. Id. sess. 2. c. 9. s. 16.
h. Laws U. S. con. 1. sess. 2. c. 9. s.16.

the United States, or any domestick or domestick servant of any such minister, may be arrested or imprisoned, or his goods seized.[i] 32. The violation of any safe conduct or passport duly obtained under the authority of the United States.[j] 33. The assaulting, striking, wounding, imprisoning, or, in any other manner, infracting the laws of nations by offering violence to the person of a publick minister.[k]

In the foregoing catalogue, murder, manslaughter, robbery, piracy, forgery, perjury, bribery, and extortion are mentioned as crimes and offences; but they are neither defined nor described. For this reason, we must refer to some *preexisting* law for their definition or description. To what preexisting law should this reference be made?

This is a question of immense importance and extent. It must receive an answer; but I cannot, in this address, assign my reasons for the answer which I am to give—The reference should be made to the *common law.*

To the common law, then, let us resort for the definition or description of the crimes and offences, which, in the laws of the United States, have been named, but have not been described or defined. You will, in this manner, gentlemen, he furnished with a legal standard, by the judicious application of which you may ascertain, with precision, the true nature and qualities of such facts and transactions as shall become the objects of your consideration and research.

In our law books, murder is thus described: it is when a person, of sound memory and of the age of discretion, unlawfully killeth any reasonable creature with malice aforethought, express or implied. Manslaughter is described as—the unlawful killing of another, without malice, either express or implied. The distinction strongly marked between murder and manslaughter is, that the former is committed with, the latter, without malice aforethought. It is essential, therefore, to know clearly and accurately the true and legal import of this characteristick distinction.

There is a very considerable difference between that sense, which is conveyed by the expression, malice, in common language, and that, to which the term is appropriated by the law. In common language, it is most fre-

i. Id. s. 25. 26.
j. Id. s. 28.
k. Id. ibid.

quently used to denote a sentiment or passion of strong malevolence to a particular person; or a settled anger and desire of revenge in one person against another. In law, it means the dictate of a wicked and malignant heart; of a depraved, perverse, and incorrigible disposition. Agreeably to this last meaning, many of the cases, which are arranged under the head of implied malice, will be found to turn upon this single point; that the fact has been attended with such circumstances—particularly the circumstances of deliberation and cruelty concurring—as betray the plain indications and genuine symptoms of a mind grievously depraved, and acting from motives highly criminal; of a heart regardless of social duty, and fatally bent upon mischief. This is the true notion of *malice* in the *legal* sense of the word. The mischievous and vindictive spirit denoted by it must always be collected and inferred from the circumstances of the transaction. On the circumstances of the transaction, the closest attention should, for this reason, be bestowed. Every circumstance may weigh something in the scale of justice.

Robbery is a felonious and violent taking, from the person of another, of money or goods to any value, putting him in fear. From this definition it appears, that to constitute a robbery, the three following ingredients are indispensable. 1. A felonious intention, or *animus furandi*. 2. Some degree of violence and putting in fear. 3. A taking from the *person* of another. Upon each of these three points there is much learned disquisition in the books of the law.

Piracy is robbery and depredation upon the high seas. The word *pirate*, says my Lord Coke,[1] in Latin *pirata*, is derived from the Greek word πειρατης, which is again fetched from πειραι *a transcundo mari*, or roving upon the sea; and, therefore, in English, a pirate is called a *rover* or *robber* upon the sea.

Piracy is a crime against the universal law of society: a pirate is *hostis humani generis*, an enemy of the whole human race. By declaring war against all mankind, he has laid all mankind under the necessity of declaring war against him. He has renounced the benefits and protection of government and society: he has abandoned himself to a savage state of

1. 3. Ins. 113.

nature. The consequence is, that, by the laws of selfdefence, every community has a right to inflict upon him that punishment, which, in a state of nature, every individual would be entitled to inflict for any invasion of his person or personal property.

"If any *person*," says a law of the United States, "shall commit, upon the high seas, or in any river, haven, basin, or bay, out of the jurisdiction of any particular state, *murder*, or *robbery*, or *any other* offence, which, if committed within the *body of a county*, would, by the laws of the United States, be punishable with death; every such offender shall be deemed, taken, and adjudged to be a *pirate and felon*, and being thereof convicted, shall suffer death."[m]

Placed in the high and responsible office of a judge of the United States, I feel myself under an official obligation to state some doubts, which arise in my mind upon this part of the law. Impressed, as I ought to be, both as a citizen and a judge, with the strongest regard for the legislative authority of the United States, I propose those doubts most respectfully, and with the greatest degree of diffidence.

Piracy, as we have seen, is a crime against the universal law of society. By that law, it may be punished by every community. But the description of piracy, according to *that* law, is a *robbery* and *depredation* on the high seas. Is a *murder*, committed upon the high seas, a *piracy* within the description of that law? "If a pirate, at sea,[n] assault a ship, but, by force, is prevented entering her; and, in the *attempt*, the pirate *kill* a person in the other ship; they are all principals in such a *murder*, if the common law have jurisdiction of the offence; but by the law *maritime*, if the parties be known, they *only* who gave the wound shall be *principals*, and the rest, *accessories*." From this authority and the foregoing description of piracy, taken jointly into our consideration, we might, perhaps, be naturally led to infer, 1. That a murder perpetrated in the *attempt* to commit a piracy, is not a piracy. 2. That *this* crime perpetrated in *such* an attempt, is, by the *maritime law* to be tried and punished as a *murder*, in which those, who *all* attempted the *piracy*, shall be considered as criminal in *different* degrees, according to the part, which they *severally* acted with regard to the *homicide*.

m. Laws U. S. 1. con. 2. sess. c. 9. s. 8.
n. Molloy. c. 4. s. 13.

The maritime law is not the law of any particular country: it is the general law of nations. "Non erit alia lex Romae, alia Athenis; alia nunc, alia posthac; sed et apud omnes gentes et omni tempore una eademque lex obtinebit."[o 3]

The law of nations has its foundation in the principles of natural law, applied to states; and in voluntary institutions, arising from custom or convention. This law is universal in its authority over the civilized part of the world; and is supported by the consideration of its general utility, as well as that of its obligatory force. This universal system has always been most liberally recognized in that country, from which we derive the boasted inheritance of the common law. According to the clear opinion declared by the great Lord Chancellor Talbot,[4] the law of nations is, in *its full extent,* a part of the law of England.[p]

True it is, that, so far as the law of nations is *voluntary* or *positive,* it may be altered by the municipal legislature of any state, in cases affecting *only* its own citizens. True it is also, that, by a treaty, the voluntary or positive law of nations may be altered so far as the alteration shall affect *only* the contracting parties. But equally true it is, that no state or states can, by treaties or municipal laws, alter or abrogate the law of nations any farther. This they can no more do, than a citizen can, by his single determination, or two citizens can, by a private contract between them, alter or abrogate the laws of the community, in which they reside.

Now the doubts, to which I have alluded, appear directly before us. Is a *person, not* a citizen of the United States, who shall commit a murder upon the high seas, liable, *under this law,* to be deemed, taken and adjudged to be a *pirate* and felon, and, as *such,* to suffer death? This question may be divided into two subordinate ones. 1. Was it the intention of the legislature, that this law should extend, in its operation, to persons not citizens of the United States? In the very next section, the phrase is altered, and instead of saying, if any *person* shall commit, it is said, if any *citizen* shall

o. 2. Burr. 887.

3. There will not be one law in Rome, another in Athens; one now, another later, but both among all peoples and at every time one and the same law will prevail.

4. Charles Talbot, the first Baron Talbot of Hensol (1685–1737), was a famous English politician and jurist.

p. 3. Burr. 1481.

commit any piracy, &c. Shall the construction be, that the legislature mean the same thing, when they use expressions so very different? 2. On the supposition, that the law was designed to extend, in its operation, to persons not citizens of the United States; can this design be carried into effect, consistently with the predominant authority of the law of nations, and of the universal law of society?

The case may very probably happen, and come before a grand jury for their official investigation. It was proper to suggest my doubts concerning it. I hope I have suggested them in the manner which I proposed to myself.

I return to the definitions and descriptions given, by the common law, of the crimes and offences mentioned, but not described or defined, in the laws of the United States.

To forge, says my Lord Coke, is metaphorically taken from the smith, who beateth upon his anvil, and forgeth what fashion or shape he will. The offence is called *crimen falsi;* the crime of falsehood; and the offender, *falsarius,* a falsifier. And this is properly taken when the act is done in the name of another person.[q] With regard, however, to this last part of the description of forgery, it has been since adjudged repeatedly and very solemnly to be too narrow. It expresses, indeed, the most obvious meaning of the word, and comprehends that species of forgery which is most commonly practised; but there are other species, which will not come within the letter of that description. An alteration in the name or quantity of land conveyed, or in the sum of money secured, is of this kind, and comes within the legal notion of forgery.

Wilful and corrupt perjury is a crime committed, when a lawful oath is administered, in some judicial proceeding, by one who has authority, to a person who swears absolutely and falsely, in a matter material to the issue or cause in question.

"An oath," says my Lord Coke, "is so sacred, and so deeply concerns the consciences of men, that it cannot be administered *to* any one, unless it be allowed by the common law, or by act of parliament; nor *by* any one, who has not authority by common law, or by act of parliament: neither can any oath, allowed by the common law, or by act of parliament, be altered,

q. 3. Ins. 169.

unless by act of parliament."[r] For these reasons, it is much to be doubted whether any magistrate is justifiable in administering voluntary affidavits unsupported by the authority of law. It is more than possible, that, by such idle oaths, a man may frequently incur the guilt, though he evade the temporal penalties of perjury.

It is a part of the foregoing definition of perjury, that it must be when the person swears *absolutely*. In addition to this, it has been said, that the oath must be *direct,* and not, as the deponent thinks, or remembers, or believes.[s] This doctrine has, however, been lately questioned, and, it seems, on solid principles. When a man swears, that he believes what, in truth, he does not believe, he pronounces a falsehood as much as when he swears absolutely, that a thing is true, which he knows not to be true. My Lord Chief Justice De Grey,[5] in a late case, said, that it was a mistake, which mankind had fallen into, that a person could not be convicted of perjury for deposing on oath, according to his belief.[t] It is certainly true, says my Lord Mansfield,[6] that a man may be indicted for perjury, in swearing that he believes a fact to be true, which he must know to be false.[u]

Bribery is when a judge, or other person concerned in the administration of justice, takes any undue reward to influence his behaviour in office. He who offers or gives, as well as he who receives this undue reward, is guilty of an offence against the law.

Extortion, taken in a large sense, is any oppression by colour or pretence of right; but, in its proper sense, it is a great misprision, in wresting by any officer, under colour of his office, any money, either when none at all is due, or not so much is due, or when it is not yet due.

I have now enumerated, and, by references to the common law, have explained the crimes and offences known to the constitution and laws of the United States. It is next in order to consider the several punishments, which are annexed to those crimes and offences.

r. 3. Ins. 165.

s. Id. 166. 1. Haw. 175.

5. William de Grey (1719–1781) was an English jurist who served as Soliciter General, Attorney General, and Lord Chief Justice of the common pleas.

t. Leach. 304.

6. William Murray (1705–1793) became the Earl of Mansfield in 1776. He had a distinguished political career in the House of Commons and in 1756 was appointed chief justice of the King's bench.

u. Ibid.

These punishments are of seven different kinds: disqualification for office—fine—imprisonment—whipping—pillory—incapacity to give testimony—death. To some crimes more kinds of punishment than one are assigned. To resistance of the officers of the customs is annexed a fine.[v] To the landing of goods entered for exportation imprisonment is the punishment allotted.[w] To bribery[x] and extortion[y] the punishments of disqualification, fine, and imprisonment are assigned. To misprision of treason,[z] manslaughter,[a] misprision of felony,[b] atrocious maiming,[c] a confederacy with pirates,[d] resistance against process,[e] a rescue of persons not convicted of any capital crime,[f] serving process for arresting a publick minister,[g] the violation of a safe conduct, and violence to the person of a publick minister,[h] are assigned the punishments of fine and imprisonment. Stealing or falsifying records, and fraudulently acknowledging bail, are punished with fine, imprisonment, and whipping.[i] Fine and whipping are the punishments annexed to larceny.[j] To perjury and subornation of perjury are allotted the punishments of fine, imprisonment, the pillory, and incapacity to give testimony.[k]

It deserves to be remarked, that, in every instance of punishment by fine, imprisonment, or whipping, limits are fixed on the side of severity; none, on the side of mercy.

Against forging,[l] against procuring or assisting to forge publick securities,[m] against uttering or causing to be uttered securities, which are

v. Laws U. S. con. 1. sess. 2. c. 35. s. 50.
w. Id. s. 59.
x. Id. sess. 2. c. 9. s. 21.
y. Id. sess. 3. c. 15. s. 39.
z. Id. sess. 2. c. 9. s. 2.
a. Id. s. 7. 12.
b. Id. s. 6.
c. Id. s. 13.
d. Id. s. 12.
e. Id. s. 22.
f. Id. s. 23.
g. Id. s. 26.
h. Id. s. 28.
i. Id. s. 15.
j. Id. s. 16.
k. Id. s. 18.
l. Laws U. S. con. 1. sess. 2. c. 9. s. 14.
m. Id. ibid.

forged,[n] against the rescue of persons convicted of capital crimes,[o] against piracy,[p] against robbery,[q] against acts of hostility as specified in the law,[r] against making a revolt in a ship, against violently hindering the captain of a vessel to fight in its defence, against piratically running away with any vessel,[s] against murder,[t] and against treason,[u] the punishment of death is denounced.

Accessories before[v] the fact to murder, robbery, or other piracy upon the seas shall suffer death. Accessories after[w] the fact shall be fined and imprisoned. Receivers of stolen goods[x] shall be liable to like punishments as in the case of larceny.

It is proper to point out to a grand jury the kinds and the grades of *punishments;* because the respect due to the legislature will lead us to conclude, that there are similar kinds and well adjusted grades of *crimes;* because the probability of a crime is in the inverse proportion to its atrociousness; and because, of consequence, a grand jury will require a degree of evidence adequate to the criminality of every charge, which comes under their consideration.

No person shall be prosecuted for any capital crime, wilful murder or forgery excepted, unless the indictment for it shall be found within three years after its commission: nor shall any person be prosecuted for an offence not capital, or for a crime or forfeiture under a penal law, unless the indictment or information for it shall be found or instituted within two years after the commission of the offence, or after the fine or forfeiture has incurred. But these provisions shall not operate in favour of such as flee from justice.[y]

n. Id. ibid.
o. Id. s. 23.
p. Id. s. 8.
q. Id. ibid.
r. Id. s. 9.
s. Id. s. 8.
t. Id. s. 3.
u. Id. s. 1.
v. Id. s. 10.
w. Id. s. 11.
x. Id. s. 17.
y. Laws U. S. con. 1. sess. 2. c. 9. s. 32.

One, who is indicted of treason, shall have, at least three days before his trial, a copy of the indictment, and a list, containing the names and places of abode, of the jurors and of the witnesses to be produced on the trial. A person indicted for any other capital crime shall have, at least two entire days before his trial, such a list of the jury, and a copy of the indictment.[z]

The trial of all crimes shall be by jury.[a]

Every one indicted shall be allowed to make his full defence by counsel learned in the law. The court, or a judge of the court, before whom he is to be tried, shall, on his request, assign him counsel, such as he shall desire, but not exceeding two; and his counsel shall have free access to him at all seasonable hours. He shall also be admitted to make, in his defence, any proof, which he can produce by witnesses: to compel the attendance of his witnesses at his trial he shall have legal process, similar to that, which is granted to compel witnesses to appear on the prosecution against him.[b]

No person shall be convicted of treason, unless on the testimony of two witnesses to the same overt act, or on confession in open court.[c]

The benefit of clergy shall not be used or allowed, upon the conviction of any crime, for which, by any statute of the United States, the punishment is or shall be declared to be death.[d]

The manner of inflicting the punishment of death shall be by hanging the person convicted, by the neck, until dead.[e]

No conviction or judgment for any offence, yet punishable by the laws of the United States, shall work corruption of blood, or any forfeiture of estate.[f]

I have now, gentlemen, given you an account, plain and concise, and yet, I hope, not altogether imperfect, of the criminal code of the United States. It will be interesting and instructive to compare this code, in some of its most remarkable regulations, with that of some other country. For this comparison, I select the criminal code of England. I select it, because, in other parts of Europe, it has been proposed as a model, on account of

z. Id. s. 29.
a. Con. U. S. art. 3. s. 2.
b. Laws U. S. con. 1. sess. 2. c. 9. s. 29.
c. Con. U. S. art. 3. s. 3.
d. Laws U. S. con. 1. sess. 2. c. 9. s. 31.
e. Id. s. 33.
f. Id. s. 24.

its mildness; and because, contrasted with many systems of criminal law, it is, indeed, comparatively mild. "That the English system of jurisprudence has its abuses, I will readily agree," says a writer of a nation long the rival of England; "but that it has fewer abuses than the system of any other civilized country, is what I am able to prove."[g]

It is the opinion of some writers, highly respected for their good sense, as well as for their humanity, that capital punishments are, in no case, necessary. It is an opinion, which I am certainly well warranted in offering—that nothing but the most absolute necessity can authorize them. Another opinion I am equally warranted in offering—that they should not be aggravated by any sufferings, except those which are inseparably attached to a violent death.[h] It was worthy only of a tyrant[i]—and of a tyrant it was truly characteristick—to give standing instructions to his executioners, that they should protract the expiring moments of the tortured criminal; and should manage the butchering business with such studied and slow barbarity, as that his powers of painful sensation should continue to the very last—*ut mori se sentiat.*[7]

Hear from the mouth of a celebrated lawyer—celebrated, however, for his learning, more than for his humanity—the sentence pronounced against treason by the law of England: hear this sentence, full of horrours, represented as flowing from admirable clemency and moderation.

At the trial of the conspirators in the gun powder plot, Sir Edward Coke concluded the part which he acted as attorney general, in the following very remarkable manner.

> The conclusion shall be drawn from the admirable clemency and moderation of the king, in that, howsoever these traitors have exceeded all others their predecessors in mischief, yet neither will the king exceed the *usual* punishment of the law, nor invent any *new* torture or torment for them; but is graciously pleased to afford them as well an ordinary course of trial, as an *ordinary punishment,* much *inferiour to their offence.* And surely, worthy of observation is the punishment provided and appointed for high treason. For

g. War. The. L. Crim. 18.

h. —See they suffer death,
But in their deaths remember they are men.
Cato.

i. Caligula.

7. So that he may feel himself die.

> first, after a traitor hath had his just trial, and is convicted and attainted, he shall have his judgment to be *drawn* to the place of execution from his prison, as being not worthy any more to tread upon the face of the earth whereof he is made: also for that he hath been retrograde to nature, therefore he is to be drawn backward at a horse tail. And whereas God hath made the head of man his highest and most supreme part, as being his chief grace and ornament; he must be drawn with his head declining downward, and lying so near the ground as may be, being thought unfit to take the benefit of the common air. For which cause also he shall be strangled, being hanged up by the neck, between heaven and earth, as deemed unworthy of both, or either; as likewise that the eyes of men may behold, and their hearts contemn him. Then he is to be cut down alive: his bowels and inlayed parts taken out and burnt, who inwardly had conceived and harboured in his heart such horrible treason. After, to have his head cut off, which had imagined the mischief. And, lastly, his body to be quartered, and the quarters set up in some high and eminent place, to the view and detestation of men, and to become a prey for the fowls of the air. And this is a reward due to traitors.[j]

I relieve your feelings by a custom which was observed among the Jews. They gave wine mingled with myrrh to a criminal at the time of his execution, in order to produce a stupor, and deaden the sensibility of the pain.

By the *constitution* of the United States, no attainder of *treason* shall work corruption of blood, or forfeiture, except during the life of the person attainted. By the *law* of the United States, as it now stands, no judgment for *any* offence shall work corruption of blood or forfeiture of *any* estate.

In England, the forfeiture of a criminal's personal estate accrues immediately upon his *conviction* of treason or felony. On his *attainder* for *treason,* he forfeits to the king all his lands of inheritance, and all his rights of entry to lands and tenements. On his attainder for *felony,* he forfeits his lands in fee simple to the crown for a year and a day; and the king may, within that time, commit what waste he pleases, by cutting timber, by ploughing meadows, by extirpating gardens, and by pulling down houses.

This uncivilized regulation, hostile to the genius of publick prosperity and improvement, is not, however, attended with any additional misfortune

j. 1. St. Tri. 243.

to the children of the prisoner. Their ruin is already completed by the corruption of their parent's blood. This unnatural principle—I call it unnatural, because it dissolves, as far as human laws can dissolve, the closest and the dearest ties of nature—this unnatural principle effectually intercepts from them the descent of his lands of inheritance, which, after the king's temporary right of forfeiture is satisfied, escheat to the lord of the fee.

Corruption of blood extends both upwards and downwards. A person attainted cannot inherit lands from his ancestors: he cannot transmit them to any heir: he even obstructs all descents to his posterity, whenever they must, through him, deduce their right from a more remote ancestor.

It has been alleged, in favour of forfeiture, that, since its effects extend to the family of the criminal as well as to himself, it will have a powerful operation to restrain a person from attempts against the state, not only by the fear of personal punishment, but also by his strongest natural affections. On a farther and closer investigation, however, it may, perhaps, be found, that this policy, as certainly it is not of the most generous, so neither is it of the most enlarged kind; since forfeitures, far from preventing, may have a tendency to multiply and to perpetuate offences and crimes.

When the law says, that the children of him, who has been guilty of crimes, shall be bereaved of all their hopes and all their rights of succession; that they shall languish in perpetual indigence and distress; that their whole life shall be one dark scene of unintermitted and unabating punishment; and that death alone shall provide for them a refuge from their misery—when such is the language, or such is the effect of the law; with what sentiments must it naturally inspire those, who are doomed to become its unfortunate, though unoffending objects? With sentiments of a deadly feud against the state, which has adopted, and which enforces it. To a law of this kind we may, with peculiar propriety, apply the maxim—une loi rigoreuse produit des crimes.[8]

In the United States, a period is assigned, beyond which crimes and offences, two excepted, cannot be prosecuted. This regulation is well calculated to establish and to preserve the security of individuals, and the tranquillity of the state. "Si post intervallum accusare (accusator) velit,"

8. A rigorous law produces crimes.

says Bracton,[9] "non erit de jure audiendus, nisi docere poterit se fuisse justis rationibus impeditum."[k]

The advantages of a copy of the indictment, of counsel at the trial, and of process to compel the appearance of the prisoner's witnesses are enjoyed, in England, only in prosecutions for treason, but not in prosecutions for other crimes.

The greatness of those advantages may be easily estimated by contemplating the helpless, the forlorn and the anxious situation of a person, who is deprived of them in a trial for his life.

When the bill for regulating trials in cases of high treason was, in the reign of William the third, brought into parliament; that part of it, which allows counsel to the prisoner, was viewed, by the friends of freedom, as a matter of the last importance. The Lord Ashley,[10] afterwards earl of Shaftesbury and author of the celebrated Characteristicks, was then a member of the house of commons. Actuated by that zeal for the principles of liberty, which accompanied him through life, he composed, as he was well qualified to compose, an excellent speech in support of that important provision. When he rose to deliver it, the great and respectable audience, before which he appeared, intimidated him to such a degree, that he lost his powers of recollection, and was incapable of pronouncing what he had previously prepared. The house, eager to hear him, waited with solicitude till he should recover from his embarrassment, and, after some time, called loudly upon him to proceed. He proceeded in this manner: "If I, sir,"—addressing himself to the speaker— "If I, sir, who rise only to give my opinion on the bill now depending, am so confounded, that I am unable to express the least of what I proposed to say; what must the condition of that man be, who, without any assistance, is pleading for his life?"[l] What must his condition be! Unacquainted with the nature and with the forms of the whole proceedings against him, unassisted by counsel, "baited by crown lawyers,"

9. Henry De Bracton (d. 1268) was a prominent judge who served on what would become known as the King's bench. He is most famous for his work *De legibus et consuetudinibus Angliae* (*On the Laws and Customs of England*).

k. Brac. 118 b. "If an accuser tries to bring an accusation after a period of time, he is not lawfully to be heard unless he can show he was previously hindered for just reasons."

10. Anthony Ashley Cooper (1671–1713) was the third Earl of Shaftesbury. John Locke educated him in his early youth, and later he became a great English politician, philosopher, and author.

l. Gen. Dict. vol. 9. p. 179.

distracted by uncertainty and suspense, he finds a desperate but an eligible refuge in the awful verdict of conviction, which determines his fate.

Let us turn our eyes to a more pleasing prospect. How few are the crimes—how few are the capital crimes, known to the laws of the United States, compared with those known to the laws of England! Allowance, we own, should be made for the difference between the nature of the two governments; the objects of one being *general;* those of the other, *enumerated.* But after every allowance is made for this consideration, still we may justly say—how few are the crimes—how few are the capital crimes, known to the laws of the United States, compared with those known to the laws of England! When Sir William Blackstone[11] wrote, no fewer than one hundred and sixty actions, which men are daily liable to commit, crowded the dismal list of felonies without benefit of clergy; in other words, felonies declared to be worthy of immediate death. Actions, almost inumerable, are doomed, by the same system, to severe, though inferiour penalties.

The co-acervation of sanguinary laws is a political distemper of the most inveterate and the most dangerous kind. By such laws the people are corrupted; and when corruption arises from the laws the evil may well be pronounced to be incurable; for it proceeds from the very source, from which the remedy should flow.

This comparison between the criminal laws of England and those of the United States might be carried much farther. The contrast would become still more and more striking; and, of course, the result would become still more and more satisfactory.

"How happy would mankind be," says the eloquent and benevolent Beccaria,[12] [m] "if laws were now to be first formed!" The United States enjoy this singular happiness. Their laws are now first formed. They are formed by the legitimate representatives of free citizens and free states. Among those citizens and those states they now begin to be diffused. To those citizens and those states they are objects of the greatest and most extensive importance. I speak particularly concerning the *criminal laws.* It is on

11. William Blackstone (1723–1780) offered the first courses on English law at Oxford. His magisterial *Commentaries on the Laws of England* (4 vols. 1765–1769) provided a thorough synthesis of British common law at the time.

12. Cesare Beccaria (1738–1794) wrote *On Crimes and Punishments* (1764). He was an advocate for reform of the criminal justice system and judiciary.

m. Chap. 28.

the excellence of the criminal laws, says the celebrated Montesquieu,[n] that the liberty of the citizens principally depends. The knowledge, continues he, which has been already acquired in some countries, and that which may be hereafter acquired in others, with regard to the surest rules which can be observed in criminal judgments, is more interesting to the human kind, than any thing else in the universe. It is only, adds he, on the practice of this knowledge that liberty can be founded.

With regard to an individual, every one knows how much his fortunes and his character, his infelicity or his happiness depend on his education. What education is to the individual, the laws are to the community. "Good laws," says my lord Bacon, whose sentences are discourses, "make a whole nation to be as a well ordered college."[o] With what earnestness should every nation—with what peculiar earnestness should that nation, which boasts of liberty as the principle of her constitution—with what peculiar earnestness should she endeavour, that her laws, especially her criminal laws, should be improved to a degree of perfection as high as human policy and human virtue can carry them!

We have already seen, that the noblest end and aim of criminal jurisprudence is to prevent crimes: and we have already seen that punishments, mild, speedy, and certain, are means calculated for preventing them. But these are not the only means. Crimes may be prevented by the genius as well as by the execution of the criminal laws. Let them be few: let them be clear: let them be be simple: let them be concise: let them be consummately accurate. Let the punishment be proportioned—let it be analogous—to the crime. Let the reformation as well as the punishment of offenders be kept constantly and steadily in view: and, while the dignity of the nation is vindicated, let reparation be made to those, who have received injury. Above all, let the wisdom, the purity, and the benignity of the civil code supersede, for they are well calculated to supersede, the severity of criminal legislation. Let the law diffuse peace and happiness; and innocence will walk in their train.

I offer no apology, gentlemen, for the nature or the length of this address. A sense of duty has drawn it from me. Every member of society should have it in his power to know when he is criminal and when he is

n. Sp. L. b. 12. c. 2.
o. 4. Ld. Bac. 9.

innocent. His criminality and his innocence should be designated by the laws. The code of criminal laws, therefore, should, as far as possible, be in the hands of every citizen. In the situation, in which I have the honour to be placed, I deem it my duty to embrace every proper opportunity of disseminating the knowledge of them far and speedily. Can this be done with more propriety than in an address to a grand jury—to a grand jury summoned and returned for the body of an extensive district—a district so extensive and important as that of Virginia? These considerations induced me to lay before you an enumeration of the crimes and the punishments known to our constitution and laws. This I have endeavoured to do with the utmost conciseness.

But, if the laws deserve it, they should be the objects of *affection* as well as of *knowledge.* Thinking, as I think, concerning the high degree of regard, to which the criminal code of the United States has an undoubted claim, I am justified in expressing—I am *obliged* to express the principles, on which I conceive that claim to be founded. This I have likewise endeavoured to do with the utmost conciseness.

I mean not, however, to recommend to you an implicit and an undistinguishing approbation of the laws of your country. Admire; but admire with reason on your side.

If, for instance, you think, that the laws respecting the publick securities are more severe than is absolutely necessary for supporting their value and their credit; it will be no crime to express your thoughts decently and properly to your representatives in congress.

Permit me to suggest another method, by which our valuable code of criminal laws may be still increased in its value. Inform and practically convince every one within your respective spheres of action and intercourse, that, as excellent laws improve the virtue of the citizens, so the virtue of the citizens has a reciprocal and benign energy in heightening the excellence of the law.

How happy are the people, by whom the laws are known and rationally beloved! The rational love of the laws generates the enlightened love of our country. The enlightened love of our country is propitious to every virtue, which can adorn and exalt the citizen and the man.

The Invalid Pension Act of 1792 required federal circuit courts (comprised of Supreme Court justices riding circuit and local federal district court judges) to hear claims by Revolutionary War veterans seeking federal benefits. Justices in other circuits agreed to hear claims, but Wilson, Iredell, and district judge Peters refused to do so. They sent the following letter to President Washington explaining why. Congress changed the law, excluding judges from this duty. *Hayburn's Case* was considered by many contemporaries, and is thought by many scholars today, to be the first instance of a federal court declaring an act of Congress to be unconstitutional.

Hayburn's Case, 2 U.S. 409 (1792), 411–414.

The Circuit court for the district of Pennsylvania, (consisting of WILSON, and BLAIR, *Justices,* and PETERS,[1] District Judge) made the following representation, in a letter jointly addressed to the President of the United States, on the 18th of April, 1792.

> To you it officially belongs to "take care that the laws" of the United States "be faithfully executed." Before you, therefore, we think it our duty to lay the sentiments, which, on a late painful occasion, governed us with regard to an act passed by the legislature of the union.
>
> The people of the United States have vested in Congress all *legislative* powers "granted in the constitution."
>
> They have vested in one Supreme court, and in such inferior courts as the Congress shall establish, "the *judicial* power of the United States."
>
> It is worthy of remark, that in Congress the *whole* legislative power of the United States is not vested. An important part of that power was exercised by the people themselves, when they "ordained and established the Constitution."
>
> This Constitution is "the Supreme Law of the Land." This supreme law "all judicial officers of the United States are bound, by oath or affirmation, to support."
>
> It is a principle important to freedom, that in government, the *judicial* should be distinct from, and independent of, the legislative department. To this important principle the people of the United States, in forming their Constitution, have manifested the highest regard.

1. Richard Peters, Jr. (1744–1828) was a Pennsylvania attorney and politician. He served as a federal district court judge for Pennsylvania from 1792 to 1828.

They have placed their *judicial* power not in Congress, but in "*courts.*" They have ordained that the "Judges of those courts shall hold their offices during good behaviour," and that "during their continuance in office, their salaries shall not be diminished."

Congress have lately passed an act, to regulate, among other things, "the claims to invalid pensions."

Upon due consideration, we have been unanimously of opinion, that, under this act, the Circuit court held for the Pennsylvania district could not proceed;

1st. Because the business directed by this act is not of a judicial nature. It forms no part of the power vested by the Constitution in the courts of the United States; the Circuit court must, consequently, have proceeded *without* constitutional authority.

2d. Because, if, upon that business, the court had proceeded, its *judgments* (for its *opinions* are its judgments) might, under the same act, have been revised and controuled by the legislature, and by an officer in the executive department. Such revision and controul we deemed radically inconsistent with the independence of that judicial power which is vested in the courts; and, consequently, with that important principle which is so strictly observed by the Constitution of the United States.

These, Sir, are the reasons of our conduct. Be assured that, though it became necessary, it was far from being pleasant. To be obliged to act contrary, either to the obvious directions of Congress, or to a constitutional principle, in our judgment equally obvious, excited feelings in us, which we hope never to experience again.

The Circuit court for the district of North Carolina, (consisting of IREDELL,[2] *Justice,* and SITGREAVES,[3] District Judge) made the following representation in a letter jointly addressed to the President of the United States, on the 8th of June, 1792.

We, the judges now attending at the Circuit court of the United States for the district North Carolina, conceive it our duty to lay before you some important observations which have occurred to us in the consideration of an act of Congress lately passed, entitled "an act to provide for the settlement of the claims of widows and orphans barred by the limitations heretofore established, and to regulate the claims to invalid pensions.

2. James Iredell (1751–1799) from North Carolina served in the Supreme Court from 1790 to 1799.

3. John Sitgreaves (1757–1802) served as a federal district court judge from 1790 to 1794.

We beg leave to premise, that it is as much our inclination, as it is our duty, to receive with all possible respect every act of the Legislature, and that we never can find ourselves in a more painful situation than to be obliged to object to the execution of any, more especially to the execution of one founded on the purest principles of humanity and justice, which the act in question undoubtedly is. But, however lamentable a difference in opinion really may be, or with whatever difficulty we may have formed an opinion, we are under the indispensable necessity of acting according to the best dictates of our own judgment, after duly weighing every consideration that can occur to us; which we have done on the present occasion.

The extreme importance of the case, and our desire of being explicit beyond the danger of being misunderstood, will, we hope, justify us in stating our observations in a systematic manner. We therefore, Sir, submit to you the following:

1. That the Legislative, Executive, and Judicial departments, are each formed in a separate and independent manner; and that the ultimate basis of each is the Constitution only, within the limits of which each department can alone justify any act of authority.

2. That the Legislature, among other important powers, unquestionably possess that of establishing courts in such a manner as to their wisdom shall appear best, limited by the terms of the constitution only; and to whatever extent that power may be exercised, or however severe the duty they may think proper to require, the Judges, when appointed in virtue of any such establishment, owe implicit and unreserved obedience to it.

3. That at the same time such courts cannot be warranted, as we conceive, by virtue of that part of the Constitution delegating *Judicial power,* for the exercise of which any act of the legislature is provided, in exercising (even under the authority of another act) any power not in its nature *judicial,* or, if *judicial,* not provided for upon the terms the Constitution requires.

4. That whatever doubt may be suggested, whether the power in question is properly of a judicial nature, yet inasmuch as the decision of the court is not made final, but may be at least suspended in its operation by the Secretary at War, if he shall have cause to suspect imposition or mistake; this subjects the decision of the court to a mode of revision which we consider to be unwarranted by the Constitution; for, though Congress may certainly establish, in instances not yet provided for, courts of appellate jurisdiction, yet such courts must consist of judges appointed in the manner the Constitution requires, and holding their offices by no other tenure than that of

their good behaviour, by which tenure the office of Secretary at War is not held. And we beg leave to add, with all due deference, that no decision of any court of the United States can, under any circumstances, in our opinion, agreeable to the Constitution, be liable to a reversion, or even suspension, by the Legislature itself, in whom no judicial power of any kind appears to be vested, but the important one relative to impeachments.

These, sir, are our reasons for being of opinion, as we are at present, that this Circuit court cannot be justified in the execution of that part of the act, which requires it to examine and report an opinion on the unfortunate cases of officers and soldiers disabled in the service of the United States. The part of the act requiring the court to sit five days, for the purpose of receiving applications from such persons, we shall deem it our duty to comply with; for, whether in our opinion such purpose can or cannot be answered, it is, as we conceive, our indispensable duty to keep open any court of which we have the honor to be judges, as long as Congress shall direct.

The high respect we entertain for the Legislature, our feelings as men for persons, whose situation requires the earliest, as well as the most effectual relief, and our sincere desire to promote, whether officially or otherwise, the just and benevolent views of Congress, so conspicuous on the present as well as on many other occasions, have induced us to reflect, whether we could be justified in acting, under this act, personally in the character of commissioners during the session of a court; and could we be satisfied that we had authority to do so, we would cheerfully devote such part of our time as might be necessary for the performance of the service. But we confess we have great doubts on this head. The power appears to be given to the court only and not to the Judges of it; and as the Secretary at War has not a discretion in all instances, but only in those where he has cause to suspect imposition or mistake, to with-hold a person recommended by the court from being named on the pension list, it would be necessary for us to be well persuaded we possessed such an authority, before we exercised a power, which might be a means of drawing money out of the public treasury as effectually as an express appropriation by law. We do not mean, however, to preclude ourselves from a very deliberate consideration, whether we can be warranted in executing the purposes of the act in that manner, in case an application should be made.

No application has yet been made to the court, or to ourselves individually, and therefore we have had some doubts as to the propriety of giving an opinion in a case which has not yet come regularly and judicially before us.

None can be more sensible than we are of the necessity of judges being in general extremely cautious in not intimating an opinion in any case extra-judicially, because we well know how liable the best minds are, notwithstanding their utmost care, to a bias, which may arise from a pre-conceived opinion, even unguardedly; much more deliberately, given: But in the present instance, as many unfortunate and meritorious individuals, whom Congress have justly thought proper objects of immediate relief, may suffer great distress even by a short delay, and may be utterly ruined by a long one, we determined at all events to make our sentiments known as early as possible, considering this as a case which must be deemed an exception to the general rule, upon every principle of humanity and justice; resolving however, that so far as we are concerned individually, in case an application should be made, we will most attentively hear it; and if we can be convinced this opinion is a wrong one, we shall not hesitate to act accordingly, being as far from the weakness of supposing that there is any reproach in having committed an error, to which the greatest and best men are sometimes liable, as we should be from so low a sense of duty, as to think it would not be the highest and most deserved reproach that could be bestowed on any men (much more on Judges) that they were capable, from any motive, of persevering against conviction, in apparently maintaining an opinion, which they really thought to be erroneous.

James Wilson's Opinion in *Chisholm* v. *State of Ga.*, 2 U.S. 419 (1793), 453–466.

Wilson, Justice

1. This is a case of uncommon magnitude. One of the parties to it is a State; certainly respectable, claiming to be sovereign. The question to be determined is, whether this State, so respectable, and whose claim soars so high, is amenable to the jurisdiction of the Supreme Court of the United States? This question, important in itself, will depend on others, more important still; and, may, perhaps, be ultimately resolved into one, no less radical than this "do the people of the United States form a Nation?"

A cause so conspicuous and interesting; should be carefully and accurately viewed from every possible point of sight. I shall examine it; 1st. By the principles of general jurisprudence. 2nd. By the laws and practice of particular States and Kingdoms. From the law of nations little or no illustration of this subject can be expected. By that law the several States and Governments spread over our globe, are considered as forming a society, not a NATION. It has only been by a very few comprehensive minds, such as those of Elizabeth[1] and the Fourth Henry, that this last great idea has been even contemplated. 3rdly. and chiefly, I shall examine the important question before us, by the Constitution of the United States, and the legitimate result of that valuable instrument.

I. I am, first, to examine this question by the principles of general jurisprudence. What I shall say upon this head, I introduce by the observation of an original and profound writer, who, in the philosophy of mind, and all the sciences attendant on this prime one, has formed an era not less remarkable, and far more illustrious, than that formed by the justly celebrated Bacon, in another science, not prosecuted with less ability, but

1. Elizabeth I (1533–1603) was queen of England from 1558–1603.

less dignified as to its object; I mean the philosophy of matter. Dr. Reid,[2] in his excellent enquiry into the human mind, on the principles of common sense, speaking of the sceptical and illiberal philosophy, which under bold, but false, pretentions to liberality, prevailed in many parts of Europe before he wrote, makes the following judicious remark: "The language of philosophers, with regard to the original faculties of the mind, is so adapted to the prevailing system, that it cannot fit any other; like a coat that fits the man for whom it was made, and shews him to advantage, which yet will fit very aukward upon one of a different make, although as handsome and well proportioned. It is hardly possible to make any innovation in our philosophy concerning the mind and its operations, without using new words and phrases, or giving a different meaning to those that are received." With equal propriety may this solid remark be applied to the great subject, on the principles of which the decision of this Court is to be founded. The perverted use of genus and species in logic, and of impressions and ideas in metaphysics, have never done mischief so extensive or so practically pernicious, as has been done by States and sovereigns, in politics and jurisprudence; in the politics and jurisprudence even of those, who wished and meant to be free. In the place of those expressions I intend not to substitute new ones; but the expressions themselves I shall certainly use for purposes different from those, for which hitherto they have been frequently used; and one of them I shall apply to an object still more different from that, to which it has hitherto been more frequently, I may say almost universally, applied. In these purposes, and in this application, I shall be justified by example the most splendid, and by authority the most binding; the example of the most refined as well as the most free nation known to antiquity; and the authority of one of the best Constitutions known to modern times. With regard to one of the terms State this authority is declared: With regard to the other sovereign the authority is implied only: But it is equally strong: For, in an instrument well drawn, as in a poem well composed, silence is sometimes most expressive.

To the Constitution of the United States the term SOVEREIGN, is totally unknown. There is but one place where it could have been used with

2. Dr. Thomas Reid (1710–1796) was a Scottish philosopher. Dr. Reid took over the chair of moral philosophy at Glasgow in 1764 upon Adam Smith's resignation. His most important works include *An Inquiry into the Human Mind on the Principles of Common Sense* (1764), *Essays on the Intellectual Powers of Man* (1785), and *Essays on the Active Powers of Man* (1788).

propriety. But, even in that place it would not, perhaps, have comported with the delicacy of those, who ordained and established that Constitution. They might have announced themselves 'SOVEREIGN' people of the United States: But serenely conscious of the fact, they avoided the ostentatious declaration.

Having thus avowed my disapprobation of the purposes, for which the terms, State and sovereign, are frequently used, and of the object, to which the application of the last of them is almost universally made; it is now proper that I should disclose the meaning, which I assign to both, and the application, which I make of the latter. In doing this, I shall have occasion incidently to evince, how true it is, that States and Governments were made for man; and, at the same time, how true it is, that his creatures and servants have first deceived, next vilified, and, at last, oppressed their master and maker.

Man, fearfully and wonderfully made, is the workmanship of his all perfect Creator: A State; useful and valuable as the contrivance is, is the inferior contrivance of man; and from his native dignity derives all its acquired importance. When I speak of a State as an inferior contrivance, I mean that it is a contrivance inferior only to that, which is divine: Of all human contrivances, it is certainly most transcendantly excellent. It is concerning this contrivance that Cicero[3] says so sublimely, "Nothing, which is exhibited upon our globe, is more acceptable to that divinity, which governs the whole universe, than those communities and assemblages of men, which, lawfully associated, are denominated States."

Let a State be considered as subordinate to the People: But let every thing else be subordinate to the State. The latter part of this position is equally necessary with the former. For in the practice, and even at length, in the science of politics there has very frequently been a strong current against the natural order of things, and an inconsiderate or an interested disposition to sacrifice the end to the means. As the State has claimed precedence of the people; so, in the same inverted course of things, the Government has often claimed precedence of the State; and to this perversion in the second degree, many of the volumes of confusion concerning sovereignty owe their existence. The ministers, dignified very properly

3. Marcus Tullius Cicero (106–43 B.C.) was a Roman orator, attorney, statesman, and political thinker.

by the appellation of the magistrates, have wished, and have succeeded in their wish, to be considered as the sovereigns of the State. This second degree of perversion is confined to the old world, and begins to diminish, even there: but the first degree is still too prevalent, even in the several States, of which our union is composed. By a State I mean, a complete body of free persons united together for their common benefit, to enjoy peaceably what is their own, and to do justice to others. It is an artificial person. It has its affairs and its interests: It has its rules: It has its rights: And it has its obligations. It may acquire property distinct from that of its members: It may incur debts to be discharged out of the public stock, not out of the private fortunes of individuals. It may be bound by contracts; and for damages arising from the breach of those contracts. In all our contemplations, however, concerning this feigned and artificial person, we should never forget, that, in truth and nature, those, who think and speak, and act, are men.

Is the foregoing description of a State a true description? It will not be questioned but it is. Is there any part of this description, which intimates, in the remotest manner, that a State, any more than the men who compose it, ought not to do justice and fulfil engagements? It will not be pretended that there is. If justice is not done; if engagements are not fulfilled; is it upon general principles of right, less proper, in the case of a great number, than in the case of an individual, to secure, by compulsion, that, which will not be voluntarily performed? Less proper it surely cannot be. The only reason, I believe, why a free man is bound by human laws, is, that he binds himself. Upon the same principles, upon which he becomes bound by the laws, he becomes amenable to the Courts of Justice, which are formed and authorised by those laws. If one free man, an original sovereign, may do all this; why may not an aggregate of free men, a collection of original sovereigns, do this likewise? If the dignity of each singly is undiminished; the dignity of all jointly must be unimpaired. A State, like a merchant, makes a contract. A dishonest State, like a dishonest merchant, wilfully refuses to discharge it: The latter is amenable to a Court of Justice: Upon general principles of right, shall the former when summoned to answer the fair demands of its creditor, be permitted, proteus-like, to assume a new appearance, and to insult him and justice, by declaring I am a Sovereign State? Surely not. Before a claim, so contrary, in its first appearance, to the general principles of right and equality, be sustained by a just and impartial tribunal, the person, natural or artificial, entitled to make such claim, should certainly be well known and authenticated. Who, or what, is a sovereignty? What is his or its sovereignty? On this subject, the errors and the mazes are endless and inexplicable. To enumerate all, therefore, will not be expected: To take notice of some will be necessary to the full illustration of the present important cause. In one sense, the term sovereign has for its correlative, subject. In this sense, the term can receive no application; for it has no object in the Constitution of the United States. Under that Constitution there are citizens, but no subjects. "Citizen of the United States." "Citizens of another State." "Citizens of different States." "A State or citizen thereof." The term, subject, occurs, indeed, once in the instrument; but to mark the contrast strongly, the epithet "foreign" is prefixed. In this sense, I presume the State of Georgia has no claim upon her own citizens: In this sense, I am certain, she can have no claim upon the citizens of another State.

In another sense, according to some writers, every State, which governs itself without any dependence on another power, is a sovereign State. Whether, with regard to her own citizens, this is the case of the State of Georgia; whether those citizens have done, as the individuals of England are said, by their late instructors, to have done, surrendered the Supreme Power to the State or Government, and reserved nothing to themselves; or whether, like the people of other States, and of the United States, the citizens of Georgia have reserved the Supreme Power in their own hands; and on that Supreme Power have made the State dependent, instead of being sovereign; these are questions, to which, as a Judge in this cause, I can neither know nor suggest the proper answers; though, as a citizen of the Union, I know, and am interested to know, that the most satisfactory answers can be given. As a citizen, I know the Government of that State to be republican; and my short definition of such a Government is, one constructed on this principle, that the Supreme Power resides in the body of the people. As a Judge of this Court, I know, and can decide upon the knowledge, that the citizens of Georgia, when they acted upon the large scale of the Union, as a part of the "People of the United States," did not surrender the Supreme or Sovereign Power to that State; but, as to the purposes of the Union, retained it to themselves. As to the purposes of the Union, therefore, Georgia is NOT a sovereign State. If the Judicial decision of this case forms one of those purposes; the allegation, that Georgia is a sovereign State, is unsupported by the fact. Whether the judicial decision of this cause is, or is not, one of those purposes, is a question which will be examined particularly in a subsequent part of my argument. There is a third sense, in which the term sovereign is frequently used, and which it is very material to trace and explain, as it furnishes a basis for what I presume to be one of the principal objections against the jurisdiction of this Court over the State of Georgia. In this sense, sovereignty is derived from a feudal source; and like many other parts of that system so degrading to man, still retains its influence over our sentiments and conduct, though the cause, by which that influence was produced, never extended to the American States. The accurate and well informed President Henault,[4] in his excellent chronological abridgment of the History of France, tells us, that, about the end of the second race of Kings, a new kind of possession was acquired, under the name of Fief. The Governors of Cities and Provinces usurped equally the property of land, and the administration of justice; and established themselves as proprietary Seigniors over those places, in which they had been only civil magistrates or military officers. By this means, there was introduced into the State a new kind of authority, to which was assigned the appellation of sovereignty. In process of time the feudal system was extended over France, and almost all the other nations of Europe: And every Kingdom became, in fact, a large fief. Into England this system was introduced by the conqueror: and to this era we may, probably, refer the English maxim, that the King or sovereign is the fountain of Justice. But, in the case of the King, the sovereignty had a double operation. While it vested him with jurisdiction over others, it excluded all others from jurisdiction over him. With regard to him, there was no superior power; and, consequently, on feudal principles, no right of jurisdiction. "The law," says Sir William Blackstone, "ascribes to the King the attribute of sovereignty: he is sovereign and independent within his own dominions; and owes no kind of objection to any other potentate upon earth. Hence it is, that no suit or action can be brought against the King, even in civil matters; because no Court can have jurisdiction over him: for all jurisdiction implies superiority of power." This last position is only a branch of a much more extensive principle, on which a plan of

4. Charles-Jean François Hénault (1685–1770) was councillor of the Parlement of Paris.

systematic despotism has been lately formed in England, and prosecuted with unwearied assiduity and care. Of this plan the author of the Commentaries was, if not the introducer, at least the great supporter. He has been followed in it by writers later and less known; and his doctrines have, both on the other and this side of the Atlantic, been implicitly and generally received by those, who neither examined their principles nor their consequences. The principle is, that all human law must be prescribed by a superior. This principle I mean not now to examine. Suffice it, at present to say, that another principle, very different in its nature and operations, forms, in my judgment, the basis of sound and genuine jurisprudence; laws derived from the pure source of equality and justice must be founded on the CONSENT of those, whose obedience they require. The sovereign, when traced to his source, must be found in the man.

I have now fixed, in the scale of things, the grade of a State; and have described its composure: I have considered the nature of sovereignty; and pointed its application to the proper object. I have examined the question before us, by the principles of general jurisprudence. In those principles I find nothing, which tends to evince an exemption of the State of Georgia, from the jurisdiction of the Court. I find everything to have a contrary tendency.

II. I am, in the second place, to examine this question by the laws and practice of different States and Kingdoms. In ancient Greece, as we learn from Isocrates,[5] whole nations defended their rights before crouded tribunals. Such occasions as these excited, we are told, all the powers of persuasion; and the vehemence and enthusiasm of the sentiment was gradually infused into the Grecian language, equally susceptible of strength and harmony. In those days, law, liberty, and refining science, made their benign progress in strict and graceful union: The rude and degrading league between the bar and feudal barbarism was not yet formed. When the laws and practice of particular States have any application to the question before us; that application will furnish what is called an argument a fortiori; because all the instances produced will be

5. An ancient Athenian philosopher, Isocrates (436–338 B.C.) studied under Socrates and Gorgias. A great teacher of rhetoric, he is mainly known for his belief in the ethical obligation of the rhetor.

instances of subjects instituting and supporting suits against those, who were deemed their own sovereigns. These instances are stronger than the present one; because between the present plaintiff and defendant no such unequal relation is alledged to exist. Columbus atchieved the discovery of that country, which, perhaps, ought to bear his name. A contract made by Columbus furnished the first precedent for supporting, in his discovered country, the cause of injured merit against the claims and pretentions of haughty and ungrateful power. His son Don Diego wasted two years in incessant, but fruitless, solicitation at the Court of Spain, for the rights which descended to him in consequence of his father's original capitulation. He endeavoured, at length, to obtain, by a legal sentence, what he could not procure from the favour of an interested Monarch. He commenced a suit against Ferdinand before the Council, which managed Indian affairs; and that Court, with integrity which reflects honour on their proceedings, decided against the King, and sustained Don Diego's claim. Other States have instituted officers to judge the proceedings of their Kings: Of this kind were the Ephori of Sparta:[6] of this kind also was the mayor of the Palace, and afterwards the constable of France. But of all the laws and institutions relating to the present question, none is so striking as that described by the famous Hottoman, in his book entitled Francogallia.[7] When the Spaniards of Arragon elect a King, they represent a kind of play, and introduce a personage, whom they dignify by the name of LAW, la Jusliza, of Arragon. This personage they declare, by a public decree, to be greater and more powerful than their King; and then address him in the following remarkable expressions. "We, who are of as great worth as you, and can do more than you can do, elect you to be our King, upon the conditions stipulated: But between you and us there is one of greater authority than you." In England, according to Sir William Blackstone, no suit can be brought against the King, even in civil matters. So, in that Kingdom, is the law, at this time, received. But it was not always so. Under the Saxon Government, a very different doctrine was held to be orthodox. Under that Government, as we are informed

6. The magistrates of Sparta.

7. François Hotman (1524–1590) was a French academic and author. His most famous work, *Franco-Gallia* (1573), promotes representative government.

by the Mirror of Justice, a book said, by Sir Edward Coke, to have been written, in part, at least, before the conquest; under that Government it was ordained, that the King's Court should be open to all Plaintiffs, by which, without delay, they should have remedial writs, as well against the King or against the Queen, as against any other of the people. The law continued to be the same for some centuries after the conquest. Until the time of Edward I. the King[8] might have been sued as a common person. The form of the process was even imperative. "Pracipe Henrico Regi Anglia" etc. ("Command Henry King of England" etc.) Bracton, who wrote in the time of Henry III,[9] uses these very remarkable expressions concerning the King "in justitia recipienda, minimo de regno suo comparetur" "in receiving justice, he should be placed on a level with the meanest person in the Kingdom." True it is, that now in England the King must be sued in his Courts by petition, but even now, the difference is only in the form, not in the thing. The judgments or decrees of those Courts will substantially be the same upon a precatory as upon a mandatory process. In the Courts of Justice, says, the very able author of the considerations on the laws of forfeiture, the King enjoys many privileges; yet not to deter the subject from contending with him freely. The Judge of the High Court of Admiralty in England made, in a very late cause, the following manly and independent declaration. "In any case, where the Crown is a party, it is to be observed, that the Crown can no more withhold evidence of documents in its possession, than a private person. If the Court thinks proper to order the production of any public instrument; that order must be obeyed. It wants no Insignia of an authority derived from the Crown." "Judges ought to know, that the poorest peasant is a man as well as the King himself: all men ought to obtain justice; since in the estimation of justice, all men are equal, whether the Prince complain of a peasant, or a peasant complain of the Prince." These are the words of a King, of the late Frederic of Prussia. In his Courts of Justice, that great man stood his native greatness; and disdained to mount upon the artificial stilts of sovereignty.

Thus much concerning the laws and practice of other States and King-

8. Edward I (1239–1307) was king of England from 1272 to 1307. He is known mainly for his military prowess in conquering Wales and dominating Scotland.

9. Henry III (1207–1272) was king of England from 1216 to 1272.

doms. We see nothing against, but much in favour of, the jurisdiction of this Court over the State of Georgia, a party to this cause.

III. I am, thirdly, and chiefly, to examine the important question now before us, by the Constitution of the United States, and the legitimate result of that valuable instrument. Under this view, the question is naturally subdivided into two others. 1. Could the Constitution of the United States vest a jurisdiction over the State of Georgia? 2. Has that Constitution vested such jurisdiction in this Court? I have already remarked, that in the practice, and even in the science of politics, there has been frequently a strong current against the natural order of things; and an inconsiderate or an interested disposition to sacrifice the end to the means. This remark deserves a more particular illustration. Even in almost every nation, which has been denominated free, the state has assumed a supercilious preeminence above the people, who have formed it: Hence the haughty notions of state independence, state sovereignty and state supremacy. In despotic Governments, the Government has usurped, in a similar manner, both upon the state and the people: Hence all arbitrary doctrines and pretensions concerning the Supreme, absolute, and incontrolable, power of Government. In each, man is degraded from the prime rank, which he ought to hold in human affairs: In the latter, the state as well as the man is degraded. Of both degradations, striking instances occur in history, in politics, and in common life. One of them is drawn from an anecdote, which is recorded concerning Louis XIV.[10] who has been stiled the grand Monarch of France. This Prince, who diffused around him so much dazzling splendour, and so little vivifying heat, was vitiated by that inverted manner of teaching and of thinking, which forms Kings to be tyrants, without knowing or even suspecting that they are so. The oppression, under which he held his subjects during the whole course of his long reign, proceeded chiefly from the principles and habits of his erroneous education. By these, he had been accustomed to consider his Kingdom as his patrimony, and his power over his subjects as his rightful and undelegated inheritance. These sentiments were so deeply and strongly imprinted on his mind, that when one of his Ministers represented to him the miserable condition, to

10. Louis XIV (1638–1715) was king of France from 1643 to 1715. He reportedly exclaimed, "*L'État, c'est moi*" (I am the state), a claim to which Wilson refers above.

which those subjects were reduced, and, in the course of his representation, frequently used the word L'Etat, the state, the King, though he felt the truth and approved the substance of all that was said, yet was shocked at the frequent repetition of the expression L'Etat; and complained of it is as an indecency offered to his person and character. And, indeed, that Kings should imagine themselves the final causes, for which men were made, and societies were formed, and Governments were instituted, will cease to be a matter of wonder or surprise, when we find that lawyers, and statesmen, and philosophers, have taught or favoured principles, which necessarily lead to the same conclusion. Another instance, equally strong, but still more astonishing, is drawn from the British Government, as described by Sir William Blackstone and his followers. As described by him and them, the British is a despotic Government. It is a Government without a people. In that Government, as so described, the sovereignty is possessed by the Parliament: In the Parliament, therefore, the supreme and absolute authority is vested: In the Parliament resides that incontrolable and despotic power, which, in all Governments, must reside somewhere. The constituent parts of the Parliament are the King's majesty, the Lords Spiritual, the Lords Temporal, and the Commons. The King and these three Estates together form the great corporation or body politic of the Kingdom. All these sentiments are found; the last expressions are found verbatim in the commentaries upon the laws of England. The Parliament form the great body politic of England! What, then, or where, are the People? Nothing! No where! They are not so much as even the "baseless fabric of a vision!" From legal contemplation they totally disappear! Am I not warranted in saying, that, if this is a just description; a Government, so and justly so described, is a despotic Government? Whether this description is or is not a just one, is question of very different import.

In the United States, and in the several States, which compose the Union, we go not so far: but still we go one step farther than we ought to go in this unnatural and inverted order of things. The states, rather than the People, for whose sakes the States exist, are frequently the objects which attract and arrest our principal attention. This, I believe, has produced much of the confusion and perplexity, which have appeared in several proceedings and several publications on state-politics, and on the politics, too, of the United States. Sentiments and expressions of this inaccurate kind prevail in our common, even in our convivial, language. Is a toast asked? "The United States," instead of the "People of the United States," is the toast given. This is not politically correct. The toast is meant to present to view the first great object in the Union: It presents only the second: It presents only the artificial person, instead of the natural persons, who spoke it into existence. A State I cheerfully fully admit, is the noblest work of Man: But, Man himself, free and honest, is, I speak as to this world, the noblest work of God.

Concerning the prerogative of Kings, and concerning the sovereignty of States, much has been said and written; but little has been said and written concerning a subject much more dignified and important, the majesty of the people. The mode of expression, which I would substitute in the place of that generally used, is not only politically, but also (for between true liberty and true taste there is a close alliance) classically more correct. On the mention of Athens, a thousand refined and endearing associations rush at once into the memory of the scholar, the philosopher, and the patriot. When Homer,[11] one of the most correct, as well as the oldest of human authorities, enumerates the other nations of Greece, whose forces acted at the siege of Troy, he arranges them under the names of their different Kings or Princes: But when he comes to the Athenians, he distinguishes them by the peculiar appellation of the PEOPLE of Athens. The well known address used by Demosthenes,[12] when he harrangued and animated his assembled countrymen, was "O Men of Athens." With the strictest propriety, therefore, classical and political, our national scene opens with the most magnificent object, which the nation could present. "The PEOPLE of the United States" are the first personages introduced. Who were those people? They were the citizens of thirteen States, each of which had a separate Constitution and Government, and all of which were connected together by articles of confederation. To the purposes of public strength and felicity, that confederacy was totally inadequate. A requisition on the several States terminated its Legislative authority: Executive or Judicial authority it had none. In order, therefore, to form a

11. Homer was the legendary Greek poet who composed the *Iliad* and the *Odyssey* in the eighth or seventh century B.C.

12. Demosthenes (384–322 B.C.) was a prominent Athenian statesman and orator.

more perfect union, to establish justice, to ensure domestic tranquillity, to provide for common defence, and to secure the blessings of liberty, those people, among whom were the people of Georgia, ordained and established the present Constitution. By that Constitution Legislative power is vested, Executive power is vested, Judicial power is vested. The question now opens fairly to our view, could the people of those States, among whom were those of Georgia, bind those States, and Georgia among the others, by the Legislative, Executive, and Judicial power so vested? If the principles, on which I have founded myself, are just and true; this question must unavoidably receive an affirmative answer. If those States were the work of those people; those people, and, that I may apply the case closely, the people of Georgia, in particular, could alter, as they pleased, their former work: To any given degree, they could diminish as well as enlarge it. Any or all of the former State powers, they could extinguish or transfer. The inference, which necessarily results, is, that the Constitution ordained and established by those people; and, still closely to apply the case, in particular by the people of Georgia, could vest jurisdiction or judicial power over those States and over the State of Georgia in particular.

The next question under this head, is, Has the Constitution done so? Did those people mean to exercise this, their undoubted power? These questions may be resolved, either by fair and conclusive deductions, or by direct and explicit declarations. In order, ultimately, to discover, whether the people of the United States intended to bind those States by the Judicial power vested by the national Constitution, a previous enquiry will naturally be: Did those people intend to bind those states by the Legislative power vested by that Constitution? The articles of confederation, it is well known, did not operate upon individual citizens; but operated only upon states. This defect was remedied by the national Constitution, which, as all allow, has an operation on individual citizens. But if an opinion, which some seem to entertain, be just; the defect remedied, on one side, was balanced by a defect introduced on the other: For they seem to think, that the present Constitution operates only on individual citizens, and not on States. This opinion, however, appears to be altogether unfounded. When certain laws of the States are declared to be "subject to the revision and controul of the Congress;" it cannot, surely, be contended that the Legislative power of the national Government was meant to have no operation on the several States. The fact, uncontrovertibly established in one instance, proves the principle in all other instances, to which the facts will be found to apply. We may then infer, that the people of the United States intended to bind the several States, by the Legislative power of the national Government.

In order to make the discovery, at which we ultimately aim, a second previous enquiry will naturally be: Did the people of the United States intend to bind the several States by the Executive power of the national Government? The affirmative answer to the former question directs, unavoidably, an affirmative answer to this. Ever since the time of Bracton, his maxim, I believe, has been deemed a good one: "Supervacuum esset leges condere, nisi esset qui leges tueretur." "It would be superfluous to make laws, unless those laws, when made, were to be enforced." When the laws are plain, and the application of them is uncontroverted, they are enforced immediately by the Executive authority of Government. When the application of them is doubtful or intricate, the interposition of the judicial authority becomes necessary. The same principle, therefore, which directed us from the first to the second step, will direct us from the second to the third and last step of our deduction. Fair and conclusive deduction, then, evinces that the people of the United States did vest this Court with jurisdiction over the State of Georgia. The same truth may be deduced from the declared objects, and the general texture of the Constitution of the United States. One of its declared objects is, to form an union more perfect, than, before that time, had been formed. Before that time, the Union possessed Legislative, but uninforced Legislative power over the States. Nothing could be more natural than to intend that this Legislative power should be enforced by powers Executive and Judicial. Another declared object is, "to establish justice." This points, in a particular manner, to the Judicial authority. And when we view this object in conjunction with the declaration, "that no State shall pass a law impairing the obligation of contracts;" we shall probably think, that this object points, in a particular manner, to the jurisdiction of the Court over the several States. What good purpose could this Constitutional provision secure, if a State might pass a law impairing the obligation of its own contracts; and be amenable, for such a violation of right, to no controuling judiciary power? We have seen, that on the principles of general jurisprudence, a State, for the breach of a contract, may be liable for damages. A third declared object is "to ensure domestic tranquillity." This tranquillity is most likely to be disturbed by controversies between States. These consequences will be most peaceably and effectually decided by the establishment and by the exercise of a superintending judicial authority. By such exercise and establishment, the law of nations; the rule between contending States; will be enforced among the several States, in the same manner as municipal law.

Whoever considers, in a combined and comprehensive view, the general texture of the Constitution, will be satisfied, that the people of the United States intended to form themselves into a nation for national purposes. They instituted, for such purposes, a national Government, complete in all its parts, with powers Legislative, Executive and Judiciary; and, in all those powers, extending over the whole nation. Is it congruous, that, with regard to such purposes, any man or body of men, any person natural or artificial, should be permitted to claim successfully an entire exemption from the jurisdiction of the national Government? Would not such claims, crowned with success, be repugnant to our very existence as a nation? When so many trains of deduction, coming from different quarters, converge and unite, at last, in the same point; we may safely conclude, as the legitimate result of this Constitution, that the State of Georgia is amenable to the jurisdiction of this Court. But, in my opinion, this doctrine rests not upon the legitimate result of fair and conclusive deduction from the Constitution: It is confirmed, beyond all doubt, by the direct and explicit declaration of the Constitution itself. "The judicial power of the United States shall extend, to controversies between two States." Two States are supposed to have a controversy between them: This controversy is supposed to be brought before those vested with the judicial power of the United States: Can the most consummate degree of professional ingenuity devise a mode by which this "controversy between two States" can be brought before a Court of law; and yet neither of those States be a Defendant? "The judicial power of the United States shall extend to controversies, between a state and citizens of another State." Could the strictest legal language; could even that language, which is peculiarly appropriated to an art, deemed, by a great master, to be one of the most honorable, laudable, and profitable things in our law; could this strict and appropriated language, describe, with more precise accuracy, the cause now depending before the tribunal? Causes, and not parties to causes, are weighed by justice, in her equal scales: On the former solely, her attention is fixed: To the latter, she is, as she is painted, blind.

I have now tried this question by all the touchstones, to which I proposed to apply it. I have examined it by the principles of general jurisprudence; by the laws and practice of States and Kingdoms; and by the Constitution of the United States. From all, the combined inference is; that the action lies.

Gideon Henfield seized a French ship and was charged by American prosecutors for engaging in acts hostile to nations at peace with the United States. Although no statute explicitly forbade this action, Wilson contended that Henfield could be charged with violating the common law of federal crimes. Although he was acquitted by the jury, Wilson's charge contributed to the eventual, though short-lived, acceptance of criminal common law claims by the federal courts.

Henfield's Case
Case No. 6,360
Circuit Court, D. Pennsylvania
11 F. Cas. 1099 (1793).

Judge Wilson (with whom were Judge Iredell and Judge Peters) charged the jury as follows:

This is, gentlemen of the jury, a case of the first importance. Upon your verdict the interests of four millions of your fellow-citizens may be said to depend. But whatever be the consequence, it is your duty, it is our duty, to do only what is right.

(After stating the substance of the charges against the defendant, the learned judge proceeded:)

It has not been contended, on the present occasion, that the defendant has any peculiar exclusive right to take a part in the present war between the European powers, in relation to all whom the United States are in a state of peace and tranquillity. If he has no peculiar or exclusive right, it naturally follows, that what he may do every other citizen of the United States may also do. If one citizen of the United States may take part in the present war, ten thousand may. If they may take part on one side, they may take part on the other; and thus thousands of our fellow-citizens may associate themselves with different belligerent powers, destroying not only those with whom we have no hostility, but destroying each other. In such a case, can we expect peace among their friends who stay behind? And will not a civil war, with all its lamentable train of evil, be the natural effect? Yet what is right must be done, independent of the consequences, which I have only stated, in order to lay before you the necessity of seriously considering the case entrusted to you before you decide upon it.

Two principal questions of fact have arisen, and require your determination. The first is, that the defendant, Gideon Henfield, has committed an act of hostility against the subjects of a power with whom the United States are at peace: this has been clearly established by the testimony. The second object of inquiry is, whether Gideon Henfield was at that time a citizen of the United States. This he explicitly acknowledged to Mr. Baker; and, if he declared true, it was at that time the least of his thoughts to expatriate himself.

The questions of law coming into joint consideration with the facts, it is the duty of the court to explain the law to the jury, and give it to them in direction. It is the joint and unanimous opinion of the court, that the United States, being in a state of neutrality relative to the present war, the acts of hostility committed by Gideon Henfield are an offence against this country, and punishable by its laws. It has been asked by his counsel, in their address to you, against what law has he offended? The answer is, against many and binding laws. As a citizen of the United States, he was bound to act no part which could injure the nation; he was bound to keep the peace in regard to all nations with whom we are at peace. This is the law of nations; not an ex post facto law, but a law that was in existence long before Gideon Henfield existed. There are, also, positive laws, existing previous to the offence committed, and expressly declared to be part of the supreme law of the land. The constitution of the United States has declared that all treaties made, or to be made, under the authority of the United States, shall be part of the supreme law of the land. I will state to you, gentlemen, so much of the several treaties in force between America and any of the powers at war with France, as applies to the present case. The first article of the treaty with the United Netherlands, declares that there shall be a firm, inviolable, and universal peace and sincere friendship between the States General of the United Netherlands and the United States of America, and between the subjects and inhabitants of the said parties. The seventh article of the definitive treaty of peace between the United States and Great Britain, declares that there shall be a firm and perpetual peace between his Britannic Majesty and the United States, and between the subjects of the one and the citizens of the other. And the first article of the treaty with Prussia declares that there shall be a firm, inviolable, and universal peace and sincere friendship between his Majesty the

King of Prussia and his subjects, on the one part, and the United States of America and their citizens on the other. It may be observed, that the treaty would not be less sufficient in relation to the present question, if "subjects" and "citizens" had not been mentioned. These treaties were in the most public, the most notorious existence, before the act for which the prisoner is indicted was committed. The notoriety may, indeed, be said to have been greater than that of the general acts of congress; since, besides the same mode of publication, they are expressly referred to in the constitution. Much has been said on this occasion, by the defendant's counsel, in support of the natural right of emigration; but little of it is truly applicable to the present question. Emigration is, undoubtedly, one of the natural rights of man. Yet it does not follow from thence that every act inconsistent with the duty is inconsistent with the state of a citizen. Nothing is more inconsistent with the duty of a citizen than treason; but it is because he still continues a citizen that he is liable to punishment.

The Treaty of Paris (1783) protected the right of British creditors to collect loans made before the Revolution. However, Virginia had passed a law in 1777 effectively abolishing those debts. A unanimous Supreme Court voided the Virginia law, thus helping to establish the supremacy of federal treaties over state law. Wilson's seriatim opinion is printed below.

James Wilson's Opinion in *Ware* v. *Hylton*, 3 U.S. 199 (1796), 281

Wilson, Justice. I shall be concise in delivering my opinion, as it depends on a few plain principles. If Virginia had a power to pass the law of October 1777, she must be equally empowered to pass a similar law in any future war; for, the powers of Congress were, in fact, abridged by the articles of confederation; and in relation to the present Constitution, she still retains her sovereignty and independence as a State, except in the instances of express delegation to the Federal Government. There are two points involved in the discussion of this power of confiscation: The first arising from the rule prescribed by the law of nations; and the second arising from the construction of the treaty of peace. When the United States declared their independence, they were bound to receive the law of nations, in its modern state of purity and refinement. By every nation, whatever is its form of government, the confiscation of debts has long been considered disreputable: and, we know, that not a single confiscation of that kind stained the code of any of the European powers, who were engaged in the war, which our revolution produced. Nor did any authority for the confiscation of debts proceed from Congress (that body, which clearly possessed the right of confiscation, as an incident of the powers of war and peace) and, therefore, in no instance can the act of confiscation be considered as an act of the nation. But even if Virginia had the power to confiscate, the treaty annuls the confiscation. The fourth article is well expressed to meet the very case: it is not confined to debts existing at the time of making the treaty; but is extended to debts heretofore contracted. It is impossible by any glossary, or argument, to make the words more perspicuous, more conclusive, than by a bare recital. Independent, therefore, of the Constitution of the United States, (which authoritatively inculcates the obligation of contracts) the treaty is sufficient to remove every impediment founded on the law of Virginia. The State made the law; the State was a party to the making of the treaty: a law does nothing more than express the will of a nation; and a treaty does the same. Under this general view of the subject, I think the judgment of the Circuit Court ought to be reversed.

Wilson penned the following plan in the mid-1790s. Two handwritten versions are contained in the Wilson notebooks at the Free Library of Philadelphia. The following text comes from a handwritten copy found in Benjamin Rush's papers at the Library Company of Philadelphia.

"On the Improvement and Settlement of Lands in the United States," mid-1790s.

In the United States there is an immense Quantity of Land, rich, well-situated and in a salubrious Climate. This Land lies useless and unimproved from the Want of Labour and Capital and Stock.

In Europe there is an Abundance of Labour and Capital and Stock; but rich and well-situated Land cannot be obtained, unless at a very high Price.

A Plan, by which the surplus Labour and Stock and Capital of Europe would be employed on the unimproved Lands of the United States, must be eminently advantageous to both.

It might be carried on to an Extent, and with a Degree of Certainty and System unknown to Transactions of any other Kind: And the Profits of it would be greater than those, which could be expected from any continued Series of mercantile Speculations—even those to the Indies not excepted.

Another Consideration, which highly recommends this Plan, is, that it would be greatly conducive to the Freedom, Ease, Independence and Happiness of those employed in its Execution.

The Extent of the Plan may be measured by the Millions of Acres, which could be furnished by the United States; and by the Millions of Men and of Money which could be furnished by Europe.

From the present Situation and Prospect of Affairs in that Part of the Globe, there is the strongest Reason to conclude, that the Numbers of Men and the Quantity of unemployed Money will rapidly encrease.

Adapted to this Situation and this Prospect in Europe are the Situation and the Prospect in the United States.

We have formed and now enjoy a Constitution, excellent in its Organization, and still more excellent in its diffusive Principles.

One Quality, for which it deserves the Attention and Attachment of those, who wish to come and reside among us, is this—the Nature of our

Government is so contrived as to expand in just and accurate Proportion to the Settlement of the Country.

New Accessions of Inhabitants run no Risque of becoming the distant, the neglected, the unprotected, the despised or the oppressed Appendages of old Governments. As new Settlements are made and encreased, new States will be formed and established. Those new States will, according to their Numbers, enjoy every Degree of Advantage and Importance, which is enjoyed by the most ancient States in the Union.

If the Encrease of the new Settlements shall be rapid and uniform; many generous Souls in Europe, who are now depressed by the extrinsic Advantages, which others enjoy on Account of their Birth and Interest and not of their Talents and Virtues, may, in the Course of a few Years—much fewer than is generally imagined—fill the first Offices in the States, which they shall have contributed to found and form. By a natural Gradation, they may be raised to Places of great Dignity and Consequence in the extended and the growing Government of the United States. In this Manner, they may acquire a just Importance, which will enable them to behold with perfect Equality, perhaps, with conscious Superiority, those, who now treat them with undeserved Severity, or with supercilious Contempt.

The late Instances of *Vermont* and *Kentucky*, and, indeed, the whole Genius of our public Policy, and the most obvious Considerations of public Interest prove that every Encouragement will be given to the Settlement, the Establishment and the Prosperity of new Governments.

Not only those, who aspire after the more elevated Ranks of Life, but those also, who, with humbler Views, wish to provide and to secure the Blessings of Liberty, Plenty and Independence, will have those Views fully accomplished by settling under the free Constitution, and on the rich Lands of the United States. Those Blessings they will be able to provide and to secure not only for themselves, but likewise for their Posterity through a long Succession of Ages.

Let us suppose that an European can purchase Lands of good Quality in the United States at the Price of   for each Acre. If he possesses Skill in Agriculture, and can command sufficient Capital and Labour and Stock; it is, by no Means, an unreasonable Calculation, that, at the End of eight Years, he may, after maintaining his Family in Comfort and Plenty, replace all the Capital, which he has expended; carry off a Stock of Cattle larger than that, which he, at first, furnished; and sell his Land at eight Times the Price, which he paid for it.

The Expence and Labour of clearing Land is often represented as grievous and almost unsurmountable. It is true, that they are great: But it is equally true, that a Tract of Land, covered with Timber, can, in less Time, with less Expence, and with more intermediate Advantage, be converted into a valuable and highly-cultivated Farm, than the waste naked Lands in Europe can be so converted.

Waste and naked Lands are generally poor and barren: Lands covered with Timber and annually meliorated by the Falling of the Leaves are generally rich and fertile. Their Surface presents a *Stratum* of *Virgin Soil;* and what is, at first, considered as a mighty Obstacle in the Way of Improvement is found, on Trial, to render that Improvement easy and rapid.

The Timber, that formidable Object to an ignorant or a weak handed Settler, becomes, in the Hands of one, who knows what he should do, and who can do what he knows, A Source of Ease, Wealth and Pleasure.

This Timber furnishes him, at an easy Rate, with Fences, and with his Materials for Building, and for the Utensils of Farming. What is more than sufficient for those Purposes may be reduced to Ashes. The Ashes will produce Pot and Pearl Ash, which, in many Places, will re-imburse all the Expences of clearing and fencing the Land. After the Pot and Pearl Ash are made, the refuse Ashes are still an excellent Manure for quickening and strengthening Vegetation.

If the Planter feels a Taste for the Ornaments as well as an Attachment to the Profits of Agriculture; his Taste may be completely gratified by selecting the Spots and Fields proper for being cleared and cultivated, and blending them judiciously with those, which should be left in their natural and unimproved State.

Even a *Farm ornée* may be planted and completed with less Expence, with greater Profit, and much more speedily n the Wilderness of America, than it can be done in the smooth and unvariegated Plains of Europe.

What has been said of *one* Settlement, of one Improvement and of one Farm may, with the same Propriety, be said of *Millions* of Settlements and Improvements and Farms.

Indeed it may be said with *more* Propriety: For every *preceding* Settlement, Improvement and Farm *prepares* the Way for those, which shall *succeed:* And every *subsequent* Settlement, Improvement and Farm bestows an *additional* Value upon those, which have *preceded* it.

By this pleasing and profitable Arrangement of Things, the Skill and Labour and Capital of every Settler are employed not only in producing Emolument to himself, but also in diffusing Benefits to all around him, to all who have gone before him, and to all who shall come after him.

During every successive Season, the surplus Grain and Stock and Labour, which can be spared from the Plantations, whose Culture has been carried to a considerable Height, will be wanted in those Plantations, whose Improvement is just begun.

A constant Market will thus be regularly opened and regularly supplied; and the alternate Vicissitudes of Want and excessive Plenty will be equally unknown. Every Thing produced will find a sufficient Demand for its Consumption; and every Demand for Consumption will find Produce in sufficient Quantities to supply it.

The reciprocal and encreasing Advantages of progressive and extending Settlements may be carried to a Height and with a Degree of Rapidity not easily conceived.

Many on the Frontiers of this Country have witnessed much on this Subject. They have seen, however, but little, compared with what would be seen on a proper Union of the Labour and Capitals of *Europe* with the fertile and unimproved Soil of *America.*

But notwithstanding all the Advantages, which I have mentioned, there are many Objections, which will arise in the Minds, and have Influence upon the Conduct of those, who meditate an Emigration to America—especially of those, who are married and have Families.

The Fatigue, the Inconveniencies and the Danger of a long Voyage are all Objects of a very uninviting Nature. The Prospect of them will make an Impression, peculiarly deep, upon one, who has a Wife, and young Children, for the Delicacy of whose Age and Sex he tenderly feels.

The Vessel may [be] insufficient: The Commander may be hard-hearted: The Accommodations on Board may be bad: The Season may be unfavourable: The Provisions may be of an ordinary Kind: The Water may be scarce: An improper Number of Passengers may be crowded together: Sickness and infectious Disorders may be the Consequence. From all, or many, or some, or even one of these Circumstances great Distress may be the Lot of those, whose Years or Constitution render them very unfit to encounter it.

Even if all these Difficulties should, in Imagination, be surmounted, others behind them will still appear in View, and spread an obscure and comfortless Scene before the doubting Emigrant.

When he and his Family shall be landed in a strange and distant Country, he will have no Friend or Acquaintance, on whom he can rely for immediate Aid or Advice or Information.

Some Time must elapse before he can come to a Determination concerning that Part of the country, on which he shall fix for his Residence. During this Time, his Family must be maintained, perhaps at a high Rate in a City.

When, at last, he shall be obliged to move towards the Place, on which, after much Hesitation and Uncertainty, his Choice has *happened* to fall, he will find no previous Preparations made for the Convenience of his Wife and Children, *during the Journey*. To *purchase*, at its *Commencement*, every Thing necessary for carrying them comfortable to its *Conclusion* will be intolerably expensive: To *hire* Things occasionally, as he shall stand in Need of them, will be absolutely impracticable.

Under these Circumstances, a Journey of some hundred Miles by Land will appear little less formidable than a Voyage of some thousand Miles by Sea: And the Impression made by *each* will be strengthened by the Impression made by the *other*.

He will next look forward to what is likely to be his Situation, when both his Voyage and his Journey shall, after many Embarrassments, at last, receive a Termination.

Incumbered with his Family and Servants, he will arrive at the Spot, of which he has made Choice—if it can be called a *Choice*, when he has had no satisfactory Information concerning the Object, on which it has fallen. He will find, perhaps, in the Neighbourhood, twenty others, to which he would have given the Preference, had he seen any just Account or Description of them.

On this Spot, degraded as it is by a Comparison with others, he has neither House nor Home. Where shall he find a Place for his Wife and Children?—How, in a frontier or unsettled Country, and, perhaps, at an unfavourable Season of the Year, shall he provide for them, till he can build a House, and raise the Means of their Subsistance on the Land, which he has purchased?

I have represented him as making the Supposition, that he would bring his *Servants,* as well as his Wife and Children, with him. On a closer Inspection, however, he will be apt to doubt whether this will be the Case.

Unforeseen Delays, unforeseen Expenses, unforeseen Difficulties may have such an unfortunate Effect in draining his Funds, as to lay him under the Necessity of parting with his Domestics, on whose Labour and Assistance he proposed to lay the Foundation of his future Improvements and Prosperity.

The Consequence of such a Situation would be—and he would perceive it in Prospect—that, at the melancholy Conclusion of his Adventure, he would find himself totally disabled from pursuing the Principle, on which it was originally undertaken—*that of uniting the Land in America with the Capital and Labour brought from Europe.* He would have the Land, indeed; but the Capital and the Sources of Labour would be gone.

Those, who are forced by dire Necessity, or impelled by resistless Ambition, weight not distant Consequences. But on those, whose Condition of Life is tolerably easy, though they indulge the natural Wish to improve it, the remotest Chance of being thrown into a Situation of such accumulated Distress as has been mentioned, will have a powerful Effect in preventing the first, but *irrevocable* Steps, which, by a Possibility, may lead to a Catastrophe, so dismal.

It is, however, by those of *this* Description, that the Settlement of a new Country can be expected to be made on the best Terms, with the greatest Expedition, and with the largest Share of private and public Felicity.

To *such,* an easy and secure Plan, by which an Emigration from Europe to the United States can be begun, carried on and completed, and by which the Ends of an Emigration can certainly and successfully be accomplished, would be a Present of the most valuable and acceptable Kind.

Those, who could devise and execute such a Plan, would perform a most precious Service to Individuals and to Society; and would merit a rich Compensation for their Exertions and Labours.

Of such a Plan I attempt the Outlines. Much *Consideration* and even EXPERIENCE will be requisite to bring all its Parts to full Perfection.

The Land-Office of the *United States* will soon be opened for the Disposal of a most extensive Territory.

The Country proposed for the general Scene of Operations should be viewed and examined. Large and well-situated, well-selected and well-located Tracts should be accurately surveyed, and purchased on the Terms offered by the Public.

The *best* Parts of those Tracts should be subdivided into Surveys of one, two or three hundred Acres each.

Correct Descriptions, representing the Lands to be neither better nor worse than in Truth, they are, should be carefully made.

The Draughts and Maps and Titles should be completed in a Manner, the most clear, regular and satisfactory.

All this must be done on *this* Side of the *Atlantic.* But to do all this with Ease and Security, and on a Scale sufficiently large, good Connexions must be formed, and ample Funds must be provided on the *other* Side of the *Atlantic.*

The first Axiom in this Plan is—*never to be in Want of Money.*

To Capitalists Inducements should be offered, sufficient to determine them to take such a Share in the Business as shall be agreed on, and to advance Proportions of the necessary Funds.

Those Capitalists should be allowed a reasonable Proportion of the Lands purchas'd, or of their net Proceeds; and a very handsome Commission on the Land, which they shall sell, and for which they shall receive Payment in Europe.

They should also be allowed a Share of the Profits of Passage-Money, arising from Vessels fitted out by them.

This last Proportion ought to be very great; and, indeed, the strongest Reason, which occurs to me, why they should not have the *Whole* is, that, by attempting to gain too much on the Passage of Emigrants, they might injure the more material Objects proposed, *here,* by the Emigration. An Interest in the Passage-Money would entitle to a Voice in its Rate, and in the proper Accommodation and Treatment of the Passengers.

The Lands purchased in the United States should be mortgaged for the Sums advanced to execute the Plan. The Money paid, in Europe, by Purchasers should be applied, in the first Place, to the Discharge of those Sums. The Surplus should be deposited at the Order of those on this and on the other Side of the Atlantic, in just Proportions.

The European Directors in this Plan should be Men of known and established Character as well as Property—such as will *attract* and *deserve* the Confidence of those, who propose to emigrate with their Families and nearest Connexions.

The Vessels employed in this Service should be strong and good and sea-worthy in every Respect: They should sail well: They should be fitted out in the most complete Manner: They should be abundantly supplied with every Thing necessary and comfortable: They should be under the Command of Officers distinguished by their Humanity as well as by their nautical Abilities.

When the Emigrants arrive in the United States, they should be immediately provided with proper Accommodations on Shore.

So soon as they are refreshed from the Fatigues of the Voyage, they should be conducted in a cheap and convenient Manner, and by easy Stages, to the Place of their Destination.

On their Arrival at the Land, which they have purchased, they should find, for their Use, a House already built, a Garden already made, an Orchard already planted, a Portion of Land already cleared, and Grain already growing or reaped. For all these Conveniencies they should pay at a reasonable Rate.

They should have the Opportunity of purchasing Stock as near as possible to the Place of their Residence; that the Trouble and Expence of driving them a long Distance may be avoided.

When such Arrangements are made, and *known* to be made from the Commencement, through the Progress and to the very Conclusion of an Emigration from Europe to the United States, those, who wish to improve their own Situation and that of their Children, will view such an Emigration in a Light very different from that, in which, hitherto, it has been generally considered. The Obstacles will appear to be smoothed; the Dangers and Difficulties will evanish; and the happy Issue of the Adventure will rise in pleasing Prospect before the Adventurer.

The same inviting Circumstances, which induce *one*, will induce many to embark in the Enterprise. The Consequence will be, that a Number of Families, acquainted and connected with one another, may emigrate from the same Place, at the same Time, in the same Vessel, to the same Neighbourhood in the United States; and may gain for themselves and secure for their Posterity the Possession and Inheritance of Liberty, Property,

Plenty and Independence, without having been obliged to sacrifice, for a single Moment, the Comforts of Life or Society in making the important Acquisition.

I have already intimated that Attention should be paid to the Characters of those, who are to take a Share of this Business in Europe. Much, I think, will depend on this Circumstance. When a Man himself and his Wife and Children, as well as his Property, are to be staked on the Issue of an Enterprise, he will be peculiarly solicitous concerning the Character of those, to whom he commits the Charge of such an important Deposit. Confidence must be the Soul of a Plan so enlarged and so interesting as this is.

The Ports in Europe, at which the Embarkations should take Place, are Objects, which should be wisely and judiciously selected. I would propose *Amsterdam* for the United and Austrian Netherlands, for the Southern and Western Parts of Germany, and for the Eastern and Northern Parts of France. For Ireland I would propose Dublin, Cork, Belfast, Londonderry and Limerick.

To fix upon a healthy Climate and convenient Situation; and to *select* and *secure* Tracts of Land *peculiarly* fertile, are Points of vast Importance to the Success of this Plan.

The last Points, in particular, will require much Information and much practical Knowledge both in the Direction and in the Execution; in examining and surveying the Country; and in superintending the Proceedings in the Land Office from the first Commencement, through the whole Progress, to the Conclusion of the *Titles.*

Good *Land* and a good *Title* are, with Emigrants, prevailing Inducements in Favour of any particular Spot. The utmost Care should, for this Reason, be employed to lay the surest Foundations of those Inducements, in *Fact* and in *Law.*

Persons of undoubted Integrity and Industry, well acquainted with the Woods, good Judges of Land, and Proficients in practical Surveying should be employed in proper Districts, and under proper Instructions, to reconnoitre the Country and make Locations of Land.

Much might be said upon the Subject of their Instructions; but, at present, it is unnecessary. Two Conditions, however, should be indispensable—that they should not be interested in a single Foot of Land in the District proposed to be surveyed—and that, while they shall be engaged in this Business, they shall make no Surveys or Locations for others, nor communicate to others Information for making Surveys or Locations.

This Business of examining the Country and making Locations in the proper Places and the proper Manner will be very expensive, and will be attended with much Trouble; but I conceive it to be essential to the Advantage, to the Success, and to the Reputation of the Plan.

The general Situations, which would first attract my Attention, are those to the Westward and Northward of Pennsylvania, on the Southern and Western Shores of Lake *Erie,* and on the River *Miami,* which falls into that Lake.

I have always thought that the most ELIGIBLE (and under this Epithet I comprise many different Views of the Subject) Communication between the Eastern and Western Territory of the United States is by the Rivers Delaware and Susquehannah and Lake Erie and the other great Lakes.

I enter not, now, upon the Reasons of this Opinion; but I would act upon it.

The Situations, which I have mentioned, are all contiguous to this great and eligible Line of Communication; and contain according to particular Information in my Possession, Tracts of Land highly valuable indeed, especially on the Western Shore of Lake *Erie* and the Rout to *Detroit.*

The Situations on the River *Miami* are attended with another Advantage, of great Service in the Accomplishment of the general Plan. They lead to the River *Wabash,* which falls into the *Ohio;* to the River *Illinois,* which falls into the Mississippi; and to the River St Joseph, which falls into Lake Michigan.

It now appears what a vast Prospect opens upon us.

The *Climate* of this long Line of Communication is not less inviting than the Situation and the Soil. The Country is in the same Latitudes with the States of Massachussets, Connecticut, New York, New Jersey and Pennsylvania. By every Information we are led to believe, that the Severity of Heat in Summer and of Cold in Winter decreases in Proportion as Progress is made to the Westward. This will become the Case more and more, as the Country shall be more and more improved.

Many Reasons, public as well as private, satisfy me, after long and deliberate Reflexion on the Subject, that it will be the Interest of the United States as well as of Individuals to pursue the Settlement of Farms and the Establishment of States in the Direction of the great Line, which I have described.

In a great political View, it will be found to be the Line of *Union* and the Line of *Strength*. But I cannot, at this Time, expatiate upon this immense Object. It is sufficient for the present Purpose, that this Line is recommended by the Salubrity of the Climate, the Convenience of the Situation, and the Fertility of the Soil, through which it extends.

Connected with this Line, there is another, which richly deserves Attention—the Line from Lake *Michigan* to the *Mississippi* by the *Fox* and the *Ouisconsing* Rivers. By *this* Communication there is only one Portage—and that one Portage is only of three Miles—from the Mississippi to the Eastern End of Lake *Erie*. It lies through a Country described by the latest and best Accounts to be very rich and very level; and it is said to lead directly to the most valuable and extensive Scene of Fur Trade, which can be found in America—that on the Head Waters of the Mississippi, and on the Waters to the Westward and Northward of it.

It may seem surprising, that I have taken no Notice of the Country immediately on the Northern Banks of the *Ohio;* nor of that lying between it and the Southern Boundary of the United States.

The Truth is, that I do not think those Countries, as to Situation, or Climate, to be on a Footing of Equality with those other Countries, which I have pointed out.

The *Soil* of the former is, indeed, equally rich with that of the latter; but the *Climate* is less healthy; and the *Communication* with the *Atlantic* and its Waters is not so *convenient,* nor is it likely to be so *permanent.*

If, however, farther and more minute Enquiry and Information should lead to a contrary Conclusion; there is evidently Nothing in what I point out, which will prevent such Conclusion from being adopted and pursued, either separately, or jointly with what I propose.

This Plan, it is obvious, is uncommonly extensive: But the Inference should not be made, that it is, *therefore,* extravagant. The very *Extent* may sometimes aid the *Execution* of a System. With Regard to the present one, this, I believe, will, on Reflexion and Experience, be found to be the Case.

There are some Parts of it, which are of peculiar Importance, and, for this Reason, will deserve peculiar and repeated Consideration—I mean those, which relate to the *Safety,* the *Convenience* and the *Cheapness* of the *Voyage* by Sea; and the *Journey* by Land—and those, which relate to the *Goodness of the Lands,* the *Improvements* begun upon them, and the Validity of the *Titles,* by which they are held.

On that Part, which relates to the Safety, the Convenience and the Cheapness of a Voyage from Europe to the United States, it is unnecessary for me to be particular.

I shall only hint, in Connexion with the Voyages, that Masts and Spars, *long* Ship-Plank, Lumber of the most valuable Kinds, Pot and Pearl Ash, ground Bark and the Essence of Bark for Dyers and Tanners, Biscuit finer than what is generally used, and Beef and Pork of superior Quality and excellently cured might, perhaps, be improved into Articles for profitable Return-Cargoes.

With Regard to the Journey by Land, I suggest the following Remarks.

When the *best* and *nearest* Rout shall be once ascertained, it will be proper, so soon as possible, to rent or purchase a Chain of Houses and Farms at convenient Distances for Stages along the whole Line of Communication. The first of these Stages should be established at the Place where the Passengers shall land. There they ought to find every Thing conducing to their Refreshment after their Voyage; and every Thing necessary to accommodate them in setting out on their Journey.

At the End of about *ten* Miles they should find another Stage and suitable Accommodations.

In this Manner, they should proceed from Stage to Stage, till their Arrival at the Lands destined for their Settlement.

Along this Line, and especially towards the Western End of it, they should find, at reasonable Prices, a Supply of Horses, Oxen, Cows, Sheep, Hogs and Poultry, all of the best Breeds; and farming Utensils of the best Kinds and Construction.

The Establishment of this Line of Stages would be very expensive at first: But the rising Value of the Plantations, which ought to be larger and larger as we advance westward; the gradual Increase of the Stock and Improvements on them; and the constant Market for every Thing, which they could produce, would, in a short Time, be Sources of great Profit to the Proprietors, as well as of great Convenience to the Emigrants.

I cannot insist too much upon the Propriety and Importance of small Improvements being made on the different Places of Settlement, before the Emigrants shall respectively arrive at them. These Improvements, though small, are every Thing to a new Settler. His Family will derive great Resource from even a *Patch* of Potatoes, Carrots, Turnips, Cabbages and other Vegetables. Instead of *losing his Time,* and wasting the scanty Remains of his Stock in *Cash* in *searching* and *procuring* the necessary Sustenance of his Family, he has the Satisfaction to find the Means of Subsistance *provided* for him on the most easy Terms, and placed within his Reach.

At first, those Improvements will require very considerable Advances in Money: But the Lands, on which they shall be made, will be an ample Security for the Re-imbursement of the Sums advanced; and, after the first Series of Settlements shall be made, those in every *preceding* Series will find their Account in making for *others,* Improvements similar to those, which were made for *themselves,* and in receiving, after a short Interval, the Return of a Sum equal to that, which they have previously been obliged to expend.

No Expence or Pains ought to be spared in *examining, surveying* and *laying off* the Lands with the utmost *Fairness* and *Correctness;* and in *obtaining* in order to be able to *give* a just Account of their Quality and Situation, and of the Timber growing upon them.

Correctness and Candour in this Part of the Business will diffuse Certainty and Satisfaction over all its succeeding Stages.

Though a large Tract may be obtained at the Land Office by one Purchase, and though to complete the Title to the Land purchased, it may be sufficient to comprehend the whole Tract in a single Survey; yet, for the Execution of *this* Plan, it will be absolutely necessary that the *best Parts* of the large Tract be accurately subdivided, and not merely upon Paper, into Surveys of one, two or three hundred Acres each, whose Boundaries should be regularly and distinctly marked.

This will prevent Confusion and Contention in the future Settlement and Improvement of the Farms. It will also put it in the Power of the Proprietors to offer for Sale *only* such Surveys as can be recommended on the best and most sufficient Foundation.

The Surveyors should be scrupulously exact and minute in making Notes, as they go along, of the Nature and Kinds and Qualities of the Soil and Timber; and also of every other Circumstance, which can throw Light upon the Subject.

By tracing and comparing those Notes, taken at short Distances and in every Direction, one, without seeing the Tract, may be able to form a very adequate Judgment concerning the Value and Situation of the Land; and to *reject* or postpone the Purchase of such as shall be of an inferior Quality.

The particular Steps proper and requisite for *completing* and authenticating the *Titles* and *Title-Deeds* it is unnecessary to enumerate here.

Every *third* Survey should be reserved, *by Lot*, for the Proprietors. This Measure will be eligible for many Reasons.

1. It is obvious that it will be profitable; as it will secure to the Proprietors an Interest in that Value, which Land, even uncultivated, will gradually acquire from the Cultivation of the Country around it.

2. It will enable them to exhibit, in particular Places, the most instructive Examples of every Species of agricultural Improvement.

3. It will stimulate them to make the strongest Exertions in promoting every Plan which can accelerate the Growth and Value of the Settlements, and the Prosperity and Happiness of the Settlers.

4. If any Survey, purchased by a Settler, should unexpectedly happen to be much inferior, in Quality or Value, to what it is represented to be; the Proprietors can, on just Terms, exchange it for another in the Neighbourhood.

5. A similar Exchange can be made, if the Title to any particular Survey should turn out to be invalid or even doubtful.

6. If a Settler should feel a *partial* or a *well-founded* Preference for a reserved Survey; he may obtain it at a reasonable Price, or may exchange it, on reasonable Terms, in the Place of that, which he has already purchased. This will encrease greatly the *Choice* among the particular Surveys, and the *Pleasure* resulting from *Judgment,* from Taste, or even from *Caprice* in making that Choice.

7. It will be in the Power of the Proprietors to *lease,* at easy and advantageous Rates, Farms to those, who shall have come out on Contracts of Service, and shall have honestly performed the Conditions of their Contracts. An easy and advantageous *Lease* will naturally pave the Way to a *Purchase;* and, thus, the most beneficial Prospects will be opened even to those, who possess Nothing but their own Labour and honest Industry.

This I deem to be of the last Importance to the general Utility and Vigour of the System.

I have said, that the Extent of a System may sometimes aid its Execution; and have expressed my Opinion, that the Remark is applicable to the present Plan. Of this I adduce *one* Illustration. From its very Extent, the Plan will obviously admit of an handsome Compensation to all, who shall be employed in its several Parts. The Compensation will be not only handsome, but permanent and encreasing. A Compensation, handsome, permanent and encreasing, will command a Choice of Characters, well recommended by their Integrity and their Skill. Characters, so recommended, will engage the Confidence of every one, whose Interest can be affected by their Conduct. This Confidence will operate as a powerful Motive for taking an Interest in a System, which will be thus skilfully and honestly carried into Execution.

The final drafts of Wilson's law lectures are contained in notebooks labeled "Introductory" and then 1–49. There is also a notebook labeled 50 which contains Wilson's unfinished "On the history of property." Because of its close association with the law lectures, it is reproduced here. For further discussion of this and the other notebooks, see pages 401–413 of this volume.

On the History of Property.

Property is the right or lawful power, which a person has to a thing. Of this right there are three different degrees. The lowest degree of this right is a right merely to possess a thing. The next degree of this right is a right to possess and to use a thing. The next and highest degree of this right is a right to possess, to use, and to dispose of a thing.

This right, in all its different degrees, may be vested in one, or it may be vested in more than one man. When this right is vested in more than one man, it may be vested in them either as a number of individuals, or as a body politick.

Concerning the origin and true foundation of property, or the right of persons to things, many opinions have been formed and entertained. With regard to property in land, Mr. Paley declares, that the real foundation of it is municipal law.[a] Others consider property as a natural right; but as a right, which may be extended or modified by positive institutions.[b]

The general property of man in animals, in the soil, and in the productions of the soil, is the immediate gift of the bountiful Creator of all. "God created man in his own image; in the image of God created he him: male and female created he them. And God blessed them; and God said unto them, be fruitful and multiply, and replenish the earth, and subdue it: and have dominion over the fish of the sea, and over the fowl of the air, and over every living thing that moveth upon the earth."[c] Immediately after the deluge, the great charter of general property was renewed. "God blessed Noah and his sons, and said unto them, be fruitful and multiply, and replenish the earth. And the fear of you and the dread of you shall be upon every beast of the earth, and upon every fowl of the air, and upon all

a. 1. Paley. 133. 138.
b. Ins. 2. 1. 11. El. Jur. 15.
c. Gen. i. 27. 28.

that moveth upon the earth, and upon all the fishes of the sea; into your hand are they delivered. Every moving thing that liveth shall be meat for you; even as the green herb have I given you all things."[d]

The information which is expressly revealed is congenial to those inferences, which may be drawn by sound and legitimate reasoning. Food, raiment, and shelter are necessary and useful to us. Things proper for our food, raiment, and shelter are provided around us. It is natural to conclude, that those things were provided to supply our wants and necessities. The same train of reasoning will apply to the enjoyments, as well as to the necessities of man.

While men were few, and the supplies of every thing were abundant, it is probable that many things were possessed and used in common. With regard to the possession and use of some things, however, this could never be strictly the case. In the fruit plucked or gathered by one for his subsistence; in the spot which he occupied for his shelter or repose; in the bow which he has made for ensuring his safety, or procuring his subsistence; in the skin which he has obtained by his skill and swiftness in the chace, and which covers his body from the inclemency of the weather, he gains a high degree of exclusive right; and of this right he cannot be dispossessed without a proportioned degree of injustice. "A publick theatre," says Cicero,[e] with his usual luminous propriety, "is common to all the citizens; but the seat which each occupies may, during the entertainment, be denominated his own." But, in the early period of society, concerning which we now speak, things, in general, would be viewed as belonging equally to all; in other words, to those who should first have occasion to use or possess them.

In this situation, we have reason to believe, society continued after the deluge, while "the whole earth was of one language and of one speech."[f] On the confusion of languages, and the dispersion of families, when mankind dwelt no longer in "the same plain,"[g] this general society was dissolved,

d. Gen. ix. 1, 2, 3.

e. De fin. l. 3. c. 20.

f. Gen. xi. 1. Erant omnia communia et indivisa omnibus, veluti unum cunctis patrimonium esset.[1] Just. l. 43. c. 1.

g. Gen. xi. 2.

1. To all men everything was in common and without separation, just as if they all had a single inheritance.

and no one subject of property could, in this new situation, be reasonably deemed as belonging equally to all. The different families and associations, however, who diverged from the common centre of emigration, would still consider many things, and particularly the country in which they commenced their new settlements, as common to each family or association.

The things most immediately necessary to the subsistence of life would become the first objects of exclusive property. The next objects would be such as ministered to its conveniency and comfort. Personal property, or property in movables, would become separate; while real property, or property in land, would continue common. When the association became too numerous, and the personal property of its members became too large, to subsist or live commodiously together; then a separation of landed possessions necessarily took place. Of these remarks we have a strong and striking illustration in the history of Abram and Lot. "Abram was very rich in cattle: Lot also had flocks, and herds, and tents. And the land was not able to bear them that they might dwell together; for their substance was great. And there was a strife between the herdmen of Abram's cattle and the herdmen of Lot's cattle. And Abram said unto Lot, let there be no strife, I pray thee, between thee and me, and between my herdmen and thy herdmen; for we be brethren. Is not the whole land before thee? Separate thyself, I pray thee, from me: if thou wilt take the left hand, then will I go to the right: or if thou depart to the right hand, then I will go to the left. And Lot lifted up his eyes, and beheld all the plain of Jordan, that it was well watered every where. Then Lot chose him all the plain of Jordan: and they separated themselves the one from the other."[h]

Even after agriculture became known and was practised in some imperfect degree, still the land continued to be the common property of the association. Cecrops, who emigrated from civilized Egypt, was the first to teach the wandering hunters or shepherds of Attica to unite in villages of husbandmen. After their union, their agricultural labours were carried on in common; and the soil, together with its immediate productions, corn, and wine, and oil, were regarded as a common property.[i] Agreeably to the same spirit and the same policy, we are told, that during the heroick ages

h. Gen. xiii. 2. 5.–11.
i. 1. Gill. 8.

of Greece, when a tribe sallied from its woods and mountains to take possession of a more fertile territory, the soldiers fought and conquered, not for their leaders, but for themselves—that the land acquired by their joint valour was their common right—and that it was cultivated by the united labour and assiduity of all the members of the tribe.[j]

In this stage of society, land was considered as the property of the community, rather than of individuals; and the inhabitants were connected with the country which they inhabited, only as members of the same association.[k] In this view of things, the famed establishment of a community of property, which Lycurgus made at Sparta, may be deemed nothing more than a renewal of their primitive institutions, of which some traces probably remained among the simple Spartans.[l]

The Scythians, it is well known, appropriated their cattle and tents, but occupied their land in common. Such, to this day, are the laws and customs of the Tartars.

Of the Suevi,[m] the largest and most powerful tribe of the ancient Germans, we are informed by Caesar, that they had no private or separate property in their land; that, every year, they sent out a proportion of their warriours in order to make war; while the rest remained at home, and cultivated the ground for all; that these warlike enterprises and peaceful occupations were pursued, in alternate years, by the different divisions of the warriours; that the tribe continued only one year in the same place; that they used corn very little; but lived chiefly on milk and flesh; and were

j. Id. 48.

k. Id. 68.

l. 1. Gill. 96.

m. Suevorum gens est longe maxima et bellicosissima Germanorum omnium—privati ac separati agri apud eos nihil est—quotannis singula millia armatorum, bellandi causa, suis ex finibus educunt: reliqui domi manent; pro se atque illis colunt. Hi rursus invicim anno post in armis sunt: illi domi remanent—neque longius anno remanere uno in loco, incolendi causa, licet; neque multum frumento, sed maximam partem lacte atque pecore vivunt, multumque sunt in venationibus.[2] Caes. l. 4. c. 1. l. 6. c. 21.

2. The nation of the Suevi is by far the largest and most warlike of all the Germans—among them there is no privately owned or separate farmland—each year they lead out of their own territory a thousand armed men in order to make war; the rest remain at home, cultivating the land for themselves and the others. The next year the latter serve their turn in arms and the former remain at home—and they may not stay in one place for the sake of dwelling in it for longer than a year, nor do they live on grain very much, but for the most part on milk and their herds, and they spend a great deal of time in hunting.

much employed in hunting. From the pen of Tacitus[n] we have nearly the same description. They change, says he, from spot to spot; and make new appropriations according to the number of hands, and to the condition and quality of each. As the plains are very spacious, the allotments are easily assigned: for though they shift their situation annually, they have still lands to spare.

In Tacitus, however, we begin to discover some appearances, among the Germans, of a private property in lands. To a certain class of their slaves, we are told, their masters assigned habitations; and from them, as from tenants, demanded in return a certain quantity of grain, or cattle, or cloth.[o] This presupposes, in the masters, a separate property in the lands let to those slaves.

In the Highlands of Scotland, we are told, common possession of the cultivated soil, as well as of the pasture grounds, is known to this day. The arable lands are divided into as many parts, as there are tenants entitled to an equal share of possession. The stock of cattle belonging to each tenant is considered as equal: the advantages accruing to the several partitions from manure are deemed also to be equivalent; yet some portion of these divisions shifts annually from one possessor to another, in such a manner, that, in a certain period of years, every tenant of the village has occupied and reaped crops from all the lands belonging to the village.[p]

It is said, that, among the Indians of Peru, the territory occupied was the property of the state, and was regulated by the magistrate; and that, when individuals were permitted to possess particular spots, these, in default of male issue, returned to the community.[q] Formerly, says Mr. Adair, the Indian law obliged every town to work together in one body, in sowing

n. Agri pro numero cultorum ab universis per vices occupantur, quos mox inter se secundum dignationem partiuntur. Facilitatem partiendi camporum spatia prestant. Arva per annos mutant; et superest ager.[3] Tac. de mor. Ger. c. 26.

o. Servis utuntur. Suam quisque sedem, suos penates regit. Frumenti modum dominus, aut pecoris, aut vestis, ut colono injungit.[4] Tac. de. mor. Gor. c. 25.

p. Grant's Ess. 97.

q. Stu. V. 158. cites Com. Per. b. 5. c. 1. 3.

3. Land is occupied by them as a whole through the villages in proportion to the number of cultivators; this is soon apportioned among them according to their ranks, the area of the fields making division easy. They change their fields through the years, and there is farmland left over.

4. They have slaves, but each slave is master of his own household. The master makes him pay an amount of grain, cattle, or clothing, like a tenant.

or planting their crops; though their fields are divided by proper marks, and their harvest is gathered and appropriated separately.[r] The ideas and opinions of private and exclusive property are, as we have reason to believe, extending gradually among the Indians; though their uncultivated territory is still considered as the common property of the nation or tribe.

From the detail which we have given, we are justified in deducing this general remark—that in the early and rude periods of society among all nations, the same family or association enjoyed and were understood to enjoy in many things a community of property, especially of landed property; and that, as to individuals, property was conceived to extend no farther than to those degrees, which comprehend the right of possession and temporary use of the soil.

But agriculture, and the industry attendant on agriculture, introduced gradually a new scene of things, and a new train of sentiments. This first of arts was not unknown to the restorer of mankind. Noah, after the deluge, began to be a husbandman, and he planted a vineyard.[s] Before the confusion of languages, the whole human race dwelt in the plain of Shinar. In that plain and its neighbourhood, the knowledge of agriculture was never entirely lost. Among the Babylonians, it is traced to the most early periods of their history. In the fertile territories of Egypt, watered by the Nile, the soil was cultivated with much assiduity and success.[t] When a famine, in the days of Abram, was grievous in the land of Canaan, the patriarch went down into Egypt to sojourn there.[u] On a similar occasion, Jacob said to his sons, who, with unavailing anguish, beheld the distressed situation of the family—Why do ye look one upon another? I have heard that there is corn in Egypt; get ye down thither, and buy for us from thence, that we may live, and not die.[v]

From Egypt, as we have already seen, the art of agriculture was transplanted into Attica by Cecrops. Before his arrival, the inhabitants had relied on the reproductions of the uncultivated soil for their annual sub-

r. Id. ibid.

s. Gen. ix. 20.

t. Osiris, one of the kings of Egypt, is regarded as the inventor of the plough. Primus aratra manu solerti fecit Osiris.[5] Tibul. l. 1. Eleg. 7. v. 29.

u. Gen. xii. 10.

v. Gen. xlii. 1, 2.

5. First Osiris made ploughs with dexterous hand.

sistence; but, by the example of the Egyptians, skilled in agriculture, they were induced to submit to labour, and contract habits of useful industry.[w]

It is the observation of Cicero, that the greatest part of the arts and discoveries, which are necessary or ornamental to life and society, were derived from the Athenians into the other parts of Greece, and then into foreign countries, for the general advantage and refinement of the human race.[x] Agriculture, in particular, was brought from Greece into Italy, according to the account of this matter given by the Romans themselves.[y] As the Egyptians taught the Greeks; so the Greeks communicated their knowledge to the Italians. For many ages, the Romans knew no other form of a plough, than that which, to this day, is used in some districts of the higher Egypt.[z]

The wise and virtuous Numa[6] was the patron of agriculture. He distributed the Romans into pagi or villages, and over each placed a superintendant to prevail with them, by every motive, to improve the practice of husbandry. To inspire their industry with redoubled vigour, he frequently condescended to be their overseer himself. This wise and judicious policy had a most happy influence upon the subsequent manners and fortunes of Rome. Our consuls, says the Roman Orator,[a] were called from the plough. Those illustrious characters, who have most adorned the commonwealth, and have been best qualified to manage the reins of government with dignity and success, dedicated a part of their time and of their labour to the cultivation of their landed estates. In those glorious ages of the republick, the farmer, the judge, and the soldier were to each other a reciprocal ornament. After having finished the publick business with glory and advantage to himself and to his country, the Roman magistrate descended,

w. 1. Anac. 6.

x. 1. Pot. Ant. 138.

y. 1. Gog. Or. Laws. 88.

z. Id. 90.

6. Numa Pompilius ruled from 715 to 673 B.C. According to legend, Numa Pompilius was the second of the kings of Rome succeeding Romulus and was credited with dividing the immediate territory of Rome into *pagi* and establishing the traditional occupational guilds of Rome.

a. Ab aratro arcessebantur, qui consules fierent—Apud majores nostros, summi viri, clarissimique homines, qui omni tempore ad gubernacula reipublicae sedere debebant, tamen in agris quoque colendis aliquantum operae temporisque consumserint.[7] Cic. pro Ros. Am. c. 18.

7. From the plough men were summoned to become consuls—in the days of our ancestors, those most excellent and distinguished men, who, though they should have sat at the helm of the state all the time, nonetheless devoted a certain amount of time and effort to cultivating their farms.

with modest dignity, from the elevation of office; and reassumed, with contentment and with pleasure, the peaceful labours of a rural and independent life.

When agriculture was once introduced, and its utility was known and experienced; it became natural to search and adopt the measures necessary for distinguishing possessions permanently; that every one who laboured and who excelled in this fundamental profession, might be secured in enjoying the fruits of his labours and his improvements. Hence the foundation of laws, which instituted and regulated the division and stable possession of the soil. Hence, too, the origin and the importance of land marks. In the early period in which Job lived, it was part of the description of a turbulent and wicked man, that he removed the land marks, and violently took away flocks.[b] The inspired legislator of the Jews speaks of them as of an institution, which, even in his time, was anciently established in Canaan. "Thou shalt not remove thy neighbour's land mark, which they of old time have set in thy inheritance, which thou shalt inherit in the land that the Lord thy God giveth thee to possess it."[c] Numa, mild as he was, ordered those who were guilty of this crime, to suffer a capital punishment.[d]

The inference which we draw from this long detail of facts is—that agriculture gave rise to that degree of property in land, which consists in the right of exclusive and permanent possession and use.

We have seen that among the ancient Germans, this degree of property was altogether unknown. The Saxons, who emigrated into England, and made a conquest there, were a part of the ancient German nation. Their settlement in England produced, with regard to the present subject, a considerable change in their sentiments and habits. After they settled in England, instead of continuing to be hunters, they became husbandmen. In pursuing this occupation, they ceased to wander annually from spot to spot; they became habituated and attached to a fixed residence; they acquired a permanent and an exclusive degree of property in land. This degree, among them, as among other nations, proceeded from their improvement in agriculture.[e]

We have good reason for believing, that, for some time after the settle-

b. Job xxiv. 2.
c. Deut. xix. 14.
d. 1. Gog. Or. Laws. 32.
e. Millar, 50.

ment of the Saxons in England, the landed estates acquired by individuals were, in general, but of a small extent. Inexpert in agriculture when they first arrived, their progress in the separate appropriation of land was, therefore, slow. This slow appropriation met, besides, with obstructions and interruptions from the vigorous opposition of the Britons, who, for centuries, disputed every inch of ground with the invaders of their country. Conformably to this opinion, we find that, from the beginning of the Saxon government, the land was divided into hides. A hide comprehended as much as could be cultivated by a single plough. The general estimation of real property, by this small and inaccurate measure, points, with sufficient clearness, to the leading circumstance, which originally marked and regulated the greatest number of landed estates.[f]

But we have also good reason for believing, that, among the Saxons, the smallness of their landed property was compensated by its independence. They were freemen; and their law of property was, that they might challenge a power to do what they pleased with their own.[g] But this degree and quality of property will be considered afterwards.

Having traced property, and especially property in land, from its general to its separate and exclusive state, it will now be proper to consider the advantages, which the latter state possesses over the former.

This superiority of separate over common property has not been always admitted: it has not been always admitted even in America. In the early settlement of this country, we find two experiments on the operation and effects of a community of goods. The issue of each, however, was very uncomfortable.

The first was made in Virginia. An instruction was given to the colonists, that, during five years next after their landing, they should trade jointly; that the produce of their joint industry should be deposited in a common magazine; and that, from this common magazine, every one should be supplied under the direction of the council. What were the consequences? I relate them in the words of the Historian of Virginia. "And now the English began to find the mistake of forbidding and preventing private property; for whilst they all laboured jointly together, and were fed out of the common store, happy was he that could slip from his labour, or

f. Id. 85. 144. 181.
g. Bac. on Gov. 123.

slubber over his work in any manner. Neither had they any concern about the increase; presuming, however the crop prospered, that the publick store must maintain them. Even the most honest and industrious would scarcely take so much pains in a week, as they would have done for themselves in a day."[h]

The second experiment was made in the colony of New Plymouth. During seven years, all commerce was carried on in one joint stock. All things were common to all; and the necessaries of life were daily distributed to every one from the publick store. But these regulations soon furnished abundant reasons for complaint, and proved most fertile sources of common calamity. The colonists were sometimes in danger of starving; and severe whipping, which was often administered to promote labour, was only productive of constant and general discontent. This absurd policy became, at last, apparent to every one; and the introduction of exclusive property immediately produced the most comfortable change in the colony, by engaging the affections and invigorating the pursuits of its inhabitants.[i]

The right of separate property seems to be founded in the nature of men and things; and when societies become numerous, the establishment of that right is highly important to the existence, to the tranquillity, to the elegancies, to the refinements, and to some of the virtues of civilized life.

Man is intended for action. Useful and skilful industry is the soul of an active life. But industry should have her just reward. That reward is property; for of useful and active industry, property is the natural result.

Exclusive property multiplies the productions of the earth, and the means of subsistence. Who would cultivate the soil, and sow the grain, if he had no peculiar interest in the harvest? Who would rear and tend flocks and herds, if they were to be taken from him by the first person who should come to demand them?

By exclusive property, the productions of the earth and the means of subsistence are secured and preserved, as well as multiplied. What belongs to no one is wasted by every one. What belongs to one man in particular is the object of his economy and care.

Exclusive property prevents disorder, and promotes peace. Without its

h. Stith. 39.
i. Chal. 89. 90.

establishment, the tranquillity of society would be perpetually disturbed by fierce and ungovernable competitions for the possession and enjoyment of things, insufficient to satisfy all, and by no rules of adjustment distributed to each.

The conveniencies of life depend much on an exclusive property. The full effects of industry cannot be obtained without distinct professions and the division of labour. But labour cannot be divided, nor can distinct professions be pursued, unless the productions of one profession and of one kind of labour can be exchanged for those of another. This exchange implies a separate property in those who make it.

The observations concerning the conveniencies of life, may be applied with equal justness to its elegancies and its refinements.

On property some of the virtues depend for their more free and enlarged exercise. Would the same room be left for the benign indulgence of generosity and beneficence—would the same room be left for the becoming returns of esteem and gratitude—would the same room be left for the endearing interchange of good offices, in the various institutions and relations of social life, if the goods of fortune lay in a mass, confused and unappropriated?

For these reasons, the establishment of exclusive property may justly be considered as essential to the interests of civilized society. With regard to land, in particular, a separate and exclusive property in it is a principal source of attachment to the country, in which one resides. A person becomes very unwilling to relinquish those well known fields of his own; which it has been the great object of his industry, and, perhaps, of his pride, to cultivate and adorn. This attachment to private landed property has, in some parts of the globe, covered barren heaths and inhospitable mountains with fair cities and populous villages; while, in other parts, the most inviting climates and soils remain destitute of inhabitants, because the rights of private property in land are not established or regarded.[k]

k. The foregoing observations were intended to compose a part of those lectures, in which the Author designed "to trace the history of property from its lowest rude beginnings to its highest artificial refinements." [Vol. 1. p. 50.] It will be perceived that the piece is indeed but a fragment; as, however, the history of property is so far completed as to trace it from its general to its separate and exclusive state, it is thought worthy of insertion. *Ed.*

PART 2

Lectures on Law

BIBLIOGRAPHICAL ESSAY
HISTORY OF JAMES WILSON'S LAW LECTURES

Mark David Hall[1]

When James Wilson wrote and delivered his lectures on law at the College of Philadelphia, he was addressing two audiences. After the introductory lecture, the first audience was the fifteen young men who attended the lectures. The second, and in Wilson's mind the far more significant audience, was the American republic. One of Wilson's greatest ambitions was to be remembered as America's Blackstone. To achieve such fame, he planned to publish his lectures as the definitive treatise on American law.[2] Accordingly, he carefully and neatly penned final versions of the lectures in what eventually numbered fifty-two notebooks.

As Kermit Hall notes in his introduction, James Wilson was unable to publish his lectures. However, his son, Bird, published them in 1804. His edition was the last to take advantage of the notebook manuscripts—until the present edition. In this essay I briefly consider the origins of the law lectures and their publication history. I then compare the notebook manuscripts to the current edition of the lectures, noting significant similarities and differences.

1. Herbert Hoover Distinguished Professor of Political Science, George Fox University. I am grateful to Joel Sartorius and his colleagues in the Rare Books Department of The Free Library of Philadelphia for their assistance, and to Rachel Sparks and Lee Nash for reading drafts of this work. I would also like to thank George Fox University for providing funds that allowed me to spend time at the Free Library and writing this essay. An earlier version of this essay was published as "James Wilson's Law Lectures" by *The Pennsylvania Magazine of History and Biography* CXXVIII (January 2004): 63–76. I am grateful to the journal for permission to revise and publish the piece, and to its editor, Tamara G. Miller, for her contributions to the original research note.

2. Mark David Hall, *The Political and Legal Philosophy of James Wilson, 1742–1798* (Columbia: University of Missouri Press, 1997), esp. pp. 27–30, 167.

The Original Plan

On July 10, 1790, the Board of Trustees of the College of Philadelphia (now the University of Pennsylvania) debated a motion to create a "law professorship." At the following meeting, board members Edward Shippen, James Wilson, and Mr. Hare were appointed to a committee "to consider the propriety & utility of establishing a law professorship & to report the duties thereof."[3] The committee's report, which was almost certainly drafted by Wilson,[4] was issued on August 14, 1790:

> The object of a system of law lectures in this country should be to explain the Constitution of the United States—its principles—its parts—its powers & the distribution & operation of these powers,—to ascertain the merits of that Constitution by comparing it with the Constitutions of other states—with the principles of government, with the rights of men—to point out the spirit, the design & the probable effect of the laws & treaties of the United States—to mark, particularly and distinctly, the rules and decisions of the Federal Courts in matters of both law and practice.
>
> To examine, legally, critically, & historically, the constitutions & laws of the several states in the union—to compare those constitutions and laws one with another and with the general rules of law and government—to investigate the nature, the properties & the extent of that connection which subsists between the general government & and each state severally, & of consequence, between each of those states & each & all of the others.
>
> To illustrate the genesis, the elements, the originals, & the rules of the common law in its theory and in its practice—to trace, as far as possible, that law to its foundations, to the laws and customs of the Normans, the Saxons, the Britons, the ancient Germans, the Romans, and perhaps, in some instances, the Grecians.
>
> Under this head it is to be observed that the common law, in its true extent, includes the law of nations, the civil law, the maritime law, the law of

3. MSS Minutes of the Board of Trustees of the College of Philadelphia, vol. 2, 1768–1791, University of Pennsylvania Archives, p. 212. Spelling and capitalization have been modernized in this and other quotations taken from the minutes.

4. Page Smith, in his biography of Wilson, asserts that Wilson was the author of the plan. Given Wilson's expertise, and the similarities between this plan and Wilson's lectures, Smith is probably correct. However, Smith does not provide any evidence to support his claim, and I have been unable to find any. Charles Page Smith, *James Wilson: Founding Father* (Chapel Hill: University of North Carolina Press, 1956), p. 307.

mercantile & the law of each particular country, in all cases in which those laws are particularly applicable.

All the forgoing subjects of discussion should be contrasted with the practice and institutions of other countries—they should be fortified by reasons, by examples, & by authorities. They should be weighed & appreciated by the precepts of natural and revealed laws.

The obvious design of such a plan is to furnish a rational and a useful entertainment to gentlemen of all professions, but particularly to assist in forming the legislator, the magistrate, & the lawyer.

The lectures and exercises may be so arranged and prepared as to suit the different views of those who shall attend them.[5]

After approving the report, the trustees "resolved that a professorship of law be established in this institution, and that a professor be appointed, whose duty it shall be to deliver, annually, in the College, at least twenty four lectures agreeably to the forgoing principles." On September 7, James Wilson was unanimously elected to be this professor of law. After this date, the minutes contain relatively little about Wilson, who resigned his position on the board upon accepting the professorship, other than to note that the trustees accepted his invitation to the first lecture and voted to grant him (along with Edward Shippen and Francis Hopkinson) a doctorate of law.[6]

On December 15, 1790, James Wilson stood before "the President of the United States, with his lady—also the Vice-President, and both houses of Congress, the President and both houses of the Legislature of Pennsylvania, together with a great number of ladies and gentlemen . . . the whole comprising a most brilliant and respectable audience," to present the first in a series of lectures on American law.[7] This lecture, which was published as a pamphlet (the only part of the lectures to be published in Wilson's lifetime), made it clear that Wilson had a grand vision for his lectures.[8]

5. MSS Minutes of the Board of Trustees of the College of Philadelphia, vol. 2, 1768–1791, University of Pennsylvania Archives, pp. 212–14.

6. Ibid., pp. 214, 216, 220, 223.

7. *Pennsylvania Packet* and *Daily Advertiser* (Philadelphia, December 25, 1790).

8. James Wilson, "An Introductory Lecture to a Course of Law Lectures, To Which is Added a Plan of the Lectures" (Philadelphia: T. Dobson, 1791). The lecture appears as the first chapter of Lectures on Law, in the present volume.

Simply put, he hoped to codify American law, thus gaining a place in history as the American Blackstone.

Wilson's first course of lectures ran for fifty-eight lectures, which went significantly beyond the minimum of twenty-four contemplated by the proposal approved by the College of Philadelphia trustees. These are printed in the first thirteen chapters of the present edition. The second course is printed in the remaining twenty-two chapters of the present edition. Although Wilson clearly intended to publish the lectures, his duties on the Supreme Court and worsening financial condition prevented him from doing so.

Six years after his father's death in 1798, Bird Wilson, relying on his father's notebooks, published the first edition of the lectures. In the preface to this work, he claimed not to have altered "the language of the Author," although he confessed to having divided them into "parts and chapters, according to the subjects."[9] Subsequent editions of the lectures edited by James De Witt Andrews (1896), Robert G. McCloskey (1967), and the present volume, have relied on Bird's edition.[10] Although no evidence suggested that Bird grossly distorted his father's lectures, students of James Wilson obviously want to have confidence in the integrity of the lectures' texts. Until recently, this has not been possible.[11]

The history of the notebooks containing Wilson's draft lectures is scanty at best. Prior to 2001, the only record of a scholar being able to see the manuscripts comes from the early 1950s, when Wilson's biographer Page Smith was able to see them. Smith used them to shed light on questions that Wilson had his students debate, and he mentioned in a footnote that the notebooks were in the possession of "James Alan Montgomery, Jr., of Philadelphia," that they "contain early drafts of the lectures," and that a "'spot check' of the MSS and the published texts revealed no significant

9. Page 423 of the current edition. All references to Wilson's lectures are to the present edition. The volumes were originally published as *The Works of the Honourable James Wilson, L.L.D.*, ed. Bird Wilson, 3 vols. (Philadelphia: Lorenzo Press, 1804).

10. James DeWitt Andrews, ed., *The Works of James Wilson* (Chicago: Callahan and Company, 1896), 2 vols. Robert G. McCloskey, ed., *The Works of James Wilson* (Cambridge: Harvard University Press, 1967), 2 vols. As well, Randolph G. Andrews published a selection of Wilson's works in *Selected Political Essays of James Wilson* (New York: Alfred A. Knopf, 1930).

11. I discuss reasons for suspecting Bird Wilson's edition in "James Wilson's Law Lectures," *The Pennsylvania Magazine of History and Biography* CXXVIII (January 2004): 63–76.

differences."[12] Smith's claim allowed Wilson scholars to have some confidence in Bird's edition, but his admission that he only "spot checked" the lectures remained a cause for concern.

James Montgomery donated the notebooks to the Free Library of Philadelphia in 1968 and 1969. Although the Free Library issued a press release about the notebooks in 1969, they were never listed in the *National Union Catalog* or elsewhere, and their location remained a mystery to Wilson scholars.[13] Their discovery in 2001 allows scholars to evaluate the accuracy of Bird's edition of the lectures. In the following sections, I provide an overview of the notebooks and suggest important similarities and differences between them and the printed versions of the lectures.

The Notebooks

The James Wilson Notebooks at the Free Library of Philadelphia consist of sixty-nine notebooks. Of these, nine contain early drafts of the lectures, fifty-two contain final versions of the lectures, and eight contain a miscellaneous collection of questions he asked his law students along with their responses, draft grand jury charges, early versions of his "Plan for Improving the United States," and copies of a few letters. In some places the final versions are heavily edited, with some sections crossed out and other passages clearly added at a later date.

The first eighteen notebooks are roughly paired, with one notebook containing very rough drafts of lectures for every notebook containing the final version. The nine notebooks containing drafts correspond to Wilson's first thirty-three law lectures, which are reprinted in the first eight chapters of the current edition of Wilson's lectures (the correspondence between the lecture and chapter numbers is discussed below). In many places they consist of a string of quotations from legal and moral

12. Smith, *James Wilson,* p. 408.

13. The press release, which is dated February 13, 1969, mentions only the first thirty-six notebooks. However, the Free Library's ascension numbers indicate that the volumes were donated in 1968 and 1969. The press release is on file in the Rare Books Collection at the Free Library of Philadelphia.

philosophers. Some of these quotes and citations survive in Wilson's final drafts, but most do not. However, there is often a substantive connection between the quotations and the final lectures.

Scholars have long known that Wilson read and cited authorities such as Thomas Reid, William Blackstone, Francis Hutcheson, Hugo Grotius, Richard Hooker, and Samuel Pufendorf. The drafts of the lectures enable them to trace the influence of each thinker on Wilson's first thirty-three lectures, lectures that contain some of his most important philosophical work. The drafts are particularly useful as Wilson, following common practice, did not always quote or cite his sources in the final versions of his works. For instance, in his lecture on the law of nature, Wilson quoted an entire paragraph from Thomas Reid's *Essay on Intellectual Power*, but neglected to put the passage in quotation marks or provide a citation.[14] Such borrowing might go unnoticed by scholars who are not intimately familiar with Reid, but a scholar who compares the drafts to the final copies could easily discover it.[15]

Beginning roughly at Wilson's thirty-fourth lecture (chapter nine in the current edition), there are no notebooks that are used solely for drafting lectures. It is possible that such notebooks existed but were lost.[16] All of the remaining notebooks with final versions of the lectures, however, contain at least some of James Wilson's editing marks, and some are extensively edited, which suggests that he abandoned his practice of creating a very rough draft of the lectures. Certainly it would be less necessary for him to do so as he moved from the more philosophical lectures to those involving more mundane issues of law. Nevertheless, the editorial changes to the final notebooks are revealing.

14. The passage to which I am referring begins, "Moral truths," and is found at p. 513.

15. Shannon C. Stimson notes several of these passages in "'A Jury of the Country': Common Sense Philosophy and the Jurisprudence of James Wilson," in *Scotland and America in the Age of the Enlightenment,* ed. Richard B. Sher and Jeffrey R. Smitten (Princeton: Princeton University Press, 1990), p. 208.

16. It is also possible that they exist today, but their location is unknown. However, in the first eighteen notebooks, Wilson often distinguished between the draft notebooks and the final editions. For instance, the first three draft notebooks (after "Introductory") are labeled "No. 1," "No. 2," and "No. 3," whereas the first three notebooks containing the final versions are labeled "F No. 1," "F No. 2," "F No. 3." Beginning with notebook 14, no notebook contains an "F" in its label.

The Final Drafts

Fifty-two of the notebooks in the Free Library's collection contain the final drafts of the law lectures.[17] Most of these are in Wilson's hand, although a small percentage of them are in a far neater script that is clearly not his. Page Smith speculated, and he was probably correct, that James had Bird write out some of the final lectures.[18] In any case, the neat handwriting always correlates with rough drafts, so there is no question that anyone other than James Wilson is the author of the final draft of the law lectures.

The final drafts reveal that Bird Wilson was, in many respects, a faithful editor. Even though Bird's introduction suggests that he rearranged some of the lectures, and even though the lectures do not follow exactly the plan laid out by Wilson in his first lecture, Bird did not rearrange any of his father's lectures.[19] He did, however, combine many of them. Throughout the notebooks Wilson numbered the lectures as he intended to deliver them. He labeled what Bird has as his first chapter "Introductory," and then offered what Bird has as chapter two in three lectures, clearly marked "L1," L2," and "L3." These labels continue through the first course of lectures, running, with some gaps, from "Introductory" to "L58." The lectures are reprinted in exactly the order they were delivered in the first thirteen chapters of Bird's edition. Wilson began labeling the second course of lectures in a similar manner, but he stopped doing so with "L7" (which covers the first two and a half chapters of the second part of Bird's edition).

Bird published the lectures in the order in which they were delivered, and he was faithful to the substance of the original text. He rarely altered his father's prose, eliminated passages, elaborated on them, or inaccurately transcribed handwriting, although I found examples of all these things. In most instances these departures are not significant, but several

17. This count treats notebook 50 as part of the law lectures rather than one of the miscellaneous notebooks (this issue is discussed later).

18. Smith, *James Wilson,* p. 314.

19. Wilson provided a general outline of his lectures on pp. 456–63. He departed from it primarily by covering the topics "philosophy of evidence" and "comparison of U.S. with Great Britain" approximately nine chapters (by Bird's division) earlier than his plan indicated (Cf. pp. 460, vi–vii).

are noteworthy. For example, in notebook 15, Wilson clearly crossed out the majority of a paragraph dealing with factions. Bird Wilson ignored this and included it anyway. The paragraph, which begins "How easily is the esprit du corps generated" and ends with "application of esprit du corps!" emphasizes the ease with which factions are formed and the powerful conflicts in which they engage.[20] Wilson may have changed his mind about the truth of the passage, or, more likely, he decided that he did not want to emphasize the point. Whatever his reasoning, Wilson scholars should be aware that he did not intend the passage to be included in the published version of the lectures.

Conversely, Bird left out the last two sentences in Wilson's final draft of his last lecture. These sentences, which would have followed "Pennsylvania," read: "To man and to Society the Subject is truly important. We took a general view of it in Prospect, before we entered upon Particulars: Now let us turn and take a retrospective Survey of the Ground, which we have passed."[21] These sentences show that Wilson considered his lectures to be complete (with the exception of the "retrospective," which he presumably did not compose, unless it is his "History of Property," discussed below). This finding is significant because Wilson's lectures are sometimes described as "unfinished" or "abandoned."[22] It is the case that Wilson did not deliver them all, and they certainly become sketchy toward the end of the lecture series, but these sentences indicate that Wilson had, in fact, covered the ground that he intended to cover in his lectures.

Bird Wilson was a good editor, but he did consistently change his father's text in three ways. First, and least significant, he often combined short paragraphs into longer ones, but his combinations almost always make sense and never alter the meaning of the text. Second, he did not capitalize many of the words that his father capitalized. In many cases Bird's changes conform to modern usage, but there are occasions that might lead a careful reader of the text to wonder why James did not follow eighteenth-century (and in some cases contemporary) practices. For instance,

20. Notebook 15, p. 23.
21. Notebook 49, pp. 16–17.
22. See, for instance, Bird Wilson, p. 417; Smith, *James Wilson,* p. 346.

James capitalized, but Bird's edition of the lectures often does not capitalize, words like "Revelation," "Scripture," and "Christian."[23] Similarly, Bird sometimes, but not always, capitalized words that are clearly referring to God, such as "Author" and "Observer."[24] Conversely, Bird capitalized each letter of "MAN" on page 583 of the lecture, whereas Wilson had merely capitalized and underlined the word, as he did for the words "subject" and "author," which immediately follow it. Such editorial choices leave a text that might suggest intellectual influences that the original text does not.

The third major change Bird consistently made is that he did not emphasize many of the words his father did. From a modern perspective, James Wilson underlined far too many words. Bird reduced the number of words that are emphasized, but his edition, like the current one, does emphasize some words, usually by italicizing them. For instance, in the very first paragraph of his "Introductory" lecture, Wilson underlined the following words: "this," "first," "fair," "brilliant," "Whole," "very respectable," "Politeness," and "Brilliancy," whereas the Bird edition only italicizes "fair" (and, note, does not capitalize "Whole," "Politeness," and "Brilliancy"). These changes are not particularly significant, and they arguably make the text easier to read for the modern reader.

In some cases, however, Bird's deletion of emphasis might be significant. For instance, in his discussion of the difference between public and private liberty, Wilson wrote that public liberty is well secured, but that "*the most formidable Enemy to private Liberty,* is, at this Moment, *the Law of the Land.*"[25] This emphasis went well beyond his usual practice of underlining individual words (and, in fact, "private" and "Law" are underlined twice). The current edition, following Bird's, merely puts "private" in italics.[26]

Even with the exceptions just noted, it is fair to say that Bird Wilson did a reasonable job reproducing his father's lectures largely as he wrote

23. Compare Notebook F4, p. 16, with *Works*, p. 521.

24. Compare Notebook F2, pp. 30–31, with *Works*, p. 498.

25. Notebook 44, p. 36.

26. Page 1130. Similarly, in a passage only a few pages away from this one, Wilson underlined the long sentence on p. 1132 that begins "Every wanton, or careless, or unnecessary act of authority" and ends with "esse possimus," an emphasis that is not reflected in the text. Notebook 44, pp. 38–44.

them. Nevertheless, he understandably did not include material that his father wanted eliminated or indicate last-minute changes or additions. These changes, however, shed light on the development of Wilson's ideas and his thought process.

Virtually all of the notebooks contain ninety pages. Wilson wrote on every other page, so that every page of text faces a blank page. He numbered the pages he planned to write on, but not the blank pages. This method left room for him to go back and edit the text by crossing out material he wanted to eliminate and placing material that he wanted to add on the blank page across from where he wanted it (he indicated where it should go with a variety of editorial marks). In many notebooks, Wilson only crossed out and/or added a few words, phrases, or sentences. Occasionally, however, he added page after page of new text, or crossed out large portions of the existing text.

As might be expected, many of Wilson's changes are simply matters of style. Many crossed-out sentences are extraneous, and much of the added material simply covers more thoroughly particular areas of law. Occasionally, however, changes are intriguing. For instance, in describing the nature of the federal union, Wilson originally wrote: "Let us turn our most scrutinizing attention to the Situation in which, on the Principles of that System, the States, and the People of the States, composing the American Union stand with Regard to one another. . . ." He then crossed out "of the States," which leaves the sentence, by my transcription, as: "Let us turn our most scrutinizing attention to the Situation in which, on the Principles of that System, the States, and the People composing the American Union, stand with Regard to one another. . . ." In Bird's edition, however, the sentence reads, "Let us turn our most scrutinizing attention to the situation in which, on the principles of that system, the states and the people, composing the American union, stand with regard to one another. . . ."[27] It is likely that the first version of the sentence placed too much emphasis on the centrality of the states for Wilson. Accordingly, he altered it to emphasize the role of both the states and the American people in America's federal system. Some of this clarity is lost, however, by Bird's version of the sentence.

27. Notebook 16, p. 30.

Bird seldom made a mistake transcribing his father's editorial changes, but the editorial changes themselves are often revealing. For instance, in a discussion of checks and balances, Wilson originally wrote that "The General Assembly of Pennsylvania is entrusted with the legislative Power of the Commonwealth," but that this power is subject to checks by the executive and that it is "subject to another given degree of control by the judicial department, whenever the laws, though in fact passed, are found to be contradictory to the constitution." Wilson then altered the first sentence to read: "The Congress is entrusted with the legislative Power of the United States."[28] Wilson may have made this change to emphasize to his audience that the Supreme Court has the ability to strike down an act of Congress, a controversial proposition at the time.

These relatively small changes in Wilson's final drafts show that the notebooks can shed light on Wilson's work. As well, there are a variety of longer passages that may interest students of the founding. For instance, Wilson crossed out a lengthy paragraph in which he argued that societies should be judged by how they treat women.[29] Scholars interested in his epistemological views may want to read the long passage on the importance of affections, or the sentence in a longer passage borrowed from Thomas Reid, that he deleted.[30] Similarly, Wilson quoted and then eliminated a long passage from Locke's *Essay Concerning Human Understanding* toward the end of his lectures.[31] And, as one might expect, Wilson struck out numerous passages on legal or political matters, such as an abstract discussion on the importance of an energetic executive or a more specific examination of cabinet officials.[32]

28. Notebook 18, p. 5; p. 707.

29. Notebook "Introductory," p. 46. This would have appeared after "peculiarly important" p. 498.

30. Notebook F3, pp. 36–40, 40. The lengthy passage would have appeared after "affections, and actions" on p. 512; the passage from Reid after "last." in the unattributed Reid quote on p. 513.

31. Notebook 24, pp. 5–6 (the passage would have appeared after "doubt and suspicion" on p. 794). See also the miscellaneous notebook entitled "Letters concerning the Digest and Charge No. 4 and Letters to P.U.S.," p. 10.

32. Notebook 17, p. 28. The paragraph would have followed "enlightened" on p. 698. Wilson wrote two paragraphs on the subordinate officers in the executive branch. He then crossed them out and moved on to the judicial branch. See notebook 30, p. 9; p. 884.

Miscellaneous Notebooks

The final drafts of Wilson's law lectures are contained in notebooks labeled "Introductory" and then 1–49.[33] Interestingly, there is a notebook labeled "50" which contains Wilson's unfinished "On the History of Property," which was published by Bird Wilson, James Andrews, and Robert McCloskey, as the first document in their collections of "Miscellaneous Papers" following the end of the law lectures.[34] Given its placement, it is possible that Wilson intended the piece to be the beginning of his "retrospective Survey of the Ground" covered in the law lectures (promised in the very last sentence of his law lectures that was deleted by Bird), rather than a separate document.[35] Like the lectures, Wilson's draft is faithfully reproduced in Bird's edition (with the sort of exceptions noted earlier).

The remaining eight notebooks in the Free Library's collection are not numbered, but are labeled roughly according to content. They include: "Questions No. 1 Digest," "Questions No. 2," "Questions No. 3, charge [?]," "Questions No. 4, Digest," "Letters concerning the Digest and Charge No. 4 and Letters to P.U.S.," "Improvements," "Improvements of the U.S.," "Charge Number 7." Some of the material in these notebooks has been published before, notably the three grand jury charges, the final drafts of Wilson's proposal for writing legal digests, and his plan for improving the United States. Much of the rest of the material in these notebooks, however, has never been published.

The notebooks labeled "Questions" contain questions posed by Wilson to his law students and his summaries of their answers. Page Smith discussed these questions and answers in his biography of Wilson, and he noted that many of the questions were preceded by brief lectures. These lectures, many of which are five to seven notebook pages long, have never been published. In some cases their contents are not particularly interesting, or they overlap with material covered in the published lectures. In other instances, such as his brief lecture preceding the question "Whether

33. An "F" precedes notebooks numbered 1–4, 9–13. Beginning with notebook 14, no notebooks are preceded by "Fs." As well, there is a notebook labeled "40a" in addition to notebook "40."

34. "On the History of Property" appears as the last document in part 1 of this volume.

35. Notebook 49, p. 18; pp. 387–97.

the Produce of the Land is to be commended as the sole Source of Wealth and Revenue of a Nation; and whether, supposing it to be so, it would, upon that Supposition, be proper or prudent to impose Restraints on Manufactures or Trade?" may provide insight into his economic views. Given the prominence of many of his students, their recorded answers may be of interest to students of the early republic as well.[36]

It is well known that Wilson was a land speculator, but less well known are his plans for facilitating the development of western land. One of the most ambitious of these plans was laid out in his essay "On the Improvement and Settlement of Lands in the United States."[37] A very rough draft of this essay, along with a variety of financial calculations, can be found in his notebook labeled "Improvements." A far more detailed plan is found in the notebook "Improvements of the U.S." Like the final drafts of the law lectures, the draft of his "Improvements" essay, and his letters to the Pennsylvania Assembly and George Washington regarding his legal digest, contain editorial changes that will interest Wilson scholars.

Conclusion

The James Wilson Notebooks at the Free Library of Philadelphia contain valuable information that careful students of Wilson will want to consult. On balance, however, the notebooks reveal that Bird Wilson was a good editor, and that his edition of the lectures, which are republished here, accurately reflects his father's final intent.

36. Smith, *James Wilson,* pp. 336–41. Wilson's fifteen students included the sons of many American leaders, and several of them became influential in their own right. At least eleven of his students went on to practice law. Students included: Seth Chapman, Henry Clymer, John Clymer, Jonathan Condy, Samuel Dickinson, Charles Evans, James Gibson, Joseph Hopkinson, Cantwell Jones, Michael Keppele, Robert Morris, William White Morris, John Read, Ceasar Rodney, and Evan Thomas.

37. Pages 372–86. The essay was taken from a handwritten manuscript in the Rush Papers at the Library Company of Philadelphia. Its contents are discussed in Smith, *James Wilson,* pp. 159–68.

THE WORKS OF THE HONOURABLE

James Wilson, L. L. D.

LATE ONE OF THE ASSOCIATE JUSTICES OF
THE SUPREME COURT OF THE UNITED STATES,
AND PROFESSOR OF LAW IN THE COLLEGE
OF PHILADELPHIA.

PUBLISHED UNDER THE DIRECTION OF

Bird Wilson, Esquire.

LEX FUNDAMENTUM EST LIBERTATIS, QUA FRUIMUR.
LEGUM OMNES SERVI SUMUS, UT LIBERI ESSE POSSIMUS.

CIC.

VOL. I

PHILADELPHIA:
AT THE LORENZO PRESS, PRINTED FOR BRONSON AND CHAUNCEY.
1804.

PREFACE

The incomplete state of the lectures on law, notwithstanding the lapse of several years between the time at which those now published were delivered and the death of the Author, is a circumstance of which the publick will naturally inquire the cause. The circumstance itself is certainly much to be lamented; but its cause presents a subject of still deeper regret.

The law professorship, in the college of Philadelphia, was established in the year 1790; and the Author was appointed the first professor. The extent of his plan of lectures rendered it impossible for him to go through his whole subject in one season: three courses were necessary for the purpose. The first course, which was delivered in the winter of 1790–91, consisted of those lectures contained in what the Editor has entitled the *first part.* The second course, which was, in a great measure, delivered in the following winter, would have consisted of the remaining two parts now published. In April, 1792, the college of Philadelphia and the university of Pennsylvania were, by an act of assembly, united into one seminary, under the latter title. A law professorship was erected in the new seminary, and the Author again appointed to fill the chair; but no lectures were delivered after the union. The preceding course had been interrupted and was not completed. The causes of these circumstances are not within the Editor's knowledge. He knows, however, that, though the delivery of the lectures was discontinued, the Author designed to complete his plan for publication. From this design his attention was drawn by another object of more importance, in which he was engaged.

In March, 1791, the house of representatives in the general assembly of Pennsylvania, resolved to appoint a person to revise and digest the laws of the commonwealth; to ascertain and determine how far any British statutes extended to it; and to prepare bills, containing such alterations, additions, and improvements as the code of laws, and the principles and forms of the constitution then lately adopted might require. The Author was unanimously appointed for that purpose. The nature of the plan which he formed in consequence of this resolution, will appear from the following letter on the subject, delivered to the speaker of the house of representatives on 24th August, 1791.

Sir,

While I am employed in executing the trust committed to me by the house of representatives, it is, I conceive, my duty, from time to time, to inform them, through you, of the steps which I have taken, and of those which I mean to take, in order to accomplish the great end which is in contemplation.

From the records deposited in the rolls office, I have taken an account of all the laws made in Pennsylvania from its first settlement till the beginning of the last session of the legislature. They are in number one thousand seven hundred and two. Their titles I have entered into a book, in the order, usually chronological, in which they are recorded. On some of them, especially those of an early date, I have made and minuted remarks: and have left ample room for more, in the course of my further investigations. I have also reduced their several subjects into an alphabetical order by entering them regularly in a common place book. This process required time, and care, and a degree of minute drudgery; but it was absolutely requisite to the correct execution of the design. How can I make a digest of the laws, without having all the laws upon each head in my view? This view can in the first instance be obtained only by ranging them in an exact common place.

But something more must still be done. To rank, in a correct edition, the several laws according to their seniority or to the order of the alphabet would, by no means, be correspondent to the enlarged plan signified by the resolutions of the house. It is obvious, and it was certainly expected, that, under each head, the different regulations, however dispersed, at present, among numerous laws, should, in the digest, be collected in a natural series, and reduced to a just form. This I deem an indispensable part of my business.

But the performance of this indispensable part gives rise to a new question. In what order should the methodised collections be arranged?

A chronological order would, from the nature of those collections, be impracticable: an alphabetical order would be unnatural and unsatisfactory. The order of legitimate system is the only one, which remains. This order, therefore, is necessarily brought into my contemplation. My contemplation of it has been attended with the just degree of diffidence and solicitude. To form the mass of our laws into a body compacted and well proportioned, is a task of no common magnitude. Arduous as it is, the enlarged views of the house of representatives stimulate me to attempt it. In such an attempt it will not be dishonourable—even to fail.

Of this system, I have begun to sketch the rough outlines. In finishing them, and in filling them up, I mean to avail myself of all the assistance, which can possibly be derived from every example set before me. But, at the same time, I mean to pay implicit deference to none.

The acts of the legislature of Pennsylvania, though very numerous, compose but a small proportion of her laws. The common law is a part, and, by far, the most important part of her system of jurisprudence. Statute regulations are intended only for those cases, comparatively few, in which the common law is defective, or to which it is inapplicable: to that law, those regulations are properly to be considered as a supplement. A knowledge of that law should, for this reason, precede, or, at least, accompany the study of those regulations.

"To know what the common law was before the making of any statute," says my Lord Coke, in his familiar but expressive manner, "is the very lock and key to set open the windows of the statute."[a] To lay the statute laws before one who knows nothing of the common law, amounts, frequently, to much the same thing as laying every third or fourth line of a deed before one who has never seen the residue of it. It would, therefore, be highly eligible, that, under each head of the statute law, the common law, relating to it, should be introduced and explained. This would be a useful commentary on the text of the statute law, and would, at the same time, form a body of the common law reduced into a just and regular system.

With such a commentary, the digest which I shall have the honour of reporting to the house will be accompanied. The constitution of the United States and that of Pennsylvania, compose the supreme law of the land: they contain and they suggest many of the fundamental principles of jurisprudence, and must have a governing and an extensive influence over almost every other part of our legal system. They should, therefore, be explained and understood in the clearest and most distinct manner, and they should be pursued through their numerous and important, though remote and widely ramified effects. Hence it is proper, that they also should be attended

a. 3. Ins. 308.

with a commentary. These commentaries will not, however, form a part of my report: they must stand or fall by their own merit or insignificance.

Another question, of very considerable importance, has occurred to me: the result of my reflections upon it, I beg leave to lay before the house.

In what manner should the digest of the laws of Pennsylvania be composed? Should it imitate the style of the British acts of parliament and those statutes, which have been framed upon their model—or should it be written in the usual forms of composition?

To professional gentlemen it is well known, that, in England, all bills were anciently drawn in the form of petitions; that these petitions, with the king's answer, were entered upon the parliament rolls; and that, at the end of each parliament, they were reduced into statutes by the judges. Hence the form, "may it please your majesty, that it may be enacted" and "be it enacted, &c." This form, like many others, has been continued in England long after the reason of it has ceased. This form, like many others, has been introduced into the colonies, and, among the rest, into Pennsylvania, where the reason of it never existed. Thus almost every sentence in our acts of assembly begins with a "be it enacted."

This form, though without foundation in Pennsylvania, is not, however, without its inconveniences. To introduce every sentence under the government of a verb, gives a stiffness—to introduce every sentence under the government of the same verb, gives a monotony as well as stiffness, to the composition. To avoid the frequent reiteration of those blemishes, the sentences are lengthened. By being lengthened, they are crowded with multifarious, sometimes with heterogeneous and disjointed, circumstances and materials. Hence the obscure, and confused, and embarrassed periods of a mile, with which the statute books are loaded and disgraced.

But simplicity and plainness and precision should mark the texture of a law. It claims the *obedience*—it should be level to the *understanding* of all.

By the first assembly of Pennsylvania an act was made "for teaching the laws in the schools."[b] This noble regulation is countenanced by the authority and example of the most enlightened nations and men. Cicero[c] informs us, that when he was a boy, the laws of the twelve tables were learned "ut necessarium carmen,"[1] as a piece of composition at once necessary and entertaining. The celebrated legislator of the Cretans used all the precautions,

b. R. O. book. A. p. 22.

c. De leg. l. 2. c. 23.

1. That essential song.

which human prudence could suggest, to inspire the youth with the greatest respect and attachment to the maxims and customs of the state. This was what Plato[2] found most admirable in the laws of Minos.

If youth should be educated in the knowledge and love of the laws: it follows, that the laws should be proper objects of their attachment, and proper subjects of their study. Can this be said concerning a statute book drawn up in the usual style and form? Would any one select such a composition to form the taste of his son, or to inspire him with a relish for literary accomplishments? It has been remarked, with truth as well as wit, that one of the most irksome penalties, which could be inflicted by an act of parliament, would be, to compel the culprit to read the statutes at large from the beginning to the end.

But the knowledge of the laws, useful to youth, is incumbent on those of riper years.

From the manner, in which other law books, as well as statute laws, are usually written, it may be supposed that law is, in its nature, unsusceptible of the same simplicity and clearness as the other sciences. It is high time that law should be rescued from this injurious imputation. Like the other sciences, it should now enjoy the advantages of light, which have resulted from the resurrection of letters; for, like the other sciences, it has suffered extremely from the thick veil of mystery spread over it in the dark and scholastick ages.

Both the divinity and law of those times, says Sir William Blackstone,[d] were frittered into logical distinctions, and drawn out into metaphysical subtilties, with a skill most amazingly artificial. Law in particular, which (being intended for universal reception) ought to be a plain rule of action, became a science of the greatest intricacy; especially when blended with the new and oppressive refinements ingrafted upon feodal property: which refinements were, from time to time, gradually introduced by the Norman practitioners, with a view to supersede (as they did in a great measure) the more homely, but the more free and intelligible, maxims of distributive justice among the Saxons.

As were the divinity and the law, such likewise was the philosophy of the schools during many ages of darkness and barbarism. It was fruitful of words, but barren of works, and admirably contrived for drawing a veil over

2. Plato (428–348 B.C.), a student of Socrates and a teacher of Aristotle, was an important Greek philosopher.

d. Bl. Com. 410. 2. Id. 58.

human ignorance, and putting a stop to the progress of knowledge.[e] But at last the light began to dawn. It has dawned, however, much slower upon the law, than upon religion and philosophy. "The laws," says the celebrated Beccaria,[f] "are always several ages behind the actual improvement of the nation which they govern." If this observation is true, and I believe it to be true, with regard to law in general; it is peculiarly true, and its truth is of peculiar importance, with regard to criminal law in particular. It is the observation of Sir William Blackstone, that, in every country of Europe, the criminal is more rude and imperfect than the civil law. Unfortunate it is that this should be the case. For on the excellence of the criminal law the liberty and happiness of the citizens chiefly depend.

We are told by Montesquieu, that the knowledge, with regard to the surest rules, observed in criminal judgments, is more interesting to mankind than any other thing in the universe. We are told by him further, that liberty can be founded only on the practice of this knowledge. But how can this knowledge be acquired—how can it become the foundation of practice, if the laws, and particularly the criminal laws, are written in a manner in which they cannot be clearly known or understood.

Deeply penetrated with the truth and the force of these remarks, which are supported by the most respectable authorities, I shall not justly incur the censure of innovation, if I express my opinion, that the law should be written in the same manner, which we use when we write on other subjects, or other sciences. This manner has been already adopted, with success, in the Constitution of the United States, and in that of Pennsylvania.

As, however, the observations, which I have made and quoted, bear particularly upon the criminal code; I propose to make, in that code, the first experiment of their justness and efficacy.

The criminal law, though the most important, is by far the least voluminous part of the system; and it can be easily formed into a separate report. This I mean to do. By doing so, I shall have a fair opportunity of exhibiting a specimen of the manner and the merits both of my plan and of its execution.

To the Speaker of the House of Representatives.

In the execution of this plan, the Author made very considerable progress. It had been undertaken, however, under the authority of only one of

e. Reid. Ess. Int. 127.
f. C. 29.

the houses of the assembly, without the sanction of the other; and, in the course of its execution, it was found, that the want of legislative sanction, and of a provision for making pecuniary compensation to persons necessarily employed as assistants in a work of so much labour and importance, joined with the difficulty of obtaining many useful and necessary books connected with the subject of the work, had retarded its progress, and thrown considerable impediments in the way of its completion. An attempt was made to remove these obstacles; and a bill was passed for that purpose by the house of representatives; but it was unfortunately negatived by the senate. The design of framing a digest under the authority of the legislature was, of course, relinquished. But the Author still contemplated the execution of a similar design, as a private work; supported only by his own name; and it occupied, for a long time, his assiduous attention. He had, in a great degree, prepared the materials; but did not live to arrange them, and compose the contemplated digest.

From these causes, the lectures continued in the state, in which they now appear. The Editor has not thought himself at liberty to make any alterations in the language of the Author: the lecturing style is, therefore, retained. He has, however, been obliged to adopt a division not, perhaps, strictly in unison with that style, but the only one which was in his power—that into parts and chapters, according to the subjects. They were never divided by the Author into distinct lectures; as, according to his mode of delivering them, they were frequently attended with recapitulations, and often embraced parts of his observations on different subjects.

Of the other parts of the contents of these volumes, the tracts on the legislative authority of parliament over the colonies, and on the Bank of North America, were before published; as were also the speech in convention on 26th November, 1787, and the oration on 4th July, 1788. These, with the other speeches now published, appear to have been selected for publication by the Author himself. His charges to grand juries in the federal courts, the Editor has not thought it proper to insert; because, as they related generally to the history, powers, and duties of juries, the contents of them are to be found in the lectures. One, however, he has selected and inserted, because it contains a concise and handsome view of the criminal law of the United States, nearly as it stands at present, and many important observations not to be found in the other works.

Of the value and merit of these volumes, the Editor will say nothing. He leaves that subject to the judgment of those who can estimate them with greater impartiality. In some parts, perhaps, they want that degree of polish, which the farther attention and corrections of the Author might have bestowed on them; and repetitions, which sometimes occur, and which, in lectures delivered, are not only excusable but proper, would probably not have been met with, had they been corrected by himself for the press. On the whole, however, the Editor trusts, that they will not be thought unworthy, either in style or sentiment, of the reputation of their Author.

CONTENTS OF THE FIRST VOLUME

LECTURES ON LAW.

Part I.

LECTURES ON LAW,

DELIVERED IN THE

College of Philadelphia

IN THE YEARS ONE THOUSAND SEVEN HUNDRED AND NINETY,
AND ONE THOUSAND SEVEN HUNDRED AND NINETY ONE.

PART I

CHAPTER I.

Introductory Lecture.
Of the Study of the Law in the United States.

Ladies and Gentlemen,

Though I am not unaccustomed to speak in publick, yet, on this occasion, I rise with much diffidence to address you. The character, in which I appear, is both important and new. Anxiety and selfdistrust are natural on my first appearance. These feelings are greatly heightened by another consideration, which operates with peculiar force. I never before had the honour of addressing a *fair* audience. Anxiety and selfdistrust, in an uncommon degree, are natural, when, for the first time, I address a fair audience so brilliant as this is. There is one encouraging reflection, however, which greatly supports me. The whole of my very respectable audience is as much distinguished by its politeness, as a part of it is distinguished by its brilliancy. From that politeness, I shall receive—what I feel I need—an uncommon degree of generous indulgence.

It is the remark of an admired historian, that the high character, which the Grecian commonwealths long possessed among nations, should not be ascribed solely to their excellence in science and in government. With regard to these, other nations, he thinks, and particularly that of which he was writing the history, were entitled to a reputation, not less exalted and illustrious. But the opinion, he says, of the superiour endowments and achievements of the Grecians has arisen, in a considerable degree, from their peculiar felicity in having their virtues transmitted to posterity by writers, who excelled those of every other country in abilities and elegance.

Alexander,[1] when master of the world, envied the good fortune of Achilles, who had a Homer to celebrate his deeds.

1. Alexander the Great (356–323 B.C.) was king of Macedon from 336 to 323 B.C. He conquered most of the ancient world.

The observation, which was applied to Rome by Sallust,[2] and the force of which appears so strongly from the feelings of Alexander, permit me to apply, for I can apply it with equal propriety, to the States of America.

They have not, it is true, been long or much known upon the great theatre of nations: their immature age has not hitherto furnished them with many occasions of extending their renown to the distant quarters of the globe. But, in real worth and excellence, I boldly venture to compare them with the most illustrious commonwealths, which adorn the records of fame. When some future Xenophon[3] or Thucydides[4] shall arise to do justice to their virtues and their actions; the glory of America will rival—it will outshine the glory of Greece.

Were I called upon for my reasons why I deem so highly of the American character, I would assign them in a very few words—That character has been eminently distinguished by the love of liberty, and the love of law.

I rejoice in my appointment to this chair, because it gives me the best opportunities to discover, to study, to develop, and to communicate many striking instances, hitherto little known, on which this distinguished character is founded.

In free countries—in free countries, especially, that boast the blessing of a common law, springing warm and spontaneous from the manners of the people—Law should be studied and taught as a historical science.

The eloquent Rousseau[5] complains, that the origin of nations is much concealed by the darkness or the distance of antiquity.

In many parts of the world, the fact may be as he represents it; and yet his complaint may be without foundation: for, in many parts of the world, the origin of nations ought to be buried in oblivion. To succeeding ages, the knowledge of it would convey neither pleasure nor instruction.

With regard to the States of America, I am happy in saying, that a complaint concerning the uncertainty of their first settlements cannot be made with propriety or truth; though I must add, that, if it could be made with propriety or truth, it would be a subject of the deepest regret.

2. Gaius Sallustius Crispus (86–34 B.C.) was a Roman politician and historian.

3. Xenophon (427–355 B.C.) was a Greek historian.

4. Thucydides (c. 460–400 B.C.) was a Greek historian best known for his *History of the Peloponnesian War.*

5. Jean-Jacques Rousseau (1712–1778) was a prolific French author and political philosopher.

If the just and genuine principles of society can diffuse a lustre round the establishment of nations; that of the States of America is indeed illustrious. Fierce oppression, rattling, in her left hand, the chains of tyranny; and brandishing, in her right hand, the torch of persecution, drove our predecessors from the coasts of Europe: liberty, benevolent and serene, pointing to a cornucopia on one side, and to a branch of olive on the other, invited and conducted them to the American shores.

In discharging the duties of this office, I shall have the pleasure of presenting to my hearers what, as to the nations in the Transatlantick world, must be searched for in vain—an original compact of a society, on its first arrival in this section of the globe. How the lawyers, and statesmen, and antiquarians, and philosophers of Europe would exult, on discovering a similar monument of the Athenian commonwealth! and yet, perhaps, the historical monuments of the states of America are not, intrinsically, less important, or less worthy of attention, than the historical monuments of the states of Greece. The latter, indeed, are gilded with the gay decorations of fable and mythology; but the former are clothed in the neater and more simple garb of freedom and truth.

The doctrine of toleration in matters of religion, reasonable though it certainly is, has not been long known or acknowledged. For its reception and establishment, where it has been received and established, the world has been thought to owe much to the inestimable writings of the celebrated Locke. To the inestimable writings of that justly celebrated man, let the tribute of applause be plenteously paid: but while immortal honours are bestowed on the name and character of Locke;[6] why should an ungracious silence be observed, with regard to the name and character of Calvert?[7]

Let it be known, that, before the doctrine of toleration was published in Europe, the practice of it was established in America. A law in favour of religious freedom was passed in Maryland, as early as the year one thousand six hundred and forty nine.

When my Lord Baltimore was afterwards urged—not by the spirit of freedom—to consent that this law should be repealed; with the enlight-

6. John Locke (1632–1704) was an English philospher and political thinker. He is best known for "A Letter on Toleration" (1689), *Two Treatises of Government* (1689), and *An Essay Concerning Human Understanding* (1689).

7. Caecilius Calvert, Second Baron Baltimore (1605–1675), was Maryland's first proprietary governor (1632–1675). Under his direction the legislature passed "An Act Concerning Toleration" in 1649.

ened principles of a man and a christian, he had the fortitude, to declare, that he never would assent to the repeal of a law, which protected the natural rights of men, by ensuring to every one freedom of action and thought.

Indeed, the character of this excellent man has been too little known. He was truly the father of his country. To the legislature of Maryland he often recommended a maxim, which deserves to be written in letters of gold: "By concord a small colony may grow into a great and renowned nation; but, by dissensions, mighty and glorious kingdoms have declined and fallen[a] into nothing."

Similar to that of Calvert, has been the fate of many other valuable characters in America. They have been too little known. To those around them, their modest merits have been too familiar, perhaps too uniform, to attract particular and distinguished attention: by those at a distance, the mild and peaceful voice of their virtue has not been heard. But to their memories, justice should be done, as far as it can be done, by a just and grateful country.

In the European temple of fame, William Penn[8] is placed by the side of Lycurgus. Will America refuse a temple to her patriots and her heroes? No; she will not. The glorious dome already rises. Its architecture is of the neatest and chastest order: its dimensions are spacious: its proportions are elegant and correct. In its front a number of niches are formed. In some of them statues are placed. On the left hand of the portal, are the names and figures of Warren, Montgomery, Mercer.[9] On the right hand, are the names and figures of Calvert, Penn, Franklin. In the middle, is a niche of larger size, and decorated with peculiar ornaments. On the left side of it, are sculptured the trophies of war: on the right, the more precious emblems of peace. Above it, is represented the rising glory of the United States. It is without a statue and without a name. Beneath it, in letters very legible, are these words—"FOR THE MOST WORTHY." By the

a. Chal. 363.

8. William Penn (1644–1718) converted to Quakerism in his twenties and soon became an avid advocate of religious toleration. To settle a debt owed to his father, Charles II gave William the colony of Pennsylvania in 1681.

9. "Warren" refers to General Joseph Warren (1741–1775), a doctor and soldier who died at the Battle of Bunker Hill. "Montgomery" refers to General Richard Montgomery (1738–1775), who died attempting to take the city of Quebec during the Revolutionary War. "Mercer" refers to General Hugh Mercer (1726–1777), who died at the Battle of Princeton.

enraptured voice of grateful America—with the consenting plaudits of an admiring world, the designation is unanimously made. Late—very late—may the niche be filled.[b]

But while we perform the pleasing duties of gratitude, let not other duties be disregarded. Illustrious examples are displayed to our view, that we may imitate as well as admire. Before we can be distinguished by the same honours, we must be distinguished by the same virtues.

What are those virtues? They are chiefly the same virtues, which we have already seen to be descriptive of the American character—the love of liberty, and the love of law. But law and liberty cannot rationally become the objects of our love, unless they first become the objects of our knowledge. The same course of study, properly directed, will lead us to the knowledge of both. Indeed, neither of them can be known, because neither of them can exist, without the other. Without liberty, law loses its nature and its name, and becomes oppression. Without law, liberty also loses its nature and its name, and becomes licentiousness. In denominating, therefore, that science, by which the knowledge of both is acquired, it is unnecessary to preserve, in terms, the distinction between them. That science may be named, as it has been named, the science of law.

The science of law should, in some measure, and in some degree, be the study of every free citizen, and of every free man. Every free citizen and every free man has duties to perform and rights to claim. Unless, in some measure, and in some degree, he knows those duties and those rights, he can never act a just and an independent part.

Happily, the general and most important principles of law are not removed to a very great distance from common apprehension. It has been said of religion, that though the elephant may swim, yet the lamb may wade in it. Concerning law, the same observation may be made.

The home navigation, carried on along the shores, is more necessary, and more useful too, than that, which is pursued through the deep and expanded ocean. A man may be a most excellent coaster, though he possess not the nautical accomplishments and experience of a Cook.[10]

b. General Washington, then President of the United States, was present when this lecture was delivered. *Ed.*

10. Likely refers to Captain James Cook (1728–1779), a British explorer, navigator, and cartographer.

As a science, the law is far from being so disagreeable or so perplexed a study, as it is frequently supposed to be. Some, indeed, involve themselves in a thick mist of terms of art; and use a language unknown to all, but those of the profession. By such, the knowledge of the law, like the mysteries of some ancient divinity, is confined to its initiated votaries; as if all others were in duty bound, blindly and implicitly to obey. But this ought not to be the case. The knowledge of those rational principles on which the law is founded, ought, especially in a free government, to be diffused over the whole community.

In a free country, every citizen forms a part of the sovereign power: he possesses a vote, or takes a still more active part in the business of the commonwealth. The right and the duty of giving that vote, the right and the duty of taking that share, are necessarily attended with the duty of making that business the object of his study and inquiry.

In the United States, every citizen is frequently called upon to act in this great publick character. He elects the legislative, and he takes a personal share in the executive and judicial departments of the nation. It is true, that a man, who wishes to be right, will, with the official assistance afforded him, be seldom under the necessity of being wrong: but it is equally true, and it ought not to be concealed, that the publick duties and the publick rights of every citizen of the United States loudly demand from him all the time, which he can prudently spare, and all the means which he can prudently employ, in order to learn that part, which it is incumbent on him to act.

On the publick mind, one great truth can never be too deeply impressed—that the weight of the government of the United States, and of each state composing the union, rests on the shoulders of the people.

I express not this sentiment now, as I have never expressed it heretofore, with a view to flatter: I express it now, as I have always expressed it heretofore, with a far other and higher aim—with an aim to excite the people to acquire, by vigorous and manly exercise, a degree of strength sufficient to support the weighty burthen, which is laid upon them—with an aim to convince them, that their duties rise in strict proportion to their rights; and that few are able to trace or to estimate the great danger, in a free government, when the rights of the people are unexercised, and the still greater danger, when the rights of the people are ill exercised.

At a general election, too few attend to the important consequences of voting or not voting; and to the consequences, still more important, of voting right or voting wrong.

The rights and the duties of jurors, in the United States, are great and extensive. No punishment can be inflicted without the intervention of one—in much the greater number of cases, without the intervention of more than one jury. Is it not of immense consequence to the publick, that those, who have committed crimes, should not escape with impunity? Is it not of immense consequence to individuals, that all, except those who have committed crimes, should be secure from the punishment denounced against their commission? Is it not, then, of immense consequence to both, that jurors should possess the spirit of just discernment, to discriminate between the innocent and the guilty? This spirit of just discernment requires knowledge of, at least, the general principles of the law, as well as knowledge of the minute particulars concerning the facts.

It is true, that, in matters of law, the jurors are entitled to the assistance of the judges; but it is also true, that, after they receive it, they have the right of judging for themselves: and is there not to this right the great corresponding duty of judging *properly*?

Surely, therefore, those who discharge the important and, let me add, the dignified functions of jurors, should acquire, as far as they possibly can acquire, a knowledge of the laws of their country: for, let me add further, the dignity, though not the importance of their functions, will greatly depend on the abilities, with which they discharge them.

But in the administration of justice—that part of government, which comes home most intimately to the business and the bosoms of men—there are judges as well as jurors; those, whose peculiar province it is to answer questions of law, as well as those, whose peculiar province it is to answer questions of fact.

In many courts—in many respectable courts within the United States, the judges are not, and, for a long time, cannot be gentlemen of professional acquirements. They may, however, fill their offices usefully and honourably, the want of professional acquirements notwithstanding. But can they do this, without a reasonable degree of acquaintance with the law?

We have already seen, that, in questions of law, the jurors are entitled to the assistance of the judges: but can the judges give assistance, without knowing what answers to make to the questions which the jury may propose? can those direct others, who themselves know not the road?

Unquestionably, then, those who fill, and those who expect to fill the offices of judges in courts, not, indeed, supreme, but rising in importance and in dignity above the appellation of inferiour, ought to make the strongest efforts in order to obtain a respectable degree of knowledge in the law.

Let me ascend to a station more elevated still. In the United States, the doors of publick honours and publick offices are, on the broad principles of equal liberty, thrown open to all. A laudable emulation, an emulation that ought to be encouraged in a free government, may prompt a man to legislate as well as to decide for his fellow citizens—to legislate, not merely for a single State, but for the most august Union that has yet been formed on the face of the globe.

Should not he, who is to supply the deficiencies of the existing law, know when the existing law is defective? Should not he, who is to introduce alterations into the existing law, know in what instances the existing law ought to be altered?

The first and governing maxim in the interpretation of a statute is, to discover the meaning of those, who made it. The first rule, subservient to the principle of the governing maxim, is, to discover what the law was, before the statute was made. The inference, necessarily resulting from the joint operation of the maxim and the rule, is this, that in explaining a statute, the judges ought to take it for granted, that those, who made it, knew the antecedent law. This certainly implies, that a competent knowledge of, at least, the general principles of law, is of indispensable necessity to those, who undertake the transcendent office of legislation.

I say, a knowledge of the general principles of law: for though an accurate, a minute, and an extensive knowledge of its practice and particular rules be highly useful; yet I cannot conceive it to be absolutely requisite to the able discharge of a legislative trust.

Upon this distinction—and it is an important one—I cannot, perhaps, explain myself better, than by delivering the sentiments, which were entertained, some centuries ago, by a very learned and able judge—I mean the Lord Chancellor Fortescue.[11]

In his excellent book, which he wrote in praise of the laws of England,

11. Lord Chancellor John Fortescue (c. 1394–c. 1476) was an English politician and Lord Chief Justice. He is the author of the celebrated *De laudibus legum Angliae* (*In Praise of the Law of England*).

he uses a number of arguments with his pupil, the prince of Wales, to excite him to the study of the law. Of these arguments the prince feels and acknowledges the full force. "But," says he, "there is one thing, which agitates my mind in such a manner, that, like a vessel tossed in the tumultuous ocean, I know not how to direct my course: it is, that when I recollect the number of years, which the students of the law employ, before they acquire a sufficient degree of knowledge, I am apprehensive lest, in studies of this nature, I should consume the whole of my youth."

To relieve his pupil from this anxiety, the chancellor cites a passage from the writings of Aristotle,[12] to the following purpose: "We are then supposed to know a thing, when we apprehend its causes and its principles, as high as its original elements."

This maxim the chancellor illustrates, by a reference to several of the sciences; and then draws this general conclusion. "Whoever knows the principles and elements of any science, knows the science itself—generally, at least, though not completely." This conclusion he then applies to the science of law. "In the same manner, when you shall become acquainted with the principles and the elements of law, you may be denominated a lawyer. It will not be necessary for *you,* at a great expense of your time, to scrutinize curious and intricate points of discussion. I know the quickness of your apprehension, and the strength of your genius. Though the legal knowledge accumulated in a series of twenty years is not more than sufficient to qualify one for being a judge; yet, in one year, you will be able to acquire a degree of it sufficient for you; without, even in that year, neglecting your other studies and improvements."[c]

That a law education is necessary for gentlemen intended for the profession of the law, it would be as ridiculous to prove as to deny. In all other countries, publick institutions bear a standing testimony to this truth. Ought this to be the only country without them? Justinian,[13] who did so much for the Roman law, was, as might have been expected, uncommonly attentive to form and establish a proper plan for studying it. All the modern

12. Aristotle (384–322 B.C.), a student of Plato and a teacher of Alexander the Great, was an important Greek philosopher.

c. Fort. de Laud. c. 7. 8.

13. Flavius Justinianus (c. 483–565) was emperor of the Eastern Roman Empire from 527 to 565. He was known for his legal reforms and for commissioning *Corpus Iuris Civilis.*

nations of Europe have admitted the profession of their municipal jurisprudence, into their universities and other seminaries of liberal education.

In England, numerous and ample provisions have been made for this purpose. For young gentlemen, there are eight houses of chancery, where they learn the first elements of law. For those more advanced in their studies, there are four inns of court. "All these together," says my Lord Coke,[d] with conscious professional pride, "compose the most illustrious university in the world, for the profession of law." Here lectures have been read, exercises have been performed, and degrees in the common law have been conferred, in the same manner as degrees in the civil and canon law, in other universities.

Besides all these, the Vinerian professorship of law has, not many years ago, been established in the university of Oxford. Of this professorship, the celebrated Sir William Blackstone was the first, who filled the chair.

A question deeply interesting to the American States now presents itself. Should the elements of a law education, particularly as it respects publick law, be drawn entirely from another country—or should they be drawn, in part, at least, from the constitutions and governments and laws of the United States, and of the several States composing the Union?

The subject, to one standing where I stand, is not without its delicacy: let me, however, treat it with the decent but firm freedom, which befits an independent citizen, and a professor in independent states.

Surely I am justified in saying, that the principles of the constitutions and governments and laws of the United States, and the republicks, of which they, are formed, are materially different from the principles of the constitution and government and laws of England; for that is the only country, from the principles of whose constitution and government and laws, it will be contended, that the elements of a law education ought to be drawn. I presume to go further: the principles of our constitutions and governments and laws are materially *better* than the principles of the constitution and government and laws of England.

Permit me to mention one great principle, the *vital* principle I may well call it, which diffuses animation and vigour through all the others. The

d. 3 Rep. Pref. 20.

principle I mean is this, that the supreme or sovereign power of the society resides in the citizens at large; and that, therefore, they always retain the right of abolishing, altering, or amending their constitution, at whatever time, and in whatever manner, they shall deem it expedient.

By Sir William Blackstone, from whose Commentaries, a performance in many respects highly valuable, the elements of a foreign law education would probably be borrowed—by Sir William Blackstone, this great and fundamental principle is treated as a political chimera, existing only in the minds of some theorists; but, in practice, inconsistent with the dispensation of any government upon earth. Let us hear his own words.

> It must be owned that Mr. Locke and other theoretical writers have held, that "there remains still inherent in the people, a supreme power to alter the legislative, when they find the legislative act contrary to the trust reposed in them; for when such trust is abused, it is thereby forfeited, and devolves to those, who gave it." But, however just this conclusion may be in theory, we cannot admit it, nor argue from it, under any dispensation of government, at present actually existing. For this devolution of power to the people at large, includes a dissolution of the whole form of government established by that people; reduces all the members to their original state of equality; and, by annihilating the sovereign power, repeals all positive laws whatsoever before enacted. No human laws will therefore suppose a case, which at once must destroy all law, and compel men to build afresh upon a new foundation, nor will they make provision for so desperate an event, as must render all legal provisions ineffectual.[e]

And yet, even in England, there have been revolutions of government: there has been one within very little more than a century ago. The learned Author of the Commentaries admits the fact; but denies it to be a ground on which any constitutional principle can be established.

If the same precise "conjunction of circumstances" should happen a second time; the revolution of one thousand six hundred and eighty eight would form a precedent: but were only one or two of the circumstances, forming that conjunction, to happen again; "the precedent would fail us."[f]

e. 1 Bl. Com. 161. 162.
f. 1 Bl. Com. 245.

The three circumstances, which formed that conjunction, were these: 1. An endeavour to subvert the constitution, by breaking the original contract between the king and people. 2. Violation of the fundamental laws. 3. Withdrawing out of the kingdom.

Now, on this state of things, let us make a supposition—not a very foreign one—and see the consequences, which would unquestionably follow from the principles of Sir William Blackstone. Let us suppose, that, on some occasion, a prince should form a conjunction of only two of the circumstances; for instance, that he should only violate the fundamental laws, and endeavour to subvert the constitution: let us suppose, that, instead of completing the conjunction, by withdrawing out of his government, he should only employ some forty or fifty thousand troops to give full efficacy to the two first circumstances: let us suppose all this—and it is surely not unnatural to suppose, that a prince, who shall form the two first parts of the conjunction, will not, like James the second, run away from the execution of them—let us, I say, suppose all this; and what, on the principles of Sir William Blackstone, would be the undeniable consequence? In the language of the Commentaries, "our precedent would fail us."

But we have thought, and we have acted upon revolution principles, without offering them up as sacrifices at the shrine of revolution precedents.

Why should we not teach our children those principles, upon which we ourselves have thought and acted? Ought we to instil into their tender minds a theory, especially if unfounded, which is contradictory to our own practice, built on the most solid foundation? Why should we reduce them to the cruel dilemma of condemning, either those principles which they have been taught to believe, or those persons whom they have been taught to revere?

It is true, that the learned Author of the Commentaries concludes this very passage, by telling us, that "there are inherent, though latent powers of society, which no climate, no time, no constitution, no contract can ever destroy or diminish." But what does this prove? not that revolution principles are, in his opinion, recognized by the English constitution; but that the English constitution, whether considered as a law, or as a contract, cannot destroy or diminish those principles.

It is the opinion of many, that the revolution of one thousand six hundred and eighty eight did more than set a mere precedent, even in

England. But be that as it may: a revolution principle certainly is, and certainly should be taught as a principle of the constitution of the United States, and of every State in the Union.

This revolution principle—that, the sovereign power residing in the people; they may change their constitution and government whenever they please—is not a principle of discord, rancour, or war: it is a principle of melioration, contentment, and peace. It is a principle not recommended merely by a flattering theory: it is a principle recommended by happy experience. To the testimony of Pennsylvania—to the testimony of the United States I appeal for the truth of what I say.

In the course of these lectures, my duty will oblige me to notice some other important principles, very particularly his definition and explanation of law itself, in which my sentiments differ from those of the respecable Author of the Commentaries. It already appears, that, with regard to the very first principles of government, we set out from different points of departure.

As I have mentioned Sir William Blackstone, let me speak of him explicitly as it becomes me. I cannot consider him as a zealous friend of republicanism. One of his survivers or successours in office has characterized him by the appellation of an antirepublican lawyer. On the subject of government, I think I can plainly discover his jealousies and his attachments.

For his jealousies, an easy and natural account may be given. In England, only one specimen of a commonwealth has been exhibited to publick examination; and that specimen was, indeed, an unfavourable one. On trial, it was found to be unsound and unsatisfactory. It is not very surprising that an English lawyer, with an example so inauspicious before his eyes, should feel a degree of aversion, latent, yet strong, to a republican government.

An account, perhaps equally natural and easy, may be given for his attachments. With all reigning families, I believe, it is a settled maxim, that every revolution in government is unjustifiable, except the single one, which conducted them to the throne. The maxims of the court have always their diffusive influence. That influence, in favour of one species of government, might steal imperceptibly upon a mind, already jealous of another species, viewed as its rival, and as its enemy.

But, with all his prejudices concerning government, I have the pleasure of beholding him, in one conspicuous aspect, as a friend to the rights of men. To those rights, the author of the beautiful and animated dissertations concerning juries could not be cold or insensible.

As author of the Commentaries, he possessed uncommon merit. His manner is clear and methodical; his sentiments—I speak of them generally—are judicious and solid; his language is elegant and pure. In publick law, however, he should be consulted with a cautious prudence. But, even in publick law, his principles, when they are not proper objects of imitation, will furnish excellent materials of contrast. On every account, therefore, he should be read and studied. He deserves to be much admired; but he ought not to be implicitly followed.

This last admonitory remark should not be confined to Sir William Blackstone: it ought to be extended to all political writers—must I say?—almost without exception. This seems a severe sentence: but, if it is just, it must be pronounced. The cause of liberty, the rights of men require, that, in a subject essential to that cause and to those rights, errour should be exposed, in order to be avoided.

The foundations of political truth have been laid but lately: the genuine science of government, to no human science inferiour in importance, is, indeed, but in its infancy: and the reason of this can be easily assigned. In the whole annals of the Transatlantick world, it will be difficult to point out a single instance of its legitimate institution: I will go further, and say, that, among all the political writers of the Transatlantick world, it will be difficult to point out a single model of its unbiassed theory.

The celebrated Grotius introduces what he says concerning the interesting doctrine of sovereignty, with the following information. "Learned men of our age, each of them handling the argument, rather, according to the present interest of the affairs of his country, than according to truth, have greatly perplexed that, which, of itself, was not very clear."[g] In this, the learned men of every other age have resembled those of the age of Grotius.

Indeed, it is astonishing, in what intricate mazes politicians and philosophers have bewildered themselves upon this subject. Systems have been formed upon systems, all fleeting, because all unfounded. Sovereignty has

g. Gro. b. i. c. 3. s. 5.

sometimes been viewed as a star, which eluded our investigation by its immeasurable height: sometimes it has been considered as a sun, which could not be distinctly seen by reason of its insufferable splendour.

In Egypt, the Nile is an object truly striking and grand. Its waters, rising to a certain height, and spreading to a certain distance, are the cause of fertility and plenty: swelling higher, and extending further, they produce devastation and famine. This stupendous stream, at some times so beneficial, at other times so destructive, has, at all times, formed a subject of anxious inquiry. To trace its source has been the unceasing aim of the mighty and the learned. Kings, attended with all the instruments of strength; sages, furnished with all the apparatus of philosophy, have engaged, with ardour, in the curious search; but their most patient and their most powerful enterprises have been equally vain.

The source of the Nile continued still unknown; and because it continued still unknown, the poets fondly fabled that it was to be found only in a superiour orb; and, of course, it was worshipped as a divinity.

We are told, however, that, at last, the source of the Nile has been discovered; and that it consists of—what might have been supposed before the discovery—a collection of springs small, indeed, but pure.

The fate of sovereignty has been similar to that of the Nile. Always magnificent, always interesting to mankind, it has become alternately their blessing and their curse. Its origin has often been attempted to be traced. The great and the wise have embarked in the undertaking; though seldom, it must be owned, with the spirit of just inquiry; or in the direction, which leads to important discovery. The source of sovereignty was still concealed beyond some impenetrable mystery; and, because it was concealed, philosophers and politicians, in this instance, gravely taught what, in the other, the poets had fondly fabled, that it must be something more than human: it was impiously asserted to be divine.

Lately, the inquiry has been recommenced with a different spirit, and in a new direction; and although the discovery of nothing very astonishing, yet the discovery of something very useful and true, has been the result. The dread and redoubtable sovereign, when traced to his ultimate and genuine source, has been found, as he ought to have been found, in the free and independent man.

This truth, so simple and natural, and yet so neglected or despised, may be appreciated as the first and fundamental principle in the science of government.

Besides the reasons, which I have already offered; others may be suggested, why the elements of a law education ought to be drawn from our own constitutions and governments and laws.

In every government, which is not altogether despotical, the institution of youth is of some publick consequence. In a republican government, it is of the greatest. Of no class of citizens can the education be of more publick consequence, than that of those, who are destined to take an active part in publick affairs. Those who have had the advantage of a law education, are very frequently destined to take this active part. This deduction clearly shows, that, in a free government, the principles of a law education are matters of the greatest publick consequence.

Ought not those principles to be congenial with the principles of government? By the revolution in the United States, a very great alteration—a very great improvement—as we have already seen, has taken place in our system of government: ought not a proportioned alteration—ought not a proportioned improvement to be introduced into our system of law education?

We have passed the Red Sea in safety: we have survived a tedious and dangerous journey through the wilderness: we are now in full and peaceable possession of the promised land: must we, after all, return to the flesh pots of Egypt? Is there not danger, that when one nation teaches, it may, in some instances, give the law to another?

A foundation of human happiness, broader and deeper than any that has heretofore been laid, is now laid in the United States: on that broad and deep foundation, let it be our pride, as it is our duty, to build a superstructure of adequate extent and magnificence.

But further; many parts of the laws of England can, in their own nature, have neither force nor application here. Such are all those parts, which are connected with ecclesiastical jurisdiction and an ecclesiastical establishment. Such are all those parts, too, which relate to the monarchical and aristocratick branches of the English constitution. Every one, who has perused the ponderous volumes of the law, knows how great a proportion of them is filled with the numerous and extensive titles relating to those different subjects. Surely they need not enter into the elements of a law education in the United States.

I mean not, however, to exclude them from the subsequent investigation of those, who shall aspire at the character of accomplished lawyers. I only mean, that they ought not to be put into the hands of students, as deserving the same time and the same attention with other parts, which are to have a practical influence upon their future conduct in their profession.

The numerous regulations, in England, respecting the poor, and the more artificial refinements and distinctions concerning real estates, must be known; but known as much in order to be avoided as to be practised. The study of them, therefore, need not be so minute here as in England.

Concerning many other titles of the English law, similar observations might be made. The force and the extent of each will increase day after day, and year after year.

All combine in showing, that the *foundation,* at least, of a separate, an unbiassed, and an independent law education should be laid in the United States.

Deeply impressed with the importance of this truth, I have undertaken the difficult, the laborious, and the delicate task of contributing to lay that foundation. I feel most sensibly the weight of the duty, which I have engaged to perform. I will not promise to perform it successfully—as well as it might be performed: but I will promise to perform it faithfully—as well as I can perform it. I feel its full importance.

It may be asked—I am told it has been asked—is it proper, that a judge of the supreme court of the United States should deliver lectures on law? It will not surely be suspected, that I deem too lightly of the very dignified and independent office, which I have the honour to hold, in consequence of the favourable sentiments entertained concerning me by those, whose favourable sentiments are indeed an honour. Had I thought that the dignity of that seat could be disparaged by an alliance with this chair, I would have spurned it from me. But I thought, and I still think in a very different manner. By my acceptance of this chair, I think I shall certainly increase my usefulness, without diminishing my dignity, as a judge; and I think, that, with equal certainty, I shall, as a judge, increase my usefulness, I will not say my dignity, in this chair. He, who is well qualified to teach, is well qualified to judge; and he, who is well qualified to judge, is well qualified to teach. Every acquisition of knowledge—and it is my duty to acquire much—can, with equal facility, and with equal propriety, be applied to either office: for let it be remembered, that both offices view the same science as their common object.

Any interference as to the times of discharging the two offices—the only one that strikes me as possible—will be carefully avoided.

But it may be further asked—ought a judge to commit himself by delivering his sentiments in a lecture? To this question I shall give a very explicit answer: and in that answer I shall include the determination, which I have taken both as a professor and as a judge. When I deliver my sentiments from this chair, they shall be my honest sentiments: when I deliver them from the bench, they shall be nothing more. In both places I shall make—because I mean to support—the claim to integrity: in neither shall I make—because in neither, can I support—the claim to infallibility.

My house of knowledge is, at present, too small. I feel it my duty, on many accounts, to enlarge it. But in this, as in every other kind of architecture, I believe it will be found, that he, who adds much, must alter some.

When the greatest judges, who ever adorned or illuminated a court of justice, have candidly and cheerfully acknowledged their mistakes; shall *I* be afraid of committing myself?

The learned and indefatigable Spelman,[14] after all the immense researches, which enabled him to prepare and publish his Glossary, published it with this remarkable precaution: "under the protestation of adding, retracting, correcting, and polishing, as, upon more mature consideration, shall seem expedient."[h]

I hope I have now shown, that my acceptance of this chair, instead of diminishing, is calculated to increase my usefulness, as a judge. Does it derogate from my dignity? By no means, in my opinion.

Let things be considered as they really are. As a judge, I can decide whether property in dispute belongs to the man on my right hand, or to

14. Sir Henry Spelman (1562–1641) was an English antiquary who is most famous for writing *Glossarium Archaiologicum,* a glossary of Anglo-Saxon and Latin legal terms.

h. Sub protestatione de addendo, retrahendo, corrigendo, poliendo, prout opus fuerit et consultius videbitur. Sir H. Spelman.

the man on my left hand. As a judge, I can pass sentence on a felon or a cheat. By doing both, a judge may be eminently useful in preserving peace, and in securing property.

Property, highly deserving security, is, however, not an end, but a means. How miserable, and how contemptible is that man, who inverts the order of nature, and makes his property, not a means, but an end!

Society ought to be preserved in peace; most unquestionably. But is this all? Ought it not to be improved as well as protected? Look at individuals: observe them from infancy to youth, from youth to manhood. Such is the order of Providence with regard to society. It is in a progressive state, moving on towards perfection. How is this progressive state to be assisted and accelerated? Principally by teaching the young "ideas how to shoot," and the young affections how to move.

What intrinsically can be more dignified, than to assist in preparing tender and ingenuous minds for all the great purposes, for which they are intended! What, I repeat it, can intrinsically be more dignified, than to assist in forming a future Cicero, or a future Bacon, without the vanity of one, and without the meanness of theother!

Let us see how things have been considered in other ages and in other countries.

Philip of Macedon,[15] a prince highly distinguished by his talents, though not by his virtues, was fully sensible of the value of science. An heir was born to his kingdom and his throne. Could any thing be more interesting to a father and a king? There was, it seems, a circumstance, which, in his opinion, enhanced the importance even of this event. His heir was born at a time, when he could receive a most excellent education.

Philip wrote to Aristotle the following letter: "You are to know that a son hath been born to us. We thank the gods, not so much for having bestowed him on us, as for bestowing him, at a time when Aristotle lives. We assure ourselves, that you will form him a prince worthy to be our successour, and a king worthy of Macedon."[i]

On Aristotle, accordingly, was devolved the charge of superintending

15. Philip of Macedon (382–336 B.C.) was king of Macedon and father of Alexander the Great.

i. 1 Lel. L. Phil. 98.

the education of the young prince, "that he may be taught," said Philip, "to avoid those errours, which I have committed, and of which I now repent."

What price Alexander the Great set upon his education, before his mind was fatally poisoned by the madness of ambition, will appear by a letter from him to Aristotle, in which we find this sentiment: "I am not so anxious to appear superiour to the rest of mankind in power, as in the knowledge of excellent things."[k] We see here the impetus of strong ambition; but it had not then taken its pernicious direction.

In the most shining periods of the Roman republick, men of the first distinction made the science of law their publick profession, and taught it openly in their houses as in so many schools. The first of these publick professors was Tiberius Coruncanius,[16] who was raised to the office of chief pontiff—the highest in the whole scale of Roman honours. His example was followed by many distinguished characters, among whom we find the celebrated names of the two Scevolae, of Cato, of Brutus, and of others well known to such as are conversant with the writers of the classical ages. Even Cicero himself, after he had been consul of Rome, after he had had kings for his clients, projected this very employment, as his future "honour and ornament."[l]

Whether, therefore, we consider the intrinsick or the external dignity of this chair; we shall find that it is, by no means, beneath an alliance with the highest offices and the highest characters.

If any example, set by me, can be supposed to have the least publick influence; I hope it will be in raising the care of education to that high degree of respectability, to which, every where, but especially in countries that are free, it has the most unimpeachable title.

I have been zealous—I hope I have not been altogether unsuccessful—in contributing the best of my endeavours towards forming a system of government; I shall rise in importance, if I can be equally successful—I will not be less zealous—in contributing the best of my endeavours towards forming a system of education likewise, in the United States. I shall rise in importance, because I shall rise in usefulness.

k. 2 Lel. L. Phil. 126.

16. Tiberius Coruncanius was the first plebian Pontifex Maximus (or head of the Roman religion) and was the first of the Jurisconsulti (public professors of the law).

l. Decus et ornamentum. De orat. l. 1. c. 45.

What are laws without manners? How can manners be formed, but by a proper education?[m]

Methinks I hear one of the female part of my audience exclaim—What is all this to us? We have heard much of societies, of states, of governments, of laws, and of a law education. Is every thing made for your sex? Why should not we have a share? Is our sex less honest, or less virtuous, or less wise than yours?

Will any of my brethren be kind enough to furnish me with answers to these questions?—I must answer them, it seems, myself? and I mean to answer them most sincerely.

Your sex is neither less honest, nor less virtuous, nor less wise than ours. With regard to the two first of these qualities, a superiority, on our part, will not be pretended: with regard to the last, a pretension of superiority cannot be supported.

I will name three women; and I will then challenge any of my brethren to name three men superiour to them in vigour and extent of abilities. My female champions are, Semiramis of Nineveh;[17] Zenobia,[18] the queen of the East; and Elizabeth of England. I believe it will readily be owned, that three men of superiour active talents cannot be named.

You will please, however, to take notice, that the issue, upon which I put the characters of these three ladies, is not that they were *accomplished;* it is, that they were *able* women.

This distinction immediately reminds you, that a woman may be an able, without being an accomplished female character.

In this latter view, I did not produce the three female characters I have mentioned. I produced them as women, merely of distinguished abilities—of abilities equal to those displayed by the most able of our sex.

But would you wish to be tried by the qualities of our sex? I will refer you to a more proper standard—that of your own.

All the three able characters, I have mentioned, had, I think, too much

m. The ancient wisdom of the best times did always make a just complaint, that states were too busy with their laws; and too negligent in point of education. 2. Ld. Bacon 423.

17. Semiramis was a legendary Assyrian queen.

18. Zenobia, or Xenobia, ruled as queen of Palmyra from 267 to 272. Although she ruled for only a short time, she embarked on military campaigns that led to her ruling Egypt and much of Syria and Asia Minor.

of the masculine in them. Perhaps I can conjecture the reason. Might it not be owing, in a great measure—might it not be owing altogether to the masculine employments, to which they devoted themselves?

Two of them were able warriours: all of them were able queens; but in all of them, we feel and we regret the loss of the lovely and accomplished woman: and let me assure you, that, in the estimation of our sex, the loss of the lovely and accomplished woman is irreparable, even when she is lost in the queen.

For these reasons, I doubt much, whether it would be proper that you should undertake the management of publick affairs. You have, indeed, heard much of publick government and publick law: but these things were not made for themselves: they were made for something better; and of that something better, you form the better part—I mean society—I mean particularly domestick society: there the lovely and accomplished woman shines with superiour lustre.

By some politicians, society has been considered as only the scaffolding of government; very improperly, in my judgment. In the just order of things, government is the scaffolding of society: and if society could be built and kept entire without government, the scaffolding might be thrown down, without the least inconvenience or cause of regret.

Government is, indeed, highly necessary; but it is highly necessary to a fallen state. Had man continued innocent, society, without the aids of government, would have shed its benign influence even over the bowers of Paradise.

For those bowers, how finely was your sex adapted! But let it be observed, that every thing else was finished, before Heaven's "last best gift" was introduced: let it be also observed, that, in the pure and perfect commencement of society, there was a striking difference between the only two persons, who composed it. His "large fair front and eye sublime" declared that, "for contemplation and for valour he was formed."

"For softness, she, and sweet attractive grace.
Grace was in all her steps, Heav'n in her eye;
In every gesture, dignity and love.
A thousand decencies unceasing flow'd
From all her words and actions, mixt with—
—mild compliance."

Her accomplishments indicated her destination. Female beauty is the expression of female virtue. The purest complexion, the finest features, the most elegant shape are uninteresting and insipid, unless we can discover, by them, the emotions of the mind. How beautiful and engaging, on the other hand, are the features, the looks, and the gestures, while they disclose modesty, sensibility, and every sweet and tender affection! When these appear, there is a "Soul upon the countenance."

These observations enhance the value of beauty; and show, that to possess and to admire it, is to possess and to admire the exhibition of the finest qualities, intellectual and moral. These observations do more: they show how beauty may be acquired, and improved, and preserved. When the beauties of the mind are cultivated, the countenance becomes beautifully eloquent in expressing them.

I know very well, that mere complexion and shape enter into the composition of beauty: but they form beauty only of a lower order. Separate them from animation—separate them from sensibility—separate them from virtue: what are they? The ingredients that compose a beautiful picture or a beautiful statue. I say too much; for the painters and the statuaries know, that expression is the soul of mimick as well as of real life.

As complexion and shape will not supply the place of the higher orders of beauty; so those higher orders have an independent existence, after the inferiour influence of complexion and shape are gone. Though the bloom of youth be faded; though the impressions of time be distinctly marked; yet, while the countenance continues to be enlivened by the beaming emanations of the mind, it will produce, in every beholder possessed of sensibility and taste, an effect far more pleasing, and far more lasting, than can be produced by the prettiest piece of uninformed nature, however florid, however regular, and however young.

How many purposes may be served at once, if things are done in the proper way! I have been giving a recipe for the improvement and preservation of female beauty; but I find that I have, at the same time, been delivering instructions for the culture and refinement of female virtue; and have been pointing at the important purposes, which female virtue is fitted and intended to accomplish.

If nature evinces her designs by her works; you were destined to embellish, to refine, and to exalt the pleasures and virtues of social life.

To protect and to improve social life, is, as we, have seen, the end of government and law. If, therefore, you have no share in the formation, you have a most intimate connexion with the effects, of a good system of law and government.

That plan of education, which will produce, or promote, or preserve such a system, is, consequently, an object to you peculiarly important.

But if you would see such a plan carried into complete effect, you must, my amiable hearers, give it your powerful assistance. The pleasing task of forming your daughters is almost solely yours. In my plan of education for your sons, I must solicit you to cooperate. Their virtues, in a certain proportion—the refinement of their virtues, in a much greater proportion, must be moulded on your example.

In your sex, too, there is a natural, an easy, and, often, a pure flow of diction, which lays the best foundation for that eloquence, which, in a free country, is so important to ours.

The style of some of the finest orators of antiquity was originally formed on that of their mothers, or of other ladies, to whose acquaintance they had the honour of being introduced.

I have already mentioned the two Scevolae among the illustrious Roman characters. One of them was married to Laelia,[19] a lady, whose virtues and accomplishments rendered her one of the principal ornaments of Rome. She possessed the elegance of language in so eminent a degree, that the first speakers of the age were ambitious of her company. The graces of her unstudied elocution were the purest model, by which they could refine their own.

Cicero was in the number of those, who improved by the privilege of her conversation. In his writings, he speaks in terms of the warmest praise concerning her singular talents. He mentions also the conversation of her daughters and grand daughters, as deserving particular notice.

The province of early education by the female sex, was deemed, in Rome, an employment of so much dignity, that ladies of the first rank did not disdain it. We find the names of Aurelia[20] and Attia,[21] the mothers of

19. Likely refers to Laelia, the daughter of C. Laelius Sapiens, Roman consul in 140 B.C.
20. Aurelia Cotra (120–54 B.C.) was the mother of Julius Caesar.
21. Atia Balba Caesar (85–43 B.C.) was the mother of Augustus.

Julius Caesar[22] and of Augustus,[23] enumerated in the list of these honourable patronesses of education.

The example of the highly accomplished Cornelia,[24] the daughter of the great Africanus,[25] and the mother of the Gracchi,[26] deserves uncommon attention. She shone, with singular lustre, in all those endowments and virtues that can dignify the female character.

She was, one day, visited by a lady of Campania, who was extremely fond of dress and ornament. This lady, after having displayed some very rich jewels of her own, expressed a wish to be favoured with the view of those which Cornelia had; expecting to see some very superb ones, in the toilet of a lady of such distinguished birth and character. Cornelia diverted the conversation, till her sons came into the room: "These are my jewels," said she, presenting them to the Campanian lady.

Cicero had seen her letters: his expressions concerning them are very remarkable. "I have read," says he, "the letters of Cornelia, the mother of the Gracchi; and it appears, that her sons were not so much nourished by the milk, as formed by the style of their mother."[n]

You see now, my fair and amiable hearers, how deeply and nearly interested you are in a proper plan of law education. By some of you, whom I know to be well qualified for taking in it the share, which I have described, that share will be taken. By the younger part of you, the good effects of such a plan will, I hope, be participated: for those of my pupils, who themselves shall become most estimable, will treat you with the highest degree of estimation.

22. Gaius Julius Caesar (100–44 B.C.) was the Roman military and political leader who overthrew the Roman Republic and instituted the Roman Empire.

23. Gaius Julius Caesar Octavianus, known as Augustus after 27 B.C., (63 B.C.–A.D. 14) was Roman Emperor from 27 B.C. to A.D. 14.

24. Cornelia Africana (c. 190–100 B.C.) was a Roman woman of high esteem and education who, upon the death of her husband, refused many offers of marriage and devoted her time to the education of her children, the Gracchi.

25. Publius Corneluis Scipio Africanus (235–183 B.C.), the elder, was a great Roman general who defeated Hannibal.

26. Tiberius Sempronius Gracchus (163–133 B.C.) and Gaius Sempronius Gracchus (153–121 B.C.) were sons of Cornelia and Tiberius Sempronius Gracchus. The Gracchi were enormously popular among the common people, pushed for egalitarian reforms, and were subsequently hated by the aristocracy of Rome. They both met tragic ends.

n. Legimus epistolas Corneliae, matris Gracchorum: apparet filios non tam in gremio educatos, quam in sermone matris. Cic. declar. orat. c. 58.

PLAN.

Gentlemen,

Permit me, at this time, to address, in a very few words, the younger and more inexperienced part of those who attend my lectures—I say the younger and more inexperienced part; because my lectures are honoured with the presence of some, whose learning, talents, and experience fit them for communicating instead of receiving instruction here. For the honour of their presence, I must consider myself indebted to the importance of my subject; and to a desire, generous and enlightened, of countenancing and encouraging every attempt, however feeble, to diffuse knowledge on a subject so important.

You have seen, my young friends, in what a high point of view I consider your education. Is this on your own account? Partly it is—that you may be great and good men. But solely it is not; for more extended hopes are entertained concerning you: you are designated by your education, and by your country, to be great and good citizens.

In no other part of the world, and in no former period, even in this part of it, have youth ever beheld so glorious and so sublime a prospect before them. Your country is already respectable for its numbers; it is free; it is enlightened; it is flourishing; it is happy: in numbers; in liberty; in knowledge; in prosperity; in happiness it is receiving great and rapid accessions. Its honours are already beginning to bud: in a few years, they will "blossom thick" upon you. You ought certainly, by proper culture, to qualify yourselves in such a manner, that when the blossoms fade and fall, the fruit may begin to appear. Remember that, in a free government, every honour implies a trust; that every trust implies a duty; and that every duty ought to be performed.

I mean not, that such of you as are designed for the practice of the law, should be inattentive to the emoluments of your profession; but I mean that you should consider it as something higher than a mere instrument of private gain. By being fitted for higher purposes, it will not be less fit, it will be more fit for accomplishing this.

It is peculiarly necessary, that you should, as soon as possible, form proper conceptions of what ought to be your objects in your course of study. Let them not be fixed too low: the higher your aims, the higher your attainments will be. To assist you in fixing those aims, let me lay before you the sentiments of a writer, who wrote on some subjects most excellently, and on others most contemptibly—I mean Lord Bolingbroke. When he wrote on politicks or business, he wrote well; because he wrote on what he knew: when he wrote concerning religion, he wrote ill; because he wrote concerning that, of which he was ignorant. The passage, I am about to quote to you is vouched by the respectable authority of Lord Kaims,[27] who considered it, and justly, as a master piece of expression and thought.

"I might instance," says he, "in other professions, the obligations men lie under of applying themselves to certain parts of history; and I can hardly forbear doing it in that of the law, in its nature, the noblest and most beneficial to mankind, in its abuse and debasement, the most sordid and the most pernicious. A lawyer now is nothing more, I speak of ninety nine in a hundred at least" (the proportion in this country, I believe, is much smaller) "to use some of Tully's[28] words, 'nisi liguleius quidam cautus, et acutus praeco actionum, cantor formularum, auceps syllabarum:'[29] but there have been lawyers that were orators, philosophers, historians: there have been Bacons and Clarendons. There will be none such any more, till, in some better age" (I hope that better age has found you, my young friends) "true ambition or the love of fame prevail over avarice; and till men find leisure and encouragement for the exercise of this profession, by climbing up to the vantage ground, so my Lord Bacon calls it, of science,[o] instead of groveling all their lives below, in a mean but gainful application to all the little arts of chicane. Till this happen, the profession

27. Lord Henry Home Kames (or Kaims) (1696–1782) was a Scottish jurist, philosopher, and author.

28. Tully is another name of Cicero, derived from his proper name, Marcus Tullius Cicero.

29. Wilson paraphrased a statement by Cicero which may be translated "A lawyer is of himself nothing except a kind of cautious and cunning pettifogger, a mere announcer of cases, a reciter of procedures, a bird-catcher for syllables." *De Oratore,* 1.16–20.

o. It is not possible to discover the more remote, and deeper parts of any science, if you stand but upon the level of the same science, and ascend not to a higher science. 2. Ld. Bac. 432.

of law will scarce deserve to be ranked among the learned professions: and whenever it happens, one of the vantage grounds, to which men must climb, is metaphysical, and the other, historical knowledge." By metaphysical knowledge, his lordship evidently means the philosophy of the human mind; for he goes on in this manner. "They must pry into the secret recesses of the human heart, and become well acquainted with the whole moral world, that they may discover the abstract reason of all laws: and they must trace the laws of particular states, especially of their own, from the first rough sketches to the more perfect draughts; from the first causes or occasions that produced them, through all the effects, good and bad, that they produced."[p]

Such, my young friends, are the great prospects before you; and such is the general outline of those studies, by which you will be prepared to realize them. Suffer me to recommend most earnestly this outline to the utmost degree of your attention. It comes to you supported with all the countenance and authority of Bacon, Bolingbroke, Kaims—two of them consummate in the practice, as well as in the knowledge of the law—all of them eminent judges of men, of business, and of literature; and all distinguished by the accomplishments of an active, as well as those of a contemplative life. The propriety, the force, and the application of their sentiments will be gradually unfolded, fully explained, and warmly urged to you in the course of my lectures.

It is by no means an easy matter to form, to digest, and to arrange a plan of lectures, on a subject so various and so extensive as that of law. With great deference to some of you, with anxious zeal for the information of others, I lay before you the following analysis: reserving, however, to myself, the full right and force of the protestation, which I have already borrowed from Sir Henry Spelman, of adding, retracting, correcting, and polishing, as, on more mature consideration, shall appear to me to be expedient.[q]

I begin with the general principles of law and obligation. These I shall investigate fully and minutely; because they are the basis of every legal system; and because they have been much misrepresented, or much misunderstood.

p. Boling. of the Study of History. let. 5. p. 149.

q. Some alterations, as the reader will observe, were afterwards made in the plan; but they are neither numerous nor important and need not be here particularized. *Ed.*

Next, I shall proceed to give you a concise and very general view of the law of nature, of the law of nations, and of municipal law.

I shall then consider man, who is the subject of all, and is the author as well as the subject of the last, and part of the second of these species of law. This great title of my plan, dignified and interesting as it is, must be treated in a very cursory manner in this course. I will, however, select some of the great truths which seem best adapted to a system of law. I will view man as an individual, as a member of society, as a member of a confederation, and as a part of the great commonwealth of nations.

His situation, under the third relation, is, in a great measure, new; and, to an American, peculiarly important: It will, therefore, merit and obtain peculiar attention.

The proper discussion of this title will draw on a discussion of the law of nations, under an aspect, almost wholly new. How far, on the principles of the confederation, does the law of nations become the municipal law of the United States? The greatness of this question is selfevident: it would be very unwise, at present, even to hint at an answer.

After having examined these important preparatory topicks, I shall trace the causes, the origin, the progress, the history, the kinds, the parts, and the properties of government.

Under this title, I shall have occasion to treat concerning legislative, executive, and judicial power; and to investigate and compare the simple and the mixt species of governments and constitutions—one, particularly, that is simple in its principle, though diversified in its form and operations.

This will lead me to a particular examination of the constitution and government of the United States, of Pennsylvania, and of her sister commonwealths.

By this time, we shall be qualified to enter, with proper advantage, upon the illustration of the different parts of our municipal law. The common law is the first great object, which will here present itself. I shall think it my duty to investigate very carefully its principles, its nature, and its history; particularly the great event of its transmigration from Europe to America; and the subsequent juridical history of the American States.

Our municipal law, I shall consider under two great divisions. Under the first, I shall treat of the law, as it relates to persons: under the second, I shall treat of it, as it relates to things.

The division of the United States into circuits, districts, states, counties, and townships will, probably, be introduced here, with some remarks concerning the causes, the operation, and the consequences of those divisions.

In considering the law as it relates to persons, the legislative department of the United States will occupy the first place; the executive department, the second; and the judicial department, the third.

Under the first, the institution and powers of congress will come into view. The principles on which the senate and house of representatives are separately established, will be carefully discriminated; and the necessary remarks will be made on the great doctrine of representation. The importance and the manner of legislation will also claim a portion of our regard.

In considering the executive authority of the United States, the appointment, the powers, and the duties of the president, will first attract our notice. We will then proceed to consider the number and the nature of the subordinate executive departments. We shall here have an opportunity of taking a very general view of the civil, commercial, fiscal, maritime, and military establishments of the United States.

When we come to the judicial department, our attention will be first drawn to the supreme court of the United States. Its establishment and its jurisdiction will be particularly considered; as also the establishment and jurisdiction of the circuit and district courts.

Here the nature, the history, and the jurisdiction of courts in general; and the powers and duties of judges, juries, sheriffs, coroners, counsellors, and attornies will be naturally introduced.

Perhaps this may be the proper place, likewise, for some general observations on the nature and philosophy of evidence; a proper system of which is the greatest desideratum in the law.

The investigation of the different parts of the constitution and government of the United States, will lay the foundation of a very interesting parallel between them and the pride of Europe—the British constitution.

If the consideration of the legislative, executive, and judicial departments of the sister states can, without intricacy or confusion, be severally arranged under the three corresponding articles in the constitution of the United States; the parts of my plan will be considerably reduced in their number. I hope, but I am not confident, that this can be done. Upon this, as upon every other part of my plan, I shall be thankful for advice.

Bodies politick and inferiour societies will be described and distinguished.

The relations of private and of domestick life will pass in review before us; and after these, the rights and duties of citizens will come under consideration.

Here the important principles of election will receive the merited attention.

The rights, privileges, and disabilities of aliens will then be examined.

Happy would it be, if the great division of the law, which relates to persons, could be closed here. But it cannot be done. We are under the sad necessity of viewing law as sometimes violated, and man as sometimes guilty. Hence the ungracious doctrine of punishment and crimes.

I will introduce this disagreeable part of my system with general observations concerning the nature of crimes, and the necessity and the proportion of punishments: next, I will descend into a particular enumeration and description of each: and I will afterwards point out the different steps prescribed by the law for apprehending, detaining, trying, and punishing offenders.

Here warrants, arrests, attachments, bail, commitments, imprisonment, appeals, informations, indictments, presentments, process, arraignments, pleas, trials, verdicts, judgments, attainders, pardons, forfeitures, corruption of blood, and executions will be considered.

With regard to criminal law, this observation may be made even in a summary: it greatly needs reformation. In the United States, the seeds of reformation are sown.

As to the second great division of our municipal law, which relates to things; it may be all comprehended under one word—property. Claims, it is true, may arise from a variety of sources, almost infinite: but the declaration of every claim concludes by alleging a damage or a demand; and the decision of every successful claim concludes by awarding a satisfaction or a restitution in property.

I shall trace the history of property from its lowest rude beginnings to its highest artificial refinements; and, by that means, shall have an opportunity of pointing out the defects of the first, and the excesses of the last.

Property is of two kinds; publick and private. Under publick property, common highways, common bridges, common rivers, common ports are included. In the United States, and in the states composing the Union, there is much land belonging to the publick.

Private property is divided into two kinds; personal and real: things moveable are comprehended under the first division: things immoveable, under the second.

Estates in real property are measured by their duration. An estate of the greatest duration, is that which is in fee, or "to a man and his heirs," in the language of the common law. Real property of shorter duration is known by the names of estates tail, estates in tail after possibility of issue extinct, estates by the curtesy of England, estates in dower, estates for life, estates for years, estates by sufferance, and estates at will.

Estates may be either absolute or conditional. Under the title of conditional estates, the excellent law of Pennsylvania with regard to mortgages will deserve particular consideration.

Estates may be in possession or in expectancy. Under the last head, reversions, remainders, vested and contingent, and executory devises will be treated.

Property may be joint or cotemporary, as well as separate and successive. Here we will treat concerning coparceners, partners, joint tenants, and tenants in common.

Property may be acquired by occupancy, conveyance, descent, succession, will, custom, forfeiture, judgment in a court of justice. In much the greatest number of instances, the acquisition of property by one is accompanied with the transfer of it by another.

Conveyances are by matter of record; as a fine, a common recovery, a deed enrolled: or by matter in pais; as livery, deed: here the nature and different kinds of deeds, at common law, and by virtue of statutes, will be particularly considered.

Property may consist of things in possession, or of things in action.

Land, money, cattle, are instances of the first kind; debts, rights of damages, and rights of action are instances of the second kind.

These are prosecuted by suit.

You have heard much concerning the forms of process, and proceedings, and pleadings. Much has been written in praise, and much has been written in ridicule, of this part of law learning. It has certainly been abused: in some hands, it has become, and daily does become ridiculous. And what is there that has been exempted from a similar fate! religion herself, elegant and simple as she is, yet, when dressed in the tawdry or tattered robes put upon her by the false taste of her injudicious friends, assumes an awkward and ridiculous appearance.

Law has experienced the same treatment with her elder sister. But though the learning with regard to pleas and pleading has been abused, it may certainly be employed for the most excellent purposes.

When properly directed and properly used, the science of well pleading is, indeed, in the language of Littleton, "one of the most honourable, laudable, and profitable things in our law."[r] Let me also adduce, in its favour, the weighty testimony of Earl Mansfield.[s] "The substantial rules of pleading," says this very able judge, "are founded in strong sense, and in the soundest and closest logick; and so appear when well understood and explained: though, by being misunderstood and misapplied, they are too often made use of as the instruments of chicane."

Permit me to add, that some of the forms of writs and pleas, particularly those that are most ancient, are models of correct composition, as well as of just sentiment.

The history of a suit at law, from its commencement, through all the different steps of its progress, to its conclusion, presents an object very interesting to a mind sensible to the beauty of strict and accurate arrangement. The dispositions of the drama are not made with more exactness and art. Every thing is done by the proper persons, at the proper time, in the proper place, in the proper order, and in the proper form.

This history may be comprised under the following titles—original writ, process, return, appearance—in person, by guardian, by next friend, by attorney—bail, declaration, profert, oyer, imparlance, continuance, pleas—in abatement and bar—replication, rejoinder, issue, demurrer, trial, demurrer to evidence, bill of exceptions, verdict, new trial, judgment, appeal, writ of error, execution.

r. Litt. s. 534.
s. 1. Burr. 319.

CHAPTER II.
Of the General Principles of Law and Obligation.

Order, proportion, and fitness pervade the universe. Around us, we see; within us, we feel; above us, we admire a rule, from which a deviation cannot, or should not, or will not be made.

On the inanimate part of the creation, are impressed the continued energies of motion and of attraction, and other energies, varied and yet uniform, all designated and ascertained. Animated nature is under a government suited to every genus, to every species, and to every individual, of which it consists. Man, the *nexus utriusque mundi,*[1] composed of a body and a soul, possessed of faculties intellectual and moral, finds or makes a system of regulations, by which his various and important nature, in every period of his existence, and in every situation, in which he can be placed, may be preserved, improved, and perfected. The celestial as well as the terrestrial world knows its exalted but prescribed course. This angels and the spirits of the just, made perfect, do "clearly behold, and without any swerving observe." Let humble reverence attend us as we proceed. The great and incomprehensible Author, and Preserver, and Ruler of all things—he himself works not without an eternal decree.

Such—and so universal is law. "Her seat," to use the sublime language of the excellent Hooker,[t2] "is the bosom of God; her voice, the harmony of the world; all things in heaven and earth do her homage; the very least as feeling her care, and the greatest as not exempted from her power. Angels and men, creatures of every condition, though each in different sort and

1. Meeting place between both worlds.

t. Hooker 34.

2. Richard Hooker (1554–1600) was an English theologian and author, who wrote the *Of the Laws of Ecclesiastical Policy.*

manner, yet all with uniform consent, admiring her as the mother of their peace and joy."

Before we descend to the consideration of the several kinds and parts of this science, so dignified and so diversified, it will be proper, and it will be useful, to contemplate it in one general and comprehensive view; and to select some of its leading and luminous properties, which will serve to guide and enlighten us in that long and arduous journey, which we now undertake.

It may, perhaps, be expected, that I should begin with a regular definition of law. I am not insensible of the use, but, at the same time, I am not insensible of the abuse of definitions. In their very nature, they are not calculated to extend the acquisition of knowledge, though they may be well fitted to ascertain and guard the limits of that knowledge, which is already acquired. By definitions, if made with accuracy—and consummate accuracy ought to be their indispensable characteristick—ambiguities in expression, and different meanings of the same term, the most plentiful sources of errour and of fallacy in the reasoning art, may be prevented; or, if that cannot be done, may be detected. But, on the other hand, they may be carried too far, and, unless restrained by the severest discipline, they may produce much confusion and mischief in the very stations, which they are placed to defend.

You have heard much of the celebrated distribution of things into genera and species. On that distribution, Aristotle undertook the arduous task of resolving all reasoning into its primary elements; and he erected, or thought he erected, on a single axiom, a larger system of abstract truths, than were before invented or perfected by any other philosopher. The axiom, from which he sets out, and in which the whole terminates, is, that whatever is predicated of a genus, may be predicated of every species contained under that genus, and of every individual contained under every such species.[u] On that distribution likewise, the very essence of scientifick definition depends: for a definition, strictly and logically regular, "must express the genus of the thing defined, and the specifick difference, by which that thing is distinguished from every other species belonging to that genus."[v]

u. 1. Gill. (4to.) 690.
v. Reid's Ess. Int. 10. 11.

From this definition of a definition—if I may be pardoned for the apparent play upon the word—it evidently appears that nothing can be defined, which does not denote a species; because that only, which denotes a species, can have a specifick difference.

But further: a specifick difference may, in fact, exist; and yet language may furnish us with no words to express it. Blue is a species of colour; but how shall we express the specifick difference, by which blue is distinguished from green?

Again: expressions, which signify things simple, and void of all composition, are, from the very force of the terms, unsusceptible of definition. It was one of the capital defects of Aristotle's philosophy, that he attempted and pretended to define the simplest things.

Here it may be worth while to note a difference between our own abstract notions, and objects of nature. The former are the productions of our own minds; we can therefore define and divide them, and distinctly designate their limits. But the latter run so much into one another, and their essences, which discriminate them, are so subtile and latent, that it is always difficult often impossible, to define or divide them with the necessary precision. We are in danger of circumscribing nature within the bounds of our own notions, formed, frequently, on a partial or defective view of the object before us. Fettered thus at our outset, we are restrained in our progress, and govern the course of our inquiries, not by the extent or variety of our subject, but by our own preconceived apprehensions concerning it.

This distinction between the objects of nature and our own abstract notions suggests a practical inference. Definitions and divisions in municipal law, the creature of man, may be more useful, because more adequate and more correct, than in natural objects.

By some philosophers, definition and division are considered as the two great nerves of science. But unless they are marked by the purest precision, the fullest comprehension, and the most chastised justness of thought, they will perplex, instead of unfolding—they will darken, instead of illustrating, what is meant to be divided or defined. A defect or inaccuracy, much more an impropriety, in a definition or division, more especially of a first principle, will spread confusion, distraction, and contradictions over the remotest parts of the most extended system.

Errours in science, as well as in life, proceed more frequently from wrong principles, than from ill drawn consequences. *Prava regula prima*[3] may be the parent of the most fatal enormities.

The higher an edifice is raised, the more compactly it is built, the more precisely it is carried up in a just direction—in proportion to all these excellencies, a rent in the foundation will increase and become dangerous.

The case is the same with a radical errour at the foundation of a system. The more accurately and the more ingeniously men reason, and the farther they pursue their reasonings, from false principles, the more numerous and the more inveterate will their inconsistencies, nay, their absurdities be. One advantage, however, will result—those absurdities and those inconsistencies will be more easily traced to their proper source. When the string of a musical instrument has a fault only in one place, you know immediately how and where to find and correct it.

Influenced by these admonitory truths, I hesitate, at present, to give a definition of law. My hesitation is increased by the fate of the far greatest number of those, who have hitherto attempted it. Many, as it is natural to suppose, and laboured have been the efforts to infold law within this scientifick circle; but little satisfaction—little instruction has been the result. Almost every writer, sensible of the defects, the inaccuracies, or the improprieties of the definitions that have gone before him, has endeavoured to supply their place with something, in his own opinion, more proper, more accurate, and more complete. He has been treated by his successours, as his predecessors have been treated by him: and his definition has had only the effect of adding one more to the lengthy languid list. This I know, because I have taken the trouble to read them in great numbers; but because I have taken the trouble to read them, I will spare you the trouble of hearing them—at least, the greatest part of them.

Some of them, indeed, have a claim to attention: one, in particular, will demand it, for reasons striking and powerful—I mean that given by the Commentator on the laws of England.

Let us proceed carefully, patiently, and minutely to examine it. If I am not deceived, the examination will richly compensate all the time, and trouble, and investigation, that will be allotted to it; for it will be

3. Deformed first principles.

uncommonly fruitful in the principles, and in the consequences of the great truths and important disquisitions, which it will lead in review before us.

"Law," says he, "in its most general and comprehensive sense, signifies a rule of action."[w] In its proper signification, a rule is an instrument; by which a right line—the shortest and truest of all—may be drawn from one point to another. In its moral or figurative sense, it denotes a principle or power, that directs a man surely and concisely to attain the end, which he proposes.

Law is called a rule, in order to distinguish it from a[x] sudden, a transient, or a particular order: uniformity, permanency, stability, characterize a law.

Again; law is called a rule, to denote that it carries along with it a power and principle of obligation. Concerning the nature and the cause of obligation, much ingenious disputation has been held by philosophers and writers on jurisprudence. Indeed the sentiments entertained concerning it have been so various, that an account of them would, in the estimation of my Lord Kaims, be a "delicate historical morsel."

This interesting subject will claim and obtain our attention, next after what we have to say concerning law in general.

When we speak of a rule with regard to human conduct, we imply two things. 1. That we are susceptible of direction. 2. That, in our conduct, we propose an end. The brute creation act not from design. They eat, they drink, they retreat from the inclemencies of the weather, without considering what their actions will ultimately produce. But we have faculties, which enable us to trace the connexion between actions and their effects; and our actions are nothing else but the steps which we take, or the means which we employ, to carry into execution the effects which we intend.

Hooker, I think, conveys a fuller and stronger conception of law, when he tells us, that "it assigns unto each thing the kind, that it moderates the force and power, that it appoints the form and measure of working."[y] Not the direction merely, but the kind also, the energy; and the proportion of actions is suggested in this description.

w. 1. Bl. Com. 38.
x. 1. Bl. Com. 44.
y. Hooker 1. 2.

Some are of opinion, that law should be defined[z] "a rule of acting or not acting;" because actions may be forbidden as well as commanded. But the same excellent writer, whom I have just now cited, gives a very proper answer to this opinion, and shows the addition to be unnecessary, by finely pursuing the metaphor, which we have already mentioned. "We must not suppose that there needeth one rule to know the good, and another to know the evil by. For he that knoweth what is straight, doth even thereby discern what is crooked. Goodness in actions is like unto straightness; wherefore that which is well done, we term right."[a]

After this dry description of the literal and metaphorical meaning of a rule, permit me to relax your strained attention by a critical remark. In the philosophy of the human mind, it is impossible altogether to avoid metaphorical expressions. Our first and most familiar notions are suggested by material objects; and we cannot speak intelligibly of those that are immaterial, without continual allusions to matter and the qualities of matter.

Besides, in teaching moral science, the use of metaphors is not only necessary, but, if prudent, and honest, and guarded, it is highly advantageous. Nature has endowed us with the faculty of imagination, that we may be enabled to throw warming as well as enlightening rays upon truth—to embellish, to recommend, and to enforce it. Truth may, indeed, by reasoning, be rendered evident to the understanding; but it cannot reach the heart, unless by means of the imagination. To the imagination metaphors are addressed.

From this short excursion into the field of criticism, let us return to our legal tract. Law is a rule "prescribed." A simple resolution, confined within the bosom of the legislator, without being notified, in some fit manner, to those for whose conduct it is to form a rule, can never, with propriety, be termed a law.

There are many ways by which laws may be made sufficiently known. They may be printed and published. Written copies of them may be deposited in publick libraries, or other places, where every one interested may have an opportunity of perusing them. They may be proclaimed in general meetings of the people. The knowledge of them may be disseminated by

z. Daws. Orig. Laws, 4. 14.
a. Hooker 11.

long and universal practice. "Confirmed custom," says a writer on Roman jurisprudence, "is deservedly considered as a law. For since written laws bind us for no other reason than because they are received by the judgment of the people; those laws, which the people have approved, without writing, are also justly obligatory on all. For where is the difference, whether the people declare their will by their suffrage, or by their conduct? This kind of law is said to be established by[b] manners."[c]

Of all yet suggested, the mode for the promulgation of human laws by custom seems the most significant, and the most effectual. It involves in it internal evidence, of the strongest kind, that the law has been introduced by common *consent;* and that this consent rests upon the most solid basis—experience as well as opinion. This mode of promulgation points to the strongest characteristick of liberty, as well as of law. For a consent thus practically given, must have been given in the freest and most unbiassed manner.

With pleasure you anticipate the prospect of a species of law, to which these remarks have already directed your attention. If it were asked—and it would be no improper question—who of all the makers and teachers of law have formed and drawn after them the most, the best, and the most willing disciples; it might be not untruly answered—custom.

Laws may be promulgated by reason and conscience, the divine monitors within us. They are thus known as effectually, as by words or by writing: indeed they are thus known in a manner more noble and exalted. For, in this manner, they may be said to be engraven by God on the hearts of men: in this manner, he is the promulgator as well as the author of natural law.

If a simple resolution cannot have the force of a law before it be promulgated; we may certainly hazard the position—that it cannot have the force of a law, before it be made: in other words, that *ex post facto* instruments, claiming the title and character of laws, are impostors.

Peculiarly striking, upon, this subject, are the sentiments of the criminal and unfortunate Strafford.[4] I call him criminal, because he acted; I

b. D. l. 1. t. 3. 32. p. 1.

c. The first written laws in Greece were given only six centuries before the Christian era.—1. Gill. 7. (4to.)

4. Most likely refers to Thomas Wentworth, the first Earl of Strafford (1593–1641) and a most capable statesman, who vigorously supported Charles I through his struggles with Parliament. Parliament passed a bill of attainder requiring his execution even though he was not convicted of a Capital crime.

call him unfortunate, because he suffered, against the laws of his country. His sentiments must make a deep impression upon others: because, when he spoke them, he must have been deeply impressed with them himself. When he spoke them, he stood under a bill of attainder, suspended only by the slender thread of political justice, and ready, like the sword of Damocles,[5] to fall on his devoted head. "Do we not live by laws? And must we be punished by laws before they are made? Far better were it to live by no laws at all, than to put this necessity of divination upon a man, and to accuse him of the breach of a law, before it be a law at all."[d]

In criminal jurisprudence, a Janus statute,[6] with one face looking backward, and another looking forward, is a monster indeed.

The definition of law in the Commentaries proceeds in this manner. "Law is that rule of action, which is prescribed by some superiour, and which the inferiour is bound to obey." A superiour! Let us make a solemn pause—Can there be *no* law without a superiour? Is it *essential* to law, that inferiority should be involved in the obligation to obey it? Are these distinctions at the root of *all* legislation?

There is a law, indeed, which flows from the Supreme of being—a law, more distinguished by the goodness, than by the power of its allgracious Author. But there are laws also that are human; and does it follow, that, in these, a character of superiority is inseparably attached to him, who makes them; and that a character of inferiority is, in the same manner, inseparably attached to him, for whom they are made? What is this superiority? Who is this superiour? By whom is he constituted? Whence is his superiority derived? Does it flow from a source that is human? Or does it flow from a source that is divine?

From a human source it cannot flow; for no stream issuing from thence can rise higher than the fountain.

5. Damocles was a courtier of Dionysius II of Syracuse; he remarked that the king must be content and happy because of the power and authority he enjoyed. Dionysius offered to exchange places with Damocles for one day. He did so, and at the end of the day a banquet was held. At the end of the meal Damocles looked up to see a sword dangling above his head held by the strength of one horsehair. The sword of Damocles represents the perilous position of those with great power.

d. Whitlocke 230.

6. Janus is the Roman god of doorways and of beginnings and endings. In this case, Janus is referenced because a doorway faces both forward and backward.

If the prince, who makes laws for a people, is superiour, in the terms of the definition, to the people, who are to obey; how comes he to be vested with the superiority over them?

If I mistake not, this notion of superiority, which is introduced as an *essential* part in the definition of a law—for we are told that a law *always*[e] supposes some superiour, who is to make it—this notion of superiority contains the germ of the divine right—a prerogative impiously attempted to be established—of princes, arbitrarily to rule; and of the corresponding obligation—a servitude tyrannically attempted to be imposed—on the people, implicitly to obey.

Despotism, by an artful use of "superiority" in politicks; and scepticism, by an artful use of "ideas" in metaphysicks, have endeavoured—and their endeavours have frequently been attended with too much success—to destroy all true liberty and sound philosophy. By their baneful effects, the science of man and the science of government have been poisoned to their very fountains. But those destroyers of others have met, or must meet, with their own destruction.

We now see, how necessary it is to lay the foundations of knowledge deep and solid. If we wish to build upon the foundations laid by another, we see how necessary it is cautiously and minutely to examine them. If they are unsound, we see how necessary it is to remove them, however venerable they may have become by reputation; whatever regard may have been diffused over them by those who laid them, by those who built on them, and by those who have supported them.

But was Sir William Blackstone a votary of despotick power? I am far from asserting that he was. I am equally far from believing that Mr. Locke was a friend to infidelity. But yet it is unquestionable, that the writings of Mr. Locke have facilitated the progress, and have given strength to the effects of scepticism.

The high reputation, which he deservedly acquired for his enlightened attachment to the mild and tolerating doctrines of christianity, secured to him the esteem and confidence of those, who were its friends. The same high and deserved reputation inspired others of very different views and characters, with a design to avail themselves of its splendour, and, by that

e. 1. Bl. Com. 43.

means, to diffuse a fascinating kind of lustre over their own tenets of a dark and sable hue. The consequence has been, that the writings of Mr. Locke, one of the most able, most sincere, and most amiable assertors of christianity and true philosophy, have been perverted to purposes, which he would have deprecated and prevented, had he discovered or foreseen them.

Berkeley, the celebrated bishop of Cloyne,[7] wrote his Principles of human Knowledge—a book intended to disprove the existence of matter—with the express view of banishing scepticism both from science and from religion. He was even sanguine in his expectations of success. But the event has proved that he was egregiously mistaken; for it is evident, from the use to which later authors have applied it, that his system leads directly to universal scepticism.

Similar, though in an inferiour degree, have been, and may be, the fate and the influence of the writings and character of Sir William Blackstone; even admitting that he was as much a friend to liberty, as Locke and Berkeley were friends to religion.

But in prosecuting the study of law on liberal principles and with generous views, our business is much less with the character of the Commentaries or of their author, than with the doctrines which they contain. If the doctrines, insinuated in the definition of law, can be supported on the principles of reason and science; the defence of other principles, which I have thought to be those of liberty and just government, becomes—I am sorry to say it—a fruitless attempt.

Sir William Blackstone, however, was not the first, nor has he been the last, who has defined law upon the same principles, or upon principles similar and equally dangerous.

This subject is of such radical importance, that it will be well worth while to trace it as far as our materials can carry us; for errour as well as truth should be examined historically, and pursued back to its original springs.

By comparing what is said in the Commentaries on this subject, with what is mentioned concerning it in the system of morality, jurisprudence, and politicks written by Baron Puffendorff, we shall be satisfied that, from the sentiments and opinions delivered in the last mentioned performance,

7. George Berkeley (1685–1753) was an Irish philosopher who advanced the theory of immaterialism.

those in the first mentioned one have been taken and adopted. "A law," says Puffendorff, "is the command of a superiour."[f] "A law," says Sir William Blackstone, "always supposes some superiour, who is to make it."[g]

The introduction of superiority, as a necessary part of the definition of law, is traced from Sir William Blackstone to Puffendorff. This definition of Puffendorff is substantially the same with that of Hobbes.[8] "A law is the command of him or them, that have the sovereign power, given to those that be his or their subjects."[h] It is substantially the same also with that of Bishop Saunderson.[9] "Law is a rule of action, imposed on a subject, by one who has power over him."[i]

Let us now inquire what is meant by superiority, that we may be able to ascertain and recognise those qualities, inherent or derivative, which entitle the superiour or sovereign to the transcendent power of imposing laws.

We can distinguish two kinds of superiority. 1. A superiority merely of power. 2. A superiority of power, accompanied with a right to exercise that power. Is the first sufficient to entitle its possessor to the character and office of a legislator? If we subscribe to the doctrines of Mr. Hobbes, we shall say, that it is. "To those," says he, "whose power is irresistible, the dominion of all men adhereth naturally, by their excellence of power."[k]

This position, strange as it is, has had its advocates in ancient as well as in modern times. Even the accomplished Athenians, who excluded it from their municipal code, seem to have considered it as part of the received law of nations. "We follow," says their ambassadour in the name of his commonwealth, "the common nature and genius of mankind, which appoints those to be masters, who are superiour in strength. We have not made this law; nor are we the first, who have appealed to it. We received it from antiquity: we are determined to transmit it to the most distant futurity: and we claim and use it in our own case."[l]

f. Puff. B. 1. c. 2. s. 6. p. 16. B. 1. c. 6. s. 1. 2. p. 56. 57.

g. 1. Bl. Com. 43.

8. Thomas Hobbes (1588–1679) was an English philosopher who is best known for his 1648 book *Leviathan.*

h. 3. Dagge 95. 96.

9. Robert Sanderson (1587–1663) was an English theologian and casuist. He was appointed Bishop of Lincoln in 1660.

i. Daws. Orig. L. 3. cites Saund. Prael. 5. s. 3.

k. De Cive 187. (Puff. 64.)

l. Puff. 65. (Thucyd. l. 5. c. 105) 1. Anac. 351.

Brennus,[10] at the head of his victorious and ferocious Gauls, with more conciseness, and with a less striking inconsistency of character, tells the vanquished Romans "omnia fortium esse."[m] Every thing belongs to the bold and the strong.

The prudent Plutarch thinks it "the first and principal law of nature, that he whose circumstances require protection and deliverance, should admit him for his ruler, who is able to protect and deliver him."[n]

For us, it is sufficient, as men, as citizens, and as states, to say, that power is nothing more than the right of the strongest, and may be opposed by the same right, by the same means, and by the same principles, which are employed to establish it. Bare force, far from producing an obligation to obey, produces an obligation to resist.

Others, unwilling to rest the office of legislation and the right of sovereignty simply on superiority of power, have to this quality superadded preeminence or superiour excellence of nature.

Let it be remembered all along, that I am examining the doctrine of superiority, as applied to human laws, the proper and immediate object of investigation in these lectures. Of the law that is divine, we shall have occasion, at another time, to speak, with the reverence and gratitude which become us.

"It is a law of nature," says Dionysius[11] of Halicarnassus, "common to all men, and which no time shall disannul or destroy, that those, who have more strength and *excellence,* shall bear rule over those, who have less."[o] The favourers of this opinion are unfortunate, both in the illustrations, by which they attempt to evince it; and in the inferences, to which they contend it gives rise.

Because Cicero, by a beautiful metaphor, describes the government of the other powers of the mind as assigned, by nature, to the understanding; does it follow that, in strict propriety of reasoning, the right of legislation is annexed, without any assignment, to superiour excellence?

10. Refers to the Brennus, a leader of the Celtic Gauls who sacked Rome in roughly 390 B.C. and uttered "Vae victus" (woe to the conquered).

m. Puff. 65. (Livy.)

n. Puff. 65. (Plut. in Pelop.)

11. Dionysius of Halicarnassus was a Greek historian and rhetor who lived during the reign of Augustus. His *Roman Antiquities* was one of the few accounts of early Roman history and covers the mythical period to the first Punic War.

o. Puff. 65. (Dion. Hal. b. 1. c. 5.)

Aristotle, it seems, has said, that if a man *could* be found, excelling in *all* virtues, such an one would have a *fair title* to be king. These words may well be understood as conveying, and probably were intended to convey, only this unquestionable truth—that excellence, in every virtue furnished the strongest recommendation, in favour of its happy possessor, *to be elected* for the exercise of authority. If so, the opinion of Aristotle is urged without a foundation properly laid in the fact.

But let us suppose the contrary: let us suppose it to be the judgment of Aristotle, that the person, whom he characterizes, derived his right to the exercise of power, not from the donation made to him by a voluntary election, but solely from his superiour talents and excellence; shall the judgment of Aristotle supersede inquiry into its reasonableness? Shall the judgment of Aristotle, if found, on inquiry, to be unreasonable, silence all reprehension or confutation? Decent respect for authority is favourable to science. Implicit confidence is its bane. Let us adopt—for it is necessary, in the cause of truth and freedom, that we should adopt—the manly expostulation, which the ardent pursuit of knowledge drew from the great Bacon—"Why should a few received authors stand up like Hercules's columns, beyond which there should be no sailing or discovery?"

To Aristotle, more than to any other writer, either ancient or modern, this expostulation is strictly applicable. Hear what the learned Grotius says on this subject. "Among philosophers, Aristotle deservedly holds the chief place, whether you consider his method of treating subjects, or the acuteness of his distinctions, or the weight of his reasons. I could only wish that the authority of this great man had not, for some ages past, degenerated into tyranny; so that truth, for the discovery of which Aristotle took so great pains, is now oppressed by nothing more than by the very name of Aristotle."[p]

Guided and supported by the sentiments and by the conduct of Grotius and Bacon, let us proceed, with freedom and candour combined, to examine the judgment—though I am very doubtful whether it was the judgment—of Aristotle, that the right of sovereignty is founded on superiour excellence.

p. Gro. Prel. 28.

To that superiority, which attaches the right to command, there must be a corresponding inferiority, which imposes the obligation to obey. Does this right and this obligation result from every kind and every degree of superiority in one, and from every kind and every degree of inferiority in another? How is excellence to be rated or ascertained?

Let us suppose three persons in three different grades of excellence. Is he in the lowest to receive the law immediately from him in the highest? Is he in the highest to give the law immediately to him in the lowest grade? Or is there to be a gradation of law as well as of excellence? Is the command of the first to the third to be conveyed through the medium of the second? Is the obedience of the third to be paid, through the same medium, to the first? Augment the number of grades, and you multiply the confusion of their intricate and endless consequences.

Is this a foundation sufficient for supporting the solid and durable superstructure of law? Shall this foundation, insufficient as it is, be laid in the contingency—allowed to be improbable, not asserted to be even possible—"if a man can be found, excelling in *all* virtues?"

Had it been the intention of Providence, that some men should govern the rest, without their consent, we should have seen as indisputable marks distinguishing these superiours from those placed under them, as those which distinguish men from the brutes. The remark of Rumbald,[12] in the nonresistance time of Charles the second, evinced propriety as well as wit. He could not conceive that the Almighty intended, that the greatest part of mankind should come into the world with saddles on their backs and bridles in their mouths, and that a few should come ready booted and spurred to ride the rest to death.[q] Still more apposite to our purpose is the saying of him, who declared that he would never subscribe the doctrine of the divine right of princes, till he beheld subjects born with bunches on their backs, like camels, and kings with combs on their heads, like cocks; from which striking marks it might indeed be collected, that the former were designed to labour and to suffer, and the latter, to strut and to crow.[r]

These pretensions to superiority, when viewed from the proper point of sight, appear, indeed, absurd and ridiculous. But these pretensions, absurd

12. Richard Rumbald (1622?–1685).

q. 1. Burgh. Pol. Dis. 3.

r. Boling. Rem. 209.

and ridiculous as they are, when rounded and gilded by flattery, and swallowed by pride, have become, in the breasts of princes, a deadly poison to their own virtues, and to the happiness of their unfortunate subjects. Those, who have been bred to be kings, have generally, by the prostituted views of their courtiers and instructors, been taught to esteem themselves a distinct and superiour species among men, in the same manner as men are a distinct and superiour species among animals.

Lewis the fourteenth was a strong instance of the effect of that inverted manner of teaching and thinking, which forms kings to be tyrants, without knowing or even suspecting that they are so. That oppression, under which he held his subjects, during the whole course of his long reign, proceeded chiefly from the principles and habits of his erroneous education. By this, he had been accustomed to consider his kingdom as his patrimony, and his power over his subjects as his rightful and undelegated inheritance. These sentiments were so deeply and strongly imprinted on his mind, that when one of his ministers represented to him the miserable condition to which those subjects were reduced, and, in the course of his representation, frequently used the word "l'etat," the state; the king, though he felt the truth, and approved the substance of all that was said, yet was shocked at the frequent repetition of the word "l'etat," and complained of it as an indecency offered to his person and character.

And, indeed, that kings should imagine themselves the final causes, for which men were made, and societies were formed, and governments were instituted, will cease to be a matter of wonder or surprise, when we find that lawyers, and statesmen, and philosophers have taught or favoured principles, which necessarily lead to the same conclusions.

Barbeyrac,[13] whose commentaries enrich the performances of the most distinguished philosophers, at one time, taught and favoured principles, which necessarily led to the conclusions, so degrading and so destructive to the human race. On this subject, it will be worth while to pursue his train of thought.

In the formation of societies and civil governments, three different con-

13. Jean Barbeyrac (1674–1744) was a French jurist whose fame chiefly lies with his preface and notes of his translation of Pufendorf's *The Duty of Man and Citizen According to Natural Law*. He also translated works by Grotius and Richard Cumberland.

ventions or agreements are supposed, by Puffendorff and many other writers, to have taken place. The first convention is an engagement, by those who compose the society or state, to associate together in one body; and to regulate, with one common consent, whatever regards their preservation, their security, their improvement, and their happiness. The second convention is, to specify the form of government, that shall be established among them. The third convention is an engagement between the following parties; that is to say, the person or persons, on whom the sovereignty, or superiority, or majesty—for it is called by all these names—is conferred, on one hand; and, on the other hand, those who have conferred this sovereignty, this superiority, this majesty; and are now, by that step, as it seems, become subjects. By this third convention, the sovereign engages to consult the common security and advantage of the subjects; and the subjects engage to observe fidelity and allegiance to the sovereign. From this last convention, the state is supposed to receive its final completion and perfection.

This account of the origin of society and government will be fully considered afterwards. I introduce it now, in order to show the force and import of Barbeyrac's observation concerning it. "The first convention," says he, "is only, with regard to the second, what scaffolding is with regard to the building, for whose construction it was erected."[s]

And is it so? Is society nothing more than a scaffolding, by the means of which government may be erected; and which, consequently, may be prostrated, as soon as the edifice of civil government is built? If this is so, it must have required but a small portion of courtly ingenuity to persuade Lewis the fourteenth, that, in a monarchy, government was nothing but a scaffolding for the king.

For the honour of Barbeyrac, however, let not this account be concluded, till it be told, that this did not continue to be always his sentiment; that, on consideration and reflection, this sentiment was changed; and that, when it was changed, he, as every other great and good man will do on similar occasions, freely and nobly retracted it. But although it has been retracted by Barbeyrac, it has neither been retracted nor abandoned by some others.

s. Puff. 641. note to b. 7. c. 2. s. 8.

To evince that I speak not without foundation, and to show, what will not be suspected till they are shown, the extravagant notions which have been entertained on this head, I will adduce a number of sentences and quotations, which Grotius[t] has collected together, in order to combat the sentiments of those, who hold that the supreme power is, always and without exception, in the people.

Historians and philosophers, poets and princes, bishops and fathers, are all summoned to oppose the dangerous doctrine.

When Tacitus says, "that, as we must bear with storms, barrenness, and the inconveniences of nature, so we must bear with the luxury or avarice of princes;" Grotius tells us, "'tis admirably said." Marcus Antoninus,[14] the philosopher, is produced as an authority, "that magistrates are to judge of private persons, princes of magistrates, but God alone of princes." King Vitigis[15] declares, that "what regards the royal power is to be judged by the powers above; because it is derived from heaven, and is accountable to heaven alone." Ireneus,[16] we are informed, says excellently, "by whose orders men are born, by his command kings are ordained." The same doctrine is contained in the constitutions of Clement. "You shall fear the king, knowing that he is chosen of God."

In a tragedy of Aeschylus, the suppliants use this language to the king. "Sir, you are the city and the publick; you are an independent judge. Seated upon your throne as upon an altar, you alone govern all by your absolute commands."

Here we have the very archetype of the idea of Lewis the fourteenth, sanctioned by the name of Grotius. If the king was the city and the publick; to mention "l'etat" in his presence, as something separate and distinct, was certainly an indecency; because it contained an implied though distant limitation of his power.

The reverend bishop of Tours[17] addresses the king of France in this very

t. Grotius 68–71.

14. Marcus Aurelius Antoninus (121–180) was Roman Emperor from 161 to 180. He was also a Stoic philosopher.

15. A Gothic king who reigned from 536 to 540.

16. St. Irenaeus (130–202) was an early Christian theologian who is recognized as the second bishop of what is now Lyons, France.

17. Possibly Gregory of Tours (c. 538–594).

remarkable manner: "If any of us, O king! should transgress the bounds of justice, he may be punished by you: but if you yourself should offend, who shall call you to account? When we make representations to you, if you please, you hear us: but if you will not, who shall condemn you? There is none but he, who has declared himself to be justice itself."

Let me also mention what Heineccius[18] says, in much more recent times, in his System of Universal Law. "The doctrine,[u] which makes the people superiour to the king or prince, and places in the former the real, and in the latter only personal majesty, is a most petulant one. It is the doctrine of Hottoman, Sidney,[19] Milton,[20] and others. Since a people, when they unite into a republick, renounce their own will, and subject themselves to the will of another, with what front can they call themselves superiour to their sovereign?"

And yet Heineccius himself allows, that "Grotius (1. 3. 8.) is thought by not a few, to have given some handle to the doctrine of passive obedience and nonresistance."

Indeed, the lawyers of almost all the states of Europe represent kings as legislators: and we know, that, in the dictionaries of many, legislative and unlimited power are synonimous terms. To unlimited power, the correlative is passive obedience.

Even Baron de Wolfius,[21] the late celebrated philosopher of Hall, lays down propositions concerning patrimonial kingdoms, without rejecting or contradicting a distinction, so injurious to the freedom and the rights of men.

Domat,[22] in his book on the civil law, derives the power of governours from *divine* authority. "It is always he (God) who places them in the seat of authority: it is from him alone that they derive all the power and au-

18. Johann Gottlieb Heineccius (1681–1741) was a German jurist who thought of law as a rational science rather than a system of explicit rules.

u. 2. Hein. 120. 121.

19. Algernon Sidney (1622–1683) was an English politician who sided with the Parliament during the English Civil War and penned the *Discourses on Government.* He was later executed on a charge of treason.

20. John Milton (1608–1674) was an English poet best known for *Paradise Lost* and his essay "Areopagitica" (1644).

21. Christian Wolff, or Wolfius (1679–1754), was a German philosopher.

22. Jean Domat (1625–1696) was a French jurist and author who published *Le Droit public,* a work that attempts to found law on religious or ethical principles.

thority that they have; and it is the ministry of his justice that is committed to them. And seeing it is God himself whom they represent, in the rank which raises them above others; he will have them to be considered as holding his place in their functions. And it is for this reason, that he himself gives the name of gods to those, to whom he communicates the right of governing and judging men."[v]

To diminish the force of the foregoing citations, it may be said, that, in all probability, Lewis the fourteenth—and the same may be said of other princes equally ignorant—never read the tragedies of Aeschylus, nor the history of Gregory of Tours.[23] It is highly probable that he never did: but it is equally probable, that their sentiments were known in his court, and found the way, through the channels of flattery, to the royal ear. But the writings of Grotius must have been well known in France, and probably to Lewis the fourteenth himself. This very book of the Rights of War and Peace was dedicated to his father, Lewis the thirteenth; and its author, we are told, had credit with some of the ministers of that prince.

Every plausible notion in favour of arbitrary power, appearing in a respectable dress, and introduced by an influential patron, is received with eagerness, protected with vigilance, and diffused with solicitude, by an arbitrary government. The consequence is, that, in such a government, political prejudices are last of all, if ever, overcome or eradicated.

But these doctrines, it may be replied, are not now believed, even in France. But they have been believed—they have been believed, even in France, to the slavery and misery of millions. And if, happily, they are not still believed there; unfortunately, they are still believed in other countries.

But I ask—why should they be believed at all? I ask further: if they are not, and ought not to be believed; why is their principle suffered to lie latent and lurking at the root of the science of law? Why is that principle continued a part of the very definition of law?

The pestilent seed may seem, at present, to have lost its vegetating power: but an unfriendly season and a rank soil may still revive it. It ought

v. 1. Domat XXII.

23. Gregory of Tours (c. 538–594) was a historian and the bishop of Tours. He wrote *The History of the Franks* and is the main source of contemporary knowledge of Merovingian history.

to be finally extirpated. It has, even within our own remembrance, done much real mischief. The position, that law is inseparably attached to superiour power, was the political weapon used, with the greatest force and the greatest skill, in favour of the despotick claims of Great Britain over the American colonies. Of this, the most striking proofs will appear hereafter. Let me, at present, adopt the sentiments expressed, on a similar subject, by Vattel. "If the base flatterers of despotick power rise up against my principles; I shall have, on my side, the friend of laws, the true citizen, and the virtuous man."[w]

Let us conclude our observations upon this hypothesis concerning the origin of sovereignty, by suggesting, that were it as solid as it is unsound in speculation, it would be wholly visionary and useless in practice. Where would minions and courtly flatterers find the objects, to which they could, even with courtly decency, ascribe superiour talents, superiour virtue, or a superiour nature, so as to entitle them, even on their own principles, to legislation and government?

We have now examined the inherent qualities, which have been alleged as sufficient to entitle, to the right and office of legislation, the superiour, whose interposition is considered as essential to a law. We have weighed them in the balance, and we have found them wanting.

If this superiour cannot rest a title on any inherent qualities; the qualities, which constitute his title, if any title he has, must be such as are derivative. If derivative; they must be derived either from a source that is human, or from a source that is divine. "Over a whole grand multitude," says the judicious[x] Hooker, "consisting of many families, impossible it is, that any should have complete lawful power, but by consent of men, or by immediate appointment of God." We will consider those sources separately.

How is this superiour constituted by *human* authority? How far does his superiority extend? Over whom is it exercised? Can any person or power, appointed by human authority, be superiour to those by whom he is appointed, and so form a necessary and essential part in the definition of a law?

w. Vattel Pref. 14.
x. Hooker. b. 1. s. 10. p. 18.

On these questions, a profound, I will not say a suspicious silence is observed. By the Author of the Commentaries, this superiour is announced in a very questionable shape. We can neither tell who he is, nor whence he comes. "When society is once formed, government results of course"—I use the words[y] of the Commentary—"as necessary to preserve and to keep that society in order. Unless some superiour be constituted, whose commands and decisions all the members are bound to obey, they would still remain as in a state of nature, without any judge upon earth to define their several rights, and redress their several wrongs. But as all the members of the society are naturally equal, it may be asked"—what question may be asked? The most natural question, that occurs to me, is—how is this superiour, without whom, there can be no law, without whom there can be no judge upon earth—how is this superiour to be constituted? This is the question, which, on this occasion, I would expect to see proposed: this is the question, to which I would expect to hear an answer. But how suddenly is the scene shifted! Instead of the awful insignia of superiority, to which our view was just now directed, the mild emblems of confidence make their appearance. The person announced was a dread superiour: but the person introduced is a humble trustee. For, to proceed, "it may be asked, in whose hands are the reins of government to be *intrusted?*"

I very well know how "a society once formed" constitute a trustee: but I am yet to learn, and the Commentator has not yet informed me, how this society can constitute their superiour. Locke somewhere says that "no one can confer more power on another, than he possesses himself."[z]

If the information, how a superiour is appointed, be given in any other part of the valuable Commentaries; it has escaped my notice, or my memory. Indeed it has been remarked by his successour in the chair of law, that Sir William Blackstone "declines speaking of the origin of government."[a]

The question recurs—how is this superiour constituted by human authority? Is he constituted by a law? If he is, that law, at least, must be made without a superiour; for by that law the superiour is constituted. If there can be no law without a superiour, then the institution of a superiour, by human authority, must be made in some other manner than by a

y. 1. Bl. Com. 48.
z. Lock. Gov. p. 2. s. 6.
a. El. Jur. 23.

law. In what other manner can human authority be exerted? Shall we say, that it may be exerted in a covenant or an engagement? Let us say, for we may say justly, that it may. Let us suppose the authority to be exerted, and the covenant or engagement to be made. Still the question recurs—can this authority so exerted, can this covenant or engagement so made, produce a superiour?

If he is now entitled to that appellation, he must be so by virtue of some thing, which he has received. But has he received more than was given? Could more be given than those, who gave it, possessed?

We can form clear conceptions of authority, original and derived, entire and divided into parts; but we have no clear conceptions how the parts can become greater than the whole; nor how authority, that is derived, can become superiour to that authority, from which the derivation is made.

If these observations are well founded; it will be difficult—perhaps we may say, impossible—to account for the institution of a superiour by human *authority*.

Is there any other human source, from which superiority can spring? 'Tis thought there is: 'tis thought that human *submission* can effectuate a purpose, for the accomplishment of which human authority has been found to be unavailing.

And is it come to this! Must submission to an equal be the yoke, under which we must pass, before we can diffuse the mild power, or participate in the benign influence of law? If such is, indeed, our fate, let resignation be our aim: but before we resign ourselves, let us examine whether our fate be so hard.

That I may be able to convey a just and full representation of opinions, which have been entertained on this subject, I shall give an abstract of the manner, in which Puffendorff has reasoned concerning it, in his chapter on the generation of civil sovereignty.

His object is, "to examine whence that sovereignty or supreme command, which appears in every state, and which, as a kind of soul, informs, enlivens, and moves the publick body, is immediately produced."

In this inquiry, he supposes that civil authority requires natural strength and a title. "Both these requisites," says he, "immediately flow from those pacts, by which the state is united and subsists." With regard to the former—natural strength—he observes, "that since all the members of the state, in submitting their wills to the will of a single director; did, at the same time, thereby oblige themselves to nonresistance, or to obey him in all his desires and endeavours of applying their strength and wealth to the good of the publick; it appears that he, who holds the sovereign rule, is possessed of sufficient force to compel the discharge of the injunctions, which he lays."

"So, likewise," adds he, "the same covenant affords a full and easy title, by which the sovereignty appears to be established, not upon violence, but in a lawful manner, upon the voluntary consent and *subjection* of the respective members."

"This, then," continues he, "is the nearest and immediate, cause, from which sovereign authority, as a moral quality, doth result. For if we suppose *submission* in one party, and, in another, the *acceptance* of that submission; there accrues, presently, to the latter, a right of imposing commands on the former; which is what we term sovereignty or rule. And as, by private contract, the right of any thing which we possess, so, by *submission,* the right to dispose of our strength and our liberty of acting, may be conveyed to another."

He illustrates this immediate cause of sovereign authority, by the following instance. "If any person should voluntarily and upon covenant deliver himself to me in servitude, he thereby really confers on me the power of a master." "Against which way of arguing, to object the vulgar maxim, *quod quis non habet, non potest in alterum transferre,*[b][24] is but a piece of trifling ignorance."[c]

Shall we, for a moment, suppose all this to be done? What is left to the

b. Puff. b. 7. c. 3. s. 1. p. 654. 655.

24. That which someone does not consider, does not afterwards carry over.

c. All this, it is true, has been done, in fact. This act of legal suicide has been often perpetrated; and, in the history of some periods, we find the prescribed form, by which liberty was extinguished—a form truly congenial with the transaction—a form expressed in terms the most disgraceful to the dignity of man. "Licentiam habeatis, mihi qualemcunque volueritis disciplinam ponere, vel venumdare, aut quod vobis placuerit de me facere."[25] (6. Gibbon 361. cites Marculf. Formul.) But these periods were the periods which introduced and established the feudal law. "The majesty of the Roman law protected the liberty of the citizen against his own distress or despair." 6. Gibbon. 360.

25. Take every liberty, place whatever restriction you wish upon me, or sell me as a slave, or do whatever you please with me.

people? Nothing. What are they? Slaves. What will be their portion? That of the beasts—instinct, compliance, and punishment. So true it is, that in the attempt to make one person more than man, millions must be made less.

We now see the price, at which law must be purchased; for we see the terms, on which a superiour, of such absolute necessity to a law, is constituted, according to the hypothesis, of which I have given an account. We see the covenants which must be entered into, the consent which must be given, the submission which must be made, the subjection which must be undergone, the state, analogous to servitude, which must be supposed, before this system of superiority can be completed. Has this been always done—must this be always done, in every state, where law is known or felt?

Without examining its incongruity with reason, with freedom, and with fact; without insisting on the incoherence of the parts, and the unsoundness of the whole, I shall, again, for a moment, take it all for granted: and, on that supposition, I shall put the question—Is even all this sufficient to constitute a superiour? Is it in the power of the meanest to prostitute, any more than it is in the power of the greatest to delegate, what he does not possess?[d] The arguments, therefore, which we used with regard to the appointment of a superiour by human authority, will equally apply to his appointment by human submission. The manner may be different: the result will be the same.

Indeed, the author of this system betrays a secret consciousness, that it is too weak and too disjointed to stand without an extrinsick support. "Yet still," says he, "to procure to the supreme command an especial efficacy, and a sacred respect, there is need of another additional principle, besides the submission of the subjects. And therefore he who affirms sovereignty to result immediately from compact, doth not, in the least, detract from

d. Let individuals, in any number whatever, become severally and successively subject to one man, they are all, in that case, nothing more than master and slaves; they are not a people governed by their chief; they are an aggregate, if you will; but they do not form an association; there subsists among them neither commonwealth nor body politick. Such a superiour, though he should become master of half the world, would be still a private person, and his interest, separate and distinct from that of his people, would be still no more than a private interest. Rousseau's Orig. Comp. 17. 18.

the *sacred* character of civil government; or maintain that princes bear rule, by human right *only,* and not by divine."[e]

It deserves remark, that, in this passage, Puffendorff assumes the divine right of princes to bear rule, as an admitted principle; and seems only solicitous to show, that the account, which he has given, of the origin of sovereignty, is not inconsistent with their sacred character.

After some further observations with regard to the source of government and the cause of sovereignty, the author acknowledges, that there is very little difference between his sentiments on the subject, and those of Boecler.[26] What Boecler's sentiments were, we learn from the account given of them by our author. "The supreme authority,"[f] says Boecler, "is not to be derived from the bare act of man, but from the command of God, and from the law of nature; or from such an act of men; by which the law of nature was followed and obeyed."

So far Puffendorff seems willing to go. He adopts a kind of compromising principle. He founds the right of the sovereign immediately upon the submission of the subjects; but, to complete the efficacy of supreme command, he calls in the aid of an additional principle, the sacred character of civil government, and the divine right of princes to bear rule. Further he was unwilling to proceed.

It has been often the fate of a compromise between two parties, that it has given entire satisfaction to neither. Such has been the fate of that adopted by Puffendorff. Some will certainly think, that he has given too much countenance to the claim, which princes have boldly made, of a divine right to rule. Others have thought, that, into his composition of a sovereign, he has infused too great a proportion of human authority. They pursue the source of sovereignty further than he is willing to accompany them, and maintain, that it is the Supreme Being, who confers immediately the supreme power on princes, without the intervention or concurrence of man.

This doctrine, in some countries, and at some periods, has been carried, and is still carried, to a very extravagant height, and has been supported

e. Puff. 655. b. 7. c. 3. s. 1.—2. Burl. 39.

26. Johann Heinrich Boecler (1611–1672) was a German scholar of history and politics.

f. Puff. 655. b. 7. c. 3. s. 1.

and propagated, and still is supported and propagated, with uncommon zeal. It has been, and still is, a favourite at courts; and has been, and still is, treated with every appearance of profound respect by courtiers, and, in too many instances, by philosophers and by statesmen, who have imitated, and still imitate courtiers in their practice of the slavish art. In the reign of James the second,[27] "the immediate emanation of divine authority" was introduced on every occasion, and ingrafted, often with the strangest impropriety, on every subject. Even in the present century, a book has been burnt by the hangman, because its author maintained, "that God is not the immediate cause of sovereignty."[g]

It cannot escape observation, that, in one particular, those who carry this doctrine the furthest, seem to challenge, with some success, the palm of consistency from those, who refuse to accompany them. Both entertain the same sentiments—and they are certainly overcharged ones—concerning sovereignty and superiority. Thus far they march together. But here, one division halt. The other proceed, and, looking back on those behind them, demand, why, having gone so far, they refuse to accomplish the journey. They insist, that all human causes are inadequate to the production of that superiority or sovereignty, about the august and sacred character of which they are both agreed. They say that neither particular men, nor a multitude of men, are themselves possessed of this sovereignty or superiority; and that, therefore, they cannot confer it on the prince. The consequence is, that, as this superiority is admitted to exist, and as it cannot be conferred by men, it must derive its origin from a higher source.

It is in this manner that Domat reasons concerning the origin of sovereignty and government. "As there is none but God alone who is the natural sovereign of man; so it is likewise from him that they who govern derive all their power and authority. It is one of the ceremonies in the coronation of the kings of France, for them to take the sword from the altar; thereby to denote, that it is immediately from the hand of God that they derive the sovereign power, of which the sword is the principal emblem."[h]

27. James II (1633–1701) was king of England from 1685 until the Glorious Revolution of 1688.

g. Puff. 656. note to b. 7. c. 3. s. 3.

h. 2. Domat 298, 299.

In the same train of sentiment, Bishop Taylor[i][28] observes, "that the legislative or supreme power is not the servant of the people, but the minister, the trustee, and the representative of God: that all just human power is given from above, not from beneath; from God, not, from the people."

Indeed, on the principle of superiority, Caligula's[29] reasoning was concise and conclusive. "If I am only a man, my subjects are something less: if they are men, I am something more."[j]

The answer to the foregoing reasoning appears to me to be more ingenious than solid, and to be productive of amusement, rather than of conviction. I shall deliver it from Burlamaqui, who, on this subject, has followed the opinions of Puffendorff. "This argument," says he, "proves nothing. It is true, that neither each member of the society, nor the whole multitude collected, are formally invested with the supreme authority; but it is sufficient that they possess it virtually; that is, that they have within themselves all that is necessary to enable them, by the concurrence of their free will and consent, to produce it in the sovereign. Since every individual has a natural right of disposing of his own natural freedom, according as he thinks proper; why should he not have a power of transferring to another, that right which he has of directing himself? Now is it not manifest, that, if all the members of the society agree to transfer this right to one of their fellow members, this cession will be the nearest and immediate cause of sovereignty? It is, therefore, evident, that there are, in each individual, the seeds, as it were, of the supreme power. The case is here very near the same, as in that of several voices collected together, which, by their union, produce a harmony, that was not to be found separately in each."[k]

The metaphors from vegetation and musick may illustrate and please; but they cannot prove nor convince. The notion of virtual sovereignty is as unsatisfactory to me, on this occasion, as that of virtual representation has been, on many others. Indeed, I see but little difference between a claim

i. Rule of Conscience 429.

28. Jeremy Taylor (1613–1667) was an English clergyman and prolific writer.

29. Gaius Julius Caesar Augustus Germanicus, or Caligula, (12–41) was Roman Emperor from 37 to 41.

j. Rous. Or. Com 6.

k. 2. Burl. 41, 42.

to derive from another that, which he is willing to give, but of which he is not possessed, and a claim to derive from him that, which he possesses, but which he has not given, and will not give.

Besides; let me repeat the questions, which I formerly put.—Have these degrading steps been always taken? must they be always taken, in every state, where law is known or felt? For let it not be forgotten, that superiority is introduced as a *necessary* part of the definition of law.

I will not attempt to paint the hideous consequences that have been drawn, nor the still more hideous practices that have claimed impunity, indulgence, and even sanction, from the pretended principle of the divine right of princes. Absolute, unlimited, and indefeasible power, nonresistance, passive obedience, tyranny, slavery, and misery walk in its train.

On this subject—its importance cannot be overrated—let us receive instruction from a well informed and a well experienced master—from one, who, probably, in some periods of his life, had felt what he so feelingly describes—from one, who had been bred to the trade of a prince, and who had been perfectly initiated in all the mysteries of the profession—from the late Frederick of Prussia.

"If my reflections," says he,

> shall be fortunate enough, to reach the ears of some princes, they will find among them certain truths, which they never would have heard from the lips of their courtiers and flatterers. Perhaps they will be struck with astonishment, to see such truths placed, by their side, on the throne. But it is time, that, at last, they should learn, that their false principles are the most empoisoned source—*la source la plus empoisonée*—of the calamities of Europe.
>
> Here is the errour of the greatest part of princes. They believe that God has expressly, and from a particular attention to their grandeur, their happiness, and their pride, formed their subjects for no other purpose, than to be the ministers and instruments of their unbridled passions. As the principle, from which they set out, is false; the consequences cannot be otherwise than infinitely pernicious. Hence the unregulated passion for false glory—hence the inflamed desire of conquest—hence the oppressions laid upon the people—hence the indolence and dissipation of princes—hence their ambition, their injustice, their inhumanity, their tyranny—hence, in short, all those vices, which degrade the nature of man.
>
> If they would disrobe themselves of these erroneous opinions; if they would ascend to the true origin of their appointment; they would see, that

> their elevation and rank, of which they are so jealous, are, indeed, nothing else than the work of the people; they would see, that the myriads of men, placed under their care, have not made themselves the slaves of one single man, with a view to render him more powerful and more formidable; have not submitted themselves to a fellow citizen, in order to become the sport of his fancies, and the martyrs of his caprice; but have chosen, from among themselves, the man, whom they believed to be the most just, that he might govern them; the best, that he might supply the place of a father; the most humane, that he might compassionate and relieve their misfortunes; the most valiant, that he might defend them against their enemies; the most wise, that he might not engage them inconsiderately in ruinous and destructive wars; in one word, the man the most proper to represent the body of the state, and in whom the sovereign power might become a bulwark to justice and to the laws, and not an engine, by the force of which tyranny might be exercised, and crimes might be committed with impunity.
>
> This principle being once established, princes would avoid the two rocks, which, in all ages, have produced the ruin of empires, and distraction in the political world—ungoverned ambition, and a listless inattention to affairs."[l] "They would often reflect that they are men, as well as the least of their subjects—that if they are the first judges, the first generals, the first financiers, the first ministers of society; they are so, for the purpose of fulfilling the duties, which those names import. They will reflect, that they are only the first servants of the state, bound to act with the same integrity, the same caution, and the same entire disinterestedness, as if, at every moment, they were to render an account of their administration to the citizens."[m]

I will not charge to the authors, whose opinions I have examined, all the consequences that have been drawn, practically as well as theoretically, from their principles. From their principles, however, admitted by themselves without due caution and scrutiny, those consequences have been drawn by others, and drawn too accurately and too successfully for the peace, liberty, and happiness of men.

After all, I am much inclined, for the honour of human nature, to believe, that all this doctrine concerning the divine right of kings was, at first, encouraged and cherished by many, from motives, mistaken certainly, but pardonable, and even laudable, and that it was intended not so much to

l. K. Prus. works. v. 6. p. 48. 50.
m. Id. p. 83. 84.

introduce the tyranny of princes, as to form a barrier against the tyranny of priests.

One of them, at the head of a numerous, a formidable, and a well disciplined phalanx, claimed to be the Almighty's vicegerent upon earth; claimed the power of deposing kings, disposing crowns, releasing subjects from their allegiance, and overruling the whole transactions of the christian world. Superstition and ignorance dreaded, but could not oppose, the presumptuous claim. The Pope had obtained, what Archimedes wanted, *another* world, on which he placed his ecclesiastical machinery; and it was no wonder that he moved *this* according to his will and pleasure. Princes and potentates, states and kingdoms were prostrate before him. Every thing human was obliged to bend under the incumbent pressure of divine control.

It is not improbable, that, in this disagreeable predicament, the divine right of kings was considered as the only principle, which could be opposed to the claims of the papal throne; and as the only means, which could preserve the civil, from being swallowed by the ecclesiastical powers.

This conjecture receives a degree of probability from a fact, which is mentioned in the history of France.

In a general assembly of the states of the kingdom, it was proposed to canonize this position—"that kings derive their authority immediately from God." That such a proposition was made in an assembly of the states, the most popular body known in the kingdom, will, no doubt, occasion surprise. This surprise will be increased, when it is mentioned, that the proposition was patronized by the most popular part of that assembly: it was the third estate, which wished to pass it into a law. But every thing is naturally and easily accounted for, when it is mentioned further, that the principal object, which the third estate had in view by this measure, was to secure the sovereign authority from the detestable maxims of those, who made it depend upon the pope, by giving him a power of absolving subjects from their oath of allegiance, and authorizing those who assassinated their princes as hereticks.[n]

The proposal did not pass into a law; because, among other reasons, the question was thought proper for the determination of the schools. But this

n. Puff. 656. n.

much may safely be inferred, that what was thought proper by the third estate to be passed into a law, would be generally received through the kingdom, as popular and wholesome doctrine.

I confess myself pleased with indulging the conjecture I have mentioned.

When I entered upon the disquisition of the doctrine of a superiour as necessary to the very definition of law; I said, that, if I was not mistaken, this notion of superiority contained the germ of the divine right of princes to rule, and of the corresponding obligation on the people implicitly to obey. It may now be seen whether or not I have been mistaken; and, if I have not been mistaken, it appears, how important it is, carefully and patiently to examine a first principle; to trace it, with attention, to its highest origin; and to pursue it, with perseverance, to its most remote consequences. I have observed this conduct with regard to the principle in question. The result, I think, has been, that, as to human laws, the notion of a superiour is a notion unnecessary, unfounded, and dangerous; a notion inconsistent with the genuine system of human authority.

Now that the will of a superiour is discarded, as an improper principle of obligation in human laws, it is natural to ask—What principle shall be introduced in its place? In its place I introduce—the consent of those whose obedience the law requires. This I conceive to be the true origin of the obligation of human laws. This principle I shall view on all its sides; I shall examine it historically and legally; I shall consider it as a question of theory, and as a question of fact.

Let us ascend to the first ages of societies. Customs, for a long time, were the only laws known among them. The Lycians[o] had no written laws; they were governed entirely by customs. Among the ancient Britons also, no written laws were known: they were ruled by the traditionary—and if traditionary, probably, the customary—laws of the Druids.

Now custom is, of itself, intrinsick evidence of consent. How was a custom introduced? By voluntary adoption. How did it become general? By the instances of voluntary adoption being increased. How did it become lasting? By voluntary and satisfactory experience, which ratified and

o. 1. Gog. Or. Laws. 8.

confirmed what voluntary adoption had introduced. In the introduction, in the extension, in the continuance of customary law, we find the operations of consent universally predominant.

"Customs," in the striking and picturesque language of my Lord Bacon, "are laws written in living tables."[p] In regulations of justice and of government, they have been more effectual than the best written laws. The Romans, in their happy periods of liberty, paid great regard to customary law. Let me mention, in one word, every thing that can enforce my sentiments: the common law of England is a customary law.

Among the earliest, among the freest, among the most improved nations of the world, we find a species of law prevailing, which carried, in its bosom, internal evidence of consent. History, therefore, bears a strong and a uniform testimony in favour of this species of law.

Let us consult the sentiments[q] as well as the history of the ancients. I find a charge against them on this subject—"that they were not accurate enough in their expressions; because they frequently applied to laws the name of *common agreements.*"[r] This, it is acknowledged, they do almost every where in their writings. He, however, who accuses the ancient writers of inaccuracy in expression, ought himself to be consummately accurate. "Let those teach others, who themselves excel." Whether the Baron Puffendorff was entitled to be a teacher in this particular, we stay not to examine. It is of more consequence to attend to the ground of his accusation.

One reason, why he urges their expressions to be inaccurate, is, that "neither the divine positive laws, nor the laws of nature had their rise from the agreement of men." All this is, at once, admitted; but the present disquisition relates only to laws that are human. What is said with regard to

p. 4. Ld. Bac. 5.

q. Mens, et animus, et consilium, et sententia civitatis posita est in legibus. Ut corpora nostra sine mente; sic civitas sine lege, suis partibus, ut nervis, ac sanguine, et membris, uti non potest. Legum ministri, magistratus; legum interpretes, judices: legum denique idcirco omnes servi sumus, ut liberi esse possimus.[30] Cicero pro Cluen. c. 53.

r. Puff. 59. b. 1. c. 6. s. 7.

30. The mind, the soul, the wisdom, and the judgment of the state rests in the laws. Just as we cannot use our bodies without the mind, so that state, without the law, cannot use its own parts, as though they were nerves, blood, and limbs. The laws' administrators are the magistrates; their interpreters the judges; we are all the laws' slaves, so that we may be free.

them? With regard to them it is said, that "the Grecians, as in their other politick speeches, so in this too, had an eye to their own democratical governments; in which, because the laws were made upon the proposal of the magistrate, with the knowledge, and by the command, of the people, and so, as it were, in the way of bargain and stipulation; they gave them the name of covenants and agreements."

I am now unsolicitous to repel the accusation: it seems, it was conceived to arise from a reference, by the ancients, to their democratical governments. Let them be called covenants, or agreements, or bargains, or stipulations, or any thing similar to any of those, still I am satisfied; for still every thing mentioned, and every thing similar to every thing mentioned, imports consent. Here history and law combine their evidence in support of consent.

Law has been denominated "a general convention of the citizens:" such is the definition of it in the Digest: for the Roman law was not, in every age of Rome, the law of slavery. A similar mode of expression has been long used in England. Magna Charta was made "by the common assent of all the realm."[s]

Let us listen to the judicious and excellent Hooker: what he says always conveys instruction. "The lawful power of making laws to command whole politick societies of men, belongeth so properly unto the same entire societies, that for any prince or potentate of what kind soever upon earth, to exercise the same of himself, and not either by express commission immediately and personally received from God, or else by authority derived, at the first, from their consent, upon whose persons they impose laws, it is no better than mere tyranny. Laws they are not, therefore, which publick approbation hath not made so."[t] "Laws human, of what kind soever, are available by consent."[u]

My Lord Shaftesbury, who formed his taste and judgment upon ancient writers and ancient opinions, delivers it as his sentiment, "That no people in a civil state can possibly be free, when they are otherwise

s. Sulliv. Pref. 18.

t. Hooker. b. 1. s. 10. p. 19.

u. Id. p. 20.

governed, than by such laws as they themselves have constituted, or to which they have freely given consent."[v]

This subject will receive peculiar illustration and importance, when we come to consider the description and characters of municipal law. I will not anticipate here what will be introduced there with much greater propriety and force.

Of law there are different kinds. All, however, may be arranged in two different classes. 1. Divine. 2. Human laws. The descriptive epithets employed denote, that the former have God, the latter, man, for their author.

The laws of God may be divided into the following species.

I. That law, the book of which we are neither able nor worthy to open. Of this law, the author and observer is God. He is a law to himself, as well as to all created things. This law we may name the "law eternal."

II. That law, which is made for angels and the spirits of the just made perfect. This may be called the "law celestial." This law, and the glorious state for which it is adapted, we see, at present, but darkly and as through a glass: but hereafter we shall see even as we are seen; and shall know even as we are known. From the wisdom and the goodness of the adorable Author and Preserver of the universe, we are justified in concluding, that the celestial and perfect state is governed, as all other things are, by his established laws. What those laws are, it is not yet given us to know; but on one truth we may rely with sure and certain confidence—those laws are wise and good. For another truth we have infallible authority—those laws are strictly obeyed: "In heaven his will is done."

III. That law, by which the irrational and inanimate parts of the creation are governed. The great Creator of all things has established general and fixed rules, according to which all the phenomena of the material universe are produced and regulated. These rules are usually denominated laws of nature. The science, which has those laws for its object, is distinguished by the name of natural philosophy. It is sometimes called, the philosophy of body. Of this science, there are numerous branches.

v. 3. Shaft. 312.

IV. That law, which God has made for man in his present state; that law, which is communicated to us by reason and conscience, the divine monitors within us, and by the sacred oracles, the divine monitors without us. This law has undergone several subdivisions, and has been known by distinct appellations, according to the different ways in which it has been promulgated, and the different objects which it respects.

As promulgated by reason and the moral sense, it has been called natural; as promulgated by the holy scriptures, it has been called revealed law.

As addressed to men, it has been denominated the law of nature; as addressed to political societies, it has been denominated the law of nations.

But it should always be remembered, that this law, natural or revealed, made for men or for nations, flows from the same divine source: it is the law of God.

Nature, or, to speak more properly, the Author of nature, has done much for us; but it is his gracious appointment and will, that we should also do much for ourselves. What we do, indeed, must be founded on what he has done; and the deficiencies of our laws must be supplied by the perfections of his. Human law must rest its authority, ultimately, upon the authority of that law, which is divine.

Of that law, the following are maxims—that no injury should be done—that a lawful engagement, voluntarily made, should be faithfully fulfilled. We now see the deep and the solid foundations of human law.

It is of two species. 1. That which a political society makes for itself. This is municipal law. 2. That which two or more political societies make for themselves. This is the voluntary law of nations.

In all these species of law—the law eternal—the law celestial—the law natural—the divine law, as it respects men and nations—the human law, as it also respects men and nations—man is deeply and intimately concerned. Of all these species of law, therefore, the knowledge must be most important to man.

Those parts of natural philosophy, which more immediately relate to the human body, are appropriated to the profession of physick.

The law eternal, the law celestial, and the law divine, as they are disclosed by that revelation, which has brought life and immortality to light, are the more peculiar objects of the profession of divinity.

The law of nature, the law of nations, and the municipal law form the objects of the profession of law.

From this short, but plain and, I hope, just statement of things, we perceive a principle of connexion between all the learned professions; but especially between the two last mentioned. Far from being rivals or enemies, religion and law are twin sisters, friends, and mutual assistants. Indeed, these two sciences run into each other. The divine law, as discovered by reason and the moral sense, forms an essential part of both.

From this statement of things, we also perceive how important and dignified the profession of the law is, when traced to its sources, and viewed in its just extent.

The immediate objects of our attention are, the law of nature, the law of nations, and the municipal law of the United States, and of the several states which compose the Union. It will not be forgotten, that the constitutions of the United States, and of the individual states, form a capital part of their municipal law. On the two first of these three great heads, I shall be very general. On the last, especially on those parts of it, which comprehend the constitutions and publick law, I shall be more particular and minute.

CHAPTER III.
Of the Law of Nature.

In every period of our existence, in every situation, in which we can be placed, much is to be known, much is to be done, much is to be enjoyed. But all that is to be known, all that is to be done, all that is to be enjoyed, depends upon the proper exertion and direction of our numerous powers. In this immense ocean of intelligence and action, are we left without a compass and without a chart? Is there no pole star, by which we may regulate our course? Has the all-gracious and all-wise Author of our existence formed us for such great and such good ends; and has he left us without a conductor to lead us in the way, by which those ends may be attained? Has he made us capable of observing a rule, and has he furnished us with no rule, which we ought to observe? Let us examine these questions—for they are important ones—with patience and with attention. Our labours will, in all probability, be amply repaid. We shall probably find that, to direct the more important parts of our conduct, the bountiful Governour of the universe has been graciously pleased to provide us with a law; and that, to direct the less important parts of it, he has made us capable of providing a law for ourselves.

That our Creator has a supreme right to prescribe a law for our conduct, and that we are under the most perfect obligation to obey that law, are truths established on the clearest and most solid principles.

In the course of our remarks on that part of Sir William Blackstone's definition of law, which includes the idea of a superiour as essential to it, we remarked, with particular care, that it was only with regard to human laws that we controverted the justness or propriety of that idea. It was incumbent on us to mark this distinction particularly; for with regard to laws which are divine, they truly come from a superiour—from Him who is supreme.

Between beings, who, in their nature, powers, and situation, are so perfectly equal, that nothing can be ascribed to one, which is not applicable to the other, there can be neither superiority nor dependence. With regard to such beings, no reason can be assigned, why any one should assume authority over others, which may not, with equal propriety, be assigned, why each of those others should assume authority over that one. To constitute superiority and dependence, there must be an essential difference of qualities, on which those relations may be founded.[a]

Some allege, that the sole superiority of strength, or, as they express it, an irresistible power, is the true foundation of the right of prescribing laws. "This superiority of power gives," say they, "a right of reigning, by the impossibility, in which it places others, of resisting him, who has so great an advantage over them."[b]

Others derive the right of prescribing laws and imposing obligations from superiour excellence of nature. "This," say they, "not only renders a being independent of those, who are of a nature inferiour to it; but leads us to believe, that the latter were made for the sake of the former." For a proof of this, they appeal to the constitution of man. "Here," they tell us, "the soul governs, as being the noblest part." "On the same foundation," they add, "the empire of man over the brute creation is built."[c]

Others, again, say, that "properly speaking, there is only one general source of superiority and obligation. God is our creator: in him we live, and move, and have our being: from him we have received our intellectual and our moral powers: he, as master of his own work, can prescribe to it whatever rules to him shall seem meet. Hence our dependence on our Creator: hence his absolute power over us. This is the true source of all authority."[d]

With regard to the first hypothesis, it is totally insufficient; nay, it is absolutely false. Because I cannot resist, am I obliged to obey? Because another is possessed of superiour force, am I bound to acknowledge his will as the rule of my conduct? Every obligation supposes motives that influence the conscience and determine the will, so that we should think it

a. 1. Burl. 82.
b. 1. Burl. 83.
c. Id. 83.
d. Id. 83. 87.

wrong not to obey, even if resistance was in our power. But a person, who alleges only the law of the strongest, proposes no motive to influence the conscience, or to determine the will. Superiour force may reside with predominant malevolence. Has force, exerted for the purposes of malevolence, a right to command? Can it impose an obligation to obey? No. Resistance to such force is a right; and, if resistance can prove effectual, it is a duty also. On some occasions, all our efforts may, indeed, be useless; and an attempt to resist would frustrate its own aim: but, on such occasions, the exercise of resistance only is suspended; the right of resistance is not extinguished: we may continue, for a time, under a constraint; but we come not under an obligation: we may suffer all the external effects of superiour force; but we feel not the internal influence of superiour authority?[e]

The second hypothesis has in it something plausible; but, on examination, it will not be found to be accurate. Wherever a being of superiour excellence is found, his excellence, as well as every other truth, ought, on proper occasions, to be acknowledged; we will go farther; it ought, as every thing excellent ought, to be esteemed. But must we go farther still? Is obedience the necessary consequence of honest acknowledgment and just esteem? Here we must make a pause: we must make some inquiries before we go forward. In what manner is this being of superiour excellence connected with us? What are his dispositions with regard to us? By what effects, if by any, will his superiour excellence be displayed? Will it be exerted for our happiness; or, as to us, will it not be exerted at all? We acknowledge—we esteem excellence; but till these questions are answered, we feel not ourselves under an obligation to obey it.[f] If the opinion of Epicurus[1] concerning his divinities—that they were absolutely indifferent to the happiness and interests of men—was admitted for a moment;[g] the

e. 1. Burl. 85. 86.

f. 1. Burl. 86. 87.

1. Epicurus (341–270 B.C.) was a Greek philosopher who founded the school of thought known as Epicureanism.

g. Epicurus re tollit, oratione relinquit deos. Deinde, si maxime talis est deus, ut nulla gratia, nulla hominum caritate teneatur: valeat. Quid enim dicam, propitius sit?[2] Cic. de Nat. Deo. l. 1. c. 44.

2. Epicurus in fact takes away the gods, though he professes to leave them. In fine, if god is precisely such as is held by no sense of gratitude, by no love of mankind, then goodbye to him! for why should I say "may he be gracious toward me"?

inference would unquestionably be—that they were not entitled to human obedience.

The third hypothesis contains a solemn truth, which ought to be examined with reverence and awe. It resolves the supreme right of prescribing laws for our conduct, and our indispensable duty of obeying those laws, into the omnipotence of the Divinity. This omnipotence let us humbly adore. Were we to suppose—but the supposition cannot be made—that infinite goodness could be disjoined from almighty power—but we cannot—must not proceed to the inference. No, it never can be drawn; for from almighty power infinite goodness can never be disjoined.

Let us join, in our weak conceptions, what are inseparable in their incomprehensible Archetype—infinite power—infinite wisdom—infinite goodness; and then we shall see, in its resplendent glory, the supreme right to rule: we shall feel the conscious sense of the perfect obligation to obey.

His infinite power enforces his laws, and carries them into full and effectual execution. His infinite wisdom knows and chooses the fittest means for accomplishing the ends which he proposes. His infinite goodness proposes such ends only as promote our felicity. By his power, he is able to remove whatever may possibly injure us, and to provide whatever is conducive to our happiness. By his wisdom, he knows our nature, our faculties, and our interests: he cannot be mistaken in the designs, which he proposes, nor in the means, which he employs to accomplish them. By his goodness, he proposes our happiness: and to that end directs the operations of his power and wisdom. Indeed, to his goodness alone we may trace the principle of his laws. Being infinitely and eternally happy in himself, his goodness alone could move him to create us, and give us the means of happiness. The same principle, that moved his creating, moves his governing power. The rule of his government we shall find to be reduced to this one paternal command—Let man pursue his own perfection and happiness.

What an enrapturing view of the moral government of the universe! Over all, goodness infinite reigns, guided by unerring wisdom, and supported by almighty power. What an instructive lesson to those who think, and are encouraged by their flatterers to think, that a portion of divine right is communicated to their rule. If this really was the case; their power ought to be subservient to their goodness, and their goodness should be employed in promoting the happiness of those, who are intrusted to their care. But princes, and the flatterers of princes, are guilty, in two respects, of the grossest errour and presumption. They claim to govern by divine institution and right. The principles of their government are repugnant to the principles of that government, which is divine. The principle of the divine government is goodness: they plume themselves with the gaudy insignia of power.

Well might nature's poet say—

> ——————— Could great men thunder,
> As Jove himself does, Jove would ne'er be quiet;
> For every pelting, petty officer
> Would use his heaven for thunder;
> Nothing but thunder. Merciful heaven!
> Thou rather with thy sharp and sulphurous bolt
> Split'st the unwedgeable and gnarled oak,
> Than the soft myrtle: O, but man, proud man,
> Dressed in a little brief authority,
> Most ignorant of what he's most assured,
> His glassy substance; like an angry ape,
> Plays such fantastick tricks before high heaven,
> As make the angels weep.
>
> *Shak. Meas. for Meas. Act II.*

Where a supreme right to give laws exists, on one side, and a perfect obligation to obey them exists, on the other side; this relation, of itself, suggests the probability that laws will be made.

When we view the inanimate and irrational creation around and above us, and contemplate the beautiful order observed in all its motions and appearances; is not the supposition unnatural and improbable—that the rational and moral world should be abandoned to the frolicks of chance, or to the ravage of disorder? What would be the fate of man and of society, was every one at full liberty to do as he listed, without any fixed rule or principle of conduct, without a helm to steer him—a sport of the fierce gusts of passion, and the fluctuating billows of caprice?

To be without law is not agreeable to our nature; because, if we were without law, we should find many of our talents and powers hanging upon us like useless incumbrances. Why should we be illuminated by reason, were we only made to obey the impulse of irrational instinct? Why should we have the power of deliberating, and of balancing our determinations, if we were made to yield implicitly and unavoidably to the influence of the first impressions? Of what service to us would reflection be, if, after reflection, we were to be carried away irresistibly by the force of blind and impetuous appetites?

Without laws, what would be the state of society? The more ingenious and artful the twolegged animal, man, is, the more dangerous he would become to his equals: his ingenuity would degenerate into cunning; and his art would be employed for the purposes of malice. He would be deprived of all the benefits and pleasures of peaceful and social life: he would become a prey to all the distractions of licentiousness and war.

Is it probable—we repeat the question—is it probable that the Creator, infinitely wise and good, would leave his moral world in this chaos and disorder?

If we enter into ourselves, and view with attention what passes in our own breasts, we shall find, that what, at first, appeared probable, is proved, on closer examination, to be certain; we shall find, that God has not left himself without a witness, nor us without a guide.

We have already observed, that, concerning the nature and cause of obligation, many different opinions have been entertained, and much ingenious disputation has been held, by philosophers and writers on jurisprudence. It will not be improper to take a summary view of those opinions.

Some philosophers maintain, that all obligation arises from the relations of things;[h] from a certain proportion or disproportion, a certain fitness or unfitness, between objects and actions, which give a beauty to some, and a deformity to others. They say, that the rules of morality are founded on the nature of things; and are agreeable to the order necessary for the beauty of the universe.[i]

Others allege, that every rule whatever of human actions carries with it a moral necessity of conforming to it; and consequently produces a sort of obligation. Every rule, say they, implies a design, and the will of attaining a certain end. He, therefore, who proposes a particular end, and knows

h. 1. Ruth. 9.
i. Gro. 10.

the rule by which alone he can accomplish it, finds himself under a moral necessity of observing that rule. If he did not observe it, he would act a contradictory part; he would propose the end, and neglect the only means, by which he could obtain it. There is a reasonable necessity, therefore, to prefer one manner of acting before another; and every reasonable man finds himself engaged to this, and prevented from acting in a contrary manner. In other words, he is obliged: for obligation is nothing more than a restriction of liberty produced by reason. Reason, then, independent of law, is sufficient to impose *some* obligation on man, and to establish a system of morality and duty.[j]

But, according to others, the idea of obligation necessarily implies a being, who obliges, and must be distinct from him, who is obliged. If the person, on whom the obligation is imposed, is the same as he who imposes it; he can disengage himself from it whenever he pleases: or, rather, there is no obligation. Obligation and duty depend on the intervention of a superiour, whose will is manifested by law. If we abstract from all law, and consequently from a legislator; we shall have no such thing as right, obligation, duty, or morality.[k]

Others, again, think it necessary to join the last two principles together, in order to render the obligation perfect.[l] Reason, say they, is the first rule of man, the first principle of morality, and the immediate cause of all primitive obligation. But man being necessarily dependent on his Creator, who has formed him with wisdom and design, and who, in creating him, has proposed some particular ends; the will of God is another rule of human actions, another principle of morality, obligation, and duty. On this distinction, the kinds of obligation, external and internal, are founded. These two principles must be united, in order to form a complete system of morality, really founded on the nature and state of man. As a rational being, he is subject to reason: as a creature of God, to his supreme will. Thus, reason and the divine will are perfectly reconciled, are naturally connected, and are strengthened by their junction.[m]

j. Hein. 63. 1. Burl. 207. 210. 212. Puff. 17. b. 1. c. 2. s. 6.
k. 1. Burl. 210. 212. 202. Hein. 10.
l. 1. Ruth. 9.
m. 1. Burl. 214. 216. 219. 220.

The cause of obligation is laid, by some philosophers, in utility.[n] Actions, they tell us, are to be estimated by their tendency to promote happiness. Whatever is expedient, is right. It is the utility, alone, of any moral rule, which constitutes its obligation.

Congenial with this principle, is another, which has received the sanction of some writers—that sociability, or the care of maintaining society properly, is the fountain of obligation and right: for to every right, there must be a corresponding obligation. From this principle the inference is drawn, that every one is born, not for himself alone, but for the whole human kind.[o]

Further—many philosophers derive our obligation to observe the law of nature from instinctive affections, or an innate moral sense.[p] This is the sense, they tell us, by which we perceive the qualities of right and wrong, and the other moral qualities in actions.

With regard, then, both to the meaning and the cause of obligation, much diversity of sentiment, much ambiguity, and much obscurity have, it appears, prevailed. It is a subject of inquiry, however, that well deserves to be investigated, explained, illustrated, and placed in its native splendour and dignity. In order to do this, it will be proper to ascertain the precise state of the question before us. It is this—what is the efficient cause of moral obligation—of the eminent distinction between right and wrong? This has been often and injudiciously blended with another question, connected indeed with it, but from which it ought to be preserved separate and distinct. That other question is—how shall we, in particular instances, learn the dictates of our duty, and make, with accuracy, the eminent distinction, which we have just now mentioned? The first question points to the *principle* of obligation: the second points to the *means* by which our obligation to perform a specified action, or a series of specified actions, may be deduced. The first has been called by philosophers—principium essendi—the principle of existence; the principle which *constitutes* obligation. The second has been called by them—principium cognoscendi—the principle of knowing it; the principle by which it may be *proved* or *perceived.* In a commonwealth, the distinction between these two questions

n. 1. Paley 82. Hein. 51.

o. Hein. 50. Gro. Prel. 17. Puff. 139. b. 2. c. 3. s. 15.

p. 1. Ruth. 9.

is familiar and easy. If the question is put—what is the efficient cause of the obligation upon the citizens to obey the laws of the state?—the answer is ready—the will of those, by whose authority the laws are made. If the other question is put—how shall we, in a particular instance, or in a series of particular instances, ascertain the laws, which the citizens ought to obey?—reference is immediately made to the code of laws.

Having thus stated the question—what is the efficient cause of moral obligation?—I give it this answer—the will of God. This is the supreme law.[q] His just and full right of imposing laws, and our duty in obeying them, are the sources of our moral obligations. If I am asked—why do you obey the will of God? I answer—because it is my duty so to do. If I am asked again—how do you know this to be your duty? I answer again—because I am told so by my moral sense or conscience. If I am asked a third time—how do you know that you ought to do that, of which your conscience enjoins the performance? I can only say, I *feel* that such is my duty. Here investigation must stop; reasoning can go no farther. The science of morals, as well as other sciences, is founded on truths, that cannot be discovered or proved by reasoning. Reason is confined to the investigation of unknown truths by the means of such as are known. We cannot, therefore, begin to reason, till we are furnished, otherwise than by reason, with some truths, on which we can found our arguments. Even in mathematicks, we must be provided with axioms perceived intuitively to be true, before our demonstrations can commence. Morality, like mathematicks, has its intuitive truths, without which we cannot make a single step in our reasonings upon the subject.[r] Such an intuitive truth is that, with which we just now closed our investigation. If a person was not possessed of the feeling before mentioned; it would not be in the power of arguments,

q. Principem legem illam et ultimam, mentem esse dicebant, omnia ratione aut cogentis, aut vetantis dei.[3] Cic. de leg. l. 2. c. 4.

r. Quae est gens, aut quod genus hominum, quod non habeat sine doctrina anticipationem quandam, id est, anticeptam animo rei quandam informationem, sine qua nec intelligi quidquam, nec quaeri, nec disputari potest.[4] Cic. de nat. Deor. l. 1. c. 16.

3. That first and final law, they used to say, is the mind of God, who forces or prohibits everything by reason.

4. What nation, what species of man is there which does not have, without teaching, some sort of foreknowledge, that is, a certain image of the thing conceived beforehand by the mind, without which nothing can be understood, investigated or discussed?

to give him any conception of the distinction between right and wrong. These terms would be to him equally unintelligible, as the term *colour* to one who was born and has continued blind. But that there is, in human nature, such a moral principle, has been felt and acknowledged in all ages and nations.

Now that we have stated and answered the first question; let us proceed to the consideration of the second—how shall we, in particular instances, learn the dictates of our duty, and make, with accuracy, the proper distinction between right and wrong; in other words, how shall we, in particular cases, discover the will of God? We discover it by our conscience, by our reason, and by the Holy Scriptures. The law of nature and the law of revelation are both divine: they flow, though in different channels, from the same adorable source. It is, indeed, preposterous to separate them from each other. The object of both is—to discover the will of God—and both are necessary for the accomplishment of that end.

I. The power of moral perception is, indeed, a most important part of our constitution. It is an original power—a power of its own kind; and totally distinct from the ideas of utility and agreeableness. By that power, we have conceptions of merit and demerit, of duty and moral obligation. By that power, we perceive some things in human conduct to be right, and others to be wrong. We have the same reason to rely on the dictates of this faculty, as upon the determinations of our senses, or of our other natural powers. When an action is represented to us, flowing from love, humanity, gratitude, an ultimate desire of the good of others; though it happened in a country far distant, or in an age long past, we admire the lovely exhibition, and praise its author. The contrary conduct, when represented to us, raises our abhorrence and aversion. But whence this secret chain betwixt each person and mankind? If there is no moral sense, which makes benevolence appear beautiful; if all approbation be from the interest of the approver;

"What's Hecuba to us, or we to Hecuba?"[s]

The mind, which reflects on itself, and is a spectator of other minds, sees and feels the soft and the harsh, the agreeable and the disagreeable,

s. Hamlet (paraphase).

the foul and the fair, the harmonious and the dissonant, as really and truly in the affections and actions, as in any musical numbers, or the outward forms or representations of sensible things. It cannot withhold its approbation or aversion in what relates to the former, any more than in what relates to the latter, of those subjects. To deny the sense of a sublime and beautiful and of their contraries in actions and things, will appear an affectation merely to one who duly considers and traces the subject. Even he who indulges this affectation cannot avoid the discovery of those very sentiments, which he pretends not to feel. A Lucretius[5] or a Hobbes cannot discard the sentiments of praise and admiration respecting some moral forms, nor the sentiments of censure and detestation concerning others. Has a man gratitude, or resentment, or pride, or shame? If he has and avows it; he must have and acknowledge a sense of something benevolent, of something unjust, of something worthy, and of something mean. Thus, so long as we find men pleased or angry, proud or ashamed; we may appeal to the reality of the moral sense. A right and a wrong, an honourable and a dishonourable is plainly conceived. About these there may be mistakes; but this destroys not the inference, that the things are, and are universally acknowledged—that they are of nature's impression, and by no art can be obliterated.

This sense or apprehension of right and wrong appears early, and exists in different degrees. The qualities of love, gratitude, sympathy unfold themselves, in the first stages of life, and the approbation of those qualities accompanies the first dawn of reflection. Young people, who think the least about the distant influences of actions, are, more than others, moved with moral forms. Hence that strong inclination in children to hear such stories as paint the characters and fortunes of men. Hence that joy in the prosperity of the kind and faithful, and that sorrow upon the success of the treacherous and cruel, with which we often see infant minds strongly agitated.

There is a natural beauty in figures; and is there not a beauty as natural in actions? When the eye opens upon forms, and the ear to sounds; the beautiful is seen, and harmony is heard and acknowledged. When actions

5. Titus Lucretius Carus (99–55 B.C.) was a Roman poet and Epicurean philosopher who wrote *De Rerum Natura* (*On the Nature of Things*).

are viewed and affections are discerned, the inward eye distinguishes the beautiful, the amiable, the admirable, from the despicable, the odious, and the deformed. How is it possible not to own, that as these distinctions have their foundation in nature, so this power of discerning them is natural also?

The universality of an opinion or sentiment may be evinced by the structure of languages. Languages were not invented by philosophers, to countenance or support any artificial system. They were contrived by men in general, to express common sentiments and perceptions. The inference is satisfactory, that where all languages make a distinction, there must be a similar distinction in universal opinion or sentiment. For language is the picture of human thoughts; and, from this faithful picture, we may draw certain conclusions concerning the original. Now, a universal effect must have a universal cause. No universal cause can, with propriety, be assigned for this universal opinion, except that intuitive perception of things, which is distinguished by the name of common sense.

All languages speak of a beautiful and a deformed, a right and a wrong, an agreeable and disagreeable, a good and ill, in actions, affections, and characters. All languages, therefore, suppose a moral sense, by which those qualities are perceived and distinguished.

The whole circle of the arts of imitation proves the reality of the moral sense. They suppose, in human conduct, a sublimity, a beauty, a greatness, an excellence, independent of advantage or disadvantage, profit or loss. On him, whose heart is indelicate or hard; on him, who has no admiration of what is truly noble; on him, who has no sympathetick sense of what is melting and tender, the highest beauty of the mimick arts must make indeed, but a very faint and transient impression. If we were void of a relish for moral excellence, how frigid and uninteresting would the finest descriptions of life and manners appear! How indifferent are the finest strains of harmony, to him who has not a musical ear!

The force of the moral sense is diffused through every part of life. The luxury of the table derives its principal charms from some mixture of moral enjoyments, from communicating pleasures, and from sentiments honourable and just as well as elegant—

> "The feast of reason, and the flow of soul."

The chief pleasures of history, and poetry, and eloquence, and musick, and sculpture, and painting are derived from the same source. Beside the pleasures they afford by imitation, they receive a stronger charm from something moral insinuated into the performances. The principal beauties of behaviour, and even of countenance, arise from the indication of affections or qualities morally estimable.

Never was there any of the human species above the condition of an idiot, to whom all actions appeared indifferent. All feel that a certain temper, certain affections, and certain actions produce a sentiment of approbation; and that a sentiment of disapprobation is produced by the contrary temper, affections, and actions.

This power is capable of culture and improvement by habit, and by frequent and extensive exercise. A high sense of moral excellence is approved above all other intellectual talents. This high sense of excellence is accompanied with a strong desire after it, and a keen relish for it. This desire and this relish are approved as the most amiable affections, and the highest virtues.

This moral sense, from its very nature, is intended to regulate and control all our other powers. It governs our passions as well as our actions. Other principles may solicit and allure; but the conscience assumes authority, it must be obeyed. Of this dignity and commanding nature we are immediately conscious, as we are of the power itself. It estimates what it enjoins, not merely as superiour in degree, but as superiour likewise in kind, to what is recommended by our other perceptive powers. Without this controlling faculty, endowed as we are with such a variety of senses and interfering desires, we should appear a fabrick destitute of order: but possessed of it, all our powers may be harmonious and consistent; they may all combine in one uniform and regular direction.

In short; if we had not the faculty of perceiving certain things in conduct to be right, and others to be wrong; and of perceiving our obligation to do what is right, and not to do what is wrong; we should not be moral and accountable beings.

If we be, as, I hope, I have shown we are, endowed with this faculty; there must be some things, which are immediately discerned by it to be right, and others to be wrong. There must, consequently, be in morals, as in other sciences, first principles, which derive not their evidence from any antecedent principles, but which may be said to be intuitively discerned.

Moral truths may be divided into two classes; such as are selfevident, and such as, from the selfevident ones, are deduced by reasoning. If the first be not discerned without reasoning, reasoning can never discern the last. The cases that require reasoning are few, compared with those that require none; and a man may be very honest and virtuous, who cannot reason, and who knows not what demonstration means.

If the rules of virtue were left to be discovered by reasoning, even by demonstrative reasoning, unhappy would be the condition of the far greater part of men, who have not the means of cultivating the power of reasoning to any high degree. As virtue is the business of all men, the first principles of it are written on their hearts, in characters so legible, that no man can pretend ignorance of them, or of his obligation to practise them. Reason, even with experience, is too often overpowered by passion; to restrain whose impetuosity, nothing less is requisite than the vigorous and commanding principle of duty.

II. The first principles of morals, into which all moral argumentation may be resolved, are discovered in a manner more analogous to the perceptions of sense than to the conclusions of reasoning. In morality, however, as well as in other sciences, reason is usefully introduced, and performs many important services. In many instances she regulates our belief; and in many instances she regulates our conduct. She determines the proper means to any end; and she decides the preference of one end over another. She may exhibit an object to the mind, though the perception which the mind has, when once the object is exhibited, may properly belong to a sense. She may be necessary to ascertain the circumstances and determine the motives to an action; though it be the moral sense that perceives the action to be either virtuous or vicious, after its motive and its circumstances have been discovered. She discerns the tendencies of the several senses, affections, and actions, and the comparative value of objects and gratifications. She judges concerning subordinate ends; but concerning ultimate ends she is not employed. These we prosecute by some immediate determination of the mind, which, in the order of action, is prior to all reasoning; for no opinion or judgment can move to action, where there is not a previous desire of some end.—This power of comparing the several enjoyments, of which our nature is susceptible, in order to discover which are most important to our happiness, is of the highest consequence and necessity to corroborate our moral faculty, and to preserve our affections in just rank and regular order.

A magistrate knows that it is his duty to promote the good of the commonwealth, which has intrusted him with authority. But whether one particular plan or another particular plan of conduct in office, may best promote the good of the commonwealth, may, in many cases, be doubtful. His conscience or moral sense determines the end, which he ought to pursue; and he has intuitive evidence that his end is good: but the means of attaining this end must be determined by reason. To select and ascertain those means, is often a matter of very considerable difficulty. Doubts may arise; opposite interests may occur; and a preference must be given to one side from a small over-balance, and from very nice views. This is particularly the case in questions with regard to justice. If every single instance of justice, like every single instance of benevolence, were pleasing and useful to society, the case would be more simple, and would be seldom liable to great controversy. But as single instances of justice are often pernicious in their first and immediate tendency; and as the advantage to society results only from the observance of the general rule, and from the concurrence and combination of several persons in the same equitable conduct; the case here becomes more intricate and involved. The various circumstances of society, the various consequences of any practice, the various interests which may be proposed, are all, on many occasions, doubtful, and subject to much discussion and inquiry. The design of municipal law (for let us still, from every direction, open a view to our principal object) the design of municipal law is to fix all the questions which regard justice. A very accurate reason or judgment is often requisite, to give the true determination amidst intricate doubts, arising from obscure or opposite utilities.

Thus, though good and ill, right and wrong are ultimately perceived by the moral sense, yet reason assists its operations, and, in many instances, strengthens and extends its influence. We may argue concerning propriety of conduct: just reasonings on the subject will establish principles for judging of what deserves praise: but, at the same time, these reasonings must always, in the last resort, appeal to the moral sense.

Farther; reason serves to illustrate, to prove, to extend, to apply what our moral sense has already suggested to us, concerning just and unjust, proper and improper, right and wrong. A father feels that paternal tenderness is refined and confirmed, by reflecting how consonant that feeling is to the relation between a parent and his child; how conducive it is to the happiness, not only of a single family, but, in its extension, to that of all mankind. We feel the beauty and excellence of virtue; but this sense is strengthened and improved by the lessons, which reason gives us concerning the foundations, the motives, the relations, the particular and the universal advantages flowing from this virtue, which, at first sight, appeared so beautiful.

Taste is a faculty, common, in some degree, to all men. But study, attention, comparison operate most powerfully towards its refinement. In the same manner, reason contributes to ascertain the exactness, and to discover and correct the mistakes, of the moral sense. A prejudice of education may be misapprehended for a determination of morality. 'Tis reason's province to compare and discriminate.

Reason performs an excellent service to the moral sense in another respect. It considers the relations of actions, and traces them to the remotest consequences. We often see men, with the most honest hearts and most pure intentions, embarrassed and puzzled, when a case, delicate and complicated, comes before them. They feel what is right; they are unshaken in their general principles; but they are unaccustomed to pursue them through their different ramifications, to make the necessary distinctions and exceptions, or to modify them according to the circumstances of time and place. 'Tis the business of reason to discharge this duty; and it will discharge it the better in proportion to the care which has been employed in exercising and improving it.

The existence of the moral sense has been denied by some philosophers of high fame: its authority has been attacked by others: the certainty and uniformity of its decisions have been arraigned by a third class.[t] We are told, that, without education, we should have been in a state of perfect indifference as to virtue and vice; that an education, opposite to that which we have received, would have taught us to regard as virtue that which we now dislike as vice, and to despise as vice that which we now esteem as virtue. In support of these observations, it is farther said, that moral sentiment is different in different countries, in different ages, and under different forms of government and religion; in a word, that it is as much the effect of custom, fashion, and artifice, as our taste in dress, furniture, and the modes of conversation.

t. 1. Paley 12–24. Kaims Pr. Eq. 8.

Facts and narratives have been assembled and accumulated, to evince the great diversity and even contrariety that subsists concerning moral opinions. And it has been gravely asked, whether the wild boy, who was caught in the woods of Hanover, would feel a sentiment of disapprobation upon being told of the conduct of a parricide. An investigation of those facts and narratives cannot find a place in these lectures; though the time bestowed on it might be well employed. It may, however, be proper to observe, that it is but candid to consider human nature in her improved, and not in her most rude or depraved forms. "The good experienced man," says Aristotle, "is the last measure of all things."[u] To ascertain moral principles, we appeal not to the common sense of savages, but of men in their most perfect state.

Epicurus, as well as some modern advocates of the same philosophy, seem to have taken their estimates of human nature from its meanest and most degrading exhibitions; but the noblest and most respectable philosophers of antiquity have chosen, for a much wiser and better purpose, to view it on the brightest and most advantageous side. "It is impossible," says the incomparable Addison,[v6] "to read a passage in Plato or Tully, and a thousand other ancient moralists, without being a greater and a better man for it. On the contrary, I could never read some modish modern authors, without being, for some time, out of humour with myself, and at every thing about me. Their business is to depreciate human nature, and consider it under its worst appearances. They give mean interpretation and base motives to the worthiest actions—in short, they endeavour to make no distinction between man and man, or between the species of men and that of brutes." True it is, that some men and some nations are savage and brutish; but is that a reason why their manners and their practices should be generally and reproachfully charged to the account of human nature? It may, perhaps, be somewhat to our purpose to observe, that in many of these representations, the picture, if compared with the original, will be found to be overcharged. For, in truth, between mankind, considered even in their rudest state, and the *mutum et turpe pecus*,[7] a very wide difference

u. 1. Hutch. 237. 121.

v. Tatler No. 103.

6. Joseph Addison (1672–1719) was an English writer and politician who founded *The Spectator*.

7. Dumb and ugly herd.

will be easily discovered. In the most uninformed savages, we find the *communes notitiae,* the common notions and practical principles of virtue, though the application of them is often extremely unnatural and absurd. These same savages have in them the seeds of the logician, the man of taste, the orator, the statesman, the man of virtue, and the saint. These seeds are planted in their minds by nature, though, for want of culture and exercise, they lie unnoticed, and are hardly perceived by themselves or by others. Besides, some nations that have been supposed stupid and barbarous by nature, have, upon fuller acquaintance with their history, been found to have been rendered barbarous and depraved by institution. When, by the power of some leading members, erroneous laws are once established, and it has become the interest of subordinate tyrants to support a corrupt system; errour and iniquity become sacred. Under such a system, the multitude are fettered by the prejudices of education, and awed by the dread of power, from the free exercise of their reason. These principles will account for the many absurd and execrable tenets and practices with regard to government, morals, and religion, which have been invented and established in opposition to the unbiassed sentiments, and in derogation of the natural rights of mankind. But, after making all the exceptions and abatements, of which these facts and narratives, if admitted in their fullest extent, would justify the claim, still it cannot be denied, but is even acknowledged, that some sorts of actions command and receive the esteem of mankind more than others; and that the approbation of them is general, though not universal. It will certainly be sufficient for our purpose to observe, that the dictates of reason are neither more general, nor more uniform, nor more certain, nor more commanding, than the dictates of the moral sense. Nay, farther; perhaps, upon inquiry, we shall find, that those obliquities, extravagancies, and inconsistencies of conduct, that are produced as proofs of the nonexistence or inutility of the moral sense, are, in fact, chargeable to that faculty, which is meant to be substituted in its place. We shall find that men always approve upon an opinion—true or false, but still an opinion—that the actions approved have the qualities and tendencies, which are the proper objects of approbation. They suppose that such actions will promote their own interest; or will be conducive to the publick good; or are required by the Deity; when, in truth, they have all the contrary properties—may be forbidden by the Deity, and may be detrimental both to publick and to private good. But when all this happens, to what cause is it to be traced? Does it prove the nonexistence of a moral sense, or does it prove, in such instances, the weakness or perversion of reason? The just solution is, that, in such instances, it is our reason, which presents false appearances to our moral sense.

It is with much reluctance, that the power of our instinctive or intuitive faculties is acknowledged by some philosophers. That the brutes are governed by instinct, but that man is governed by reason, is their favourite position. But fortunately for man, this position is not founded on truth. Our instincts, as well as our rational powers, are far superiour, both in number and in dignity, to those, which the brutes enjoy; and it were well for us, on many occasions, if we laid our reasoning systems aside, and were more attentive in observing the genuine impulses of nature. In this enlarged and elevated meaning, the sentiment of Pope[w] receives a double portion of force and sublimity.

"And reason raise o'er instinct as you can,
In this, 'tis God directs, in that, 'tis man."

This sentiment is not dictated merely in the fervid glow of enraptured poetry; it is affirmed by the deliberate judgment of calm, sedate philosophy. Our instincts are no other than the oracles of eternal wisdom; our conscience, in particular, is the voice of God within us: it teaches, it commands, it punishes, it rewards. The testimony of a good conscience is the purest and the noblest of human enjoyments.

It will be proper to examine a little more minutely the opinions of those, who allege reason to be the sole directress of human conduct. Reason may, indeed, instruct us in the pernicious or useful tendency of qualities and actions: but reason alone is not sufficient to produce any moral approbation or blame. Utility is only a tendency to a certain end; and if the end be totally indifferent to us, we shall feel the same indifference towards the means. It is requisite that *sentiment* should intervene, in order to give a preference to the useful above the pernicious tendencies.

Reason judges either of relations or of matters of fact. Let us consider some particular virtue or vice under both views. Let us take the instance

w. Ess. on Man. Ep. 3. v. 99

of *ingratitude.* This has place, when good will is expressed and good offices are performed on one side, and ill will or indifference is shown on the other. The first question is—what is that matter of fact, which is here called a vice? Indifference or ill will. But ill will is not always, nor in all circumstances a crime: and indifference may, on some occasions, be the result of the most philosophick fortitude. The vice of ingratitude, then, consists not in matter of fact.

Let us next inquire into the relations, which reason can discover, among the materials, of which ingratitude is composed. She discovers good will and good offices on one side, and ill will or indifference on the other. This is the relation of *contrariety.* Does ingratitude consist in this? To which side of the contrary relation is it to be placed? For this relation of contrariety is formed as much by good will and good offices, as by ill will or indifference. And yet the former deserves praise as much as the latter deserves blame.

If it shall be said, that the morality of an action does not consist in the relation of its different parts to one another, but in the relation of the whole actions to the rule; and that actions are denominated good or ill, as they agree or disagree with that rule; another question occurs—What is this rule of right? by what is it discovered or determined? By reason, it is said. How does reason discover or determine this rule? It must be by examining facts or the relations of things. But by the analysis which has been given of the particular instance under our consideration, it has appeared that the vice of ingratitude consists neither in the matter of fact, nor in the relation of the parts, of which the fact is composed. Objects in the animal world, nay inanimate objects, may have to each other all the same relations, which we observe in moral agents; but such objects are never supposed to be susceptible of merit or demerit, of virtue or vice.

The *ultimate* ends of human actions, can never, in any case, be accounted for by reason. They recommend themselves entirely to the sentiments and affections of men, without dependence on the intellectual faculties. Why do you take exercise? Because you desire health. Why do you desire health? Because sickness is painful. Why do you hate pain? No answer is heard. Can one be given? No. This is an ultimate end, and is not referred to any farther object.

To the second question, you may, perhaps, answer, that you desire health, because it is necessary for your improvement in your profession. Why are you anxious to make this improvement? You may, perhaps, answer again, because you wish to get money by it. Why do you wish to get money? Because, among other reasons, it is the instrument of pleasure. But why do you love pleasure? Can a reason be given for loving pleasure, any more than for hating pain? They are both ultimate objects. 'Tis impossible there can be a progress *in infinitum;* and that one thing can always be a reason, why another is hated or desired. Something must be hateful or desirable on its own account, and because of its immediate agreement or disagreement with human sentiment and affection.

Virtue and vice are ends; and are hateful or desirable on their own account. It is requisite, therefore, that, there should be some sentiment, which they touch—some internal taste or sense, which distinguishes moral good and evil, and which embraces one, and rejects the other. Thus are the offices of reason and of the moral sense at last ascertained. The former conveys the knowledge of truth and falsehood: the latter, the sentiment of beauty and deformity, of vice and virtue. The standard of one, founded on the nature of things, is eternal and inflexible. The standard of the other is ultimately derived from that supreme will, which bestowed on us our peculiar nature, and arranged the several classes and orders of existence. In this manner, we return to the great principle, from which we set out. It is necessary that reason should be fortified by the moral sense: without the moral sense, a man may be prudent, but he cannot be virtuous.

Philosophers have degraded our senses below their real importance. They represent them as powers, by which we have sensations and ideas only. But this is not the whole of their office; they judge as well as inform. Not confined to the mere office of conveying impressions, they are exalted to the function of judging of the nature and evidence of the impressions they convey. If this be admitted, our moral faculty may, without impropriety, be called the *moral sense.* Its testimony, like that of the external senses, is the immediate testimony of nature, and on it we have the same reason to rely. In its dignity, it is, without doubt, far superiour to every other power of the mind.

The moral sense, like all our other powers, comes to maturity by insensible degrees. It is peculiar to human nature. It is both intellectual and active. It is evidently intended, by nature, to be the immediate guide and director of our conduct, after we arrive at the years of understanding.

III. Reason and conscience can do much; but still they stand in need of support and assistance. They are useful and excellent monitors; but, at some times, their admonitions are not sufficiently clear; at other times, they are not sufficiently powerful; at all times, their influence is not sufficiently extensive. Great and sublime truths, indeed, would appear to a few; but the world, at large, would be dark and ignorant. The mass of mankind would resemble a chaos, in which a few sparks, that would diffuse a glimmering light, would serve only to show, in a more striking manner, the thick darkness with which they are surrounded. Their weakness is strengthened, their darkness is illuminated, their influence is enlarged by that heaven-descended science, which has brought life and immortality to light. In compassion to the imperfection of our internal powers, our all-gracious Creator, Preserver, and Ruler has been pleased to discover and enforce his laws, by a revelation given to us immediately and directly from himself. This revelation is contained in the holy scriptures. The moral precepts delivered in the sacred oracles form a part of the law of nature, are of the same origin, and of the same obligation, operating universally and perpetually.

On some important subjects, those in particular, which relate to the Deity, to Providence, and to a future state, our natural knowledge is greatly improved, refined, and exalted by that which is revealed. On these subjects, one who has had the advantage of a common education in a christian country, knows more, and with more certainty, than was known by the wisest of the ancient philosophers.

One superiour advantage the precepts delivered in the sacred oracles clearly possess. They are, of all, the most explicit and the most certain. A publick minister, judging from what he knows of the interests, views, and designs of the state, which he represents, may take his resolutions and measures, in many cases, with confidence and safety; and may presume, with great probability, how the state itself would act. But if, besides this general knowledge, and these presumptions highly probable, he was furnished also with particular instructions for the regulation of his conduct; would he not naturally observe and govern himself by both rules? In cases, where his instructions are clear and positive, there would be an end of all farther deliberation. In other cases, where his instructions are silent, he would supply them by his general knowledge, and by the information, which he could collect from other quarters, concerning the counsels and systems of the commonwealth. Thus it is with regard to reason, conscience, and the holy scriptures. Where the latter give instructions, those instructions are supereminently authentick. But whoever expects to find, in them, particular directions for every moral doubt which arises, expects more than he will find. They generally presuppose a knowledge of the principles of morality; and are employed not so much in teaching new rules on this subject, as in enforcing the practice of those already known, by a greater certainty, and by new sanctions. They present the warmest recommendations and the strongest inducements in favour of virtue: they exhibit the most powerful dissuasives from vice. But the origin, the nature, and the extent of the several rights and duties they do not explain; nor do they specify in what instances one right or duty is entitled to preference over another. They are addressed to rational and moral agents, capable of previously knowing the rights of men, and the tendencies of actions; of approving what is good, and of disapproving what is evil.

These considerations show, that the scriptures support, confirm, and corroborate, but do not supercede the operations of reason and the moral sense. The information with regard to our duties and obligations, drawn from these different sources, ought not to run in unconnected and diminished channels: it should flow in one united stream, which, by its combined force and just direction, will impel us uniformly and effectually towards our greatest good.

We have traced, with some minuteness, the efficient principle of obligation, and the several means, by which our duty may be known. It will be proper to turn our attention back to the opinions that have been held, in philosophy and jurisprudence, concerning this subject. On a review of them, we shall now find that, in general, they are defective rather than erroneous; that they have fallen short of the mark, rather than deviated from the proper course.

The fitness of things denotes their fitness to produce our happiness: their nature means that actual constitution of the world, by which some things produce happiness, and others misery. Reason is one of the means, by which we discern between those things, which produce the former, and those things, which produce the latter. The moral sense feels and operates to promote the same essential discriminations. Whatever promotes the greatest happiness of the whole, is congenial to the principles of utility and sociability: and whatever unites in it all the foregoing properties, must be agreeable to the will of God: for, as has been said once, and as ought to be said again, his will is graciously comprised in this one paternal precept—Let man pursue his happiness and perfection.

The law of nature is immutable; not by the effect of an arbitrary disposition, but because it has its foundation in the nature, constitution, and mutual relations of men and things. While these continue to be the same, it must continue to be the same also. This immutability of nature's laws has nothing in it repugnant to the supreme power of an all-perfect Being. Since he himself is the author of our constitution; he cannot but command or forbid such things as are necessarily agreeable or disagreeable to this very constitution. He is under the glorious necessity of not contradicting himself. This necessity, far from limiting or diminishing his perfections, adds to their external character, and points out their excellency.

The law of nature is universal. For it is true, not only that all men are equally subject to the command of their Maker; but it is true also, that the law of nature, having its foundation in the constitution and state of man, has an essential fitness for all mankind, and binds them without distinction.

This law, or right reason, as Cicero[x] calls it, is thus beautifully described by that eloquent philosopher. "It is, indeed," says he, "a true law, conformable to nature, diffused among all men, unchangeable, eternal. By its commands, it calls men to their duty: by its prohibitions, it deters them from vice. To diminish, to alter, much more to abolish this law, is a vain attempt. Neither by the senate, nor by the people, can its powerful obligation be dissolved. It requires no interpreter or commentator. It is not one law at Rome, another at Athens; one law now, another hereafter: it is the same eternal and immutable law, given at all times and to all nations: for God, who is its author and promulgator, is always the sole master and sovereign of mankind."

"Man never *is,*" says the poet, in a seeming tone of complaint, "but always *to be* blest." The sentiment would certainly be more consolatory, and, I think, it would be likewise more just, if we were to say—man ever *is; for* always to be blest. That we should have more and better things before us,

x. De Rep. l. 3.

than all that we have yet acquired or enjoyed, is unquestionably a most desirable state. The reflection on this circumstance, far from diminishing our sense or the importance of our present attainments and advantages, produces the contrary effects. The present is gilded by the prospect of the future.

When Alexander had conquered a world, and had nothing left to conquer; what did he do? He sat down and wept. A well directed ambition that has conquered worlds, is exempted from the fate of that of Alexander the Great: it still sees before it more and better worlds as the objects of conquest.

It is the glorious destiny of man to be always progressive. Forgetting those things that are behind, it is his duty, and it is his happiness, to press on towards those that are before. In the order of Providence, as has been observed on another occasion, the progress of societies towards perfection resembles that of an individual. This progress has hitherto been but slow: by many unpropitious events, it has often been interrupted: but may we not indulge the pleasing expectation, that, in future, it will be accelerated; and will meet with fewer and less considerable interruptions.

Many circumstances seem—at least to a mind anxious to see it, and apt to believe what it is anxious to see—many circumstances seem to indicate the opening of such a glorious prospect. The principles and the practice of liberty are gaining ground, in more than one section of the world. Where liberty prevails, the arts and sciences lift up their heads and flourish. Where the arts and sciences flourish, political and moral improvements will likewise be made. All will receive from each, and each will receive from all, mutual support and assistance: mutually supported and assisted, all may be carried to a degree of perfection hitherto unknown; perhaps, hitherto not believed.

"Men," says the sagacious Hooker, "if we view them in their spring, are, at the first, without understanding or knowledge at all. Nevertheless, from this utter vacuity, they grow by degrees, till they become at length to be even as the angels themselves are. That which agreeth to the one now, the other shall attain to in the end: they are not so far disjoined and severed, but that they come at length to meet."[y]

y. Hooker, b. 1. s. 6. p. 8.

Our progress in virtue should certainly bear a just proportion to our progress in knowledge. Morals are undoubtedly capable of being carried to a much higher degree of excellence than the sciences, excellent as they are. Hence we may infer, that the law of nature, though immutable in its principles, will be progressive in its operations and effects. Indeed, the same immutable principles will direct this progression. In every period of his existence, the law, which the divine wisdom has approved for man, will not only be fitted, to the cotemporary degree, but will be calculated to produce, in future, a still higher degree of perfection.

A delineation of the laws of nature, has been often attempted. Books, under the appellations of institutes and systems of that law, have been often published. From what has been said concerning it, the most finished performances executed by human hands cannot be perfect. But most of them have been rude and imperfect to a very unnecessary, some, to a shameful degree.

A more perfect work than has yet appeared upon this great subject, would be a most valuable present to mankind. Even the most general outlines of it cannot, at least in these lectures, be expected from me.

CHAPTER IV.
Of the Law of Nations.

The law of nature, when applied to states or political societies, receives a new name, that of the law of nations. This law, important in all states, is of peculiar importance in free ones. The States of America are certainly entitled to this dignified appellation. A weighty part of the publick business is transacted by the citizens at large. They appoint the legislature, and, either mediately or immediately, the executive servants of the publick. As the conduct of a state, both with regard to itself and others, must greatly depend upon the character, the talents, and the principles of those, to whom the direction of that conduct is intrusted; it is highly necessary that those who are to protect the rights, and to perform the duties of the commonwealth, should be men of proper principles, talents, and characters: if so, it is highly necessary that those who appoint them should be able, in some degree at least, to distinguish and select those men, whose principles, talents, and characters are proper. In order to do this, it is greatly useful that they have, at least, some just and general knowledge of those rights that are to be protected, and of those duties that are to be performed. Without this, they will be unable to form a rational conjecture, concerning the future conduct of those whom they are to elect. Nay, what is more; without some such general and just knowledge, they will be unable to form a rational judgment, concerning the past and present conduct of those whom they have already elected; and, consequently, will be unable to form a rational determination whether, at the next election, they should reappoint them, or substitute others in their place. As the practice of the law of nations, therefore, must, in a free government, depend very considerably on the acts of the citizens, it is of high import that, among those citizens, its knowledge be generally diffused.

But, if the knowledge of the law of nations is greatly useful to those who appoint, it must surely be highly necessary to those who are appointed, the publick servants and stewards of the commonwealth. Can its interests be properly managed, can its character be properly supported, can its happiness be properly consulted, by those who know not what it owes to others, what it owes to itself, what it has a right to claim from others, and what it has a right to provide for itself? In a free commonwealth, the path to publick service and to publick honour is open to all. Should not all, therefore, sedulously endeavour to become masters of such qualifications, as will enable them to tread this path with credit to themselves, and with advantage to their country?

In the United States, a system of republicks, the law of nations acquires an importance still more peculiar and distinguished. In the United States, the law of nations, operates upon peculiar relations, and upon those relations with peculiar energy. Well am I justified, on every account, in announcing the dignity and greatness of the subject, upon which I am now to enter.

On all occasions, let us beware of being misled by names. Though the law, which I am now to consider, receives a new appellation; it retains, unimpaired, its qualities and its power. The law of nations, as well as the law of nature, is of obligation indispensable: the law of nations, as well as the law of nature, is of origin divine.

The opinions of many concerning the law of nations have been very vague and unsatisfactory; and if such have been the opinions, we have little reason to be surprised, that the conduct of nations has too often been diametrically opposite to the law, by which it ought to have been regulated. In the judgment of some writers, it would seem, for instance, that neither the state which commences an unjust war, nor the chief who conducts it, derogates from the general sanctity of their respective characters. An ardent love of their country they seem to have thought a passion too heroick, to be restrained within the narrow limits of systematick morality; and those have been too often considered as the greatest patriots, who have contributed most to gratify the publick passion for conquest and power. States, as well as monarchs, have too frequently been blinded by ambition. Of this there is scarcely a page in ancient or in modern history, relating to national contentions, but will furnish the most glaring proofs. The melancholy truth is, that the law of nations, though founded on the most solid principles of natural obligation, has been but imperfectly viewed in theory, and has been too much disregarded in practice.

The profound and penetrating Bacon was not inattentive to the imperfect state, in which he found the science of the law of nations. As, in another science, that enlightened philosophical guide pointed to the discoveries of a Newton;[1] so in this, in all probability, he laid a foundation for the researches of a Grotius. For we have reason to believe, as we are told by Barbeyrac,[a] that it was the study of the works of Lord Bacon, that first inspired Grotius with the design of writing a system concerning the law of nations. In this science Grotius did much; for he was well qualified to do much. Extensive knowledge, prodigious reading, indefatigable application to study, all these were certainly his. Yet with all these, he was far from being as successful in law, as Sir Isaac Newton was in philosophy. He was unfortunate in not setting out on right and solid principles. His celebrated book of the Rights of War and Peace is indeed useful; but it ought not to be read without a due degree of caution: nor ought all his doctrines to be received, without the necessary grains of allowance. At this we ought not to wonder, when we consider the extent, the variety, and the importance of his subject, and that, before his time, it was little known, and much neglected. His opinion concerning the source and the obligation of the law of nations is very defective. He separates that law from the law of nature, and assigns to it a different origin. "When many men," says he, "at different times and places, unanimously affirm the same thing for truth; this should be ascribed to a general cause. In the subjects treated of by us, this cause can be no other than either a just inference drawn from the principles of nature, or a universal consent. The first discovers to us the law of nature, the second the law of nations."[b] The law of nations, we see, he traces from the principle of universal consent. The consequence of this is, that the law of nations would be obligatory only upon those by whom the consent was given, and only by reason of that consent. The farther consequence would be, that the law of nations would lose a part, and the

1. Sir Isaac Newton (1643–1727) was an English physicist, mathematician, and astronomer.

a. Pref. to Puff. s. 29. p. 79.

b. Gro. Prel. s. 41.

greatest part, of its obligatory force, and would also be restrained as to the sphere of its operations. That it would lose the greatest part of its obligatory force, sufficiently appears from what we have said at large concerning the origin and obligation of natural law, evincing it to be the will of God. That it would be restrained as to the sphere of its operations, appears from what Grotius himself says, when he explains his meaning in another place. He qualifies the universality of his expression by adding these words, "at least the most civilized nations;" and he afterwards says that this addition is made "with reason."[c] On the *least* civilized nations, therefore, the law of nations would not, according to his account of it, be obligatory.

I admit that there are laws of nations—perhaps it is to be wished that they were designated by an appropriate name; for names, after all, will have their influence on operations—I freely admit that there are laws of nations, which are founded altogether upon consent. National treaties are laws of nations, obligatory solely by consent. The customs of nations become laws solely by consent. Both kinds are certainly voluntary. But the municipal laws of a state are not more different from the law of nature, than those voluntary laws of nations are, in their source and power, different from the law of nations, properly so called. Indeed, those voluntary laws of nations are as much under the control of the law of nations, properly so called, as municipal laws are under the control of the law of nature. The law of nations, properly so called, is the law of nature applied to states and sovereigns. The law of nations, properly so called, is the law of states and sovereigns, obligatory upon them in the same manner, and for the same reasons, as the law of nature is obligatory upon individuals. Universal, indispensable, and unchangeable is the obligation of both.

But it will naturally be asked, if the law of nations bears, as from this account it bears, the same relation to states, which the law of nature bears to individuals; if the law of nature and the law of nations are accompanied with the same obligatory power, and are derived from the same common source; why should the law of nations have a distinct name? Why should it be considered as a separate science? Some have thought that the difference was only in name; and if only in name, there could surely be no solid reason for establishing even that difference. Of those, who thought

c. Gro. 14.

so, Puffendorff was one. "Many," says he,[d] "assert the law of nature and of nations to be the very same thing, differing no otherwise than in external denomination. Thus Mr. Hobbes divides natural law, into the natural law of men, and the natural law of states, commonly called the law of nations. He observes, that the precepts of both are the same; but that as states, when once instituted, assume the personal properties of men, what we call the law of nature, when we speak of particular men, we denominate the law of nations, when we apply it to whole states, nations, or people. This opinion," continues Puffendorff, "we, for our part, readily subscribe to; nor do we conceive, that there is any other voluntary or positive law of nations, properly vested with a true and legal force, and obliging as the ordinance of a superiour power." By the way, we may here observe, that, with regard to the law of nations, Grotius and Puffendorff seem to have run into contrary extremes. The former was of opinion, that the whole law of nations took its origin and authority from consent. The latter was of opinion, that every part of the law of nations was the same with the law of nature, that no part of it could receive its obligatory force from consent; because, according to his favourite notion of law, no such thing could exist without the intervention of a superiour power. The truth seems to lie between the two great philosophers. The law of nations, properly so called, or, as it may be termed, the natural law of nations, is a part, and an important part, of the law of nature. The voluntary law of nations falls under the class of laws that are positive. If a particular name had been appropriated to this last species of law, it is probable that much confusion and ambiguity, on this subject, would have been avoided; and the distinction between the different parts of that law, comprehended, at present, under the name of the law of nations, would have been as clearly marked, as uniformly preserved, and as familiarly taken, as the well known and well founded distinction between natural and municipal law. But to return.

As Puffendorff thought that the law of nature and the law of nations were precisely the same, he has not, in his book on these subjects, treated of the law of nations separately; but has every where joined it with the law of nature, properly so called. His example has been followed by the greatest part of succeeding writers. But the imitation of it has produced

d. Puff. p. 149. b. 2. c. 3. s. 23.

a confusion of two objects, which ought to have been viewed and studied distinctly and apart. Though the law of nations, properly so called, be a part of the law of nature; though it spring from the same source; and though it is attended with the same obligatory power; yet it must be remembered that its application is made to very different objects. The law of nature is applied to individuals: the law of nations is applied to states. The important difference between the objects, will occasion a proportioned difference in the application of the law.[e] This difference in the application renders it fit that the law of nature, when applied to states, should receive an appropriate name, and should be taught and studied as a separate science.

Though states or nations are considered as moral persons; yet the nature and essence of these moral persons differ necessarily, in many respects, from the nature and essence of the individuals, of whom they are composed. The application of a law must be made in a manner suitable to its object. The application, therefore, of the law of nature to nations must be made in a manner suitable to nations: its application to individuals must be made in a manner suitable to individuals. But as nations differ from individuals; the application of the law suitable to the former, must be different from its application suitable to the latter. To nations this different application cannot be made with accuracy, with justness, and with perspicuity, without the aid of new and discriminating rules. These rules will evince, that, on the principles themselves of the law of nature, that law, when applied to nations, will prescribe decisions different from those which it would prescribe, when applied to individuals. To investigate those rules; to deduce, from the same great and leading principles, applications differing in proportion to the difference of the persons to which they are applied, is the object of the law of nations, considered as a science distinct and separate from that of the law of nature.

Having given you this general idea and description of the law of nations; need I expatiate on its dignity and importance? The law of nations is the law of sovereigns. In free states, such as ours, the sovereign or supreme power resides in the people. In free states, therefore, such as ours, the law of nations is the law of the people. Let us again beware of being misled

e. Vat. Pref. 1.

by an ambiguity, sometimes, such is the structure of language, unavoidable. When I say that, in free states, the law of nations is the law of the people; I mean not that it is a law made by the people, or by virtue of their delegated authority; as, in free states, all municipal laws are. But when I say that, in free states, the law of nations is the law of the people; I mean that, as the law of nature, in other words, as the will of nature's God, it is indispensably binding upon the people, in whom the sovereign power resides; and who are, consequently, under the most sacred obligations to exercise that power, or to delegate it to such as will exercise it, in a manner agreeable to those rules and maxims, which the law of nature prescribes to every state, for the happiness of each, and for the happiness of all. How vast—how important—how interesting are these truths! They announce to a free people how exalted their rights; but, at the same time, they announce to a free people how solemn their duties are. If a practical knowledge and a just sense of these rights and these duties were diffused among the citizens, and properly impressed upon their hearts and minds; how great, how beneficial, how lasting would be their fruits! But, unfortunately, as there have been and there are, in arbitrary governments, flatterers of princes; so there have been and there are, in free governments, flatterers of the people. One distinction, indeed, is to be taken between them. The latter herd of flatterers persuade the people to make an improper use of the power, which of right they have: the former herd persuade princes to make an improper use of power, which of right they have not. In other respects, both herds are equally pernicious. Both flatter to promote their private interests: both betray the interests of those whom they flatter.

It is of the highest, and, in free states, it is of the most general importance, that the sacred obligation of the law of nations should be accurately known and deeply felt. Of all subjects, it is agreeable and useful to form just and adequate conceptions; but of those especially, which have an influence on the practice and morality of states. For it is a serious truth, however much it has been unattended to in practice, that the laws of morality are equally strict with regard to societies, as to the individuals of whom the societies are composed. It must be owing either to ignorance, or to a very unjustifiable disregard to this great truth, that some transactions of publick bodies have often escaped censure, nay, sometimes have received applause, though those transactions have been such, as none of the individuals composing those bodies would have dared to introduce into the management of his private affairs; because the person introducing them would have been branded with the most reproachful of names and characters. It has been long admitted, by those who have been the best judges of private life and manners, that integrity and sound policy go hand in hand. It is high time that this maxim should find an establishment in the councils of states, and in the cabinets of princes. Its establishment there would diffuse far and wide the most salutary and benign effects.

Opinions concerning the extent of the law of nations have not been less defective and inadequate, than those concerning its origin and obligatory force. Some seem to have thought, that this law respects and regulates the conduct of nations only in their intercourse with each other. A very important branch of this law—that containing the duties which a nation owes itself—seems to have escaped their attention. "The general principle," says Burlamaqui,[f] "of the law of nations, is nothing more than the general law of sociability, which obliges nations to the same duties as are prescribed to individuals. Thus the law of natural equality, which prohibits injury and commands the reparation of damage done; the law of beneficence, and of fidelity to our engagements, are laws respecting nations, and imposing, both on the people and on their respective sovereigns, the same duties as are prescribed to individuals." Several other writers concerning the law of nations appear to have formed the same imperfect conceptions with regard to its extent. Let us recur to what the law of nature dictates to an individual. Are there not duties which he owes to himself? Is he not obliged to consult and promote his preservation, his freedom, his reputation, his improvement, his perfection, his happiness? Now that we have seen the law of nature as it respects the duties of individuals, let us see the law of nations as it respects the duties of states, to themselves: for we must recollect that the law of nations is only the law of nature judiciously applied to the conduct of states. From the duties of states, as well as of individuals, to themselves; a number of corresponding rights will be found to arise.

A state ought to attend to the preservation of its own existence. In what does the existence of a state consist? It consists in the association of the individuals, of which it is composed. In what consists the preservation of

f. 2. Burl. 3. 4. 1. Burl. 196.

this existence? It consists in the duration of that association. When this association is dissolved, the state ceases to exist; though all the members, of whom it was composed, may still remain. It is the duty of a state, therefore, to preserve this association undissolved and unimpaired. But in this, as in many other instances, a difference between the nature of states and the nature of individuals will occasion, for the reasons already mentioned, a proportioned difference in the application of the law of nature. Nations, as well as men, are taught by the law of nature, gracious in its precepts, to consider their happiness as the great end of their existence. But without existence there can be no happiness: the means, therefore, must be secured, in order to secure the end. But yet, between the duty of self-preservation required from a state, and the duty of self-preservation required from a man, there is a most material difference; and this difference is founded on the law of nature itself. A nation has a right to assign to its existence a voluntary termination: a man has not. What can be the reasons of this difference? Several may be given. By the voluntary act of the individuals forming the nation, the nation was called into existence: they who bind, can also untie: by the voluntary act, therefore, of the individuals forming the nation, the nation may be reduced to its original nothing. But it was not by his own voluntary act that the man made his appearance upon the theatre of life; he cannot, therefore, plead the right of the nation, by his own voluntary act to make his exit. He did not make; therefore, he has no right to destroy himself. He alone, whose gift this state of existence is, has the right to say when and how it shall receive its termination.

Again; though nations are considered as moral persons, and, in that character, as entitled, in many respects, to claim the rights, and as obliged, in many respects, to perform the duties of natural persons; yet we must always remember that of natural persons those moral persons are composed; that for the sake of natural persons those moral persons were formed; and that while we suppose those moral persons to live, and think, and act, we know that they are natural persons alone, who really exist or feel, who really deliberate, resolve, and execute. Now none of these observations resulting from the nature and essence of the nation, can be applied, with any degree of propriety, to the nature and essence of the man: and, therefore, the inferences drawn from these observations, with regard to the case of the nation, are wholly inapplicable to the case of the man.

One of these inferences is, that as it was for the happiness of the members that the moral existence of the nation was produced; so the happiness of the members may require this moral existence to be annihilated. Can this inference be applied to the man?

Further; there may be a moral certainty, that, of the voluntary dissolution of the nation, the necessary consequence will be an increase of happiness. Can such a consequence be predicted, with moral certainty, concerning the voluntary death of the man?

This instance shows, in a striking manner, how, on some occasions, the law of nature, when applied to a nation, may dictate or authorize a measure of conduct very different from that, which it would authorize and dictate with regard to a man.

As it is, in general, the duty of a state to preserve itself; so it is, in general, its duty to preserve its members. This is a duty which it owes to them, and to itself. It owes it to them, because their advantage was the final cause of their joining in the association, and engaging to support it; and they ought not to be deprived of this advantage, while they fulfil the conditions, on which it was stipulated. This duty the nation owes to itself, because the loss of its members is a proportionable loss of its strength; and the loss of its strength is proportionably injurious both to its security, and to its preservation. The result of these principles is, that the body of a nation should not abandon a country, a city, or even an individual, who has not forfeited his rights in the society.

The right and duty of a state to preserve its members are subject to the same limitations and conditions, as its right and duty to preserve itself. As, for some reasons, the society may be dissolved; so, for others, it may be dismembered. A part may be separated from the other parts; and that part may either become a new state, or may associate with another state already formed. An illustration of this doctrine may be drawn from a recent instance, which has happened in the commonwealth of Virginia. The district of Kentucky has, by an amicable agreement, been disjoined from the rest of the commonwealth, and has been formed into a separate state. It is a pleasure, perhaps I may add it is a laudable pride, to be able to furnish, to the world, the first examples of carrying into practice the most sublime parts of the most sublime theories of government and law.

When a nation has a right, and is under an obligation to preserve itself and its members; it has, by a necessary consequence, a right to do every thing, which, without injuring others, it can do, in order to accomplish and secure those objects. The law of nature prescribes not impossibilities: it imposes not an obligation, without giving a right to the necessary means of fulfilling it. The same principles, which evince the right of a nation to do every thing, which it lawfully may, for the preservation of itself and of its members, evince its right, also, to avoid and prevent, as much as it lawfully may, every thing which would load it with injuries, or threaten it with danger.

It is the right, and generally it is the duty, of a state, to form a constitution, to institute civil government, and to establish laws. If the constitution formed, or the government instituted, or the laws established shall, on experience, be found weak, or inconvenient, or pernicious; it is the right, and it is the duty of the state to strengthen, or alter, or abolish them. These subjects will be fully treated in another place.

A nation ought to know itself. It ought to form a just estimate of its own situation, both with regard to itself and to its neighbours. It ought to learn the excellencies, and the blemishes likewise of its own constitution. It ought to review the instances in which it has already attained, and it ought to ascertain those in which it falls short of, a practicable degree of perfection. It ought to find out what improvements are peculiarly necessary to be promoted, and what faults it is peculiarly necessary to avoid. Without a discriminating sagacity of this kind, the principle of imitation, intended for the wisest purposes in states as well as in individuals, would be always an uncertain, sometimes a dangerous guide. A measure extremely salutary to one state, might be extremely injurious to another. What, in one situation, would be productive of peace and happiness, might, in another, be the unfortunate cause of infelicity and war. Above all things, the genius and manners of the people ought to be carefully consulted. The government ought to be administered agreeably to this genius and these manners; but how can this be done, if this genius and these manners are unknown? This duty of self-knowledge is of vast extent and of vast importance, in nations as well as in men.

To love and to deserve honest fame, is another duty of a people, as well as of an individual. The reputation of a state is not only a pleasant, it is also a valuable possession. It attracts the esteem, it represses the unfriendly inclinations of its neighbours. This reputation is acquired by virtue, and by the conduct which virtue inspires. It is founded on the publick transactions of the state, and on the private behaviour of its members.

A state should avoid ostentation, but it should support its dignity. This should never be suffered to be degraded among other nations. In transactions between states, an attention to this object is of much greater importance than is generally imagined. Even the marks and titles of respect, to which a nation, and those who represent a nation, are entitled, ought not to be considered as trivial: they should be claimed with firmness: they should be given with alacrity. The dignity, the equality, the mutual independence, and the frequent intercourse of nations render such a tenour of conduct altogether indispensable.

It is the duty of a nation to intrust the management of its affairs only to its wisest and best citizens. The immense importance of this duty is easily seen; but it is not sufficiently regarded. The meanest menial of a family will not be received without examination and cautious inquiry. The most important servants of the publick will be voted in without consideration and without care. In electioneering, as it is called, we frequently find warm recommendations and active intrigues in favour of candidates for the highest offices, to whom the recommenders and intriguers would not, if put to the test, intrust the management of the smallest part of their own private interest. An election ground, the great theatre of original sovereignty, on which nothing but inviolable integrity and independent virtue should be exhibited, is often and lamentably transformed into a scene of the vilest and lowest debauchery and deception. An election maneuvre, an election story, are names appropriated to a conduct, which, in other and inferiour transactions, would be branded, and justly branded, with the most opprobrious appellations. Even those, who may be safely trusted every where else, will play false at elections. The remarks, which I have made concerning general elections, may be too often made, with equal truth, concerning other appointments to offices. But these things ought not to be. When the obligation and the importance of the great national duty required at elections—a duty prescribed by him who made us free—a duty prescribed that we may continue free—when all this shall be sufficiently diffused, and known, and felt; these things will not be. The people will then elect conscientiously; and will require conscientious conduct from those whom they elect.

A nation ought to encourage true patriotism in its members. The first step towards this encouragement is to distinguish between its real and its pretended friends. The discrimination, it is true, is often difficult, sometimes impracticable: but it is equally true, that it may frequently be made. Let the same care be employed, let the same pains be taken, to ascertain the marks of deceit and the marks of sincerity in publick life, and in intriguing for publick office, which are usually taken and employed in private life, and in solicitations for acts of private friendship. The care and pains will sometimes, indeed, be fruitless; but they will sometimes, too, be successful; at all times, they will be faithful witnesses, that those, who have employed them, have discharged their duty.

If a nation establish itself, or extend its establishment in a country already inhabited by others; it ought to observe strict justice, in both instances, with the former inhabitants. This is a part of the law of nations, that very nearly concerns the United States. It ought, therefore, to be well understood. The whole earth is allotted for the nourishment of its inhabitants; but it is not sufficient for this purpose, unless they aid it by labour and culture. The cultivation of the earth, therefore, is a duty incumbent on man by the order of nature. Those nations that live by hunting, and have more land than is necessary even for the purposes of hunting, should transfer it to those who will make a more advantageous use of it: those who will make this use of it ought to pay, for they can afford to pay, a reasonable equivalent. Even when the lands are no more than sufficient for the purposes of hunting, it is the duty of the new inhabitants, if advanced in society, to teach, and it is the duty of the original inhabitants, if less advanced in society, to learn, the arts and uses of agriculture. This will enable the latter gradually to contract, and the former gradually to extend their settlements, till the science of agriculture is equally improved in both. By these means, the intentions of nature will be fulfilled; the old and the new inhabitants will be reciprocally useful; peace will be preserved, and justice will be done.

It is the duty of a nation to augment its numbers. The performance of this duty will naturally result from the discharge of its other duties: by discharging them, the number of persons born in the society will be increased;

and strangers will be incited to wish a participation in its blessings. Among other means of increasing the number of citizens, there are three of peculiar efficacy. The first is, easily to receive all strangers of good character, and to communicate to them the advantages of liberty. The state will be thus filled with citizens, who will bring with them commerce and the arts, and a rich variety of manners and characters. Another means conducive to the same end is, to encourage marriages. These are the pledges of the state. A third means for augmenting the number of inhabitants is, to preserve the rights of conscience inviolate. The right of private judgment is one of the greatest advantages of mankind; and is always considered as such. To be deprived of it is insufferable. To enjoy it lays a foundation for that peace of mind, which the laws cannot give, and for the loss of which the laws can offer no compensation.

A nation should aim at its perfection. The advantage and improvement of the citizens are the ends proposed by the social union. Whatever will render that union more perfect will promote these ends. The same principles, therefore, which show that a man ought to pursue the perfection of his nature, will show, likewise, that the citizens ought to contribute every thing in their power towards the perfection of the state. This right involves the right of preventing and avoiding every thing, which would interrupt or retard the progress of the state towards its perfection. It also involves the right of acquiring every thing, without which its perfection cannot be promoted or obtained.

Happiness is the centre, to which men and nations are attracted: it is, therefore, the duty of a nation to consult its happiness. In order to do this, it is necessary that the nation be instructed to search for happiness where happiness is to be found. The impressions that are made first, sink deepest; they frequently continue through life. That seed, which is sown in the tender minds of youth, will produce abundance of good, or abundance of evil. The education of youth, therefore, is of prime importance to the happiness of the state. The arts, the sciences, philosophy, virtue, and religion, all contribute to the happiness, all, therefore, ought to receive the encouragement, of the nation. In this manner, publick and private felicity will go hand in hand, and mutually assist each other in their progress.

When men have formed themselves into a state or nation, they may reciprocally enter into particular engagements, and, in this manner, contract new obligations in favour of the members of the community; but they cannot, by this union, discharge themselves from any duties which they previously owed to those, who form no part of the union. They continue under all the obligations required by the universal society of the human race—the great society of nations. The law of that great and universal society requires, that each nation should contribute to the perfection and happiness of the others. It is, therefore, a duty which every nation owes to itself, to acquire those qualifications, which will fit and enable it to discharge those duties which it owes to others. What those duties are, we shall now very concisely and summarily inquire.

The first and most necessary duty of nations, as well as of men, is to do no wrong or injury. Justice is a sacred law of nations. If the law of the great society of nations requires, as we have seen it to require, that each should contribute to the perfection and happiness of others; the first degree of this duty surely is, that each should abstain from every thing, which would positively impair that perfection and happiness. This great principle prohibits one nation from exciting disturbances in another, from seducing its citizens, from depriving it of its natural advantages, from calumniating its reputation, from debauching the attachment of its allies, from fomenting or encouraging the hatred of its enemies. If, however, a nation, in the necessary prosecution of its own duties and rights, does what is disagreeable or even inconvenient to another, this is not to be considered as an injury; it ought to be viewed as the unavoidable result, and not as the governing principle of its conduct. If, at such conduct, offence is taken, it is the fault of that nation, which takes, not of that nation, which occasions it.

But nations are not only forbidden to do evil; they are also commanded to do good to one another. The duties of humanity are incumbent upon nations as well as upon individuals. An individual cannot subsist, at least he cannot subsist comfortably, by himself. What is true concerning one, is true concerning all. Without mutual good offices and assistance, therefore, happiness could not be procured, perhaps existence could not be preserved. Hence the necessity of the duties of humanity among individuals. Every one is obliged, in the first place, to do what he can for himself; in the next, to do what he can for others; beginning with those with whom he is most intimately connected. The consequence is, that each man is obliged to give to others every assistance, for which they have a real occasion, and which he can give without being wanting to himself. What each is obliged to perform for others, from others he is entitled to receive. Hence the advantage as well as the duty of humanity. These principles receive an application to states as well as to men. Each nation owes to every other the duties of humanity. It is true, there may be some difference in the application, in this as well as in other instances: but the principles of the application are the same. A nation can subsist by itself more securely and more comfortably than an individual can; therefore the duty of mutual assistance will not, at all periods, be equally indispensable, or return with equal frequency. But when it becomes, as it may become, equally indispensable; and when it returns, as it may return, with equal frequency; it ought, in either case, to be equally performed. One individual may attack another daily: a longer time is necessary for the aggression of one nation upon another. The assistance, therefore, which ought to be given to the individual daily, will be necessary for the nation only at more distant intervals of time. But between nations, what the duties of humanity lose in point of frequency, they gain in point of importance, in proportion, perhaps, to the difference between a single individual, and all those individuals of whom the nation is composed.

One nation ought to give to another, not only the assistance necessary to its preservation, but that also which is necessary to its perfection, whenever it is wanted, and whenever, consistently with other superiour duties, it can be given. The cases in which assistance ought to be demanded, and those in which it ought to be given, must be decided respectively by that nation which demands, and by that of which the demand is made. It is incumbent on each to decide properly; not to demand, and not to refuse, without strong and reasonable cause.

It may, perhaps, be uncommon, but it is certainly just, to say that nations ought to love one another. The offices of humanity ought to flow from this pure source. When this happily is the case, then the principles of affection and of friendship prevail among states as among individuals: then nations will mutually support and assist each other with zeal and ardour; lasting peace will be the result of unshaken confidence; and kind and generous principles, of a nature far opposite to mean jealously, crooked policy, or cold prudence, will govern and prosper the affairs of men. And why should not this be the case? When a number of individuals, by the social union, become fellow citizens, can they, by that union, devest themselves of that relation, which subsists between them and the other—the far greater—part of the human species? With regard to those, can they cease to be men?

The love of mankind is an important duty and an exalted virtue. Much has been written, much has been said concerning the power of *intellectual* abstraction, which man possesses, and which distinguishes him so eminently from the inferiour orders of animals. But little has been said, and little has been written, concerning another power of the human mind, still more dignified, and, beyond all comparison, more amiable—I may call it the power of *moral* abstraction.

All things in nature are individuals. But when a number of individuals have a near and striking resemblance, we, in our minds, class them together, and refer them to a species, to which we assign a name. Again; when a number of species have a resemblance, though not so near and striking, we, in the same manner, class them also together, and refer them to a genus, to which we likewise assign a name. Different genera may have a resemblance, though still less close and striking; we refer them to a higher genus, till we arrive at *being,* the highest genus of all. This is the progress of intellectual abstraction.

We are possessed of a moral power, similar in its nature and in its progress—a principle of good will as well as of knowledge. This principle of benevolence is indeed primarily and chiefly directed towards individuals, those especially, with whom we are or wish to be most intimately connected. But this principle, as well as the other, is capable of abstraction, and of embracing general objects. The culture, the improvement, and the extension of this principle ought to have made, in the estimation of philosophers, as important a figure among the moral, as the other has made among the intellectual powers and operations of the mind; for it is susceptible of equal culture, of equal improvement, and of equal extension.

"After having," says the illustrious Neckar, in his book concerning the importance of religious opinions,[g] "proved myself a citizen of France, by my administration, as well as my writings, I wish to unite myself to a fraternity still more extended, that of the whole human race. Thus, without

g. Pref. 19.

dispersing our sentiments, we may be able to communicate ourselves a great way off, and enlarge, in some measure, the limits of our circle. Glory be to our thinking faculties for it! to that spiritual portion of ourselves, which can take in the past, dart into futurity, and intimately associate itself with the destiny of men of all countries and of all ages!"

To the same purpose is the sentiment of Cicero, in his beautiful treatise on the nature and offices of friendship.[h] "In tracing the social laws of nature," says he, "it seems evident, that man, by the frame of his moral constitution, is supposed to consider himself as standing in some degree of social relation to the whole species in general; and that this principle acts with more or less vigour, according to the distance at which he is placed with respect to any particular community or individual of his kind."

This principle of benevolence and sociability, which is not confined to one sect or to one state, but ranges excursive through the whole expanded theatre of men and nations, instead of being always acknowledged and always recommended, as it ought to have been, has been altogether omitted by some philosophers: by some, its existence seems to have been doubted or denied.

"Some sort of union," says Rutherforth,[2] in his institutes of natural law,[i] "there is between all nations: they are all included in the collective idea of mankind, and are frequently spoken of under this general name. But this is not a social union: the several parts of the collective idea, whether we consider the great body of mankind as made up of individuals or of nations, are not connected, as the several parts of a civil society are, by compact among themselves: the connexion is merely notional, and is only made by the mind, for its own convenience."

The very enlarged active power, concerning which I speak, is, to this day, so far as I know, without an appropriated name. The term *philanthropy* approaches near, but does not reach it. We sometimes call it *patriotism,* by a figurative extension of that term, which, in its proper meaning, denotes a circle of benevolence limited by the state, of which one is a member. When

h. c. 5.

2. Thomas Rutherforth (1712–1771) was an English author and Regius Professor of Divinity at Cambridge.

i. Vol. 2. 463. 464.

we speak of the most exalted of all characters, of the man who possesses this virtue, we generally describe him, by a metaphor, a "citizen of the world." A "man of the world," which would be the more natural expression, though it is in common use, is used to convey a very different idea.

If the general observations, which I have before made concerning the nature, the structure, and the evidence of language, be well founded, the particular remarks I have now made will appear to be striking and just.

This power of moral abstraction should be exercised and cultivated with the highest degree of attention and zeal. It is as necessary to the progress of exalted virtue, as the power of intellectual abstraction is to the progress of extensive knowledge. The progress of the former will be accompanied with a degree of pleasure, of utility, and of excellence, far superiour to any degree of those qualities, which can accompany the latter. The purest pleasures of mathematical learning spring from the source of accurate and extended intellectual abstraction. But those pleasures, pure as they are, must yield the palm to those, which arise from abstraction of the moral kind.

By this power, exerted in different proportions, the commonwealth of Pennsylvania, the empire of the United States, the civilized and commercial part of the world, the inhabitants of the whole earth, become objects of a benevolence the warmest, and of a spirit the most patriotick; for custom, the arbitress of language, has not yet authorized a more appropriate epithet. By this power, a number of individuals, who, considered separately, may be so minute, so unknown, or so distant, as to elude the operations of our benevolence, yet, comprehended under one important and distinguished aspect, may become a general and complex object, which will warm and dilate the soul. By this power the capacity of our nature is enlarged; men, otherwise invisible, are rendered conspicuous; and become known to the heart as well as to the understanding.

This enlarged and elevated virtue ought to be cultivated by nations with peculiar assiduity and ardour. The sphere of exertion, to which an individual is confined, is frequently narrow, however enlarged his disposition may be. But the sphere, to the extent of which a state may exert herself, is often comparatively boundless. By exhibiting a glorious example in her constitution, in her laws, in the administration of her constitution and laws, she may diffuse reformation, she may diffuse instruction, she may diffuse happiness over this whole terrestrial globe.

How often and how fatally are expressions and sentiments perverted! How often and how fatally is perverted conduct the unavoidable and inveterate effect of perverted sentiment and expression! What immense treasures have been exhausted, what oceans of human blood have been shed, in France and England, by force of the expression "natural enemy!" 'Tis an unnatural expression. The antithesis is truly in the thought: for natural enmity forms no title in the genuine law of nations, part of the law of nature. It is adopted from a spurious code.

The foregoing rules and maxims of national law, though they are the sacred, the inviolable, and the exalted precepts of nature, and of nature's Author, have been long unknown and unacknowledged among nations. Even where they have been known and acknowledged, their calm still voice has been drowned by the solicitations of interest, the clamours of ambition, and the thunder of war. Many of the ancient nations conceived themselves to be under no obligations whatever to other states or the citizens of other states, unless they could produce in their favour a connexion formed and cemented by a treaty of amity.

At last, however, the voice of nature, intelligible and persuasive, has been heard by nations that are civilized: at last it is acknowledged that mankind are all brothers: the happy time is, we hope, approaching, when the acknowledgment will be substantiated by a uniform corresponding conduct.

How beautiful and energetick are the sentiments of Cicero on this subject. "It is more consonant to nature," that is, as he said a little before, to the law of nations, "to undertake the greatest labours, and to undergo the severest trouble, for the preservation and advantage of all nations, if such a thing could be accomplished, than to live in solitary repose, not only without pain, but surrounded with all the allurements of pleasure and wealth. Every one of a good and great mind, would prefer the first greatly before the second situation in life." "It is highly absurd to say, as some have said, that no one ought to injure a parent or a brother, for the sake of his own advantage; but that another rule may be observed concerning the rest of the citizens: such persons determine that there is no law, no bonds of society among the citizens, for the common benefit of the commonwealth. This sentiment tends to dissolve the union of the state. Others, again, admit that a social regard is to be paid to the citizens, but deny that this regard ought to be extended in favour of foreigners: such persons would destroy the common society of the human race; and if this common society were destroyed, the destruction would involve, in it, the fate also of beneficence, liberality, goodness, justice. Which last virtue is the mistress and the queen of all the other virtues."[j] By justice here, Cicero clearly means that universal justice, which is the complete accomplishment of the law of nature.

It has been already observed, that there is one part of the law of nations, called their voluntary law, which is founded on the principle of consent: of this part, publick compacts and customs received and observed by civilized states form the most considerable articles.

Publick compacts are divided into two kinds—treaties and sponsions. Treaties are made by those who are empowered, by the constitution of a state, to represent it in its transactions with other nations. Sponsions are made by an inferiour magistrate or officer, on behalf of the state, but without authority from it. Such compacts, therefore, do not bind the state, unless it confirms them after they are made. These take place chiefly in negotiations and transactions between commanding officers, during a war.

Though the power of making treaties is usually, it is not necessarily annexed to sovereign power. Some of the princes and free cities of Germany, though they hold of the emperour and the empire, have nevertheless the right of making treaties with foreign nations: this right, as well as several other rights of sovereignty, the constitution of the empire has secured to them.

With a policy, wiser and more profound, because it shuts the door against foreign intrigues with the members of the union, no state comprehended within our national government, can enter into any treaty, alliance, or confederation.[k]

It is in the constitution or fundamental laws of every nation, that we must search, in order to discover what power it is, which has sufficient authority to contract, with validity, in the name of the state.

A treaty is valid, if there has been no essential defect in the manner, in which it has been made; and, in order to guard against essential defects,

j. Cic. de off. l. 3. c. 5. 6.
k. Cons. U. S. art. 1. s. 10.

it is only necessary that there be sufficient power in the contracting parties, that their mutual consent be given, and that that consent be properly declared.

It is a truth certain in the law of nature, that he who has made a promise to another, has given to that other a perfect right to demand the performance of the promise. Nations and the representatives of nations, therefore, ought to preserve inviolably their treaties and engagements: by not preserving them, they subject themselves to all the consequences of violating the perfect right of those, to whom they were made. This great truth is generally acknowledged; but too frequently an irreligious disregard is shown to it in the conduct of princes and states. But such a disregard is weak as well as wicked. In publick as in private life, among sovereigns as among individuals, honesty is the best policy, as well as the soundest morality. Among merchants, credit is wealth; among states and princes, good faith is both respectability and power.

A state, which violates the sacred faith of treaties, violates not only the voluntary, but also the natural and necessary law of nations; for we have seen that, by the law of nature, the fulfilment of promises is a duty as much incumbent upon states as upon men. Indeed it is more incumbent on the former than on the latter; for the consequences both of performing and of violating the engagements of the former, are generally more important and more lasting, than any which can flow from engagements performed or violated by individuals. Hence the strict propriety, as well as the uncommon beauty of the sentiment—that if good faith were banished from every other place, she should find an inviolable sanctuary at least in the bosoms of princes.

Every treaty should be illuminated by perspicuity and candour. A tricking minister is, in real infamy, degraded as much below a vulgar cheat, as the dignity of states is raised above that of private persons. Ability and address in negotiation may be used to avoid, never to accomplish a surprise.

Fraud in the subsequent interpretation, is equally base and dishonourable as fraud in the original structure of treaties. In the scale of turpitude, it weighs equally with the most flagrant and notorious perfidy.

Treaties and alliances are either personal or real. The first relate only to the contracting parties, and expire with those who contract. The second relate to the state, in whose name and by whose authority the contract was made, and are permanent as the state itself, unless they determine, at another period, by their own limitation.

Every treaty or alliance made with a commonwealth is, in its own nature, real; for it has reference solely to the body of the state. When a free people make an engagement, it is the nation which contracts. Its stipulations depend not on the lives of those, who have been the instruments in forming the treaty: nor even on the lives of those citizens, who were alive when the treaty was formed. They change; but the commonwealth continues the same.

Hence the stability and the security of treaties made with commonwealths. By the faithful observance of their treaties, the Cantons of Switzerland have rendered themselves respectable and respected over all Europe. Let it be mentioned to the honour of the parliament of Great Britain, that it has frequently thanked its king for his zeal and attachment to the treaties, in which he has engaged the nation.

The corruption of the best things and institutions, however, always degenerates into the worst. The citizens of Carthage prostituted the character of their republick to such a degree, that, if we may believe the testimony of an enemy, *Punica fides*[3] became proverbial, over the ancient world, to denote the extreme of perfidy.

As the United States have surpassed others, even other commonwealths, in the excellence of their constitution and government; it is reasonably to be hoped, that they will surpass them, likewise, in the stability of their laws, and in their fidelity to their engagements.

In the great chart of the globe of credit, we hope to see American placed as the very antipode of Carthaginian faith.

3. Carthaginian loyalty or faith.

CHAPTER V.
Of Municipal Law.

I now proceed to the consideration of municipal law—that rule, by which a state or nation is governed. It is thus defined by the learned Author of the Commentaries on the Laws of England: "A rule of civil conduct, prescribed by the *supreme power* of the state, commanding what is right and prohibiting what is wrong."[a] In my observations upon Sir William Blackstone's definition of law in general, I did him the justice to mention, that he was not the first, and that he has not been the last, who has defined law upon the same principles, or upon principles similar, and equally dangerous. Here it is my duty to mention, and, in one respect, I am happy in mentioning, that he was the first, though, I must add, he has not been the last, who has defined municipal law, as applied to the law of England, upon principles, to which I must beg leave to assign the epithets, dangerous and unsound. It is of high import to the liberties of the United States, that the seeds of despotism be not permitted to lurk at the roots of our municipal law. If they shall be suffered to remain there, they will, at some period or another, spring up and produce abundance of pestiferous fruit. Let us, therefore, examine, fully and minutely, the extent, the grounds, the derivation, and the consequences of the abovementioned definition.

"Legislature," we are told, "is the greatest act of superiority, that can be exercised by one being over another. Wherefore it is requisite to the very essence of a law, that it be made by the supreme power. Sovereignty and legislature are, indeed, convertible terms; one cannot subsist without the other."[b] "There must be in every government, however it began, or by whatsoever right it subsists, a supreme, irresistible, absolute, uncontrolled

a. 1. Bl. Com. 44.
b. 1. Bl. Com. 46.

authority, in which the *jura summi imperii,* or the rights of sovereignty reside." "By sovereign power is meant the making of laws; for wherever that power resides, all others must conform to and be directed by it, whatever appearance the outward form and administration of the government may put on. For it is at any time in the option of the legislature to alter that form and administration, by a new edict or rule, and to put the execution of the laws into whatever hands it pleases: and all the other powers of the state must obey the legislative power in the execution of their several functions, or else the constitution is at an end."[c] "In the British parliament, is lodged the sovereignty of the British constitution."[d] "The power of making laws constitutes the supreme authority."[e] "In the British parliament," therefore, which is the legislative power, "the supreme and absolute authority of the state is vested."[f] "This is the place, where that absolute despotick power, which must, in all governments, reside somewhere, is intrusted by the constitution of these kingdoms." "Its power and jurisdiction is so transcendent and absolute, that it cannot be confined, either for causes or persons, within any bounds."[g] "It can change and create afresh even the constitution of the kingdom and of parliaments themselves. It can, in short, do every thing that is not naturally impossible." "What the parliament doth, no authority upon earth can undo."[h] "So long as the English constitution lasts, we may venture to affirm, that the power of parliament is absolute and without control."[i] "Hence the known apothegm of the great Lord Treasurer Burleigh,[1] that England could never be ruined but by a parliament."[j]

It is obvious, that though this definition of municipal law, and this account of legislative authority be applied particularly to the law of England and the legislature of Great Britain; yet they are, in their terms and

c. Id. 48. 49.
d. Id. 51.
e. Id. 52.
f. 1. Bl. Com. 147.
g. Id. 160.
h. Id. 161.
i. Id. 162.
1. William Cecil, the first Baron Burghley (1520–1598), was the chief advisor to the first Queen Elizabeth for most of her reign.
j. Id. 161.

in their meaning, extended to every other state or nation whatever—"to every government, however it began, or by whatever right it subsists." Indeed, the opinion of Mr. Locke and other writers, "that there remains still inherent in the people a supreme power to remove and alter the legislature," is considered to be so merely theoretical, that "we cannot adopt it, nor argue from it, under any dispensation of government at present actually existing."[k]

The doctrines contained in the foregoing quotations from the Commentaries on the laws of England, may be comprised under the two general propositions, which follow. 1. That in every state, there is and must be a supreme, irresistible, absolute, uncontrolled authority, in which the rights of sovereignty reside. 2. That this authority, and these rights of sovereignty must reside in the legislature; because "sovereignty and legislature are convertible terms," and because "it is requisite to the very essence of a law, that it be made by the supreme power." In the first general proposition, I have the pleasure of agreeing entirely with Sir William Blackstone. Its truth rests on this broad and fundamental principle—that, by the constitutions of nature, men and nations are equal and free. In the second general proposition, I am under the necessity of differing altogether from the learned Author of the Commentaries. I differ from him, not only in the opinion, that the foregoing chain of reasoning must be applicable to every government and to every system of municipal law; I differ from him likewise in the opinion, that the foregoing chain of reasoning can be justly applied even to the government of Great Britain and to the municipal law of England. I think I can safely pledge myself to show, that, in both, I differ from him on the most solid and satisfactory grounds.

It deserves to be remarked, that, for his definition of municipal law, he cites the authority of no English court, nor of any English preceding writer, lawyer, or judge. Indeed, so far as I know, he could cite no such authority. So far as I have examined the English law books and authorities, upon this important subject—and I have examined them, as it has been my duty to do, with no small degree of attention—this definition stands entirely unsupported in point of authority. I may, however, be mistaken—I pretend not to have read, far less to remember, every thing in the law. If

k. Id. 161.

I am mistaken, I will thank the friendly monitor, that will advise me of the mistake. As at present advised, I can say, that, so far as I know, this definition is unsupported by authority in the English law. I shall hereafter have occasion to show that, concerning acts of parliament, to which the definition is particularly applied, our law authorities hold, and even parliament itself holds, a very different language.

The introduction of the principle of superiority into the definition of law in general, we traced, when we examined that subject, from Sir William Blackstone to Baron Puffendorff. The introduction of the same principle into the definition of municipal law, can be traced to the same source. "Human laws," says he, "are nothing else, but the decrees of the supreme power, concerning matters to be observed by the subjects."[l] The celebrated Heineccius, in his system of Universal Law, gives a definition much to the same purpose—"Civil laws," says he, "are the commands of the supreme power in a state."[m] Why was this principle transplanted into the law of England?

It deserves to be further remarked, that, for all the strong sentiments and expressions concerning the necessary connexion, and indeed the convertibility of the sovereign and the legislative powers, no authority is produced from the English law; and—I speak under the guard as before—so far as I know, none could be produced, except in one instance, of which I shall soon take notice. The observation, which I have already made with regard to the definition of municipal law, may, therefore, be applied, with equal propriety, to the necessary connexion between the sovereign and the legislative powers. This connexion is not attempted to be supported by authority in the English law. I excepted one instance. It is this—"The power and jurisdiction of parliament is so transcendent and absolute, that it cannot be confined, either for causes or persons, within any bounds."[n] For this, the authority of my Lord Coke in his fourth Institute is quoted. I have examined the passage. It stands thus. "Of the power and jurisdiction of the parliament, *for making of laws in proceeding by bill,* it is so

l. Puff. 688. b. 7. c. 6. s. 3.
m. 2. Heln. s. 150. p. 152.
n. 1. Bl. Com. 160.

transcendent and absolute, as it cannot be confined, either for causes or persons, within any bounds."[o] From this authority, I think it may be fairly and justly inferred—that, by the British constitution, the legislative authority of that nation is, without any exception of causes or persons, vested in the British parliament. In the same manner, by the constitution of Pennsylvania, the legislative power of this commonwealth is vested in a general assembly. But can it be inferred from this authority, that the sovereign power of Great Britain is vested in her parliament? Can it be inferred from the constitution of Pennsylvania, that her sovereign power is vested in her general assembly? I think, therefore, I may now venture to say, that both in his definition of municipal law, and in his opinion concerning the convertibility of the legislative and the sovereign authority, Sir William Blackstone stands unsupported by authority. Is he supported by reason and by principle? By neither, in my humble opinion.

The discussion of this question necessarily leads me to consider the establishment of government, and the division of its powers. That this subject may be fully understood,—for, in the United States, it ought to be understood fully—I shall examine the sentiments, which have been generally entertained and received concerning it, and then compare those sentiments with what I consider as the true state of things. No sooner is government mentioned, than the fine flattering images of power, dominion, and sovereignty dance in the fancy, as the beautiful and magnificent effects of its establishment. But the truth is, that sovereignty, dominion, and power are the parents, not the offspring of government. Let us, however, see what has been thought, and what ought to be thought, concerning those splendid objects.

The theory of the establishment of government has been generally such as I am about to explain.

It has been supposed, that, if a multitude of people, who had formerly lived independent of each other, wished to unite in a political society, and to establish a government, they would find it necessary to take the following steps. 1. Each individual would engage with all the others to join in one body, and to manage, with their joint powers and wills, whatever

o. 4. Ins. 36.

should regard their common preservation, security, and happiness. In consideration of this engagement, made by each individual with all the others, all those others would engage with each individual to protect and defend him from injury, and to secure him in the prosecution of every just and laudable pursuit. These reciprocal engagements from each individual to all the others, and from all the others to each individual form the political association. Those who do not enter into them are not considered as a part of the society.

The society being formed, some measures must be taken in order to regulate its operations; otherwise it could never adopt or pursue a system of measures for promoting, jointly and effectually, the publick security and happiness. These measures involve the formation of government.

A third step, we are told, must also be taken, before government can be completed. In addition to the engagement of political association, another engagement must be made: to that engagement, there must be a new party. What he is—whence he comes—from what source his equal and independent powers of contracting originate, have never, to this moment, been explained. Such an account of him as I have received, I will give: if it is not satisfactory, you must not blame me. "This party is one or more persons, on whom the supreme authority is conferred," says one.[p] By another, we are told, that this party is one or more persons, on whom "the sovereignty is conferred."[q] The sovereignty or supreme authority! How has it started up all of a sudden? Why does it make its first appearance in a derivative state? Where do we find it originally?—for it must exist originally before it can be conferred. To these questions we receive no explicit answer. We are told at one time; that "there are, in each individual, the seeds, as it were, of the supreme power."[r] We are told, more cautiously, at another time, that the voluntary consent and subjection of the respective members of the society, is the "nearest and immediate cause, from which sovereign authority, as a moral quality, results."[s] But, to make the most of these different pieces of information, let us suppose that this cause will

p. 2. Burl. 28.
q. Puff. 640. b. 7. c. 2. s. 8.
r. 2. Burl. 42.
s. Puff. 654. b. 7. c. 3. s. 1.

produce its proper effects; that these seeds will yield, in due time, their natural fruits; and that this conferred sovereignty existed originally in those who conferred it. What is this sovereignty? Is it divisible or indivisible? Was the whole or only a part of it conferred? Was it conferred unconditionally, or upon certain conditions? Was it conferred gratuitously, or for a valuable consideration? Why hear we nothing concerning these important steps, which, upon the opinion generally received, must have been taken previously to the complete formation of a government? This, I confess, is far from being satisfactory: let us, however, take it as it is; and proceed to the remaining step, which, we are told, is taken for the complete establishment of government. This is an engagement by those, who are to be the future governours, that they will consult most carefully and act most honestly for the common security and happiness; and a reciprocal engagement by those, who are, in future, to be governed, that they will observe fidelity and allegiance to those invested with the sovereign authority.

It is admitted not to be probable, that, in the formation of the several governments, these three steps have been actually and regularly taken; yet, we are told, in every just institution of power, there must have been such transactions as implicitly contain the full force and import of all of them.[t]

That the two first steps have been sometimes taken, and must be always supposed, in the regular structure of a government, I readily agree; because it is not easy to discover how a government could be formed without them. But with regard to the third, I see no necessity for it: I see no propriety in it: it is derogatory, in my humble judgment, from the genuine principles of legitimate sovereignty, and inconsistent with the best theory, and the best exercise too, of supreme power. But the full illustration of these dignified subjects is reserved for another place.

With regard, however, to the British constitution, we must allow the supposition, that a contract took place at its establishment. For this we have high political authority. A full assembly of the lords and commons, met in convention in the year 1688, declared that James the second had

t. 2. Hutch. 227.

broke the original contract between the king and people.[u] What the terms of that contract were, at what time it was made, and what duties it enjoined, have been subjects of dark and doubtful disputation. For this reason, as we are told by Sir William Blackstone, it was, after the revolution, judged proper to declare these duties expressly, and to reduce that contract to a plain certainty. So that, whatever doubts might be formerly raised, by weak and scrupulous minds, about the existence of such an original contract, they must now entirely cease; especially with regard to every prince, who has reigned since that revolution.[v]

But, after all, what will this prove with regard to the supreme power of parliament? Do we hear, in the British constitution, of any contract between *them* and the people? How came *they* to be invested with such immense authority? The usual theories of government support no hypothesis of this kind, even in favour of the British legislature; far less, in favour of the legislature of every other government, "however formed, or by whatever right subsisting."

Let us trace this matter a little farther: let us endeavour to form some just conceptions concerning this supreme and sovereign power, concerning which so much has been said, and concerning which so little has been said justly. Let us turn our eyes, for a while, from books and systems: let us fix them upon men and things. While those, who were about to form a society, continued separate and independent men, they possessed separate and independent powers and rights. When the society was formed, it possessed jointly all the previously separate and independent powers and rights of the individuals who formed it, and all the other powers and rights, which result from the social union. The aggregate of these powers and these rights composes the sovereignty of the society or nation. In the society or nation this sovereignty originally exists. For whose benefit does it exist? For the benefit of the society or nation. Is it necessary for the benefit of the society or nation, that, the moment it exists, it should be transferred?—This question ought, undoubtedly, to be seriously considered, and, on the most solid grounds, to be resolved in the affirmative, before the transfer is made. Has this ever been done? Has it ever been evinced, by unanswerable arguments,

u. 1. Bl. Com. 211. 212.
v. Id. 233.

that it is necessary to the benefit of a society to transfer all those rights and powers, and the results of all those rights and powers, which the members once possessed separately, but which the society now possess jointly? I think such a position has never been evinced to be true. Those powers and rights were, I think, collected to be exercised and enjoyed, not to be alienated and lost. All these powers and rights, indeed, cannot, in a numerous and extended society, be exercised personally; but they may be exercised by representation. One of those powers and rights is to make laws for the government of the nation. This power and right may be delegated for a certain period, on certain conditions, under certain limitations, and to a certain number of persons. I ask—Is it necessary that, along with this power and this right, all the other powers and rights of the nation should be delegated to the same persons? I ask farther—is it necessary, that all those other powers and rights should be delegated without any right of resumption?—Another of those powers and rights is that of carrying the laws into execution. May not the society delegate this right for another period, on other conditions, with other limitations, and to other persons? A third right and power of the society is that of administering justice under the laws. May not this right be delegated for still another period, on still other conditions, under still other limitations, and to still other persons? Or may not this power and right be partly delegated and partly retained in personal exercise? For, in the most extended communities, an important part of the administration of justice may be discharged by the people themselves. All this certainly may be done. All this certainly has been done, as I shall have the pleasure of showing, when I come to examine the American governments, and to point out, by an enumeration and comparison of particulars, how beautifully, how regularly, and how usefully we have established, by our practice in this country, principles concerning the reservation, the distribution, the arrangement, the direction, and the uses of publick authority, of which even the just theory is still unknown in other nations.

Let us now pause and reflect. After what we see can be done, after what we see has been done, in the delegation and distribution of the rights and powers of society; can we subscribe to the doctrine of the Commentaries—that the authority, which is legislative must be *supreme?* Can we consent, that this doctrine should form a first principle in our system of municipal law? Certainly not. This definition is not calculated for the meridian of the United States.

I go farther—It is not calculated for the meridian of Great Britain. In order to show this, as it ought to be shown, it will be necessary to enter into a disquisition concerning the component parts and powers of the British parliament, and the origin, kinds, and properties of the English municipal law; the greatest and best proportion of which was never made by a parliament at all.

The British parliament consists of three distinct branches; the king, the house of lords, and the house of commons. To that species of English law, which is called a statute, the assent of all the three branches is necessary. When it has received the assent of all the three, it becomes a law and is obligatory upon the nation; but it is obligatory upon different parts of it for different reasons. "An act of parliament," says my Lord Hale, "is made, as it were, a tripartite indenture, between the king, the lords, and commons; for without the concurrent consent of all those three parts of the legislature, no such law is or can be made."[w] What is an indenture? The Commentaries will tell us, that it is a species of deed, to which there are more parties than one.[x] What is the first requisite of a deed? The Commentaries will also tell us, "that there be persons able to contract, and be contracted with."[y] If a deed is a contract or agreement; if an indenture is a species of deed, to which there are more parties than one; if an act of parliament may be called an indenture tripartite, because there are three parties to it—the king, the lords, and the commons; we find, that an act, which, considered indistinctly and dignified by the name of law, requires the whole supreme power of the nation to give it birth, is, when viewed more closely and analyzed into the component parts of its authority, properly arranged under the class of contracts. It is a contract, to which there are three parties; those, who constitute one of the three parties, not acting even in publick characters. A peer represents no one; he votes for himself; and when he is absent, he may transfer his right of voting to another. This

w. Hale's Hist. 2.
x. 2. Bl. Com. 295.
y. Id. 296.

may be thought a very free way of treating what is represented as necessarily an emanation of sovereign authority; but it is treating it truly; and give me leave to add, it is treating it accurately. Besides; I shall not be ashamed of treading in a path, though even a foot path, to which I am directed by the finger of the enlightened Lord Hale. That path, to which he points, will lead to instruction. Let us pursue it—To this indenture there are three parties: to an indenture the power of contracting in each of the parties is necessary. What is the power of contracting in the different parts? The king contracts for himself, and as representing the executive authority of the nation. The peers engage in their private and personal rights. The members of the house of commons bind themselves and those whom they represent. They represent, or are supposed—how justly is immaterial to our present argument—to represent "all the commons of the whole realm."[z] We all know, that one may execute an instrument, either in person, or by an attorney: we all know that an instrument may be executed by a person in his own right and as attorney also. Perhaps it would not be improper if, on some occasions at least, the forms, as well as the principles, of private, were copied into publick, transactions. Permit me to mention an instance, in which this was lately done. In the ratification of the constitution of the United States by the convention of Pennsylvania, the distinct characters, in which the members of that convention acted, are distinctly marked. "We the delegates of the people of the commonwealth of Pennsylvania, in general convention assembled, do, in the name and by the authority of the same people, and for ourselves, assent to and ratify the foregoing constitution for the United States of America."

The foregoing, though a very familiar, must, I think, be admitted to be a very intelligible and satisfactory illustration and analysis of the manner, in which acts of parliament are made and become obligatory. For my own part, I cannot conceive how the truth, or the real dignity of a subject, can suffer by being closely inspected. When the exclamation—procul este[2]—is made, I am led to suspect, that a secret conscious want of dignity or integrity is the cause. The plain and simple analysis, which I have given, of

z. 4. Ins. 1.
2. Be far away.

the nature and obligation of acts of parliament is evidently countenanced by the expressive legal language of my Lord Hale—It is supported and confirmed by the very respectable authority of my Lord Hardwicke.[3] "The binding force—" I use his very words, as they are reported—"the binding force of these acts of parliament arises from that prerogative, which is in the king, as our sovereign liege lord; from that personal right, which is inherent in the peers and lords of parliament to bind themselves and their heirs and successours in their honours and dignities; and from the delegated power vested in the commons, as the representatives of the people; and, therefore, Lord Coke says, 4. Inst. 1. these represent the whole commons of the realm, and are trusted for them. By reason of this representation, every man is said to be a party to, and the consent of every subject is involved in, an act of parliament."[a] "Every man in England," says the Author of the Commentaries himself, "is, in judgment of law, party to the making of an act of parliament, being present thereat by his representatives."[b] What is there in all this, that necessarily implies the irresistible energy of power, which is sovereign and supreme, without limits and without control?

We have already seen all the parties to an act of parliament. Let us, again, take a deliberate and distinct view of them: where shall we find the sovereign and supreme power? In the king? It is true, that he is called by my Lord Hardwicke "sovereign liege lord," and that his prerogative, as such, is assigned, and with much propriety, as one of the sources, from which "the binding force of acts of parliament arises." The legal and constitutional import of the expressions, sovereign liege lord, is well known. They present the king to his subjects as the object of their allegiance: they present him to foreigners as exercising the whole authority of the nation in foreign transactions. To foreign transactions, the British parliament is no party: to foreign nations, the British parliament is totally unknown. Alliances, treaties of peace, even declarations of war, are made in the name, and by the constitutional authority, of the king alone. But, it has

3. Philip Yorke, first Earl of Hardwicke (1690–1764), was an English politician and Lord Chief Justice who is most famous for his equity decisions.

a. 2. Atk. 654.

b. 1. Bl. Com. 185.

never been pretended, that the prerogative of the king, as sovereign liege lord, extended so far as to bind his subjects by his laws. Even Henry the eighth, tyrant as he was, knew that an act of parliament was necessary, if even that could be sufficient, to endow his proclamations with legal obligatory force. But the king, by assenting to an act of parliament, can bind himself; and he can bind all that portion of the sovereign power of the nation, which is intrusted to his management and care. And it is certainly proper, that, as he represents the executive and the foreign powers of the nation, he should be consulted in the making of the national laws. From this short and clear deduction, we evidently see, that the absolute, uncontrolled power, mentioned by Sir William Blackstone as inseparable from legislative authority, is not to be found in the king. Is it to be found in the house of lords? That will not be pretended. Their votes bind not a single person in the nation, except themselves and the heirs and successours of their honours and dignities. Let us go to the house of commons: is this supreme power, which elsewhere we have searched for in vain, to be found among the members of this house? In what character? In their own right? This will not be alleged. As representatives? As representatives, they act, not by their own power, but by the power of those whom they represent. This power, therefore, whatever it is, cannot be found among the members of the house of commons, it must be looked for among their constituents. There, indeed, we shall find it: and the moment we find it, we shall discover its nature and extent. The king and the commons assembled in parliament are invested by the whole nation, except the house of lords, who act in their own right, not with "transcendent and absolute power and jurisdiction" *generally,* as one would naturally conclude from the unqualified expressions of Sir William Blackstone; but with this "transcendent and absolute power and jurisdiction for the *making of laws,*" as we find in the determinate language of my Lord Coke. To the making of laws, this power and jurisdiction of the British parliament is strictly and rigidly confined. A single law the British parliament cannot execute: in a single cause, the British parliament cannot administer justice. Why then should "absolute despotick power," to use the language of the Commentaries, be ascribed to the British parliament? Has this doctrine a solid foundation? I presume it has not. But though it has not a solid foundation, it has produced, as I shall hereafter show, the most pernicious effects. I will acknowledge freely, that the bounds, which circumscribe the authority of the British parliament, are not sufficiently accurate: I will acknowledge farther, that they are not sufficiently strong. But can this suggest a reason or a motive for denying their existence? It strongly suggests, indeed, reasons and motives of a very different kind. It suggests the strongest reasons and motives for circumscribing the authority of the British parliament by limits more accurate, for fortifying those limits with an additional degree of strength, and for rendering the practice more conformable than it now is, to the theory of its institution—for rendering the house of commons in fact, what it is presumed to be in law, "a representation of all the commons of the whole realm." If any thing coming from this chair could be supposed, by possibility, to produce the smallest effect in that nation, I would warmly recommend to it the accomplishment of those great objects, as consummations most devoutly to be wished. The maxim of the great Lord Burleigh has prevailed long enough: let it make way for a better. Instead of saying, that "England can never be ruined but by a parliament;" let it be said, and truly said, that "England can never be ruined but by herself."

The learned Author of the Commentaries distinguishes between a law and a counsel; and also between a law and an agreement. I will examine the principle of these distinctions, in order that its strength or weakness may appear. It will be necessary to mention what is said in the Commentaries upon this subject. "Municipal law is called a *rule,* to distinguish it from *advice* or *counsel,* which we are at liberty to follow or not, as we see proper, and to judge of the reasonableness or unreasonableness of the thing advised: whereas our obedience to the law depends not upon our approbation, but upon the maker's will. Counsel is only matter of persuasion; law is matter of injunction: counsel acts only upon the willing; law upon the unwilling also.

"It is also called a *rule,* to distinguish it from a *compact* or *agreement:* for a compact is a promise proceeding *from* us; law is a command directed *to* us. The language of a compact is, 'I will, or will not, do this;' that of a law is, 'thou shalt, or shalt not, do this.' It is true, that there is an obligation, which a compact carries with it, equal, in point of conscience, to that of a law; but then the original of the obligation is different. In compacts, we ourselves determine and promise what shall be done, before we are obliged to do it; in laws, we are obliged to act, without ourselves determining or promising any thing at all."[c]

The examination of the principle, which lies at the root of these distinctions, is an interesting subject indeed. If these distinctions can be supported, we may bid a last adieu to the maxim which I have always deemed of prime importance in the science of government and human laws—a free people are governed by laws, of which they approve. Before we part from this darling position, let us, at least, cast behind us, a "longing, lingering look."

Upon these passages in the Commentaries, I make remarks similar to those, which I made upon the passages examined some time ago. No authority in the English law is adduced—none, so far as I know, could be adduced to support them. These sentiments concerning law, as well as the definitions of municipal law, and law in general, may be traced to the performance of Baron Puffendorff. Let us see what this performance says. "*Law* differs from *counsel* in this, that by the latter a man"—"has no proper power, so as to lay any direct obligation on another; but must leave it to his pleasure and choice whether he will follow the counsel or not." "But law, though it ought not to want its reasons, yet these reasons are not the cause why obedience is paid to it, but the power of the exacter, who, when he has signified his pleasure, lays an obligation on the subject to act in conformity to his decree." "We obey laws, not principally on account of the matter of them, but upon account of the legislator's will. And thus law is the injunction of him, who has a power over those, to whom he prescribes; but counsel comes from him, who has no such power." "Counsel is only given to those, who are willing to have it; but law reaches the unwilling."[d]

"Neither are those ancients accurate enough in their expressions, who frequently apply to laws the name of *common agreements*." "The points of distinction between a compact or covenant and a law, are obvious. For a *compact* is a *promise*, but a *law* is a *command*. In *compacts*, the form of speaking is, I will do so and so; but in *laws*, the form runs, do thou so, after an imperative manner. In *compacts*, since they depend, as to their original, on

c. 1. Bl. Com. 44. 45.
d. Puff. 58. 59. b. 1. c. 6. s. 1.

our will, we first determine what is to be done, before we are obliged to do it; but in *laws,* which suppose the power of others over us, we are, in the first place, obliged to act, and afterwards the manner of acting is determined. And, therefore, he is not bound by a *compact,* who did not freely tie himself by giving his consent: but we are, for this reason, obliged by a *law;* because we owed an antecedent obedience to its author."[e]

You now see, that these distinctions between a law and an agreement, a law and a compact are adopted from Baron Puffendorff: whence he derived them, it is immaterial to inquire. But it is material to show, as I think I can do unanswerably, that these distinctions, if they could be supported, would overturn the beautiful temple of liberty from its very foundations. It is material also to show, as I think I can do unanswerably, that the fair temple of liberty stands unshaken and undefaced; and that the sole legitimate principle of obedience to human laws is human consent. This consent may be authenticated in different ways: in its different stages of existence, it may assume different names—approbation—ratification—experience: but in all its different shapes—under all its different appellations, it may easily be resolved into this proposition, simple, natural, and just—All human laws should be founded on the consent of those, who obey them. This great principle I shall, in the course of these lectures, have occasion to follow in a thousand agreeable directions. My present business, while I examine the principles of municipal law as delivered in the Commentaries, is to apply them and the examination of them to the law of England. In that law, we shall find the stream of authority running, from the most early periods, uniform and strong in the direction of the principle of consent—consent, given originally—consent, given in the form of ratification—and, what is most satisfactory of all, consent given after long, approved, and uninterrupted experience. This last, I think, is the principle of the common law. It is the most salutary principle of obedience to human laws, that ever was diffused among men. With such a Byzantium before him, is it not astonishing, indeed, that the attention—must I say the attachment?—of Sir William Blackstone should have been attracted towards a Chalcedon?[f]

e. Puff. 59. b. 1. c. 6. s. 2.
f. 3. Gibbon. 6. 7. Tac. Ann. XII. 62.

The ancient coronation oath of the kings of England obliged them, to the utmost of their power, to cause those laws to be observed, "which the men of the people have made and chosen."[g]

Let us next pay the respect, which is due to the celebrated sentiment of the English Justinian, Edward the first. "Lex justissima, ut quod omnes tangit, ab omnibus approbetur." It is a most just law, that what affects all should be approved by all. This golden rule is, with great propriety, inserted in his summons to his parliament. The Lord Chancellor Fortescue, in his most excellent tractate concerning the English laws, informs his royal pupil, that the statutes of England are framed, not by the will of the prince, but by that and by the assent of the whole kingdom. "Angliae statuta, nedum principis voluntate, sed et totius regni assensu, ipsa conduntur." And if a statute, though passed with the greatest caution and solemnity, should be found, on experience, not to reach those purposes, which were intended by its framers, it can soon be reformed; but not without the same assent of the peers and commonalty of the kingdom, from which it originally flowed. "Et si statuta haec, tanta solennitate et prudentia edita, efficaciae tantae, quantae conditorum cupiebat intentio, non esse contingant, correcto reformari ipsa possunt; et non sine communitatis et procerum regni illius assensu, quali ipsa primitus emanarunt."[h4] "To an act of law, statute or common, every man," says Lord Chief Justice Vaughan,[5] "is as much consenting, and more solemnly, than he is to his own private deed."[i] Authorities to the same purpose might, without end, be heaped upon authorities from the law books. I forbear to trouble you with any more of them. Let us have recourse to what I may properly call a perpetually standing authority upon this very important subject—the writ for choosing members of parliament. It commands the sheriff of each county to cause two knights, the most fit and discreet of the county, and two citizens from every city, and two burgesses from every borough within the county, to be chosen according to law—"So that the said knights have full and

g. 1. Bl. Com. 236, note. "que lez gentez du people avont faitez et esliez."[6]

h. Fortes. c. 18.

4. See translation in text.

5. Sir John Vaughn (1608–1674) was Chief Justice of the Court of Common Pleas from 1668 to 1674.

i. Vaugh. 392.

6. Which the men of the people have made and chosen.

sufficient power for themselves,[j] and the commonalty of the said county, and the said citizens and burgesses for themselves and the commonalty[k] of the said cities and boroughs, severally from them, to do and consent to those things, which, by the favour of God, shall happen to be ordained by the common council of the kingdom: so that for default of such power, or through improvident election of the said knights, citizens, or burgesses, the said affairs remain not undone."[1] Can language be more explicit to show the principle, upon which acts of parliament must be made, and consequently the principle, upon which alone they ought to be obeyed? It is directed, that the members have full and sufficient powers *for themselves,* and for their constituents *from their constituents.* This is precisely according to the analysis, which we have already given of the power of parliament. Why are those powers necessary? To do and *consent* to those things, which shall be ordained by parliament. Those powers are absolutely necessary; for, without them, the business of the nation would remain undone. Is it possible, that any one, who has ever seen this venerable and authentick legal instrument, could suppose, that the sovereign power of the nation was vested in the parliament of Great Britain? Is it possible, that one who has seen this writ could forget the rock, from which the members were hewn, and the hole of the pit from which they were dug? The humble servants, who must come furnished with "full and sufficient power from" their masters "the commonalty of the county, and the burgesses and the citizens separately—" "*Divisim,*" one by one—have those humble servants, when assembled together, the uncontrolled powers of the nation in their hands? When they are intrusted with the legislative, may they, therefore, assume also the executive and the judicial powers of their country?

j. It is the wisdom of the English law, that acts of parliament are equally binding to the makers of them as to the rest of the people. The makers are empowered for themselves, as well as for their constituents; and themselves, as well as their constituents must taste the sweet or bitter fruits of their own works. This suggests a powerful motive for caution and justice in their determinations (2. Whitlocke 87.) But this doctrine ill agrees with the new and foreign theory, introduced into the Commentaries—"A law always supposes some superiour, who is to make it." 1. Bl. Com. 43.

k. It is a great trust reposed in members of parliament, to have the power of the whole commonalty of a county, or city, or borough conferred on them. The acts of the members are the acts of the commonalty, from whom they have their power, and who are bound by them. 2. Whitlocke 89.

l. 1. Whitlocke 2. 3.

We now see, in a very striking point of view, the strong and expressive import of the language of my Lord Hale, when he says, that an act of parliament is, as it were, a tripartite indenture, between the king, the lords, and the commons. They form three parties: each party has power to contract. The king contracts in his own right—for the king is also a man—and in consequence of the powers devolved on him by that original contract, long supposed, but, at the revolution of 1688, expressly recognized to have been made between him and the people. The lords of parliament contract solely in their own right. The members of the house of commons contract in their own right, for themselves, and in right of their constituents, for the commonalty of the whole realm. Thus we find every party and every power to form a contract, a compact, or an agreement—for these terms are synonimous—in the strictest and most proper sense of the words. The vital principle of every contract is the consent of the mind. My Lord Hale did not draw the obligatory principle of an act of parliament from a foreign fountain: he drew it, pure and clear, from its native springs.

Sir William Blackstone tells us, that the original of the obligation, which a compact carries with it, is different from that of a law. The original of the obligation of a compact we know to be consent: the original of the obligation of an act of parliament we have traced minutely to the very same source.

But acts of parliament are not the only—let us add, they are not the principal—species of law, known and obligatory in England. That kingdom boasts in the common law. In the countenance of that law, every lovely feature beams consent. This law is of vast importance. By it, the proceedings and decisions of courts of justice are regulated and directed. It guides the course of descents and successions to real estates, and limits their extent and qualifications: it appoints the forms and solemnities of acquiring, of securing, and of transferring property: it prescribes the manner and the obligation of contracts: it establishes the rules, by which contracts, wills, deeds, and even acts of parliament are interpreted.[m] This law is founded on long and general custom. A custom, that has been long and generally observed, necessarily carries with it intrinsick evidence of consent. Caution and prudence are universally recommended in the

m. Hale's Hist. 24.

introduction of new laws: can caution and prudence be so strongly exemplified—can their fruits be so certainly reaped in any other laws, as in those that are established by custom? The prospect of convenience invites to the first experiment: a first experiment, successful, encourages to make a second. The successful experiments of one man or one body of men induce another man or another body of men to venture upon similar trials. The instances are multiplied and extended, till, at length, the custom becomes universal and established. Can a law be made in a manner more eligible? Experience, the faithful guide of life and business, attends it in its every step. Other laws demand to be taken upon trust: a good countenance is their only recommendation. Those, who introduce them, can only say, in their favour, that they look well. A customary law, with a modesty appropriate to conscious merit, asks for admittance only upon trial, and claims not to be considered as a part of the political family, till she can establish a character, founded on a long and intimate acquaintance. The same means, by which the character of one law is known and approved, are employed to try and discriminate the character of every other. In favour of every one that is recommended, it can be said, not only, that it has lived unexceptionably by itself, but also that it has lived in peace and harmony with all the others. In this manner, a system of approved and concording laws is gradually, though slowly, collected and formed. By a process of this kind, the immortal Newton collected, arranged, and formed his just and beautiful system of experimental philosophy. By the same kind of process, our predecessors and ancestors have collected, arranged, and formed a system of experimental law, equally just, equally beautiful, and, important as Newton's system is, far more important still. This system has stood the test of numerous ages: to every age it has disclosed new beauties and new truths. In improvement, it is yet progressive; and what has been said poetically on another occasion, may be said in the strictest form of asseveration on this,—it acquires strength in its progress. From this system, we derive our dearest birthright and richest inheritance. The rise, the progress, the history, and the component parts of this invaluable system; its extension to America, and the principles of its establishment in the several states and in the national government, it will be my duty and my pleasure to trace and to exhibit in the course of these lectures. My present business is, to ascertain the origin of its obligatory force. Surely, this may be done with ease. The common law is founded on long and general custom. On what can long and general custom be founded? Unquestionably, on nothing else, but free and voluntary *consent.* The regions of custom afford a most secure asylum from the operations of absolute, despotick power. To the cautious, circumspect, gradual, and tedious probation, which a law, originating from custom, must undergo, a law darted from compulsion will never submit.

"Sic volo, sic jubeo, stet pro ratione voluntas,"[7] is the motto of edicts, proclaimed, in thunder, by the voice of a human superiour. Far dissimilar are the sentiments expressed in calm and placid accents by a customary law. I never intruded upon you: I was invited upon trial: this trial has been had: you have long known me: you have long approved me: shall I now obtain an establishment in your family? A customary law carries with it the most unquestionable proofs of freedom in the country, which is happy enough to be the place of its abode.

Some truths are too plain to be proved. That a law, which has been established by long and general custom, must have received its origin and introduction from free and voluntary consent, is a position that must be evident to every one, who understands the force and meaning of the terms, in which it is expressed. My object is to imprint, as well as to prove, this great political doctrine. Perhaps this cannot be done better, than by laying before you the sentiments, which an English parliament held upon this subject, above two hundred years ago. You will see how strongly they support the principle—that the obligation of human laws arises from consent. The sentiments were expressed on an occasion similar to one, which will still suggest matter of very interesting recollection to many minds—They were expressed when an attempt was made to establish, in England, a foreign jurisdiction. With becoming indignation against it, the parliament declare—"This realm is free from subjection to any man's laws, but only to such as have been devised, made, and obtained within this realm, for the wealth of the same, or to such as, by sufferance of your grace and your progenitors, the people of this your realm have taken at their free liberty, with their *own consent* to be used amongst them, and have *bound themselves* by *long use and custom* to the observance of the same, not as to

7. Thus I will, thus I command, let my will stand as the reason.

the observance of laws of any foreign prince, potentate, or prelate, but as to the customed and ancient laws of this realm, originally established as laws of the same, by the said sufferance, consents, and customs, and none otherwise." [n]

Some writers, when they describe that usage, which is the foundation of common law, characterize it by the epithet *immemorial.* The parliamentary description is not so strong. "Long use and custom" is assigned as the criterion of law, "taken by the people at their free liberty, and by their own consent." And this criterion is surely sufficient to satisfy the principle: for consent is certainly proved by long, though it be not immemorial usage.

That consent is the probable principle of the common law, is admitted by the Author of the Commentaries himself. "It is one of the characteristick marks of English liberty," says he,[o] "that our common law depends upon custom, which carries this internal evidence of freedom along with it, that it probably was introduced by the voluntary consent of the people." I search not for contradictions: I wish to reconcile what is seemingly contradictory. But, if the common law could be introduced, as it is admitted it probably was, by the voluntary consent of the people; I confess I can not reconcile with this—certainly a solid—principle, the principle that "A law always supposes some superiour, who is to make it," nor another principle, that "sovereignty and legislature are indeed convertible terms."

A power, far beneath the sovereign power, may be invested with legislative authority; and its laws may be as obligatory as any other human laws. Of this, instances occur even in the government of Great-Britain.

It is necessarily and inseparably incident to all corporations, to make by-laws, or private statutes, for their government. These laws are binding upon themselves, unless contrary to the laws of the land, and then they are void.[p] From these positions, we clearly infer, that laws, obligatory upon those for whom they are made, may be enacted by a power, so far from being absolute and supreme, that its laws are void, when contrary to those enacted by a superiour power: so far do sovereignty and legislature, in this instance at least, appear to be from convertible terms: so far

n. St. 25. H. 8. c. 21. s. 1.
o. 1. Bl. Com. 74.
p. 1. Bl. Com. 475.

is it from being requisite to the very essence of a law, that it be made by the supreme power. Sir William Blackstone tells us, that in the provincial establishments in America, the assemblies had the power of making local ordinances; that subordinate powers of legislation subsisted in the proprietary governments; and that, in the charter governments, the assemblies made laws, suited to their own emergencies:[q] and yet, in these instances, he certainly did not admit, that "by sovereign power is meant the making of laws."

I hope I have now shown, that the definition of municipal law in the Commentaries is not calculated even for the meridian of Great-Britain: it is still less calculated for that of many other governments: for, in many other governments, the distinction is still more strongly marked between the sovereign and legislative powers.

In the original constitution of Rome, the sovereign power, the *dominium eminens,* as it is called by the civilians, always resided in the collective body of the people. But the laws of Rome were not always made by that collective body. To the senate was indulged a privilege of legislation; partial and subordinate, it is true; but still a privilege of legislation. An act of the senate was not considered as a permanent law; but it was allowed to continue in force for one year; not longer, unless it was ratified by the people. To the plebeians, exclusive of the senators and patricians, a privilege of legislation was also indulged; but their laws bound only themselves. While we are taking notice of the different bodies, that possessed the power of legislation in Rome, it is proper to mention one very great defect, which existed in the constitution of that celebrated republick. A power, inferiour to that which made a law, could dispense with it. The senate, by its own decree, could dispense with a law, made by the whole collective body of the people. This power, dangerous in every free government, was often exercised, in Rome, to accomplish the most pernicious purposes.[r]

q. 1. Bl. Com. 108.

r. In the government of Media, an opposite extreme prevailed. When an edict was once published, it was not in the power of the legislator to alter or repeal it. The same power, which is sufficient to make, should be sufficient to abrogate a law. 3. Gog. Or. Laws. 11.

In the United States, and in each of the commonwealths, of which the union is composed, the legislative is very different from the supreme power. Instead of being uncontrollable, the legislative authority is placed, as it ought to be, under just and strict control. The effects of its extravagancies may be prevented, sometimes by the executive, sometimes by the judicial authority of the governments; sometimes even by a private citizen, and, at all times, by the superintending power of the people at large. These different points will afterwards receive a particular explication. At present, perhaps, this general position may be hazarded—That whoever would be obliged to obey a constitutional law, is justified in refusing to obey an unconstitutional act of the legislature—and that, when a question, even of this delicate nature, occurs, every one who is called to act, has a right to judge: he must, it is true, abide by the consequences of a wrong judgment.

Puffendorff, from whom the idea of a superiour, as forming a necessary ingredient in the idea of law, seems to have been transplanted into the Commentaries, insists much upon what he calls a maxim—*that a person cannot oblige himself;* "and this maxim," he tells us, "is not confined to single men, but extends to whole bodies and societies:"[s] "for a person to oblige himself under the notion of a lawgiver, or of a superiour, is an impossibility."[t] Hence the inference seems to be drawn, that "obligations are laid on human minds by a superiour." To different minds, the same things, sometimes, appear in a very different manner. If I was to make a maxim upon this subject, it would be precisely the reverse of the maxim of Baron Puffendorff. Instead of saying, that a man cannot oblige himself; I would say, that no other person upon earth can oblige him, but that he certainly can oblige himself. Consent is the sole principle, on which any claim, in consequence of human authority, can be made upon one man by another. I say, in consequence of human authority; for, in consequence of the divine authority, numerous are the claims that we are reciprocally entitled to make, numerous are the duties, that we are reciprocally obliged to perform. But none of these can enter into the present question. We speak of authority merely human. Exclusively of the duties required by the law of nature, I can conceive of no claim, that one man can make upon

s. Puff. 63. b. 1. c. 6. s. 7.
t. Id. 688. b. 7. c. 6. s. 3.

another, but in consequence of his own consent. Let us, upon this occasion, as we have done upon some others, simplify the object by a plain and distinct analysis. Let us take for the subject of our analysis the very question we are upon—Whether a man can be bound by any human authority, except his own consent? Let us suppose, that one demands obedience from me to a certain injunction, which he calls a law, by performing some service pointed out to me: I ask him, why am I obliged to obey it? He says it is just I should do it. Justice, I tell him, is a part of the law of nature; give me a reason drawn from human authority. He tells me, he had promised it. Very well, perform your promise. Suppose he rises in his tone, and tells me, he orders it. Equal and free, I see no reason for obeying the order of one, who is only equal and free. Repelled from this attack upon my independence, he assails me on a very different quarter; and, softening his accents, represents how generous, nay how humane, it would be, to do as he desires. Humanity is a duty; generosity is a virtue; but neither is to be referred to human authority. Let invention be put upon the rack, and the severest torture will not draw from it a discovery of any external human authority, by which I am obliged to obey the supposed law, or to perform the supposed service. He tells me, next, that I promised to do it. Now, indeed, I discover a human source of obligation. If I promised to do it, I am bound to do it; unless the promise is either unlawful, or discharged; dissolved by an equal, or prohibited by a superiour authority. But this promise originated from consent; for if it was the abortion of compulsion—the effect sometimes of exterior and superiour human *power,* but never of human *authority*—I am not bound to consider it as my act and deed.

Let us now vary the supposition a little. Suppose this demand to be made upon me by one, of whose superiour judgment and unimpeached veracity I had the strongest and best founded belief: suppose me at that period of life—for there is such a period of life—when I should believe implicitly whatever was taught me by one, whom I knew I could so well trust: suppose this person, respected for his knowledge and integrity, should tell me, that he really thought it my duty to comply with the demand. I think I should probably feel a sense of obligation arise within me. But why? because this respectable person says it? No. But for a reason, which may be easily mistaken for this: because I believe, that what this respected person says must be true. Here, indeed, is a species of external human authority, exerted and obeyed for the wisest purposes: But this is very different from that external human authority, which is assigned by some as the source of obligation in human laws. This species of authority is said to have been carried to a very great height by Pythagoras,[8] the celebrated philosopher. He delivered it as a maxim, and it was received as such in his school, that whatever he said must be true. *Ipse dixit*[9] was an undisputed authority. But if folly and falsehood had been as inseparably associated with the character of Pythagoras, as veracity and wisdom were, in the minds of his followers, I ask—would his *ipse dixit* have been received as an undisputed authority? I presume not. To recur, then, to the supposition, which I last made; I should feel the sense of obligation arise in me, not because I should think it his will, that I should comply with the demand; but because I should believe in his opinion, that it was my duty to do so. This refers to a very different source. For let me suppose a little farther, that, after feeling this sense of obligation arise within me, I should come to learn, either from my own observation, or from authority still superiour to that of the person in whom I placed confidence, that this confidence was misplaced; that what he told me proceeded either from mistake, or from something worse than mistake; his will might continue the same, and my opinion concerning it might continue the same, but my sense of obligation would be greatly altered. These remarks, I hope, will be sufficient to show, that no exterior human authority can bind a free and independent man.

The next question is—can a man bind himself? Baron Puffendorff lays it down as a maxim, that he cannot: and on this maxim, applied to publick bodies as well as private individuals, he builds a very interesting series of argumentation—just, indeed, and unanswerable, if the basis, on which it rests, be solid and sound.

We have, at last, reached the bottom of the business. We are now come to the important question, the resolution of which must, in my opinion, decide the fate of all human laws. I say, in my opinion; for I have already given my reasons for thinking, that if a man cannot bind himself, no human authority can bind him. For one man, equal and free, cannot be bound by another, who is no more. The consequence necessarily is, that

8. Pythagoras (c. 582–507 B.C.) was a Greek mathematician and philosopher. He is best known for the Pythagorean theorem.

9. He himself said it. Refers to an assertion made but not proved.

if a man can be bound by any human authority, it must be by himself. A farther consequence necessarily is, that if he cannot bind himself, there is an end of all human authority, and of all human laws. How differently, sometimes, things turn out, from what was expected from them! The idea of superiority, it was probably thought, would strengthen the obligation of human laws. When traced minutely and accurately, we find, that it would destroy their very existence. If no human law can be made without a superiour; no human law can ever be made.

First principles ought to be admitted with caution indeed. When you first read, in the Commentaries, this principle—"a law always supposes some superiour, who is to make it;" you did not suspect, I presume, that this principle is subversive of all human laws. You now perceive, that, if a man can be bound by human authority, it must be by his own. But is he his own superiour? The creative imagination of a Theobald[10] himself could not suggest the fancy. He could only go so far as to say

> "None but himself can be his *parallel*."

Even the master of a show, who boasted, that his elephant was "the greatest elephant in the world," thought it necessary, for preventing mistakes, to add—except himself.

But to resume seriously the important question—can a man bind himself? Simple facts have sometimes led to the greatest discoveries. The sublime theory of gravitation was first suggested to Newton by an apple falling from a tree.

At the end of the second volume of the Commentaries are precedents of some useful instruments, known to the law of England. Among others, there is a precedent of a common bond. In that bond, there are these words written—*I bind myself.* This form of a bond has been known and used and approved in England from time immemorial. If a man cannot bind himself, then all the bonds, which have been executed in England, have been mere nullities. The substantial parts of that bond are parts of the common law of England. The part, which I have mentioned, is certainly a most substantial one. All parts of the precedent are not substantial: many of them may be omitted or altered without vitiating the force of the bond. The law does not require any particular form of words: but one

10. Lewis Theobald (1688–1744) was an English Shakespearean editor and playwright.

thing it strictly requires—such words as declare the intention of the party, and denote his being bound: such words will be sufficient: such words will be carried into effect by the judgment of the law.

Let us examine the obligatory principle of a bond by legal tests, by triers at the common law. Suppose one applies to a court of justice to enforce the obligation of a bond, and proposes it as the foundation of his demand. In what manner is he directed by the law to express the legal import of the instrument? He is directed to declare, that, by this instrument, the party who executed it, "acknowledged himself to be bound,"[u] or "bound himself."[v] The precedents are in both forms. When the action is properly instituted, the party, against whom it is instituted, is next called upon, with all legal solemnity, to make his defence—for against no man ought a decision to be pronounced till he has an opportunity of being heard. He appears: the instrument is produced. What can he say, why a decision should not be pronounced against him? The common law furnishes him with forms to suit almost every case, certainly every case that has been brought before a court of justice. If the case of the present defendant is so very peculiar, that nothing similar to it ever happened before; the common law will protect him in forming a defence, suited to his very peculiar case. Among all the different kinds of pleas, fitted for every case that has happened, for almost every case that can happen, are there any furnished, which bear towards this principle—that the defendant could not oblige himself? There are. But they are furnished only for those, who, by reason of their infancy, or any other cause, appear to want a common degree of understanding. For without understanding it, no obligation can be legitimately formed. There are others too, that respect another situation, which it will be proper to examine particularly; because it is probable, that it will throw much light upon the principle of obligation to human laws. The understanding, though necessary, is not, of itself, sufficient to form a legitimate obligation: in a legitimate obligation, the *will* must concur; compulsion will not be received as a substitute for consent. The common law is a law of liberty. The defendant may plead, that he was compelled to execute the instrument. He cannot, indeed, deny the execution of it; but

u. Boh. Ins. Leg. 102.
v. 2. Mod. Ent. 178.

he can state, in his plea, the circumstances of compulsion attending its execution;[w] and these circumstances, if sufficient in law, and established in fact, will procure a decision in his favour, that, in such circumstances, he did not bind himself. If he never executed the instrument at all; he can state the fact; and unless the execution of it be proved against him, he will, upon this plea likewise, obtain a decision, that he did not bind himself. But if he can do none of these things—if he executed the instrument; if he executed it voluntarily; if he executed it knowingly; the law will pronounce, that he bound himself. This has been the regular course of the law during time immemorial—a course, uninterrupted and unrepealed. In the municipal law of England, therefore, the doctrine is established—that a man can bind himself. This doctrine is established by strict legal inference from the principles and the practice of the common law. The consequence is, that, on the principles of the municipal law of England, a superiour is not necessary to the existence of obligation. A man can bind himself. But is his bond a law? Yes, it is a law binding upon himself. Farther it ought not to bind. But shall a private contract be viewed in the venerable light of a law? Why not, if it has all its essential properties? Suppose this contract to have been made by millions, contracting on each side: it would have been dignified by the name of a treaty: as such, had the United States been the contractors on one side, it would have become a law of the land: as such, it would have become an important part of the law of nations. Is the act of millions more binding upon those millions, than the act of one is binding upon that one? Light will break in upon us by degrees.

By the law of England, a man can bind himself. The law of England speaks not a language contrary to that of the law of nature. By this law also, a man can bind himself. "If among men," says Barbeyrac,[x] "the immediate reason why one ought to be subject to the command of another is ordinarily this, that he has voluntarily consented to it"—and we have shown, that this is not only *ordinarily,* but *always* the reason—"then," continues he, "this consent, and all other engagements whatever are only obligatory through that maxim of natural law, which tells us, that every one ought to observe what he has engaged himself to." This maxim is,

w. 5. Rep. 119.
x. Puff. 67. n. 2. to b. 1. c. 6. s. 12.

indeed, a part of the law of a superiour; but this maxim is founded upon the previous truth—that a man can engage himself: I need not surely prove, that an engagement must be made before it can be observed. "That we should be faithful to our engagements," says the very learned President Goguet,[y][11] "is one of those maxims, which derive their origin from those sentiments of equity and justice, which God has engraven on the hearts of all men: they are taught us by that internal light, which enables us to distinguish between right and wrong." The same important lesson is delivered to nations, as well as to men.[z]

We see now, that, both by the law of England, and by the superiour law of nature, men and nations can bind themselves. Can they be bound without their consent? Is it necessary to dig for another foundation, on which the obligatory force of human laws can be laid? Can any other solid foundation be found?

That this foundation is sufficient to support the whole beautiful structure of human law, will abundantly appear.

"The union of families," says the same respectable author, whom I quoted just now, "could not have taken place but by an agreement of wills. When we view society as the effect of unanimous concord, it necessarily supposes certain covenants. These covenants imply conditions. These conditions are to be considered as the first laws."[a] We have already seen the sentiments of the excellent Hooker—that "human edicts, derived from any other human source, than the consent of those, upon whom they are imposed, are nothing better than mere tyranny. Laws they are not, because they have not the publick approbation."[b] "The mother of civil law," says Grotius,[c] "is that very obligation, which arises from consent." "So that the civil law," says his commentator, Barbeyrac,[d] "is, at the bottom, no more than a consequence of that inviolable law of nature—every man is obliged to a religious observance of his promise." "The legislative power

y. 1. Gog. Or. Laws. 7. 8 .

11. Antoine Yves Goguet (1716–1758) was a French historian and Chancellor to the Paris Parliament.

z. Vat. Pref. 12.

a. 1. Gog. Or. Laws. 7.

b. Hooker. b. 1. s. 10. p. 19. 20.

c. Pref. 20. s. 16.

d. Id. note to s. 16.

of a civil society," says Dr. Rutherforth, in his Institutes of Natural Law,[e] "is acquired by the immediate and direct consent of the several individuals, who make themselves members of such society. And the legislative body acquires it, as by the immediate and direct consent of the collective body of the society, so by the remote and indirect consent of the several members."

I hope I have now performed my engagement: I hope I have evinced, from authority and from reason, from precedent and from principle, that *consent* is the sole obligatory principle of human government and human laws. To trace the varying but powerful energy of this animating principle through the formation and administration of every part of our beautiful system of government and law, will be a pleasing task in the course of these lectures. Can any task be more delightful than to pursue the circulation of liberty through every limb and member of the political body? This kind of anatomy has a peculiar advantage—it traces, without destroying, the principle of life.

Before I conclude, it will be proper to take a concise view of the consequences, necessarily resulting from the doctrine, that the legislative power must be "absolute, uncontrolled, irresistible, and supreme." 1. The power, which makes the laws, cannot be accountable for its conduct; it cannot be submitted either to human judgment, or to human punishment. For both these, says Puffendorff,[f] suppose a superiour; but a superiour to the supreme, in the same order of men, and the same notion of government, is a contradiction. 2. If to every human law, a superiour is necessary: and if the power, which makes a human law, must be supreme; the consequence unquestionably is, that that power cannot be bound by the laws, which it makes: for where shall we find a superiour to what is supreme? "When a civil power," says Puffendorff,[g] "is constituted supreme, it must, on this very score, be supposed exempt from human laws; or, to speak more properly, above them. Human laws are nothing else but the decrees of the supreme power, concerning matters to be observed, by the subjects, for the publick good of the state. That no such edicts can directly oblige

e. Vol. 2. 222.
f. B. 7. c. 6. s. 2. p. 687.
g. B. 7. c. 6. s. 3. p. 688.

the sovereign is manifest; because his very name and title supposeth, that no bond or engagement can be laid on him by any other mortal hand: and for a person to oblige himself, under the notion of a lawgiver, or of a superiour, is an impossibility." 3. If the legislative power be absolute, uncontrolled, and supreme; all opposition to its acts must be unlawful. This, indeed, is not so much a consequence, as a part of the doctrine. In the language of the Commentaries, this power is "irresistible,"[h] Many recollect the numerous and the extravagant inferences, which, at a former period, were drawn from the supposed absolute, irresistible, uncontrolled, and supreme power of the British parliament. They will fall under our notice, when we come to examine the principles, the rise, and the progress of the American constitutions and governments.

I have already mentioned, that though Sir William Blackstone was the first, he has not been the last, who defined municipal law, as applied to the law of England, upon unsound and dangerous principles. This doctrine has been adopted by his successour in the Vinerian chair, though with some degree of apparent hesitation. "Every state," says he, "must, like individuals, be subject to certain rules." "The necessity of rules infers the necessity of political superiours."[i] "The giving of laws to a people, forms the most exalted degree of human sovereignty; and is, perhaps, in effect, or in strict propriety of speech, the only truly supreme power of the state."[j] The sensible and decided Mr. Paley,[12] in his principles of moral and political philosophy, has propagated the same doctrine without limitation and without reserve. "As a series of appeals" says he, "must be finite, there necessarily exists, in every government, a power, from which the constitution has provided no appeal; and which power, for that reason, may be termed absolute, omnipotent, uncontrollable, arbitrary, despotick; and is alike so, in all countries. The person, or assembly, in whom this power resides, is called the sovereign or the supreme power of the state. Since to the same power universally appertains the office of establishing publick laws, it is

h. 1. Bl. Com. 49.
i. El. Jur. (4to) 26. 27.
j. El. Jur. (4to) 43.
12. William Paley (1743–1805) was an English philosopher and theologian.

also called the legislature of the state."[k] It is not improbable, that the doctrine is disseminated wherever the Commentaries are generally received as authority.

I have already intimated, that there is a period in our lives, when we receive implicitly whatever we are taught, especially by those, in whom, we think, we can confide. "It is the intention of nature," says the ingenious Dr. Reid,[l] "that we should be carried in arms before we are able to walk upon our legs; and it is likewise the intention of nature, that our belief should be guided by the authority and reason of others, before it can be guided by our own reason." At this very period of life, the Commentaries, as a book of authority, are put into the hands of young gentlemen, to form the basis of their law education. Is it surprising, that the reception of its doctrines should be indiscriminate, as well as implicit? indeed the former is the unavoidable consequence of the latter. But doctrines received implicitly, at this period of life, are not so easily dismissed in its subsequent stages. "For," says the same experienced judge of human nature,[m] "the novelty of an opinion, to those who are too fond of novelties; the gravity and solemnity, with which it is introduced; the opinion we have entertained of the author; and, above all, its being fixed in our minds at that time of life, when we receive implicitly what we are taught; may cover its absurdity, and fascinate the understanding for a time"—I will add—for a long time. These observations explain, and, while they explain, they justify my conduct in examining, so fully and so minutely, the definitions of law in general and of municipal law given in the Commentaries on the laws of England. This full and minute examination has, at the same time, given me a fit opportunity of discovering, of illustrating, and, I hope, of establishing very different principles, as the foundation of the science of law. In this, as in every other science, it is all important, that the foundation be properly and surely laid.

Permit me to close this subject with the sentiments, which a very learned and ingenious judge expressed, on an occasion somewhat similar

k. 2. Paley 185.
l. Inq. 433.
m. Reid. Ess. In. 568.

to this, and in a situation somewhat similar to mine. The principles of the revolution in England have been dear to whigs: they have been opposed inveterately and pertinaciously by tories. Some passages in the law performances of the great and good Lord Chief Justice Hale were conceived, on both sides, and justly, to militate against the principles of that revolution. These passages were cited with uncommon exultation, and were, no doubt, disseminated by the votaries of the abdicated family with extraordinary zeal. Seventy years after the revolution, and sixteen years after the last rebellion, which was raised in order to overturn its happy establishment, Mr. Justice Foster[13] thought it his duty to publish some observations on those passages, with a view to detect and expose their mistakes, which were great, and to defend the principles, on which the revolution and the subsequent establishment were founded. Concerning these observations, and their publication, he thus speaks,

> The cause of the Pretender seems now to be absolutely given up. I hope in God it is so. But whether the root of bitterness, the principles which gave birth, and growth, and strength to it, and have been, twice within our memory, made a pretence for rebellion, at seasons very critical, whether those principles be totally eradicated, I know not. These I encounter, by showing that certain historical facts, which the learned Judge hath appealed to in support of them, either have no foundation in truth, or, were they true, do not warrant the conclusions drawn from them.
>
> The passages I animadvert upon have been cited with an uncommon degree of triumph by those, who, to say no worse of them, from the dictates of a misguided conscience, have treated the revolution and present establishment as founded in usurpation and rebellion; and they are in every student's hand. Why, therefore, may not a good subject, be it in season or out of season, caution the younger part of the profession against the prejudices, which the name of Lord Chief Justice Hale, a name ever honoured and esteemed, may otherwise beget in them? I, for my part, make no apology for the freedom I have taken with the sentiments of an author, whose memory I can love and honour, without adopting any of his mistakes on the subject of government.
>
> It cannot be denied, and I see no reason for making a secret of it, that the learned Judge hath, in his writings, paid no regard to the principles, upon

13. Sir Michael Foster (1689–1763) was Judge of the Court of Kings Bench.

which the revolution and present happy establishment are founded. The prevailing opinion of the times, in which he received his first impressions, might mislead him. And it is not to be wondered at, if the detestable use the parliamentary army made of its success in the civil war did contribute to fix him in the prejudices of his early days. For, in the competition of parties, extremes, on one side, almost universally produce their contraries on the other. And even honest minds are not always secured against the contagion of party prejudice.

But, it matters not with us, whether his opinion was the effect of prejudices early entertained, or the result of cool reflection; since the opinion of no man, how great or good soever, is or ought to be the sole standard of truth.[n]

The next great title in my course of lectures is MAN, the subject of all, and the author, as well as the subject of part of those kinds of law, of which I have now given a general and summary view. Man I shall consider as an individual, as a member of society, as a member of a confederation, and as a part of the great commonwealth of nations.

On a slight glance of this subject, it may seem, perhaps, not to be very intimately connected with a system of lectures on law. And, indeed, it must be owned, that as law, or what is called law, is sometimes taught, and sometimes practised, there is but a slender and very remote alliance between law and man. But, in the real nature of things, the case is very different.

You have not, I am sure, forgotten, that, in an early address, which I made to you, I recommended, most earnestly, to the utmost degree of your attention, an outline of study, supported with all the countenance and authority of three distinguished and experienced characters—Bacon, Bolingbroke, Kaims: it will not, I am sure, be forgotten, that metaphysical knowledge, or the philosophy of the human mind, formed a very conspicuous part of that outline; one of those "vantage grounds," which every one must climb, who aims to be really a master in the science of law.

"Natura juris a natura hominis repetenda est,"[14] is the judgment of Cicero. It is a judgment, not more respectable on account of the high

n. Fost. Pref. 6. 7.
14. The nature of the law is to be sought from the nature of man himself.

authority, which pronounces it, than on account of its intrinsick solidity and importance.

You have heard me mention, that a proper system of evidence is the greatest *desideratum* in the law. From a distinct and accurate knowledge of the human mind, and of its powers and operations, the principles and materials of such a system must be drawn and collected.

Whatever produces belief may be comprehended under the name of evidence. Belief is a simple and undefinable operation of the mind; but, by the constitution of our nature, it is intimately and inseparably associated with many other powers and operations. This association should be minutely traced: all its properties and consequences should be distinctly marked. Belief attends on the perceptions of our external senses, on the operations of our internal consciousness, on those of memory, on those of intuition, on those of reason: it is attendant, likewise, on the veracity, the fidelity, and the judgment of others. Hence the evidence of sense, the evidence of recollection, the evidence of consciousness, the evidence of intuition, the evidence of demonstration, probable evidence, the evidence of testimony, the evidence of engagements, the evidence of opinion, and many other kinds of evidence; for this is, by no means, a complete enumeration of them.

It is difficult, perhaps it is impossible, to discover any common principle, to which all these different kinds of evidence can be reduced. They seem to agree only in this, that, by the constitution of our nature, they are fitted to produce belief.

It is superfluous to add, that the social operations of the mind should be well known and studied by him, who wishes to reach the genuine principles of legal knowledge.

CHAPTER VI.

Of Man, as an Individual.

"Know thou thyself," is an inscription peculiarly proper for the porch of the temple of science. The knowledge of human nature is of all human knowledge the most curious and the most important. To it all the other sciences have a relation; and though from it they may seem to diverge and ramify very widely, yet by one passage or another they still return.

In every art and in every disquisition, the powers of the mind are the instruments, which we employ; the more fully we understand their nature and their use, the more skilfully and the more successfully we shall apply them. In the sublimest arts, the mind is not only the instrument, but the subject also of our operations and inquiries. The poet, the orator, the philosopher work upon man in different ways and for different purposes. The statesman and the judge, in pursuit of the noblest ends, have the same dignified object before them. An accurate and distinct knowledge of his nature and powers, will undoubtedly diffuse much light and splendour over the science of law. In truth, law can never attain either the extent or the elevation of science, unless it be raised upon the science of man.

The knowledge of human nature is not more distinguished by its importance, than it is by its difficulty. Though the mind—the noblest work of God, which reason discovers—is of all objects the nearest to us, and seems the most within our view; yet it is no easy matter to attend to its operations and faculties, in such a manner as to obtain clear, full, and distinct conceptions concerning them. The consequence has been, that in no branch of knowledge have greater errours, and even absurdities, insinuated themselves, than in the philosophy of the human mind. Instead of proceeding slowly and cautiously by observation and experience, those who have written on this subject have adopted the more easy, but the less certain mode of process by hypothesis and analogy. The event has been such as might have been expected: those who have cultivated other sciences, have made progress, because they have set out in the right road, and have consulted the proper guides: those who have speculated on human nature have, too many of them, been involved in a dark and inextricable labyrinth, because they commenced their journey in an improper direction, and have listened to the information of those, whose information was the result of conjecture and not of experience. But this darkness will not last for ever. Some future sun of science will arise, and illuminate this benighted part of the intellectual globe. When the powers of the human mind shall be delineated truly and according to nature, those, whose vision is not distorted by prejudice, will recognise their own features in the picture. They will be surprised that things, in themselves so clear, could be so long involved in absurdity; and, when the truth is to be found in their own breasts, that they have been led so far from it by false systems and theories.

The only instrument, by which we can have any distinct notion of the faculties of our own and of others minds, is reflection. By this power, the mind makes its own operations the object of its attention, and views and examines them on every side. This power of reflection or self-examination, so absolutely indispensable in the investigation of what is so near and so important to us, is neither soon nor easily acquired or exerted. The mind, like the eye, contemplates, with facility, every object around it; but is with difficulty turned inward upon its own operations. Whoever has attempted to experiment on the philosophy of the mind—the only legitimate way in which a knowledge of it can be acquired—must have found how utterly impossible it is to make any clear and distinct observations on our faculties of thought, unless the passions, as well as the imagination, be silent and still. The materials on which we reflect are so minute, so mixed, and so volatile, that the strongest minds alone can, in any degree, arrange them, even in their quietest state. The least breath of passion moves and agitates them, so as to render every thing distorted and deformed.

Reflection, like all our other powers, is greatly improved by exercise: it thus becomes habitual; the difficulty attending it daily diminishes; and the advantages resulting from it are many and great. One who is accustomed habitually to reflection, can think and speak with accuracy on every subject; and can judge and discriminate for himself in many cases, in which others must trust to notions borrowed, confused, and indistinct.

Assisting and subservient to accurate reflection, is the structure of language, which is of much use in developing the operations of the mind. The language of mankind is expressive of their thoughts. The various operations of the understanding, will, and passions have various forms of speech corresponding to them, in all languages; a due attention to the signs, throws light on the things signified by them. There are, in all languages, modes of speech, by which men signify their judgment, or give their testimony, or accept, or refuse, or command, or threaten, or supplicate, or ask information or advice, or plight their faith in promises or contracts. If such operations were not common to mankind, we should not find, in all languages, forms of speech by which they are expressed.

A system of human nature is not expected from this chair. The undertaking, indeed, is too vast for me; it is too vast for any one man, however great his genius or abilities may be. But it comes directly within our plan, to consider it so far as to have just conceptions of man in two most important characters, as an author, and as a subject of law; as accountable for his own conduct, as capable of directing the conduct both of himself and of others. The laws, which God has given to us, are strictly agreeable to our nature; they are adjusted with infallible correctness to our perfection and happiness. On those, which we make for ourselves, the same characters, as deeply and as permanently as possible, ought to be impressed. But how, unless we study and know our nature, shall we make laws fit for it, and calculated to improve it?

I mean not—for it would be uninstructive—to give you an account of the divisions and subdivisions, into which metaphysicians have attempted to class and arrange our mental powers and principles. No division has been more common, and, perhaps, less exceptionable, than, that of the powers of the mind into those of the understanding and those of the will. And yet even this division, I am afraid, has led into a mistake. The mistake I believe to be this; it has been supposed, that in the operations ascribed to the will, there was no employment of the understanding; and that in those ascribed to the understanding, there was no exertion of the will. But this is not the case. It is probable, that there is no operation of the understanding, in which the mind is not in some degree active; in other words, in which the will has not some share. On the other hand, there can be no energy of the will, which is not accompanied with some act of the understanding. In the operations of the mind, both faculties generally, if not always, concur; and the distinction between them can be of no farther use, than to arrange each operation under that faculty, which has the largest share in it. Thus by the perceptive powers, we are supposed to acquire knowledge, and by the powers of volition, we are said to exert ourselves in action.

If even this division, long and generally received as it has been, has given occasion to a mistake; we have no great reason to indulge a partiality for others. The truth is, that they have been generally superficial and inaccurate; they have depended more on fancy than on nature; and have proceeded more from presumptuous attempts to accommodate the mind to a system, than from respectful endeavours to accommodate a system to the mind. Abhorrent from the first, restrained by propriety from aiming at the second; let my humble task be to select and make such observations concerning our powers, our dispositions, our principles, and our habits, as will illustrate the intimate connexion and reciprocal influence of religion, morality, and law.

Simplicity is the favourite object of system. In the material world, attachment to this simplicity misled the penetrating Des Cartes.[1] Even the great Newton, patient, faithful, and attentive as he was in tracing Nature's footsteps, was, on one occasion, almost seduced, by the same attachment, to follow hypothesis, the ape of Nature. A body of morality, pretending to be complete, has sometimes been built on a single pillar of the inward frame: the entire conduct of life has been accounted for, at least the attempt has been made to account for it, from a single quality or power. Many systems of this kind have appeared, calculated merely to flatter the mind. According to some writers, man is entirely selfish; according to others, universal benevolence is the highest aim of his nature. One founds morality upon sympathy solely: another exclusively upon utility. But the variety of human nature is not so easily comprehended or reached. It is a complicated machine; and is unavoidably so, in order to answer the various and important purposes, for which it is formed and designed.

How wretched are oftentimes the representations and the imitations of Nature's works! A puppet may make a few motions and gesticulations; but how unlike it is to that, which it represents! How contemptible, when

1. René Descartes (1596–1650) was an important French philosopher, mathematician, and scientist.

compared to the body of a man, whose structure the more we know, the more we discover its wonders, and the more sensible we are of our ignorance! Is the mechanism of the mind so easily comprehended, when that of the body is so difficult? Yet, by some systems, which are offered to us, with pretensions the most lofty and magnificent, a few laws of association, joined to a few original feelings, explain the whole mechanism of sense, imagination, memory, belief, and of all the actions and passions of the mind. Is this the man that Nature made? It is a puppet surely, contrived to mimick her work. The more we know of other parts of nature, the more we approve and admire them. But when we look within, and consider the mind itself, which makes us capable of all our prospects and enjoyments; if it is indeed what some late systems of high pretensions make it, we find we have only been in an enchanted castle, imposed upon by spectres and apparitions. We blush to think how we have been deluded; we are ashamed of our frame; and can hardly forbear expostulating with our destiny. Is this thy pastime, O Nature, to put such tricks upon a silly creature, and then take off the mask, and show him how he has been befooled? If this is the philosophy of human nature; my soul! enter thou not into her secrets. It is surely the forbidden tree of knowledge: I no sooner taste of it, than I perceive myself naked.—Such, in substance, has been the well founded expostulation[a] against some of the late and famed theories concerning the human mind. The theory, which we adopt, because we think it grounded in truth and reality, will open very different—the most enrapturing prospects.

The mind itself, indeed, is *one* internal principle: but its operations many, various, connected, and complicated: its perceptions are mixed, compounded, and decompounded, by habits, associations, and abstractions: its powers both of action and perception, on account either of a diversity in their objects, or in their manner of operating, are considered as separate and distinct faculties. This I take to be a just state of things with regard to the mind, and its perceptions, operations, and powers. But I think it is highly probable, that, in opposition to this account, the mind has been too often considered as distributed into different divisions and departments: and that the operations, in each department, have been considered as simple and unmixed. Each one of you, by recalling to remembrance your

a. Reid's Inq. 26. 28.

manner of thinking upon these subjects, will be able to say whether this has not been the case.

Again; the mind is an *active* principle. It has been the opinion of some modern philosophers, that, in thinking and sensation, the mind is merely passive. In all ages, and in all languages, the various modes of thinking have been expressed by words of active signification; such as seeing, hearing, reasoning, willing. It seems, therefore, to be the natural judgment of mankind, that the mind is active in its various ways of thinking; and for this reason, they are called its operations, and are expressed by active verbs. Sensation, imagination, memory, and judgment have, in all ages, been considered, by the vulgar, as *acts* of the mind. This is shown by the manner, in which they are expressed in all languages. When the mind is much employed in them, we say it is very active; whereas, if they were impressions only, as the *ideal* philosophy would lead us to conceive, we ought, in such a case, rather to say, that the mind is very passive. The paper which I hold in my hand was not active, when it received the characters written on it.

Man is composed of a body and a soul intimately connected; but at what time and in what manner connected, we do not know. In consequence of this connexion, the body lives and performs the functions necessary to life for a certain time; increases for a certain time in stature and in strength; is nourished with food, and is refreshed by sleep. In consequence of the same connexion, the body moves; the hands fulfil their various and active offices; the tongue expressive speaks; and the eyes sometimes still more expressive look. The body, and the things of the body, are far from being beneath our regard. In its present state, it is a mansion well fitted for the temporary residence of its noble inhabitant: in its renewed state, it will be endowed with the power of retaining that fitness for ever.

The fabrick of the human mind, however, is more astonishing still. The faculties of this are, with no less wisdom, adapted to their several ends, than the organs of the other. Nay, as the mind is of an order higher than that of the body, even more of the wisdom and skill of the divine Architect is displayed in its structure. In all respects, fearfully and wonderfully are we made.

From experience we find, that when external things are within the sphere of our perceptive powers, they affect our organs of sensation, and are perceived by the mind. That they are perceived we are conscious; but the manner in which they are perceived, we cannot explain; for we cannot trace the connexion between our minds and the impressions made on our organs of sense; because we cannot trace the connexion which subsists between the soul and the body. Frequent and laborious have been the attempts of philosophers to investigate the manner, in which things external are perceived by the mind. Let us imitate them, neither in their fruitless searches to discover what cannot be known; nor in framing hypotheses which will not bear the test of reason, or of intuition; nor in rejecting selfevident truths, which, though they cannot be proved by reasoning, are known by a species of evidence superiour to any that reasoning can produce.

Many philosophers allege that our mind does not perceive external objects themselves; that it perceives only *ideas* of them; and that those ideas are actually in the mind. When it has been intimated to them, that, if this be the case; if we perceive not external objects themselves, but only ideas; the necessary consequence must be, that we cannot be certain that any thing, except those ideas, exists; the consequence has been admitted in its fullest force. Nay, it has been made the foundation of another theory, in which it has been asserted, that men and other animals, the sun, moon, and stars, every thing which we think we see, and hear, and feel around us, have no real existence; that what we dignify with such appellations, and what we suppose to be so permanent and substantial, are nothing more than "the baseless fabrick of a vision"—are nothing more than ideas perceived in the mind. The theory has been carried to a degree still more extravagant than this; and the existence of mind has been denied, as well as the existence of body. We shall have occasion to examine these castles, which have not even air to support them. Suffice it, at present, to observe, that the existence of the objects of our external senses, in the way and manner in which we perceive that existence, is a branch of intuitive knowledge, and a matter of absolute certainty; that the constitution of our nature determines us to believe in our senses; and that a contrary determination would finally lead to the total subversion of all human knowledge. For this belief we cannot, we pretend not to assign an argument; it is a simple and original, and therefore an inexplicable act of the mind. It can neither be described nor defined. But one thing we shall engage to do, though, at present, we are not prepared for it. When those philosophers prove by argument, that we ought to receive the testimony of reason; we then will prove, by argument, that we ought to receive the testimony of sense. Till that time, let us receive the testimony of both, as of faculties, with which we have been endowed, for wise and benevolent purposes, by him who is all-true. The senses were intended by him to give us all that information of external objects, which he saw to be proper for us in our present state. This information they convey without reasoning, without art, without investigation on our part. They are five in number. Tastes are referred to the sense of tasting: odours, to that of smelling: sounds, to that of hearing: light and colours, to that of seeing: all other bodily sensations, to that of touch.

Our external senses are not indeed the most exalted of our powers; but they are powers of real use and importance; and, to powers of a more dignified nature, they are most serviceable and necessary instruments. It has been the endeavour of some philosophers to degrade them below that rank, in which they ought to be placed. They have been represented as powers, by which we receive sensations only of external objects. Even this part of their service is far from being unimportant. The perception of external objects is a principal link of that mysterious chain, which connects the material with the intellectual world. But this, as I before mentioned,[b] is not the whole of the functions discharged by the senses: they judge, as well as inform: they are not confined to the task of conveying impressions; they are exalted to the office of deciding concerning the nature and the evidence of the impressions, which they convey.

The senses are the vehicles of pleasures, less elevated indeed than those which are intellectual, still less elevated than those which are moral, but pleasures not beneath the regard of a rational and a moral mind. The pleasures of sense, it is true, ought, like every thing else that is subordinate, to be prevented from transgressing their natural and proper bounds: but that is no reason why they should be either neglected or despised. To be without the senses even of tasting and smelling, would be a real misfortune, because it would be a real inconvenience, and would be attended with the loss of sensations innocent and agreeable. The organ of smelling is often the speediest and the surest instrument to prevent or to recover a

b. Ante. p. 520.

person from a fainting fit. The senses are susceptible of improvement; and they ought to be improved; for they are the sources both of pleasures and of advantage. Some of the senses are the sources of pleasures of a very elegant kind. The ear is the welcome messenger of melody and harmony, as well as of sound: the eye, of beauty, as well as of light and colours: and the man who feels not agreeable emotions from the contemplation of beauty, and is not moved with concord of sweet sounds—I will not finish the fine poetical description—I will only say, that he has no reason to exult in the absence of those enjoyments. Both the eye and the ear are capable of being refined to a very great height. For this I need only appeal to judges of musick, of painting, of statuary, of architecture. In many mechanick arts, a good eye, as it is called, is of excellent service. Gentlemen of the military profession—a profession which has something singular in it; a profession which should be learned, that it may never be used—know the importance of a military eye.

It is not without design that I have said thus much concerning the utility and importance of our senses. It has been the custom of certain philosophers, and, I must here add, of certain divines, to represent human nature as in a state of hostility endless and uninterrupted, internal as well as external. According to these philosophers, and according to these divines, he is at war with all the world, as well as with himself. The senses have been considered as incorrigible rebels, who aspired to be tyrants: the inference has been, that they ought to be treated as the vilest slaves. The monk, who built a dead wall before his window, that he might not be seduced by the beauties of creation, introduced no new doctrine; he only carried to an unusual height a doctrine already received. This doctrine embraces the two vicious extremes, and excludes the golden mean. Whence this sombre system derives its origin, I care and inquire not. Of one thing I am certain; it is not that wisdom which cometh from above: for the ways of that wisdom are the ways of pleasantness, and all her paths are peace. Our senses ought to be deemed, as they really are, and as they are intended to be, the useful and pleasing ministers of our higher powers. Let it be remembered, however, that, of the pleasures of sense, temperance and prudence are the necessary and inseparable guides and guardians; detached from whom, those pleasures lose themselves in another nature and in other names: they become vices and pains.

As the external senses convey to us information of what passes without us; we have an internal sense, which gives us information of what passes within us. To this we appropriate the name of consciousness. It is an immediate conception of the operations of our own minds, joined with the belief of the existence of those operations. In exerting consciousness, the mind, so far as we know, makes no use of any bodily organ. This operation seems to be purely intellectual. Consciousness takes knowledge of every thing that passes within the mind. What we perceive, what we remember, what we imagine, what we reason, what we judge, what we believe, what we approve, what we hope, all our other operations, while they are present, are objects of this.

This, like many other operations of the mind, is simple, peculiar, inaccessible equally to definition and analysis. For its existence every one must make his appeal to himself. Are you conscious that you remember, or that you think? We have already seen, that the existence of the objects of sense is one great branch of intuitive knowledge: of the same kind of knowledge, the existence of the objects of consciousness is another branch, more extensive and important still. When a man feels pain, he is certain of the existence of pain; when he is conscious that he thinks, he is certain of the existence of thought. If I am asked to prove that consciousness is a faithful and not a fallacious sense; all the answer which I can give is—I feel, but I cannot prove; I can find no previous truth more certain or more luminous, from which this can derive either evidence or illustration. But some such antecedent truth is necessarily the first link in a chain of proof. For proof is nothing else than the deduction of truths less known or less believed, from others that are more known or better believed. "What can we reason, but from what we know?"[c] The immediate and irresistible conviction, which I have of the real existence of those things, of whose existence I am conscious, is a conviction produced by intuition, not by reason. He who doubted, or pretended to doubt, concerning every other information, deemed himself justified in taking for granted the veracity of that information, which was given to him by his consciousness. He was conscious that he thought; and therefore he was satisfied that he really thought.—"Cogito"[2] was a first

c. Pope's Ess. on Man. Ep. 1. v. 18.

2. Cogito is short for Descartes's famous first principle "*Cogito ergo sum*" (I think, therefore I am).

principle, which he who pronounced it dangerous and unphilosophical to assume any thing else, judged it safe and wise to assume. And when he had once assumed that he thought, he gravely set to work to prove, that because he thought he existed. His existence was true, but he could not prove it; and all his attempts to prove it have been shown, by a succeeding philosopher, to be inconsistent with the rules of sound and accurate logick. But even this succeeding philosopher, who showed that Des Cartes had not proved his existence, and who, from the principles of his own philosophy could not assume this existence without proof—even this philosopher has assumed the truth of the information given by consciousness. "Mr. Hume,[3] after annihilating body and mind, time and space, action and causation, and even his own mind, acknowledges the reality of the thoughts, sensations, and passions, of which he is conscious."[d] He has left them—how philosophically I will not pretend to say—to "stand upon their own bottom, stript of a subject, rather than call in question the reality of their existence."[e] Let us felicitate ourselves, that there is, at least, one principle of common sense, which has never been called in question. It is a first principle, which we are required and determined, by the very constitution of our nature and faculties, to believe. Perhaps we shall find other first principles, which, by the same constitution of our nature and faculties, we are equally required and determined to believe. Such principles are parts of our constitution, no less than the power of thinking: reason can neither make nor destroy them: like a telescope, it may assist, it may extend, but it cannot supply natural vision.

Possessed of the senses and of consciousness; and believing, as we must believe, the truth of the information, which they give, we cannot complain that our knowledge is a *baseless* fabrick; but if we were possessed only of those powers, we might well complain, that our knowledge was a *fleeting* fabrick. The moment that an external object is removed from the operation of our senses, that moment our perception of it is lost: the moment our attention is withdrawn from the consideration of any of the powers of the mind, that moment our immediate conception of it is gone. The

3. David Hume (1711–1776) was an important Scottish philosopher, economist, and historian.

d. Reid's Ess. Int. 579.

e. Reid's Inq. 39. 139.

external object may, indeed, return; but it will return as a stranger: the internal power may become again the object of our consciousness; but it will appear as an object hitherto unknown. As to the purpose of accumulating knowledge, every succeeding moment would be as the first moment of our existence. We should perceive what is present; but we should have no power of connecting what is present, with what is past. Without this connecting power, we should have no means of forming any conjecture concerning what is to come. But the divine hand that made us, leaves not its workmanship unfinished. We are endowed with a power, by which we have an immediate knowledge of things past. We are provided with a storehouse, fitted to preserve things new and old. And of this storehouse it is the extraordinary property, that the more it is filled with treasure, the more capacious and retentive it becomes. You know I speak of the memory. Much might be usefully said concerning this necessary and important power; but my plan, which comprehends such a variety of parts, forbids me to enlarge upon each of them.

Of the immediate cause of remembrance we know nothing: and all attempts to trace and discover that cause have, to say the least of them, proved vain and illusory: it is one of those things, of which we must be contented to remain ignorant. But while of some things we ought to acquiesce in our ignorance; of others, we should be satisfied with our knowledge: though we cannot assign a cause *why* we remember, we know the fact that we *do* remember; and we know likewise another fact, that our remembrance is true. What we distinctly remember, we believe as strongly as what we distinctly perceive. To give a reason why we believe the information of our perceptions, I have already declared myself incapable: the same declaration I now make, concerning the information of our memory. By the constitution of our nature, it is always accompanied with belief.

I had occasion to rescue the senses from the unjust disparagement, which they have sometimes suffered: let me now perform the same just office to the memory. You know it to be the fashion of some to exclaim, with a degree of affectation, how wretched their memories are. The design is not declared; but it is obvious. At the expense of their memory, they insinuate a compliment to their judgment: for it has somehow been received as an opinion, that a strong memory and a strong judgment have seldom been united in the same mind. Perhaps the beautiful lines of Mr. Pope may have contributed to give a currency to this sentiment: but the sentiment is ill founded. I will, indeed, admit, on one hand, that a great memory is often found without a great genius: but I will not admit, on the other, that a great genius is often found without a great memory. The contrary I believe to be generally, I will not say always, the case. Men of the most extensive abilities have been men also of the most extensive memories: witness Themistocles, Cicero, Caesar, Bolingbroke. If these remarks be true, the compliment to judgment at the cost of memory is but a left-handed one. Instead of being rivals, judgment and memory are mutual assistants. Memory furnishes the materials which judgment selects, adjusts, and arranges. Those materials selected, adjusted, and arranged are more at the call of memory than before: for it is a well known fact, that those things, which are disposed most methodically and connected most naturally, are the most distinct, as well as the most lasting objects of remembrance: hence, in discourse, the utility as well as beauty of order. Strength, as well as clearness in our perceptions greatly aids the memory: hence, in discourse, the utility as well as beauty of vivacity. Agreeable emotions, attending our perceptions, contribute to render them both clear and strong: hence, in discourse, the utility as well as beauty of every chaste and elegant ornament. That which is conveyed through the channel of two senses makes a stronger and more lasting impression, than that which is conveyed through the channel of one: hence, in discourse, the utility as well as beauty of just and expressive action. To associate the pleasing with the useful, is Nature's example as well as precept.

I have already intimated that memory is greatly susceptible of improvement: it is so to a surprising degree. This improvement is acquired by vigorous but prudent exercise; and by habitual but lively attention. I assign limitations both to exercise and attention, because both are liable to run into excess. A memory overloaded will make but little useful progress either in literature or business. An attention overstrained is apt to degenerate into what is, with singular propriety, termed absence of thought. To counterfeit this absent kind of thoughtfulness, has been the affectation of those, who wish to be deemed deep thinkers, without the trouble of thinking. To feel it is frequently the lot of those, who think too much. But it is a failing, not an excellence: it is to be avoided, not to be courted. When it begins to steal upon a studious person, he should relieve his attention by changing its object.

In all the ways, in which the objects of our thoughts have hitherto presented themselves to us, they have been necessarily attended with the act or operation of belief. But they may be presented to us in another way, unaccompanied with that act or operation. Let me exemplify this by a set of very familiar instances: for things may be exemplified, that cannot be defined. You see this handkerchief. You are necessarily determined to believe that you see it. You remember that, but a moment ago, I showed you a handkerchief. You are now necessarily determined to believe that you saw it. In the first instance, the handkerchief was seen: that was necessarily accompanied with the belief of its then present existence. In the second instance, the handkerchief was remembered: that was necessarily accompanied with the belief of its past existence. You may hereafter think of a handkerchief, certainly without seeing, probably without recollecting, the handkerchief, which I just now showed you. In the first instance, the perception was accompanied with the belief of present existence: in the second instance, the remembrance was accompanied with the belief of past existence: in the third and last instance, the conception is not accompanied with any belief at all. Conception is an operation of the mind, by which we apprehend a thing, without any belief or judgment concerning it, without referring it to present or past existence. Every one is conscious that he can conceive a thousand things, of whose present or past existence he has not the least belief. You have seen a mountain: you have seen gold: you can conceive a golden mountain: but can you believe its existence?

Conception enters into every operation of the mind. Our senses and our consciousness cannot convey to us information concerning any object, without, at the same time, giving some conception of that object. If we remember any thing, we must have some conception of that, which we remember. In conception there is neither truth nor falsehood; for conception neither affirms nor denies. But though all the other operations of the mind include conception; conception itself may exist, detached from all the others, excepting consciousness. By logicians, conception is frequently called *simple apprehension.*

The powers of sensation, of consciousness, and of memory are exerted upon objects which exist, or have existed. Conception is often exerted upon objects, which have neither past, nor present, nor even future existence. The creative powers of conception and description possessed by

Shakespeare were, by no means, confined to actual existence, past, present, or to come.

Judgment is an important operation of the mind; and is employed upon the materials of perception and knowledge. It is generally described to be, that act of the mind, by which one thing is affirmed or denied of another. But this description is, in one respect, too limited; in another, it is too extensive. It is too limited in this respect, that though our judgments, when expressed, are indeed expressed by affirmation or denial, yet it is not necessary to a judgment that it be expressed at all. Men may judge without affirming or denying any thing; nay, they may judge contrary to what they affirm or deny. The description is too extensive in this respect, that it includes testimony as well as judgment. When a judge pronounces his decree, he delivers it in the affirmative or negative: when a witness delivers his testimony, he uses the affirmative or negative likewise. Judgment and testimony are, however, operations very different from one another: wrong judgment is only an errour: false testimony is something more.

In persons arrived at the years of discretion, their perceptions, their consciousness, their memory are objects of their judgment. Evidence is the ground of judgment; and where evidence is, it is impossible not to judge.

To every determination of the mind concerning what is true or what is false, the name of judgment may be assigned. Some consider knowledge[f] as a separate faculty, conversant about truth and falsehood: perhaps it is more accurate to consider it as a species of judgment; for without judgment, how can there be any knowledge? Judgments are intuitive, as well as discursive, founded on truths that are selfevident, as well as on those that are deduced from demonstration, or from reasoning of a less certain kind. The former, or intuitive judgments, may, in the strictest sense, be called the judgments of nature.

Sense and judgment are sometimes used, especially by some modern philosophers, in contradistinction to each other—very improperly. In common language, and in the writings of the best authors, sense always implies judgment: a man of sense is a man of judgment: common sense is that degree of judgment, which is to be expected in men of common education and common understanding.

f. Locke on Hum. Und. b. 4. c. 14.

With the power of judging, the power of reasoning is very nearly connected. Both powers are frequently included under the general appellation of reason. But reasoning is strictly the process, by which we pass from one judgment to another, which is the consequence of it. In all reasoning, there must be one proposition, which is inferred, and another, at least, from which the inference is made.

Reason, as well as judgment, has truth and falsehood for its objects: both proceed from evidence; both are accompanied with belief.

The power of reasoning is frequently selected as the characteristick quality, which distinguishes the human race from the inferiour part of the creation. From nature the capacity of reasoning is unquestionably derived; but it may be wonderfully strengthened, improved, and extended by art. Imitation and exercise are the two great instruments of improvement.

In a chain of reasoning, the evidence must proceed regularly and without interruption from link to link: the evidence of the last conclusion can be no greater than that of the weakest link in the chain; because if even the weakest link fails, the whole chain is broken.

In reasoning, the most useful and the most splendid talent is the invention of intermediate proofs. In all productions of the understanding, invention is entitled to the highest praise. It implies a luminous view of the object proposed, and sagacity and quickness in discerning, selecting, and employing, to the utmost advantage, the means that are best fitted for accomplishing that object. In the assemblage of those qualities consists that superiority of understanding, which is denominated genius.

Reasoning is distinguished into two kinds; that, which is demonstrative; and that, which is only probable. In demonstrative reasoning there are no degrees; the inference, in every step of the series, is necessary; and it is impossible but that, from the premises, the conclusion must flow. Hence demonstrative reasoning can be applied only to such truths as are necessary; not to such as are contingent.

With regard to reasoning, which is only probable, the connexion between the premises and the conclusion is not a necessary connexion. Probability is susceptible of numerous and widely differing degrees of strength and weakness. The degrees of evidence are measured by their effect upon a clear, a sound, and an unprejudiced understanding. Every degree of evidence produces a proportioned degree of knowledge and belief.

Probable evidence may be distributed into a number of different kinds.

One, and a very important one, is that of human testimony. On this a great part of human knowledge depends. History and law resort to it for the materials of decision and faith. To examine, to compare, and to appreciate this kind of evidence is the business of the judge, the juryman, the counsel, and the party. Without some competent discernment concerning it, no man can act with common prudence or safety in the ordinary occurrences of life.

Another kind of probable evidence is, the opinion of those, who are professional judges of the point in question. In England, a reference is sometimes made to the judges for their opinions in a matter of law. On a trial, recourse is frequently had to the professional sentiments of a physician. A shoemaker could point out to Apelles[4] himself a defect in the picture of a shoe. A tyrant, nurtured and practised in the tyrant's art, could, at the first glance, discover a mistake in the representation of a decollated head.

A third kind of probable evidence is that, by which we recognise the identity of the same thing, and the diversity of different things. This kind of evidence is of the greatest consequence in the affairs of life. By it, the identity of persons and things is determined in courts of justice. In acquiring, retaining, and applying this kind of evidence, there is a wonderful diversity of talents in different men. Some will recollect and distinguish almost all the faces they have ever seen: others are much more slow, and much less retentive in this species of recollection and discrimination.

There are many other kinds of probable evidence, that well deserve the study of the lawyer, the philosopher, and the man. But this is not the proper occasion to attempt an enumeration of them.

Every free action has two causes, which cooperate in its production. One is moral; the other is physical: the former is the will, which determines the action; the latter is the power, which carries it into execution. A paralytick may will to run: a person able to run, may be unwilling: from the want of will in one, and the want of power in the other, each remains in his place.

Our actions and the determinations of our will are generally accompanied with liberty. The name of liberty we give to that power of the mind, by which it modifies, regulates, suspends, continues, or alters its deliberations and actions. By this faculty, we have some degree of command over

4. Apelles (c. 352–308 B.C.) was a famous painter in ancient Greece.

ourselves: by this faculty we become capable of conforming to a rule: possessed of this faculty, we are accountable for our conduct.

But the existence of this faculty has been boldly called in question. It has been asserted, that we have no sense of moral liberty; and that, if we have such a sense, it is fallacious.

With regard to the first question, let every one ask it of himself. Have I a sense of moral liberty? Have I a conviction that I am free? If you have; this sense—this conviction is a matter of fact, or an object of intuition; and vain it is to reason against its truth or existence.

If it exists; why is it to be deemed fallacious? Are there peculiar marks of deception discoverable in it? Can any reason be assigned why we should suspect it, and not every other sense or power of our nature? He that made one, made all. If we are to suspect all; we ought to believe nothing.

But by what one especial power are we told that we ought to suspect all others? On which is this exclusive character of veracity impressed? If Nature is fallacious; how do we learn to detect the cheat? If she is a juggler by trade; is it for us to attempt to penetrate the mysteries of her art, and take upon us to decide when it is that she presents a true, and when it is that she presents a false appearance? If she is false in every other instance, how can we believe her, when she says she is a liar?

But she does not say so. She is, and she claims to be honest; and the law of our constitution determines us to believe her. When we feel, or when we perceive by intuition, that we are free; we may assume the doctrine of moral liberty, as a first and selfevident, though an undemonstrable principle.

I have frequently mentioned *first principles*. The evidence, on which they ought to be received, well deserves discussion and attention. This is a subject which has been greatly misunderstood, and, perhaps, misrepresented. It is a subject, in which inferences, destructive of all knowledge and virtue, have been drawn, with all the pomp and parade of metaphysical sagacity. It is a subject, concerning which proper conceptions are essentially necessary to the progress of all science, that is truly valuable. They are peculiarly necessary in the study of law, in which evidence bears such an active and distinguished part. To believe our senses—to give credit to human testimony, has been considered as unphilosophical, and, consequently, irrational, if not absurd. The connexion, on this subject, between the principles of law, of philosophy, and of human nature has never, so far as I know, been sufficiently traced or explained.

Of some philosophers of no small fame, and of no small influence in propagating a certain fashionable—creed, I was going to say; but that would be peculiarly improper—system I will call it, by a particular indulgence—Of such philosophers it has been the favourite doctrine, that reason is the supreme arbitress of human knowledge; that by her solely we ought to be governed; that in her solely we ought to place confidence; that she can establish first principles; that she can ascertain and correct the mistakes of common sense.

Reason is a noble faculty, and when kept within its proper sphere, and applied to its proper uses, exalts human creatures almost to the rank of superiour beings. But she has been much perverted, sometimes to vile, sometimes to insignificant purposes. By some, she has been chained like a slave or a malefactor; by others, she has been launched into depths unknown or forbidden.

Are the dictates of our reason more plain, than the dictates of our common sense? Is there allotted to the former a portion of infallibility, which has been denied to the latter? If reason may mistake; how shall the mistake be rectified? shall it be done by a second process of reasoning, as likely to be mistaken as the first? Are we thus involved, by the constitution of our nature, in a labyrinth, intricate and endless, in which there is no clue to guide, no ray to enlighten us? Is this true philosophy? is this the daughter of light? is this the parent of wisdom and knowledge? No. This is not she. This is a fallen kind, whose rays are merely sufficient to shed a "darkness visible" upon the human powers; and to disturb the security and ease enjoyed by those, who have not become apostates to the pride of science. Such degenerate philosophy let us abandon: let us renounce its instruction: let us embrace the philosophy which dwells with common sense.

This philosophy will teach us, that first principles are in themselves apparent; that to make nothing selfevident, is to take away all possibility of knowing any thing; that without first principles, there can be neither reason nor reasoning; that discursive knowledge requires intuitive maxims as its basis; that if every truth would admit of proof, proof would extend to infinity; that, consequently, all sound reasoning must rest ultimately on the principles of common sense—principles supported by original and intuitive evidence.

In the investigation of this subject, we shall have the pleasure to find, that those philosophers, who have attempted to fan the flames of war between common sense and reason, have acted the part of incendiaries in the commonwealth of science; that the interests of both are the same; that, between them, there never can be ground for real opposition: that, as they are commonly joined together in speech and in writing, they are inseparable also, in their nature.

We assign to reason two offices, or two degrees. The first is, to judge of things selfevident. The second is, from selfevident principles, to draw conclusions, which are not selfevident. The first of these is the province, and the sole province, of common sense, and, therefore, in its whole extent, it coincides with reason; and is only another name for one branch or one degree of reason. Why then, it may be said, should it have a particular name assigned to it, since it is acknowledged to be only a degree of reason? To this it may be answered, why would you abolish a name, which has found a place in all civilized languages, and has acquired a right by prescription? But this degree of reason ought to be distinguished by a particular name, on two accounts. 1. In the greatest part of mankind, no other degree of reason is to be found. It is this degree of reason, and this only, which makes a man capable of managing his own affairs, and answerable for his conduct towards others. 2. This degree of reason is purely the gift of heaven; and where heaven has not given it, no education can supply it; though, where it is given, it may, in a certain degree, be improved. But the second degree of reason is learned by practice and rules, where the first is wanting.

From the age of Plato down to the present century, it has been the opinion of philosophers, that nothing is perceived but what is in the mind which perceives it: that the mind takes no direct cognizance of external things; but that it perceives them through the medium of certain shadows or images of them: those images were called by the ancients *species, forms, phantasms;* by the moderns they are called *ideas.*

On this foundation the systems of Des Cartes and Locke have been built. The doctrines of Mr. Locke have been received, not only in England, but in many other parts of Europe, with unbounded applause; and to his theory of the human understanding the same kind of respect and deference has been paid, as to the discoveries of Sir Isaac Newton in the natural world.

The school of Mr. Locke has given rise to two sects: at the head of one are Berkely and Hume: at the head of the other are Hartley[5] and Priestley.[6]

In the extension of Mr. Locke's principles, the Bishop of Cloyne[7] conceived that he saw reason to deny the reality of matter; and to resolve all existence into mind. In his own sublime language, he thought he discovered, "that all the choir of heaven and furniture of the earth; all those bodies that compose the frame of the universe, are merely ideas, and exist only in the mind."

Mr. Hume, proceeding on the same principles of reasoning, advances boldly a step farther: he thinks he sees reason for denying the existence of mind as well as of matter; he annihilates spirit as well as body; and reduces mankind—I use his own words—to "a bundle or collection of different perceptions, which succeed each other with an inconceivable rapidity, and are in a perpetual flux and movement." "There is properly no simplicity in the mind at one time; nor identity in it at different times; whatever natural propensity"—tis indeed natural—"we may have to imagine that simplicity and identity: they are successive perceptions only, that constitute the mind."[g]

On the other hand, Dr. Hartley, assuming the existence of an immaterial principle, and of an external world, has endeavoured to trace the connexion between them. By a chain of hypotheses, he has attempted to illustrate the nature of the impressions, which the senses receive from external objects; the laws, by which those impressions influence our ideas; and the rules of association, by which these ideas are connected in our mind. He has thus formed a system, which, in the opinion of some enlightened men, explains, in a satisfactory manner, most of the operations of the thinking faculty.

5. David Hartley (1705–1757) was an English philosopher and physician who founded the Associationist school of psychology.

6. Joseph Priestley (1733–1804) was an English author, chemist, educator, and dissenting clergyman.

7. I.e. George Berkeley.

g. Tr. on hum. nat. 439. 440.

Dr. Priestley has embraced these doctrines with his usual warmth; and has propagated them with his well known zeal. He is of opinion, however, that they ought to be further simplified. A principle, separate from body, he contends is an incumbrance on Dr. Hartley's system. On the principles of deduction, satisfactory to him, he asserts, that to matter, we should ascribe the capacity of intelligence, as well as the property of gravitation. Thought he believes to arise necessarily from a certain organization of the brain; and, resting on this, he denies the existence of an immaterial principle.

Different—exceedingly different indeed—nay, totally irreconcilable are these illustrious men in the conclusions, which they draw. But however widely they differ, however impracticable it may be to reconcile them with regard to their conclusions; they all agree concerning their fundamental principles. They all agree in *assuming* the *existence* of *ideas*. This is the fundamental principle of Mr. Locke's philosophy.

Strange has been the fate of this principle! Strange have been the vicissitudes, with which it has been attended! Strange have been the revolutions, which it has been thought capable of producing! What a powerful engine it has been! In skilful and experienced hands, how tremendous have been its operations! Wielded by one philosopher, it attaches itself solely to matter, and destroys mind. Wielded by another, it attaches itself solely to mind, and destroys matter. Wielded by a third, it becomes equally fatal to matter and mind: by a single fiat of uncreating omnipotence, it strikes body and spirit, time and space into annihilation; and leaves nothing remaining but impressions and ideas!

We have hitherto been apt, perhaps, with unphilosophick credulity, to imagine, that thought supposed a thinker; and that treason implied a traitor. But correct philosophy, it seems, discovers, that all this is a mistake; for that there may be treason without a traitor, laws without a legislator, punishment without a sufferer. If, in these cases, the *ideas* are the traitor, the legislator, the sufferer; the author of this discovery ought to inform us, whether ideas can converse together; whether they can possess rights, or be under obligations; whether they can make promises, enter into covenants, fulfil, or break them; whether, if they break them, damages can be recovered for the breach. If one set of ideas make a covenant; if another successive set—for be it remembered they are all in succession—break the covenant; and if a third successive set are punished for breaking it; how can we discover justice to form any part of this system? These professional questions naturally suggest themselves.

Will these philosophers forgive me, if, from this dreary prospect—if a view of nothing can be called a prospect—I turn my eyes, and direct them to another scene, not indeed so solemn or awful, but such as, in one particular, bears to it a certain strong, though, perhaps, a ridiculous analogy. I would wish to pay all becoming deference to a system, venerable by its high antiquity, and fortified by the authority of philosophers without number. The images, and species, and phantasms of the ancients, and the ideas of the moderns, I wish to contemplate and treat with all imaginable respect. But there is an unlucky object of comparison, which constantly presents itself to my view. I cannot think of this doctrine of ideas, so versatile in its nature and application, without thinking, at the same time, of another doctrine, which has likewise been uncommonly powerful in its operations and effects. Shall I be forgiven?—I repeat the question—if, upon this occasion, I introduce—my Lord Peter's brown loaf.[8] His lordship presented it once: it was excellent mutton. He presented it a second time: it was delicious beef. He presented it a third time: it was exquisite plumb pudding.

Shall I be permitted to ask one question—I think, a very natural one—did the brown loaf ever exist? If it never existed at all; my Lord Peter was equally infallible, when he called it mutton, as when he called it plumb pudding; and when he called it plumb pudding, as when he called it mutton or beef.

Shall I be permitted to ask another question—equally natural as the former? These images, and species, and phantasms of the ancients; these ideas of the moderns—did they ever exist? You will unquestionably be surprised when I tell you, that though, from the time of Plato and Aristotle to the time of Berkely and Hume, ideas and species have been supposed to lie at the foundation of the philosophy of the human mind, and, consequently, of all philosophy and knowledge; yet that foundation has never, till lately, been examined; but that the existence of ideas and species has always been assumed as a doctrine taken for granted. You will,

8. Lord Peter is a proverbial character who threatens his brothers with a terrible curse if they don't believe the lies he tells them. He then sets a loaf of brown bread before them and declares it to be mutton.

perhaps, be further surprised, on being told, that, when lately the rubbish, which, during the long course of two thousand years, had covered and concealed the foundations of philosophy, was removed; and when those foundations were examined by an architect of uncommon discernment and skill; no such things as the ideas of the moderns, or the species of the ancients were to be discovered there.

"I acknowledge," says the enlightened and candid Dr. Reid,[h] "that I never thought of calling in question the principles commonly received with regard to the human understanding, until the Treatise of Human Nature was published." This is the performance of Mr. Hume, from which I cited a passage a little while ago. It appeared in the year 1739. "The ingenious author," continues Dr. Reid, "of that treatise, upon the principles of Locke, who was no sceptick, hath built a system of scepticism, which leaves no ground to believe any one thing rather than its contrary. His reasoning appeared to me to be just: there was, therefore, a necessity to call in question the principles, upon which it was founded; or admit the conclusion.

"But can any ingenious mind admit this sceptical system without reluctance? I truly could not: for I am persuaded that absolute scepticism is not more destructive of the faith of a christian, than of the science of a philosopher, and of the prudence of a man of common understanding."—I may add—or the sound principles of a lawyer or statesman. "I am persuaded," continues the Doctor, "that the unjust live by faith, as well as the just; and that, if all belief could be laid aside, piety, patriotism, friendship, parental affection, and private virtue would appear as ridiculous as knight errantry; and that the pursuits of pleasure, of ambition, and of avarice must be grounded upon belief, as well as those that are honourable and virtuous.

"For my own satisfaction, I entered into a serious examination of the principles, upon which this sceptical system is built; and was not a little surprised to find, that it leans with its whole weight upon a hypothesis, which is ancient indeed and hath been very generally received by philosophers; but of which I could find no solid proof. The hypothesis I mean is, that nothing is perceived but what is in the mind, which perceives it; that we do not really perceive things that are external, but only certain images

h. Inq. Ded. 4–8.

and pictures of them imprinted upon the mind, which are called *impressions* and *ideas*.

"If this be true; supposing certain impressions and ideas to exist in my mind, I cannot, from their existence, infer the existence of any thing else; my impressions and ideas are the only existences, of which I can have any knowledge or conception, and they are such fleecting and transitory beings, that they can have no existence at all, any longer than I am conscious of them. So that, upon this hypothesis, the whole universe about me, bodies and spirits, sun, moon, stars and earth, friends and relations, all things without exception which I imagined to have a permanent existence, whether I thought of them or not, vanish at once,

And like the baseless fabrick of a vision,
Leave not a track behind.

"I thought it unreasonable, upon the authority of philosophers, to admit a hypothesis, which, in my opinion, overturns all philosophy, all religion and virtue, and all common sense; and finding that all the systems concerning the human understanding, which I was acquainted with, were built upon this hypothesis, I resolved to inquire into this subject anew, without regard to any hypothesis."

The fruits of his inquiries have been published; and richly deserve your perusal and attention. Others have sown and cultivated the same seeds of knowledge, with the most encouraging success; and there is reason to hope, that the philosophy of human nature will not much longer continue the reproach of the human understanding.

Monopoly and exclusive privilege are the bane of every thing—of science as well as of commerce. The sceptical philosophers claim and exercise the privilege of assuming, without proof, the very first principles of their philosophy; and yet they require, from others, a proof of every thing by reasoning. They are unreasonable in both points. Some things, which ought to be believed, ought to be believed without proof. The first principle of their philosophy—the existence of ideas—is none of those things. If it be true; it is a discursive, not an intuitive truth; and, therefore, it can be proved. For this reason, unless it be proved, it should not be believed.

After having mentioned the sceptical philosophers, it is with a degree of reluctance that I so soon introduce the respected name of Mr. Locke.

I introduce him not as one of those philosophers, but as one, who has unfortunately given a sanction to principles, the consequences of which he certainly did not foresee. But from his principles, those consequences have been ably and unanswerably drawn by others. His principles, therefore, ought to be minutely examined, that we may see whether, on a strict examination, they will stand the test.

I shall examine his leading principle by the very test, which he himself proposes for its trial. Cautious and candid as he was, it is very remarkable, that, while he recommends it to others to be careful in the admission of principles, he admits his own leading principle without sufficient examination and care. "I take leave to say"—I use his own words[i]—"I take leave to say, that every one ought very carefully to beware what he admits for a principle, to examine it strictly, and see whether he certainly knows it to be true of itself by its own evidence; or whether he does only, with assurance, believe it to be so upon the authority of others." And yet he begins his observations on ideas and their original, by assuming their existence, as his leading principle. "Every man being conscious to himself that he thinks; and that which his mind is applied about, whilst thinking, being the *ideas* that are *there,* tis past doubt, that men have in their minds several ideas." "It is, in the *first* place, then, to be inquired *how* he comes by them."[j]

With all deference for the character and talents of Mr. Locke—and I have, indeed, a high respect for them—I think that a previous inquiry ought to have been made—*Does* he come by them? To assume, without proving, that the things, which the mind is applied about, whilst thinking, are the ideas that are *there*; is certainly to assume too much.

In another place,[k] he expresses a hope, that it will be received as an intuitive truth—as one of that species of intuitive truths, which arise from consciousness. "I presume," says he, "it will be easily granted me, that there are such ideas in men's minds." Why so easily granted? Why should the leading principle of a philosophy, which, if true, necessarily draws us to such consequences as have been represented—why should such a leading principle be taken on trust? "Because," continues Mr. Locke,[l] "every one is conscious of them in himself."

i. On Hum. Und. b. 4. c. 20. s. 8.
j. Id. b. 2. c. 1. s. 1.
k. Id. Introd.
l. On Hum. Und. b. 1. c. 1. s. 8.

Here is a fair and candid appeal: for if every one is conscious of ideas in his own mind, he must believe that such ideas are *there:* for consciousness is unquestionably a first principle of evidence. In this appeal I have the pleasure of joining with Mr. Locke. In one thing we certainly agree—the object of both is to discover the truth. Of this truth, you shall be the judges, or rather the triers between us; for consciousness is a matter of fact.

But before we enter upon the trial of this appeal, let us be sure that the point to be tried is clearly ascertained and understood: let us not be misled by verbal ambiguity, nor drawn into the field of verbal disputation. Many errours, and some of no inconsiderable importance, have arisen from the vague, the doubtful, or the inaccurate application of the term *idea.*

By ideas are sometimes meant the acts or operations of our minds in perceiving, remembering, or imagining objects. In this sense, the existence of ideas is far from being called in question. We are conscious of them every day and every hour of our lives.

Sometimes *idea* is used to denote *opinion*—Thus, when we speak of the ideas of Cicero; we mean his opinions or doctrines.

But there is a third sense, in which the term *idea* has been used. It has been used to denote those images and pictures of things, which, and not the things themselves, are the immediate objects perceived by the mind. Those, who speak the most intelligibly, explain their doctrine in this manner. Suppose me to look at a mirrour; and, while I am looking at it, suppose a person to come behind me; I see, in the mirrour, not the person himself, but his image. In the same manner, when, without a mirrour, I am supposed to see a house or a tree; I see only an image of those objects in my mind. This image is the immediate object of my perception.

It is in this last sense, now explained, that an appeal is made to your consciousness for the truth of the existence of ideas.

You look at me: now I call for your conscious verdict. Are you conscious, that you really see me: or are you conscious, that you see, not me, but only a certain image or picture of me, imprinted upon your own minds? If the latter; your consciousness decides in favour of Mr. Locke: if the former; it decides in favour of me. In whose favour does your verdict decide? Before you finally declare it, it may, perhaps, be urged, that you perceive me by means of intervening resemblances of me, distinctly painted on the retinae of your eyes.

This shows, that I am willing to give the cause an impartial trial, nay, an advantageous one, on the side of my admired antagonist. From those parts only of our knowledge, which are disclosed by the sense of seeing, could this objection be urged.

I admit, that the resemblances mentioned are distinctly painted on the retinae of your eyes. But suffer me to ask you—do you *perceive* those resemblances, *so* painted? I presume you do not: for the existence of those resemblances was never, so far as I know or have heard, perceived by any of the innumerable race of men: it was not so much as suspected, till in the last century. Then the discovery was made by Kepler: but even to Kepler the discovery was not disclosed by consciousness:[9] it was the result of deep and accurate researches into the philosophy of vision.

But I have not yet done with my answer to this objection. That you do not perceive me by the intervention of any perception of the resemblances painted on the retinae of the eyes, is evident from two circumstances. In the first place, the resemblances of me are painted on the retinae of both eyes: therefore, if you saw me through the intervention of those resemblances, you would see me double. In the second place, the resemblances of me on the retinae are inverted: therefore, if you saw me through the intervention of those resemblances, you would see me turned upside down.

Are you now ready finally to declare your verdict? Do you perceive me? or do you only perceive, in your own minds, an image or picture of me?

I presume I may say, that the existence of ideas is not the dictate of consciousness. Is the existence of ideas entitled, in any other manner, or from any other source, to be considered as an intuitive truth? I have not heard it suggested. If it is a truth, and not an intuitive one; it is a truth capable of being proved: if it is capable of being proved; it ought to be proved, as we have already said, before it be believed.

A proof has been attempted: let us examine it. "No being, it is said, can act or be acted upon, but where it is; and, consequently, our mind cannot act upon, or be acted upon by any subject at a distance."[m]

This argument possesses one eminent advantage: its obscurity, like that

9. Johannes Kepler (1571–1630) was a German mathematician and astronomer. He is best known for his laws of planetary motion, but he also made significant discoveries in the realm of optics.

m. Reid's Ess. Int. 203. 2 Elem. Crit. 513. n.

of an oracle, is apt to impose on the hearer, who is willing to consider it as demonstration, because he does not, at first, discover its fallacy. Let it undergo a fair examination; let it be drawn out of its obscurity: let it be stated and analyzed in a clear point of view. Then it will appear as follows.

"No subject can be perceived, unless it acts upon the mind, or is acted upon by the mind: but no distant object can act upon the mind, or be acted upon by the mind; for no being can act but where it is: therefore the immediate object of perception must be something in the mind, so as to be able to act upon, or to be acted upon by the mind."

Now you see, fairly stated in all its parts, the argument, which is supposed to prove the necessity of phantasms or ideas in the mind, as the only objects of perception. It is singularly unfortunate for this argument, that it concludes directly against the very hypothesis, of which it is the only foundation: for how can phantasms or ideas be raised in the mind by things at a distance, if things at a distance cannot act upon, or be acted upon by the mind.

Again; the argument assumes a proposition as true, without evidence—that no distant subject can act upon, or be acted upon by the mind. This proposition requires evidence; for it is not intuitively certain. Till this proposition, therefore, be proved, every man may rationally rely upon the conviction of his senses, that he sees and hears objects at a distance.

But further; to render the foregoing argument conclusive, it ought to be proved, that when we perceive objects, either they act upon us, or we act upon them. This is not selfevident; nor is it proved. Indeed reasons may be well offered against its admission.

When we say, that one being acts upon another, we mean that some power is exerted by the agent, which produces, or tends to produce a change in the thing acted upon. Now, there appears no reason for asserting, that, in perception, either the object acts upon the mind, or the mind upon the object. An object, in being perceived, does not act at all. I perceive the desk before me; but it is perfectly inactive; and, therefore, cannot act upon my mind. Neither does the mind, in perception, act upon the object. To perceive an object is one thing: to act upon it is another thing. To say, that I act upon the paper before me, when I look at it, is an abuse of langauge. We have, therefore, no evidence, that, in perception, the mind acts upon the object, or the object upon the mind; but strong evidence to the contrary. The consequence is, that the very foundation of the only argument brought to prove the existence of ideas is sandy and unsound.

Thus the first principle of the ideal philosophy is supported neither by intuition nor by proof. On what pretension, then, can it lay any just claim to our regard?

And yet this principle, unsupported, absurd, and unphilosophical as it is, will, I believe, be found to be the sole foundation laid, so far as any is laid, in our law books, for the philosophy of the law of evidence. My Lord Chief Baron Gilbert,[10] the most approved, and deservedly the most approved writer on this part of the law, grounds his general observations on the doctrine of Mr. Locke, that knowledge is nothing but the perception of the agreement or disagreement of our *ideas.*[n]

In one of my early lectures,[o] I made the following observations. "Despotism, by an artful use of 'superiority' in politicks; and scepticism, by an artful use of 'ideas' in metaphysicks, have endeavoured—and their endeavours have frequently been attended with too much success—to destroy all true liberty and sound philosophy. By their baneful effects, the science of man and the science of government have been poisoned to their very fountains. But those destroyers of others have met, or must meet with their own destruction." I have put you in possession of materials to judge for yourselves whether these observations are or are not well founded.

At first sight, it would seem strange that the principles of law, as they are laid down in a book, which is very generally received for authority, should be destructive of liberty; and that the principles of the philosophy of the human mind, as they likewise are generally received and taught, should be subversive of all truth and knowledge. But after what we have seen; is it not as true as strange?

This investigation has cost me some trouble: to you I hope it will be attended with some advantage. I thought it my duty to make and to communicate it; because, without it, any superstructure of system, which I could build, would not satisfy me as resting on a solid foundation. Could I have been justified in palming upon you a system leaning on such principles as do not satisfy myself?

10. Sir Geoffrey Gilbert (1674–1726) was an English judge and author.

n. Gilb. Ev. 1–3.

o. Ante. p. 472.

I know very well, that, in the business of life, the dictates of common sense will always, and that in the business of government, the spirit of liberty will sometimes prevail over false theories of politicks and philosophy. But is this a reason why those false theories should be received, or encouraged, or propagated? Ought not our conduct as men and as citizens to receive benefit instead of detriment from the systems of our education? One, whose practice is in diametrical opposition to his principles, stands always in an awkward, often in a painful, sometimes in a dangerous situation.

I have said, that the spirit of liberty will sometimes prevail over false theories of politicks. Unhappily I could not say more: I could not say, generally: far less could I say, always. Let us look around us and behold the sons of men, who inhabit this globe. What an immense proportion of them are the wretched slaves of perverted opinion, of perverted system, of perverted education, and of perverted example in matters relating to the principles of society, and the rights of the human kind!

I hope I have now shown, that the philosophers before mentioned unreasonably claimed the exclusive privilege of assuming the first principle of their philosophy, without proof: I now proceed to show, that they are equally unreasonable in requiring, from others, a proof of every thing by reasoning.

The defects and blemishes of the received philosophy, which have most exposed it to ridicule and contempt, have been chiefly owing to a prejudice of the votaries of this philosophy in favour of reason. They have endeavoured to extend her jurisdiction beyond its just limits; and to call before her bar the dictates of common sense. But these will not submit to this jurisdiction: they plead to its authority; and disdain its trial; they claim not its aid; they dread not its attacks.

In this unequal contest between reason and common sense, the former will always be obliged to retreat both with loss and with dishonour; nor can she ever flourish, till this rivalship is dropt, till these encroachments are given up, and till a cordial friendship is restored. For, in truth, reason has no other root than the principles of common sense: it grows out of them: and from them it draws its nourishment.

There are some common principles, which are the foundation of all science, and of all reasoning. Before men can argue together, they must agree in such principles; for it is impossible for two to reason, but from principles held by them in common. Such common principles seldom admit of direct proof; they need none; they are such as men of common understanding will acknowledge as soon as they are proposed and understood.

Such principles, when we have occasion to use them in science, are called *axioms.* Upon such, the finest, the most elaborate, and the most sublime reasonings in mathematicks are founded.

In every other science, as well as in mathematicks, there are some common principles, upon which all the reasonings in that science are grounded, and into which they may be resolved. If these were pointed out and considered, we should be better able to judge concerning the strength and certainty of the conclusions in that science.

It is not impossible, that what is only a vulgar prejudice may be mistaken for a first principle. Nor is it impossible, that what is really a first principle, may, by the enchantment of words, have such a mist thrown about it, as to hide its evidence, and make a man of candour doubt concerning it.

The peripatetick philosophy,[11] instead of being deficient, was redundant in first principles; instead of rejecting those, which are truly such, it adopted, as such, many vulgar prejudices and rash judgments. This seems, in general, to have been the spirit of ancient philosophy.

How naturally one extreme produces its opposite! Des Cartes, at the head of modern reformers in philosophy, anxious to avoid the snare, in which Aristotle and the peripateticks had been caught—that of admitting things too rashly as first principles—resolved to doubt of every thing, till it was clearly proved. He would not assume, as a first principle, even his own existence. In what manner he supposed nonexistence could institute, or desire to institute a series of proof to prove existence or any thing else, we are not informed.

He thought he could prove his existence by his famous enthymem—Cogito, ergo sum. I think, therefore, I exist. Though he would not assume the existence of *himself* as a first principle, he was obliged to assume the existence of his *thoughts* as a first principle. But is this entitled to any degree of preference? Can one, who doubts whether he exists, be certain that

11. I.e. Aristotelian philosophy.

he thinks? And may not one, who, without proof, takes it for granted that he thinks—may not such an one, without the imputation of unphilosophick credulity, take it for granted, likewise without proof, that he exists?

In every just proof, a proposition less evident is inferred from one, which is more evident. How is it more evident that we think, than that we exist? Both are equally evident: one, therefore, ought not to be first assumed, and then used as a proof of the other.

But further; if we attend to the strict rules of proof; the existence of Des Cartes was not legitimately inferred from the existence of his thoughts. If the inference is legitimate; it must become legitimate by establishing this proposition—that thought cannot exist without a thinking being. But did Des Cartes, or has any of his followers proved this proposition? They have not proved it: they cannot prove it. Mr. Hume has denied it; and has triumphantly challenged the world to establish it by proof. The basis of his philosophy is, as we have already seen—"that a train of successive perceptions constitute the mind."

Let me not here be misunderstood. When I say, that the existence of a thinking principle, called the mind, has not been and cannot be proved; I am far from saying, that it is not true, that such a thinking principle exists. I know—I feel—it to be true; but I know it not from proof: I know it from what is greatly superiour to proof: I *see* it by the shining light of intuition.

Why will philosophers, by a preposterous pride, wish and endeavour to be indebted, for the discovery of every thing, to the feeble and glimmering rays of their own tapers, when they have only to throw the window open, and they will behold every thing illuminated by the splendour of the meridian sun?

Let me, upon this subject, further, observe, that strongly as Des Cartes was seized with this phobia of first principles, he was obliged, in one instance at least, to suffer the detested liquid to touch his lips. Cogito, says he: I think. You think! How do you prove that?. You, who will not believe your own existence without proof—can you consistently dispense with the proof of the existence of your thoughts? He is obliged to submit to the inconsistency. He assumes the existence of his thoughts, as a first principle. Why did he not pursue the same course with regard to other intuitive truths?

As the last observation on this subject, I beg leave to take notice, that, in this remarkable enthymem, Des Cartes assumed the very thing to be proved. Cogito. *I* think. Who *are you*? Existence is implied in the very proposition, that *one* thinks.

To the distinction between first principles and those principles, which may be ascribed to the power of reasoning, it is not a just objection, that there may be some judgments, concerning which we may be doubtful, to which class they should be referred. In painting and in nature, two colours, very different, may so run into one another, as to render it difficult to perceive where one ends and the other begins.

Let us then conclude—for we may safely conclude—that all knowledge, obtained by reasoning, must be built on first principles. When we examine, by analysis, the evidence of any proposition; we find, either that it is selfevident; or that it rests upon one or more propositions, which support it. The same thing may be said of the propositions, which support it; and of those again, which support them. But we cannot go back, in this tract, to infinity. Where, then, must the analysis stop? When we come to propositions, which support all that are built upon them, but are themselves supported by none: in other words, when we come to selfevident propositions.

All first principles must be the immediate dictates of our natural faculties; nor is it possible that we should have any other evidence of their truth. In different sciences, the faculties, which dictate these first principles, are very different: the eye, in astronomy and opticks: the ear, in musick: the moral sense, in morals.

Some first principles yield conclusions, which are certain; others yield such only as are probable. In just reasoning, the strength or weakness of the conclusion will always correspond to the strength or weakness of the principles, on which it is grounded. But the lowest degree of probability, as well as absolute certainty, must be grounded ultimately on first principles.

After hearing so much concerning first principles, the question will naturally suggest itself—are they ascertained and pointed out? That they were so, is most ardently to be desired. In mathematicks, they have been so, as far back as the annals of literature can carry us. And the consequence has been, that, in mathematicks, we find no sects, or contrary systems. This science, founded upon first principles, as upon a rock, has been increased from age to age, till it has become the loftiest and most solid fabrick, which human reason can boast.

Till within these two hundred years, natural philosophy was in the same fluctuating state with the other sciences. Every new system pulled up the old one by the roots. The great Lord Bacon first marked out the only foundation, on which natural philosophy could be built. His celebrated successour, Sir Isaac Newton, gave the first and noblest examples of that chaste induction, of which his guide in the principles of science could only delineate the theory. He reduced the principles of Lord Bacon into a few axioms, which he calls "regulae philosophandi,"—rules of philosophising. From these, together with the phenomena observed by the senses, which he likewise assumes as first principles, he deduces, by strict reasoning, the propositions of his philosophy; and, in this manner, has erected an edifice, which stands immovable upon the basis of first and self-evident principles. This edifice has been enlarged by the accession of new discoveries, made since his time; but it has not been subjected to alterations in the plan.

The other sciences have not, as yet, been so fortunate as those of mathematicks and natural philosophy. Indeed the other sciences, compared with these, have this disadvantage, that it is more difficult to form distinct and determinate conceptions of the objects, about which they are employed. But this difficulty, though great, is not insurmountable: it may afford a reason why the other sciences have had a longer infancy; but it can afford none, why they may not, at last, arrive at maturity by the same steps as those of a quicker growth.

If the same unanimity concerning first principles could be introduced into the other sciences, as in those of mathematicks and natural philosophy; this might be considered as a new era in the progress of human reason.[p]

Some first principles I have already had occasion to notice: in the course of my system, others will come forward into view; and will receive

p. Reid's Inq. 483.

particular attention; especially in the important law of evidence, upon which the practical use of the whole municipal law entirely rests. For the facts must be ascertained by evidence, before they are susceptible of an application of the law. "Ex facto oritur jus."[12] How can facts be satisfactorily established, unless the genuine philosophy of evidence be known?

Investigation will, perhaps, disclose to us, that this part of philosophy has been best known, where the knowledge of it has been least expected.

12. Law arises from fact.

CHAPTER VII.

Of Man, as a Member of Society.

"It is not fit that man should be alone," said the all-wise and all-gracious Author of our frame, who knew it, because he made it; and who looked with compassion on the first solitary state of the work of his hands. Society is the powerful magnet, which, by its unceasing though silent operation, attracts and influences our dispositions, our desires, our passions, and our enjoyments. That we should be anxious to share, and, by sharing, to divide our afflictions, may, to some, appear by no means strange, because a certain turn of thinking will lead them to ascribe this propensity to the selfish rather than to the social part of our nature. But will this interested solution account for another propensity, equally uniform and equally strong? We are no less impatient to communicate our pleasures than our woes. Does self-interest predominate here? No. Our social affection acts here unmixed and uncontrolled.

There's not a blessing individuals find,
But some way leans and hearkens to the kind.
No bandit fierce, no tyrant mad with pride,
No caverned hermit rests self-satisfied.
Who most to shun or hate mankind pretend,
Seek an admirer, or would fix a friend.
Abstract what others feel, what others think,
All pleasures sicken, and all glories sink.[a]

In all our pictures of happiness, which, at certain gay and disengaged moments, appear, in soft and alluring colours, to our fancy, does not a partner of our bliss always occupy a conspicuous place? When, on the other hand, phantoms of misery haunt our disturbed imaginations, do not

a. Pope's Ess. Man. Ep. 4. v. 39.

solitary wanderings frequently form a principal part of the gloomy scenes? It is not an uncommon opinion, and, in this instance, our opinions must be vouched by our feelings, that the most exquisite punishment, which human nature could suffer, would be, in total solitude, to languish out a lengthened life.

"These deep solitudes" is the circumstance that first bursts from the labouring bosom of the cloistered Eloisa, when she describes the "awful cells," where "ever musing melancholy reigns."

How various and how unwearied are the workings of the social aim! Deprived of one support, it lays hold on another: deprived of that other, it lays hold on another still. While an intelligent, or even an animate being can be found, it will find an object for its unremitted pursuit and attachment.

We may extract sweet lessons of liberty and sociability from the prison of barbarous and despotick power. A French nobleman was long immured in a dreary and solitary apartment. When he had uttered many an unavailing sigh after society, he, at last, was fortunate enough to discover a spider, who had taken up his abode in the same room. Delighted with the acquisition, he immediately formed a social intercourse with the joint inhabitant of his sequestered mansion. He enjoyed, without molestation, this society for a considerable time. But the correspondence was, at last, discovered by his keeper, long tutored and accustomed to all the ingenious inventions and refinements of barbarity. By an effort, which evinced him a consummate master of his art, he killed the spider, and reduced his prisoner again to absolute solitude. The nobleman, after his release, used frequently to declare, that he had seldom experienced more poignant distress, than what he had suffered from the loss of his companion in confinement.

Some philosophers, however, have alleged, that society is not natural, but is only adventitious to us; that it is the mere consequence of direful necessity; that, by nature, men are wolves to men; not wolves to wolves; for between them union and society have a place; but as wolves to sheep, destroyers and devourers. Men, say they, are made for rapine; they are destined to prey upon one another: each is to fight for victory, and to subdue and enslave as many of his fellow creatures, as he possibly can, by treachery or by force. According to these philosophers, the only natural principles of man are selfishness, and an insatiable desire of tyranny and dominion. Their conclusion is, that a state of nature, instead of being a state of kindness, society, and peace, is a state of selfishness, discord, and war. By a strange perversion of things, they would so explain all the social passions and natural affections, as to denominate them of the selfish species. Humanity and hospitality towards strangers or those in distress are represented as selfishness, only of a more deliberate kind. An honest heart is only a cunning one; and good nature is a well regulated self-love. The love of posterity, of kindred, of country, and of mankind—all these are only so many different modifications of this universal self-love.

But if we attend to our nature and our state; if we listen to the operations of our own minds, to our dispositions, our sensations, and our propensities; we shall be fully and agreeably convinced, that the narrow and hideous representation of these philosophers is not founded on the truth of things; but, on the contrary, is totally repugnant to all human sentiment, and all human experience. Indeed, an appeal to themselves will evince, that their philosophy is not consistent even with the instinctive principles of their own hearts—principles, of which the native lustre will, at some times, beam forth, notwithstanding all the care employed to cover or extinguish it. The celebrated Sage of Malmesbury,[1] savage and unsociable as he would make himself and all mankind appear, took the utmost pains that, during his life, and even after his death, others might be kindly rescued from the unhappy delusions, by which they were prevented from discovering the truth.[b] He told us "that both in religion and in morals, we were imposed on by our governours; that there is nothing, which, by nature, inclines us either way; and that nothing naturally draws us to the love of what is without or beyond ourselves." And yet he was the most laborious of all men in composing and publishing systems of this kind—*for our use.*

To such philosophers, animated with this preposterous zeal, this answer, in the spirit of their own doctrines, is plain and easy. If there is nothing to carry you without yourselves; what are we to you? From what motives do you give yourselves all this concern about us? What can induce

1. Thomas Hobbes of Malmesburg (1588–1679), author of *Leviathan*, notorious in Wilson's time for his egoistic account of human nature.

b. 1. Shaft. Char. 90.

you to trim your midnight lamp, and waste your spirits in laborious vigils, for our instruction? You disclaim all social connexion with your species; what, then, we say again, are we to you?

But a subject, in itself so material to the sciences of philosophy and of law, merits a serious, a full, and a patient discussion. For it is of high practical importance, that the principles of society should be properly explained and well understood. It has been one of the happy characteristicks of the present age, both on this and on the other side of the Atlantick, that the spirit of philosophy has been wisely directed to the just investigation of those principles; and that the spirit of patriotism has been vigorously exerted in their support.

In a very early part of these lectures,[c] it was observed, concerning definitions and divisions, that by them we are in danger of circumscribing nature within the limits of our own notions, formed frequently on partial and defective views. A very remarkable instance of this occurs in the subject, on the examination of which we now enter.

The intellectual powers of the mind have been commonly divided into simple apprehension, judgment, and reasoning. This division has received the sanction of high antiquity, and of a very extensive adoption; yet it is far from being complete. From it many of the operations of the understanding are excluded, such as consciousness, moral perception, taste, memory, and our perception of objects by means of our external senses. But, besides all these, there is a whole class, and a very important one too, of our intellectual operations, which, because they were not fortunate enough to be included within the foregoing division, have been overlooked by philosophers, and have not even yet been distinguished by a name. Some operations of the mind may take place in a solitary state: others, from their very nature, are social; and necessarily suppose a communication with some other intelligent being. In a state of absolute solitude, one may apprehend, and judge, and reason. But when he bears or hears testimony; when he gives or receives a command; when he enters into an engagement by a promise or a contract; these acts imply necessarily something more than apprehension, judgment, and reasoning; they imply necessarily a society with other beings, social as well as intelligent.

c. Ante. p. 466.

Simple apprehension is unaccompanied with any judgment or belief, concerning the object apprehended. Judgment is formed, as these philosophers say, by comparing ideas, and by perceiving their agreements and disagreements. Reasoning is an operation, by which, from two or more judgments, we deduce a conclusion. Now, from this account of these three operations of the mind, it appears unquestionably, that testimony is neither apprehension, nor judgment, nor reasoning. The same observation will apply, with the same propriety, to a promise, to an agreement, to a contract. Testimony, agreements, contracts, promises form very distinguished titles in that law, which it is the object of these lectures to delineate: perhaps it has already been evinced to your satisfaction, that some of them form its very basis.

That system of human nature must, indeed, appear extremely inadequate and defective, by which articles of such vast importance, both in theory and in the business of life, are left without a place, and without a name.

The attempts of some philosophers to reduce the social operations under the common philosophical divisions, resemble very much the attempts of others, to reduce all our social affections to certain modifications of self love. The Author of our existence intended us to be social beings; and has, for that end, given us social intellectual powers. They are original parts of our constitution; and their exertions are no less natural than the exertions of those powers, which are solitary and selfish.

Our social intellectual operations appear early in life, and before we are capable of reasoning; yet they suppose a conviction of the existence of other intelligent and social beings. A child asks a question of his nurse, and waits for her answer: this implies a conviction that she is intelligent and social; that she can receive and return a communication of thoughts and sentiments.

All languages are fitted to express the social as well as the solitary operations of the mind. To express the former is indeed the primary and the direct intention of language. A man, who had no interchange of sentiments with other social and intelligent beings, would be as mute as the irrational animals that surround him. By language, we communicate to others that, which we know: by language, we learn from others that, of which we are ignorant: by language, we advise, persuade, console, encourage, sooth, restrain: in consequence of language, we are united by political societies, government, and laws: by means of language, we are raised from a situation, in which we should be as rude and as savage as the beasts of the woods.

In the more imperfect societies of mankind, such as those composed of colonies scarcely settled in their new seats, it might pass for sufficient good fortune, if the people proved only so far masters of language, as to be able to understand one another, to confer about their wants, and to provide for their common necessities. Their exposed and indigent state would not afford them either that leisure or that easy disposition, which is requisite for the cultivation of the fine arts. They, who were neither safe from violence, nor secure from want, would not be likely to engage in unnecessary pursuits. It could not be expected that they would turn their attention towards the numbers of their language, or to its best and most perfect application and arrangement. But when, in process of time, the affairs of the society were settled on an easy and secure foundation; when debates and discourses, on the subjects of common interest and of publick good, were become familiar; when the speeches of distinguished characters were considered and compared; then there would be observed, between one speaker and another, a difference, not only with regard to a more agreeable measure of sound, but to a happier and more easy arrangement of sentiment.

The attention paid to language is one distinguishing mark of the progress of society towards its most refined period: as society improves, influence is acquired by the means of reasoning and discourse: in proportion as that influence is felt to increase, in proportion will be the care bestowed upon the methods of expressing conceptions with propriety and elegance. In every polished community, this study has been considered as highly important, and has possessed a place in every plan of liberal education.

In all languages, a question, a promise, a contract, which are social acts, can be expressed as easily and as properly, as a judgment, which is a solitary act. The expression of a judgment has been dignified with a particular appellation; it has been denominated a *proposition.* It has been analyzed, with great logical parade, into its several parts: its elements of subject, predicate, and copula have been exhibited in ostentatious arrangement: their various modifications have been traced and examined in laborious and voluminous tracts. The expression of a question, of a covenant, or of a promise is as susceptible of analysis as the expression of a judgment: but this has not been attempted; these operations of the mind have not been honoured even with a distinct and appropriate name. Why has so much pains been taken, why has so much labour been bestowed in analyzing, and assigning appropriate names to the solitary operations, and the expression of the solitary operations of the understanding; while so little attention has been allotted to such of its operations as are social? Perhaps it will be difficult to assign any other reason than this: in the divisions, which have been made of the operations of the mind, the social ones have been omitted; and, consequently, have not been introduced to notice or regard.

Our moral perceptions, as well as the other powers of our understanding, indicate, in the strongest manner, our designation for society. Veracity, and its corresponding quality, confidence, show this, in a very striking point of view. If we were intended for solitude, those qualities could have neither operation nor use. On the other hand, without those qualities, society could not be supported. Without the latter, the former would be useless: without the former, the latter would be dangerous. Without confidence in promises, for instance, we must, in the greatest part of our conduct, proceed entirely upon the calculations of chance: but there could be no confidence in promises, if there was no principle, from which their performance might be reasonably expected.

Some may imagine, that though this principle did not exist, yet human affairs might, perhaps, be carried on as well; for that general caution and mutual distrust would be the necessary result; and where no confidence would be reposed, no breach of it could happen. But, not to mention the uneasiness and anxiety which would unavoidably attend such a situation, it is not considered how much, in every hour of our lives, we trust to others; and how difficult, if not entirely impracticable, it would be to perform the most common as well as the most important business of human life, without such trust. The conclusion is, that the performance of promises is essential to society.

Deeply laid in human nature, we now behold the basis of one of the principal pillars of private municipal law; that, which enforces the obligation of promises, agreements, and covenants.

Again; the moral sense restrains us from harming the innocent: it teaches us, that the innocent have a right to be secure from harm. These are two great principles, which prepare us for society; and, with regard to them, the moral sense discovers peculiar inflexibility: it dictates, that we should submit to any distress or danger, rather than procure our safety and relief by violence upon an innocent person.

Similar to the restraint, respecting personal safety and security, is the restraint, which the moral sense imposes on us, with regard to property. Robbery and theft are indulged by no society: from a society even of robbers, they are strictly excluded.

The necessity of the social law, with regard to personal security, is so evident, as to require no explanation. Its necessity, with regard to property, will be explained and made evident by the following remarks.

Man has a natural propensity to store up the means of his subsistence: this propensity is essential, in order to incite us to provide comfortably for ourselves, and for those who depend on us. But this propensity would be rendered ineffectual, if we were not secured in the possession of those stores which we collect; for no one would toil to accumulate what he could not possess in security. This security is afforded by the moral sense, which dictates to all men, that goods collected by the labour and industry of individuals are their property; and that property ought to be inviolable.

We beheld, a little while ago, one of the principal pillars of *civil* law founded deeply in our nature: we now perceive the great principles of *criminal* law laid equally deep in the human frame. Violations of property and of personal security are, as we shall afterwards show particularly, the objects of that law. To punish, and, by punishing, to prevent them, is or ought to be the great end of that law, as shall also be particularly shown.

That we are fitted and intended for society, and that society is fitted and intended for us, will become evident by considering our passions and affections, as well as by considering our moral perceptions, and the other operations of our understandings. We have all the emotions, which are necessary in order that society may be formed and maintained: we have tenderness for the fair sex: we have affection for our children, for our parents, and for our other relations: we have attachment to our friends: we have a regard for reputation and esteem: we possess gratitude and compassion: we enjoy pleasure in the happiness of others, especially when we have been instrumental in procuring it: we entertain for our country an animated and vigorous zeal: we feel delight in the agreeable conception of the improvement and happiness of mankind.

The centre mov'd, a circle straight succeeds,
Another still, and still another spreads.
Friend, parent, neighbour first it will embrace,
His country next, and next all human race;
Wide and more wide, th' o'erflowings of the mind
Take ev'ry creature in, of ev'ry kind;
Earth smiles around, with boundless bounty blest,
And heav'n beholds its image in his breast.[d]

How naturally, and sometimes how strongly, are our passions communicated from one to another, without even the least knowledge of the cause, by which they were originally produced! They are conveyed by aspect: the very countenance is infectious: the emotion flies from face to face: it is no sooner seen than experienced: like the electrick shock, it is felt instantaneously by a whole multitude; though, perhaps, only one of them knows from whence it proceeds. Such is the force of society in the passions.

This sympathy is an important quality of many of our passions: in particular, it invites and produces a communication of joys and sorrows, hopes and fears. Spirits, the most generous and the most susceptible of strong impressions, are the most social and combining. They delight most to move in concert; and feel, in the strongest manner, the force of the confederating charm.

The social powers and dispositions of our minds discover themselves in the earliest periods of life. So soon as a child can speak, he can ask, and he can answer a question: before he can speak, he shows signs of love, of resentment, and of other affections necessarily pointed to society. He is capable of social intercourse long before he is capable of reasoning. We behold this charming intercourse between his mother and him, before he is a year old. He can, by signs, ask and refuse, threaten and supplicate. In danger, he clings to his mother—for I will not, on this occasion, distinguish between the mother and the nurse—he enters into her joy and grief, is happy in her caresses, and is unhappy in her displeasure.

As sociability attends us in our infancy; she continues to be our companion through all the variegated scenes of our riper years. By an irresistible charm, she insinuates herself into the hearts of every rank and class

d. Pope's Ess. on Man. Ep. 4. v. 365.

of men, and mixes in all the various modes and arrangements of human life. Let us suppose a man of so morose and acrimonious a disposition, as to shun, like Timon of Athens,[2] all communication with his species; even such a misanthropist would wish for at least one associate, into whose bosom he might discharge the rancour and virulence of his own heart.

Society is necessary as well as natural to us. To support life, to satisfy our natural appetites, to obtain those agreeable enjoyments of which our nature is susceptible, many external things are indispensable. In order to live with any degree of comfort, we must have food, clothing, habitations, furniture, and utensils of some sort. These cannot be procured without much art and labour; nor without the friendly assistance of our fellows in society.

Let us suppose a man of full strength, and well instructed in all our arts of life, to be reduced suddenly to solitude, even in one of the best of soils and climates: could he procure the grateful conveniences of life? It will not be pretended. Could he procure even its simple necessaries? In an ingenious and excellent romance, we are told this has been done. But it will be remembered, that the foundation of Robinson Crusoe's future subsistence, and of all the comforts which he afterwards provided and collected, was laid in the useful instruments and machines, which he saved from his shipwreck. These were the productions of society.

Could one, uninstructed in our arts of life, and unfurnished with the productions of society, subsist in solitude, though he were of full age, and possessed of health and strength? the probabilities would run strong against him.

Could one subsist in solitude during the weak, uninformed, and inexperienced period of his infancy? This he could not do, unless, like another Romulus and Remus, he owed his subsistence to the social aid of the wolves.

But let us, for a moment, suppose, that food, raiment, and shelter were supplied even by a miracle; a solitary life must be continually harassed by dangers and fears. Suppose those dangers and fears to be removed; could he find employment for the most excellent powers and instincts of his mind? Could he indulge affection or social joy? could he communicate, or could he receive social pleasure or social regard? Dispositions very dif-

2. Timon of Athens lived during the Peloponnesian War and had a reputation for misanthropy.

ferent indeed—sour discontentment, sullen melancholy, listless languor—must prey upon his soul.

The reciprocal assistance of those, who compose a single family, may procure many of the necessaries of life; and may diminish its dangers. In this state some room will be afforded for social enjoyments, and for the finer operations of the mind. Still greater pleasures and advantages would be obtained by the union of a few families in the same neighbourhood. They would undertake and execute laborious works for the common good of all; and social emotions would operate in a less contracted circuit. Associations, still larger, will enlarge the sphere of pleasure and enjoyment; and will furnish more diversified and delightful exercise to our powers of every kind. Knowledge is increased: inventions are discovered: experience improves them: and the inventions, with their improvements, are spread over the whole community. Designs of durable and extensive advantage are boldly formed, and vigorously carried into effect. The social and benevolent affections range in an ample sphere; and attain an eminent degree of strength and refinement.

On what does our security—on what do our enjoyments depend? On our mutual services and sympathetick pleasures. Other animals have strength or speed sufficient for their preservation and defence. Man is, in all states, encompassed with weakness and dangers: but the strength and safety, which he wants by himself, he finds, when he is united with his equals. Nature has endowed him with a principle, which gives him force and superiority, where otherwise he would be helpless and inferiour. By sociability, they, who separately could make no effectual resistance, conquer and tame the various kinds of the brute creation. Society is the cause, that, not satisfied with the element on which he was born, man extends his dominion over the sea. Society supplies him with remedies in his diseases, with comfort in his afflictions, and with assistance in his old age. Take away society, and you destroy the basis, on which the preservation and happiness of human life are laid.

"There is nothing more certain," says Cicero,[e] "than the excellent maxim of Plato—that we are not intended solely for ourselves; but that our friends and our country claim a portion of our birth. Since, according to the doctrine of the stoicks, the productions of the earth are designed for men, and

e. De off. l. 1. c. 7.

men are designed for the mutual aid of one another; we should certainly pursue the design of Nature, and promote her benign intention, by contributing our proportion to the general interest, by mutually performing and receiving good offices, and by employing our care, our industry, and even our fortune, in order to strengthen the love and friendship, which should always predominate in human society."

In point of dignity, the social operations and emotions of the mind rise to a most respectable height. The excellency of man is chiefly discerned in the great improvements, of which he is susceptible in society: these, by perseverance and vigour, may be carried on progressively to degrees higher and higher, above any limits which we can now assign.

Our social affections and operations acquire still greater importance, in another point of view: they promote and are necessary to our happiness. "If we could suppose ourselves," says Cicero,[f] who knew so well how to illustrate law by philosophy—"if we could suppose ourselves transported by some divinity into a solitude, replete with all the delicacies which the heart of man could desire, but excluded, at the same time, from every possible intercourse with our kind, there is not a person in the world of so unsocial and savage a temper, as to be capable, in these forlorn circumstances, of relishing any enjoyment." "Nothing," continues he, "is more true, than what the philosopher Archytas[3] is reported to have said: If a man were to be carried up into heaven, and see the beauties of universal nature displayed before him, he would receive but little pleasure from the wonderful scenes, unless there was some person, to whom he could relate the glories, which he had viewed. Human nature is so constituted, as to be incapable of solitary satisfactions. Man, like those plants which are formed to embrace others, is led, by an instinctive impulse, to recline on those of his own kind."

> Man, like the gen'rous vine, supported lives;
> The strength he gains is from th' embrace he gives.[g]

The observations, which we make in common life, vouch the justness of these sentiments. We see those persons possess the greatest share of happiness, who have about them many objects of love and endearment.

f. De Amic. 23.

3. Archytas (428–347 B.C.) was a Greek philosopher, mathematician, and statesman. He was a close friend to Plato.

g. Pope's Ess. on Man. Ep. 3. v. 311.

To the want of these objects, may be ascribed the moroseness of monks, and of those who, without entering into any religious order, lead the lives of monks.

Of the same nature with the indulgence of domestick affections, and equally refreshing to the spirit, is the pleasure, which flows from acts of beneficence, either in bestowing pecuniary favours, or in imparting, to those who want it, the benefit of our advice, or the assistance of our professional skill. The last consideration is urged, with peculiar propriety, by the professor of law. Innumerable instances occur, in which gentlemen of the bar, who possess abilities and character, can bestow what may be called favours, even on those, who are both able and willing to pay well for their services. When a client has an important business depending, entire confidence in the integrity and talents of his counsel diffuses over his mind a degree of composure and serenity, against which a fee, weighed in the balance, would be found wanting. This is particularly the case, when the life or the reputation of the client is at stake.

The foregoing observations may also be applied to publick services done for the state, by assisting her in her councils, or by defending or prosecuting her interests. Even if no suitable return, as it sometimes happens, should be received from the state for such services; yet a mind, nurtured to the refined and enlarged exercise of the social passion, will find no trivial pleasure in the reflection that it has performed them, and that those, for whom they were performed, enjoy the advantages resulting from them. Virtue, in such an instance, will prove herself her own reward. A man, whose soul vibrates in unison with the benevolent affections, will always find within him an encouragement, and a compensation too, for discharging his duty—an encouragement and a compensation, of which ingratitude itself cannot deprive him.

I will not appeal to vanity, and ask, if any thing can be more flattering, than to *obtain* the praises and acclamations of others. But I will appeal to conscious rectitude, and ask, whether any thing can be more satisfactory, than to *deserve* their regard and esteem.

The possession of science is always attended with pleasure: but science, believe me, acquires an increased relish, when we have an opportunity of pouring it into the bosoms of others. We receive a redoubled satisfaction from the agreeable, though, perhaps, the flattering opinion, that we communicate entertainment and instruction; and from the opinion, better founded, that even weak attempts to communicate entertainment and instruction are received with reflected social emotions.

What can be more productive of happiness than even those wants, which are the foundations of so many blessings—love and friendship, generosity and reliance, kindness and gratitude? The gratifications even of sense lose their relish, if not heightened by the "spes mutui credula animi"[4]—corresponding social emotions.

Our esteem of others, too, arising from the approbation of their conduct, is a most pleasing affection. The contemplation of a great and good character warms the heart, and invigorates the whole frame.

The wisest and most benign constitution of a rational and moral system is that, in which the degree of private affection, most useful to the individual, is, at the same time, consistent with the greatest interest of the system; and in which the degree of social affection, most useful to the system, is, at the same time, productive of the greatest happiness to the individual. Thus it is in the system of society. In that system, he who acts on such principles, and is governed by such affections, as sever him from the common good and publick interest, works, in reality, towards his own misery: while he, on the other hand, who operates for the good of the whole, as is by nature and by nature's God appointed him, pursues, in truth, and at the same time, his own felicity.

Regulated by this standard, extensive, unerring, and sublime, self-love and social are the same.

To a state of society, then, we are invited from every quarter. It is natural; it is necessary; it is pleasing; it is profitable to us. The result of all is, that for a state of society we are designated by Him, who is all-wise and all-good.

Society may be distinguished into two kinds, natural and civil. This distinction has not been marked with the accuracy, which it well merits. Indeed some writers have given little or no attention to the latter kind; others have expressly denied it, and said, that there can be no civil society without civil government. But this is certainly not the case. A state of civil society must have existed, and such a state, in all our reasonings on this subject, must be supposed, before civil government could be regularly formed and established. Nay, 'tis for the security and improvement of such

4. Literally, "the trusting hope of mutual feeling," but a clearer sense of the tone is "the naive hope that love will be requited." The phrase is from Horace, *Odes,* 4.1.29.

a state, that the adventitious one of civil government has been instituted. To civil society, indeed, without including in its description the idea of civil government, the name of *state* may be assigned, by way of excellence. It is in this sense that Cicero seems to use it, in the following beautiful passage. "Nothing, which is exhibited on our globe, is more acceptable to that divinity, which governs the whole universe, than those communities and assemblages of men, which, lawfully associated,—jure sociati—are denominated states."[h]

How often has the end been sacrificed to the means! Government was instituted for the happiness of society: how often has the happiness of society been offered as a victim to the idol of government! But this is not agreeable to the true order of things: it is not consistent with the orthodox political creed. Let government—let even the constitution be, as they ought to be, the handmaids; let them not be, for they ought not to be, the mistresses of the state.

A state may be described—a complete body of free persons, united together for their common benefit, to enjoy peaceably what is their own, and to do justice to others. It is an artificial person: it has an understanding and a will peculiar to itself: it has its affairs and its interests: it deliberates and resolves: it has its rules; it has its obligations; and it has its rights. It may acquire property, distinct from that of its members: it may incur debts, to be discharged out of the publick stock, not out of the private fortunes of individuals: it may be bound by contracts, and for damages arising *quasi ex contractu.*[5]

In order to constitute a state, it is indispensably necessary, that the wills and the power of all the members be united in such a manner, that they shall never act nor desire but one and the same thing, in whatever relates to the end, for which the society is established. It is from this union of wills and of strength, that the state or body politick results. The only rational and natural method, therefore, of constituting a civil society, is by the convention or consent of the members, who compose it. For by a civil society we properly understand, the voluntary union of persons in the same end, and in the same means requisite to obtain that end. This union is a benefit, not a sacrifice: civil is an addition to natural order.

h. Somn. Scip. c. 3.

5. As if from contract. An expression applied to obligations that are not contractual.

This union may rationally be supposed to be formed in the following manner: if a number of people, who had hitherto lived independent of each other, wished to form a civil society, it would be necessary to enter into an engagement to associate together in one body, and to regulate, with one common consent, whatever regards their preservation, their security, their improvement, their happiness.

In the social compact, each individual engages with the whole collectively, and the whole collectively engage with each individual. These engagements are obligatory, because they are mutual. The individuals who are not parties to them, are not members of the society.

Smaller societies may be formed within a state by a part of its members. These societies also are deemed to be moral persons; but not in a state of natural liberty: their actions are cognizable by the superiour power of the state, and are regulated by its laws. To these societies the name of corporations is generally appropriated, though somewhat improperly; for the term is strictly applicable to supreme as well as to inferiour bodies politick.

The foregoing account of the formation of civil society, which refers it to original engagements; and consequently resolves the duty of submission to the laws of the society, into the universal obligation of fidelity in the performance of promises, is warmly attacked by a sensible and ingenious writer.[i] He represents it, as founded on a supposition, false in fact; as insufficient, if it was true, for the purposes, for which it is produced; and as leading to dangerous consequences. He acknowledges, however, that, in the United States, transactions have happened, which bear the nearest resemblance to this political idea, of any, of which history has preserved the account or the memory. This subject has already received some; it will afterwards receive more attention and examination. At present, it is sufficient, and it is proper, to intimate to you the point of discussion; for it is a very important one in the science of government.

In civil society, previously to the institution of civil government, all men are equal. Of one blood all nations are made; from one source the whole human race has sprung.

When we say, that all men are equal; we mean not to apply this equality to their virtues, their talents, their dispositions, or their acquirements. In

i. 2. Paley 140.

all these respects, there is, and it is fit for the great purposes of society that there should be, great inequality among men. In the moral and political as well as in the natural world, diversity forms an important part of beauty; and as of beauty, so of utility likewise. That social happiness, which arises from the friendly intercourse of good offices, could not be enjoyed, unless men were so framed and so disposed, as mutually to afford and to stand in need of service and assistance. Hence the necessity not only of great variety, but even of great inequality in the talents of men, bodily as well as mental. Society supposes mutual dependence: mutual dependence supposes mutual wants: all the social exercises and enjoyments may be reduced to two heads—that of giving, and that of receiving: but these imply different aptitudes to give and to receive.

Many are the degrees, many are the varieties of human genius, human dispositions, and human characters. One man has a turn for mechanicks; another, for architecture; one paints; a second makes poems: this excels in the arts of a military; the other, in those of civil life. To account for these varieties of taste and character, is not easy; is, perhaps, impossible. But though their efficient cause it may be difficult to explain; their final cause, that is, the intention of Providence in appointing them, we can see and admire. These varieties of taste and character induce different persons to choose different professions and employments in life: these varieties render mankind mutually beneficial to each other, and prevent too violent oppositions of interest in the same pursuit. Hence we enjoy a variety of conveniences; hence the numerous arts and sciences have been invented and improved; hence the sources of commerce and friendly intercourse between different nations have been opened; hence the circulation of truth has been quickened and promoted; hence the operations of social virtue have been multiplied and enlarged.

Heaven, forming each on other to depend,
Bids each on other for assistance call,
'Till one man's weakness grows the strength of all.
Wants, frailties, passions closer still ally
The common interest, or endear the tie:
To these we owe true friendship, love sincere,
Each home-felt joy, that life inherits here.[j]

j. Pope. Ess. Man. Ep. 2. v. 249.

How insipidly uniform would human life and manners be, without the beautiful variety of colours, reflected upon them by different tastes, different tempers, and different characters!

But however great the variety and inequality of men may be with regard to virtue, talents, taste, and acquirements; there is still one aspect, in which all men in society, previous to civil government, are equal. With regard to all, there is an equality in rights and in obligations; there is that "jus aequum," that equal law, in which the Romans placed true freedom. The natural rights and duties of man belong equally to all. Each forms a part of that great system, whose greatest interest and happiness are intended by all the laws of God and nature. These laws prohibit the wisest and the most powerful from inflicting misery on the meanest and most ignorant; and from depriving them of their rights or just acquisitions. By these laws, rights, natural or acquired, are confirmed, in the same manner, to all; to the weak and artless, their small acquisitions, as well as to the strong and artful, their large ones. If much labour employed entitles the active to great possessions, the indolent have a right, equally sacred, to the little possessions, which they occupy and improve.

As in civil society, previous to civil government, all men are equal; so, in the same state, all men are free. In such a state, no one can claim, in preference to another, superiour right: in the same state, no one can claim over another superiour authority.

Nature has implanted in man the desire of his own happiness; she has inspired him with many tender affections towards others, especially in the near relations of life; she has endowed him with intellectual and with active powers; she has furnished him with a natural impulse to exercise his powers for his own happiness, and the happiness of those, for whom he entertains such tender affections. If all this be true, the undeniable consequence is, that he has a right to exert those powers for the accomplishment of those purposes, in such a manner, and upon such objects, as his inclination and judgment shall direct; provided he does no injury to others; and provided some publick interests do not demand his labours. This right is natural liberty. Every man has a sense of this right. Every man has a sense of the impropriety of restraining or interrupting it. Those who judge wisely, will use this liberty virtuously and honourably: those, who are less wise, will employ it in meaner pursuits: others, again, may, perhaps, indulge it in what may be justly censured as vicious and dishonourable. Yet, with regard even to these last, while they are not injurious to others; and while no human institution has placed them under the control of magistrates or laws, the sense of liberty is so strong, and its loss is so deeply resented, that, upon the whole, more unhappiness would result from depriving them of their liberty on account of their imprudence, than could be reasonably apprehended from the imprudent use of their liberty.

The right of natural liberty is suggested to us not only by the selfish parts of our constitution, but by our generous affections; and especially by our moral sense, which intimates to us, that in our voluntary actions consist our dignity and perfection.

The laws of nature are the measure and the rule; they ascertain the limits and the extent of natural liberty.

In society, when the sentiments of the members are not unanimous, the voice of the majority must be deemed the will of the whole. That the majority, by any vote, should bind not only themselves, but those also who dissent from that vote, seems, at first, to be inconsistent with the well known rules—that all men are naturally equal; and that all men are naturally free. From these rules, it may be alleged, that no one can be bound by the act of another, without his own consent. But it is to be remembered, that society is constituted for a certain purpose; and that each member of it consents that this purpose shall be carried on; and, consequently, that every thing necessary for carrying it on shall be done. Now a number of persons can jointly do business only in three ways—by the decision of the whole, by the decision of the majority, or by the decision of the minority. The first case is not here supposed, nor is there occasion to make a question concerning it. The only remaining question, then, which can be proposed, is, which is most reasonable and equitable—that the minority should bind the majority—or that the majority should bind the minority? The latter, certainly. It is most reasonable; because it is not so probable, that a greater number, as that a smaller number, concurring in judgment, should be mistaken. It is most equitable; because the greater number are presumed to have an interest in the society proportioned to that number. Besides; though, in the case supposed, the minority are bound without their *immediate* consent; they are bound by their consent originally given to the establishment of the society, for the purposes which it was intended to accomplish. For it has been already observed, that those, who enter not into the original engagement forming the society, are not to be considered as members: all the members, therefore, must have originally given their consent.

The rule, which we have mentioned, may be altered and modified by positive institution. In some cases, the consent of a number larger than a mere majority: in others, even unanimity may be required.

This is the proper place for considering a question of very considerable importance in civil society, and concerning which there has been much diversity in the sentiments of writers, and in the laws and practice of states: has a state a right to prohibit the emigration of its members? may a citizen dissolve the connexion between him and his country?

On the principles of the compact of association, which I have already stated, there seems to be but little doubt that one article of it may be, that each individual binds himself indissolubly to the society, while the society performs, on its part, the stipulated conditions. This engagement each individual may make for himself: [k] but can he make it for his children and his posterity? must they be and continue bound by the act of their father and ancestor?

The notion of natural, perpetual, and unalienable allegiance from the citizen to the society, or to the head of the society, of which he was born a member, has, by some writers and in some countries, been carried very far indeed: and their practice has been equally rigorous with their principles. The well known maxim, which the writers upon the law of England have adopted and applied to this case is,[l] "Nemo potest exuere patriam."[6] It is not, therefore, as is holden by that law, in the power of any private subject to shake off his allegiance, and to transfer it to a foreign prince. Nor is it in the power of any foreign prince, by naturalizing or employing a subject of Great Britain, to dissolve the bond of allegiance between that subject

k. Connecticut was originally settled by emigrants from the neighbourhood of Boston. They applied to the general court of Massachussetts for permission to go in quest of new adventures: and could not be satisfied, until they had obtained the leave of the court. For it was the general sense, as we are assured, that the inhabitants were all mutually bound to one another by the oath of a freeman, as well as the original compact; so as not to be at liberty to separate without the consent of the whole. Chal. 286.

l. Fost. 184.

6. No one can cast off his country.

and the crown. Hence it has been adjudged, that a cartel for the exchange or ransom of prisoners of war cannot extend to the case of a subject born, though clothed with a commission from the party to the cartel. The reason assigned is, that by the laws of all nations, subjects taken in arms against their lawful prince are not considered as prisoners of war, but as rebels; and are liable to the punishments ordinarily inflicted on rebels.[m] This doctrine was, so late as the year one thousand seven hundred and forty seven, applied to the case of a native of Great Britain, who had received his education in France from his early infancy; and who had spent his riper years in a profitable employment in that kingdom, where all his hopes were centred.[n]

The reasons in favour of the position, that a citizen cannot dissolve the political connexion between him and his country, may be stated in the following manner. Every citizen, as soon as he is born, is under the protection of the state, and is entitled to all the advantages arising from that protection: he, therefore, owes obedience to that power, from which the protection, which he enjoys, is derived. But while he continues in infancy and nonage, he cannot perform the duties of obedience. The performance of them must be respited, till he arrive at the years of discretion and maturity. When he arrives at those years, he owes obedience, not only for the protection, which he then enjoys, but also for that, which, from his birth, he has enjoyed. Obedience now becomes a duty founded upon principles of gratitude, as well as upon principles of interest: it becomes a debt, which nothing but the performance of the duties of citizenship, during a whole life, will discharge.[o]

But, notwithstanding this train of thought and reasoning, there are certainly cases, in which a citizen has an unquestionable right to renounce his country, and go in quest of a settlement in some other part of the world. One of these cases is, when, in his own country, he cannot procure a subsistence. Another is, when the society neglects to fulfil its obligations to the citizen. A third is, when the society would establish laws, on things, to which the original social compact cannot oblige the citizen to submit.[p]

m. Id. 60.
n. Fost. 59.
o. 2. P. Wms. 123. 124.
p. Vat. 96. b. 1. s. 223–225.

In answer to the inferences drawn from principles of gratitude, it may be observed, that every man being born free, a native citizen, when he arrives at the age of discretion, may examine whether it be convenient for him to join in the society, for which he was destined by his birth. If, on examination, he finds, that it will be more advantageous to him to remove into another country, he has a right to go, making to that which he leaves a proper return for what it has done in his favour, and preserving for it, as far as it shall be consistent with the engagements, which his new situation and connexions may require, the sentiments of respect and attachment.

The sentiments of Mr. Locke on this subject go much further. "'Tis plain," says he,[q] "by the law of right reason, that a child is born a subject of no country or government. He is under his father's tuition and authority, till he comes to the age of discretion; and then he is a freeman, at liberty what government he will put himself under; what body politick he will unite himself to."

"O glorious regulations!" says Cicero,[r] "originally established for us by our ancestors of Roman name; that no one of us should be obliged to belong to more than one society, since a dissimilitude of societies must produce a proportioned variety of laws; that no one, contrary to his inclination, should be deprived of his right of citizenship; and that no one, contrary to his inclinations, should be obliged to continue in that relation. The power of retaining and of renouncing our rights of citizenship, is the most stable foundation of our liberties."

In the digest of the Roman law,[s] it is laid down as a rule, that every one is at liberty to choose the state, of which he wishes to be a member.

Indeed, excepting in some very particular cases, every one ought to be at liberty to leave the state. This general liberty is not only just, but may be productive of much generous emulation among states, and of extensive advantages to their citizens. Those states, which manage their affairs best, will offer the strongest inducements to their own citizens to remain, and to others to incorporate among them. On the other hand, it is both inhuman and unjust to convert the state into a prison for its citizens, by

q. On Civ. Gov. s. 118.
r. Pro. Balb. c. 13.
s. Dig. l. 49. t. 15.

preventing them from leaving it on a prospect of advantage to themselves. True it is, that they ought to make compensation for any advantages, which they have derived from the state at its expense: but equally true it is, that this compensation is generally made, by their having contributed annually, during their past residence, towards the publick revenue, by paying taxes on property, as all men, even minors, do; and by consuming goods, on which imposts or duties have been levied.

Emigration may arise from various causes. It may be occasioned by the population of a country. In this case, great numbers may be constantly leaving the state, and yet the state may be increasing in population. It has been suggested by some writers, that the right of exposing children has been one cause of the populousness of China. Surely the prospect that they will be comfortably provided for, if not in their own, yet in another country, must be a much more powerful, as well as more humane incentive to marriages.

Insecurity, hardships, oppression may be the causes of emigration. A nation whose inhabitants are in a predicament so disagreeable, may be in declining circumstances; but those circumstances, indicating a decline, are not the effects of emigration; they are the effects of the evils and calamities which occasion it. Two things, which are commonly considered as cause and effect, are often no more than two collateral effects of the same cause.

Independently, therefore, of the question of right, there can be but few cases, in which emigration could be prohibited on the sound principles of policy. Emigration, it is true, may be a symptom of languor and decay; but it may also be an evidence and a consequence of the overflowing vigour and prosperity of the state.

Permit me to suggest a still further reason—to me it appears a strong one—in favour of unrestrained emigration. In a free state, the consent of every citizen to its institution and government ought to be evinced either by express declarations, or by the strongest and justest presumptions. When a state is formed, the residence of a citizen is presumed a sufficient evidence of his assent and acquiescence in its institutions: to reside in any country is universally deemed a submission to its authority. But that these presumptions may be fairly drawn, we must be understood as speaking of a state, from which the citizens have liberty to depart with their effects at pleasure. Where this liberty is not enjoyed, the considerations of family, of property, and many other considerations that are without a name, may detain a man, much against his inclination, in a country, in which he finds himself trammelled. In such case, his residence is no reasonable evidence of his consent to the formation, the constitution, the government, or the laws of the state.

Upon the whole it appears, that the right of emigration is a *right,* advantageous to the citizen, and generally useful even to the state. It may, however, in the fundamental laws, be reduced to a certainty. The citizens of Neufchatel in Switzerland may quit the country, and carry off their effects, in whatever manner they please, without paying any duties.[t] By the constitution of Pennsylvania,[u] it is declared "that emigration from the state shall not be prohibited."

These remarks on the rights and principles of emigration, prepare the way for remarks, more important, on the principles and rights of colonization, which will form the subject of inquiry in a future part of our lectures.

t. Vat. 96. b. 1. s. 225.
u. Art. 9. s. 25.

CHAPTER VIII.

Of Man, as a Member of a Confederation.

A number of states or societies may associate or confederate together for their mutual security and advantage. In some respects, such confederacies are to be considered as forming only one nation: in other respects, they are to be considered as still retaining their separate political capacities, characters, rights, and powers. Associations of this kind have made their appearance but seldom on the great theatre of human affairs; and when they have appeared, the part they have acted has generally been but a short one; and even that short part has, in most instances, been defaced, or mutilated, or rendered obscure by the effect of all-corroding time. The appearance, however, of personages, so peculiarly interesting to the United States, well deserves to be marked, to be traced, to be distinguished, with the most sedulous precision and exactness.

The first association of this kind, of which we have any information from history, is that of the Amphyctionick Council, so called from Amphyction, by whom it was instituted. In the time of this wise and patriotick prince, the condition of Greece demanded his most serious and deep reflection. That country was divided into a great number of small independent sovereignties. That division was likely to occasion controversies, and produce ruinous intestine wars. Weakness and confusion, the inseparable concomitants of such wars, might invite the attacks of the barbarous nations, by whom Greece was surrounded. Her destruction, total and irretrievable, might prove the necessary consequence.

To prevent calamities, so probable and so great, Amphyction meditated and formed the plan of uniting all the different states of Greece in one common bond, as well as in one common interest; that, availing themselves of the advantages and strength acquired by this union, they might labour together in maintaining their internal peace and security, and in rendering themselves respectable, and, if necessary, formidable to the neighbouring nations. With this view, and on these principles, he formed a league among twelve Grecian cities, whose deputies were to meet twice a year at Thermopylae, where Amphyction reigned.[a] Difference of times and circumstances produced many successive alterations in this assembly; but the general intention and invariable object of all its modellers and directers was, to form a complete representation of all Greece.[b]

Each city sent two deputies; and had, of consequence, two votes in their deliberations, without distinction or preeminence.

We should consider the Council of the Amphyctions as the Congress of the United States of Greece. The delegates, who composed that august assembly, represented the body of the nation; and were invested with full power to deliberate and resolve upon whatever appeared to them to be most conducive to the publick prosperity.[c] Besides those laws, by which each particular city was governed, others were enacted by the Council of Amphyctions, of general force and obligation on all. Those were called Amphyctionick laws. All contests between the Grecian states and cities came under the particular cognizance of the Amphyctions. To their tribunal, an appeal also lay in all private controversies.[d] To the same tribunal, individuals were amenable for their publick crimes.[e] Their authority extended to the raising of forces, and to compel the obstinate to submit to the execution of their decrees. The three religious wars, undertaken by the order of the Amphyctions, are striking instances of the extent of their power.[f]

Among the Grecians, it was esteemed a high honour to have a right to send delegates to this kind of states general. The least mark of infidelity to their country was sufficient to prevent their admission, or to procure their expulsion. The Lacedemonians, however important, and the Phocians were, for some time, excluded; and could not obtain a readmission, till, by unequivocal proofs of service and attachment to the publick, they had made reparation for the fault, which they had committed.

a. 2. Gog. Or. Laws. 26.
b. Lel. L. P. Prel. 43.
c. 2. Gog. Or. Laws. 27.
d. Lel. L. P. Prel. 39. 53.
e. Lel. Dem. Int. to oration de corona.
f. 2. Gog. Or. Laws. 27.

The effects, produced by the Council of the Amphyctions, fully answered the most sanguine expectations of the prince, by whom it was instituted. From the moment of its establishment, the interests of their country became the common concern of all the people of Greece. The different states, of which the union was composed, formed only one and the same republick: and this union it was, which made the Greeks so formidable afterwards to the barbarians.[g] To the Amphyctions we may ascribe the salvation of Greece from the invasion of Xerxes. It was by means of this association, that she performed such wonderful actions, and supported, for so long a time, the character of the pride of nations.

Amphyction ought to be esteemed one of the greatest men, that Greece ever produced; and the establishment of the Council of the Amphyctions should be admired, as a great master-piece in human politicks.

While the generous principles, on which the Council of the Amphyctions was formed, continued to preserve their due vigour, that illustrious body was respectable, august, and powerful. But when Greece herself began to degenerate, her representative body was contaminated with the general corruption. The decline of this council we may date particularly from the time, when Philip of Macedon, artful and intriguing, practised on its venal members by bribes, and succeeded in having his kingdom annexed to the Hellenick Body. It continued, however, for ages after the destruction of Grecian liberty, to assemble, and to exercise some remains of its authority.[h]

The next confederacy, which claims our attention, is that of the Lycians. In this republick, the just rights of suffrage were observed with great accuracy. It was an association of twenty three towns. These were arranged into three classes, in proportion to their strength. In the first class, six states were included. The numbers of which the second and third classes were composed, are uncertain. Every city had its own magistrates and government, and managed its own internal affairs. But all, uniting together, formed only one common republick, and had one common council. In that council, they deliberated and resolved concerning war, concerning peace, concerning alliances; in a word, concerning the general

g. 2. Gog. Or. Laws. 28.
h. Lel. L. P. Prel. 56. 57.

interests and welfare of the Lycians. The towns of the first class had three votes; the towns of the second class had two votes; and the towns of the third class had one vote, in the common council. In the same proportion, they contributed to the publick expenses, and appointed the publick magistrates of the union.

This republick was celebrated for its moderation and justice. Respected and unimpaired, it continued till the Romans, by their extending conquests, overpowered every thing in Asia.

Concerning the Lycians, one observation is made, which merits our particular notice. They observed customs more than written laws.[i]

"Was I to give," says the celebrated Montesquieu,[j] "the model of an excellent confederate republick, I would select that of Lycia." The happy experience, however, of the United States, has evinced, that, even upon that model, immense improvements have been made.

The Achaean League[1] comes now in review before us. The cities composing it retained, like those of Lycia, the government of their interiour police, and appointed their own magistrates and publick officers. The senate, in which they were represented, had the sole and exclusive right of declaring war and making peace; of receiving and sending ambassadours; of entering into treaties, and forming alliances. It appointed a chief magistrate, called a pretor, who commanded their armies, and who, assisted by a council of ten of the senators, not only administered the government during the recess of the senate; but, when the senate was assembled, had also a large share in its deliberations. At first, there were two pretors; but experience taught them to prefer one.

In Achaia, all the cities had the same money, the same weights and measures, the same customs and laws. The popular government, we are told, was not so tempestuous in the cities of Achaia, as in some of the other cities of Greece; because, in Achaia, it was tempered by the authority and laws of the confederacy. Indeed it is unquestionable, that, in this confederacy, there was much more moderation and justice, than was to be found in any of the cities exercising singly all the prerogatives of sovereignty.

i. 2. Ub. Em. 320. 323.
j. Sp. Laws. b. 9. c. 3.
1. A confederation of Greek city states in Achaea in the fifth and fourth centuries B.C.

When Lacedaemon[2] was admitted into the Achaean League; she was obliged to abolish the institutions of Lycurgus, and to adopt the laws of the Achaeans. But Lacedaemon had been long a member of the Amphyctionick Council; and, during all the time, she had been left in the full possession of her own government and laws. This circumstance discloses a very important difference between those two confederate systems.[k]

The Aetolian League[3] was similar to that of the Achaeans; and therefore it is unnecessary to make particular observations concerning it.[l]

The Germanick Body has been generally considered as a confederate state. From the feudal system, which has itself many of the important features of a confederacy, the federal system, which constitutes the empire of Germany, has grown. Its powers are vested in a diet, representing the component members of the confederacy; in the emperour, who is the executive magistrate, with a negative on the decrees of the diet; and in the imperial chamber and aulick council, two tribunals possessed of supreme jurisdiction in controversies, which concern the empire, or happen among its members.

The diet possesses the power of legislation for the empire, of making peace and war, contracting alliances, assessing quotas of troops and money, constructing fortresses, regulating coin, admitting new members, and subjecting disobedient members to the ban of the empire; by which the party is degraded from his sovereign rights, and his possessions are forfeited. The members of the confederacy are expressly restricted from entering into compacts prejudicial to the empire; from imposing tolls and duties on their mutual intercourse, without the consent of the emperour and diet; from altering the value of money; from doing injustice to one another; and from affording assistance or retreat to the disturbers of the publick peace. The ban is denounced against such as shall violate any of these restrictions.

The members of the diet, as such, are subject, in all cases, to be judged by the emperour and diet; and, in their private capacities, by the aulick council and imperial chamber.

2. Lacedaemon was an alternative name for Sparta.

k. 1. Pub. 114. 2. Ub. Em. 240. 243.

3. The league (or confederacy centered on the cities of Aetolia in central Greece) that was formed in 370 B.C. to oppose the Achaean League and Macedon.

l. 2. Ub. Em. 257.

The prerogatives of the emperour are numerous. The most important of them are—his exclusive right to make propositions to the diet, to negative its resolutions, to name ambassadours, to confer dignities and titles, to fill vacant electorates, to found universities, to grant privileges not injurious to the states of the empire, to receive and apply the publick revenues, and generally to watch over the publick safety. In certain cases, the electors form a council to him. In the character of emperour, he possesses no territory within the empire; and receives no revenue for his support.

The fundamental principle, on which this confederacy rests, is—that the empire is a community of sovereigns—that the diet is a representation of sovereigns—and that the laws are addressed to sovereigns.[m] The princes and free states of Germany may treat with foreign powers.[n]

The Swiss Cantons are frequently mentioned as forming a confederacy; but they are improperly mentioned in that character. They are no more than states connected together by a close and perpetual alliance. They have no common treasury; they have no national troops, even in war; they have no common coin; they have no common tribunal; they have no common characteristick of sovereignty.

When a dispute happens among the cantons, there is a provision, that the parties to that dispute shall each choose four judges out of the neutral cantons, who, in case of disagreement, choose an umpire. This tribunal, under an oath of impartiality, pronounces definitive sentence. This sentence all the cantons are bound to enforce.[o]

The United Netherlands are generally represented as a confederacy. If the term can, with propriety, be applied to them; they are a confederacy of republicks, or rather of aristocracies, of a very remarkable texture.

The union is composed of seven coequal and sovereign states or provinces;[p] and each state or province is a composition of equal and independent cities. In all important cases, not only the states, but the cities, must be unanimous.

m. 1. Pub. 119. 120.

n. Vat. 171.

o. 1. Pub. 123.

p. We may exceed the United Provinces by having, not many sovereignties *in* one commonwealth, but many commonwealths under one sovereignty. Milt. 370.

The sovereignty of the union is represented by the states-general, consisting of deputies appointed by the provinces. Some hold their seats for life; some, for six years; some, for three years, some, for one year; some, during pleasure.

The states-general have authority to enter into treaties and alliances; to make war and peace; to raise armies and equip fleets; to ascertain quotas, and demand contributions. In all these cases, however, unanimity and the sanction of their constituents are requisite. They have authority to appoint and receive ambassadours; to execute treaties and alliances already formed; to provide for the collection of duties on imports and exports; to regulate the mint, with a saving to the provincial rights; to govern, as sovereigns, the dependent territories.

The particular states or provinces are restrained, unless with the general consent, from entering into foreign treaties; from establishing imposts injurious to others; and from charging higher duties upon their neighbours than upon their own citizens.

A council of state; a chamber of accounts; and five colleges of admiralty, aid and fortify the federal administration.

The executive magistrate of the union is the stadtholder, who is now an hereditary prince. As stadtholder,[4] he is invested with very considerable prerogatives. In his civil capacity, he has power to settle disputes between the provinces; to assist at the deliberations of the states-general; to give audiences to foreign ambassadours; and to keep agents, for his particular affairs, at foreign courts. In his military capacity, he commands the federal troops; provides for garrisons; regulates military affairs; disposes of military appointments, and of the government of fortified towns. In his marine capacity, he is admiral, and superintends every thing relative to naval affairs; presides in the admiralties in person or by proxy; appoints naval officers; and establishes councils of war, whose sentences are not executed till he approve them. He is stadtholder in the several provinces, as well as in the union; and, in this provincial character, he has the appointment of town magistrates; executes provincial decrees; and presides, when he pleases, in the provincial tribunals. Throughout all, he has the power of pardon.[q]

4. The office of a viceroy or chief executive officer in the confederate provinces that would become the Netherlands.

q. 1. Pub. 125. 126.

After the independence of the United Netherlands was recognised by Spain, the individual states began to pay very little regard to the decrees of the states-general: even particular towns and lordships seemed desirous of maintaining entire independence on the states of the provinces, within which they were situated. The Dutch government, which had greatly relaxed, and was even threatened with dissolution, recovered its tone through the dangers, to which the United Provinces were exposed by the war of thirty years, which was terminated by the peace of Westphalia. Since that time, dissensions among the Dutch have prevailed, or have been composed, according as they have dreaded or trusted their ambitious neighbours.[r]

In the Saxon Heptarchy,[5] a confederacy certainly existed; though, perhaps, a confederacy weak, defective, and interrupted; and from all the confederated states a wittenagemote[6] was frequently called.[s] This general superintending body was sometimes called a *pananglicum.*

Among the ancient Germans, the genius of confederacy pervaded the whole structure of society. They sojourned in huts, which served them as strong holds, to which they carried their property in time of danger. These strong holds or *pagi,* as the Greeks and Romans called them, were the natural resort of the tribes in their neighbourhood, and seem to have been the embryos of the little states, with which ancient Europe so much abounded. A point of union being thus formed among a few tribes, it was natural that the warriours should frequently assemble at that point. In those assemblies, a king, or common leader in war, and an executive magistrate in peace, was chosen.[t] "Eliguntur," says Tacitus,[u] "in iisdem consiliis principes, qui jura per pagos vicosque reddunt."[7]

Though, in general, each pagus acknowledged no superiour, yet particular circumstances of society induced numbers of them to confederate;

r. 2. Anal. Rev. 337.

5. A possible confederacy that existed among seven Anglo-Saxon kingdoms in the seventh and eighth centuries.

6. A wittenagemote, or witenagemote, was an Anglo-Saxon council occasionally convened to advise the king.

s. Mil. 52.

t. 3. Edin. Phil. Trans. 18.

u. De mor. Germ. c. 12.

7. At the same assemblies are chosen leaders, who administer law through the towns and villages.

and, when wars happened, a common leader of the confederacy was chosen of course. When a confederacy of neighbouring pagi had subsisted for a considerable time, a sentiment of national union and of national character began, at last, to appear and operate. The common leader, occasionally chosen for a war, was so often elected, that he became a king, like the chief of a pagus; that he was a *princeps regionis*,[8] with several *principes pagorum*[9] in such a subordination under him, as the chiefs of *vici*, or of primary tribes, were originally held under the chiefs of the pagi.

These combined associates became, again, the members of a greater and less consolidated confederacy. According to Tacitus, the Suevi, one of the greatest communities of Germany, were not comprehended in a single people, but were divided into several nations, all bearing distinct names, though they were all included under the common appellation of Suevi. The Semnones, a single nation, though, indeed, the most noble and the most ancient nation, comprehended under this great confederacy, inhabited no fewer than a hundred pagi. Over the largest portion of Germany the confederacy of the Suevi extended.[v] Thus the Semnones, though but a single member of the great confederacy of the Suevi, were themselves, considered with regard to the pagi which they inhabited, a very considerable national confederacy.

Of a confederacy, whether supreme or subordinate, every member possessed, within itself, legislative, executive, and judicial powers, similar, but inferiour to those exercised by the confederacy itself. In this way the form of society was nearly indestructible.[w] The bonds of association were in just, though inverse, number and proportion to the extent and greatness of the parts associated.

Let us conclude this general view of confederacies with an account of one, which was established, where we should little expect to find it, in Iceland. That obscure and sequestered region—but what place or what people are there, from whence instruction may not be drawn—was peopled by a series of colonies from Norway. These colonists relinquished their country,

8. Chief or leading man of a region.
9. Chiefs or leading men of pagi (i.e., provincial districts, particularly in Gaul and Germany).
v. Tac. de mor. Germ. c. 38. 39.
w. 3. Edin. Phil. Trans. 22.

when it was conquered by Harold[10] with the beautiful hair, in the year eight hundred and seventy eight. In their new settlements, they formed small communities with elective chiefs. These, by degrees, combined together, and held assemblies, under a common leader, in each of the four great provinces, into which the ridges of Mount Hecla divide the island. At last, these four provinces likewise confederated, and formed, in the year nine hundred and twenty eight, a republick, under one chief magistrate.

The whole country was arranged into regular divisions, called provinces, hundreds, and reeps. The magistrates held their offices for life. Diets were held for the districts; and an alting, or great annual assembly, was held for the nation. In that assembly, besides the arrangement of political matters, appeals were received from the provincial courts, and rejudged, in its presence, and under its inspection, by the former judges. The duty of the lagman, or chief of the nation, was to carry into execution what the alting ordered and decreed. There was a succession of thirty eight lagmans, which continued till the year one thousand two hundred and sixty two, when the republick was destroyed by the Danes.

This account is taken from the Icelandick historian, Arngrimus Jonas,[11] a native of the island, and a person, who appears to have had abundance of materials for his work.[x]

On a subject of such magnitude, not only that which has been done, but also that which has been proposed to be done, well deserves attention and examination. I allude to the grand plan of a general confederacy in Europe, formed by the immense genius of Henry the Fourth of France; in which he received most essential assistance from the genius, no less penetrating and active, of Elizabeth of England.

It is very remarkable, that, by several writers, and even by some very profound ones, this very enlarged plan of government is considered as nothing better than a mere visionary project; and doubts are proposed whether it could ever engage the serious contemplation of Henry the Great. To me, I confess, the matter appears in a very different light; and I feel myself justified and supported in directing your close and earnest

10. Harald I (c. 850–c. 933) was the first king and founder of Norway.
11. An Icelandic historian, Jonas lived from 1568 to 1648.
x. 3. Edin. Phil. Trans. 23.

attention to it, when I consider the fact as authenticated by the testimony of Sully, Henry's faithful and confidential minister, and the plan itself as occupying, for a series of years, the unremitted application of Henry and Elizabeth; who were distinguished by their wisdom, as well as by their enterprise; and who knew, if ever princes knew, how to draw the important line between what is extravagant and what is great.

An investigation of this sublime system, from its commencement through the various and successive stages of its progress and preparation, must be instructive to all: to Americans, it must be interesting as well as instructive.

Sully enters upon his account of it with expressing some sagacious apprehensions, that—as, in fact, has since been the case—it would be considered as one of those darling chimeras, or idle political speculations, in which a mind susceptible of singular and uncommon conceptions, is sometimes easily engaged. He confesses, that at the first time the king suggested to him the idea of a political system, by which all Europe might be managed and governed as a single family, he received the suggestion, supposing that Henry meant by it nothing more than to amuse himself with an agreeable speculation, or, at most, to show, that his contemplations on political subjects were more profound and more extensive than those of others.

How modest is conscious merit! Henry often afterwards owned to his confidential friend, that he had long concealed even from him what he meditated upon this great subject, from a principle of shame, lest he should disclose designs, which might appear ridiculous or impracticable.

Inattentive to this great design, when it was first suggested, the cold and cautious Sully was averse to it when the suggestion was renewed. An endless series of difficulties and obstructions presented itself to his circumspect mind. The extent of a design, which supposed a union of all the states in Europe; the concatenation of events, almost infinite, that would be necessary for its accomplishment; the immense expenses, which, if it could be accomplished, would thereby be rolled upon France at a crisis, when she was scarcely able to supply her own necessities—all these considerations induced him to consider the scheme as a vain one, and even to suspect, that, in it, there was something illusory. The disposition of the princes of Europe to become jealous of France, when she should have assisted them to dissipate their fears from the overgrown power of the house of Austria, appeared, of itself, an insurmountable obstacle. His own sentiments he endeavoured to infuse into the mind of the king, with an honest desire to undeceive him, as he thought. Henry begged him to consider the plan in its several parts, and not to pass an indiscriminate sentence of condemnation upon the whole. This solicitation, so reasonable and so unassuming, it was impossible to refuse. The result of Sully's consideration was what Henry expected it would be—the conversion of the minister to the opinions of the prince. After having seen all the parts of the fabrick from their proper points of view, after having made the necessary examinations and the necessary calculations, he found himself engaged and confirmed in the sentiment, that the plan was just in its intention, and that it would be practicable in the execution, and glorious in its consequences.

Great minds frequently unite, without intercommunication, upon the same great object. This exalted system presented itself to the penetration and magnanimity of Elizabeth, before it had occurred to the expansive comprehension of Henry. Indeed it appears doubtful, whether he was not indebted to her for the first hint of the design. But between two such minds, there was no mean jealousy about the right or the merit of the prior discovery. The family of Sully is still possessed of a letter written by Henry, evidently to Elizabeth, though her name does not appear either in the superscription or in the letter itself. It is addressed to "her who merits immortal praise." In it, Henry speaks of a certain object, which he calls "the most excellent and rare enterprise that the human mind ever conceived"— "a thought rather divine than human." He mentions, with rapture, "a discourse so well connected and demonstrative of what would be necessary for the government of empires and kingdoms," and those "conceptions and resolutions," from which nothing less could be hoped, than "most remarkable issues both of honour and glory." These expressions can point, to no other person than Elizabeth—to no other object than that, in the investigation of which we are now engaged.

It is well known that Henry and Elizabeth were anxious to have a personal interview; and that, in the year 1601, the latter came to Dover and the former to Calais for this purpose. The ceremonials, established among princes, prevented the satisfaction of a conference; but those communications, which Henry could not make in person, he transmitted by the faithful Sully. This minister found that she was deeply engaged in the means, by which the great design might be happily executed; and that, notwithstanding the difficulties, which, in some points, she apprehended, she did not appear at all to doubt of success. This she chiefly expected for a reason, of the solidity and justness of which, Sully declares that he was afterwards well convinced. It was, that as the plan was, in truth, contrary only to the designs of some princes, whose ambitious views were sufficiently known to all Europe, the obstacles interposed by those princes, instead of retarding, would promote the design; since they would place its necessity in a more striking point of view.

"A very great number," says Sully, "of the articles, conditions, and different dispositions is due to this queen; and sufficiently evince, that, in respect of wisdom, penetration, and all the other perfections of the mind, she was not inferiour to any king, the most truly deserving of that title."

The death of this great princess gave such a violent shock to the whole plan, that Henry and his minister were almost induced to abandon their fondest hopes. The successour to the throne was the successour neither to the virtues nor to the talents of Elizabeth; and Henry had too much penetration to expect that assistance, which James[12] had too much pusillanimity to give. After some time, however, favourable circumstances occurred again, which induced him to reassume the plan, and to prepare, with renewed vigour, for its execution. Of its execution, he was on the very eve, when the fatal poignard of Ravaillac[13] interrupted it.

The leading object in the great design was to reduce within reasonable bounds, the formidable power of the house of Austria. With this view, it was proposed to devest that house of its possessions in Germany, Italy, and the Low Countries; and to confine it to the kingdom of Spain, bounded by the ocean, the Mediterranean, and the Pyrenean mountains. That it might, however, be equally powerful with the other sovereigns in Europe, it was intended to allot to it Sardinia, Majorca, Minorca, the Canaries, the Azores, and its possessions in Asia, Africa, and America.

"If there be any where," says Vattel,[y] "a state restless and mischievous, always ready to injure others, to traverse their designs, and to foment domestick troubles within them; it is not to be doubted, that all have a

12. James I (1566–1625) was king of England from 1603 to 1625. He was the first to call himself the king of Great Britain.

13. François Ravaillac (1578–1610) assassinated Henry IV in 1610.

y. B. 2. s. 53.

right to join in order to repress it, and deprive it of the power to molest them in future. The conduct of Philip the second of Spain[14] was adapted to unite all Europe against him; and it was from just reasons that Henry the Great formed the design of humbling a power, formidable by its forces, and pernicious by its maxims."

Between Henry and Elizabeth, it was a settled point, that neither of them should, by the different dismemberments proposed to be made, receive any thing, except the glory of distributing them with equity and impartiality. Henry even sometimes said, with equal moderation and good sense, that were the meditated dispositions once firmly established, he would have consented that the extent of France should have been determined by a majority of suffrages. With regard to England, the conduct of Elizabeth was probably influenced by an observation, which she made, that the Britannick isles, in all the different states, through which they passed, and among all the variations of their laws and policy, had never experienced great misfortunes, but when their sovereigns had interfered in matters beyond the sphere of their little continent. It seems, indeed, as if they were concentred in it, even by nature; and their happiness appears to depend entirely on themselves, provided they aim only to maintain peace in the three nations subject to them, by governing each according to its own laws and customs.

The ultimate design of the great plan was, to divide Europe equally among a certain number of powers, in such a manner, that no one might have reason for either envy or fear, from the power or possessions of the others. The number of states were reduced to fifteen. They were of three different kinds; hereditary monarchies; elective monarchies; republicks. The hereditary monarchies were six—France, Spain, Britain, Denmark, Sweden, Lombardy. The elective monarchies were five—the Empire, the Papacy, Poland, Hungary, Bohemia. The republicks were four—the Venetian, the Italian, the Helvetick, the Belgick.

There was to have been a general council, representing all the states of Europe. The establishment of this would have been the happiest invention that could have been conceived for preventing those innovations, and for applying a remedy to those inconveniences or defects, which time of-

14. Philip II (1527–1598) was king of Spain from 1556 to 1598.

ten introduces or discovers in the wisest and the most useful institutions. The model of this general council of Europe was formed on that of the ancient Amphyctions of Greece (a delineation of which I have already laid before you) with such alterations only as rendered it suitable to the alterations of customs, climate, and policy. It was to consist of a certain number of delegates from all the governments of the Christian Republick, who were to be constantly assembled as a senate. This body was to discuss the different interests, decide the controversies, and determine all the civil, political, and religious affairs of Europe, whether within itself or with its neighbours. The senate was to consist of four delegates from each of the following powers—the Emperour, the Pope, the kings of France, Spain, England, Denmark, Sweden, Lombardy, Poland, and the republick of Venice; and of two only from the other republicks and inferiour powers. All together would have composed a senate of about sixty six persons. They were to be chosen every three years. With regard to the place of meeting, it was undetermined whether it would be better for the council to be fixed or ambulatory; united in one, or divided into three. If it were divided into three, each containing twenty two magistrates, then each of them must have been fixed in such a centre as should appear to be most commodious. If it were judged more expedient not to divide the assembly, whether fixed or ambulatory, it must have been nearly in the centre of Europe.

Besides this general council, it would have been proper to have constituted subordinate councils: but whatever the number or form of those subordinate councils had been, it would have been absolutely necessary that an appeal should have lain from them to the general council, whose decisions, when considered as proceeding from the united authority of all the sovereigns, pronounced in a manner equally free and absolute; must have been regarded as so many final and irrevocable decrees.

A particular account is given by Sully of the measures taken to secure the success of this great and glorious design.

Henry was indefatigable in his negotiations in the different courts of Europe, particularly in the United Provinces, and in the circles of Germany. The council of the states-general were very soon unanimous in their determinations. The states-general were, in a short time, followed by the landgrave of Hesse, and the prince of Anhalt, to whom, as well as to the prince of Orange, the confederacy was obliged for being increased by the duke of Savoy; by all of the reformed religion in Hungary, Bohemia, and lower Austria; by many princes and towns in Germany; and by a great proportion of the Swiss Cantons. But a discovery either of the true motives, or of the full extent of the design, was cautiously avoided. It was, at first, concealed from all, without exception; and it was afterwards revealed, only to a few persons of approved discretion; and even of those, only to such as were absolutely to engage others to join the confederacy.

The king, on his side, had actually set on foot two good and well furnished armies; one of which he was to have commanded in person. It was to have consisted of twenty thousand foot, all native French, eight thousand Swiss, four thousand Lansquenets or Walloons, five thousand horse, and twenty cannons. The second was to have been commanded by Lesdiguieres, consisting of ten thousand foot, one thousand horse, and ten cannons; besides a flying camp of four thousand foot, six hundred horse, and ten cannons; and a reserve of two thousand foot to garrison places, where they might be necessary. Magazines were collected and deposited in proper places, for facilitating the execution of the enterprise: and, with the same view, manifestoes were composed with the greatest care. In them, a spirit of justice, of good policy, of honesty, of disinterestedness, and of inviolable faith was universally apparent.

It is impossible to dismiss a design, so interesting to humanity, without indulging a few observations concerning its nature, and its probable effects. That it was bold and magnificent, it will be unanimously agreed: but was it nothing more? was it not presumptuous and extravagant? We have seen that, as such, it was, at first, considered by Sully. As such, even the least difficult and most unimportant parts of it were considered by the other counsellors of France: for it was only on the least difficult and most unimportant parts, that he could venture to consult them. "Could it be imagined," says Sully, "that Henry, in his whole council, could not find one person, besides myself, to whom he could, without danger, disclose the whole of his designs; and that the respect due to him could scarce restrain those, who appeared most devoted to his service, from treating what, with the greatest circumspection, he had intrusted to them, as wild and extravagant chimeras." So true is sometimes the poet's exclamation—

Truths would you teach, or save a sinking land?
All fear, none aid you, and few understand.

But nothing discouraged that great prince, who was an abler politician and a better judge than all his council, and than all his kingdom. When he perceived that affairs, both at home and abroad, began to wear a favourable aspect, he then considered his success as infallible.

At this distance of time, and with our present imperfect knowledge of particular circumstances, it would be unwise to attempt a judgment, or even a conjecture, upon a detail of facts, existing at that age, and in the different states of Europe. But from general principles, and from our knowledge of some eminent characters, inferences, plausible and even satisfactory, may be drawn.

One inference may be drawn from the nature of the design, which Henry had formed. It was not a design inspired by mean and despicable ambition: it was not a design, guided by base and partial interests: it was a design, in the first place, to render France happy, and permanently happy: but as he well knew that France could not enjoy permanent felicity, unless in conjunction with the other parts of Europe; and as he was well pleased that the other parts of Europe should participate the felicity of France; it was the happiness of Europe in general which he laboured to procure; and to procure in a manner so solid and so durable, that nothing should afterwards be able to shake its foundations. May we not conclude, that, every thing else being equal, the probability is in favour of a great and good design? The fury and ravage of conquests have extended farther and wider, than the benevolent system of Henry the Great was meant or proposed to extend. Why should evil be more powerful or more enlarged in its operations than good? In private life, success is most frequently, though not universally, on the side of virtue: is it natural to expect a contrary rule in the administration of states and kingdoms? Is there not reason to hope that publick virtue will, on the whole, be triumphant; and that publick flagitiousness must, and should, and, at a proper time, will be degraded to the deepest abyss of humiliation?

These observations suggest general reasons in favour of the great design: other reasons may be drawn from the character, and talents, and virtues of the great man, who undertook its execution. It could not have been formed by one more eminently qualified to accomplish it. He possessed a courage capable of surmounting the greatest obstacles: he possessed a presence of mind, which saw and seized every opportunity of advantage: he possessed a prudence, which would not precipitate, but would calmly and patiently wait for the fit season of action: he possessed consummate experience, the result jointly of talents and of time. With all those great qualities as a soldier, as a statesman, and as a patriot, what was there, fair, or honest, or honourable, to which he could not form just pretensions? Had this enterprise failed in his hands, it would probably have failed for no other reason than this—that he was too great and too enlightened for the age in which he lived.

Had he been successful, the consequences of his success would, indeed, have been beneficial, lasting, and extensive. Those consequences would have reached not only his own subjects, not only the christian nations of Europe, but the whole world in general: of those consequences, the generation, at that time alive, the generations that have since succeeded, and those generations that are still to succeed, would have participated, down to the latest periods of time: those consequences would have been the source of all the sweets, which naturally flow from an uninterrupted and universal tranquillity.

Let me add another remark, which has been made in Europe, and which, with pride and joy, may be transferred to America. "Henry the Great has always had the honour of being considered as the author of the most important invention for the benefit of mankind, that has yet appeared in the world; the execution of which may, perhaps, be reserved by Providence, for the greatest and most capable of his successours." This rich succession has been reaped in America. Here the sublime system of Henry the Great has been effectually realized, and completely carried into execution.

When the political bonds, by which the American States had been connected with Great Britain, were dissolved; when they assumed, among the powers of the earth, the separate and equal station, to which the laws of nature and of nature's God entitled them, the form of government, which each should institute for herself, and that form, if any, which all should institute for all, became objects of the most serious and interesting deliberation. With regard to this last, which is the object of our present discussion, four different systems lay before them; any one of which they might have adopted. They might have consolidated themselves into one government, in which the separate existence of the states would have been entirely absorbed. They might have rejected any plan of union or association, and have acted as distinct and unconnected states. They might have formed two or more confederacies. They might have united in one federal republick.

To support, with vigour, a single government over the whole extent of the United States, would, I apprehend, demand a system of the most unqualified and the most unremitted despotism: even despotism herself, extended so far and so wide, would totter under the weight of her own unwieldiness.

Separate states, numerous as those of America are, still more numerous as they must become, contiguous in situation, unconnected and disunited in government, would, at one time, be the prey of foreign force, foreign influence, and foreign intrigue; at another, the victims of mutual rage, rancour, and revenge.

Would it have been proper to have divided the United States into two or more confederacies? It will not be unadvisable to examine this object with accuracy and attention. Some aspects, under which it may be viewed, are far from being, at first sight, uninviting. Two or more confederacies would be each more compact and more manageable, than a single one extending over the same territory. By dividing the United States into two or more confederacies, the great collision of interests, apparently or really different or contrary, in the whole extent of their dominion, would be broken, and, in a great measure, disappear in the several parts. But these advantages, which are discovered from certain points of view, are greatly overbalanced by inconveniences, which will appear on a closer inspection. Animosities and, perhaps, wars would arise from assigning the extent, the limits, and the rights of the different confederacies. The expenses of governing would be multiplied by the number of federal governments. The danger, resulting from foreign influence and mutual dissensions, would not, perhaps, be less great and alarming in the instance of different confederacies, than in the instance of different, though more numerous, unassociated states. These observations, and many others which might be made on the subject, will be sufficient to evince, that a division of the United States into a number of separate confederacies would probably be an unsatisfactory and an unsuccessful experiment.

The only remaining system, that is to be considered, is the union of the American States into one confederate republick. It will not be necessary to employ many arguments to show, that this is the most eligible system, which could have been proposed. By adopting it, the vigour and decision of a wide spreading monarchy may be associated with the freedom and beneficence of a compacted commonwealth. On one hand, the extent of territory; the diversity of climate and soil; the number, and greatness, and connexion of lakes and rivers, with which the United States are intersected and almost surrounded, all indicate an enlarged government to be fit and advantageous for them. On the other hand, the principles and dispositions of their citizens indicate, that, in this enlarged government, liberty shall reign triumphant.

Agreeably to these principles, the United States have been formed into one confederate republick; first, under the articles of confederation; afterwards, under our present national government. The weakness and inefficiency of the former; the excellencies, the advantages, and the imperfections of the latter—for it has its imperfections, though neither many nor dangerous—we shall hereafter have an opportunity of showing. Our present purpose will be best answered by taking a general view of those principles, characters, and properties, which distinguish or ought to distinguish a confederate republick and its members.

"An overgrown republick," says the Marquis of Beccaria, in the exquisite performance, with which he has enriched the treasures of legislation—"an overgrown republick can be saved from despotism, only by subdividing it into a number of confederate republicks. But how is this practicable? By a despotick dictator, who, with the courage of Sylla,[15] has as much genius for building up, as that Roman had for pulling down. If he be an ambitious man; his reward will be immortal glory: if a philosopher;

15. Lucius Cornelius Sulla Felix (c. 138–78 B.C.) was a skilled Roman general who was eventually appointed lifetime dictator of Rome.

the blessings of his fellow citizens will sufficiently console him for the loss of authority, though he should not be insensible to their ingratitude."[z] In the United States, there is no occasion for the assumption of dictatorial power, in order to be enabled to perform supereminent services for the publick. Powers amply sufficient for the performance of the greatest services, the enlightened citizens of the United States know how to give. As they know how to give those powers, so they know how to confine them within the proper and reasonable limits.

If a commonwealth is small, it may be destroyed by a foreign power; if it is extensive, it carries within it the internal causes of its destruction. This double disadvantage affects equally democracies and aristocracies, whether they are well, or whether they are ill constituted. The former disadvantage is selfevident; and, therefore, requires no illustration. The latter may be evinced from the following considerations. In a very extended commonwealth, it is difficult, if not impracticable, to provide, at the same time, the three following requisites—a number of representatives, which will not be too large; opportunities of minute and local information, which will be sufficiently frequent and convenient; and a connexion between the constituent and representative, which will be sufficiently intimate and binding. The experience of ages evinces, that, where a certain excess in numbers prevails, regularity, decency, and the convenient despatch of business are expected in vain. On the other hand, when, to avoid an excessive number of representatives, one representative is allotted to too great a number of constituents; it is improbable, that the former should possess a sufficient degree of accurate and circumstantial knowledge, or of an interest, common, and, at the same time, peculiar, with the latter, to qualify him for the zealous and well informed discharge of his confidential trust. Add to these considerations, that, in a commonwealth, the proceedings and deliberations are too complicated and too slow for the emergencies of an extended government; to whose affairs and interests, simplicity and secrecy in council, and vigour and despatch in execution are of indispensable necessity. For these reasons, it is not unlikely, that mankind would, at last, have been obliged to submit always to the government of a single person, if they had not invented the form of a constitution, which is

z. Bec. c. 26.

recommended by all the internal advantages of a republican government, and, at the same time, by all the force and energy of a government, which is monarchical. This form is a federal republick.

This form of government is a convention, by which several states consent to become citizens of a larger state, which they wish to form.[a] It is a society formed of other societies, which make a new one. This new one may be enlarged and aggrandized by the union of associates still new.

This kind of republick, fitted for resistance against exteriour attacks, is equally fitted to maintain its greatness without interiour corruption. It is formed for avoiding the inconveniences of that government, which is bad; and for securing the benefits of that, which is good.

In this kind of republick, the rights of internal legislation may be reserved to all the states, of which it is composed; while the adjustment of their several claims, the power of peace and war, the regulation of commerce, the right of entering into treaties, the authority of taxation, and the direction and government of the common force of the confederacy may be vested in the national government.

A confederate republick should consist of states, whose government is of the same nature; and it is proper that their government should be of the republican kind. Small monarchies are unfriendly to the genius of confederation. The spirit of monarchy is too often dominion and war; that of a commonwealth is more frequently moderation and peace. It is not likely, therefore, that these two kinds of government should subsist, on amicable terms, in the same confederated republick. Thus Germany, which consists of free cities and arbitrary monarchies, forms a confederacy, jarring and disjointed. Thus Greece was ruined, when the kings of Macedon obtained a seat among the Amphyctions. Hence we may see the propriety and wise policy of that article in the constitution of the United States,[b] which provides, that they shall guaranty to every state in the union a republican form of government.

When we say, that the government of those states, which unite in the same confederacy, ought to be of the same nature; it is not to be understood, that there should be a precise and exact uniformity in all their particular establishments and laws. It is sufficient that the fundamental prin-

a. Mont. Sp. Laws. b. 9. c. 1.

b. Art. 4. s. 4.

ciples of their laws and constitutions be consistent and congenial; and that some general rights and privileges should be diffused indiscriminately among them. Among these, the rights and privileges of naturalization hold an important place. Of such consequence was the intercommunication of these rights and privileges in the opinion of my Lord Bacon, that he considered them as the strongest of all bonds to cement and to preserve the union of states. "Let us take a view," says he, "and we shall find, that wheresoever kingdoms and states have been united, and that union incorporated by a bond of mutual naturalization, you shall never observe them afterwards, upon any occasion of trouble or otherwise, to break and sever again."[c] Machiavel,[16] when he inquires concerning the causes, to which Rome was indebted for her splendour and greatness, assigns none of stronger or more extensive operation than this—she easily compounded and incorporated with strangers.[d] This important subject has received a proportioned degree of attention in forming the constitution of the United States. "The citizens of each state shall be entitled to all privileges and immunities of citizens in the several states."[e] In addition to this, the congress have power to "establish a uniform rule of naturalization throughout the United States."[f]

Though a union of laws is, by no means, necessary to a union of states; yet a similarity in their code of *publick*[g] laws is a most desirable object. The publick law is the great sinew of government. The sinews of the different governments, composing the union, should, as far as it can be effected, be equally strong. "In this point," says my Lord Bacon, "the rule holdeth, which was pronounced by an ancient father, touching the diversity of rites in the church; for finding the vesture of the queen in the psalm (who prefigured the church) was of divers colours; and finding again that Christ's coat was without a seam, concludeth well, in veste varietas sit, scissura non sit."[h]

c. 4. Ld. Bac. 243.

16. Niccolò Machiavelli (1469–1527) was an Italian political thinker. He is best known for his works *The Prince* and *Discourses on Livy.*

d. Id. 214.

e. Art. 4. s. 2.

f. Art. 1. s. 8.

g. 4. Ld. Bac. 224. 225.

h. 4. Ld. Bac. 215. In clothing let there be variety, but no seam.

Non omnibus facies una; sed qualis decet esse sororum.[17]
Ovid.

In a confederated republick, consisting of states of unequal numbers, extent, and power, the influence of each ought to bear a corresponding proportion. The Lycian republick was an association of twenty three towns. The large ones had three votes in the common council, the middling ones two, the small ones one. They contributed to the national expenses according to the proportion of suffrages. "Were I to give a model," says the celebrated Montesquieu,[i] "of an excellent confederate republick, I would pitch upon that of Lycia."

No one state, comprehended within a confederated republick, should be permitted to conclude an alliance with a foreign nation. This salutary regulation subsists not in the constitution of the Germanick Body. Hence the frequent dissensions and calamities, to which that great confederacy is constantly exposed, and with which it is frequently visited, through the rashness or the ambition of a single member.

With regard to foreign transactions, and with regard to those matters, which affect the general interests of the whole union, a confederated republick should be considered and should act as a single government or nation.

A union of hearts and affections, as well as a union of counsels and interests, is the very life and soul of a confederated republick. This is a subject, on which it is almost impossible to say too much, or to speak with too much zeal. We have, in former lectures,[j] seen how strong, how active, and how persevering are the operations and aims of our social powers. They are capable of being raised to the greatest height. They are capable of being enlarged to the greatest extent. But they partake of human imperfection: in their most useful and amiable forms, they sometimes degenerate into irregularity, abuse, and what I may call an excess of concentricity: by this I mean, overstrained exertions within a narrow and contracted sphere. Faction itself is frequently nothing else than a warm but inconsiderate ebullition of our social propensities.

17. They have not all the same appearance; but such as it befits sisters to have.
i. Sp. Laws. b. 9.c. 3.
j. Ante ch. 7.

How easily is the esprit du corps generated! How powerfully is it felt! How universally does it operate! How early does it appear! How ardent we see it in boys of different schools; and of different classes in the same school! With what emulation do they strive to outshine one another in their several tasks or sports! With what eagerness do the young men of neighbouring and rival towns—rival because they are neighbouring—contend for victory in their rural and manly exercises! Let the distinction be once formed—it is immaterial on what occasion, or from what cause—and its effects will be both strong and lasting. They will be beneficial or pernicious, according to the direction, which it first receives, and the objects to which it ultimately tends. How frivolous; how fierce; how obstinate; and how bloody were the contests of the Blues and Greens in the Hippodrome of Constantinople![18] The empire was sometimes shaken to its centre; and those, who produced the strong convulsions, could tell neither what they wished, nor why they were agitated. On the other hand; how often has the reputation of a regiment been preserved or heightened—how often, in battle, has victory been obtained or retrieved, by the wise encouragement and skilful application of the esprit du corps! This spirit should not be extinguished: but in all governments, it is of vast moment—in confederated governments, it is of indispensable necessity—that it should be regulated, guided, and controlled.

"The associating genius of man," says my Lord Shaftesbury, "is never better proved, than in those very societies, which are formed in opposition to the general one of mankind, and to the real interest of the state."[k] Extensive governments are particularly exposed to this inconvenience: to this inconvenience a national government, such as ours, composed of a great number of states, powerful, extensive, and separated, to a great distance, by situation, and, sometimes too, by an opinion of interest, not only from one another, but from the superintending power, by which they are connected—to this inconvenience, I say, such a national government is, of all, the most exposed—by this inconvenience, I add, such a national

18. The Hippodrome of Constantinople was a horse-racing track and social center of the city. The Blues and Greens were different teams, whose contests sometimes heated to the point of civil war. The worst of these was the riots of Nika (532), when thirty thousand people were supposedly killed.

k. 1. Shaft. 114.

government is, of all, the most endangered. To embrace the whole, requires an expansion of mind, of talents, and of temper. To the trouble, though the generous trouble, of expanding their mind, their talents, and their temper, some will be averse from indolence, or what the indolent call moderation; others will be averse from interest, or what the interested call prudence. The former will encourage a narrow spirit by their example; the latter will encourage it by their exertions also. These last will introduce and recommend the government of their state, as a rival, for social and benevolent affection, to the government of the United States. The simplicity of some, the inexperience of others, the unsuspecting confidence, again, of others will be won by plausible and seducing representations; and, in this manner, and by these arts, the patriotick emanations of the soul, which would otherwise be diffused over the whole Union, will be refracted and converged to a very narrow and inconsiderable part of it.

Against this ungenerous application of one of the noblest propensities of our nature, the system of our education and of our law ought to be directed with the most vigorous and unremitted ardour. This application of that noble propensity is not merely ungenerous: it is no less unwise. It is unwise, as to the person, who makes it; it is unwise, as to the state, to the advantage of which it is supposed to be made. Apply and extend, in favour of the Union, the same train of reflection and argument which is used in favour of the state. With regard to the latter, will it not be allowed—will it not be urged—will it not be properly urged, that the interest of the whole should never be sacrificed to that of a part, nor the interest of a greater part to that of a part, which is smaller? Will it not be allowed—will it not be urged, that to think or act in a contrary manner, would be improper and unwise? Why should not the same reasoning and the same conduct be allowed—why should they not be urged—for they may be urged with equal propriety—in favour of the interests of the Union, or of the greater part of the Union, compared with those of a single member, of which that Union is composed?

But it will be seldom, if ever, necessary that the interest of a single state should be sacrificed to that of the United States. The laws, and government, and policy of the union operate universally and not partially; for the accomplishment of general and not of local purposes. On the other hand, the laws, and government, and policy of a particular state, compared with the Union, operate partially and not universally; for the accomplishment of purposes, which are local, and not general. If, then, on any subject, a difference should take place between the sentiments, and designs, and plans of the national government and those of the government of a single state; on whose side are justice and general utility likely to be found? It is to be presumed that they will be found on the side of the national government. That government is animated and directed by a representation of the whole Union: the government of a single state is animated and directed by a representation of only a part, inconsiderable when compared with the whole. Is it not more reasonable, as well as more patriotick, that the interests of every part should be governed, since they will be embraced, by the counsels of the whole, than that the interests of the whole should be governed, since they will not be embraced, by the counsels of a part?

Expanded patriotism is a cardinal virtue in the United States. This cardinal virtue—this "passion for the commonweal," superiour to contracted motives or views, will preserve inviolate the connexion of interest between the whole and all its parts, and the connexion of affection as well as interest between all the several parts.

Let us, then, cherish; let us encourage; let us admire; let us teach; let us practise this "devotion to the publick," so meritorious, and so necessary to the peace, and greatness, and happiness of the United States.

The central parent-publick calls
Its utmost effort forth, awakes each sense,
The comely, grand, and tender. Without this,
This awful pant, shook from sublimer powers
Than those of self, this heaven-infused delight,
This moral gravitation, rushing prone
To press the publick good, *our* system soon,
Traverse, to several *selfish* centres drawn,
Will reel to ruin.

2. Thom. Works. 158.

"—To avoid this fate,
Let worth and virtue—
Exerted full, from every quarter shine,
Commix'd in heightened blaze. Light flash'd to light,

Moral or intellectual, more intense
By giving glows. As on pure winter's eve,
Gradual, the stars effulge; fainter, at first,
They, straggling, rise: but when the radiant host,
In thick profusion poured, shine out immense,
Each casting vivid influence on each,
From pole to pole a glittering deluge plays,
And worlds above rejoice, and men below."

2. Thom. Works. 162.

CHAPTER IX.
Of Man, as a Member of the Great Commonwealth of Nations.

Every civil society, under whatever form it appears, whether governed merely by the natural laws of such a society, or by them and civil institutions superadded—every such society, not subordinate to another, is a sovereign state.

Those, who unite in society, lived, before their union, in a state of nature: a state of nature is a state of equality and liberty. That liberty and that equality, belonging to the individuals, before the union, belong, after the union, to the society, which those individuals compose. The consequence is, that a society is subjected to no power or authority without it; that it may do what is necessary for its preservation; that it may exercise all its rights, and is obliged to give an account of its conduct to no one. But these things constitute what is called sovereignty. Every state, therefore, composed of individuals, free and equal, is a state sovereign and independent. The aggregate body possesses all the rights of the individuals, of whom it is formed.

Another consequence is, that the rights of any one state are naturally the same as those of every other. States are moral persons, who live together in a natural society, under the law of nations. To give a state a right to make an immediate figure in the great society of nations, it is sufficient, if it be really sovereign and independent; that is, it must govern itself by its own authority.[a] Thus, when the United Colonies found it necessary to dissolve the political bonds, which had connected them with Great Britain, and to assume among the powers of the earth the separate and equal station, to which the laws of nature and of nature's God entitled them; they

a. Vat. b. 1. s. 4.

had a right to publish and declare, as, in fact, they did publish and declare, that "they were free and independent states; and that, as free and independent states, they had full power to levy war, to conclude peace, contract alliances, establish commerce, and to do all other acts and things, which independent states may of right do"; though, at that time, no articles of confederation were agreed upon; nor was any form of civil government instituted by them.

A number of individuals, who have formed themselves into a society or state, are, with regard to the purposes of the society, bound to consider themselves as one moral person. But the rest of mankind, who are not parties to this social compact, are under no obligation to take notice of it; and may still consider the society as a large number of unconnected persons. This personality—I know no better expression for it—of a state must, as to other nations, be derived from their consent and agreement. But when a society have once associated, and considered and announced themselves to other nations as a moral person, this consent and agreement ought not to be refused, without solid and special reasons, which will justify the refusal. On this consent and agreement, the mutual and mutually beneficial intercourse of nations is founded: whatever, therefore, promotes this intercourse, should be zealously encouraged; whatever prevents or interrupts it, should be cautiously avoided.

Though one state has, by an unequal alliance, formed a connexion with another state more powerful; still the weaker state is to be reckoned in the class of sovereigns. To the weaker state, the unequal alliance may secure the most assistance; on the stronger, it may reflect the most honour; but it leaves both the same rank among the society of nations.

We may go further; if a state, in order to provide for its own safety, finds it necessary to place itself under the protection of another; and, in consideration of that protection, stipulates to perform equivalent offices, without devesting itself of the right of self-government; such a state ceases not to preserve its place among sovereigns. The payment even of tribute, though it may diminish the dignity of the society, by no means destroys or impairs its sovereignty or its rights.

Two sovereign states may employ the same executive magistrate, or bear allegiance to the same prince, without any dependence on each other; and each may retain all its national rights, free and undiminished. This last, under the house of Stuart, was the case of England and Scotland, before the nation of Great Britain was formed by their union. This last, also, as shall be hereafter shown at large, was the case of Great Britain and the American colonies, before the political connexion between them was declared to be dissolved.

But one people who have passed under the *dominion* of another, can no longer form a state: they can no longer retain a place in the great society of nations. Of that great society, equality is the basis and the rule. To this equality, the inferiority of subjection and the superiority of command are, alike, repugnant.

This equality of nations is the great and general foundation of national rights. In this matter, no regard is had to names. On the great theatre of the world, empires, kingdoms, commonwealths, principalities, dukedoms, free towns, are all equally imperial. A society, which, without subordination to any other, exercises within itself all the essential powers of society, is sovereign, and has all the rights of a sovereign and independent state; however narrow its territories; however small its numbers may be.

Every nation deserves consideration and respect; because it makes an immediate figure in the grandest society of the human race; because it is independent of all earthly power; and because it is an assemblage of a number of men, who, doubtless, are more considerable than any individual.

With regard to precedency, or the first place among equals, power and antiquity are grounds, upon which it is claimed or allowed. Into this question, the forms of government do not enter.

The natural state of individuals we have already seen to be a state of society and peace: such also is the natural state of nations. This state, it is the duty of nations, as well as of individuals, to preserve and improve. But among nations, as well as among individuals, differences and causes of difference will, sometimes, unavoidably arise. Over independent nations there is no coercive authority, to which recourse may be had for a decision of their controversies. What, then, shall be done, in order to terminate or adjust them? Much may be done; much ought to be done, before the fatal appeal is made to the dernier resort of sovereigns.

In some peculiar situations, it is more prudent, as well as more honourable, to abandon than to claim a right; to disregard, than to resent an injury: but, by nations, even this laudable and generous conduct should be observed with great prudence and circumspection, and in such a manner as, instead of cowardice, to discover magnanimity. When this conduct can be so observed, what a glorious example does it exhibit to the world! "A king of France ought not to revenge the wrongs of a duke of Orleans," was nobly said by a monarch of an elevated mind. Might it not also be said, that it is not every petty offence, which ought to provoke the dignified energy of sovereign power? Suppose a picture, disrespectful to Lewis the fourteenth, had been exhibited in Holland; was this a sufficient occasion for drawing forth the great monarch at the head of the armies of France? Was it a sufficient occasion for drawing him forth at the head of those armies against a power, comparatively inconsiderable, and trembling to its centre from a conscious sense of its own inferiority?

Nec deus intersit, nisi nodus vindice dignus.[1]

On some occasions, it may be proper to claim a right, or take notice of an injury, merely with a determined and heroick purpose of ceding the former, and of forgiving the latter. This mode of proceeding, adopted at a proper time, in a proper manner, and by a proper person, has a great and a useful effect. It displays the good sense and superiour judgment of him, who observes it; and secures the esteem, perhaps the friendship of him, towards whom it is observed.

Controversies often happen, when neither of the parties to them is intentionally wrong: they arise from misapprehensions or mistakes. In such cases, nothing more is necessary for an amicable accommodation, than candid conference and mutual explanation. "There are two kinds of disputation," says Cicero,[b] "one, by argument and reason; the other, by violence and force. To determine controversies by the former belongs to man; by the latter, to the brutes. To the latter we ought never to have recourse, but when all hopes of success by the former are proved to be unavailing." If in every minute particular, an entire coincidence of sentiment and interest cannot take place; concessions, in the course of a negotiation, may be made on both sides; and, in this manner, a satisfactory adjustment of every difference may be effectuated.

1. Nor would God intervene, unless the predicament be worthy of a helper to untangle it.
b. De off. l. 1. c. 11.

If the parties themselves, notwithstanding their peaceful and proper inclinations, cannot finally agree upon the terms, according to which the difference should be adjusted; those terms may, in many instances, be arranged and settled by the kind and benevolent mediation of a common friend. Delicate, indeed, but highly useful is the office of a mediator. Address, prudence, a winning smoothness, but, above all, a most strict impartiality are the rare qualifications, which he ought to possess. Possessing these, he will favour what is due to justice and right; but remembering, at the same time, that his office is to conciliate, and not to judge, his leading effort will be to preserve or to procure peace, and to prevail on him, who has even justice on his side, to relax something, if such a relaxation shall be necessary for accomplishing a purpose so desirable and so humane. In the Alcoran,[2] it is delivered as an indispensable injunction, that if two nations of the faithful will go to war, the others shall interpose and force the aggressor to make satisfaction, and afterwards lay both under an obligation to live, for the future, in peace and friendship.[c]

If, unfortunately, neither negotiation nor friendly interposition of disinterested and benevolent powers shall prove effectual, for determining a controversy between two nations; there is another method remaining, by which mutual irritation and, much more, dreadful extremities may be prevented between those, who have no common judge upon earth, to whom they can appeal. This method is, to refer the matter in dispute to the award of arbitrators.

This mode of decision has been embraced by nations, the most powerful and the most wise. When the Athenians and the citizens of Megara had a dispute concerning the property of the island of Salamis, five Lacedemonian umpires were chosen to settle their contested claims. Some of the Italian states, in the early ages of Rome, submitted their controversies to the determination of the Romans. The Romans themselves, haughty and domineering as they were, and proud of the character *debellare superbos,*[3] proposed to the Samnites, that the subject of their contention should be referred to the arbitration of their common friends and allies.[d] The

2. Archaic term for the Koran.
c. Puff. 556. b. 5. c. 13. s. 7.
3. To battle down the proud. From Virgil's *Aeneid,* book VI, line 853.
d. Liv. l. 8. c. 23.

Druids, those revered ministers of a mysterious superstition, were the umpires between nations at war, and frequently brought matters to an accommodation, when the belligerent powers were on the very instant of an engagement. "It is cruel and detestable," says Thucydides, "to treat him as an enemy, who is willing to submit his case to an arbitration."[e]

In all their alliances with one another, and even in those, which they have formed with the neighbouring powers, the Swiss have used the wise precaution to ascertain, beforehand, the manner, in which their differences should be left to the award of arbitrators, in case it should prove impracticable to adjust them upon amicable terms. This prudent and judicious policy has contributed, in no small degree, to maintain the Helvetian republick in that flourishing state, which has secured its liberty, and rendered it respectable over all Europe.[f]

When the sentence of the arbitrators is given, it ought to be obeyed; unless it be flagrantly partial, manifestly unjust, or clearly beyond the powers given by the submission. If the award is upon the very point disputed, it can never be manifestly unjust, since it has been rendered doubtful by the dissension of the parties.

It has been the opinion of some very respectable and well informed writers, that it would be highly convenient, and even somewhat necessary, that congresses of a number of states should be held, in which the differences of contending parties might be determined by those altogether disinterested in them; and in which, likewise, some effectual means might be devised and carried into execution, for compelling nations at war to conclude a peace upon fair and equitable conditions. In the course of the present century, two general congresses have been held in Europe—one at Cambray; the other at Soissons: but they were nothing more than pompous farces, acted, with great parade, by those, who wished to appear solicitous for an accommodation, but who, in fact, were little solicitous to promote it.[g]

If justice cannot be obtained in any of the peaceful modes abovemen-

e. Gro. 486. 487.
f. Vat. b. 2. s. 329.
g. Vat. b. 2. s. 330. I.e.

tioned; a nation has then a right to do itself justice. But even this ought to be done, when it can possibly be done, without proceeding to the last direful necessity of commencing a war. Reprisals may be made. If one nation has got into its possession what belongs to another, and will not restore it; if it refuses to pay a just debt, or to make reparation for an injury; that other nation may seize property belonging to the first, may apply it for its own benefit, in discharge of what is due, together with interest and damages; or it may hold the property in pledge, until satisfaction be made.

The subject of reprisals is so delicate and interesting that the nature and the extent of the right to make them deserve a careful and accurate investigation.

We have already seen,[h] that a nation is to be considered as a moral person, having an understanding and will peculiar to itself: as such it is considered by the law of nations. The consequence necessarily is, that every act of this moral or collective person must, in the view of that law, be the concurrent act of its several members.

From the same principles, the property of each of the members must, with regard to other states, be deemed the property of the whole nation. In some degree, this is, in truth, the case; because the nation has power over the riches of the citizens; and because those riches form a part of the national wealth. All those, who compose a nation, making, in the consideration of foreign states, one whole, or one single person; all their property must be considered as the property of that single person. It is in the power of a nation to establish, among its citizens, a community of goods; but whether this is done, or is not done, the separate property of those citizens can neither be known nor discriminated by other states. The unavoidable result is, that, if one nation has a right to any part of the goods of another, it has a right to the goods of its citizens, till the right be satisfied or discharged. The unavoidable result, again, is, that when it is justifiable to make reprisals, they may be made on the property of any of the citizens, as well as on that of the nation. From this rule, one exception has been made, and deserves to be established. This exception is made in

h. Ante p. 635. 636.

favour of a deposit trusted to the faith of the nation, which has a right to make reprisals. This deposit has been made only in consequence of the reliance, which the owner had on this faith: this faith ought to be respected, even in the case of an open and declared war. For this reason, in France, in England, and in some other countries of Europe, the money, which hostile foreigners have placed in the publick funds, has been considered as sacred from the rights of reprisals, and even of war.

He who, for the injustice done by a nation, makes reprisals upon the property of its citizens indiscriminately, cannot be accused of seizing the property of one person in order to satisfy the debt of another. It is a demand against the state, to the discharge of which every citizen is bound to contribute his just proportion. It is the duty and business of the nation to provide, that those citizens, upon whom the reprisals fall immediately, should be indemnified for every thing beyond that share, which, on a fair assessment, they ought to pay. The nation ought to go farther: if the reprisals have been occasioned originally by the injustice or violence of some of its members; those members should be compelled to make satisfaction for every loss, which has arisen from their conduct.

Though the property of the private citizens, from the nature and the necessity of the case, must, in many, perhaps, in most instances, be considered by foreign states as liable for their demands against the nation; yet where publick property can be known and certainly distinguished, it is unquestionably proper, that such property should, in the first place, be the selected object of reprisals, if to reprisals it be easily or conveniently accessible. The principles of humanity and the dictates of magnanimity suggest, with equal force, the reasonableness and propriety of this discrimination, whenever it can be made.

As the property of a nation, or of the citizens of a nation, may be seized by reprisals, in order to compel it to do justice; so, on some occasions, the citizens themselves may be seized, in consequence of the same principles, and may be detained until full satisfaction has been received. This mode of proceeding was known among the Grecians by a name, which may be literally translated *mancatching;* 'Ανδροληψια. At Athens, the law permitted the relations of him, who had been assassinated in a foreign country, to apprehend three persons of that country, and detain them, till the assassin was punished or delivered up.

In making reprisals, three precautions should be inviolably observed. 1. They ought not to be made without the authority of the nation. Though reprisals are not war; and though their proper use is to prevent war; yet they approach to a war, and are often followed by one. They are, therefore, proceedings of too much publick moment, to be carried on under the direction and at the discretion of individuals; probably, of individuals immediately and particularly interested in them. In all civilized countries, therefore, it is the unvaried practice, that when a citizen considers himself as injured by a foreign state, he applies to the sovereign power of his nation for permission to make reprisals. 2. Reprisals ought to be made only for a demand, which is both just and certain. If it be doubtful or unliquidated, the first application should be for such steps as may be necessary to ascertain its reasonableness and its extent. 3. The reprisals should be in a due proportion to the demand. General reprisals, the grand pensionary De Wit[4] used to say, were scarcely to be distinguished from an open war.

We have now seen that the citizens, in their persons and in their fortunes, may be accountable for the conduct of the nation: so, on the other hand, the nation may sometimes be accountable for the conduct of its private citizens.

The state should protect the citizen, should defend him from injury, and should procure reparation for injuries which he has sustained. So, likewise, the nation should not suffer its citizens to commit injuries against the citizens of other states; it ought to disclaim the conduct of such as offer injuries; and ought to compel or to give satisfaction for the injuries which have been offered.

It is impossible, however, that, even in the best regulated state, the government should be able to superintend the whole conduct of all the citizens, and to restrain them within the precise bounds of duty and obedience: it would be unjust, therefore, to impute to the nation, or to the government, all the faults or offences, which its members may commit. Hence it does not necessarily follow, that one has received an injury from a nation, merely because he has received an injury from a citizen belonging to that nation. To a whole state, the follies, the injuries, or the crimes

4. John De Witt (1625–1672) was the Grand Pensionary of Holland during the wars with England from 1653 to 1672.

of a particular person ought not to be immediately ascribed: in every state, wicked and disorderly citizens are unhappily to be found: let such be held responsible for the consequences of their crimes and disorders.

This doctrine is certainly reasonable and just; but if a nation wishes not to be involved in the punishment of her citizens, she should sedulously avoid the impropriety and the offence of becoming an accomplice in their injuries and crimes. In their injuries and crimes she becomes an accomplice, when she approves or ratifies them, and when she affords protection and security to those, who have committed them. In such cases, the nation may justly be considered as even the author, and the citizens as only the instruments, of the wrong or outrage which has been done.

When the offending citizen escapes into his own country, his nation should oblige him to repair the damage, if reparation can be made; should punish him according to the measure of his offence; or, when the nature and the circumstances of the case require it, deliver him up to the offended state to meet his doom there. This is frequently done with regard to atrocious crimes, such as are equally contrary to the laws and the safety of all nations.

In states, which are most strictly connected by friendship and good neighbourhood, they go farther still. Even with regard to common injuries, which are prosecuted civilly, whether for reparation of damage, or for a slight civil punishment, the citizens of two neighbouring states are reciprocally compelled to appear before the magistrate of the country, in which they are accused of having offended. On a requisition of this magistrate, which is called a letter rogatory, they are cited judicially, and compelled by their own proper magistrates to appear. "An admirable institution!" exclaims Vattel,[i] in a tone of admiration, "by which many neighbouring states live together in peace and harmony, and seem to form but one and the same commonwealth." This institution is in force through all Switzerland.

If we could restrain, would it be proper to restrain the pleasing and animating reflection, that even the most admired institutions of Europe are improved, while they are adopted by the United States? For the trial and punishment of every kind of offence, prosecuted criminally, and,

i. B. 2. s. 76.

therefore, on common law principles, locally, the following provision is made in our national constitution.[j] "A person charged, in any state, with treason, felony, or other crime, who shall flee from justice, and be found in another state, shall, on demand of the executive authority of the state from which he fled, be delivered up, to be removed to the state, having jurisdiction of the crime." In civil causes of a transitory nature, no such provision is necessary; but a much better one is made. In Switzerland, controversies depending between citizens of different states must be decided by the magistrates of a state, of which one party, but not the other, is a citizen. But, in the United States, for controversies depending between citizens of two different states, a tribunal is formed and established, impartial, and equally independent of both.

The foregoing remarks exhibit, in a very striking point of view, the numerous, the near, and the important relations, by which states and the members of states may be connected together. We here discover the much famed institutions of Alfred the Great, extended on a national scale. In the great society of nations, we see each citizen bound for the good behaviour of all, and all bound for the good behaviour of each. As the principles of society, humanity, benevolence, and liberality shall become more and more regarded and cultivated, the rights and duties of different nations, and of the citizens of different nations, will become more and more studied, and will be better and better practised and observed. In this study, the present century has witnessed great and manifest improvements. In this study all men are interested: it is rich in delight: it is inestimable in importance: its maxims should be known by every citizen of every free state.

The relations existing between different states and the citizens of different states, and the rights and duties arising from those relations, form a constituent part of the common law. In that country, from which the common law has been brought, the law of nations has always been most respectfully and attentively adopted and regarded by the municipal tribunals, in all matters, concerning which it is proper to have recourse to that rule of decision. The law of nations, in its full extent, is a part of the law of England.[k] The infractions of that law form a portion of her code of

j. Art. 4. s. 2.
k. 3. Burr. 1481.

criminal jurisprudence. In civil transactions between the citizens of different states, that law has, in England, been received in its most ample latitude.

One branch of that law, which, since the extension of commerce, and the frequent and liberal intercourse between different nations, has become of peculiar importance, is called the law of merchants. This system of law has been admitted to decide controversies concerning bills of exchange, policies of insurance, and other mercantile transactions, both where citizens of different states, and where citizens of the same state only, have been interested in the event.[l] This system has, of late years, been greatly elucidated, and reduced to rational and solid principles, by a series of adjudications, for which the commercial world is much indebted to a celebrated judge, long famed for his comprehensive talents and luminous learning in general jurisprudence.

Another branch of the law of nations, which has also become peculiarly important by the extension of commerce, is the law maritime. In a cause depending in the court of king's bench in England, and tried at one of the assizes, my Lord Mansfield, the great judge to whom allusion has been just now made, was desirous to have a case made of it for solemn adjudication; not because he himself entertained great doubts concerning it; but in order to settle the point, on which it turned, more deliberately, solemnly, and notoriously; as it was of an extensive nature; and especially as the maritime law is not the law of a particular country, but the general law of nations: non erit alia lex Romae, alia Athenis; alia nunc, alia posthac; sed et apud omnes gentes et omni tempore, una eademque lex obtinebit.[m]

In the plan of my lectures, I proposed a question, the greatness of which is selfevident—How far, on the principles of the confederation, does the law of nations become the municipal law of the United States? I mentioned, that it would be unwise, at that time, to hint at an answer. An answer I mean not to give even now: but I deem it highly proper now to state the nature, the extent, and the importance of the question. It points to a course new and unexplored.

l. In commercial cases, all nations ought to have their laws conformable to each other. Fides servanda est; simplicitas juris gentium praevaleat. 3. Burr. 1672. "Faith must be kept; the simplicity of the law of nations must prevail."

m. 2. Burr. 887. "There will not be one law in Rome, another in Athens one now, another later; but both among all peoples and at every time one and the same law will prevail."

We have seen the divine origin; we have seen the amazing extent; we have seen the uncommon magnitude of the law of nations: we have, in part, seen, likewise, how ineffective the execution of that law, under human authority, has hitherto been.

Amicable agreement between parties in controversy has been recommended, and recommended with great propriety, where the recommendation can take effect: but controversy, which has arisen, and which, from the very supposition of the case, subsists between the parties, is certainly not the most natural guide to lead to an amicable accommodation. The mediation of a disinterested and benevolent power has been recommended likewise: but this mediation, though it enhances the merit and displays the beauty of the candid, the peaceful, and the disinterested virtues, affords no reasonable security, that the exertion of those virtues will be accompanied with the wished for effect. To arbitration recourse has been advised: but to the institution of arbitrators, the previous consent of the parties in controversy is requisite: and how, against the unwilling, is the award of the arbitrators to be enforced?

What is next to be done? The same disposition or the same mistake, which, on one of the sides, must have given birth to the controversy, will probably communicate to it vigour and perseverance. Nay, that disagreement of mind between the parties, which must have taken place when the controversy commenced, is likely to be increased, instead of being diminished, by the frequent, numerous, and mutual irritations, which will unavoidably happen in the prosecution of it. All the modes of adjustment, which have been hitherto mentioned, presuppose the reconciliation of irritated minds. But must the peaceful adjustment of controversies between states—an adjustment so salutary and so necessary to the human race—depend on events so very precarious, so very improbable? Must the alternatives in disputes and differences between the dignified assemblages of men, known by the name of nations, be the same, which are the prerogatives of savages in the rudest and most deformed state of society—voluntary accommodation, or open war, or violent reprisals, inferiour, in odium, only to war? Individuals unite in civil society, and institute judges with authority to decide, and with authority also to carry their decisions into full and adequate execution, that justice may be done and war may be prevented. Are states too wise or too proud to receive a lesson from individuals? Is the idea of a common judge between nations less admissible than that of a common judge between men? If admissible in idea, would it not be desirable to have an opportunity of trying whether the idea may not be reduced to practice? To return to the original question—has or has not our national constitution given us an opportunity of making this great and interesting trial?

Let us turn our most scrutinizing attention to the situation, in which, on the principles of that system, the states and the people, composing the American Union, stand with regard to one another; the situation, in which they stand with regard to foreign nations; and the situation, in which they stand with regard to the government of the United States.

With regard to one another, they have, by ordaining and establishing the national constitution, engaged to "form a more perfect union," "to ensure domestick tranquillity," "to establish justice:"[n] they have engaged "that the citizens of each state shall be entitled to all privileges and immunities of citizens in the several states:"[o] they have engaged that no state shall enter into "any treaty, alliance, or confederation;"[p] "nor, without the consent of congress, into any agreement or compact with another state."[q]

With regard to foreign nations, the states, composing the American Union, have made an engagement precisely in the terms of the last mentioned engagement, which they have made with regard to one another—absolutely to enter into no treaty, alliance, or confederation with foreign nations; and to enter into no agreement or compact with them, unless with the consent of congress.[r]

With regard to the government of the United States, they have engaged that the judicial power of the United States shall extend "to controversies between two or more states; between a state and the citizens of another state; between citizens of different states; between citizens of the same state claiming lands under grants of different states; and between a state, or the citizens thereof, and foreign states, citizens, or subjects."[s]

n. Preamb.
o. Art. 4. s. 2.
p. Art. 1. s. 10.
q. Ibid.
r. Ibid.
s. Art. 3. s. 2.

The law of nations respecting treaties, alliances, and confederations must be thrown entirely out of the question: these are absolutely interdicted.

The law of nations respecting agreements and compacts between two or more states; between a state and the citizens of another state; between citizens of different states; between citizens of the same state claiming lands under grants of different states; and between a state, or the citizens thereof, and foreign states, citizens, or subjects, will still be applicable, as before the national constitution was established, to controversies arising in all those different enumerated cases.

In all those different enumerated cases, the tribunals of the United States have judicial authority to decide. By what law shall their decisions be governed? Before the establishment of the national government, controversies happening in those enumerated cases, if determined at all, must have been determined by the principles and rules of the law of nations. But before that establishment, there was no power to determine them judicially by any law.

We have already seen that, in England, the courts of common law, in cases, to which the law of nations, and particularly in cases, to which one great branch of it, the law of merchants is applicable, have made approved application of that law, and have received it, in its fullest extent, as a part of the law of England. Should a similar conduct be observed by the tribunals of the United States, in the numerous and very important cases, to which the national constitution extends their judicial authority?

If a similar conduct ought to be observed by those tribunals; what an immense improvement has taken place in the application and administration of the law of nations! Hitherto that great law has been applied and administered by the force or by the pleasure of the parties in controversy: in the United States, it can now be applied and administered by impartial, independent, and efficient, though peaceful authority.

This deduction, if properly founded, places the government of the United States in an aspect, new, indeed, but very conspicuous. It is vested with the exalted power of administering judicially the law of nations, which we have formerly seen to be the law of sovereigns.

It has been already observed, that the maxims of this law ought to be known by every citizen of every free state. Reasons, and very sufficient ones, were suggested, why this should be the case. A new reason, striking and illustrious, now appears, why the maxims of this law ought to be particularly known and studied by every citizen of the United States. To every citizen of the United States, this law is not only a rule of conduct, but may be a rule of decision. As judges and as jurors, the administration of this law is, in many important instances, committed to their care.

What a beautiful and magnificent prospect of government is now opened before you! The sluices of discord, devastation, and war are shut: those of harmony, improvement, and happiness are opened! On earth there is peace and good will towards men! On contemplating such a prospect, though only by the eye of a sublime imagination, well might the ardent and elevated Henry address the congenial ardour and elevation of Elizabeth—O most excellent and rare enterprise—Thought rather divine than human!

To us this prospect is realized by happy experience: how thankful ought we to be in enjoying it! how zealous should we be to secure it to ourselves and to our latest posterity! how anxious should we be to extend its example, its influence, and its advantages to the remotest regions of the habitable globe!

CHAPTER X.
Of Government.

We have already seen, that society may exist without civil government: indeed, if we would think and reason with accuracy on the subject, we shall necessarily be led to consider, in our contemplation, the formation of society as preexistent to the formation of those regulations, by which the society mean, that their conduct should be influenced and directed.

It is necessary that this distinction be plainly made, and clearly understood. It has been controverted by some: an inattention to it has produced, in the minds of others, practical inferences, which are both ill founded and dangerous. A change of government has been viewed as a desperate event, as an object of the most terrifick aspect; because it has been thought, that government could not be changed, without tearing up the very foundations of the social establishment. It has been supposed, that, in a transition from one government to another, the body making it must be dissolved; that every thing must be reduced to a state of nature; and that the rights and obligations of the society must be lost and discharged.

In many parts of the world, indeed, the idea of revolutions in government is, by a mournful and indissoluble association, connected with the idea of wars, and of all the calamities attendant on wars.[a] But joyful experience teaches us, in the United States, to view them in a very different and much more agreeable light—to consider them only as progressive steps in improving the knowledge of government, and increasing the happiness of society and mankind.

It is true, that institutions, which depend on the form or structure of the preceding government, must fall, when that form or structure is taken away. But establishments, whose foundations rest on the society itself,

a. Changes in course of government are looked at as uncouth motions of the celestial bodies, portending judgments or dissolution. Bac. on Gov. 7.

cannot be overturned by any alteration of the government, which the society can make. The acts and compacts which form the political association, are very different from those by which the associated body, when formed, may choose to maintain and regulate itself.

But though, without government, society may exist; yet it must be admitted, that, without government, society, in the present state of things, cannot flourish; far less, can it reach perfection. In a state of nature, it is true, any one individual may act uncontrolled by others; but it is equally true, that, in such a state, every other individual may act uncontrolled by him. Amidst this universal independence, the dissensions and animosities between the interfering members of the society, would be numerous and ungovernable. The consequence would be, that each member, in such a natural state, would enjoy less liberty, and suffer more interruption and inconvenience, than he would under a civil government.

Again; it is true, that, by the fundamental laws of society, obedience is stipulated on the part of the members, and protection is stipulated on the part of the body. But the modes, and extent, and particular objects of this obedience, and the modes, and extent, and particular instruments of this protection, are all equally unascertained. Precision and certainty in these points, so important to the peace and order of society, can be obtained only by a system of government. In addition, therefore, to the rules, which necessarily enter into the formation of society, other rules—those, which compose government—have been gradually introduced into every community, which has attained any considerable degree of improvement.[b]

How the different governments, which have successively appeared in the different parts of the world, began; on what principles they were originally formed; what share in their formation should be ascribed to stratagem, what to force, what to necessity, what to conveniency, what to wisdom, what to patriotism—all these are questions, which would employ, and the answers to which would gratify curiosity: some of them would convey much pleasure and instruction: but, with regard to many of them, complete information cannot be obtained; and if it could, it would not be accompanied with a proportioned degree of satisfaction. The origin of

b. Sine imperio, nec domus ulla, nec civitas, nec gens, nec hominum universum genus stare, nec rerum natura omnis, nec ipse mundus potest.[1] Cic. de leg. l. 3. c. 1.

1. Without authority neither any house, nor state, nor nation, nor the whole human race can stand, nor physical nature, nor the very universe itself.

many governments is obliterated or obscured by the impressions of all-corroding time. Some exceptions, however, there are; and of those exceptions, some deserve to be considered with careful and patient attention: they contain matter of wise example, or of prudent caution.

From ancient history I select one instance, the particulars of which are transmitted to us with a considerable degree of accuracy and minuteness. The Medes originally were included in the great empire of Assyria: from this empire they separated themselves by a successful revolt. After their separation, they continued, for some time, without any established form of government—in a state of self command, as the expression used by Herodotus[2] denotes. Of this state, they soon began to experience the infelicities: injuries were committed; controversies arose; dissensions took place: there was no settled or acknowledged authority to repress animosities, to determine disputes, or to order reparation for injustice that had been done.

One man there was, whose integrity and wisdom taught his countrymen to revere him, and to apply to him as the judge and arbiter of their differences. This was the famed Dejoces.[3] His decisions were equitable; but the execution of them depended on the pleasure of the parties, against whom they were made. Influence, however, and reputation supplied, in some tolerable degree, the place of regular and established authority; and the Medes confided and acquiesced in the prudence and justice of Dejoces.

Stimulated by latent principles of ambition, or directed by the admonitions of sagacity, Dejoces became dissatisfied with the situation, in which he stood. Perhaps he wisely foresaw, that unless he possessed authority at the same time that he deserved confidence, he could not be long safe in his own person, or useful to his fellow citizens. Another supposition there is likewise reason to make. Perhaps his ambition suggested to him, that the influence, which he already enjoyed, might, by an easy and a certain transition, be converted into power; that the voluntary acquiescence under his awards might be improved into implicit submission to his edicts; and that the respected judge might become the splendid monarch of Media.

2. Herodotus (484–425 B.C.) was a Greek historian. He is generally considered to be the first historian.

3. Likely refers to Deioces, uniter of the seven Median tribes, who was elected to be their king in 665 B.C.

Whatever his motives were, we know what was their result. He would not exercise any longer the confidential office of administering justice among the Medes; but had recourse to a retired life, under the pretence, that he could no longer support the excessive fatigue of the business of others; and that it was now become absolutely necessary for him to devote his attention to the management of his own affairs.

The consequence, which was naturally expected, naturally followed. The disorders, which the character and influence of Dejoces had repressed, returned, upon his retirement, with redoubled violence; and increased to such a degree, that the Medes were obliged to convene a general council of the nation, in order to deliberate upon the proper methods of finding and applying a remedy to the publick miseries and dissensions. The expedient adopted by the general council was, that a king should be elected, who should have power to restrain the rage of violence, and to make laws for the government of the nation. When it was determined to elect a king; there was no hesitation concerning the person, on whom the election should fall. With common consent, Dejoces was elected king of Media.[c]

With regard to the first establishment of civil government, it is probable, that the maintenance of publick peace and the promotion of publick happiness were the ends originally proposed by the people, in many instances. It is certain, that, in every instance, they were the ends, which by all ought to have been proposed and prosecuted too. One thing is unquestionable, and this, indeed, is all that is necessary to be known upon the subject; that every man must have had his own advantage and happiness in view; and must have endeavoured, as much as possible, to preserve his natural liberty. This is founded on the constitution of mankind; and this invincible principle would operate with greater force on the first formation of government, than after it was fully established; for under established governments, the natural love of liberty is frequently counteracted by education, by prejudice, by interest, by ambition. Of this melancholy, but undeniable truth, the history of man and of government produces too many striking examples. The degeneracy of government, and the consequent degeneracy of the citizens, have been fruitful topicks of contemplation and complaint, in almost every age and country.

c. Rol. An. Hist. b. 3. c. 3. 3. Gog. Or. Laws. 8. 9.

It is a question rather of curiosity than of utility—what kind of government is the most ancient? The different kinds have different advocates in favour of their antiquity; and their different hypotheses are supported with much ingenuity and zeal. The ardour of polemical disquisition, however, upon this subject, might have been greatly softened by the obvious reflection, that it by no means follows, that the kind of government which is oldest, is the kind which is also best. That form which was most simple, and not that form which was most perfect, would, in all probability, attract the attention, and determine the choice, of a rude and inexperienced society. In many parts of the world, the science of government is even yet in a state of nonage: shall its first be deemed its most finished movements?

The most simple form of government is that of monarchy: reasonable conjecture, therefore, would lead us to presume, that this form is the most ancient. This presumption of reason is confirmed by the information of history, both sacred and profane. The most ancient nations mentioned by the inspired historian and legislator of the Hebrews—for instance, the Egyptians, the Babylonians, the Assyrians—were all under the government of kings. Homer, the true original of his own Ulysses, who knew societies as well as men, seems scarcely to have seen, or heard, or even imagined any other species of government, than that which was monarchical. The most famous states of antiquity, Athens and Rome, were monarchies at their first commencement. The history of China is said to reach a period of antiquity very remote; at the remotest period, monarchy was the form of government which prevailed in it.

But though monarchy is the most ancient form of government; monarchs were, at first, neither hereditary nor despotick. We have seen that Dejoces, the first monarch of Media, became a king by election. Crowns, in general, were originally elective. True, indeed, it is, that, from causes obvious and easy to be assigned, the office, which, at first, was elective, became afterwards hereditary.

The dominions of the first monarchs were far from being extensive. In the days of Abraham, there were five kings in the single Valley of Sodom. The kings defeated by Joshua in Palestine were thirty one in number. The different provinces, which, at present, compose the empire of China, formed anciently so many separate monarchies. "The ancient

Britons," says Bacon in his Discourses on Government,[d] "had many chiefs in a little room; whom the Romans called kings, for the greater renown of their empire." For many ages, Greece was divided into a vast number of small and inconsiderable kingdoms.

The authority of those ancient monarchs was not more extensive than their dominions. It appears from many monuments, that, by the constitutions of the first kingdoms, the people had a great share in the government. Affairs of importance were debated and determined in the general assemblies of the nations.[e] "De majoribus omnes consultant,"[4] says Tacitus[f] of the ancient Germans. The first kings were, indeed, properly no more than judges, who had no power to inflict punishments by their own authority, and without the consent of the people. Hence the poet Hesiod[5] says, that the muses give kings the art of persuasion, that they may engage the people to submit to their decisions, for which end they were placed in that exalted station.[g] "Principes jura per pagos vicosque reddunt," says Tacitus in the treatise just now cited.[h]

"In my opinion," says Cicero,[i] "it was not among the Medes only, as Herodotus informs us; but it was among our own ancestors likewise, that kings of good character were chosen, in order that the administration of justice might be enjoyed. For when the poor were oppressed by the rich, they fled for relief to some one, preeminent in virtue, who would protect the weak from injustice, and would dispense equal law to the high and to the low. If they could obtain this from the mouth of one just and good man, they were satisfied; but, as they were often disappointed in this reasonable demand, they had, afterwards, recourse to general law, which spoke one language to all."

The course of things in other nations, was similar to that, which took place in Media and in Rome. "At first," says the excellent Hooker, "when some kind of regiment was once approved; it may be, that nothing was,

d. P. 1.

e. 1. Gog. Or. Laws. 15.

4. On larger matters all consult.

f. De mor. Germ. c. 11.

5. Hesiod was a Greek poet who lived around 700 B.C.

g. Gro. 70. n. 53.

h. De mor. Germ. c. 12. "The leaders administer law through the cantons and villages."

i. De off. l. 2. c. 12.

then, further thought upon for the manner of governing; but all permitted to their wisdom and discretion, which were to rule; till, by experience, they found this, for all parts, very inconvenient, so as the thing, which they had devised for a remedy, did but increase the sore, which it should have cured. They saw, that to live by one man's will, became the cause of all men's misery. This constrained them to come unto law, wherein all men might see their duties beforehand, and know the penalties of transgressing them."[j]

This progress of government and law, we find remarkably exemplified in the history of Greece. At first, all the Grecian cities were under the government of kings, not arbitrarily, but agreeably to the laws and customs of the country. He was esteemed the best king, who was the justest and strictest observer of the laws, and who never departed from the established customs of his kingdom. This explains the true meaning of Homer, (who painted to the life) when he denominated kings, "men, who distribute justice." These small monarchies, thus limited, subsisted for a long time, as, for instance, that of the Lacedemonians. But, afterwards, some kings began to abuse their power, and to govern according to their pleasure, rather than according to the laws. This the Greeks could not endure; and, therefore, abolished the monarchical form of government, and established other kinds of government in its place.

To find out the best kind of government has been long the celebrated problem in the political world. In order to furnish some imperfect materials for the solution of this very important inquiry, let us consider and investigate the qualities and principles, by which a good government ought to be characterized.

Men, frail and imperfect as they are, must be the instruments, by which government is administered. But, in order to guard against the consequences of their frailties and imperfections, one effort, in the contrivance of the political system, is, to provide, that, for the offices and the departments of the state, the wisest and the best of her citizens be elected. A second effort is, to communicate to the operations of government as great a share as possible of the good, and as small a share as possible of the bad propensities of our nature. A third effort is, to increase, encourage, and strengthen those good propensities, and to lessen, discourage, and correct those bad ones. A fourth effort is, to introduce, into the very form of

j. Hooker. b. 1. p. 18.

government, such particular checks and controls, as to make it advantageous even for bad men to act for the publick good. When these efforts are successful, and happily united; then is accomplished what we truly mean, when we speak of a government of laws, and not of men; then every man does homage to the laws; the very least as feeling their care; the greatest as not exempted from their power.

What are the qualities in government, necessary for producing laws, properly designed, properly framed, and properly enforced? Goodness should inspire and animate the intention: wisdom should direct and arrange the means: power should render the means efficacious, by carrying the laws vigorously into execution. The more all those qualities prevail in any government, the nearer does that government approach to its perfection. In some kinds of government, one of the qualities is eminent in undue proportion: in others, another: but the best are those, in which all the qualities are happily blended in their operation, and diffuse, through the whole society, their mingled and tempered influence.

We have now taken a general view of government, and have traced the qualities, which should operate through the whole: let us descend to a more minute examination of its different parts: let us view the structure and properties of each, considered by itself; and also the mutual dependencies and controls, which each ought to possess, and to which each ought to be subject, when considered relatively to others.

The powers of government are usually, and with propriety, arranged under three great divisions; the legislative authority, the executive authority, and the judicial authority. Let us consider each, as its greatness deserves to be considered.

The first remark, which I shall make on the structure of the legislative power, is, that it ought to be *divided.* In support of this position, which is, indeed, one of the most important in both the theory and the practice of government, many arguments may be advanced. Let me introduce one, by the declaration of an admired judge, whose manly candour must charm every generous mind. "It is the glory and happiness of our excellent constitution, that, to prevent any injustice, no man is concluded by the first judgment; but that, if he apprehends himself to be aggrieved, he has another court, to which he may resort for relief. For my part, I can say, that it is a consideration of great comfort to me, that, if I do err, my judgment is not conclusive to the party; but my mistake may be rectified, and so no injustice be done."[k] Is less skill required—should less caution be observed—in making laws, than in explaining them? Are mistakes less likely to happen—are they less dangerous—is it less necessary to prevent or rectify them, in the former case, than in the latter? Which is most necessary? to preserve the streams, or to preserve the fountain from becoming turbid?

But the danger arising from mistakes and inaccuracies is not the only nor the greatest one, to be apprehended from a single body possessed of legislative power. It is impossible to restrain it in its operations. No other power in government can arrest the proceedings of that which makes the laws. Let us suppose, that this single body, in a lucky moment, should pass a law to restrain itself: in the next moment, an unlucky one, it might repeal the restraining law. Any mounds, which it might raise to confine itself, would still be within the sphere of its own motion; and whatever force should impel it, would necessarily impel those mounds along with it. To stop and to check, as well as to produce motion in this political globe, we must possess—what Archimedes wanted—another globe to stand upon.

A single legislature is calculated to unite in it all the pernicious qualities of the different extremes of bad government. It produces general weakness, inactivity, and confusion; and these are intermixed with sudden and violent fits of despotism, injustice, and cruelty.

But I will take the subject a little deeper: it is of the utmost consequence that it be fully discussed. In private life, how often and how fatally are we seduced, by our passions and by our prejudices, from those paths, which would lead us to our true interests? But are passions and prejudices less frequently to be found in publick bodies, than in individuals? Are they less powerful? Do they not become inflamed by mutual imitation and example? Will they not, if unrestrained, produce the most mischievous effects? Ye, who are versed in the science of human nature—ye, who have viewed it in the faithful mirrour of history—tell us, for you know, what answer should be given to these questions. Cannot you point out instances, in which the people have become the miserable victims of passions, operating upon their government without restraint? Cannot you point out other

k. Str. 565.

instances, in which the violence of one part of the government has been happily controlled by the constitutional interposition of another part?

There is not in the whole science of politicks a more solid or a more important maxim than this—that of all governments, those are the best, which, by the natural effect of their constitutions, are frequently renewed or drawn back to their first principles. When a single legislature is determined to depart from the principles of the constitution—and its incontrollable power may prompt the determination—there is no constitutional authority to arrest its progress. It may proceed, by long and hasty strides, in violating the constitution, till nothing but a revolution can stop its career. Far different will the case be, when the legislature consists of two branches. If one of them should depart, or attempt to depart from the principles of the constitution; it will be drawn back by the other. The very apprehension of the event will prevent the departure or the attempt.

In all the most celebrated governments both of ancient and of modern times, we find the legislatures composed of distinct bodies. Such was that formed at Athens by Solon. Such was that instituted at Sparta by Lycurgus. Such was that, which so long flourished at Rome. In our sister states, their legislatures consist of distinct bodies of men. Similar, upon this subject, is the constitution of the United States. And we can now happily say, that Pennsylvania no longer exhibits an instance to the contrary—that she no longer holds out to view a beacon to be avoided, instead of an example deserving imitation.

Thus much I have thought it necessary to say concerning that power of government, which is intrusted with the making of the laws. Let us next consider those powers, which are intrusted with their execution, and with the administration of justice under their authority. Wise and good laws are indeed essential; but though they are essential, they are so only as means. If we stop here, all that we have done is nugatory and abortive. The end is still unattained; and that can be attained only when the laws are vigorously and steadily executed; and when the administration of justice under them is unbiassed and enlightened.

Indeed, if I mistake not, an inferiour proportion of attention, in this and in most of our sister states, has been employed about these important parts of the political system. Laws have abounded: their multiplicity has been often a grievance: but their weak and irregular execution, and the unwise and unstable administration of justice, have been subjects of general and well grounded complaint.

Habits contracted before the late revolution of the United States, operate, in the same manner, since that time, though very material alterations may have taken place in the objects of their operations.

Before that period, the executive and the judicial powers of government were placed neither in the people, nor in those, who professed to receive them under the authority of the people. They were derived from a different and a foreign source: they were regulated by foreign maxims: they were directed to foreign purposes. Need we be surprised, that they were objects of aversion and distrust? Need we be surprised, that every occasion was seized for lessening their influence, and weakening their energy? On the other hand, our assemblies were chosen by ourselves: they were the guardians of our rights, the objects of our confidence, and the anchor of our political hopes. Every power, which could be placed in them, was thought to be safely placed: every extension of that power was considered as an extension of our own security.

At the revolution, the same fond predilection, and the same jealous dislike, existed and prevailed. The executive and the judicial as well as the legislative authority was now the child of the people; but, to the two former, the people behaved like stepmothers. The legislature was still discriminated by excessive partiality; and into its lap, every good and precious gift was profusely thrown.

Even at this time, people can scarcely devest themselves of those opposite prepossessions: they still hold, when, perhaps, they perceive it not, the language, which expresses them. In observations on this subject, we hear the legislature mentioned as the *people's representatives*. The distinction, intimated by concealed implication, though probably, not avowed upon reflection, is, that the executive and judicial powers are not connected with the people by a relation so strong, or near, or dear.

But it is high time that we should chastise our prejudices; and that we should look upon the different parts of government with a just and impartial eye. The executive and judicial powers are now drawn from the same source, are now animated by the same principles, and are now directed to the same ends, with the legislative authority: they who execute, and they who administer the laws, are as much the servants, and therefore as much the friends of the people, as they who make them. The character, and interest, and glory of the two former are as intimately and as necessarily connected with the happiness and prosperity of the people, as the character, and interest, and glory of the latter are. Besides; the execution of the law, and the administration of justice under the law, bring it home to the fortunes, and farms, and houses, and business of the people. Ought the executive or the judicial magistrates, then, to be considered as foreigners? ought they to be treated with a chilling indifference?

Having shown, that, on the principles of our new system, jealousies and prejudices concerning the executive and judicial departments ought to be discarded; let us now consider, in what manner those departments should be formed and constituted. We begin with the executive department.

The executive as well as the legislative power ought to be restrained. But there is a remarkable contrast between the proper modes of restraining them. The legislature, in order to be restrained, must be *divided.* The executive power, in order to be restrained, should be *one.* Unity in this department is at once a proof and an ingredient of safety and of energy in the operations of government.

The restraints on the legislative authority must, from its nature, be chiefly internal; that is, they must proceed from some part or division of itself. But the restraints on the executive power are external. These restraints are applied with greatest certainty, and with greatest efficacy, when the object of restraint is clearly ascertained. This is best done, when one object only, distinguished and responsible, is conspicuously held up to the view and examination of the publick.

In planning, forming, and arranging laws, deliberation is always becoming, and always useful. But in the active scenes of government, there are emergencies, in which the man, as, in other cases, the woman, who deliberates, is lost. Secrecy may be equally necessary as despatch. But, can either secrecy or despatch be expected, when, to every enterprise, and to every step in the progress of every enterprise, mutual communication, mutual consultation, and mutual agreement among men, perhaps of discordant views, of discordant tempers, and of discordant interests, are indispensably necessary? How much time will be consumed! and when it is consumed; how little business will be done! When the time is elapsed; when the business is unfinished; when the state is in distress, perhaps, on the verge of destruction; on whom shall we fix the blame? whom shall we select as the object of punishment?

Ruinous dissensions are not the only inconveniences resulting from a numerous executive body: it is equally liable to pernicious and intriguing combinations. When the first take place, the publick business is not done at all: when the last take place, it is done for mean or malicious purposes.

The appointment to offices is an important part of the executive authority. Much of the ease, much of the reputation, much of the energy, and much of the safety of the nation depends on judicious and impartial appointments. But are impartiality and fine discernment likely to predominate in a numerous executive body? In proportion to their own number, will be the number of their friends, favourites, and dependents. An office is to be filled. A person nearly connected, by some of the foregoing ties, with one of those who are to vote in filling it, is named as a candidate. His patron is under no necessity to take any part, particularly responsible, in his appointment. He may appear even cold and indifferent on the occasion. But he possesses an advantage, the value of which is well understood in bodies of this kind. Every member, who gives, on his account, a vote for his friend, will expect the return of a similar favour on the first convenient opportunity. In this manner, a reciprocal intercourse of partiality, of interestedness, of favouritism, perhaps of venality, is established; and, in no particular instance, is there a practicability of tracing the poison to its source. Ignorant, vicious, and prostituted characters are introduced into office; and some of those, who voted, and procured others to vote for them, are the first and loudest in expressing their astonishment, that the door of admission was ever opened to men of their infamous description. The suffering people are thus wounded and buffeted, like Homer's Ajax, in the dark; and have not even the melancholy satisfaction of knowing by whom the blows are given. Those who possess talents and virtues, which would reflect honour on office, will be reluctant to appear as candidates for appointments. If they should be brought into view; what weight will virtue, merit, and talents for office have, in a balance held and poized by partiality, intrigue, and chicane?

The person who nominates or makes appointments to offices, should be known. His own office, his own character, his own fortune should be responsible. He should be alike unfettered and unsheltered by counsellors.

No constitutional stalking horse should be provided for him to conceal his turnings and windings, when they are too dark and too crooked to be exposed to publick view. Instead of the dishonourable intercourse, which I have already mentioned, an intercourse of a very different kind should be established—an intercourse of integrity and discernment on the part of the magistrate who appoints, and of gratitude and confidence on the part of the people, who will receive the benefit from his appointments. Appointments made and sanctioned in this highly respectable manner, will, like a fragrant and beneficent atmosphere, diffuse sweetness and gladness around those, to whom they are given. Modest merit will be beckoned to, in order to encourage her to come forward. Barefaced impudence and unprincipled intrigue will receive repulse and disappointment, deservedly their portion.

If a contrary conduct should unfortunately be observed—and, unfortunately, a contrary conduct will be sometimes observed—it will be known by the citizens, whose conduct it is: and, if they are not seized with the only distemper incurable in a free government—the distemper of being wanting to themselves—they will, at the next general election, take effectual care, that the person, who has once shamefully abused their generous and unsuspecting confidence, shall not have it in his power to insult and injure them a second time, by the repetition of such an ungrateful return.

The observations, which I have made on the appointments to offices, will apply, with little variation, to the other powers and duties of the executive department.

When more than one person are engaged in the same enterprise, a difference of opinion, concerning the object or the means, is no improbable contingency. When the difference takes place among those of equal authority, where is the umpire to decide? A prevailing and undecided difference in sentiment, is the inauspicious parent of bitter and determined opposition in conduct. In business, which is merely deliberative, these differences may be concluded by a resolution or a vote: for, when a vote is taken, the majority is ascertained, and the business is done. But, in publick enterprises, the case is far otherwise. To the success of the enterprise, the zealous cooperation of the dissenting minority is no less indispensable, than that of the consenting majority. Is such cooperation to be expected? Would it be safe to calculate the motions of government upon an expectation, indeed, so extremely improbable? If we build on such a sandy foundation, will not the superstructure tumble in pieces, and bury, under its ruins, the dearest interests of the state?

If, on the other hand, the executive power of government is placed in the hands of one person, who is to direct all the subordinate officers of that department; is there not reason to expect, in his plans and conduct, promptitude, activity, firmness, consistency, and energy? These mark the proceedings of one man; at least, of one man, fit to be intrusted with the management of important publick affairs. May we not indulge, at least in imagination, the pleasing prospect, that this one man—the choice of those who are deeply interested in a proper choice—will be a man distinguished by his abilities? Will not those abilities pervade every part of his administration? Will they not diffuse their animating influence over the most distant corners of the nation?—May we not further indulge the pleased imagination in the agreeable prospect—in one instance, at least, it is realized by experience—that the publick choice will fall upon a man, in whom distinguished abilities will be joined and sublimed by distinguished virtues—on a man, who, on the necessary foundation of a private character, decent, respected, and dignified, will build all the great, and honest, and candid qualities, from which an elevated station derives its most beautiful lustre, and publick life its most splendid embellishments?

If these pleasing prospects should unhappily be blasted by a preposterous choice, and by the preposterous conduct of the magistrate chosen; still, at the next election, an effectual remedy can be applied to the mischief: and this remedy will be applied effectually, unless, as has been already intimated, the citizens should be wanting to themselves. For a people wanting to themselves, there is indeed no remedy in the political dispensary. From their power there is no appeal: to their errour there is no superiour principle of correction.

The third great division of the powers of government is the judicial authority. It is sometimes considered as a branch of the executive power; but inaccurately. When the decisions of courts of justice are made, they must, it is true, be executed; but the power of executing them is ministerial, not judicial. The judicial authority consists in applying, according to the principles of right and justice, the constitution and laws to facts and transactions in cases, in which the manner or principles of this application are disputed by the parties interested in them.

The very existence of a dispute is presumptive evidence, that the application is not altogether without intricacy or difficulty. When intricacy or difficulty takes place in the application, it cannot be properly made without the possession of skill in the science of jurisprudence, and the most unbiassed behaviour in the exercise of that skill. Clear heads, therefore, and honest hearts are essential to good judges.

As all controversies in the community respecting life, liberty, reputation, and property, must be influenced by their judgments; and as their judgments ought to be calculated not only to do justice, but also to give general satisfaction, to inspire general confidence, and to take even from disappointed suiters—for in every cause disappointment must fall on one side—the slightest pretence of complaint;[l] they ought to be placed in such a situation, as not only to be, but likewise to appear superiour to every extrinsick circumstance, which can be supposed to have the smallest operation upon their understandings or their inclinations. In their salaries and in their offices, they ought to be completely independent: in other words, they should be removed from the most distant apprehension of being affected, in their judicial character and capacity, by any thing, except their own behaviour and its consequences.

"We are," says a very sensible writer on political subjects, "to look upon all the vast apparatus of government as having ultimately no other object or purpose, but the distribution of justice. All men are sensible of the necessity of justice to maintain peace and order; and all men are sensible of the necessity of peace and order for the maintenance of society."[m] "The pure, and wise, and equal administration of the laws," says Mr. Paley;[n] "forms the first end and blessing of social union." But how can society be maintained—how can a state expect to enjoy peace and order, unless the administration of justice is able and impartial? Can such an administration be expected, unless the judges can maintain dignified and independent characters? Can dignity and independence be expected from judges, who are liable to be tossed about by every veering gale of politicks, and who can be secured from destruction, only by dexterously

l. Etiam quos contra statuit, aequos placatosque demisit;[6] says Cicero of Brutus.

m. 1. Hume's Ess. 35.

n. 2. Paley. 285.

6. Even those against whom he made decisions, he sent away unruffled and placated.

swimming along with every successive tide of party? Is there not reason to fear, that in such a situation, the decisions of courts would cease to be the voice of law and justice, and would become the echo of faction and violence?

This is a subject, which most intimately concerns every one, who sets the least value upon his own safety, or that of his posterity. Our fortunes, our lives, our reputations, and our liberties are all liable to be affected by the judgments of the courts. How distressing and melancholy must the reflection be, that, while judges hold their salaries only at pleasure, and their commissions only for the term of a few years, our liberties, our fortunes, our reputations, and our lives may be sacrificed to a party, though we have done nothing to forfeit them to the law.

Though the foregoing great powers—legislative, executive, and judicial—are all necessary to a good government; yet it is of the last importance, that each of them be preserved distinct, and unmingled, in the exercise of its separate powers, with either or with both of the others. Here every degree of confusion in the plan will produce a corresponding degree of interference, opposition, combination, or perplexity in its execution.

Let us suppose the legislative and executive powers united in the same person: can liberty or security be expected? No. In the character of executive magistrate, he receives all the power, which, in the character of legislator, he thinks proper to give. May he not, then—and, if he may, will he not then—such is the undefined and undefinable charm of power—enact tyrannical laws to furnish himself with an opportunity of executing them in a tyrannical manner? Liberty and security in government depend not on the limits, which the rulers may please to assign to the exercise of their own powers, but on the boundaries, within which their powers are circumscribed by the constitution. He who is continually exposed to the lash of oppression, as well as he who is immediately under it, cannot be denominated free.

Let us suppose the legislative and judicial powers united: what would be the consequence? The lives, liberties, and properties of the citizens would be committed to arbitrary judges, whose decisions would, in effect, be dictated by their own private opinions, and would not be governed by any fixed or known principles of law. For though, as judges, they might be bound to observe those principles; yet, Proteus-like, they might immediately assume the form of legislators; and, in that shape, they might escape from every fetter and obligation of law.

Let us suppose a union of the executive and judicial powers: this union might soon be an overbalance for the legislative authority; or, if that expression is too strong, it might certainly prevent or destroy the proper and legitimate influences of that authority. The laws might be eluded or perverted; and the execution of them might become, in the hands of the magistrate or his minions, an engine of tyranny and injustice. Where and how is redress to be obtained? From the legislature? They make new laws to correct the mischief: but these new laws are to be executed by the same persons, and will be executed in the same manner as the former. Will redress be found in the courts of justice? In those courts, the very persons who were guilty of the oppression in their administration, sit as judges, to give a sanction to that oppression by their decrees. Nothing is more to be dreaded than maxims of law and reasons of state blended together by judicial authority. Among all the terrible instruments of arbitrary power, decisions of courts, whetted and guided and impelled by considerations of policy, cut with the keenest edge, and inflict the deepest and most deadly wounds.

Let us suppose, in the last place, all the three powers of government to be united in the same man or body of men: miserable indeed would this case be! This extent of misery, however, at least in Europe, is seldom experienced; because the power of judging is generally exercised by a separate department. But in Turkey, where all the three powers are joined in the Sultan's person, his slaves are crushed under the insupportable burthen of oppression and tyranny. In some of the governments of Italy, these three powers are also united. In such there is less liberty than in the European monarchies: and their governments are obliged to have recourse to as violent measures to support themselves, as even that of the Turks. At Venice, where an aristocracy, jealous and tyrannical, absorbs every power, behold the state inquisitors, and the lion's mouth, at all times open for the secret accusations of spies and informers. In what a situation must the wretched subjects be under such a government, all the powers of which are leagued, in awful combination, against the peace and tranquillity of their minds!

But further; each of the great powers of government should be independent as well as distinct. When we say this; it is necessary—since the subject is of primary consequence in the science of government—that our meaning be fully understood, and accurately defined. For this position, like every other, has its limitations; and it is important to ascertain them.

The independency of each power consists in this, that its proceedings, and the motives, views, and principles, which produce those proceedings, should be free from the remotest influence, direct or indirect, of either of the other two powers. But further than this, the independency of each power ought not to extend. Its proceedings should be formed without restraint, but, when they are once formed, they should be subject to control.

We are now led to discover, that between these three great powers of government, there ought to be a mutual dependency, as well as a mutual independency. We have described their independency: let us now describe their dependency. It consists in this, that the proceedings of each, when they come forth into action and are ready to affect the whole, are liable to be examined and controlled by one or both of the others.

So far are these different qualities of mutual dependency and mutual independency from opposing or destroying each other, that, without one, the other could not exist. Whenever the independency of one, or more than one, is lost, the mutual dependency of the others is, that moment, lost likewise: it is changed into a constant dependency of that one part on two; or, as the case may be, of those two parts on one.

An example may illustrate the foregoing propositions. They cannot be explained too fully. The congress is intrusted with the legislative power of the United States. In preparing bills, in debating them, in passing them, in refusing to pass them, their resolutions and proceedings should be uncontrolled and uninfluenced. Here is the independency of the legislative power. But after the proceedings of the legislature are finished, so far as they depend on it, they are sent to be examined, and are subjected to a given degree of control by the head of the executive department. Here is the dependency of the legislative power. It is subject also to another given degree of control by the judiciary department, whenever the laws, though in fact passed, are found to be contradictory to the constitution.

The salutary consequence of the mutual dependency of the great powers of government is, that if one part should, at any time, usurp more power than the constitution gives, or make an improper use of its constitutional power, one or both of the other parts may correct the abuse, or may check the usurpation.

The total disjunction of these powers would, in the end, produce that very union, against which it seems to provide. The legislature would soon become tyrannical, and would assume to itself the rights of the executive and judicial powers.

The important conclusion to be drawn from the premises, which we have established, is, that, in government, the perfection of the whole depends on the balance of the parts, and the balance of the parts consists in the independent exercise of their separate powers, and, when their powers are separately exercised, then in their mutual influence and operation on one another. Each part acts and is acted upon, supports and is supported, regulates and is regulated by the rest.

It might be supposed, that these powers, thus mutually checked and controlled, would remain in a state of inaction. But there is a necessity for movement in human affairs; and these powers are forced to move, though still to move in concert. They move, indeed, in a line of direction somewhat different from that, which each, acting by itself, would have taken; but, at the same time, in a line partaking of the natural direction of each, and formed out of the natural directions of the whole—the true line of publick liberty and happiness.

The works of human invention are progressive; and frequently are not completed, till after a slow and lengthened series of gradual improvements, remotely distant from one another both in place and in time. To the theory and practice of government, this observation is applicable with peculiar justness and peculiar force. In this science, few opportunities have been given to the human mind of indulging itself in easy and unrestrained investigation: still fewer opportunities have offered of verifying and correcting investigation by experiment. An age—a succession of ages—elapses, before a system of jurisprudence rises from its first rude beginnings. When we have made a little progress, and look forward; a few eminences in prospect are fondly supposed to form the greatest elevation, which we shall be obliged to ascend. But these, once gained, disclose, behind them, new and superiour degrees of excellence, yet unattained. In beginning and continuing the pursuit of the arduous paths, through which this science leads us, we may well adopt the language of the philosophick poet;

So pleas'd, at first, the tow'ring Alps we try,
Mount o'er the vales, and seem to tread the sky.
Th' eternal snows appear already past,
And the first clouds and mountains seem the last:
But these attain'd, we tremble to survey
The growing labours of the lengthen'd way;
Th' increasing prospect tires our wand'ring eyes,
Hills peep o'er hills, and Alps on Alps arise!

If the discoveries in government are difficult and slow, how much more arduous must it be to obtain, in practice, the advantage of those discoveries, after they have been made! Of some governments, the foundation has been laid in necessity; of others, in fraud; of others, in force; of how few, in deliberate and discerning choice! If, in their commencements, they have been so unpropitious to the principles of freedom, and to the means of happiness; shall we wonder, that, in their progress, they have been equally unfavourable to advances in virtue and excellence.

Let us ransack the records of history: in all our researches, how few fair instances shall we be able to find, in which a government has been formed, whose end has been the happiness of those, for whom it was designed! how few fair instances shall we find, in which such a government has been administered with a steady direction towards that end!

To all these circumstances, we must add others, which show still further the numerous and the strong obstacles that lie in the way of improvement in jurisprudence. Government, founded in improper principles, and directed to improper objects, has a natural and powerful bias, both upon those who rule, and upon those who are ruled. Its bias upon the first will occasion no surprise: its bias upon the second, however surprising, is not, perhaps, less efficacious. How often have the vassals of absolute monarchy conceived their own dignity and happiness to be involved in the glory of their monarch! How often have they, in pursuit of projects for the accomplishment of his capricious desires, discovered a degree of courage and enthusiasm, worthy of a nobler object and a better cause! If such is the effect produced upon their conduct; will an inferiour effect be produced on their sentiments? Hence the principles of despotism become the principles of a whole nation, blinded and degraded by its pernicious influence.

But let us suppose that the light of liberty, at last, breaks in upon them; how slow must its progress; how feeble, for a long time, must its energy be! Power, splendour, influence, prejudice, fashion, all stand arranged in opposition to its operations.

Let us enlarge the sphere of our conjecture further, and suppose, that, notwithstanding all the efforts of opposition, the principles and doctrines of freedom are successfully propagated and established; yet how many and how formidable are the barriers, that remain to be surmounted, before those principles and doctrines can be carried successfully into practice? The friends of freedom, we shall suppose, are unanimous in their sentiments; does the same unanimity prevail with regard to their measures? does it prevail still farther with regard to the time and manner of pursuing them? In all these particulars, is unanimity attended with discretion, on one hand, and with decision, on the other? A failure in one circumstance, is a failure in all. Have not centuries passed without a single auspicious juncture, in which all, conjoined and cooperating, could have succeeded?

When we revolve, when we compare, when we combine the remarks, which we have been now making; when we take a slight glance of others, which might be offered; we shall be at no loss to account for the slow and small progress, which, after a lapse of ages, has been made in the science and practice of government.

Among the ancient political writers, no more than three regular forms of government were known and allowed. The first is that, in which the supreme power is lodged in the hands of a single person. This they denominated a monarchy. The second is that, in which the supreme power is vested in a select assembly, the members of which either fill up by election the vacancies of their own body, or succeed to their places by inheritance, property, tenure of lands, or in respect of some personal right or qualification. To this they gave the appellation of aristocracy. The third is that, in which the supreme power remains with the people at large, and is exercised either collectively, or by representation. On this they bestowed the name of democracy.

To each of these simple forms, conveniences and inconveniences, good and bad qualities are attached. In a democracy, publick virtue and purity of intention are likely to be found; but its counsels are often improvident, and the execution of them as frequently weak. In an aristocracy, we expect wisdom formed by education and experience; but, on the other hand, we may expect jealousies and dissensions among the nobles, and oppression of the lower orders. In a monarchy, there are strength and vigour; but there is danger, that they will not be employed for the happiness and prosperity of the state. A democracy is best calculated to direct the end of the laws; an aristocracy, to direct the means of attaining that end; a monarchy, to carry those means into execution.

The ancients considered all other species of governments as either corruptions of these three simple forms, or as reducible to some one of them. They had no idea of combining all the three together, and of uniting the advantages resulting from each. Cicero,[o] indeed, seems to have indulged a fond speculative opinion, that a government formed of the three kinds, properly blended and tempered, would, of all, be the best constituted. But this opinion was treated as visionary by his countrymen; and by Tacitus,[p] one of the wisest of them.

The example of Great Britain, however, has evinced that the sentiments of Cicero merited a very different reception; and that, if they did not point to the highest degree of excellence, they pointed, at least, to substantial improvement.

The government of that nation is composed of monarchical, aristocratical, and democratical parts. It possesses—we freely and with pleasure acknowledge—it possesses advantages over all that have preceded it: in dignity and in duration, in the maintenance of liberty, both publick and private, it has stood preeminent. But has it reached the lofty summit of perfection? In the race of excellence, has it gained a goal, which cannot be surpassed? Is it entitled, as, in less enlightened times, the columns of Hercules were thought to be, to the proud inscription of "ne plus ultra?"[7]

For the western world, new and rich discoveries in jurisprudence have been reserved. We have found that, in order to arrive, in this first of human sciences, at a point of perfection hitherto unattained, it is not necessary to intermix the different species of government. We have discovered, that one of them—the best and purest—that, in which the supreme power remains with the people at large, is capable of being formed, arranged,

o. Frag. de rep. l. 2

p. Ann. l. 4.

7. The pinnacle of excellence.

proportioned, and organized in such a manner, as to exclude the inconveniences, and to secure the advantages of all the three. On the basis of goodness, we erect the pillars of wisdom and strength.

The formation and establishment of constitutions are an immense practical improvement, introduced by the Americans into the science of government and jurisprudence. By the invigorating and overruling energy of a constitution, the force and direction of the government are preserved and regulated; and its movements are rendered uniform, strong, and safe.

It is proper that the nature and distinguishing characteristicks of a constitution should be clearly stated and explained. The sentiments and expressions, even of celebrated writers upon this subject, are uncommonly inaccurate and obscure.

By the term constitution, I mean that supreme law, made or ratified by those in whom the sovereign power of the state resides, which prescribes the manner, according to which the state wills that the government should be instituted and administered. From this constitution the government derives its power: by this constitution the power of government must be directed and controlled: of this constitution no alteration can be made by the government; because such an alteration would destroy the foundation of its own authority.

As to the people, however, in whom the sovereign power resides, the case is widely different, and stands upon widely different principles. From their authority the constitution originates: for their safety and felicity it is established: in their hands it is as clay in the hands of the potter: they have the right to mould, to preserve, to improve, to refine, and to finish it as they please. If so; can it be doubted, that they have the right likewise to change it? A majority of the society is sufficient for this purpose; and if there be nothing in the change, which can be considered as contrary to the act of original association, or to the intention of those who united under it; all are bound to conform to the resolution of the majority. If the act of original association be infringed, or the intention of those who united under it be violated; the minority are still obliged to suffer the majority to do as they think proper; but are not obliged to submit to the new government. They have a right to retire, to sell their lands, and to carry off their effects.

It may, perhaps, be asked—why is so much pains taken to prove and illustrate a principle, which, when detached from adventitious circumstances, and exhibited in its undisguised appearance, is so obvious, that few will be found disposed, in direct terms, to refuse their assent to its truth? Has it been denied, that those, who have a right to make, have a right to alter what they have made?

In England it has been denied: the successour of Sir William Blackstone in the Vinerian chair[8] expresses himself upon this subject in the following manner. "However the historical fact may be of a social contract, government ought to be, and is generally considered as founded on consent, tacit or express, on a real or *quasi* compact. This theory is a material basis of political rights; and, as a theoretical point, is not difficult to be maintained. For what gives any legislature a right to act, where no express consent can be shown? what, but immemorial usage? and what is the intrinsick force of immemorial usage, in establishing this fundamental or any other law, but that it is evidence of common acquiescence and consent? Not," adds he, "that such consent is subsequently revocable, at the will even of all the subjects of the state, for that would be making a part of the community equal in power to the whole originally, and superiour to the rulers thereof, after their establishment."[q] "I am far," says he, in another place, "from maintaining, that any consent, tacit or express, is essential to induce the duty of subjection from individuals born under an established government."[r] The evident consequence of these positions is, that though the great and animating principle of consent is considered as necessary to the first formation of government, yet it is by no means necessary in the successive periods of its establishment. The theory is admitted; but the continued right to practise according to that theory is denied. In other words, an established government is treated as superiour to those, or, at least, to others possessing all the rights of those, who originally formed its establishment.

In America, indeed, the doctrine, which I have taken some pains to prove and illustrate, has not been denied, in words; yet unwearied attempts have, on more occasions than one, been made to elude its operation, and to destroy its force.

Besides; it is of high import, that the great principles of society and government should not only be known and recognised, but also that they

8. I.e. Sir Robert Chambers (1737–1803).

q. El. Jur. (4to.) 22.

r. Id. 23.

should be so maturely considered and estimated, as, at last, to make a practical impression, deep and habitual, upon the publick mind. A proper regard to the original and inherent and continued power of the society to change its constitution, will prevent mistakes and mischiefs of very different kinds. It will prevent giddy inconstancy: it will prevent unthinking rashness: it will prevent unmanly languor.

Some have appeared apprehensive, that the introduction of this principle into our political creed would open the door for the admission of levity and unsteadiness in all our political establishments. The very reverse will be its effect. Let the uninterrupted power to change be admitted and fully understood, and the exercise of it will not be lightly or wantonly assumed. There is a *vis inertiae*[9] in publick bodies as well as in matter; and, if left to their natural propensities, they will not be moved without a proportioned propelling cause. If, indeed, the prevailing opinion should be, that the society had not the regular power of altering, on every proper opportunity, its political institutions; an occasion, favourable in appearance, but deceptive in reality, might be suddenly fixed on, as a season for action. It might be allowed not to be, in every respect, unexceptionable; but when, it would be urged, will another, less exceptionable, present itself? The consequence would be, that the juncture, however unpropitious, would be seized with premature and improvident zeal, in order to accomplish the meditated change. Disappointments, arising from the want of due preparations, would take place; disasters, very prejudicial to the publick and to individuals, would be produced; and the enterprise would prove abortive, merely because it was pursued at an unfit time, and under unfit circumstances.

On the other hand, how often and how long has degrading despotism reigned triumphant, because the enfeebled and desponding sufferers under it have not known, or, having once known, have, at last, forgotten, that they retain, during every moment of their slavery, the right of rescuing themselves from the proud and bloated authors and instruments of their oppression! Hesitation about the right will be attended with a corresponding hesitation about the expediency of redress. A revolution, surrounded, in prospect, so thickly with doubts, uncertainties, and apprehensions, will

9. Power of inactivity.

wear a gloomy and formidable appearance; and the miserable patients of tyranny will languish out their lives in excruciating and accumulated distress, merely because they will not undergo one short operation, which would not be more painful than their disease, and which would forever deliver them from all its ills and consequences.

The importance of a good constitution will, on reflection and examination, be easily conceived, deeply felt, and readily acknowledged. On the constitution will depend the beneficence, the wisdom, and the energy, or the injustice, the folly, and the weakness of the government and laws. On the good or bad qualities of the government and laws, will depend the prosperity or the decline of the state. On the same good or bad qualities will depend, on one hand, the excellence and happiness, and, on the other, the depravity and infelicity of the citizens.

A state well constituted, well proportioned, and well conducted feels her own importance, her own power, and her own vigour. Her importance, her power, and her vigour are seen by others, as well as felt by herself. What are the consequences? Internal firmness; external respect: the confidence of her citizens; the esteem of foreigners. What, again, are the consequences of these? Peace; and dignity and security in the enjoyment of peace.

Let us reverse the scene—let us view a state ill constructed, ill proportioned, and ill directed. She may exhaust every stratagem, and employ every art, to cover her weakness and her defects: but can she destroy her own knowledge of them? will her arts and stratagems be successful in concealing them from others? The very pains taken to conceal, will facilitate the discovery, and enhance its importance. Her imperfections, half seen behind the veil drawn over them, will appear greater, than if fully exposed. What will be the result of this situation, thus felt and thus viewed? Fluctuation in her councils; irresolution in her measures; pusillanimity in her attempts to execute them: the distrust and alarm of her own citizens: the contempt, and the unfriendly designs produced by the contempt, of the nations around her: the evils attending war, or the evils, little inferiour, attending a nation, which is equally incapable of securing peace and of repelling hostilities.

The influence of a good or bad constitution is not less powerful on the citizens, considered as individuals, than on the community, considered as a body politick. It is only under a good constitution that liberty—the precious gift of heaven—can be enjoyed and be secure. This exalting quality comprehends, among other things, the manly and generous exercise of our powers; and includes, as its most delicious ingredient, the happy consciousness of being free. What energetick, what delightful sensations must this enlivening principle diffuse over the whole man! His mind is roused and elevated: his heart is rectified and enlarged: dignity appears in his countenance, and animation in his every gesture and word. He knows that if he is innocent and upright, the laws and constitution of his country will ensure him protection. He trusts, that, if to innocence and integrity he adds faithful and meritorious services, his country, in addition to protection, will confer upon him honourable testimonies of her esteem. Hence he derives a cheerful and habitual confidence, this pervades and invigorates his conduct, and spreads a noble air over every part of his character. Hence, too, he is inspired with ardent affection for the publick: this stimulates and refines his strongest patriotick exertions. His heart, his head, his hands, his tongue, his pen, his fortune; all he is, and all he has, are devoted to his country's cause, and to his country's call.

A person of a very different description appears in view—pale, trembling, emaciated, faltering in his steps, not daring to look upwards, but, with marked anxiety, rolling his eager eyes on every side. Who is he? He is the slave of a bad constitution and a tyrannical government. He is afraid to act, or speak, or look. He knows that his actions and his words, however guarded, may be construed to be criminal: he knows that even his looks and countenance may be considered as the signs and evidences of treacherous thoughts and treasonable conspiracies; and he knows that the suspicion of his masters, upon any of these points, may be fatal: for he knows, that he is at the mercy of those, who, upon the slightest suspicion, may seize or hang him—who may do whatever they please with him, and with all those who are dear to him. What effects must this man's situation produce upon his mind and temper? Can his views be great or exalted? No. Such views, instead of being encouraged, would give offence; and he is well aware what would follow. Can openness and candour beam from his soul? No. Such light would be hateful to his masters; it must be extinguished. Can he feel affection for his country, its constitution, or its government? No. His country is his prison; its constitution is his curse; and its government is a rod of oppression, held continually over his head. What must this man be? He must be abject, fawning, dastardly, selfish, disingenuous, deceitful, cunning, base—but why proceed in the disgusting detail? He must receive the stamp of servility fully impressed on his person, on his mind, and on his manners.

Such are the influences of a constitution, good or bad, upon the political body: such are its influences upon the members, of which that body is composed. Surely, then, the first consideration of a state, and its most important duty, is to form that constitution, which will be best in itself; and best adapted to the genius, and character, and manners of her citizens. Such a constitution will be the basis of her preservation, her happiness, and her perfection.

CHAPTER XI.

Comparison of the Constitution of the United States, with that of Great Britain.

The British constitution has been celebrated in the most sublime and in the most elaborate strains by poets, by orators, by lawyers, and by statesmen. "As for us Britons," says the elegant Shaftesbury, comparing them, in the spirit of a fond and a just preference, with many other nations, "as for us Britons, thank heaven, we have a better sense of government, delivered to us from our ancestors. We have a notion of a publick, and a constitution; how a legislative and how an executive is modelled. We understand weight and measure in this kind; and can reason justly on the balance of power and property. The maxims we draw from hence, are as evident as those in mathematicks. Our increasing knowledge shows us every day, more and more, what common sense is in politicks."[a]

My Lord Bolingbroke,[b] in his masterly and animated style, represents this constitution as "a noble fabrick, the pride of Britain, the envy of her neighbours, raised by the labour of so many centuries, repaired at the expense of so many millions, and cemented by such a profusion of blood—a fabrick, which has resisted the efforts of so many races of giants."

You will be surprised on being told, that, if the nature and characteristick qualities, which I have described, are the true nature and characteristick qualities of a constitution; no such thing as a constitution, properly so called, is known in Great Britain. What is known, in that kingdom, under that name, instead of being the controller and the guide, is the creature and the dependent of the legislative power. The supreme power of the people is a doctrine unknown and unacknowledged in the British

a. 1. Shaft. 108.
b. Diss. on Part. let. 10. p. 151. 152.

system of government. The omnipotent authority of parliament is the dernier resort, to which recourse is had in times and in doctrines of uncommon difficulty and importance. The natural, the inherent, and the predominating rights of the citizens are considered as so dangerous and so desperate a resource, as to be inconsistent with the arrangements of any government, which does or can exist.

The order of things in Britain is exactly the reverse of the order of things in the United States. Here, the people are masters of the government; there, the government is master of the people.

That, on this very interesting subject of contrast, you may be enabled to judge for yourselves, I shall lay before you some passages from British writers of high reputation. From those passages, you can draw your own inferences.

"Most of those," says Mr. Paley, "who treat of the British constitution, consider it as a scheme of government formally planned and contrived by our ancestors, in some certain era of our national history; and as set up in pursuance of such regular plan and design. Something of this sort is secretly supposed, or referred to in the expressions of those, who speak of the principles of the constitution, of bringing back the constitution to its first principles, of restoring it to its original purity, or primitive model. Now this appears to me an erroneous conception of the subject. No such plan was ever formed; consequently no such first principles, original model, or standard exist.

"The constitution is one principal division, head, section, or title of the code of publick laws, distinguished from the rest only by the particular nature, or superiour importance of the subject, of which it treats. Therefore the terms *constitutional* and *unconstitutional,* mean *legal* and *illegal.* The distinction and the ideas, which these terms denote, are founded in the same authority with the law of the land upon any other subject; and to be ascertained by the same inquiries. The system of English jurisprudence is made up of acts of parliament, of decisions of courts of law, and of immemorial usages; consequently, these are the principles of which the constitution itself consists; the sources, from which all our knowledge of its nature and limitations is to be deduced, and the authorities, to which all appeal ought to be made, and by which every constitutional doubt or question can alone be decided. This plain and intelligible definition is the more necessary to be preserved in our thoughts, as some writers upon the subject absurdly confound what is constitutional with what is expedient; pronouncing forthwith a measure to be unconstitutional, which they adjudge in any respect to be detrimental or dangerous; whilst others again ascribe a kind of transcendent authority, or mysterious sanctity to the constitution, as if it was founded in some higher original, than that, which gives force and obligation to the ordinary laws and statutes of the realm, or were inviolable on any other account than its intrinsick utility.

"An act of parliament, in England, can never be unconstitutional, in the strict and proper acceptation of the term: in a lower sense it may; viz. when it militates with the spirit, contradicts the analogy, or defeats the provision of other laws, made to regulate the form of government. Even that flagitious abuse of their trust, by which a parliament of Henry the eighth conferred upon the king's proclamation the authority of law, was unconstitutional only in this latter sense."[c]

Sir William Blackstone uses the term, constitution, as commensurate with the law of England. "Of a constitution," says he, "so wisely contrived, so strongly raised, and so highly finished, it is hard to speak with that praise, which is justly and severely its due. It hath been the endeavour of these Commentaries, however the execution may have succeeded, to examine its solid foundations, to mark out its extensive plan, to explain the use and distribution of its parts, and from the harmonious concurrence of those several parts to demonstrate the elegant proportion of the whole."[d]

Mr. Paley uses the word in a more confined and, perhaps, a more proper sense, when applied to Great Britain; as meaning that part of the law, which relates to the designation and form of the legislature; the rights and functions of the several parts of the legislative body; the construction, office, and jurisdiction of the courts of justice.[e] In this sense I shall use the term, when I speak of the British constitution. And in this sense, the superiority of our constitution to that of Great Britain will eminently appear from the comparison, which we now institute, between their principles, their construction, their proportion, and their properties.

c. 2. Paley. 203. 205.
d. 4. Bl. Com. 435. 436.
e. 2. Paley. 203.

The extension of the theory and practice of representation through all the different departments of the state is another very important acquisition made, by the Americans, in the science of jurisprudence and government. To the ancients, this theory and practice seem to have been altogether unknown. To this moment, the representation of the people is not the sole principle of any government in Europe. Great Britain boasts, and she may boast with justice, that, by the admission of representation, she has introduced a valuable improvement into the science of jurisprudence. The improvement is certainly valuable, so far as it extends; but it is by no means sufficiently extensive.

Is the principle of representation introduced into the executive department of the constitution of Great Britain? This has never been attempted. Before the revolution of one thousand six hundred and eighty eight, some of the kings claimed to hold their thrones by divine, others by hereditary right; and even at the important era of that revolution, nothing farther was endeavoured or obtained, than the recognition of certain parts of an original contract, supposed, at some former period, to have been made between the king and the people. A contract seems to exclude, rather than to imply delegated power. The judges of Great Britain are appointed by the crown. The judicial department, therefore, does not depend upon a representation of the people, even in its remotest degree. Is representation a principle operating in the legislative department of Great Britain? It is; but it is not a predominating principle; though it may serve as a very salutary check. The legislature consists of three branches, the king, the lords, and the commons. Of these, only the latter are supposed, by the constitution, to represent the authority of the people. We now see clearly, to what a narrow corner of the British government the principle of representation is confined. In no other government in Europe does it extend farther: in none, I believe, so far. The American States enjoy the glory and the happiness of diffusing this vital principle throughout all the different divisions and departments of the government. Representation is the chain of communication between the people and those, to whom they have committed the important charge of exercising the delegated powers necessary for the administration of publick affairs. This chain may consist of one link, or of more links than one; but it should always be sufficiently strong and discernible.

As, in England, the house of commons alone represents, or is supposed to represent, the people at large; so, in that house alone are we to look for the constitutional and authoritative expression of the people's will. But even in that house, this will is but very feebly and very imperfectly expressed, for the representation in that house is very unequal and inadequate; and it is protracted through a period of time much too long.

It is very unequal and inadequate. In England, we may, from information which seems to be unexceptionable, compute six hundred and thirty nine thousand taxable inhabitants. This number would assign one representative to twelve hundred constituents. But the fact is, that a number not exceeding six thousand are sufficient to return more than one half of the members of the house of commons. This is in the proportion of twenty three constituents for one representative. The consequence is, that a majority of the house of commons may be returned by less than a fiftieth part of the constituents, that ought to be requisite for returning that majority. What is the situation of the other forty nine parts? Need I repeat, this representation is very unequal and inadequate? As to the number of electors, it certainly is.

It may, perhaps, be expected, that this deficiency in their numbers is, in some measure at least, compensated by the worth, the respectability, the independence, and the enlarged influence of the individuals, who are empowered to vote. To this expectation, the fact is directly reverse. That small part are the most dependent and the least respectable part of the commons of England. They are emphatically styled the *rotten* part of the constitution. In dignity and respectability, therefore, as well as in numbers, the representation of the commons of England is extremely inadequate and unequal.

The softness of a whisper may sometimes communicate sound with a more distinct impression than the report of a cannon. Sir William Blackstone admits that "if any alteration might be wished or suggested in the present frame of parliament, it should be in favour of a more complete representation of the people."[f]

The inequality of the representation of the people of England is evinced, in the most striking manner, by another comparative view, in which it

f. 1. Bl. Com. 172.

may be placed. Ninety two members represent the landed interest; about one hundred members represent the great cities and towns; above three hundred members represent small and inconsiderable boroughs.

But further; the representation of the commons is not renewed by them at periods sufficiently near one another. Parliaments were at first annual; they were afterwards triennial; now they are septennial. This last period is surely too long. The members will be apt to forget the source from which they have received their powers. Every government, in order to preserve its freedom, has frequent need of some new provisions in favour of that freedom. Such new provisions are most likely to spring from those, who have been recently animated by the inspiration of the people.

A representation, inadequate, unequal, and continued too long, is inconsistent with the principles of free government: for by such a representation, it is probable that the sense of the people will be misapprehended, or misrepresented, or despised. This probability has, in England, been converted into fact and experience. During many years past, the politicks of the house of commons have been moved by the direction of the court and ministers, and not by the sense of the nation. Numerous and striking instances of this might be produced. But I can only point to those paths of investigation; I cannot pursue them.

How immensely different is the state of representation in the house of commons, from that which is established in the United States. With us, every freeman who possesses an attachment to the community, and a common interest with his fellow citizens, and is in a situation not necessarily dependent, is entitled to a vote for members. With us, no preference is given to any party, any interest, any situation, any profession, or any description over another. With us, those votes, equally, freely, and universally diffused, will have their frequent and powerful operation and influence. With us, therefore, it may be expected, that the voice of the representatives will be the faithful echo of the voice of the people.

Having seen that the house of representatives of the United States will not suffer by being compared, in its proportion and in its duration, with the house of commons of Great Britain; let us proceed to a comparison of the senate with the house of lords.

That house is divided into two orders; the lords spiritual, and the lords temporal. The lords spiritual are composed of the archbishops and bishops. All these hold, or are supposed to hold, certain ancient baronies under the crown; and, in right of succession to those baronies, which were inalienable from their respective dignities, they obtained their seats in the house of lords. With the other lords they intermix in their votes; and the majority of such intermixture binds both estates. The lords temporal consist of all the peers of the realm, by whatever title of nobility they are distinguished. Of these, some sit by descent, as all ancient peers; others, by creation, as all new made ones; others, since the union with Scotland, by election of the nobility of that country. The number of peers is indefinite; and may be increased at the pleasure of the crown.

The writers on the British constitution view the distinctions of rank and honours as necessary in every well governed state, in order to reward such as are eminent for their services to the publick; exciting thus a laudable ardour in others; and diffusing, by such ardour, life and vigour through the whole community. A body of nobility, they say, creates and preserves that gradual scale of dignity, which proceeds from the peasant to the prince; rising, like a pyramid, from a broad foundation, and diminishing as it rises, till, at last, it terminates in a single point. It is this ascending and contracting proportion, they conclude, which adds stability to any government.

That eminent services ought to be rewarded, that devotion to the publick ought to receive the warmest encouragement, will not be denied here. But does this encouragement—do these rewards grow only in an aristocratick soil? Has republicanism no rewards or honours for her meritorious sons? She is accused, it is true, of ingratitude. But the facts, which have given rise to the accusation, have not, we hope, been owing peculiarly to her disposition or principles, but have sprung from a spirit of envy and malevolence, predominating, alas! too much in all communities, and discovering too often more activity and zeal in doing mischief, than the opposite qualities display in doing good. Besides; instances have not been unfrequent, in which publick gratitude has been expressed by commonwealths, most generously and most effectually, both in words and actions. It is true, that the publick testimonials of gratitude and esteem have no hereditary descent among republicans; because it is true, that no regular course of descent is established in the qualities and services which merit them.

The nobility, we are told, are necessary in the British constitution, to form a barrier against the mutual encroachments of the king and of the people. In the government of the United States, separate orders of men do not exist; no encroachments of this kind can take place; and there is no occasion to provide barriers against them. The pyramid of government may certainly be raised with all the graces of fair proportion, and also with the more substantial qualities of firmness and strength, although the materials, of which it is constructed, be not an assemblage of different and dissimilar kinds. These are more likely to recal to our minds the composition and the fate of a heterogeneous and disjointed piece of workmanship, so well described by the prophet Daniel. But to drop the idea of approving and disapproving by metaphor; we find that, in Britain, there being two orders, the king and the people, it was necessary that there should be a third, to hold the balance between them. But different orders, we apprehend, may well be dispensed with in a good and perfect government.

Wisdom, it is said, is found in an aristocracy. Why? Because its members are formed by education, and matured by experience, for the discharge of their duty. Education and experience, it will be readily allowed, are excellent for forming and finishing the habits and characters of statesmen. But on whom will the best education be probably bestowed? On whom will it be likely to produce the strongest and most beneficial influence? On him, whose parents know, and who himself will soon know, that, whether he receive it or not, or, receiving it, whether he improve it or not, still he must succeed to all the preeminences of aristocratick power?—or on him, whose parents foresee, and who himself will be soon sensible, that his prospects of success in publick life must depend on the qualities, acquired as well as natural, which he can bring into publick life along with him? Whom will experience best teach? Him, who sees, that, as estimable acquirements have not been necessary for introducing him to the dignities of the state, they are as little necessary for continuing him in the enjoyment of them? or him, who is aware, that, as the good opinion of his fellow citizens concerning his talents and virtues procured him admission to the honours of his country, his continuance in the possession of those honours must depend on his justifying that good opinion, on his improving it into confidence, and on his showing, by a progressive display of services and accomplishments, that his conduct becomes daily more and more worthy of publick sanction and esteem? He is, it is true, in some measure, dependent: but his dependence is not of an irrational or illiberal kind. It is of a kind, which, instead of depressing, will rouse and elevate the temper and character.

We thus seize the strong outworks of aristocracy, and successfully turn on herself her most formidable batteries.

In drawing a contrast between the executive magistrates of the United States and Great Britain, I wave every degree of comparison with regard to some of the characters applied to the latter, in the description given of him by the British law and the British lawyers. They ascribe to him certain qualities as inherent in his royal capacity, distinct from and superiour to those of any other individual in the nation: they assign to him certain properties of a great and transcendent nature: by these means, it is thought, the people will consider him in the light of a superiour being; and will pay him that awful respect, which may enable him, with greater ease, to carry on the business of government. The law clothes him with the attributes of sovereignty, of ubiquity, and of absolute perfection: he can do no wrong: he can think no wrong: in him no folly—in him no weakness can be found: royal wisdom is ascribed to the infant of a span long, as much as to the experienced sire, who has seen three generations: the man dies; but the king satisfies the wish of eastern adulation: he lives for ever!

Prepossessions long entertained, habits long formed, and practices long established may, possibly, have interwoven those ideas into the system of the British constitution in such a manner, that it would be difficult now to disentangle them, without tearing or injuring some more useful parts of the fabrick. But in forming a new system, it is certainly neither necessary nor proper to introduce into it qualities and pretensions so disproportioned to the sober consideration and management of human affairs. Power may be conferred without mystery; and may be exercised, for every wise and benevolent purpose, without challenging attributes, to which our frail and imperfect state of humanity stands in daily and marked contradiction.

On what foundation is the monarchical part of the British constitution supported? Are the rights of the monarch supposed, by it, to flow from the authority of those, over whom he is placed? Is the majesty of the people recognised as the august parent of the prerogative of the prince?

No. Such principles have never received the sanction of the British constitution. Concerning the origin of the powers and rights of their monarchs, very different opinions have, at different times, been entertained and propagated. The dark foundations of conquest have, in some reigns, been uncovered and exposed to view. Divine right has, in others, been impiously summoned to sanctify claims and pretensions, too exorbitant to have derived their source from human authority. At some periods, the title to the crown has been supposed to be founded on hereditary right, a right derived, by succession, from a long list of ancestors. But, in tracing this succession upwards, we necessarily come, at last, in fact, or in idea, to some one, who was the first possessor. How did he acquire his possession? The solution, now received, of this question, is, that it was in consequence of an original contract, made, at some former distant period, between the king and the people. The terms of this contract have, indeed, been the subject of frequent and doubtful disputation. At the revolution, however, some of them were reduced to a certainty: and the existence of the contract itself was explicitly recognised. But a contract does not imply the idea of *derivative* power; it seems rather to imply an equality between the parties contracting. Besides; the crown, on whomever it may be devolved by virtue of this contract, still retains its descendible quality, and becomes hereditary in the wearer. Even in this enlightened century, the most determined champions of liberty in Great Britain have not instituted the claim, that the power of every part of government, the monarchical not excepted, should be founded on the authority of the people. Hear in what a humiliating manner one of their boldest and most energetick writers has described their power on this interesting subject. "The British liberties are not the grants of princes. They are original rights, conditions of original contracts, coequal with the prerogative, and coeval with the government."[g]

How different is this language, and how different are these sentiments, from the language and sentiments, which, under our improved systems of government, we are entitled to hold and express! We have no occasion to enter a caveat against the supposition, that our liberties are the grants of princes. With us, the powers of magistrates, call them by whatever

g. Bol. Rem. let. 4.

name you please, are the grants of the people. With us, no prerogative or government can be set up as coequal with the authority of the people. The supreme power is in them; and in them, even when a constitution is formed, and government is in operation, the supreme power still remains. A portion of their authority they, indeed, delegate; but they delegate that portion in whatever manner, in whatever measure, for whatever time, to whatever persons, and on whatever conditions they choose to fix.

Those, who have traced and examined the subject of the appointment of governours, find, or think they find, an irreconcilable opposition between the principles of what they admit to be sound theory, and the rules of what they contend to be exclusively the safe and eligible practice. That what appears right in theory may be wrong in practice, is, no doubt, a possible case: but I am apt to believe that, generally, this contrariety is more apparent than real: and proceeds either from inaccurate investigation, or from improper conduct.

It has been the sentiment of many writers, that to have elective governours is best in speculation; but that to have hereditary ones is best in fact. The sense of nations has often, on this subject, coincided with the sentiments of writers; and therefore, they have trusted to chance rather than to choice, the succession of those, who hold the reins of power over them. They admit, that the chance is even a bad one. They admit that one born to govern is, by education, generally disqualified, both in body and mind, rather than qualified for government. They admit, that he will probably be debased by ignorance, enervated by pleasure, intoxicated by flattery, and corrupted by pride. They admit, that this chance may give them a fool, a madman, a tyrant, or a monster: and yet they hold it safer to depend on all the caprices of this very chance, than to commit their fortune and their fate to the discernment of choice.

And whence this strong antipathy to choice? Popular clamours, popular disturbances, popular distractions, popular tumults, and popular insurrections are ever present to their view. The unfortunate and fluctuating example of Poland dances perpetually before their eyes. They reflect not on the cause of this example. Poland is composed only of slaves, headed and commanded by a few despots. Those despots have private purposes to serve; and they head their slaves as the instruments for executing those private purposes. In Poland, we search in vain for a people. Need we be surprised, that, at an election in Poland, where there are only tyrants and slaves, all the detestable and pernicious extremes of tyranny and slavery should unite?

But surely, in the United States, we have no occasion to be apprehensive of such an odious and destructive union. In the United States, we have freemen and fellow citizens. To freemen and fellow citizens, and to those selected, for this very purpose, by freemen and fellow citizens, we may trust the appointment of our first and most important magistrate. In this appointment, no one can participate, either immediately or indirectly, who does not possess a common interest with the community. We are justified, therefore, in abandoning chance, and confiding in choice: our practice corresponds with our theory; and our theory is admitted to be just. An election made by those, whom we have described, authorized by the constitution, directed by the laws, held on the same day and for the same purpose, but at different and at distant places—such an election may certainly be carried on with fairness and with regularity; and its event may be considered as the genuine production of design, and not as the casual result of a "lottery."[h]

In one important particular—the unity of the executive power—the constitution of the United States stands on an equal footing with that of Great Britain. In one respect, the provision is much more efficacious.

The British throne is surrounded by counsellors. With regard to their authority, a profound and mysterious silence is observed. One effect, we know, they produce; and we conceive it to be a very pernicious one. Between power and responsibility, they interpose an impenetrable barrier. Who possesses the executive power? The king. When its baneful emanations fly over the land; who are responsible for the mischief? His ministers. Amidst their multitude, and the secrecy, with which business, especially that of a perilous kind, is transacted, it will be often difficult to select the culprits; still more so, to punish them. The criminality will be diffused and blended with so much variety and intricacy, that it will be almost impossible to ascertain to how many it extends, and what particular share should be assigned to each.

But let us trace this subject a little further. Though the power of the king's counsellors is not, as far as I can discover, defined or described in

h. See Bol. Pat. King. 89.

the British constitution; yet their seats are certainly provided for some purpose, and filled with some effect. What is wanting in authority may be supplied by intrigue; and, in the place of constitutional influence, may be substituted that subtle ascendency, which is acquired and preserved by deeply dissembled obsequiousness. To so many arts, secret, unceasing, and well directed, can we suppose that a prince, in whose disposition is found any thing weak, indolent, or accommodating, will not be frequently induced to yield? Hence spring the evils of a partial, an indecisive, and a disjointed administration.

In the United States, our first executive magistrate is not obnubilated behind the mysterious obscurity of counsellors. Power is communicated to him with liberality, though with ascertained limitations. To him the provident or improvident use of it is to be ascribed. For the first, he will have and deserve undivided applause. For the last, he will be subjected to censure; if necessary, to punishment. He is the dignified, but accountable magistrate of a free and great people. The tenure of his office, it is true, is not hereditary; nor is it for life: but still it is a tenure of the noblest kind: by being the man of the people, he is invested; by continuing to be the man of the people, his investiture will be voluntarily, and cheerfully, and honourably renewed.

The president of the United States has such powers as are strictly and properly executive; and, by his qualified negative on the legislature, is furnished with a guard to protect his powers against their encroachments. Such powers and such a guard he ought to possess: but a just distribution of the powers of government requires that he should possess no more. In this important aspect, the constitution of the United States has much more regular, more correct, and better proportioned features, than are those of the constitution of Great Britain. It will be well worth while to trace this observation through various instances: its truth and its interesting consequences will, by this means, clearly appear.

As the king is the sole fountain of honour; he has, without limitation, the constitutional prerogative of creating peers; and of exalting to higher dignities those already created. He has also the power of appointing and promoting the bishops and archbishops. Those lords spiritual and temporal form one branch of the legislature. The number, therefore, and the rank of the members composing that branch depend entirely on the pleasure of the crown. This is a reprehensible dependency of the legislative on the executive power. Indeed, experience has proved it to be so. A single century has not yet revolved, since twelve peers were created at one time, with the avowed purpose of securing, by their necessary votes, the success of a favourite court system. A conviction, that, on any great crown emergency, recourse can be had to a similar expedient, will naturally lead the house of lords to be cautious, in an undue degree, of giving pointed opposition to the crown, however just or well grounded such opposition might be.

Another instance of the dependency of the house of lords on the king deserves to be mentioned: the speaker of that house, whose office it is to preside there and manage the forms of their business, is the lord chancellor, whose appointment and commission are at the pleasure of the crown.

Indeed, this undue and dangerous dependency of the house of lords seems to be acknowledged and dreaded—for, in one instance, provision is made against its effects—by the British constitution itself. It is the indisputable right of the house of commons—a right, over which they have constantly watched with a jealous solicitude—that all grants of parliamentary aid begin in their house. Several reasons have been assigned for this exclusive privilege—but the true one, arising from the spirit of the constitution, is this. The lords, being created, at pleasure, by the king, are supposed more liable to be influenced by the crown; and, being a permanent hereditary body, are, when once influenced, supposed more likely to continue so, than the commons, who are a temporary body elected by the people. It would, therefore, be extremely dangerous to give the lords any power of framing new taxes for the subject: it suffices that they have the power of rejecting, if they think the commons too lavish or improvident in their grants.

By the constitution of the United States, money bills originate in the house of representatives: the reason is, that as that house are more numerous than the other, and its members are elected more frequently; the most local and recent information of the circumstances of the people may be found there. But, as the senate derive their authority ultimately from the same origin with the other house; they have a right to propose and concur in amendments in these as well as in other bills.

But further; the power of conferring nobility is a source of influence, which the crown possesses over the house of commons, as well as over the house of lords. A coronet, and all the proud preeminences and gilded glories which encircle a coronet, are objects of ambition, whose tempting charms, few—very few indeed—are capable of resisting. Even the great commoner wishes and sighs to be something more. Will not his views be directed to that power, by which alone his wishes can be gratified? Will not his conduct receive a bias from the longing, expecting turn of his mind? When his towering hopes of elevation are suspended on the crown; will he easily run the risk of seeing them dashed to the ground, by speaking, and voting, and acting in opposition to its views and measures?

We are now arrived, in our progress, at another fountain, from which, in Great Britain, the waters of bitterness have plentifully flowed—I mean the fountain of office. We reprehend not the nature of this power, nor the place, where, by the British constitution, it is deposited. In every government there must be such a power; and it is proper, that it should be lodged in the hands of him, who is placed at the head of the executive department. What we censure is, that this power is not circumscribed by the necessary limitations. It may be—it is exercised in favour of the members of both houses of parliament. Offices of trust and profit are scattered, with a lavish hand, among those, by whom a return, very dangerous to the liberties of the nation, may be made; and from whom such a return is but too often expected.

This is the box of Pandora, which has been opened on Britain. To its poisonous emanations have been owing the contaminated and contaminating scenes of venality, of prostitution, and corruption, which have crowded and disgraced her political theatre. To the same efficacy have been owing the indiscriminate profligacy and universal degeneracy, which have been diffused through every channel, into which the treasures of the publick have procured admission. In the house of lords, this stream of influence may flow without measure and without end. Some attempts have been made to confine it in the house of commons; but they have been feeble and unavailing. If any member of that house accepts an office under the crown, his seat, it is true, is vacated; but he may be immediately reelected. This provision, flimsy as it is, extends not to officers in the army or navy accepting new commissions. The ardent aspirations after military preferment are thus left to be exerted, with all their energetick vigour, in promoting the designs of the crown, or of the ministers of the crown.

But fears, as well as hopes, operate in favour of the influence, which we have been tracing in so many directions. For the members hold their offices and commissions, and, consequently, may be dismissed from them, at the pleasure of the crown.

Indeed, this influence has been so great and so uniform, that for more than a century past, it has been found, that reliance could be placed on it implicitly. Accordingly, during that whole period, the king has never once been under the disagreeable necessity of interposing his negative to prevent the passing of an obnoxious law. It has been discovered to be a less ungracious, though not a less efficacious method, to stop its progress in one of the two houses of parliament.

To the power of the crown to confer offices on members of parliament, we may also ascribe those numerous and violent dissensions, which, on so many occasions, and some of them very critical ones, have convulsed the national councils, and sacrificed the national interests. Ample though the means are, which the crown can employ in gaining and securing members, by the offices in its gift, they are insufficient to gratify all. To a sure majority, the object must be confined. But of a majority, gained by the interest of the court, the necessary consequence is, a minority in opposition to its measures.[i]

The above is a plain and simple account of the manner, in which the parties in parliament have been formed, and in which they have, without interruption, been continued; though, on both sides, a very different account has been uniformly attempted to be palmed upon the publick. Neither side has chosen to give a true history and character either of themselves or of their antagonists: each finds its interest in appearing, and in representing the other, under a borrowed dress. While the influence of the crown, produced by offices of trust and profit bestowed upon members of parliament, shall continue, this state of formed and irreconcilable parties will continue also.

The result is, that a provision, by which the members of the legislature will be precluded, while they remain such, from offices, finds, with great propriety, a place in the constitution of the United States. In this

i. It was the saying of King William, that if he had places enough to give, the names of whig and tory would soon be lost.

important particular, it has a decided superiority over the constitution of Great Britain.

Perhaps the qualified negative of the president of the United States on the proceedings of the senate and house of representatives in congress, possesses advantages over an absolute negative, such as that vested in the crown of Great Britain over the proceedings of the lords and commons. To this last, recourse would not be had, unless on occasions of the greatest emergency. A determination not to interpose it without the last necessity, would prevent the exercise of it in many instances, in which it would be proper and salutary. In this manner, it would remain, like a sword always in the scabbard, an instrument, sometimes of distant apprehension, but not of present or practical utility. The exercise of the qualified negative is not an experiment of either dangerous or doubtful issue. A small bias it turns without noise or difficulty. To the operation of a powerful bias, which cannot be safely checked or diverted, it decently and leisurely gives way.

The qualified negative will be highly advantageous in another point of view: it will form an index, by which, from time to time, the strength and height of the current of publick opinions and publick movements may, with considerable exactness, be ascertained. Whenever it is exercised, the votes of all the members of both the houses must be entered on their journals. The single point, that there is a majority, will not be the only one, which will appear: it will be evinced also, how great that majority is. If it consists of less than two thirds of both houses, it seems reasonable, that the dissent of the executive department should suspend a business, which is already so nearly in equilibrio. On the other hand, if, after all the discussion, investigation, and consideration, which must have been employed upon a bill in its different stages, before its presentment to the prèsident of the United States, and after its return from him with his objections to it, two thirds of each house are still of sentiment, that it ought to be passed into a law; this would be an evidence, that the current of publick opinion in its favour is so strong, that it ought not to be opposed. The experiment, though doubtful, ought to be made, when it is called for so long and so loudly.

Besides; the objections of the president, even when unsuccessful, will not be without their use. If the law, notwithstanding all the unfavourable appearances, which accurate political disquisition discovered against it, proves, upon trial, to be beneficial in practice; it will add one to the many instances, in which feeling may be trusted more than argument. If, on the contrary, experience shows the law to be replete with all the inconveniences, which sagacious scrutiny foresaw in its operations, the disease will no sooner appear, than the remedy will be known and applied.

Another advantage, of very general and extensive import, will flow from the qualified negative possessed by the president of the United States. His observations upon the bills and acts of the legislature will, in a series of time, gradually furnish the most valuable and the best adapted materials for composing a practical system of legislation. In every successive period, experience and reasoning will go hand in hand; and will, jointly, produce a collection of accurate and satisfactory knowledge, which could be the separate result of neither.

By the British constitution, the power of judging in the last resort is placed in the house of lords. It is allowed, by an English writer on that constitution, that there is nothing in the formation of the house of lords; nor in the education, habits, character, or professions of the members who compose it; nor in the mode of their appointment, or the right, by which they succeed to their places in it, that suggests any intelligible fitness in the nature of this regulation.[j] Ecclesiasticks, courtiers, naval and military officers, young men, just of age, born to their elevated station, in other words, placed there by chance, are, for the most part, the members, who compose this important and supreme tribunal. These are the men, authorized and assigned to revise and correct the decisions, pronounced by the sages of the law, who have been raised to the seat of justice on account of their professional eminence, and have employed their lives in the study and practice of the jurisprudence of their country. There is surely something, which, at least in theory, appears very incongruous in this establishment of things. The practical consequences of its impropriety are, in a considerable degree, avoided, by placing in the house of lords some of the greatest law characters in the kingdom; by calling to their assistance the opinions of the judges upon legal questions, which come before the house for its final determination; and by the great deference which those, who are uninformed, naturally pay to those, who are distinguished by their

j. 2. Paley. 282. 283.

information. After all, however, there is a very improper mixture of legislative and judicial authority vested and blended in the same assembly. This is entirely avoided in the constitution of the United States.

It may, perhaps, be objected, that, by this constitution, one branch of the legislature is to present, and the other is to try impeachments. The answer is obvious. Impeachments, and offences and offenders impeachable, come not, in those descriptions, within the sphere of ordinary jurisprudence. They are founded on different principles, are governed by different maxims, and are directed to different objects: for this reason, the trial and punishment of an offence on an impeachment, is no bar to a trial and punishment of the same offence at common law.

In the judicial establishments of Great Britain, there is, we cheerfully confess, much to admire, and much to imitate. The judges are the grand depository of the fundamental laws of the kingdom; and have gained a known and stated jurisdiction, regulated by certain and established rules, which cannot be altered, but by act of parliament. By the statute 13. W. III. c. 2. "An act for the further limitation of the crown, and better securing the rights and liberties of the subject," provision is made, that after the said limitation shall take effect, the commissions of the judges shall be, not, as formerly, "durante bene placito," but "quamdiu bene se gesserint;"[1] that their salaries shall be ascertained and established; but that it may be lawful to remove them on the address of both houses of parliament.

Though, in virtue of this law, the judges received commissions to hold their offices during their good behaviour; it was supposed, that their seats were immediately vacated by the demise of the crown. When their seats were vacated, their salaries terminated. A new commission, it is true, might be given, and, if given, must be given during good behaviour; but a new commission might also be refused, by the successour to the throne. Under the new commission, if given, a different salary might be assigned. In this state of dependence, not so degrading, indeed, as it had been, but still very precarious, and, as it respected the heir apparent of the throne, very embarrassing and humiliating, the judges of England continued till the first year of the reign of George the third.[2]

That Prince, soon after his accession, declared, from the throne, to

1. "Not during good pleasure," but "as long as they conduct themselves well."
2. George III (1783–1820) was king of England from 1760 to 1820.

both houses of parliament, that he looked upon the independency and uprightness of judges as essential to the impartial administration of justice, as one of the best securities to the rights and liberties of the subjects, and as most conducive to the honour of his crown. He, therefore, recommended it to the consideration of parliament, to make further provision for continuing the judges in the enjoyment of their offices during their good behaviour, notwithstanding the demise of the crown; and for enabling him to secure their salaries during the continuance of their commissions. Provision was accordingly made, by parliament, for both those purposes. But the judges are still liable to be removed by the king, upon the address of both houses of parliament.

This establishment for the administration of justice appears, in the opinion of Mr. Paley, no undiscerning judge of the subject, to approach so near to perfection, as to justify him in declaring, that a politician, who should sit down to delineate a plan for the dispensation of publick justice, guarded against all access to influence and corruption, and bringing together the separate advantages of knowledge and impartiality, would find, when he had done, that he had been transcribing the judicial constitution of England.[k] "It may teach," continues he, "the most discontented among us to acquiesce in the government of his country, to reflect that the pure, wise, and equal administration of the laws forms the first end and blessing of social union; and that this blessing is enjoyed by him in a perfection, which he will seek in vain in any other nation of the world."

Notwithstanding this high encomium, pronounced from a motive of which I cannot but approve, I hesitate not to institute a comparison between the judicial establishment of England, and that which is introduced by the constitution of the United States. Nay, I am sanguine, that, on a just comparison, the latter will be found to contain many very useful and valuable improvements on the former.

The laws, in England, respecting the independency of the judges, have been construed as confined to those in the superiour courts.[l] In the United States, this independency extends to judges in courts inferiour as well as supreme. This independency reaches equally their salaries and their commissions.

k. 2. Paley. 284. 285.
l. 1. Bl. Com. 267.

In England, the judges of the superiour courts do not now, as they did formerly, hold their commissions and their salaries at the pleasure of the crown; but they still hold them at the pleasure of the parliament: the judicial subsists, and may be blown to annihilation, by the breath of the legislative department. In the United States, the judges stand upon the sure basis of the constitution: the judicial department is independent of the department of legislature. No act of congress can shake their commissions or reduce their salaries. "The judges, both of the supreme and inferiour courts, shall hold their offices during good behaviour, and shall, at stated times, receive for their services a compensation, which shall not be diminished during their continuance in office." [m] It is not lawful for the president of the United States to remove them on the address of the two houses of congress. They may be removed, however, as they ought to be, on conviction of high crimes and misdemeanors.

The judges of the United States stand on a much more independent footing than that on which the judges of England stand, with regard to jurisdiction, as well as with regard to commissions and salaries. In many cases, the jurisdiction of the judges of the United States is ascertained and secured by the constitution: as to these, the power of the judicial is coordinate with that of the legislative department. As to the other cases, by the necessary result of the constitution, the authority of the former is paramount to the authority of the latter.

It will be proper to illustrate, at some length, the nature and consequences of these important doctrines concerning the judicial department of the United States; and, at the same time, to contrast them with the doctrines held concerning the same department in England. Much useful and practical information may be drawn from this comparative review.

It is entertaining, and it may be very instructive, to trace and examine the opinions of the English courts and lawyers concerning the decision, which may be given, in the judicial department, upon the validity or invalidity of acts of parliament.

In some books we are told plainly, and without any circumlocution or disguise—that an act of parliament against law and reason is, therefore,

m. Con. U. S. art. 3. s. 1.

void[n]—that, in many cases, the common law will control acts of parliament; and sometimes adjudge them to be utterly void: for when an act of parliament is against common right and reason, or repugnant, or impossible to be performed; the common law will control it, and adjudge such act to be void. Some statutes are made against law and right, which those who made them perceiving, would not put them in execution[o]—that an act of parliament made against natural equity, as to make a man judge in his own cause, is void in itself; for *jura naturae sunt immutabilia*, and they are *leges legum*.[p]

My Lord Chief Justice Holt expresses himself, upon this delicate and embarrassing subject, in his usual blunt and decided manner: "It is a very reasonable and true saying, that if an act of parliament should ordain, that the same person should be a party and a judge, or, which is the same thing, judge in his own cause; it would be a void act of parliament; for it is impossible that one should be judge and party; for the judge is to determine between party and party, or between the government and the party; and an act of parliament can do no wrong; though it may do several things, that look pretty odd."[q]

These doctrines and sayings, however reasonable and true they appear to be, have been, nevertheless, deemed too bold; for they are irreconcilable with the lately introduced positions concerning the supreme, absolute, and uncontrollable power of the British parliament. Accordingly, Sir William Blackstone, on the principles of his system, expresses himself in the following manner, remarkably guarded and circumspect, as to the extent of the parliamentary power. "If there arise *out* of acts of parliament, *collaterally*, any absurd consequences, *manifestly* contradictory to common reason; they are, with regard to *those collateral* consequences, void. I lay down the rule with these restrictions; though I know it is generally laid down more largely—that acts of parliament contrary to reason are void. But if the parliament will *positively* enact a thing to be done, which is unreasonable; I know of no power that can control it: and the examples usually alleged in support of this sense of the rule do none of them prove, that, where the

n. 4. Rep. 13.
o. 8. Rep. 118.
p. Hob. 87. "The laws of nature are immutable, and they are the laws of laws."
q. 12. Mod. 687. 688.

main object of a statute is unreasonable, the judges are at liberty to reject it: for that were to set the judicial power above that of the legislature, which would be subversive of all government." "No court has power to defeat the intent of the legislature, when couched in such evident and express words, as to leave no doubt concerning its intention."[r]

The successour of Sir William Blackstone in the Vinerian chair walks in his footsteps. "It is certain," he admits, "no human authority can rightfully infringe or abrogate the smallest particle of natural or divine law; yet a British judge, of highly deserved estimation, seems in some measure unguarded in asserting from the bench, that an act of parliament made against natural equity, is void in itself. The principle is infallibly true; the application of it, and the conclusion, dangerous. We must distinguish between right and power; between moral fitness and political authority. We cannot expect that all acts of legislators will be ethically perfect; but if their proceedings are to be decided upon by their subjects, government and subordination cease."[s]

It is very true—we ought to "distinguish between right and power:" but I always apprehended, that the true use of this distinction was, to show that power, in opposition to right, was devested of every title, not that it was clothed with the strongest title, to obedience. Is it really true, that if "the parliament will positively enact an unreasonable thing—a thing manifestly contradictory to common reason—there is no power that can control it?" Is it really true that such a power, vested in the judicial department, would set it above the legislature, and would be subversive of all government? If all this is true; what will the miserable, but unavoidable consequence be? Is it possible, in the nature of things, that all which is positively enacted by parliament can be decreed and enforced by the courts of justice? It will not be pretended. The words in two different laws may be clearly repugnant to one another. The law supposes that, sometimes, this is the case; and accordingly has provided, as we are told in the Commentaries, that, in this case, the later law takes place of the elder. "Leges posteriores, priores contrarias abrogant,"[3] we are told, and properly told, is a maxim of universal law, as well as of the English constitutions.[t]

r. 1. Bl. Com. 91.
s. El. Jur.(4to.) 48.
3. "Later laws annul earlier laws to the contrary."
t. 1. Bl. Com. 59.

Suppose two such repugnant laws to be produced in the same cause, before the same court: what must it do? It must control one, or obey neither. In this last instance, the remedy would be worse than the disease: but there is not the least occasion to have recourse to this desperate remedy. The rule which we have cited from the Commentaries, shows the method that should be followed. In the case supposed, the first law is repealed by the second: the second, therefore, is the only existing law.

Two contradictory laws, we have seen, may flow from the same source: and we have also seen, what, in that case, is to be done. But two contradictory laws may flow likewise from different sources, one superiour to the other: what is to be done in this case ?

We are informed, in another part of the Commentaries, that, "on the two foundations of the law of nature, and the law of revelation, all human laws depend; that is to say, no human laws should be suffered to contradict these"—"that, if any human law should enjoin us to commit what is prohibited by these, we are bound to transgress that human law, or else we must offend both the natural and the divine.[u] What! are we bound to transgress it?—And are the courts of justice forbidden to reject it? Surely these positions are inconsistent and irreconcilable.

But to avoid the contradiction, shall it be said, that we are bound to suppose every thing, positively and plainly enacted by the legislature, to be, at least, not repugnant to natural or revealed law? This may lead us out of intricate mazes respecting the omnipotence; but, I am afraid, it will lead us into mazes equally intricate and more dangerous concerning the infallibility of parliament. This tenet in the political creed will be found as heterodox as the other.

"I know of no power," says Sir William Blackstone, "which can control the parliament." His meaning is obviously, that he knew no *human* power sufficient for this purpose. But the parliament may, unquestionably, be controlled by natural or revealed law, proceeding from *divine* authority. Is not this authority superiour to any thing that can be enacted by parliament? Is not this superiour authority binding upon the courts of justice? When repugnant commands are delivered by two different authorities, one inferiour and the other superiour; which must be obeyed? When the courts of justice obey the superiour authority, it cannot be said with

u. Id. 42. 43.

propriety that they control the inferiour one; they only declare, as it is their duty to declare, that this inferiour one is controlled by the other, which is superiour. They do not repeal the act of parliament: they pronounce it void, because contrary to an overruling law. From that overruling law, they receive the authority to pronounce such a sentence. In this derivative view, their sentence is of obligation paramount to the act of the inferiour legislative power.

In the United States, the legislative authority is subjected to another control, beside that arising from natural and revealed law; it is subjected to the control arising from the constitution. From the constitution, the legislative department, as well as every other part of government, derives its power: by the constitution, the legislative, as well as every other department, must be directed; of the constitution, no alteration by the legislature can be made or authorized. In our system of jurisprudence, these positions appear to be incontrovertible. The constitution is the supreme law of the land: to that supreme law every other power must be inferiour and subordinate.

Now, let us suppose, that the legislature should pass an act, manifestly repugnant to some part of the constitution; and that the operation and validity of both should come regularly in question before a court, forming a portion of the judicial department. In that department, the "judicial power of the United States is vested" by the "people," who "ordained and established" the constitution. The business and the design of the judicial power is, to administer justice according to the law of the land. According to two contradictory rules, justice, in the nature of things, cannot possibly be administered. One of them must, of necessity, give place to the other. Both, according to our supposition, come regularly before the court, for its decision on their operation and validity. It is the right and it is the duty of the court to decide upon them: its decision must be made, for justice must be administered according to the law of the land. When the question occurs—What is the law of the land? it must also decide this question. In what manner is this question to be decided? The answer seems to be a very easy one. The supreme power of the United States has given one rule: a subordinate power in the United States has given a contradictory rule: the former is the law of the land: as a necessary consequence, the latter is void, and has no operation. In this manner it is the right and it is the duty of a court of justice, under the constitution of the United States, to decide.

This is the necessary result of the distribution of power, made, by the constitution, between the legislative and the judicial departments. The same constitution is the supreme law to both. If that constitution be infringed by one, it is no reason that the infringement should be abetted, though it is a strong reason that it should be discountenanced and declared void by the other.

The effects of this salutary regulation, necessarily resulting from the constitution, are great and illustrious. In consequence of it, the bounds of the legislative power—a power the most apt to overleap its bounds—are not only distinctly marked in the system itself; but effectual and permanent provision is made, that every transgression of those bounds shall be adjudged and rendered vain and fruitless. What a noble guard against legislative despotism!

This regulation is far from throwing any disparagement upon the legislative authority of the United States. It does not confer upon the judicial department a power superiour, in its general nature, to that of the legislature; but it confers upon it, in particular instances, and for particular purposes, the power of declaring and enforcing the superiour power of the constitution—the supreme law of the land.

This regulation, when considered properly, is viewed in a favourable light by the legislature itself. "It has been objected," said a learned member[v] of the house of representatives, in a late debate, "that, by adopting the bill before us, we expose the measure to be considered and defeated by the judiciary of the United States, who may adjudge it to be contrary to the constitution, and therefore void, and not lend their aid to carry it into execution. This gives me no uneasiness. I am so far from controverting this right in the judiciary, that it is my boast and my confidence. It leads me to greater decision on all subjects of a constitutional nature, when I reflect, that, if from inattention, want of precision, or any other defect, I should do wrong, there is a power in the government, which can constitutionally prevent the operation of a wrong measure from affecting my constituents. I am legislating for a nation, and for thousands yet unborn; and it is the

v. Mr. Elias Boudinot.[4]

4. Elias Boudinot (1740–1821) was a prominent American politician and lawyer. He served in the U.S. House of Representatives for New Jersey and as president of the Continental Congress in 1782–1783.

glory of the constitution, that there is a remedy for the failures even of the legislature itself."

It has already appeared, that the laws, in England, respecting the independency of the judges, have been construed as confined to those in the superiour courts. In many courts, nay in almost all the courts, which have jurisdiction in criminal, even in capital cases, the judges are still appointed and commissioned occasionally, and at the pleasure of the crown. Those courts, though possessing only a local jurisdiction, and confined to particular districts, are yet of a general nature, and are universally diffused over the kingdom. Such are the courts of oyer and terminer and general gaol delivery. They are held twice in every year in every county of the kingdom, except the four northern ones, in which they are held only once, and London and Middlesex, in which they are held eight times. By their commissions, the judges of those courts have authority to hear and determine all treasons, felonies, and misdemeanors; and to try and deliver every prisoner who shall be in the gaol, when they arrive at the circuit town, whenever indicted, or for whatever crime committed. Sometimes also, upon particular emergencies, the king issues a special or extraordinary commission of oyer and terminer and gaol delivery, confined to those offences which stand in need of immediate inquiry and punishment. Those courts are held before the king's commissioners, among whom are usually—but not necessarily, as it would seem—two judges of the courts at Westminster.[w]

It is somewhat surprising, that, in a nation where the value of liberty and personal security has been so long and so well known, less care has been taken to provide for the independency of the judges in criminal than in civil jurisdiction. Is property of more consequence than life or personal liberty? Is it more likely to become the selected and devoted object of ministerial vengeance or resentment? If peculiar precaution was necessary or proper to ensure the independence of the judges on the crown, one would think it most reasonable to apply that precaution to the independence of those judges, who exercise criminal jurisdiction. Even treason may be tried before judges, named, for the occasion, and during pleasure, by him, who, in law, is supposed to be personally as well as politically offended.

w. 4. Bl. Com. 266. 267.

To the constitution of the United States, and to those who enjoy the advantages of that constitution, no judges are known, but such as hold their offices during good behaviour.

With regard to the institution and establishment of juries, as well as those of judges, an advantage is possessed under the constitution of the United States, greater than what is possessed under the constitution of Great Britain. This subject deserves to be placed in the clearest and strongest point of view.

To be tried only by men of one's own condition, is one of the greatest blessings—to know that one can be tried only by such men, is one of the greatest securities—which can be enjoyed under any government.

If the trial of causes was committed entirely to one selected body of men, deprived, by their situation, of having many opportunities of knowing particularly the circumstances and characters of the parties, who come before them; it could not be expected, that the proper and practical adjustment of facts to persons would, in every instance, be made. The transactions of life will be best investigated by a competent number of sensible and unprejudiced jurymen, summoned and assembled for each particular cause. Such men will be triers not only of the facts; but also of the credibility of the witnesses. They will know whom and what to believe, as well as whom and what to hear. Truth will be estimated by the character, and not by the number, of those, who give their testimony. The testimony of one witness will not be rejected merely because it stands single; nor will the testimony of two witnesses be believed, if it be encountered by reason and probability. These advantages of a trial by jury are important in all causes: in criminal causes, they are of peculiar importance.

In criminal causes, the accusation charges not only the particular fact, which has been committed, but also the motive or design, to which it owed its origin, and from which it receives its complexion. This design is often so closely interwoven with the transaction, that the elucidation of both depends on a collected view of particulars, arising not merely from the testimony, but also from the conduct and character of the witnesses, and sometimes likewise from the character and conduct of the person accused. Of such conduct and character, men of the same condition with that person, and probably of the same condition with the witnesses too, are the best qualified to make the proper comparison and estimate; and consequently to determine, upon the whole, whether the conduct of the prisoner, comprehending both the fact and the motives, is, or is not, within the meaning of the law, upon which the accusation against him is founded.

This institution does honour to human policy: it is the most excellent method for the investigation and discovery of truth; and the best guardian of both publick and private liberty, which has been hitherto devised by the ingenuity of man. We are told by the celebrated Montesquieu, that Rome, that Sparta, that Carthage—states, once so free and so prosperous—have lost their liberties, and have perished. Their fate he holds up to the view of other states, as a memento of their own. But there is one consolatory distinction, which he did not take, and which we will apply in our favour. In Rome, in Sparta, in Carthage, the trial by jury did not exist, or was not preserved. Liberty can never be insecure in that country, in which "the trial of all crimes is by jury."[x]

Is it not, then, of the last consequence, that, in criminal causes, this most excellent mode of trial should be placed on the most solid and permanent foundation? Is it enough that its establishment be legal,—supported by the legislature? Is it not proper that it should be constitutional—supported by authority superiour to that of the legislature? Such an establishment it has not in Great Britain; but it has in the United States.

I have now finished the parallel between the pride of Europe—the British constitution—and the constitution of the United States. Let impartiality hold the balance between them: I am not solicitous about the event of the trial.

THE END OF THE FIRST VOLUME.

x. Con. U. S. art. 3. s. 2.